# Perspectives on Education and Development

*Revisiting Education Commission and After*

# PERSPECTIVES ON EDUCATION AND DEVELOPMENT

*Revisiting Education Commission and After*

*Edited by*

VED PRAKASH
K. BISWAL

NUEPA

SHIPRA

Rs 1500, US$ 50

ISBN: 978-81-7541-420-4

2024 PoD Impression
(2012, First Published 2008)

*Perspectives on Education and Development:*
*Revisiting Education Commission and After*



Published by:
**SHIPRA PUBLICATIONS**
LG 18-19, Pankaj Central Market
I.P. Ext., Patparganj, Delhi 110092, India
11 47322068; 2223 5152; 96500 28065
info@shiprapublication.com
www.shiprapublication.com

# Foreword

The Education Commission (1964-66) was constituted at a critical time when, as an emerging democratic society, the country was engaged in public debates on models of development appropriate for a society faced with issues and tensions relating to land reforms, cooperatives, foreign aid, religious and linguistic identities, status of women, caste conflicts and education. The jobs assigned to the Commission in its Terms of Reference reflected these dilemmas and development challenges. The contemporary development discourse was also recognizing education as a powerful instrument of social transformation and nation building. Education was seen critical for poverty alleviation, reduction of inequalities, promotion of social harmony and strengthening of national unity. In this context and driven by the vision of building a self-reliant India, the Commission was assigned the task of recommending a national system of education encompassing all stages of education.

Inspired by the Indian freedom struggle and guided by the principles enshrined in the Constitution coupled with the changing context of development, the Commission made a number of recommendations for building a national system of education. The Commission submitted its report in 1966, which provided a clear vision of education for modernization and national unity. The Commission saw education critical for increasing productivity, promoting national unity, consolidating democracy, modernizing the country and developing scientific, moral and spiritual values. Education was perceived as a powerful instrument to create the 'new society'. The Commission attempted to establish a strong relationship between education and national development. One of the unique features of the Commission was that it looked beyond the expansion and quality improvement concerns, and provided a set of recommendations to bring about transformation of the existing education system. Although, for some reasons, some of the important recommendations could not be implemented fully, the Commission, however, became the landmark in the policy planning process. Its recommendations were fed into the subsequent Education Policies of 1968 and 1986.

Since the Commission submitted its report in 1966, very few scholars have attempted to critically examine the impact of the Commission's recommendations on policy planning and development of education. Keeping this in view, the National University of Educational Planning and Administration (NUEPA), New Delhi organized a three-day *National Seminar on the Education Commission: Revisiting the Commission's Premises, Vision and Impact on Policy Formulation* in New Delhi from December 26-28, 2006. The seminar has made an attempt to examine the Commission's underlying premises, vision and recommendations and their impact on policy planning at a time when the educational terrain is undergoing fast changes, particularly in the context of globalization and emergence of knowledge economy. Besides, the seminar identified gaps in the implementation of the Commission's recommendations; examined their relevance in the changing context; and reflected on possible strategies to deal with emerging development challenges. The seminar provided a platform to rethink 'the basic idea of change' envisaged by the Education Commission and to initiate a national debate on its continuing relevance and the need to evolve a new framework for policy planning in the future.

The present volume on *Perspectives on Education and Development: Revisiting Education Commission and After,* which includes 23 papers contributed by eminent educationists, provides a reflective assessment of the impact of the Education Commission on policy planning. I would like to place on record my deep appreciation for the NUEPA for initiating this national debate. I would like to thank all the contributors to this volume for their sincere engagement in bringing to the forefront critical issues of human resource development. I would also like to thank Prof. Ved Prakash and Dr. K. Biswal for their hard work in making this volume available to all of us. I am sure people engaged with educational endeavours at all levels will find this book very useful.

**Sudeep Banerjee**
Formerly Secretary to the Government of India, and
Chancellor
NUEPA

February 6, 2008
New Delhi

# Preface

There are times in history when a new direction has been sought to be given by every country to develop "its system of education to express and promote its unique socio-cultural identity and also to meet the challenges of the times". Such moments came to Indian education, particularly after Independence, which called for addressing multi-dimensional facets of the country's envisioned educational future through various Commissions on Education and the formulation of a National Policy on Education.

Although, the nation provided the constitutional mandate through its original Article 45 for compulsory education for all children up to the age of 14, within ten years of the commencement of the Constitution, higher education was the first to receive discrete attention through the setting up of the University Education Commission in 1948, under the chairmanship of Dr. S. Radhakrishnan. This was followed by the Secondary Education Commission in 1952, under the chairmanship of Dr L. Lakshmanswamy Mudaliar which gave a new direction to school education in Independent India. Indian education did face substantive new challenges in school and higher education as a consequence of the above two Commissions.

However, the first comprehensive effort in giving a new orientation to education as a whole was the setting up of the Education Commission (EC) in 1964 with Professor D. S. Kothari as its Chairman and Shri J. P. Naik as its Member Secretary, the two doyens of Indian education, whose contributions will be remembered for long. The mandate of the Commission was to advise the government on the national pattern of education and the principles and policies for the development of education at all stages and in all its aspects. This was the first Commission in our educational history which looked comprehensively at all aspects of education. It was also the first Commission to be charged with achieving a national system of education. The Education Commission report aptly titled, "Education and National Development", turned out to be a landmark in many ways. The first National Policy on Education, 1968, was an embodiment of the recommendations contained in the Education Commission Report. Forty years down the time, several things had happened in the field of education and it was time that a realistic stock taking was done, academically, of the various recommendations of the Commission.

It may not be out of context to state that during the last 40 years since the Education Commission submitted its report in 1966 very few educational discourses have attempted to critically look into the impact of the Commission on policy, planning and development of education. Since the education system has undergone a lot of transformation, we thought it may be very useful to reflect on the Education Commission's premises and the multi-dimensional aspects which concern and dominate the Indian educational scenario. The organization of the "National Seminar on the Education Commission: Revisiting the Commission's Premises, Vision and Impact on Policy Formulation" was the outcome of this introspection.

The deliberations and the papers contributed by eminent educationists touch a wide spectrum of issues and concerns in Indian education which have been reviewed. This volume contains the essence of the thinking of scholars in Indian education who have articulated their academic insight in the papers that have been included. It is our fervent hope that the papers have brought out the focus on such recommendations as have not only stood the test of time but need to be further nurtured for enabling education to play a role in educational development as visualized by the Education Commission. It is also felt that we need to re-examine the recommendations which could not be implemented but whose relevance is as valid today as it was when the recommendations were made. We also feel that transformation in Indian education and in the changing scenario in which education has to also play its role in today's context, we should include such issues and concerns which need to be articulated afresh for the national development. It may be a wishful thinking that another concerted effort by a group of socially and educationally committed thinkers, rooted in the ground realities of Indian education, can present a fresh vision for new ideas which emanate from this volume, for intense debate and dialogue.

This volume would not have been possible but for the contributions from leading scholars and thinkers, whose names appear on thematic papers, and I would place on record my sense of deep appreciation at their involvement in this effort. In particular, I would like to record my deep appreciation for Shri Sudeep Banerjee, Chancellor, NUEPA for his guidance and overall encouragement in planning this seminar. My grateful thanks are also due to Prof. Anil Sadgopal, who was greatly instrumental in enabling my thinking towards conceptualizing this seminar and for various suggestions for its successful organization. Such an important work needed careful scrutiny to bring this volume in the present shape and I am grateful to Prof. A.K. Sharma and Prof. C. Seshadri for undertaking this task.

Dr. K. Biswal discharged the responsibility of overall coordination and management of this effort and I am very happy to acknowledge the support that he has provided me all through in this regard.

Mrs. Sushma Asija, Shri Anil Gupta and Shri Sudhir Dagar provided invaluable administrative support so important for executing a task of this order. I place on record my appreciation for their contribution.

January, 2008
New Delhi

**Ved Prakash**
Vice-Chancellor, NUEPA

# Contents

## Part III
## Curriculum, Pedagogy and Knowledge



## Part IV
## Planning and Governance



## Part V
## Resources and National Economy



## Part VI
## Education Commission's Perception of Knowledge

## Part VII
## Contemporary Concerns and Future Challenges

# Introduction

VED PRAKASH

The report of the Education Commission (1964-66), chaired by Prof. D.S. Kothari, is possibly the last education policy-related document of the Nehruvian era. The very timing of the decision to constitute the Commission lent a special significance and critical perspective to the report. This was the time when the emerging democratic society had gained the initial experience of five-year developmental planning. This was also the time when the agenda of ushering in a scientific age was looked upon as a means to transform the traditional society into a modern one by way of alleviating poverty, minimizing inequalities and institutionalizing democratic and forward looking education.

At the same time, the immediate backdrop of the Commission was provided by a historic food crisis that called for questioning the very notion of agricultural productivity and the role of science and technology in rural development. The policy makers were also engaged in a public debate on various models of development. Issues relating to land reforms, co-operatives, foreign aid, federal structure of Indian polity, religious and linguistic identities, status of women, caste conflicts and the medium of education were sources of major tensions. These dilemmas and challenges faced by the nation were reflected in the Terms of Reference as well as in the composition of the Commission. This is also the first Commission in the post-Independence India to be assigned the task of recommending a national system of education from pre-primary stage to professional and higher education.

## Commission's Premises

The vision of the Commission was inspired by the Indian freedom struggle against imperialism and embedded deeply in the principles enshrined in the Constitution. In order to decipher the various elements that comprised the Commission's vision and its recommendations, it would be necessary to identify and examine the underlying premises. A study of the Commission's report reveals, among others, the following set of important premises:

(i) Education is a powerful means of social transformation and nation building;

(ii) The heritage of the Indian freedom struggle must continue to inspire our children and youth;

(iii) Education shall promote human, moral and scientific values;

(iv) The education system must be designed to build a democratic, egalitarian, secular and forward-looking society as envisaged in the Constitution;

(v) The education system must be rooted in the principles of social justice and equality enshrined in the Constitution;

(vi) Alleviation of poverty, reduction of inequalities (related to class, caste, religion, region, gender and language), promotion of social harmony and strengthening of national unity shall be the central concerns of education;

(vii) Educational goals can be achieved only through a national system of education that is based upon certain critical notions, structures and institutionalized processes;

(viii) An immediate objective of education should be to increase national productivity (particularly in agriculture) and develop scientific and technological base for this purpose;

(ix) The State has a constitutional obligation as well as a key role in educational planning, development and mobilization of resources;

(x) The national economy needs to be reprioritized to mobilize the necessary resources for achieving the objectives of education;

(xi) Teachers have a central role in education and therefore, their status in society, quality of teacher education and teaching environment are matters of critical concern;

(xii) Language is a means of political, social and cultural empowerment;

(xiii) Higher education has a key role in nation-building which must be a priority concern of the Government;

(xiv) A nation-wide system of promoting excellence at all stages of education, combined with accessibility to various sections of society, needs to be institutionalized;

(xv) Education thrives best in a democratic environment—both inter-institutional and intra-institutional; and

(xvi) Any form of organization and governance that are not in tune with the educational goals must be replaced by a rational alternative.

There is a need to study whether these premises, which formed the essential basis of the Commission's vision and recommendations, continue to influence the development policy in the country. Since the presentation of the Commission's report to the nation in 1966, the education system has undergone a lot of transformation. It is time now to examine these premises from different perspectives with a view to:

(a) Placing these premises in the historical, political and socio-economic context of the Commission;
(b) Studying the consonance, partial divergence and contradiction between the premises and recommendations of the Commission;
(c) Analyzing the reasons of partial divergence or contradiction, if any;
(d) Deciphering the rationale for both acceptance and non-acceptance of the Commission's recommendations;
(e) Reviewing the premises in the context of the neoliberal economic policies, pursuit of global hegemony, identity conflicts and other contemporary challenges facing the nation; and
(f) Modifying the premises accordingly to define a new framework and thereby, move towards a futuristic vision of education.

## The Seminar: Expectations and Objectives

It is in this perspective that the National University of Educational Planning and Administration (NUEPA) organized a three-day *"National Seminar on the Education Commission: Revisiting the Commission's Premises, Vision and Impact on Policy Formulation"* in December 2006, which was also the centenary year of Prof. D. S. Kothari, the Chairperson of the Commission. The Seminar was organized as a tribute to Prof. D. S. Kothari. About 100 participants including academics, policy-makers, planning experts and practitioners were drawn from all over India. The seminar adopted various modes of presentation and discussion, including plenary and parallel sessions, and panel discussion.

The seminar gave us an opportunity to rethink "the basic idea of change" as envisaged by the Commission, modify the basic premises and the recommendations wherever necessary and move on to build a new framework to meet the contemporary challenges. While undertaking this exercise, we have gained by reviewing the policy and programmatic documents of the intervening four decades, analyzing the impact of the global economic order and examining the prevailing policy discourse.

Specifically, the seminar attempted the following:

(i) To undertake a critical review of the key recommendations of the Education Commission (1964-66) in terms of its underlying premises, vision and impact on policy formulation during the past four decades;
(ii) Given the constitutional obligations and principles, to examine the relevance of major concerns and recommendations of the Commission in the context of emerging global economic order and the need to respond to the developmental challenges ahead; and

(iii) To provide a platform to rethink "the basic idea of change" as envisaged by the Commission and to initiate a national debate on its continuing relevance and the need to evolve a new framework for policy formulation for the future.

### *Scope of the Seminar*

The seminar looked at the Commission's recommendations covering all stages and aspects of education—from pre-primary to professional and higher education—and their implications for national development and contemporary challenges. The attempt was to take an integral view rather than to fragment or compartmentalize our understanding in terms of various stages or functional aspects. The seminar dealt with philosophical, political, socio-economic, cultural, curricular and pedagogical dimensions of the Commission's concerns and recommendations.

Presentations in the Seminar had covered seven broad themes as under:

- *Perspectives, goals and values*: with emphasis on the Commission's views on society, education and national development; goals of education; and values and education;
- *Equality and social justice*: particularly, regional imbalances in educational development; education of the backward sections of society (SC, ST and minorities); and inclusive education;
- *Curriculum, pedagogy and knowledge:* the Commission's vision of the development of science, mathematics, social sciences and humanities; relationship between productive work and education; curriculum; and teacher education;
- *Planning and governance*: examining organization and governance of education; decentralization and public participation in educational planning; and autonomy of educational institutions;
- *Resources and national economy*: financing of education and mobilization of resources for education;
- *Education Commission's as well as current perception of knowledge*: knowledge as perceived by the commission and the present perception of knowledge; and
- *Contemporary concerns and future challenges*: the Commission's vision of institutionalizing new ideas with focus on curricular transformation, vocational education, adult education, research and development and agricultural education.

Keeping in view the seven broad themes outlined above, the NUEPA had commissioned eminent people in their respective fields to contribute papers focusing on the premises of the Education Commission, their relevance or otherwise in the contextual realities of the present day Indian education and to make suggestions and directions for understanding future deliberations in the true spirit of revisiting the Education Commission. The university had the unique privilege of an overwhelming response to the preparation and submission of thematic papers as well as participation in the seminar. The list of contributors to the thematic papers and the list of participants are given in Annexure I and II respectively.

As many as 23 papers have been included in this volume and an analytical review of all these papers is being made here to give an overview of what follows in the detailed papers of the contributing authors. The sequence of the review as given below follows the same sequence as given in the seven themes referred to earlier.

C. Seshadri, in his paper, *Perspectives on Society, Education and Values: The Education Commission and After*, presents a constructive critique of the theoretical formulations of the Education Commission (EC) report from the perspective of philosophy of education. As such, the discussion is centred on the EC's perspectives on the "society", "education", "values", "equality" and "knowledge". These themes constitute the corner stones of the EC's educational philosophy. They are also of critical significance to the on-going and future educational policy discourses and practical action. The approach adopted by Seshadri is to present the EC position on these themes, critically examine them from the perspective of the basic premises and vision of the EC, developments in educational thinking during the intervening period and the emerging educational scenario in the context of globalization and neo-liberal economic policies.

Seshadri's paper is organized around five sections—*Society, Education, Values, Equality and Knowledge,* and the EC in the New Context. In the first four sections, the EC position in relation to each theme is explained and critiqued. This is followed by an account of how these themes were treated and worked upon in the intervening years of educational theorizing leading up to modern times. In the last section, the EC vision and its central concerns are revisited and critiqued with reference to their contemporary relevance.

The EC vision of the future *Society* as a democratic, secular, egalitarian and modernized society driven by a harmonious blend of science and spirituality is articulated with the help of vision statements extracted from the Report. The vision is critiqued with reference to its historical and philosophical foundations, the view of "development" it embodies, the place of science and technology and the EC's interpretations of the notions of democracy, egalitarianism, secularism and spiritual and cultural heritage. The concern in the paper is to examine their theoretical bases and consistency with EC's normative prescriptions and judgments.

The EC's view of *Education* and its relationship with national development, the individual and the society and the role of education as an instrument of change are critically examined. The EC's die-hard optimism in the power of education to transform society is particularly brought under focus and critiqued with reference to findings from sociology of education.

The Commission's recommendations on social, moral and spiritual education are examined with reference to rationale and theoretical formulation of the proposal; objectives and content; sources and pedagogy of value education. Special focus is turned on the Commission's recommendations on direct teaching of values, education about religions, our cultural heritage as a storehouse of values, science as the paradigm of values, using the regular subjects of the curriculum as vehicles of value development and relationship between moral and spiritual education. How the EC's insights triggered and impacted the discourse on value education in later years is also reviewed and critiqued.

The EC's position on *Equality*—its bold proclamation of egalitarian ideology and recommendation of the Common School—is explained and critiqued. It is pointed out that the EC's treatment of equality is far from adequate; it did not take equality as a problematic issue but accepted it as an unanalyzed notion; it concerned itself with equality of opportunity, a diluted egalitarian demand; it attributed inequality to external sources and causes (of lack of access, poverty, habitat, gender and caste); it did not ask the question why children fail and whether education led to empowerment of the individual. Also, the contribution of the EC in bringing the issue of equality into the open and widening the terms of the egalitarian debate and impacting policy discourse in later years is discussed.

The EC's scattered references to different aspects of *Knowledge*—explosion of knowledge, appropriate pedagogy, the primacy of science, integration of science and spirituality are brought together and explored with reference to their epistemological and sociological dimensions. Using the EC's insights as benchmarks, a critical account is given of the enlargement of the knowledge discourse in later years, encompassing such issues as the pedagogical fallout of the knowledge explosion phenomenon, celebration of science as the paradigm of knowledge, school-bag load problem, multiple ways of "knowing", knowledge aim in the Information and Communication Technology (ICT) ambience and sociology of knowledge.

The EC's themes of *Society, Education, Values, Knowledge* and *Equality* discussed before are revisited to examine their *Contemporary Relevance* and significance in the context of globalization, economic liberalization, privatization and the ICT. The issues discussed cover: key pointers for visioning the future, aims of education, the egalitarian ideal, value education and knowledge aim in the ICT ambience.

*Revisiting the Education Commission: Perspectives, Goals and Values*, by M. Anandakrishnan, analyses aspects of the Commission's report on perspective, goals and values. It also discusses the extent to which these aspects have been implemented, the progress achieved, the persisting shortfalls and the reasons thereof. The main thrust of the review is to provide a framework for new policy initiatives in education in the vastly changed circumstances—education in the concurrent list, growing aspirations especially of the underprivileged sections, resulting issues of access rate, equity, affordability and supply levels and availability of new technological pedagogic innovations, international influences and new spheres of knowledge and skills.

Under the *perspectives*, the author states the basic premises of the Commission and its key recommendations. As regards later developments, he regrets that there has been a kind of policy vacuum relating to education and especially higher education. The hope created by the Commission has been frustrated on the grounds of short term pressures. The supply side of the educational system is heavily distorted and unbalanced. Increased allocation to education of six per cent of the GDP has not materialized so far. The regulatory system for education has become defunct.

The author underscores the Commission's recommendations on goals, objectives and values and says they are even more relevant today than in the sixties. He endorses the Commission's position on National Objectives and Life, Needs and Aspirations—Common School System, Medium of Instruction, Knowledge Society, Affiliation System, College-School Synergy, Adult and Continuing Education situating the discussion in the changed context, etc.

On the Commission's emphatic assertion on education being the main instrument of change, he regrets that education has been de-linked from all other national endeavours. He cites statistics to show the correlation of education with economic indicators: Population Growth and Literacy, Economic Growth Performance, Disparities among States in Net State Domestic Product (NSDP), Below Poverty Line (BPL) and School Enrolment and Gross Enrollment Ratio (GER) in Higher Education. As regards increasing productivity, he says, our record in implementing the Commission's suggestions is tardy, distorted and inadequate pointing to imbalances in the availability of skill development facilities and decline in research, in quality and quantity.

He reiterates the current significance of Social and National Integration and the attributes of Modernization. He says establishing the knowledge society is the foremost challenge in the immediate future. "Knowledge" will not only be the driver of the Indian economy but also the source for attaining satisfactory quality of life and living conditions of every society. While ushering in such a society, it is necessary to ensure that justice and human values prevail and its social goals are kept in focus. It should emphasize context-oriented knowledge, healthy social values, work experience and aesthetic expression.

The author then goes on to describe the structure and growth strategies of education at different levels with respect to enrolment, participation, discipline-wise distribution and other aspects with the help of Tables and Charts.

By way of conclusion the author says: The rationale for new directions should be articulated along with the modalities for action. The guiding principles should relate to such factors as access, affordability, excellence, competence, knowledge base, skill base, and international standards. The educational opportunities should be available to all those who can benefit through a system of social justice for fair access. The measures for inclusion are in the overall national interest to recognize and foster the potential wherever it is found and should not be viewed as a charity from those with entrenched privileges. Concomitantly the, efforts to promote educational equity will require evolution of a new curriculum framework which is relevant, flexible and context-oriented to attract and retain the underprivileged students. It is also necessary to demonstrate that equity measures can be undertaken while preserving at the same time high quality and academic excellence.

On an optimistic note the author says that extensive support is growing for national level consensus for including large sections of underprivileged population into the mainstream development domains, particularly education. In order to overcome the apprehensions and resistance from the privileged sections about the interference effects, there is a need to evolve policy dialogue with different stakeholders and progressive policy changes.

In *The Education Commission's Perspectives on Society, Education and Development,* M. S. Yadav situates the genesis, constitution and terms of reference of the Commission in the context of socio-economic life and system of governance during the years just before and after Independence. He describes the adoption by the new notion of planned development and the main features of the Five Year Plans—their objectives, thrusts, social welfare, community development and rural extension. He draws attention to the point that the Plans are aimed at development not in the existing framework but at changing the framework itself to enable the fruits of development to reach all the people.

To give an idea of the problems and challenges faced in "educational reconstruction" and the nature of public discourse in education in the country, he presents views of Abul Kalam Azad, Zakir Husain, Gandhi, Nehru and Ambedkar. Their observations, he says, pertained mainly to the purposive dimension of education as related to socio-cultural aspects of Indian society and national development as visualized during the freedom struggle and the experiential dimension of the endeavour of reconstruction of education post-Independence. He says, though there was considerable experimentation in education during freedom struggle, there was no single model of education which could be accepted on conceptual adequacy and feasibility for the country as a whole. Gandhi's Basic Education had become controversial from the point of feasibility. The Education Commission, therefore, faced the challenge of devising an appropriate model for establishing the national system of education covering all stages.

Yadav then presents his analysis of the three key concepts of education, society and national development and also as perceived by the Education Commission. Education is a socially devised process for the benefit of the people, individually and also collectively; it derives its strength in terms of its content and sustenance from its social purpose. It is a continual process and evolves through time. Society as envisioned for Free India is as described in the Constitution: a secular democracy characterized by equality, social justice and social cohesiveness and socialistic pattern of society. Yadav observes that the view of national development and the role of education to promote it represent a paradigm shift in perspective. This perspective amounts to seeking knowledge and its significance in the context of its relevance to life and society. Thus, contribution to national development seems to have become the destination for knowledge and education to arrive at and a criterion to assess their relevance and worth.

Yadav then describes the Commission's approach to address its task of advising on the development of a national system of education. One significant parameter of its approach was to relate education with the Indian society and its progress through national development. The relationship of education with society and national development thus identified was treated as basic and fundamental to derive all principles and policies for the development of a national education system. Yadav then deals with aims and objectives of education formulated by the Commission and its important recommendations towards educational development.

Arjun Dev, in his paper on *Education Commission and After: A Segregated School System,* quotes extensively from the report of the Education Commission (1964-66). There are several issues in education, which have defied solution in spite of the backing of the considered views of various Commissions and Committees on education. One such issue with which we have lived since the Education Commission's report is the debate surrounding the Common School System and its related neighbourhood school concept. The strong and unequivocal support of the Education Commission and subsequent policy resolutions have failed to create conducive climate in the country for its implementation. Perhaps the system is not in tune with the changing perceived social realities on the ground. The social ethos of present day India, particularly of urban Indian society, at the moment, is characterised by fierce competition among individuals that is carried out to educational institutions providing education of different levels of quality. The institutions said to be providing quality education are patronised by those sections of the society who have strong urge for vertical mobility and who have a capacity to pay exorbitant fees of these schools. The beneficiaries of this system do not bother about its social consequences so long as it enables them to maintain their social, political, economic and cultural hegemony in the society. These are the people who dismiss the idea of the Common School System as a utopia, not in tune with the concepts of globalisation, liberalisation, privatisation, which are the hallmarks of many developing societies to achieve the goal of modernisation.

The present day status of the Common School System raises some fundamental questions which merit serious consideration. Is the concept of Common Schools System still relevant and valid? If so, is it amenable to easy and smooth implementation? Or, has the idea been rendered as un-implementable? If so, what purpose does it serve in reiterating it, time and again, in policy documents? Arjun Dev has made an insightful analysis of this important recommendation of the Education Commission. As he mentions, it may not be inappropriate to consider linking the issue of the Common School System with "direct action for social transformation" and to treat the battle for it as "essentially political" which "will have to be decided politically".

R. Govinda, in his paper: *"Literacy and Elementary Education: Regional Imbalances and Social Inequities"*, says that the issue of balancing the demands of quantity, quality and equality in developing the education system of the country was highlighted by J.P. Naik. Unfortunately, one finds discourses converging on almost the same issues even now. Based on an insightful analysis of persisting inequalities in the spread of education in different parts of the country and among different sections of the society, Naik emphatically pleaded for plurality of perspective in the delivery mechanisms as well as in the structure and contents of the school system. It is in this backdrop that Govinda's paper attempts to explore the current status of literacy and elementary education in different parts of the country. The main aim is to examine persisting interstate disparities and review the state of educational development among different social groups.

The paper also examines the policies and programmes promoted at the national level to overcome such disparities and presents some proposals. Describing regional imbalances and social inequities in education as twin problems of the Indian education system, it is argued that even though there has been considerable improvement in literacy rate that helped in generating demand for school education, provision of equitable access to quality education for all irrespective of caste, class and gender has remained elusive. This has resulted in the continuation of imbalances, inequities and disparities in the educational system.

A few States continue to have large concentration of illiterates and out of school children. The situation is deplorable in rural areas and particularly among girls, Scheduled Castes and Scheduled Tribes. The paper highlights the need for adopting policies that are explicitly pro-poor and inclusive with special measures to reach quality education to schools attended by the poor and regions inhabited by them. It is necessary to prepare focused action plans for educationally backward states and districts, promotion of fairness of provisions for overcoming social inequities, giving a clear shape to the involvement of private providers in the Plan framework along with establishment of a Common School System envisaged by the Education Commission.

It is also essential to pay attention to educational needs of out-of-school youth and adolescents considering the fact that a large number of children are still dropping out without completing even the primary cycle of schooling and most of these belong to marginalized social groups. There is also a need for re-examining the framework of Centre-State partnership in financing if a sustainable system of elementary education is to emerge. Govinda advocates an education development programme emphasizing a sustained action leading to cumulative change in the ground reality instead of undertaking *ad hoc* measures which cannot drive long-term progress.

R.P. Singh, in his paper, *Regional Imbalances in Educational Development,* quotes R.A. Gopalaswami, Member, Education Commission, (Minute of Supplementation) who stated that "planned-economy within the framework of a free, democratic and quasi-federal policy is a pioneering venture. The Education Commission (1964-66) felt concerned about the pitiable state of literacy in the country and therefore, offered a plan of action. However, this was, historically speaking, next only to CABE having made a planned proposal (Sir John Sargeant Plan) earlier in 1944 to educate the entire country within the space of 20 years which did not secure political acceptance at that time.

The paper examines the recommendations made by the Education Commission against the backdrop of the nation's unfulfilled desire to become fully literate and comes to the conclusion that mere provision of either money or schools within a kilometre of the child's habitation is not enough. There are already in existence several successful models in the world and each carries a lesson or two to teach us how universal literacy within a stipulated period is possible to achieve. In a highly complex society like that of India we need to break away from the past solutions and evolve a wholly new model. It would appear that we have thus far missed the wood for the trees. A wholly new approach is overdue.

Singh has given a detailed background of the problem related to regional imbalances in educational development citing episodes from print-media. He says that for educational progress in India we could consider either adopting a model that is rightly suitable somewhere in the world or evolve one that suites our conditions. In either case, it is not possible to think of a single model that could have been successful in our case. The issue of regional imbalances has been brought out in the paper through enrolment figures of boys and girls including SCs and STs at primary, upper primary, secondary stages of education in different states of the country. The educational expenditure in different states has also been mentioned. A Plan of Action proposed in the paper suggests that in the larger interest of the country, each region should be free to strive for its best and to develop at its own pace. This will necessarily lead to some inequalities but what is needed is a balancing factor, a deliberate and sustained effort to assist the less advanced areas to come up to at least certain minimum levels so that the gap between them and the advanced areas would be reduced to the minimum. It also suggests that districts should be adopted as the basic units for educational planning and development and the disparity associated with the education of girls, scheduled castes, and disabled children is reduced by adapting appropriate strategies.

Padma Velaskar, in her paper, *National Commitment to Education of the Dalits: A Critical Commentary on the Report of the Education Commission,* takes a critical look into the Commission's ideology of development, its articulation of the assumed role of education in an egalitarian social transformation and the specific agenda for education of dalits.

She says that the EC's liberal ideology and developmental model endorsed a state programme of capitalistic development and laid more emphasis on modern economic development and less on social transformation. It failed to acknowledge the fundamental conflict of interest between rapid modernization and egalitarianism in a resource-poor country. The EC also lacked a theory of society and social transformation; it did not make an expanded critique of hierarchical social structure nor did it squarely confront the social reality of caste. No programme for ending caste discrimination in school is conceptualized despite the grand array of other programmatic recommendations.

Velaskar points out that equality of opportunity remained a decontextualized and ahistorical notion with EC's refusal to acknowledge the material and cultural reality of dalits. Its notion of equality of opportunity was that of a meritocracy and not of social justice. From the perspective of dalits, she finds Phule-Ambedkarian and other dalit subaltern ideologies and theories of democratic socialism hold greater promise of egalitarian social transformation.

The EC's Common School strategy, Velaskar says, is a bold and laudable policy initiative, but it ignores and underestimates the tremendous social resistance to social mixing that is characteristic of Indian society. What was needed was an anticipation of the brakes that would be put on equalizing processes.

She criticizes the EC for constructing gender relations in an "embarrassingly" patriarchal manner—legitimizing different spheres for men and women as normal and natural notions. Further, women were homogenized; the lives of masses of peasant, low caste, dalit, tribal women, who worked in farm and public labour did not enter the world view of the dominant classes.

The EC sees curriculum as value neutral and equal; there is absence of subaltern groups' culture and ideologies in the recommended curriculum and the dominant discourse is of a cultural majoritarian nationhood. Today, dalits challenge high caste epistemology and knowledge. The issue, Velaskar says, requires serious thinking and development of theories that are vibrant expressions of critical multiculturalism and are capable of creating a new moral order for Indian society.

The EC's entire approach to selection and transmission of values is deeply problematic. The cultural tussle between competing and contrasting visions and ideologies of Western and Nehruvian modernity and Gandhian thought (which are privileged in the EC Report) is not sorted out, leaving a lot of ambiguities and convoluted statements of value positions.

As to promoting dignity of labour and overcoming the tradition of denigrating manual work, Velaskar says that the work experience route chosen by the EC being ideological would remain superficial and notional as long as its structural basis of caste-untouchability and gender division of labour is not problematized.

On the whole, Velaskar finds that, for the dalits, the EC report is a disappointing treatise on social justice and attainment of dignity. Referring to "the current impact of a 'structurally adjusting' education and a worsening situation of opportunities" with state commitment to egalitarianism within or outside of education being almost nonexistent, she considers it pertinent for envisioning greater educational equality for these historically oppressed sections. Besides, she critically re-examines the egalitarian ideology and policy perspectives that emanated from the EC report.

Madan Mohan Jha, in his paper, *Inclusion in the Indian Education Policies: Revisiting Equality in the Kothari Commission Report,* examines the issue of equality as addressed in the report. Jha's theoretical framework for analysis is Right Based Approach (RBA) against the Need Based Approach (NBA).

Analysing the report, Jha maintains that it does not mention "inclusion" or "rights" anywhere; the conceptual back up for equalization of educational opportunity is derived from deprivation and need of children. He is critical of the EC report for being long on the equality rhetoric but short in suggesting strong solutions. While the EC stresses on quality as against expansion, the

Sargent Report talked about a "system of public education" in "a democracy" that would "provide for *all* its members, and not for a few only". Abolition of fees to help the poor in the EC report remained confined only to "tuition fees" leaving out the hidden costs. As regards universalisation of primary education, the EC report recommendation is contrary to the "organic whole" approach of the Sargent Report. It thus prepared the ground for later educational programmes like District Primary Education Programme (DPEP) confining to only five years of basic education. For overcoming differences in the standards of schools and colleges, another source of inequality, the EC does not give any specific alternative, except making a rhetorical suggestion "to evolve more reliable and egalitarian methods of selection, whether for admission to institutions or for award of scholarships" (p. 109). Jha criticizes the EC report for making "a prophetic statement of despair": "*Like all ideals in life, perfect equality of educational opportunity is probably unattainable.*" (p. 109).

On the equalization of educational opportunity for girls, Jha, like several others, criticizes the EC for adopting "a feminine", stereotyped and discriminatory approach. It restricted the significance of the education of girls to "improvement of homes, for moulding the character of children" and "reduction in fertility rate".

Jha finds the EC treatment of education of the 'backward classes' inadequate. The EC has listed only two groups: Scheduled Castes and Scheduled Tribes. The Scheduled Castes have been disposed of in one small paragraph, "by making a statement but without giving any evidence": "the problem, of reducing inequality with regard to the Scheduled Castes, has become a little easier because of the diminution of the rigor of untouchability". There is no heading of "recommendations" under education of the Scheduled Tribes.

The EC observed that "the education of the handicapped children should be an inseparable part of the general education system". It has also noted that the constitutional directive on compulsory education under Article 45 included handicapped children as well. Jha says that although the initial premise seems to be drawn from the inclusive approach built up on the RBA, the contradiction can be easily noticed as it called for "their education" to be "organized not merely on humanitarian grounds, but also on grounds of utility". Such an ambivalent approach, says Jha, can be seen in other parts of the report also. For example, it recommended that only 10 per cent of the children should be covered by 1986; and that the disabled children might "find it psychologically disturbing to be placed in an ordinary school". Jha regrets that the EC, otherwise known for its progressive ideas, "took special education in the country twenty years backwards, undid what the Sargent Report had achieved, and set up the tone of a discourse on 'their' education, which is still reverberating in Indian policies". Neither the NPE nor the modified policy in 1992 advance the cause of education of the disabled and the policy has remained unchanged as it was "hesitant in full commitment to universalisation of elementary education for this group of children". Thus the education of the children with disabilities continued to remain on the fringe, isolated from the mainstream education.

As regards institutional frameworks, Jha makes a mention of Gandhi's basic education and the Common School System of the EC. He traces later developments in policy thinking with regard to Common School and explains the current expansion of exclusive schools.

Jha discusses at length the civil society initiatives outside policy thinking for the RBA starting from Gokhale's Bill on compulsory elementary education, liberal interpretations of Article 21 by the judiciary leading to incorporation of right to education as a Fundamental Right (Article 21A) and the continued discussions on the scope of the right and manner of its realization. Jha concludes that while there is a strong constitutional foundation for rights and equity, the Commission's approach to the policies is not principled as far as rights perspective and inclusiveness are concerned.

Sudesh Mukhopadhyay's paper on *The Education Commission's Vision on Inclusive Education*: *Beginning of a Long Journey,* captures the impact of the Kothari Commission's recommendations on inclusive education from the post-1968 period till date. The author acknowledges three contributions of the Commission that influenced the future of inclusion in the country: policy direction on promoting inclusion as an approach, drawing attention to the issue of defining special education needs and estimating the size of the disabled population and visualizing a wide range of services including special schools and capacity building needs.

In her description of the context prior to 1960, she refers to the Report of Secondary Education Commission and the Five Year Plans. She holds the Sargent Report as progressive of its time—it argued for integration and for making education of the disabled a part of the "national system of education". About the period as a whole, she says that the country did not give thought to systemic interventions as emotional and sympathy orientation was stronger than political/human resource approach.

Discussing the Commission's views on the need for education of the "handicapped" children, she says that they were based not merely on humanitarian grounds but also on grounds of utility. The Commission recommended special as well as integrated education. However, its definition of the disabled, estimate of the size of the target and categorization are open to question. The Commission's action plan also was limited by requirement of teachers and financial resources. The issue of definition and numbers, the author says, still remains an elusive one. Citing the Organization for Economic

Co-operation and Development (OECD) categorization (2004), she suggests that the same can be revisited with a country specific approach.

On the post-Commission developments, the author mentions: the adoption of the recommendations in the 1968 educational policy, establishment of a Special Education Cell in the National Council of Educational Research and Training (NCERT) and launch of the scheme for Integrated Education for the Disabled Children (IEDC). The IEDC, she says, can be considered as an extension of the views of the Commission. The NPE 1986 and its reviews continued with the IEDC approach. Significant developments during this period included: starting of the Project Integrated Education of the Disabled by the NCERT, coordination with other schemes in the Ministry of Human Resource Development (MHRD) and other ministries and focus on training of administrators. Action points emerging from the NPE were visible in the Five Year Plans. The seeds sown by the Commission "were showing some significant off-shoots". Later developments in the Ninth Plan and afterwards included enactment of the Persons with Disabilities Act (1995), legal obligation in respect of education up to 18 years, restructuring of vocational programmes, broad basing of distance education, adoption of composite area approach for IEDC and launch of Sarva Siksha Abhiyan (SSA).

Commenting on the impact of the recommendations, the author says the translation of the Commission's vision into action has been limited for want of an accompanying plan of action. On the other major contemporary developments, she mentions enactment of the 86th amendment to the Constitution making education a fundamental right, the Biwako Millennium Framework for Action (2002) and National Action Plan for Inclusion in Education of Children and Youth with Disabilities (2005). She also mentions about preliminary thinking on the scheme for inclusive education in Secondary Schools. Quoting comparative figures from the Census and Sample Survey, she points out that the issue of estimating the size of the disabled population and definition of the disabled continues to defy resolution. Present efforts towards mainstreaming of the disabled, though noteworthy, are still inadequate. While regular education shows a steady growth, a rapid increase has taken place in special schools. She reports about contribution of the ministries other than education like the Social Justice and Labour ministries by way of support services and training programmes. She also notes that voluntary enterprise is substantial with more than 3500 NGOs functioning in the field and suggests that the government play a more proactive role by way of starting new programmes. As to capacity building, the country is still in need of a master plan for generating necessary manpower requirements. Also, economic rehabilitation of the disabled is yet to be addressed strongly.

Anita Ghai, in her paper, *Gender and Inclusive Education at All Levels,*reviews the educational policy statements and programmes on girls' education from the gender perspective and criticizes them for not challenging the basic issue of patriarchy and traditional gender stereotyping and for viewing girls' education in instrumental terms. As regards inclusive education, she criticizes their non-engagement with understanding of disability and their continued skepticism about integrated education. She also cautions about the insidious ways in which globalization and commoditization of education under GATS further marginalizes the weaker sections including women. She says that neither gender nor inclusion can be comprehended without the social, cultural, economic and political matrix within which they function.

Ghai says, the EC reflected the dominant paradigm of viewing women in a linear way as good wives and mothers; it did not consider the issues of patriarchy or the neglect of women's role as social producers. It argued the need to educate women for its instrumental value and not as an end. Even the NPE toed the same line. None of the policies challenged the hegemonic core of patriarchy, which prevents girls from getting their due. The Programme of Action (PoA) and SSA interventions also have not been able to address the problems of girls' education effectively.

Ghai points to the insidious ways in which globalization and free trade affect women. Globalization privileges the paradigm of profit over humanity thereby restricting the state revenue for welfare purposes including education. As an economic force globalization turns women into a marketable commodity thereby further strengthening the patriarchal stranglehold. It also leads to state organized feminism replacing feminist politics; 'Empowerment' acquires the meaning of empowering women only to the extent of harnessing women's contribution to growth. The commoditization of education under GATS further marginalizes the weaker sections including women.

Referring to inclusive education, Ghai says, the EC analysis of the education of the 'handicapped' is at best conventional and conservative; while it speaks of social justice and constitutional commitment, it looks at disability as an individual problem and not as a social category requiring serious academic engagement and research. Its argument for education of the disabled has instrumental underpinnings and runs counter to education being an inalienable right of every citizen. It is skeptical about integration although it recommended education of the handicapped to be an inseparable part of the general education system. Ghai says that every policy thereafter has continued to reflect this skepticism by non-engagement with understanding of disability. SSA negates inclusion by promoting parallel streams in education for children with disabilities. The suggestions in the Persons With Disabilities Act, 1995 belie the thrust on inclusion.

Ghai says the policy documents are totally oblivious to the paradigm shift—social oppression transforms "impairment" into "disability"—in understanding of impairment and disability. The policy on education of the disabled is guided by medical constructions that encourage cure/overcoming theories; neo-liberalism perceives the disabled person as having a deficit. When education is implicated in a process of reducing 'the human' to capital, those who are not seen as fulfilling this are marginalized. Most of the educational provisions for disabled children remain exclusionary commanding a low priority as a whole.

Ghai concludes by recommending the adoption of the Common School System with firm political conviction, acceptance of diversity as a reality to be treasured, public discourse on the aims of education and working at the societal structures to disrupt the hegemonic discourses of patriarchy as well as normality. The implications of the reduction of inequalities do not point to a single direction of change. Guaranteeing equality of access to and participation in "mainstream" education requires a change in the system. However, that will come only if we question what the children should learn, what kind of society we visualize, and finally who the 'we' is who should debate and take the discourse further.

Anil Sadgopal, in his paper, *Deciphering Policy Discourse on Place of Work in Curriculum*, has extensively cited the thinking on and relationship between work and education. In this he has quoted Mahatma Gandhi, the report of the CABE Committee, the Education Commission (1964-66), National Policy on Education 1968/1986/1992, Report of the Review Committee on the Curriculum for the 10-Year School, Challenge of Education—A Policy Perspective (1985). This has been done to analyse the policy discourse on the place of work in curriculum. The Education Commission emphasized the role of education as a powerful instrument of social, economic and political change. The Commission concluded that one of the means of achieving educational transformation leading to national development was by linking education to productive work and this link could be forged by introducing work experience as an integral part of general education. Work experience aimed at giving the citizens a keen sense of personal work dignity, efficiency and by strengthening in them the desire for self-improvement and social service. This aspect was highlighted in the "Curriculum for the 10-Year School: A Framework" (NCERT, 1976). The Review Committee, which reviewed the above document, recommended Socially Useful Productive Work (SUPW) as a distinct curricular area to provide children with opportunities of participating in social and economic activities inside and outside the classroom, thereby enabling them to understand the scientific principles and processes involved in different types of work.

Sadgopal says that the analysis of the policy discourse on the place of productive and community work in curriculum and its relationship with knowledge presents an obstacle even in incorporating the Gandhian concept in school curriculum from pre-school to senior secondary stage. This was done while keeping in mind the contemporary challenges faced by India in the context of globalization as well as the distortions that are likely to affect the concept itself due to class, caste, religion, culture, gender and disability dimensions, each of these having serious epistemic and curriculum implications. Although this has not happened thus far, there is a strong need to institutionalize the role of productive and community work as medium of knowledge acquisition, developing values and skill formation in school curriculum.

It is an accepted fact that reorganization of higher secondary education, especially its vocationalisation, is essential if education has to play a positive role in national development and social change. But there is a long transition period for accepting this in principle and implementing it in practice. This is so because the new demands not only require an internal restructuring and modification of content in education, but even more required strong links to be developed between education or the school and the departments, agencies and enterprises concerned with development such as industries and commerce, agriculture, health and community development. New consciousness in thinking are, therefore, needed both among educationists and important people from other spheres of life if work and education in school curriculum has to become a solid base for vocational education whether organized inside or outside the school.

In his paper, *Teacher Education: How far have We Traversed the Path Envisioned by the Education Commission (1964-66)*, M.A. Khader says that the tone of the Commission's recommendations was set by its recognition of the primacy of teacher in actualizing the connectivity between quality education and national development. He describes the key features of the road map traced by the Commission for improving teacher status and quality of teacher education programmes and institutions. With reference to the Commission's recommendations and the road map, the author evaluates the post-EC educational developments, especially the creation of DIETs, CTEs and IASEs under the central scheme of teacher education and the establishment of the NCTE as a statutory body to enforce quality norms and standards. Citing evidences on their ineffective functioning, Khader concludes that mere creation of structures does not ensure change or quality; what matters is their capacity to perform. He finds the overall scenario of teacher education as disappointing; the series of curriculum frameworks for teacher education have failed to take root across the country. He says that the NCTE, the system of governance, and teacher educators are partners of the prevailing trend. He suggests that the NCTE needs to move out of its number-driven approach and seriously engage itself in initiating reform in teacher education curriculum. The road to the future calls for building a culture of intellectual inquiry in teacher education involving scholars from multiple disciplines and the teacher community. This would set the stage for realizing the Commission's vision on quality teacher education. Strategic initiative on the part of the NCTE for organizing a collective thrust involving the UGC, NCERT and NUEPA opens the pathway for moving towards the vision.

Mohd. Akhtar Siddiqui in his paper, *Teacher Education: Vision of Kothari Commission and Its Realisation,* argues that the suggestions made by the Commission for revamping and strengthening teacher education still hold valid and are yet to be fully implemented. However, attempts towards improving teacher education system have to look ahead of the Commission's recommendations in order to make the system relevant and effective in the present and future contexts.

Putting before him the basic premise of the Commission that a sound programme of professional education of teachers is an essential condition for the qualitative improvement of education, Siddiqui discusses its major recommendations on teacher education and their implementation over the years citing from the successive national educational policies and teacher education curriculum frameworks. He says, the Commission's recommendation that "education" should be recognized as a social science or as an independent discipline, (p. 125) although reinforced by the successive policy documents, remains only partially implemented and education as a discipline is yet to gain general recognition. Likewise, the recommendation for making extension work an integral part of teacher education to break the isolation from schools is not fully implemented. The author suggests that specific provision be made for this in the NCTE norms. As regards breaking the isolation among teacher education programmes, the establishment of the CTEs and IASEs has helped, but this is confined to the CTEs and IASEs. The idea of State Boards of Teacher Education has not seen the light of the day till now, but it seems not relevant any more in view of the establishment of the NCTE.

The author categorizes the Commission's recommendations on quality reform of teacher education curriculum and processes as: reorientation of subject knowledge, integrated courses, revitalization of professional studies, improved methods of teaching and evaluation, teaching practice as internship, development of special courses and revision and improvement of curriculum. In-service education has drawn benefit from collaboration with universities but in pre-service teacher education this has not happened. Implementation of integrated courses is limited to RIEs and a few universities. Low status of professional studies continues for want of research emphasis in training colleges. Emphasis on varied and new methods of teaching and process oriented rather than only product oriented evaluation of teacher trainees is a major improvement. The recommendation on internship has been reiterated by later documents but internship has remained a weak and elusive step in teacher training programmes. Development of special courses is confined to special needs of teachers and teacher educators; but there are many new, emerging areas which are yet to be addressed. As regards curriculum revision, attempts at curricular reform (at school level) have not been adequately supported with efforts at teacher education. Post graduate courses continue with the same one year structure.

There is a general lack of enthusiasm for enhancing duration of courses in view of resource and infrastructure implications. In view of the increasing demand for qualified teacher educators for the rising number of teacher education institutions, the curricula of post graduate teacher education courses need to be revamped. The observations on the poor quality of training institutions have been reiterated by successive reports and the NCTE is apprised of the situation. In-service education received a fillip under the centrally sponsored scheme of teacher education but its quality still remains a matter of concern. Teachers in higher education are oriented in Academic Staff Colleges through Refresher Courses, but so far no thought has been given to their full-fledged training.

The author regrets that the Commission's advice for planned expansion of training facility has hardly received any attention except the setting up of a DIET in each district. He suggests that large scale unregulated expansion of teacher education, especially at the hands of private investors, should be met by establishing institutions on the basis of a perspective plan and institutional mapping exercise so that the expansion is more evenly distributed and becomes beneficial for trainee teachers and schools.

To make the teacher education system relevant to modern times, Siddiqui suggests that priority attention should be given to: professionalism in teacher education, development of education as a discipline, bridging the gap between school and teacher education curricula, quality control, need for qualified teacher educators, globalization of economies, media support including new technologies, continuing education of teachers and the common school system.

In his paper, *Teacher Education in the Eyes of Education Commissions: Time We Made Incisive Decisions*, A.K. Sharma, referring to the perspectives on teacher education reflected in the successive commissions and committees on education over the years identifies major areas of action towards reorganization and restructuring of teacher education. These are: professionalization of teacher education as a priority, professional development of teachers, profile of teacher educators, professional preparation of teachers in higher education, norms and standards in teacher education, manpower planning, breaking the isolation of teacher education, research in teacher education, and teachers for vocationalization of education.

The concerns of professionalization of teacher education include quality of intake, duration, curriculum, process/pedagogy, school practice/internship, training and teaching methodologies and value orientation. In relation to each of these, Sharma takes a critical look into the current practice against the background of policy recommendations made by the EC and other bodies and raises important questions. As to the current practice of admitting students on the basis of a Common Entrance Test, he wonders whether such tests really identify the right talent for a teaching career. He also mentions the distortions that the admission test has undergone defeating the very purpose of the exercise. As for duration and structure (one year, two year, four year), he suggests that the NCTE must come out with an unequivocal pronouncement on the issue. Drawing attention to the concern for relating teacher education curriculum to school education curriculum, he pleads for evolving a new National Curriculum Framework for Teacher Education. Considering that the system is utilizing the professional training in general for any level of school education, Sharma advocates a general teacher education programme, which orients a prospective teacher to the pedagogical aspects of different stages. Pedagogical training, he says, should deal with concerns such as: handling large sized classes, methodology of multi-grade setting, inclusive education, gender equality, requirements of slow learners and special concerns of gifted learners. For school practice and internship, he suggests that the NCTE should make it mandatory for institutions to ensure support of practicing schools. He refers to how this requirement is being subverted by ingenious institutions with commercial motives. He pleads for spelling out training methodologies apart from teaching methodologies as part of pedagogical orientation particularly of teacher educators. He suggests that the profile of teacher educator should be defined and a scheme for their professional development prepared. He wants the value concerns to be integrated into the curriculum instead of treating them as 'additionalities'. Referring to the national evaluation of the centrally sponsored scheme of teacher education, he calls for a well designed analysis of our failures to implement this scheme in the right perspective.

As to professional preparation of teachers in higher education, he suggests that specialized training methodologies appropriate to higher education be developed. Referring to the mushrooming of teacher education institutions, Sharma suggests that the NCTE has a to take a fresh look into existing norms, generate process norms and develop monitoring strategies for ensuring the observance of norms. He laments that no manpower survey of teacher requirement is available as would help the NCTE to address its mandate of monitoring development of teacher education. He says the EC recommendations on breaking the isolation of teacher education institutions are as valid today as they were at the time of their formulation. He laments the absence of adequate research on problems of education including pedagogy under Indian conditions.

The paper, *The Kothari Commission and Curricular Imperatives* by Vijaya S. Varma, presents an overview of the Kothari Commission Report focusing on its recommendations that relate to curricular issues. The author traces how these ideas have developed in time focusing on the new National Curriculum Framework (NCF) prepared by the NCERT in 2005 (NCF). After critiquing some of the curricular guidelines and principles of the NCF and the text books developed, the author concludes with the description of a model of curriculum development.

The author draws attention to the Commission's famous assertion that if the "change on a grand scale" that it envisioned was to be achieved without a violent revolution, education was the one and only instrument that could do it because of its potential for reaching all the people. He refers to the revolution in education that the Commission desired: changes in objectives, in content, in teaching methods, in the size and composition of the student body, in the selection and professional preparation of teachers, and in its organization.

The author mentions the two national curricular frameworks that followed the national policies on education in 1968 and 1986 as major developments in curriculum since the Kothari Commission. And he singles out the new NCF 2005 for detailed discussion. He also points out that the ideas contained in the two curricular frameworks—need for healthy, enjoyable and stress-free early childhood education, sustenance and nurturing of talent, reduction of the curricular load, empowerment of teachers by ensuring their participation in the development of curricular material and participation of parents and community in the educational process and the need to root education in the Indian milieu—are not new and can certainly be traced back to the Kothari Commission Report. He wonders why the NCF did not attempt to analyze the causes for the non-implementation of these ideas instead of repeating the same. Also the vision of the NCF remains undifferentiated; there is little discussion of what people expect from the education system and how these expectations will impact on the implementation of the vision, the processes and structures that need to be put in place to take us from where we are to where we want to be.

Referring to the constructivist view of education, a major feature of the NCF, he says that adopting constructivism as the paradigm for the whole system of school education—for all classes and all subjects—reveals a vision which is both limited and limiting. It also does not recognize the fact that very often children's own constructions of knowledge are flawed and at odds with more accurate constructions generally accepted by scientists. Sticking to a particular pedagogy will probably prove too linear and unimaginative an approach to cater to the needs of all children. He criticizes the NCF for its lack of analysis of the difficulties in the adoption of mother tongue as medium of instruction. He also points out the problems encountered in promoting community participation in education and especially curriculum planning—maintenance of quality and uniformity, likely clashes between the modern and the traditional viewpoints, risk of local vested interests and obscurantist views governing what is taught in the school. As regards local knowledge he raises the question of its validation—who will do it and how? On the Commission's recommendation on work experience and national service, he points out that there has never been any serious effort to act on them. He criticizes the NCF for giving short shrift to multi-grade schools and repeating the Commission's recommendation on common school without making any effort to explain why the proposal has not taken off.

Referring to the Commission's emphasis on science education, the author draws attention to the crisis situation facing the future of basic sciences in the country—shortage of good students, good science teachers and good research scientists. He says that we have failed to make science teaching interesting enough to attract and retain young talent. To substantiate his point he presents a detailed analysis and criticism of the new science textbooks prepared under the NCF. As an exemplar of good curricular practice he presents the Eklavya model of curriculum development which "embodies practices worth emulating".

S.C. Behar, in his paper, *Rethinking Educational Governance for Social Transformation,* has based his re-thinking of Education Commission (1964-66) extensively and specially from Naik's own critique in his book "Education Commission and After" (1979). In this paper, some of the proposed institutional reforms including district boards, the bureaucratic reforms including Indian Educational Service and reorganisation at all levels and the role of private enterprise in the era of globalisation are revisited. He feels that improvement in the existing structure and culture of administration alone will not suffice and focus has to be shifted to the totality of governance, governance at the levels of school or sub-district as crucial as any in a transformatory education.

In respect of the role of state, civil society and private enterprises, he has attempted to analyse a few relevant issues inextricably linked with the general trend of what is popularly known as liberalisation, globalisation and privatisation. He firmly supports the Education Commission that in the existing unequal society, the state has to be fully responsible for ensuring high quality education to all at all stages, totally free up to elementary and secondary and highly subsidised at tertiary level. The state cannot withdraw even to the slightest extent from this sector even if it does so from other sectors. Behar mentions that governance has far richer and wider connotation than administration or management which is inclusive of political executive in a parliamentary democracy.

The multiple systems of governance attempted in this paper flow from an optimistic perspective and are grounded in the firm belief that their contour, design, values and culture play a vital role in contributing to social change. He cites that educational governance to be an effective change agent must be based on some non-negotiable uncompromisable values such as respect for plurality, de-politicisation of education, besides de-bureaucratisation of education which includes making governance non-hierarchical, flat organisational structure, and professionalisation of the educational structure. In his view of decentralisation of authority, he focuses on autonomy and accountability, federalism, transparency, corruption-free governance and respect for dissent. Behar suggests that "All key appointments in education should be by a Committee consisting of all political parties recognised by the Election Commission of the relevant level.",

As regards structure of educational governance at the national and state levels, it suggests establishment of central and state advisory boards of education, a permanent education commission for the whole of education, not just one stage elementary, secondary or higher or sub-sector like technical for agricultural education. As regards educational governance at district and sub-district levels, it has elaborated on the role of Panchayati Raj Institutions—urban local bodies, establishment of district boards of education, district advisory board of education, school complexes (which should take over much of the inspection functions), community involvement/participation control.

The paper ventures to make suggestions about the multiple models of educational governance which includes university based integrated governance, PRI and local bodies based governance, autonomous or self-managing educational institutions, fully autonomous experimental institutions, a reversed pyramid model, a transparent accountable system promoting plurality. It advocates challenging institutional structure which is learner-centric.

Rethinking educational governance in order to revisit the Education Commission with eyes focussed on social transformation necessitates challenging boundaries. Behar mentions that it is possible to develop a blue-print for an educational revolution so passionately desired by the Commission which will initiate peaceful multiple processes for social transformation. The paper concludes by saying that "another concerted effort by a large number of socially and educationally committed thinkers, rooted on the ground realities but eyes fixed on the sky can present a fresh vision and agenda before this country for intense debate and dialogue".

Madhu Prasad, in *Autonomy, Privatization and Commercialization in Higher Education*, citing references from the Radhakrishnan and Kothari Commission Reports and the Lima Declaration on Academic freedom, says that questions relating to autonomy—of persons, disciplines, procedures and institutions—in higher education, cannot be properly addressed unless they are considered from a variety of relevant perspectives like academic freedom, equality, self-determination, liberal education, social goals, public funding and market. A selective approach focused upon current expediency like the prevailing emphasis on promoting financial autonomy of higher education institutions as a means of effecting cost efficiency may end up doing more harm than good. To advocate privatization and withdrawal of the state from this sector on the ground that only privileged groups have benefited from higher education is to confuse symptoms with the cause—elites dominate higher education because of the failure to universalize quality elementary and secondary education.

Prasad cites international experiences on reducing the reliance on state funding and moving towards market-friendly reforms and the influence of increasing commercialization and privatization and draws attention to the change it has caused in social perception of higher education. The change is reflected in the commoditization of education and a "great deal of interest in accountability" in market terms eroding what was once a widespread consensus—that higher education was a public good and not just a private benefit for sponsors or students.

Prasad expresses concern that policy makers in India today are advocating market criteria to resolve problems of efficiency and accountability. Privatization is seen as the magic wand to set the forces of profit mobilization at work. The critical and transformatory purpose of education has receded into background. The notion of autonomy takes the form of a strategy for facilitating the emergence of unit-based "providers" of a commodity called "knowledge" of varying quality. This perspective is far from the formulations and recommendations of the Kothari Commission and other bodies that once dominated policy. Prasad criticizes the selective use of the Commission's recommendations on college autonomy for defending the current campaign for a nation-wide spread of autonomous institutions.

Prasad says, the concept of administrative and financial autonomy of institutions does not rest on the specificity of academic pursuits. It reduces them to income generation and protection of consumer or stakeholder rights. Secondly, instruments of accountability are available only to stakeholders and consumers, but if services are supported with public resources then, in a democratic set up, they must also be available to those who are not presently consumers or stakeholders of the service. Finally, the question of social accountability proceeds as if it were purely a matter of finance. In the altered framework, only that education has value, or "excellence", which allows the student-consumer to fetch a good market price for the skills she has acquired.

Prasad says that the context of the contemporary debates on institutional autonomy is enormously influenced by the neo-liberal economic agenda adopted by successive governments since the early 1990's. Autonomy has come to mean that an institution is expected to mobilize its own financial resources and maximize student returns on investment in fees by assuring high market prices on acquired skills. But, says Prasad, this was not what the

Kothari Commission had in mind. Like the Commissions and Committees that preceded and followed it, the Kothari Commission had been concerned primarily with academic and decision-making autonomy, not with financial "self-sufficiency" and certainly not with the idea that institutions of higher education ought to be primarily motivated by courting markets as sources of finance for academic programs.

The question, says Prasad, has acquired greater urgency because of the entry of the WTO and GATS into the arena of higher education and the importance of retaining the system's independence from the control of global political and economic vested interests, particularly in the context of the pressure to "open up" the Indian education "market" to foreign direct investment. The developing countries have special academic needs that require to be protected. If higher education worldwide were subject to the strictures of the WTO, the idea that the university serves a broad public good would be weakened.

Jandhyala B G Tilak, in his paper, *The Kothari Commission and Financing of Education,* states that the Commission made a valuable set of recommendations on financing education in India, which he has critically reviewed in his paper starting from the premises of the recommendations, the visionary approach adopted by the Commission, the relevance, soundness and practical feasibility of the recommendations. The whole approach of the Commission to educational development in general and financing of education in particular was strongly influenced by a strong conviction of the Commission on the role of education in development. Major recommendations reviewed in the paper include, allocation of six per cent of national income to education, the most widely quoted recommendation made by the Commission on financing, "the best" pattern of intra-sectoral allocation of resources in education, i.e., allocation of resources between different levels of education, allocation to items such as scholarships, research, role of the state and mobilization of resources from other sources through fees and other measures of cost recovery, centrally sponsored schemes, grants-in-aid, etc. Contrary to the general criticism that many recommendations were made with no sound basis, it has been shown that detailed analyses of costs and financing of education formed the basis for making many recommendations including the ones relating to six per cent of national income, scholarships per student, allocation to different levels of education. Unfortunately, many of the recommendations are yet to receive serious attention of the government. It is shown how they are, even after forty years, still relevant for education development in the country. It is argued in the paper that they are relevant not just because their implementation is due; also they are relevant today for their intrinsic value, essentially because the Commission had looked into the distant future, being firmly on the ground, adopted a visionary approach, built its recommendations on strong empirical evidence and knowledge—national and international, with a strong conviction on the role of education in national development, and above all with a strong commitment to national development.

Pushpa M Bhargava, in his paper, *Knowledge for National Development*, states that a major objective—often unstated but always implied—of our National Education Policy and all the Education Commissions and programmes after Independence, has been to make India a knowledge society and democratise knowledge for development involving the entire society. The paper outlines the principles that may underlie such development using education, agriculture and traditional knowledge as specific examples. Bhargava has outlined several attributes of knowledge, which he believes define knowledge, are noteworthy in the context of a knowledge based society. He feels that for India to evolve into a knowledge-based society, one of the most important actions that our Parliament has to take is to pass a Bill enabling a ban on commercialisation of school education, college education and all higher education. But it cautions that we must distinguish between commercial private institutions, which we must eventually ban and non-commercial private institutions which we should encourage. For this to happen, a new system of assessment, accreditation and supervision of private institutions would be needed. Bhargava outlines the perception of the values that would be important for our citizens to cultivate, the minimum knowledge that they should have and the concepts of which they should have a fair understanding so that they could appreciate their implications.

According to Bhargava, to make our school education serve as a foundation for national development, we must make education up to high school a fundamental and justiciable right implementable fully by the end of a specific period, say, seven years. This is the only way to eventually end reservation in academic institutions or jobs. Besides, this would also help implementing laws against child labour. The paper cites several steps that need to be taken to make our school system responsible to social needs.

In higher education, the paper deals with its objectives, nature of higher education institutions and the issue of quality, quantity and equity. In agricultural and rural sector, the paper says that two issues need to be dealt with: (a) identifying areas where existing information should be disseminated in the agricultural sector and/or where new information needs to be generated and disseminated (research-cum-extension areas); and (b) designing information packages for panchayats that would make them and through them the Gram Sabhas knowledgeable and capable of exercising their rights and discharging their rights effectively. Bhargava has given considerable thought and space in his paper on traditional and cultural knowledge because for India to be an effective knowledge based society, it must encompass both modern and traditional knowledge. Some areas of our traditional knowledge include plant-based practice formulations, traditional agricultural practices, traditional water harvesting practices, our cultural traditions and some aspects of tourism.

Ram Takwale, in his paper, *Vision of Institutionalizing New Ideas of the Education Commission: Focus on Open and Distance Learning,* essentially concentrates on the expansion of channels of education envisaged by the Commission to increase quality, access and equity of education by linking education with national reconstruction and development. The focus of the paper is on the correspondence education or home-study, which later on took the form of open and distance education, and added non-formal mode to the system of education. The Commission could not have anticipated the fast development of the Information Revolution leading to networking of people and places all over the globe and created a situation for post-industrial society with tools and technologies, which offers decentralization and mass participation on an unprecedented scale. These processes are typical of information age and have no resemblance to any of the industrial and agrarian age. However, the ideas of the Commission rooted in development of the people, democratic decentralization and people's participation, and the bottom up approaches have all the relevance in the Information Age.

The paper considers the two programmes of generating the revolution and national system of education in the light of development of the open and distance education. The Commission has recommended the expansion of education at the school, vocational and higher education levels. This developed the system of education to include a second channel of education, the non-formal mode, through correspondence education to give access to all those who are not able to enter into formal and ful-time education. Out of many suggestions of the Commission, the one, which has been accepted widely and had great impact, is the institutionalisation of correspondence education in the form of open schools, distance education institutions of the universities and open universities. The Open and Distance Education (ODE) is changing with different generations of distance education created essentially due to communication technologies. This institutionalisation has the potential to generate the change and transformation expected in the educational revolution.

The paper discusses the aspects of quality, access and equality in the light of the Commission's recommendations and subsequent development. The idea of own-time study for school children has been implemented along with two major directions of development, the non-formal education of school drop-outs and open schooling. The open school program has not expanded to the extent of open and distance education at tertiary level in its coverage due to the target group of school children it has to address. Open schools also allow mature adults over the age of 18 years to take courses. This has created overlapping of the target groups addressed as well as the courses offered by the non-formal systems of open schools, open universities and DEIs, which is yet to be resolved. The emergence of knowledge based society is raising the minimum levels of education essential for every one in the society; and it is now common acceptance that all school children should have general education up to 10th standard and secondary education with vocational components enabling school finishers to be eligible to enter into the world of work. The forces of globalisation and knowledge economy have strengthened policies of privatization adopted to liberalize the system of education to have social participation and contribution. These policies are creating divides on the socio-economic basis and limiting the impact of education and turning it into instruments of divisive forces to create a stratified society. The goal of equity is thus getting defeated.

Institutionalization of open and distance learning (ODL) through open schools and open universities has shown a way of giving quality content for learning and enabled to solve the iron triangle of quality, access and cost, a practical version of value triangle of quality, quantity and equity. The development of ICT has now reached such a stage, that it makes quality education for all a distinct possibility. The development in ICT is continuing with creation of advance generation of technologies and the process is likely to go on for a couple of decades untill it reaches the saturation point. This global-Local linkage with participative developmental processes appropriate to the locality should be the goal of education system adopted in the UNESCO program of Decade of Education for Sustainable Development (2005-2014).

The paper refers to Technology Mediated Open and Distance Education (Tech-MODE), which is one of the models of education being developed through the consortium approach, creates a system of education that can institutionalize e-learning through distributed system of education. It is technology driven and aims at making education accessible to anyone, anytime, anywhere. It can use all the facilities and technology empowerment to enable people to participate in development through partnership programs. The goal is to develop public-private-community partnership with a win-win approach. This brings in many functionaries like teachers in institutions of public as well as private sector and community with expertise and domain knowledge, and paves the way for non-exploitative development of all partners besides bringing an end to exclusive reliance on public or private sectors.

Prof. Takwale argues that private and social contributions are necessary to increase resources for education. He also observed that the government's policy of creating more seats in leading institutions by upgrading the infrastructure facilities or by creating new national institutions might solve the existing problem, but it is not a permanent solution.

*The Vision of Institutionalizing New Ideas of the Education Commission: Focus on Open and Distance Learning*, by H. P. Dikshit, begins with an analysis of our failure in realizing the revolution in education envisioned by the Kothari Commission and attributes the failure to our inability to appreciate the concerns of the Commission to deal with education of large target groups of learners. He presents the transformations that have taken place in national efforts towards extension of education to larger target groups starting from the Commission's recommendation of Correspondence Courses—distance education, distance and open education, on-line education, omnipresent education and distributed education. He analyzes the present status, future trends and emerging directions nationally and internationally.

Dikshit traces the history of modern open learning systems to the correspondence course started by the University of Delhi in 1962. The idea gained support in the Kothari Commission Report. Its later expansion led to the setting up of the first Open University by the Government of Andhra Pradesh in 1982 and the creation of the Indira Gandhi National Open University in 1985. This was followed by the initiation of Open Schooling in 1979 which later developed into the National Institute of Open Schooling. With the dynamic growth of the ODL system, the need for maintaining standards in distance education became inevitable and an apex statutory body, the Distance Education Council (DEC) was set up.

In the context of the emergence of the knowledge society, Dikshit talks of three "very visible and vibrant" revolutions with global impact that the country has witnessed—ICT, Space and Satellite Technology and ODL system with global impact. He attaches great significance to each of these in advancing distance learning. He says that in placing India among the advanced nations in the IT sector, distance education played a crucial role by training required manpower. Secondly, the ODL system has greatly benefitted from the strides made by the Indian Space Research Organization (ISRO), especially from its pioneering satellite instructional television (SITE) experiment in 1975-76. Nearly 24,000 teachers were trained in October 1975 through multimedia packages. The Open University system continued to get expensive technological support from ISRO. Thus capability for four TV-channels and two interactive networks dedicated to education had been developed under the ISRO-IGNOU collaboration by 2002. Another development was the launching of a dedicated geo-stationary satellite for education, the EDUSAT on September 20, 2004, to support the education for all movement under the Sarva Shiksha Abhiyan (SSA).

The third revolution is the emergence of Open and Distance Learning system with global impact. Nearly 25 per cent of students in higher education are in the ODL system. The ODL system has effectively addressed the training of teachers, an important recommendation of the EC Report, in the NE region. A joint project of the IGNOU-ISRO-MHRD-State Governments is being implemented through the EDUSAT network with a HUB at Jabalpur. The project seeks to train teachers in Mathematics and Communication Skills.

In terms of international impact IGNOU has presence in thirty five countries and this is expanding. It is currently hosting the secretariat and chairing the SAARC Consortium of Open and Distance Learning. Several countries are using the ODL material produced in India. The development of a Satellite and Fiber Optic network to provide communication and connectivity for all the 53 member countries of Pan African Parliament with India is on the anvil. The Tele-education programme of IGNOU is believed to commence shortly with Ethiopia.

Dikshit says that the concern in ODL system for the convenience and requirements of learners has propelled the system to keep pace with new dimensions of technology like the use of fiber optic connections in place of the expensive Satellite Communication. He mentions mobile cell phones as a promising technology considering the increasing numbers of mobile phone users (70m) in the country. He also mentions private satellite service providers like London based INMARSAT

As regards the tasks ahead, the author says that we have to aim at increasing the participation rate in higher education to at least 40 per cent from the current seven per cent. He regrets that in spite of the Kothari Commission's specific observation about equal recognition of different forms of education, the same has not happened even after 40 years because of "closed mindsets and inertia in accepting a change". He mentions some encouraging developments like: the DEC entering into MOUs with NCTE, ICAR, DCI UGC support, use of ODL by major institutions of science and technology and the Knowledge Commission's assurance of support for the new mode of education which it has termed as Distributed Education.

Hridaya Kant Dewan, in *Adult Education*, explores the perspectives behind the macro efforts in adult education with reference to the Kothari Commission report, the kinds of processes adopted and their impact. He does this through probing into the key concepts like "education" the meaning of which varied from literacy to continuous learning and education for transformation, not only over time but also across different discourses at the same historic point. The author explores the articulations of the purpose of adult education and how it defines critically the manner in which the programmes get structured and impacts the outcomes. He also examines the design and implementation of adult education programmes over the years with reference to policy, structure and mechanism, teacher, materials, content, methods and systemic issues of politics, sociology and financial resources.

Dewan says that the Kothari Commission looks at education (and adult education) as a means to promote modernization and overcome resistance to change and clinging to the traditional forms of life. He points out that this perception and its underlying philosophy have been contested on the ground that it undermines the knowledge and wisdom the so-called illiterates possess. Examining the arguments in favour and against the "modernizing view", he says that the strong point of the Commission is that it has recognized adult education (however inadequately) as a social and political intervention rather than a welfare based "nice" activity.

The author then discusses the purpose of adult education as enunciated by different policy documents, renowned thinkers and activists in the field, the Talimi Sangh, Sewa Mandir and international experiences. He says that the issue of adult education and its relationship with poverty, social transformation and the village is still contentious and unresolved. The Commission, he observes, did not recognize the possible tension between oppression, exploitation and domination on the one hand and education for greater knowledge on the other. This absence of a statement on the socio-political and economic perspective is even starker in the 1986 policy. The NPE derived the need for adult education neither from equity nor from modernization to bring enlightenment; instead it argued for adult education to increase productivity involving the industrial houses also as partners.

The author also refers to other issues of philosophical and sociological dimensions like treating literacy as a technical issue, the view that literacy is not by itself liberative and does not give an ethical world view and the questionable belief in the ethical strength of science. He presents the cases of Talimi Sangh and Sewa Mandir and international movements. He quotes profusely from the Nicaraguan literary crusade and brings out the revolutionary character of adult education and its philosophical and epistemological bases. The author draws the conclusion that if the adults have to be motivated we cannot do so by neutral literacy alone without bringing in a social, economic and political view.

The author then passes on to the issues of content, methodology and language and reviews the position of the Kothari Commission and other policy documents and cites the experience of BJVJ and Sewa Mandir.

Just like the why of adult education, the issue of content and method also does not have a simple or clear path. Should adult education be merely literacy or it should include work education? There is also the wider question of the content including elements of understanding social injustice, exploitation, organization, group interest and struggles. What should be the knowledge that forms the basis of the program? Should it only come from the local context, constructed with the learner community or should it be knowledge that modernizes the learner community? The author examines the recommendations of the Kothari Commission and the subsequent policy statements on these issues and points out that they placed their faith on literacy, scientific knowledge, technological awareness and the state language.

As regards the teacher, the author after reviewing experiences says that identification and capacity building of those who will engage with the adult learner is an important concern. For a program not restricted to individual motivations but dealing with adult learners systematically, it becomes imperative to address the issue of identifying volunteers as well as ensuring that they have the abilities to engage the adult learners meaningfully.

As regards structure and mechanism, the author reviews the Commission's recommendation for making the school as the centre of village life and also presents analyses of experiences of mass literacy campaigns like Total Literacy Campaign and BJVJ. Citing research findings, he gives a comprehensive critique of the literacy campaigns with reference to organization and commitment, programmatic structure, the role of bureaucracy and overall functioning and achievements.

Dinesh Abrol and L. Pulamte, in their paper, *The Challenge before Indian Agricultural Universities: Impact and Relevance of the Kothari Commission's Vision and Strategy,* examine the impact of the recommendations of Education Commission (1964-66) on the organization and performance of Indian Agricultural Universities. The paper describes the challenge before Indian Agricultural Universities to be one of how to shift away from the grip of structural rigidities created during the implementation of the Education Commission vision and strategy, as they have not been able to transform the system of education to help tackle the latest concerns of the Indian agriculture. It suggests that quite a few of these structural rigidities have originated on account of the problems inherent in the vision and strategy developed by the Commission for the achievement of food security in India. It studies the changes undertaken after the adoption of the Education Commission recommendations in the Indian Agricultural Universities in respect of the integration of education, research and extension. It suggests that the vision and strategy that the Education Commission developed for the system of education for agriculture is no more appropriate and relevant in finding solutions to the problems agriculture in India is facing. It concludes that while the recommended system of education for agriculture functioned productively for selected regions in the short run, but the imprint these recommendations have left on the organization of education, research and extension has also made the same agricultural universities to fail in respect of finding appropriate agricultural technology solutions. It argues that the malfunctions had begun to develop very early and have got only rigidified further during the last thirty years. It makes the case that in spite of the advance warnings, the policymakers have failed to bring about appropriate systemic changes or innovation including education for agriculture in time. It provides an understanding of the systemic failures by looking into the structural rigidities introduced in the system of education for agriculture. It traces the inertia, resistance and pressures for change detected in the system of education for agriculture. It also investigates into the curriculum making processes and pedagogy being followed in the existing system of agricultural universities to enable the policy makers to have a better understanding of the social engineering undertaken in the course of establishment of agricultural universities in India. It seeks the inclusion of the rural institutes, community polytechnics and other related institutions into the system of education for agriculture for the benefit of the construction of a path of sustainable development in the currently prevailing Indian conditions. It addresses a new set of recommendations to the community of practitioners of educational planning on the system of education of agriculture.

The above overview may provide adequate base and stimulus for going into the details of the papers of each author to have an appropriate understanding, the logic of their intellectual insights of the Commission's premises, vision and impact on policy formulation in the chapters that follow.

# Part I

# Perspectives, Goals and Values

# 1

# Perspectives on Society, Education and Values: The Education Commission and After

C. SESHADRI

## Introduction

The Education Commission (EC) was set up by the Government of India in 1964 in the context of national concerns on developmental planning, demands of scientific age and modernization, poverty elimination, inequality, agricultural productivity and rural development. Its mandate was "to advise the government on the national pattern of education and on the general principles and policies for the development of education at all stages and in all its aspects".

The EC Report, titled, *Education and National Development,* turned out to be a landmark in many ways. The EC was the first commission in our educational history to look comprehensively at almost all aspects of education; it was also the first commission to be charged with suggesting a national system of education (J.P. Naik, 1982, *The Education Commission and After*, p. 2)[1]. The Report was also better received and better implemented than the earlier Commissions of the post-independence period (Naik, p. 195, footnote). The Commission took an integrated view of education to address the problems of national development in a holistic manner and in its sweep covered all stages, from pre-school to higher levels of education, including universities and research institutions—technical, agriculture, vocational and general. Gunnar Myrdal (1970, p. 202) referred to the EC Report as "one of the most distinguished examples of the continuation in independence time of the glorious tradition of honest, comprehensive and penetrating public investigations in British India".

The EC Report, however, had limited success in terms of the high expectations of policy changes and practical implementation it had raised—the member secretary, Naik, himself admitted this, 13 years later, in his review of post-EC happenings. But its major contribution lay in bringing to national attention the theoretical and practical issues involved in any attempt at national and educational reconstruction—visioning the future society, concepts of development and modernization, significance of education to nation building and the values that are to guide our lives and the future of the nation. So prophetic and far-reaching have been its proposals on educational reconstruction and so powerful has been the initial impetus of its theoretical formulations that they have influenced educational thinking in the country for decades and continue to function as benchmarks in modern discussions on education. On the British Plowden Report, *Children and their Primary Schools,* published around the same time (1967), Prof Peters (1969, *Preface*) observed that it soon came to be regarded as an authoritative textbook on the theory of primary education in Colleges of Education "on account of the unusual amount of educational theorizing it contained". More or less, a similar thing happened with the EC report. The Report carried extensive discussion on education and national objectives, school curriculum, teaching methods, guidance and evaluation and teacher education and virtually functioned as a standard reference document on educational theory and practice. No wonder, it was an instant hit, especially with students of education and teacher educators, and remained so for more than two decades.

## Objectives and Scope

It is this aspect of the EC Report—its underlying educational philosophy and theoretical formulations-that constitutes the focus of the present study. Its broad objective is to present a constructive critique of the report focusing on EC's perspectives on 'society', 'education' and 'values'. These themes, being of particular significance to the on-going and future educational policy discourse, are critically examined from the perspective of the basic premises and vision of the EC, developments in educational thinking during the intervening period and the emerging educational scenario in the context of globalization and neo-liberal economic policies.

The paper is organized around five sections—Society, Education, Values, Equality and Knowledge and EC in the New Context. 'Equality' and 'Knowledge' are discussed separately as they constitute major value domains in their own right and also form the corner stones of the EC educational philosophy. In the first four sections, the EC position in relation to each theme is explained and critiqued. This is followed by an account of how these themes worked in the intervening years of educational theorizing leading to modern times. In the last section, the EC vision and its central concerns are revisited and critiqued with reference to developments in the present context.

## PART I: SOCIETY

***EC Vision of the Future Society:*** The EC vision of the future (good) society and the educational system that acts as an instrument of its realization is articulated in the opening chapter. The report begins with its celebrated declaration: *The destiny of India is now being shaped in her classrooms*, and moves on to a description of the existing state of the society, problems of national development and the need for relating education to life, needs and aspirations of the people. Situating its vision within the framework of the Indian Constitution, the Commission envisions the creation of a democratic, secular, egalitarian and modernized society driven by a harmonious blend of science and spirituality. The following extracts from the Commission's Report articulate its vision:

- *The principal objective of the great enterprise of national reconstruction is to raise the standard of living of our people.* There is colossal poverty of the masses and large incidence of under or unemployment. Our goal must be to secure a rapid rate of economic growth, distribute income more equitably, control growth of population, and provide full employment. India has to raise her present standards of living and take her rightful place in the comity of nations as soon as possible, within the lifetime of a generation at the most (para 1.11).
- *We should achieve social and national integration and create an integrated and egalitarian society.* Our society is hierarchical, stratified and deficient in vertical mobility. The social distance between the different classes, the rich and the poor, the educated and the uneducated is large and widening. Developments which threaten national unity and social progress have made the situation critical (1.07). Social and national integration is a major problem, which will have to be tackled on several fronts including education...introducing a Common School System of public education, making social and national service an integral part of education at all levels, developing all modern Indian languages...promoting national consciousness (1.35).
- *We need to strengthen democracy and make it permanently viable by deepening its foundations* by the creation of an educated electorate, a dedicated and competent leadership and the cultivation of essential values like self-control, tolerance, mutual goodwill and consideration for others and make democracy a way of life (1.08).
- *The most distinctive feature of a modern society is its adoption of a science-based technology. We need to adopt science as a basic component of our education and culture.* The one great lesson of the present age of science is that, with determination and willingness to put in hard work, prosperity is within the reach of any nation which has a stable and progressive government (1.83). Science also strengthens the commitment of man to free enquiry and to the quest

for truth...loosens the bond of dogmatism and acts as a powerful dispeller of fear and superstition, fatalism and passive resignation (1.24).

- *India cannot forever remain as a receiver of knowledge;* she must make her own contribution as an intellectual and cultural equal to the eternal human endeavor to extend the frontiers of knowledge (1.10).
- *India's contribution can and should be far more than material gains. India is heir to an ancient and great civilization, which can make a contribution to human progress by striving to create the 'age of science and spirituality'.* In the developments that we envisage in the future, we hope that the pursuit of mere material affluence and power would be subordinated to that of higher values and the fulfillment of the individual (1.24). We can harness science to support rather than weaken our basic commitment to cultural and spiritual values (1.84). India has made many glorious contributions to world culture; the grandest of all is the concept and ideal of non-violence and compassion... (1.86). A new pride and a deeper faith expressed in living for the noble ideals of peace and freedom, truth and compassion are now needed (1.83). It should be our goal to re-interpret and raise to a new level of understanding the insight gained by the ancient seers as regards the fundamental problems of life (1.84).
- *We believe that India should strive to bring science and the values of the spirit together and in harmony and thereby pave the way for the eventual emergence of a society which would cater to the needs of the whole man and not only to a particular fragment of his personality* (1.80). If science and ahimsa join together in creative synthesis of belief and action, mankind will attain a new level of purposefulness, prosperity and spiritual insight (1.87).

In sum, the EC sees the future society as 'democratic', 'egalitarian', 'secular' and 'modern' and in accordance with the values of the Indian Constitution, its development fuelled by the beneficial forces of science and technology and regulated by the spiritual and humanistic values upheld in the Indian tradition.

## Critique

The EC vision of the future society and concept of education as an instrument of realizing it are inspired by a kind of idealism that claims to combine the best from Indian philosophical tradition and modern science. The basic values of democracy, equality, secularism and social justice form the connecting thread for all its recommendations. In broad outlines, the EC utopia is inspired by the values associated with the freedom movement, the consensus that had been built up on the national system of education and the fundamental values of the Indian Constitution. The Commission's thinking also represents a reiteration of the basic principles of national scheme of education proposed by Mahatma Gandhi—relating education to life, needs and aspirations of the people, work as an integral aspect of education, moral and spiritual values, national integration, neighbourhood school, rural social service and extension work and school's intimate relationship with community. Where it differed from the Gandhian dream is in its finding the future salvation of the country in large scale adoption of a science and technology-based development model (albeit, with the condition that not science alone, but a creative synthesis of science and spiritual heritage should guide our future).

The EC vision is shaped by its concern and anguish about the existing state of affairs in the economic, social and political spheres and its zeal for national reconstruction through education. It is a grand vision as visions go but it is a vision built more on noble intents, fervent hopes and reminiscences of the past and less on rigorous analysis of facts, trends and realistic evaluations and projections. Despite succeeding two earlier Commissions, UEC (University Education Commission, 1950) and SEC (Secondary Education Commission, 1953), it continues to feed on criticism of the 'strangle hold of the colonial past'. The EC cannot be faulted on this score, for the 'blame game' continued over the years and the 'colonial ghost' has not left us completely.

The EC vision statements are hortatory, emotive and inspirational in tone and fired with nationalistic fervour, as they should be, but they also need to be strong in substance and content. Some of the statements are, as Naik himself points out, plain naïve like: "prosperity is within the reach of every nation which has determination, willingness to work hard and a stable and progressive government" (1.83). "There is no doubt that in the years to come India's trade and commerce will grow, there will be more food for all; more education, better health and reasonable standard of living will be available" (1.83). These ideals constitute a mere wish, which has little meaning without explanation of *why* India has remained poor and *how* poverty is to be eliminated. The Commission had no suggestions to offer on how to deal with what Naik (pp. 172-9) called as the three worst evils of the society—elitism, hierarchical organization and poverty. A kind of helplessness also characterizes EC's situation analysis, like its reference to the federal structure, multi-party government as 'difficulties' to be overcome (1.11).

Naik rightly criticizes the Commission for its inadequate treatment of 'development', its central concern. It identifies development only with increase in productivity, social and national integration, modernization and cultivation of moral, social and spiritual values. It does not even refer to many crucial aspects of development like: skewed structure of property ownership, inegalitarian wage structure, social and cultural determinants of poverty, social, economic and political inequalities, exploitation, unemployment, concentration of economic, political and knowledge power in the hands of a minority of haves and marginalization of the vast masses (Naik, p. 56).

Even as it extolled the primacy of science and technology in the scheme of things, the EC failed to acknowledge the more important social, economic and political transformation needed to create the new society. The distinguishing feature of the modern society, it said, is its adoption of science and technology in industry and in its way of life. The EC expressed its "deep conviction that the progress, welfare and security of the nation depend critically on a rapid, planned and sustained growth in the quality and extent of education and research in science and technology"(16.01). But the Commission did not address "the problem of social, economic and political processes and structures which would place man in an appropriate relationship with society and other individuals" apart from development of science and technology. This, as rightly observed by Naik, (pp. 10-11) remained a major weakness of the EC's theoretical formulation of the problem.

## Egalitarianism

What is particularly appealing is the egalitarian perspective with which the Commission looks at the problems of education and society. It may be worthwhile here to look into its understanding of egalitarianism vis-à-vis its diagnosis of the social situation and the manner in which it proposed to deal with the problem. For the EC egalitarianism, in the context of poverty and unemployment, low level of national income and its unsatisfactory rate of growth and uneven distribution, meant more equitable distribution of income so that the more deprived sections could have a larger share (1.06). In a traditional society where work is associated with 'uneducated' lower classes and education is the privilege of upper classes, (1.27) it means the abolition of privilege through integration of work with education. In the context of a fragmented schooling system, it means bringing all able children under a Common School System (1.37) and making the 'haves' realize that their self interest lies in identifying themselves with the masses, by sharing the life and experiences of the poor. It means overcoming the deplorable gulf between the educated and uneducated, intelligentsia and the masses. It implies that the intelligentsia should try to become a real service group striving to uplift the masses and resist the temptation to become a parasitical group living for itself and perpetuating its own privileged position (1.37). It means community living in school and college and making self-help and manual work a part of the daily life and training in all types of educational institutions (1.45) and participation in programmes of community development (1.46).

Notwithstanding these highly appropriate indicators and explanations, one gets the feeling that the Commission's treatment of egalitarianism remained inadequate. First, the concept is not analyzed or explained in depth. Its exclusive chapter, *Towards Equalization of Educational Opportunity,* dealt mainly with widening access to education and not with the more basic philosophical and sociological aspects of the problem.[2] Secondly, even the wider social and economic aspects of the problem were not taken into account. As Naik (p. 56) points out, the Commission failed to highlight the 'basic problems' that hindered the egalitarian cause like the inegalitarian international economic order, extremely skewed structure of poverty ownership, inegalitarian social and cultural determinants of poverty, concentration of power in the hands of a minority of haves. Also, its educational recommendations lacked the cutting edge to combat poverty and its afflictions; it did not suggest any pro-active curricular or teaching strategies to enable education to function as a genuine instrument of empowerment. In comparison, the National Curriculum Framework (NCF) 2005, at least talks of 'critical pedagogy'. Although the Commission said that only 'the right type of education' can lead to national development,(1.16) it shied away from declaring conscious and explicit pursuit of empowerment of the poor as the overt objective of basic education. This is disappointing considering that the EC made equality and eradication of poverty its central theme and asserted its unflinching belief in the power of education to transform society.

## Democracy

The Commission, without any explanation, dismisses caste as an undemocratic institution. It considers strengthening democracy as a political challenge. It also talks of India's faith in 'democratic socialism'(1.11) and the complexity of the situation—federal constitution, multi-party system of democratic government and mixed economy (1.11). It holds that the existing position where good education is available to a small minority, who can pay and not to all eligible children is undemocratic (1.37). It says that in a democracy the individual is the end but hastens to add that individual fulfillment will come not through selfish, narrow loyalties but through dedication to wider loyalties of national development (1.14). It identifies the democratic values as scientific temper, tolerance, and respect for the culture of other national groups (1.68). It says that it is precisely in a situation of diversities that democracy can make its most significant contribution and education should consolidate democracy as a form of government and help the country to adopt it as a way of life (1.20).

The EC did not, however, address the inherent contradictions in the philosophy of democracy, in particular between freedom and equality. While it rightly held that discriminatory schooling is undemocratic it had no suggestions on how to deal with the situation where private schooling and freedom of parents to seek the kind of education they want for their children are defended in the name of democracy. EC's democracy is primarily concerned with the poor and meeting their "explosion of expectations" (1.08). Its egalitarianism is thoroughgoing in its preferring equality as the final arbiter and emphasizing the social good over individual achievement, recommending inclusive schooling, criticism of elitism and privilege and emphasis on social duties. But just why the equality claims are overriding in a conflict situation involving other democratic freedoms needs to be argued and justified.

## Secularism, Culture and Spirituality

The EC mentions 'secularism', 'cultural tradition' and 'spirituality' at several places and especially in connection with its discussion of social, moral and spiritual values (1.78, 1.80). Secularism, according to EC, means that "in political, economic and social matters all citizens irrespective of their religious faith will enjoy equality of rights, no religious community will be favoured or discriminated against and instruction in religious dogmas will not be provided in State schools" (1.78). It is not an irreligious or anti-religious policy; it gives to every citizen the fullest freedom of religious beliefs and worship and there is no contradiction between science and spirituality. There is a sense in which the walls between the secular and the spiritual are tending to break down and what is secular is seen to have spiritual roots (1.80). A vitalized study of science with its emphasis on open-mindedness, tolerance, and objectivity would inevitably lead to the development of a more secular outlook (1.80). 'Secularism' continues to remain a contentious topic with the right and left wing intellectuals (Imtiaz Ahmad, 1969, Pratibha Dixit, 1969) offering varying interpretations of what constitutes pseudo and genuine secularism. The EC has only repeated the all too familiar rhetoric on the theme without entering into any controversy.

About culture and spirituality, the EC refers to: our being 'heir to a great culture', (1.73) insight gained by the ancient seers, (1.84) glorious contributions to world culture...non-violence, compassion, (1.86) great tradition of duty without self-involvement, 'unacquisitive' temperament, tolerance and innate love of peace and reverence for all life, freedom and truth, (1.83) and creation of the 'age of science and spirituality', (1.11) "value of national culture and traditions and a pride in India's past achievements", (1.63) and "understanding and reevaluation of our cultural heritage" to deepen national consciousness (1.66). It concludes by making a fervent plea to combine the best from Western materialism and Indian spiritualism and realize the synthesis of *ahimsa* and atom—EC's metaphors for the spiritual and material (1.87). The Commission's concern is that the new society is to be built on the firm foundations of what is indigenous and ours by inheritance; the Indian tradition has always emphasized self-knowledge in the context of the need to control the destructive forces of science and technology and humane use of knowledge.

The EC observations on our spiritual and cultural heritage (which echo the views of the UEC) are a reiteration of the beliefs and value articulations of nationalist, Indian thinkers of the freedom movement—Gandhi, Tagore, Vivekananda and others. The concern of these thinkers was to restore the faith of the people in their cultural heritage and develop a sense of national pride and patriotism at a time when the imperialist rulers had questioned its very validity against the 'superior' values of European culture. Their presumption—from Ram Mohan Roy to Radhakrishnan—was that any reorientation of Indian thought which attempts a break with religion cannot go very far (Naravane, 1964, p. 16). At the same time, they realized that the needs of modernization demanded a breakaway from the dreg of tradition—superstition, ritualism, restrictive beliefs and practices. Accordingly, they sought to reinterpret Indian thought and tradition in a manner that would be supportive of modern values emphasizing a spacious, tolerant and all-embracing religious spirit. They pointed out that Indian culture springs from multiple and divergent sources and emphases and that we need to take an evolutionary and dynamic view of Indianness and not tie it down to any rigid model.

Commendable as the EC's reference to the lasting, universal values of our cultural heritage may be, it has raised more questions than it has answered. A basic question relates to the definition of *Indian* culture. It is argued that India has many cultures which have existed side by side and Indianness is a characteristic of all of them and the view that Hinduism constitutes the singular strand of the mainstream of Indian life is criticized (Imtiaz Ahmad, 1970). The EC did not probe further into the issue of 'cultural heritage'. It did not even consider it a problematic one and took it as an uncontested 'given'. This was one of its inadequacies. For, this issue (of defining Indian culture in a manner that finds general acceptance) was to later figure as a major factor in the acceptance or rejection of important recommendations. It also became a contentious issue during later years with opinions divided on what constitutes 'national culture'. Regretting this lapse, Naik (p. 56) said: "We must study Indian tradition in depth, de-link its concepts from religion and integrate it with the educational system. This is an area of darkness which calls for the labour of some of our best intellectuals for years to come."

## Modernization

The EC's account of modernization is essentially normative. In its articulation of 'modernization' (1.69) the Commission identifies different features of a modern society: explosion of knowledge, rapid social change, need for rapid advance and educational progress. The most distinctive feature of a modern society, says the EC, is its adoption of a science-based technology and adapting to attendant social and cultural changes. It says that modernization aims at creating an economy of plenty which will offer to every individual a larger way of life and a wider variety of choices (1.74). In the same breath, it cites *anasakti* (duty without self-involvement) and *aparigraha* (unacquisitive temperament) as precious assets of our cultural heritage. The Commission rightly warns that modernization does not mean refusal to inculcate necessary moral and spiritual values and self-discipline (1.74). Essentially, the modern society to the EC is a society driven by science and technology in its material and cultural aspects, with the rider that it must be harnessed by moral and spiritual values. It does not discuss at length the adaptive demands of a modern society. The EC's characterization of modern society in this fashion appears smug. However, Naik set the record straight by differentiating modernization from westernization and criticizing its identification with knowledge of English and higher education. A modernized person, he said, is one "who retains the best of his own culture and combines it with the best he adopts from others and has a secular, rational and scientific temper and commitment to the constitutional values" (p. 184). The modernizing process should be an integral part of all education including elementary and adult education (p. 185).

## The EC Vision in Later Years

The EC vision of the future society, its value presuppositions and trust in education as an instrument of its realization continued to inspire educational thinking during the post-EC period. Successive committees and commissions on education continued to refer to the more or less same concerns of educational and national development. The *NCT-I* (1983, p. 6) referred to divisive forces arising from linguistic division of the country, the reality of caste, violence sparked by religions, mixing of politics with religion, vast social and economic disparities, abject poverty and deprivation, hunger and malnutrition. It identified four national goals as having critical urgency for the well-being of our people: A United Secular India, A Modern India, A Productive People and A Humane and Caring Society. "There is today a clamour across the nation that the existing education system must be replaced by a better one" (p. 11). A review of the educational situation *Challenge of Education—A Policy Perspective* (1985, p. 13) stated that many of the changes required were anticipated by the EC and that "the problems of today are more the result of tardy and haphazard implementation and decline in the allocation of resources". The *NPE-1986* and its subsequent reviews reiterated the EC vision and its basic position with regard to national development and educational reconstruction. The *NPE* reaffirmed the EC outlines of the national system of education—basic education for all, Common School System, common structure, common core curriculum based on history of freedom movement, constitutional obligations, national identity, common cultural heritage, equality, democracy, secularism, gender justice, protection of environment, removal of social barriers, small family norm and scientific temper (pp. 5-9).

## Summing Up

The EC vision claims to combine the best from Indian philosophical tradition, modern science and the fundamental values of the Indian Constitution. It is shaped by the Commission's concern and anguish over the existing state of affairs in the economic, social and political spheres and zeal for national reconstruction through education. It is a grand vision as visions go but it is a vision built more on noble intents, exhortations, fervent hopes and desires and reminiscences of the past and less on rigorous analysis of facts, trends and realistic evaluations and projections based on critical analysis. While it is strong on identification of societal problems it had no suggestions to offer on how to deal with them. Even as it extolled the primacy of science and technology in the scheme of things, it failed to address the more important problem of social, economic and political transformation needed to create the new society. Despite its sincere proclamation of egalitarianism, its treatment of egalitarianism was far from adequate: the concept was not explained in depth, the wider social and economic aspects of the problem were not taken into account and no pro-active recommendations made to enable education to function as a genuine instrument of empowerment. It did not address the inherent contradictions in democracy, in particular between freedom and equality and just why the equality claims are overriding in a conflict situation involving other democratic freedoms. The Commission described the modern society as a society driven by science and technology in its material and cultural aspects. At the same time, it rightly warned that modernization does not mean refusal to inculcate necessary moral and spiritual values and self-discipline. The EC observations on spiritual and cultural heritage are a reiteration of the concern of nationalist thinkers of the freedom movement to restore the faith of the people in their cultural heritage and develop a sense of national pride and patriotism. The EC seeks to reinterpret Indian thought and tradition in a manner that would be supportive of modern values emphasizing a spacious, tolerant and all-embracing religious spirit. However, it did not clarify 'cultural heritage' vis a vis plurality of Indian culture.

## PART II: EDUCATION

In addressing its mandate, the EC was guided by the basic concepts of national education as it had come to be understood at the time India became free. These were: education should be based on our own traditions and suited to the life, needs and aspirations of the people, removal of illiteracy and basic education for all, integration of productive work with education, primacy for regional languages, modernization of the society and removal of poverty through science and technology, patriotism and pride in our culture and provision for moral and aesthetic education (Naik, pp. 2-4). The Commission looked upon education as the chief instrument for realizing the future society as envisioned by it—a democratic, modern, secular, egalitarian society driven by science and technology in harmony with cultural and spiritual heritage. Of particular philosophical interest in EC's perspectives on education are concept and aims of education, concepts of development and change and perception of education as an instrument of change.

## Concept and Aims of Education

Despite the prevailing skepticism, it should not be overlooked that educational aims serve important normative functions—they give direction to the educative process, motivate action on them and provide criteria for evaluating the educative process. More than anything else, they belong to that category of human thinking which we cannot do away with even if we want to—they represent the values we believe in and our vision of the true, good and beautiful. Substantive educational assertions on curriculum, methods or any other aspect, by logical necessity, involve educational aims. They may be explicitly stated or lie concealed. Rather than pretend that we could carry on without them, it is better if we lay bare our educational intentions and desires—aims, in other words. This is especially necessary at a time when schooling per se is *equated* with education (Seshadri, 2002).

It is a pity that the EC does not dwell on what education is as a concept and how it perceives the aims of education. Without any theoretical preliminaries it straightaway moves on to a discussion of education in relation to objectives of national development—self-sufficiency in food, economic growth and full employment, social and national integration and political development. National development objectives can be achieved, says the Commission, if education is related to productivity, if it strengthens social and national integration, consolidates democracy, hastens the process of modernization and builds character by cultivating social, moral and spiritual values. Education helps in the achievement of these objectives by contributing to the development of physical resources and also of human resources. It not only imparts knowledge and skills to develop human beings as productive citizens but changes the values and attitudes of the people as a whole and functions as the main instrument of change.

It can be seen that the EC's emphasis is on the *social purposes* of education and on the need to use it as a tool for realization of national aspirations. This does not, it says, imply any under-estimation of values for the individual. In a democracy, the individual is an end and the primary purpose of education is to provide him with the widest opportunity to develop his potentialities to the full. But the path to this goal lies through social reorganization and emphasis on social perspectives. In the desired socialistic pattern of society, it must be realized that individual fulfillment will come, not through selfish or narrow loyalties to personal or group interests, but through dedication of all to the wider loyalties of national development in all its parameters (1.15). The *Draft National Policy on Education, 1979* articulated the EC educational aims as: fullest development of the individual, social and human values, strong character, national unity, pride in our cultural heritage, faith in the country's future, scientific and moral values, knowledge, freedom, equality, social justice, democracy, socialism, and secularism.

In its zealous description of the social purposes of education and education-development linkage, the EC overlooks the status of education in its intrinsic goodness. When the Commission says that all education is not necessarily good, it is using 'education' in an uncommon way *for education by definition is something that we desire as worthwhile and good for all.* To be educated is a good state to be in, not in the instrumental sense, not for its extraneous benefits but simply for the reason that education is something that is good in itself. The case for Universal Elementary Education (UEE) rests as much on the intrinsic value of education as on its social and economic returns. From this angle, the EC's account of education is theoretically weak.

## Education and National Development

The Commission laid the highest emphasis on relating education to development even to the extent of naming the report as *Education and National Development.* The problems of national development, it said, have to be addressed through development of physical resources and development of human resources through a properly organized programme of education. The latter is more crucial of the two; the former is a means to an end, development of human resources is an end in itself; without it even the development of physical resources is not possible. The Commission gave detailed recommendations on how education has to be reorganized to address these two interdependent aspects of development.

The EC's account of development missed out on many of its crucial aspects. It identified self-sufficiency in food, economic growth and full employment, social and national integration and political development as problems of national development. It did not, as Naik points out, even refer to: skewed structure of property ownership, inegalitarian wage structure, social and cultural determinants of poverty, social, economic and political inequalities, exploitation, unemployment, concentration of economic, political and knowledge power in the hands of a minority of haves and marginalization of the vast masses. It also had no suggestions on specific programmes of development to deal with the problems identified by it. Its recommendation on work experience fell far short of the Gandhian conception of manual work as a pedagogic medium of education, as an essential and universal element of the curriculum (Anil Sadgopal, 2005). It eroded the very spirit of basic education (Salamathulla, 2004, p. 161). Although, the EC referred to "human change on a grand scale" in its reference to the human aspects of development, it essentially stuck to restrictive concepts of "human resource", "human capital", "investment in human resources" and "economic returns" in keeping with the economic paradigm of the times. It fell short of adopting the broader perspective of development that goes beyond income and economic returns to embrace wider aspects of quality of life, and expansion of human freedoms and choices; not to mention ethical development which modern day economists hold as indispensable for further progress in other fields in the context of developments in nuclear research, Information Technology (IT) and Bio Technology (BT) (Jean Dreze, 2002).

## Higher Education and Development

Despite its stand that education must be deliberately organized towards national development, the EC's articulation of the objectives of higher education do not reflect any pro-active actions and strategies to make it development-oriented (save its recommendation of compulsory one month rural service for all university graduates). The EC makes a distinction between "fundamental values", which do not change and "functions" of universities which change from time to time. The EC says the principal objects of universities are: to deepen man's understanding of the universe and of himself—in body, mind and spirit and to disseminate this understanding throughout society and to apply it in the service of mankind. Universities can fill this role only if they owe uncompromising loyalty to certain fundamental values of life...pursuit of truth and excellence in all its diversity, courage and fearlessness (11.01). It mentions the special responsibilities in the present state of our social and educational development as: serve as the conscience of the nation as assessors of the national way of life, (11.04) adult education and extension service (11.06) and qualitative improvement of schools (11.07). Avoiding the extremes—higher education as a crusader for development and higher education as an ivory tower—the EC plays safe when it says: do not be a community service station nor an ivory tower but a balance between commitment and detachment (11.05). The "special responsibilities" it mentions are more in the nature of general guidelines and not as focused programmes of action.

The problem of linking higher education to development has recurred time and again and the debate has been marked by differing views and contesting claims on the concept and concerns of higher education and its potential to effect changes. The Review Committee (1990) criticized the NPE

(1986) characterization of higher education as a social critic and disseminator of specialized knowledge and skills as too mild a way of stating the role of higher education in a context of increasing poverty, illiteracy, inequality, and failure of basic education and other challenges of development. More than a reflection, it said, action on the part of those receiving it is important, especially on such issues as regional development and school education including UEE. It suggested that the curriculum and the entire education process should be dynamically and integrally linked to such issues. Sadly, this perception has not been shared in subsequent policy statements, notably the CABE Committee, which said that priority should be on restoring intellectual vigour, seriousness of purpose and discipline to make higher education work. Even a perfectly reasonable proposal like compulsory social and national service for college going youth was thrown overboard. It is clear, as Naik had feared, that there are powerful forces at work against higher education becoming development oriented. Although extension is touted as "the fourth dimension" of higher education, going by the track record of NSS in colleges and universities, higher education has treated its developmental obligations with benign neglect.

## Education and Social Change

The EC perceives changes of different kinds and at different levels. It talks of social, economic and political change related to national aspirations, programmes and problems of national development. It refers to Heilbroner's condition of "human change on a grand scale" for the success of a traditional society's journey to economic development involving "a wholesale metamorphosis of habits, a wrenching reorientation of values concerning time, status, money, work and an unweaving and reweaving of the fabric of daily existence itself". The EC says these observations are applicable to advances on the social, political and cultural fronts as well.

The "educational revolution" that the Commission talks about refers to changes in objectives, content, teaching methods, programmes, size and composition of the student body, teacher selection and preparation, and organization. It refers to internal transformation to relate education to life, needs and aspirations of the nation involving changes in knowledge, skills, interests and values of the people as a whole. It also refers to changes in quality and availability of education—qualitative improvement to achieve internationally comparable standards and expansion of educational facilities on the basis of manpower needs and equality of educational opportunity.

What stands out prominently in the Commission's discussion of change is its abiding faith in the power of education to effect changes and transform society. After issuing a disclaimer that its recommendations are not necessarily the best or valid, the Commission hastened to add: "*There is, of course, one thing about which we feel no doubt or hesitation: education, science-based and in coherence with Indian culture and values, can alone provide the foundation—as also the instrument—for the nation's progress, security and welfare"* (Foreword). The Commission declared that if the "human change on a grand scale" is to be achieved there is one instrument and one instrument only that can be used, EDUCATION (1.14).

The Commission, however, qualified its assertion by taking the position that education must be *deliberately* organized towards national development. It said, the belief that *all* education is necessarily good, both for the individual and the society and necessarily leads to progress is naïve; it can be harmful as it is misplaced. There is a conceptual issue here which we have referred to previously (p. 10). Quantitatively, it can be organized to promote or retard social justice and equality of educational opportunity. Qualitatively, it can produce competent professional manpower or indifferently educated graduates. Only the right type of education can lead to national development, otherwise the results will be just the opposite (1.16).

## Critique

Notwithstanding these qualifications, the Commission's unflinching belief in the power of education to act as the lever of social change was rightly criticized as too optimistic. Gunnar Myrdal (1970, p. 206) observed that the EC's belief in "a revolution in education" setting in motion the much desired social, economic and cultural revolution is quite correct but "the initial lack of the social...revolution itself presents a tremendous inhibition for giving impetus to the revolution in education". Naik rightly points out that the areas of change identified by the Commission derive more from the political, economic and sociological analysis of the situation and only incidentally from analysis of the educational situation; in any case education was considered as the victim rather than the cause. Yet, the Commission pinned its hope on an educational revolution to usher in the larger social revolution. Despite its die hard posturing, the Commission finds itself caught on the horns of a dilemma; on the one hand it agrees that it may not be possible to make much headway in education unless the basic problems of life are squarely tackled, on the other hand it advocates breaking the vicious circle by beginning with educational reconstruction in a big way (Naik, p. 12).

The question of whether education or society is the prime mover of change was one of the most debated questions in the sixties and seventies (Gore, 1970). Emphatic assertion alone will not make a proposition true; the Commission should have addressed the question of how the dialectical process of education operates between preservation of the status quo and social transformation. The EC not only upheld the primacy of educational change, but also believed that the national system of education visualized by it could be created even within the existing political, social and economic structure "if students, teachers and educational administrators provided the needed academic leadership". As Naik admitted, this was a naïve belief and "was not theoretically correct"; it ignores the basic fact that the existing power structure "will do its damnedest to see that no radical reconstruction of education contrary to its interests takes place" (p. 57). Naik was forced to conclude that "All things considered, I believe that we must now abandon the role of primacy in social transformation...it is a hangover of the pre-independence struggle for national education and has outlived its utility" (p. 57). He added that a programme for radical reconstruction of education to succeed must take the form of a national movement accompanied by a simultaneous movement for corresponding socio-economic-political reform (p. 196).

Later educational thinking was more circumspect about the role of education as a change agent. *The Curriculum For The Ten-Year School* observed pessimistically: "It is not easy to bring about a change in the existing system to meet the requirements of national development" implied by the EC recommendations...the task is made difficult—growing number of children, rigid postures and orthodox attitudes act against new ways of teaching and learning. The *NCT-II* said (p. 6) that it would be futile to expect education alone to accomplish this nation-building task. Education can become a major force if it is asked to support the political determination of our leaders to pursue this goal single-mindedly. The National Advisory Committee on the school bag load (1993) had to admit that "the roots of the curriculum load problem, relate to our perception of knowledge and the competition-based social ethos and the phenomenon cannot be altered without altering a lot of things in our social set-up...the problems of school load need wider discussions because they are centrally connected with images of our civilization and self-esteem."

## Summing Up

To conclude, the EC sees education as the lever to effect the needed changes in the society to realize its utopia. Accordingly, it calls for an internal revolution in education. This conception of education as a prime mover of change, however, rests more on pious hope than on critical understanding of the dialectic of education. The Commission understands its dilemma but still chooses to pin its faith in education. At the same time, it fights shy of suggesting radical steps to link education with development.

## PART III: VALUES

The EC recommended introduction of moral, social and spiritual education guided by two considerations—character development through inculcation of social, moral and spiritual values as an essential feature of national education and the logic of modernization, which creates an economy of plenty and provides freedom to people to choose from a wider variety of choices.

## The EC Proposal

The EC endorsed the earlier recommendations of the UEC and Committee on Religious and Moral Instruction (CRMI) on the subject and regretted that they did not evoke enthusiastic response. At the school level it recommended education in social, moral and spiritual values which includes indirect methods, direct teaching in periods set apart for it (8.96) as well as stories from religion and accounts of religious leaders (8.97). For higher education it approved the suggestions of UEC and CRMI and recommended education about religions and silent meditation (1.76).

The EC's case for "education about religions" is that a tolerant study of all religions helps citizens to understand each other better and live amicably together; it also overcomes the widespread general ignorance and misunderstanding in religious matters (1.79). Further, it makes use of the "natural points of contact between moral values and the teachings of great religions" (8.97). Lest it be misunderstood, the Commission explains that education *about* religion should not be the same as religious education which may conflict with secularist principles. It also points out that secularism is not an irreligious or anti-religious policy. It even suggests the modus operandi for the implementation of the recommendation both at the school and higher education stages, actions to be taken by central and state governments and private institutions—time table provision, teaching to be done by teachers drawn from different communities and provision of resource support by university departments of comparative religion.

As regards the sources of values, EC suggests that we should draw freely from our own traditions—there are strands within Indian thought itself which can lead to the new outlook: willing acceptance of life with all its joys and sorrows, inspiration for social service, faith in future—as well as from the liberalizing forces of the West: dignity of the individual, equality, social justice. The EC also draws attention to the regular curriculum itself—the general subjects, co-curricular activities, work experience—as a powerful reservoir of values and wants the teacher to ensure that his/her teaching should bring out the fundamental values such as integrity and social responsibility. Science, it says, promotes open mindedness, tolerance, objectivity and will lead to a secular outlook. At the same time, it also wisely warns against using the curriculum *overtly* as an instrument of value education. Its point is to draw attention of the teacher to values that are constitutive of the discipline and to the fact that good teaching of a subject involves making explicit the inherent values. It also stresses the importance of the school atmosphere and personality of the teacher in developing values.

## Critique

***Nomenclature:*** The EC's reference to "social, moral and spiritual education" (and not just "moral education") is in keeping with the tradition; the EC's predecessors (UEC, 1950, SEC, 1953, CRMI, 1959 and CEI, 1962) did the same. The combining of the moral and spiritual is a characteristic feature of Indian thinking on moral education. It derives from a socio-philosophic tradition with roots in the deep past. Indian thought considers a purely humanistic or moral approach to life as inadequate and incomplete unless that humanism is set against the ultimate backdrop of religion (Radhakrishnan, 1959). The EC has only followed the tradition.

***Merits of the Proposal:*** The EC treatment of values has several merits: its rationale derives from a clearly articulated vision of the good society embedded in the fundamental values of the Constitution. Its approach is not xenophobic; it acknowledges sources of values from indigenous as well as Western. It is rightly critical about the absence of egalitarian values in the Hindu tradition and calls for reinterpretation and re-evaluation of traditional culture. It integrates teaching of values with the total curriculum, productive work and community living. Its value prescriptions are generally in tune with the modern outlook espoused by it. Its practical recommendations on pedagogy—use of indirect methods, emphasis on school atmosphere, pupil-teacher relationship, and teaching by general (and not specialist) teachers—are also sound. Its advice that every teacher whatever be his/her subject must necessarily accept the responsibility of moral development of students is well taken.

***Weaknesses:*** Notwithstanding these positive aspects, the Commission's theoretical formulation of the proposal suffers from some inadequacies. First, the Commission does not provide a strong rationale for the intervention other than stating that modernization demands it and that it is an element of the national system of education. It does not address the basic questions related to philosophical, sociological and psychological aspects of value learning and teaching. It makes no mention of the social context of the Indian school and the social reality under which it has to function. It takes too optimistic a view of education, glosses over its social context and cultural heterogeneity and leaves the objectives and scope of direct teaching of values unspecified. It accepts without analysis that certain curricular and pedagogical interventions in an enabling school atmosphere naturally lead to character development. It does not, for example, address the question of the point, purpose and scope of value education—the Commission talks of 'inculcation'—in organized public education. It does not address the question of what it means to 'value educate'; it should have emphasized that value education is a process of inducing learning, by putting learners in situations that make them think, reason, question, reflect, care, feel concern and act. It should have warned against didactic approaches to value learning. It does not probe into the processes of teaching and learning and suggest any new insights. The EC's glossing over of these features left the field free for the value education movement in succeeding years becoming muddled on several counts.

***School Subjects as Vehicles of Value Communication:*** The EC suggests that regular subjects of the curriculum are repositories of values and they should be taught with a conscious and explicit emphasis on their value dimensions: "He must ensure that in the teaching of his particular subject ...fundamental values such as integrity and social responsibility are brought out". Although the suggestion has many attractions, its underlying epistemological assumptions need to be looked into carefully. There are two aspects to be considered here. First, treating the disciplines as deliberate instruments of value education may in all likelihood distort their true nature. One cannot also make an absolute distinction between the academic content of a discipline and the inherent values. The truth is that in any process of genuine acquisition of knowledge both knowledge and value get intermingled. Learning a discipline the right way not only involves acquiring its knowledge content but also acquisition of skills and habits of mind and values characteristic of that discipline (Seshadri, 1988). The EC has done well to caution that "the teacher need not, we can even say that he should not, try to draw out the underlying moral all the time" (8.95).

***Romanticization of Science:*** The second aspect relates to EC's glorification of science as a fountainhead of values—open-mindedness, tolerance, objectivity, (1.80) commitment to free enquiry and quest for truth...loosens the bond of dogmatism and acts as a powerful dispeller of fear and superstition, fatalism and passive resignation (p. 1.24). Such romanticization of science "as a continuous story of unremitting courage, effort and achievement in the struggle against ignorance" (Hirst, 1974) and its virtual identification with rationality almost borders on scientism. As Hirst has asked, can science by itself provide a full moral justification for human actions? Where, in science, is respect for man as man? The point is that one needs to take a more balanced view of what science is in its material and cultural aspects and what its possibilities and potential are.

***The Moral and the Religious:*** EC's linking of moral education with religious education, again, is not free from contention. Pragmatic reasons apart, which the EC is well aware of as evidenced from its guarded approach to its implementation, the important issue here is one that relates to the autonomy of morals. Ethics, it is pointed out, is an autonomous form of knowledge and ethical values do not depend upon religion for their validity, although there may be points of intersection between the two. They are two distinct and separate realms of discourse. A moral act is essentially a rational act and a moral person is a rationally autonomous individual. Moral education does not derive its justification from religion. In other words, it is not logically necessary that a virtuous person should be a religious person interpreting 'religious' in a strictly technical sense (Seshadri, 1981). The EC does not dispute this; it only wants that the fundamental similarities among the religions and the emphasis they place on cultivation of broadly comparable moral and spiritual values be transmitted through education (1.79). It is difficult, however, to share EC's optimism that a study of religions would in fact realize the stated objectives. It may be interesting to note here that the later documents on educational policy, especially the NPE and the NCFs, carefully played down the EC recommendation in this regard. The EC has also been criticized for "glossing over the difference between religion and spiritualism, secularism and moral education" being "befogged by idealistic jargon and realistic suggestions mixed up with impracticable recommendations" (R.K. Yadav, 1983).

***The Issue of Cultural Heritage:*** Although the EC recommended a blend of the best in our culture and from Western science, it did not attempt to unpack 'our cultural heritage' other than mentioning that "the understanding and re-evaluation of our cultural heritage would be promoted by well-organized teaching of the languages and literature, philosophy, religions and history of India and by introducing the students to Indian architecture, sculpture, painting, music, dance and drama" (1.66). But the notion turned out to be a problematic one and sparked off a lively debate during later years on the related question of "Indianization" of education and "distinctly Indian values". It is not clear, also, how EC's recommendation of anasakti, aparigraha as "precious assets of our great tradition" (p. 21) go with the values associated with neo-liberal economic thinking in a globalized context.

## The EC Impact

The EC may not have given a fully worked out, satisfactory philosophy and programme of value education but it did succeed in turning national attention on the issue. The intervening four decades saw vigorous debate on the 'crisis of values' facing the Indian society and the need for educational action to deal with it. 'Value Education', a new phrase, became a buzz word and dominated educational discussions during the later years. The debate also focused on specific themes on Indian culture and tradition like uniqueness of Indian values and 'Indianization' of education. Government support came in a big way for value education activities—advocacy, resource materials, and teacher orientation. Practically, every committee that looked into educational reform in the post-EC period accorded primacy to discussion of values. The NPE said that education should foster universal and eternal values oriented towards the unity and integration of people, it should help eliminate obscurantism, religious fanaticism, violence, superstition and fatalism (8.5-8.6). The UGC policy frame on higher education suggested introduction of a Foundation Package as part of restructuring of undergraduate education. The Planning Commission accepted value education as an aspect of development planning and set up a Core Group to study and report on the issue. A Working Group was set up in 1983 by the Government to review teachers' training programme in the light of the need for value orientation of education.

*The Curriculum for the Ten-Year School,* which followed the EC Report did not mention religious education nor did it favour any direct instruction/curricular provision in social and moral values. However, it made provision in the curriculum for arts. Neither the NPE nor the national curriculum framework that accompanied it approved direct moral instruction; they also avoided reference to religious education. As to the values that should be promoted they mentioned: national integration, social justice, rational outlook, democratic values, scientific humanism, character building and human values—compassion, endurance, courage, decision making, resourcefulness, respect for others, team spirit, truthfulness, faithfulness, loyalty to duty and the common good. The NCT mentioned caring values—caring for people, for nature and for environment. It recommended Fundamental Duties mentioned in the Constitution (42nd amendment) as a good frame of reference that found ready acceptance by all sections of people (p. 8). The NCT-II concerned with higher education discussed at length a range of issues related to values of the teaching profession—world-view and values, desired world-view of teachers, categories of values, core socio-political values and core academic values. It presented a normative model, an inventory of the elements of world-view and values desirable and necessary for teachers.

## Appraisal

The hype that surrounded value education during this period is muddled on several counts. The discourse has mostly been emotive in tone and superficial lacking deeper appreciation of what it means to 'value educate'. Various proposals are made to value orient education and compendia of values are presented. Many of the 'solutions' offered are pat and simplistic. They fail to take note of the social, ideological and cultural heterogeneity of the people and the historical context of modern living. Some of the proposals are suspected to carry hidden agendas—ideological and political—and the entire issue has become contentious. The discourse is basically flawed as it overlooks the fact that values are integral to the educational process and treats them as an add-on. It is not appreciated that value teaching is not a sphere of activity that is discontinuous with teacher's regular job of teaching. Any model of value education, if it is not integrated with total content and process of education, only leads to talks and sermons. *More than anything else, value education discussions should be anchored to our vision of the just society and a schooling system that serves as an instrument to realize the vision. This framework is conspicuously missing in extant deliberations.* The merit of the EC proposal consists in its being anchored to its vision of the just society built on the values of democracy, equality, socialism and secularism and an education system that serves as a tool of social and national transformation.

## Equality and Knowledge

Equality and knowledge are two other value themes on which the EC observations are of particular significance, in the light of how they influenced educational discourse and impacted policy thinking in later years.

## The EC Perspective on Equality in Education

'Equality', in a sense, constitutes the *leit motif* of the EC report. So important did the EC consider equality that it devoted an entire chapter, *Towards Equalization of Educational Opportunity,* running to 35 pages for its discussion. The EC championed the cause of equality as the guiding principle, both of educational and social development. Equalizing opportunity, it said, is a social objective of education to enable the backward classes to use education as a lever for improvement of their condition. It accepted equality alongside democracy as a constitutional imperative. It made an impassioned plea for banishment of privilege, elitism and exclusion from education. In its treatment of notions like standards, quality and talent it never forgot to remind the nation that "a good deal of potential talent never enters school" (p. 240). The EC's recommendation of the Common School in a highly fragmented society was a daring one, because the school system reinforced the class and caste divisions of the larger society,. The failure to act on this crucial recommendation that would have spared the nation from a fractured and divisive school system continues to weigh on the national conscience. It has lent added justification to the political movement for reservations for the backward classes in higher learning institutions.

## Critique

Yet, it must be admitted that the Commission's treatment of equality was far from adequate. First, it did not take equality as a problematic issue at all; it simply accepted it as an axiom. Secondly, it concerned itself with equality of *opportunity,* (that is, of access) which is a diluted egalitarian demand. It identified the sources of inequality as lack of access, poverty, differences in educational background, home environment, habitat, gender and caste. It did not address the question why children failed and why those who went to school were none the better for it, what the point and purpose of education was and whether it led to empowerment of the individual. The extension of the equality debate to cover these aspects was to happen in later years. Also, its definition of the Common School System as one "where access to good education will depend not on wealth or class but on talent", is singularly unhelpful. As long as "good education" remains vacuous and left to individual interpretations, justification can always be adduced in favour of differences between schools on the plea that they account for 'quality' or 'good' schools. Further, the EC's suggestion that private schools generally were better schools and provided "good education" is contentious (Seshadri, 1999). On the positive side, the EC's contribution lay in its bold proclamation of egalitarian ideology and in its bringing the issue of equality into the open. The Commission also admitted that although perfect equality of educational opportunity is an unattainable ideal, in a good system of education there should be a continuous attempt to identify factors contributing to inequality and adopt measures to eliminate them (p. 109).

## The Continuing Equality Discourse

***From equality of opportunity to equality of result:*** The EC did not go beyond equating opportunity with access. Dealing with UEE it referred to problems of access, enrolment and retention; there was no reference to quality as such although it pointed to "lack of proper articulation between education and life" as an "educational weakness" (p. 161). The debate it triggered in later years was robust and in its sweep covered a wide range of issues relating to the meaning of educational equality in the context of continued afflictions of inequality—large scale drop-out, failures and ineffectiveness of education in improving the life chances of those who had completed schooling and the basic issue of non-relevance of education for the masses (Seshadri, 1978). Representing an advance in thinking, the NPE in 1986 talked of equality of opportunity "*not only in terms of access but also in conditions of success*". The NCF-86 elaborated the equality principle as "...ensuring equal access to educational facilities and ensuring that *the conditions of learning provide equal chances of success to all*". Even more explicitly, it said that "the design of the curriculum and its transaction will have to focus more on *educational effects or learning outcomes and their equalization* among children". This was a marked advance indeed. From merely making available to all the physical instruments of education, egalitarian thought had moved to zero in on the very substance of education, the curriculum. The new thesis was that educational content is not socially neutral and as such it should be designed and transacted in such a way that it did not act against the interests, especially, of the disadvantaged learners.

The EC, true to its egalitarian commitment, was deeply concerned about our smug and arrogant belief that whatever is being done in the name of education—both its content and process—is something that is good for all, when the reality is that it acted against the larger interests of the disadvantaged and the deprived masses. Referring to the 'intractability' of the problems of poverty and related cultural disadvantages, it was suggested (Shukla, 1975) that the curriculum emphasize those skills, attitudes and values, which the disadvantaged will learn as well as or better than those from the privileged strata. It was even pointed out (Karlekar, 1975) that the problem of higher education of the scheduled castes is essentially one of socialization into the dominant norms of an educational system based on learning by rote and cramming from notebooks.

***The legitimacy of the school curriculum:*** The polemical writings of Illich, Freire and others questioned the time-honoured, beliefs about education, schooling, teaching and learning entertained by mainstream educational thinkers and showed how they acted against the poor and the oppressed everywhere. Concerns like the inegalitarian division of school knowledge as high and low status, the questionable legitimacy of the curriculum and the demand for a level playing field in education were highlighted in the Indian debate in the seventies by several thinkers and notably by Naik himself in his *Equality, Quality and Quantity* and other works.

The legitimacy of the school curriculum became an important concern for sociologists and educationists in the mid sixties and later years. The basic contention of these critics was that all knowledge is socially constructed and education acts as a hegemonic device for those in positions of power. Deriving inspiration from the Marxian dictum, "in each epoch the thoughts of the ruling class are the ruling thoughts", and the egalitarian ideology and phenomenology of Alfred Schultz, they argued that the school curriculum is to be seen as "socially constructed as sets of shared meanings" representative of the dominant power structure of society. Knowing the world is not coming into possession of a set of truths about the world which is out there, but a matter of coming to perceive the world in particular ways, which are largely determined by one's interactions with a particular historical and social context. Reality exists only as a phenomena in our consciousness and not as an 'out there' pre-constituted field of objects awaiting explication. What knowledge shall be transmitted through the curriculum and in what form are decided not on the basis of epistemological theories but on the basis of normative value premises relating to the material conditions of existing social relations. Subject disciplines are not autonomous systems of knowledge but socio-historical constructs of a particular time.

An offshoot of this discussion was the demand for linking school knowledge with community knowledge—life outside the school, local occupation (farming), geography, cultural traditions, local history, community knowledge and technology. The demand was based on giving recognition to the informal knowledge the child possessed as well as on pedagogical reasons.

The NCF-2005 makes this as a major plank for curriculum revision. The principle recommended is for integrating formal knowledge taught in school with the reality of life of the child. It is pointed out that the disconnect between the formal knowledge taught to the child in the school and the informal knowledge experiences that the child undergoes outside—at home, in the community and in the work place and other informal learning situations—alienates the children, especially those coming from disadvantaged backgrounds where the tradition of informal learning is strong and acts against their interests.

***Equality and quality:*** The EC was particular that quality of education be judged with reference to its overall objectives and not in elitist, socially neutral terms. As the NCF-2005 says: Quality in education includes a concern for quality of life in all its dimensions—concern for peace, protection of environment and predisposition towards social change. They are core components of quality, not mere value premises.

The EC's concern for a level playing field for all in education, however, remained only dormant; it was not forcefully articulated. Naik, in his later writings (*Equality, Quality and Quantity*, 1975, *Policy and Performance in Indian Education*, 1975) attributed the narrow interpretation of educational quality and excellence as achievement in linguistic and cognitive areas to the middle class vested interests that had a rich tradition in them. He also held them responsible for the failure of work experience in education.

A disturbing fall out of 'marketization' of basic education is delinking of social relevance of education from discussions on quality. For example, skill development, an otherwise laudable objective of education, is looked upon as training students in vocational skills and preparation of work force for the market. As Sadgopal (2005) has said, while the objective of skill development is integral to education, the holistic purpose of education related to social relevance and pedagogic quality of education cannot be allowed to become subservient to market. Unless checked, this tendency will have an adverse impact on UEE as no child will devote 8 or 10 years of her life in an educational programme that lacks both social relevance and pedagogic quality. Sadgopal has also drawn attention to how the Government's policy of allowing international funding of primary education and giving space to private corporations especially ICT and NGOs in defining quality of education in the name of public-private partnership has begun to impact upon field practice, planning and research.

## The EC Perspectives on Knowledge

In the course of its discussion especially of modernization, educational aims, curriculum and teaching methods, the EC makes references to different aspects of knowledge—explosion of knowledge, the primacy of science, integration of science and spirituality and appropriate pedagogy. The EC account of knowledge covers its different philosophical categories: meaning, structure, forms, paradigms and pedagogy. None of these, however, is addressed directly or in depth. But even its by-the-way references are pregnant with rich insights which fuelled deeper epistemological and sociological exploration into the knowledge theme in later years.

The EC emphasizes scientific and technological knowledge as the main driving force to realize a modernized society. It holds science as the paradigm of knowledge both for its material and cultural contributions. At the same time, it points to the need for harnessing science to support rather than weaken basic commitment to cultural and spiritual values. It refers to 'explosion of knowledge' and says that in a modern society the stock of knowledge is greater and its growth quicker and one of the tasks of education is to keep pace with the advance in knowledge and contribute towards extending the frontiers of knowledge (p. 3). It did not foresee the trivialization of knowledge that was to happen in later years and the havoc it would cause on the entire system of education. But it did warn that knowledge in a modern society is not something that is received passively but actively discovered and this calls for a revolution in traditional education where the assimilative faculties tend to be emphasized to the neglect of the critical and creative ones (p. 18).

## The Continuing Knowledge Discourse

*The fall-out of 'knowledge explosion*: The Commission's reference to "explosion of knowledge" made it a catch phrase in subsequent discussions on the issue and it continued to remain in fashion for decades. Initially, "explosion of knowledge" and "extending frontiers of knowledge" appeared as emotive slogans with little explanation of what they implied by way of curricular and pedagogic actions. An initial outcome of this upsurge was the shift of emphasis from *acquisition* of knowledge to *mastering its tools*. This was, in a way, contained in EC's admonition of the traditional conception of "knowing" as "knowing by heart". Eventually, it was to lead to the articulation of a new philosophy of education centred round the concepts of "learning society", "lifelong learning", "self-learning" and "learning to learn". The challenge before the school systems the world over was how to cope with the ever expanding horizons of knowledge and accommodate it in the curricula. The Commission did not address this question in full detail but it drew attention to the danger of passive absorption of inherited knowledge and the need for change in our perception of teaching and learning. This was stimulus enough to kick start the educational establishment to work out the implications of knowledge explosion to educational objectives, curriculum content, pedagogic approaches, teaching materials and the role of students and teachers.

*The Curriculum for the Ten-Year School,* emphasizing the process of self-learning and discovery observed: Flexibility and dynamism in curriculum is necessary with the rapidly expanding frontiers of knowledge in science and technology and changing socio-economic conditions of our society. The *Challenge of Education* noted: Tomorrow's information rich and technology intensive society, calls for modifying learning processes towards developing capacity to learn, life-long learning and recurrent education. The *NCT 1983-85* observed: In the context of explosion of knowledge teachers, to remain up-to-date, have to be on their toes, learn continuously. The new methodology should emphasize: deep understanding, application of knowledge, teaching to be curious, explorative, critical, innovative, both cognitive and affective domains, multiple sources, methods and tools of learning.

*'Knowledge', 'information' and 'understanding':* The knowledge explosion phenomenon also led to the "catching up syndrome". "Explosion of knowledge" was taken as an undebatable 'given' and used as justification for increased academic burden on children. Concern on such a thing happening had been voiced earlier by the Review Committee on The Curriculum for the Ten-Year School (1977), NCERT Working Group (1984) and NPE Review Committee (1990). It was left to the National Advisory Committee (1992) to offer a fuller explanation of the school bag load phenomenon and throw light on the issues involved. In its report, *Learning Without Burden*, the Committee pointed out that the notion of knowledge explosion fails to distinguish between knowledge and information. It said that the human capacity to find new facts and store them has expanded, but the concepts and theories that assist in the generation and organization of information can hardly be said to have multiplied at an explosive rate. Like the EC earlier, (1.70) the Committee also observed, that in an ex-colonial society it looks as if all new knowledge is being produced by others and our job is simply to learn and consume this knowledge. The explosion of knowledge slogan prevents us from appreciating that learning is not the same thing as storing information; that it involves understanding the phenomenon and applying it in understanding other phenomena. Understanding is confused with acquisition of facts leading to the neglect of understanding as an aim of education.

*Is science the standard of knowledge?:* The EC, which held that the future of the country depended on its adoption of science and technology as the basis for development and modernization, extolled science as the paradigm of knowledge and gave it primacy in the curriculum. The 'science is the hope' theme was affirmed in successive educational policy documents. The *Challenge of Education* noted: New learning needs have arisen from economic, social growth and progress in science and technology.... Tomorrow's world would usher in an information-rich and technology intensive society, which calls for new approaches to learning. *The National Commission on Teachers-I*

(p. ix), observed: "We saw unusual nostalgia on the part of some to cling to the past and solve contemporary problems and issues by means of obsolete ideas and traditions. We saw this as a reminder that our goal of a brighter and better future will never be realized until we place science and technology at the centre of things."

The EC considered science as knowledge par excellence. Its romanticization of science as a paradigm of knowledge and value, (1.24, 1.80) to which reference has already been made, borders on scientism. The portrayal of science as the embodiment of truth and rationality and the deification of the scientific method has been criticized by historians and philosophers of science in the past, notably by Thomas Kuhn and Feyeraband. Further, sociologists of knowledge have also questioned the 'purity' of scientific knowledge.

To be fair, it must be admitted that the EC warned against domination by science and also pleaded for the integration of science and spirituality. In this context, it referred to our spiritual heritage and the need to strive to bring science and the values of the spirit (ahimsa and atom) together and thereby pave the way for the eventual emergence of the whole man. Such sentiments in favour of breadth of vision, awareness of history, culture and tradition, in school and higher education have received general approval.

Yet, the monolithic view that only scientific phenomena and rationality constitute knowledge in the true sense and nothing else dies hard. The other forms of human experience—liberal arts, humanistic studies, creative endeavours like music, dance, drama and so on—are considered as important too but not as *knowledge* or *pursuit of truth*. The view that empirical knowledge and *only* empirical knowledge constitutes *knowledge and truth* will not have many takers today. That human experience spans different realms of meaning and knowledge exists in different forms, that there are diverse ways of knowing and truth criteria are internal to a particular form, still remain unappreciated. It is to the credit of the *NCF 2005* to have discussed the issue from this perspective and drawn attention to the multiple dimensions of knowledge and different ways of knowing. It says the idea that objectivity, a necessary constituent of knowledge, can be achieved only if knowledge is free from emotions (care, concern and love), must be abandoned. One implication of this for education is that literary and artistic creativity is as much part of man's epistemic enterprise as is seeking knowledge through laboratory experiments or deductive reasoning. The former frequently enables us to see truth in a way that the paradigmatic scientific quest cannot *(National Focus Group on Aims of Education,* p. 5).

## Summing up

In this section the EC position on equality and knowledge are explained and critiqued. It is pointed out that despite its bold proclamation of egalitarian ideology and recommendation of the common school, the EC treatment of equality is far from adequate; it did not take equality as problematic but accepted it as an unanalyzed notion; it concerned itself with equality of *opportunity*; it attributed inequality to external sources and causes (of lack of access, poverty, habitat, gender and caste); it did not ask the question why children fail and whether education led to empowerment of the individual. The contribution of EC lies in bringing the issue of equality into the open and widening the terms of the egalitarian debate (which led to questioning the legitimacy of the school curriculum and even of the knowledge disciplines) impacting policy discourse in later years. As to knowledge, EC's scattered references to its different aspects—explosion of knowledge, appropriate pedagogy, the primacy of science, are brought together and explained. Using the EC insights as benchmarks, a critical account is given of the enlargement of the knowledge discourse in later years encompassing such issues as the pedagogical fall out of the knowledge explosion phenomenon, celebration of science as the paradigm of knowledge, school bag load problem, 'information' and 'understanding' and the many ways of 'knowing' and seeking 'truth'.

## PART IV: EC IN THE NEW CONTEXT

### The Relevance of the EC Articulations

Educational documents, by their very nature, become 'dated' after sometime. But this does not happen to writings on education that deal with its very fundamentals and deals with them in a manner that is forward looking and not confined to a time or age. There can be two ways of looking at the EC Report. The obvious one is to judge it in terms of the impact it had on the implementation of a national system of education, which was its mandate. As Naik said, the EC must be seen as the end result of a persistent search for a national system of education spread over nearly sixty years (beginning with the Indian National Congress resolution of 1906) and the success or otherwise of its efforts should be judged with reference to this aspect. In his evaluative study of post-EC developments during 1966-78, *The Education Commission and After*, which has been profusely quoted in this paper, Naik laid bare the many shortcomings of the EC Report and exposed the social and political factors that impeded its effective implementation.[3] Naik says the EC placed great trust in the body politic to share its concerns with the same intensity and provide a fair trial to its recommendations, but this unfortunately did not happen. During later years realization dawned on every one that even moderate (not to mention radical) educational reforms are very difficult to carry through even with the additional constitutional support of concurrency (which the EC, surprisingly, was not in favour of). That is the reason why the later educational policy documents were guarded in their proposals for change and more realistic in their expectations having learnt lessons from the past. The EC had no such past to learn lessons from.

A second way of judging the Report, which is as much important, if not more, is in terms of its spin-off, the influence it had on later educational thinking and policy making. Here, it must be admitted that the EC Report has had a lasting impact on subsequent movement of thought in Indian education leading to deeper understanding and appreciation of the educational phenomena—its discourse, theories and principles and generation of fresh insights. The EC insights and ideas on education-society relationship, educational equality, value education, curriculum, teaching, learning and other aspects provided the basis for educational theorizing in later years leading to their refinement and elaboration. In a way, the EC recommendations constituted a bench mark for all subsequent educational developments in policies and programmes. It speaks about the 'classic' nature of the Report that four decades later we continue to find the concepts, principles and recommendations of the EC quoted and referred to. It would be worthwhile therefore to revisit the EC themes and concepts and associated principles and theories discussed thus far and examine their contemporary relevance and significance.

## Society

In visioning the future society we may take note of the lessons drawn from the post-EC experiences of Naik. In his reflections Naik suggested that the visioning be approached by identifying "the worst aspects of the existing social order which have to be eliminated as early as possible" (p. 173). This approach, he says, will not only indicate the major features of the future society but also suggest a programme of action. He mentions three such aspects: the elitist character of society in which all power—political, economic and knowledge—is concentrated in the hands of a small elite comprising the upper castes, hierarchical organization that is inimical to democracy and social justice and poverty "which has few parallels in the world". He also mentioned threats to secularism and authoritarianism (pp. 175-6). Naik laments that the main forces of modernization—education and science and technology—have allied themselves with the elite and helped them to improve their standards of living but have not done so for the masses. *Naik could as well be describing the current times!* The point is that any attempt towards visioning of the future society has to take note of these persisting elemental problems of our society. The situation has become even more complex now with the society under the grip of globalization and economic liberalization and privatization policies.

## Education

***The point of education:*** A renewed enthusiasm to go back to the basics in education—what education is and what it is all about (which the EC, disappointingly, avoided discussing)—characterizes the contemporary engagement with education, at least among educationists. A journal, *Issues in Primary Education,* devoted an entire issue (Vol. IV, Jun.-Dec., 2002) to a discussion of aims of education. The NCF-2005 set up a National Focus Group to deal with aims of education. This is the first time, I think, that a national forum was created to discuss exclusively aims of education, the starting point of all educational activity.

The contemporary concern to go back to the fundamentals is prompted by several disturbing happenings. One of these is the general tendency of the school deviating from its central concern of *education* and the community's treatment of *schooling per se* as synonymous with education irrespective of whether it served educational aims or not. The demand today is for a kind of schooling that is centred round meeting the short term market needs rather than pursuit of genuine educational goals. As a consumer commodity, education has met the same fate as other material commodities operating in a market economy driven by the profit motive. Worse, the market forces have influenced not only the distribution of education but its very meaning. Education as an intrinsic value makes no sense in the prevailing commercial ethos. It is refreshing, however, that we hear saner voices now and then. "Today's times are far from normal and we need to remind ourselves of the purpose of education...we have lost sight of the basic purpose of education, helping individuals to develop into good human beings and good citizens" (Jagdeep S. Chhokar, 2006, Renuka Narayanan in *The New Indian Express*). The slide of the school from declared educational ideals (which has occurred throughout history and in all societies) may be indicative of the remoteness or non-relevance of ruling educational aims or even a deeper malaise in the society. In the past whenever it reached a crisis point the attention of the people was diverted back to the basic question of what education was all about and whether schools were doing their job alright. We seem to have reached such a point today.

## The Individual and the Social in Education

The individual-social dichotomy continues to torment us. The EC observed that individual fulfillment will come not through selfish loyalties but dedication to wider loyalties of national development in all parameters. Harmonization of the individual and social claims in education has been reiterated successively in all policy documents. The resolution, however, is fraught with difficulties. As the NCF-2005 points out, the lack of clarity about the notion of the individual independent of the complex matrix of relationships in which an individual is inevitably located and "all-inclusive humanity" as distinct from "this or that specific variety of humanity" creates difficulties in thinking about aims of education in our times. "Thus for instance we have to find a way out of a seeming contradiction such as: we must encourage children to cultivate the 'scientific temper' (the tendency to follow reason beyond the dictates of culture, tradition and community) and also teach them the unassailable values of humanity. Also we must find a stable room for the nation between the individual and the humanity" (*Position Paper of the National Focus Group on Aims of Education, pp. 5-6*).

## Education as a Lever of Change

An extreme optimism in the power of education to change society was the driving force behind the EC recommendations. While education by its very nature continues to remain as an ideal to be striven for, as something that is desirable in itself, perspectives on education have undergone a change. The idealism surrounding education has over the years been tempered by social and economic realities and the traditional optimism in the power of education to change society has sobered down. In his post-EC study, Naik admitted that EC's belief in the primacy of education in social transformation was not theoretically correct. As to the alternative—socio-economic revolution should come first—Naik saw, in his time, no such revolution round the corner. One wonders whether the 'economic revolution' the country has been undergoing currently carries the seed in it of bringing about qualitative social transformation on the lines the EC had envisioned.

## Values

The EC's goal of a modern society driven by a truly national system of education based on the lasting, universal values of our cultural heritage is as relevant (even more relevant) today as it was at the time it was formulated. But 'national' and 'Indian culture' continue to elude general acceptance. Whatever has been proposed in the national curricular frameworks has been criticized either as not being 'national' enough or for carrying a hidden political or cultural agenda. At a time when the reigning mood is one of assertion of small community identities and celebration of plurality, freedom and autonomy, some are wary of, and even fear, a 'national' thinking in education it may act against the diversities in lifestyles, culture, language and religions of the people. Globalization has made the context further complicated.

In a refreshing treatment of the value theme, the NCF-2005 (*Position Paper of the National Focus Group on Aims of Education, p. 7*) reminds us that values are integral to the process of education and the whole education has to be value education. "Here, we need powerful reminders of Gandhian ideas of ahimsa, peace and harmony." *Déjà vu! It is EC's atom and ahimsa all over again!*

The NCF prescription for dealing with values is Peace Education. "Education for peace is education for life, not merely training for a livelihood. Equipping individuals with the values, skills and attitudes they need to be wholesome persons who live in harmony with others and are responsible citizens is the goal of education for peace. Peace is a contextually appropriate and pedagogically gainful point of coherence for values. Educating for peace is the ideal strategy for contextualizing and operationalizing value education (*Position Paper of the National Focus Group on Peace Education, p. 185*).

## Equality

***Have we dumped the egalitarian ideal?:*** The singular, most significant contribution of the EC is its proposal for a Common School System. It was one of the EC recommendations that attracted wide attention according to Naik. Understandably, the opinion was divided on the adoption of the neighbourhood school concept and continuance of the public schools both within the Commission and the Committee of MPs that debated the proposed reform. The end result was its inclusion as a "non-controversial, ineffective and colourless statement" in the Policy document. "For all practical purposes the proposal has remained a dead letter", wrote Naik in 1982. However, he thought even its symbolic inclusion has the advantage of stimulating thinking on the subject and drawing attention to the dual and non-national character of our educational system. He concluded that the battle is essentially political and will have to be decided politically; (p. 80) and that "it is worthwhile to keep the debate going" (p. 82).

None of these hopes have been realized; neither has there been a sustained dialogue among the academics and politicians nor have new social and political forces emerged in favour of the cause. While all political parties across the spectrum are presenting a united front in favour of reservations for the backward classes in professional and higher learning and elite institutions, *lamentably there has been no similar concerted movement to attack the breeding place of inequality, the fragmented school system and make schooling inclusive in the true sense.* The scenario on the ground points to how the nation has moved further and further away from the EC vision. The existence and proliferation of myriad types of private schools is not based on any educational principle nor do they form a homogeneous category. They are the result of diverse interest groups based on caste, religion, economic class, language and ethnicity creating their own space for promoting their narrow sectarian agenda against the background of globalization, free market economy and constitutionally guaranteed educational freedoms (Anuradha De and others, 2002).

The EC's crusade for egalitarianism involved fight against elitism and promotion of people's education. Both these causes have suffered. Private schooling panders to the sectarian demands of privilege and exclusiveness at a price to those who can pay. In the process, it has done immense damage to the basic orientation and purposes of primary education. Increasingly, it is being treated more as an instrument of preparing children for book learning at the higher levels than as a self-sustaining and self-contained experience of basic education, a fundamental human right.

What is shocking is that no one seems to care about equality anymore. Worse, the society seems to have accepted the situation as inevitable "at a time when India is emerging as a superpower fuelled by economic liberalization and free trade, globalization, and privatization." *The ethics of globalization seems to have altered the sense of morality the nation had inherited from the freedom struggle as also enshrined in the Constitutional principles of equality, justice and democracy* (Anil Sadgopal, in *The New Indian Express*, 2004). Today a studied silence and inaction by the academia and the public characterizes our stand on the Common School System. Neither the NPE nor the PoA accorded any importance to it. The NPE Review made recommendations to revive the idea but they were dismissed as impractical, "although desirable" by the CABE Committee on Education. Even the otherwise progressive NCF-2005 toes a soft line on the issue. Its observation that we need to reaffirm commitment to equality "within cultural and socio-economic diversity" and promote values that foster peace, humaneness, tolerance in a multi-cultural society compromises the overriding claim of equality.

## Knowledge

***Knowledge in the ICT ambience:*** Caution about the likely distortions that knowledge explosion would cause in education and the nature of accommodation that education has to make were duly signaled by the EC—need for catching up with the "exploding field", warning against passive absorption of inherited knowledge, dangers of domination by science and emphasis on creativity and discovery. These were reiterated, elaborated and refined by successive educational committees and commissions taking note of the widening influence of ICT, the gaping digital divide notwithstanding.

IT has been hailed as the defining technology of our times leading to redefining of our notions about education, school and teacher. Flush as the society is with the euphoria created by the promise of a veritable haven of learning resources and endless opportunities for life-long learning—a utopia of learning webs, virtual classrooms and what have you—concern is also brewing about the challenges they are likely to pose to long cherished educational aims and values. With specific reference to the theory and practice of education, questions are asked on what knowledge as a core aim means in an information-rich society, how the autonomy of educational goals must be protected from the control of technology and how the liberal education ideal of pursuit of knowledge as an intrinsic value be preserved in the corporate ethos of the knowledge society.

The most immediate and serious of these questions is the celebration of information in various forms in the name of knowledge—in the media, in education and elsewhere. Attention to the misplaced emphasis on information in the name of knowledge was drawn by the National Advisory Committee more than a decade ago by pointing out the distinction between knowledge and understanding. Rightly understood, the IT revolution demands that the learner be enabled to construct his/her own knowledge, calling into aid appropriate technological devices, rather than being treated as a receptacle of knowledge handed down by teachers and books. The new pedagogy to be compatible with IT should encourage questioning, exploration, problem solving, heuristic, algorithmic strategies, decision making and group work. But available indications are not encouraging for one to hope that such a pedagogy would inform school teaching in the near future (*Facts and frictions—What have you memorized lately?* Teja Shrikant Lele in *The New Indian Express*, Dec. 21, 2004).

Secondly, the optimism of IT revolutionizing teaching and learning is rightly not shared by many educational thinkers and teachers. It is pointed out that preparation of high quality software requires very deep understanding of the impediments to the process of learning and the mechanisms by which children learn and this is a daunting task. On the contrary, doubts and fears are voiced not only about what is actually happening on the ground but also about the direction towards which current developments are leading. How could ICT revolution herald a revolution in teaching and learning when our education is increasingly being driven by market forces and teachers and parents would want the new medium to serve the demands of the market place than exploration and creative thought (Kumaraswamy, 2001). What if learning from virtual reality replaces learning from first hand experience and "real" reality? It is unfortunate that simulations on the computer screen have started replacing simple things of joy in nature (Jayaram, 2001). What if the authority that the computer carries and the electronic access to answers for every conceivable question inhibits independent thinking and search for knowledge and also undermines the educationally desirable "state of not knowing, a feeling for the unknown, the cleansing of the mind that doubt and inquiry bring..." (Mark Lee, 2001).

What we need, then, is an interpretation of knowledge that acknowledges its comprehensive and all-embracing nature that calls into play higher powers of mind than mere memorization and storage of information—conceptual thinking, understanding of principles, laws, generalizations and critical and reflective thinking. What the knowledge society needs is education that facilitates knowledge acquisition in this broader sense and attempts at the total transformation of the human personality in all its richness. The important question today is whether the advent of ICT would free education from its traditional hold and enable it to pursue knowledge in its broader sense.

***Pursuit of the liberal education ideal:*** The EC had observed (despite its all out acclamation of science) that "it would be a sad day if the present preoccupation with science and technology resulted in the neglect of the humanities..." (12.58) ... we can make great contributions on the basis of our old traditions (12.59) ... we borrow from the West for science but we contribute to the world in social, pedagogic and humanistic studies deriving from our tradition (12.59).

The EC's fears have come true. The disinterested pursuit of 'pure' knowledge as a human excellence in its own right, higher education today has come under a cloud. For want of support for learning areas, which have no 'use' for market requirements and conditions, cash-strapped universities began performance appraisal in terms of corporate values and culture. This poses a severe threat to the pursuit of knowledge as an intrinsic end. We find ourselves living in difficult times and caught on the horns of a dilemma. The challenge before us is how to fairly deal with what appear to be two equally valid value positions represented by the demands of academic, theoretical and humanistic studies on the one side and the technological, practical and utilitarian ones on the other.

## Further Pointers for Future Visioning

In his future visioning, Naik talks about the "current" debate on capitalist and socialist development models and suggests a third model that is environment friendly, appropriate technology-based and does not equate quality of life with consumerism. I wonder how he would have reacted to the current happenings on the economic and political fronts. We are told that the era of ideologies—left, right, centre—and development models is over. This is how an eminent journalist sees it: "A different sort of revolution is sweeping our country...if you... survey the entire country and indeed the rest of the world as well it is now evident that, whatever your ideology, there is only one way of economic governance. It is to embrace the global markets, be creative and competitive, fight for a larger share of the flowing capital, build better infrastructure, wealth, enterprise and thereby more jobs and money for welfare schemes.... This is the way India has been changing over the past 15 years" (Shekhar Gupta, in *The New Indian Express*, June 24, 2006).

There is joy all around about the increasing growth rates registered by the Indian economy. But this euphoria hides the stark poverty of a sizeable percentage of our people and the increasing inequalities. Sadgopal (2005, *Position Paper of the National Focus Group on Work and Education, Foot note 2, p. 318*) articulates the concern thus: It is now being increasingly acknowledged that the Indian economy has already entered the stage of advanced capitalism.... This is evident from the impact that the Indian economy is able to make on international relations and negotiations, including in the

WTO. Conscious of this transformation, the Indian ruling class is already projecting itself as becoming the "third largest economy of the world" and acquiring the status of a "Superpower by 2020"! Of course, these projections do not reflect any concern with regard to the future of the vast sections of society that are marginalized today.

Functioning in the pre-globalization period, the EC mentioned about "international understanding" for the "one world" "towards which we are moving". Education, it said, should help one learn to appreciate the fruitful diversity of the cultures of mankind and valuing with an open mind the contributions of different countries and races to human civilization. It did not refer to the economic aspect of globalization. As we understand today, globalization is an economic phenomenon, a process of integrating the nation-states by removing or minimizing the restrictions on the movement of material and financial resources, labour, technology and ideas. It affects the sovereignty of nation-states and raises political issues; free flow of ideas brings about changes in values and life styles and raises socio-cultural issues (Sreekantaradhya, 2004). The country has already started experiencing the adverse impact of globalization in education. As the NCF-2005 observes, globalization and spread of market relations have led to increasing commercialization of education, shifting of responsibility for education from the state to the community, commodification of knowledge and application of market related concepts to schools and school quality. Individual aspirations in a competitive economy had made education an instrument of material success, distorted values and ignored learning from each other. Competitive environment and aspirations of parents have led to stress and anxiety among children to the detriment of their personal growth. In the name of globalization long cherished values of educational quality and excellence are narrowly interpreted to fit the globalization paradigm.

The NCF-2005, even as it reiterates the basic concerns of education, successively pointed out by previous educational policy statements and committee reports, describes the present educational context thus: The social context of caste hierarchy, economic status and gender relations, cultural diversity, and uneven economic development continue to pose challenges. The ills of the national school system—55 lakh teachers teach 2025 lakh children in 10 lakh schools, 75 per cent schools are multi-grade, 50 per cent pass out of Class X examination, 37 per cent lack literacy skills, 53 per cent drop out at the elementary stage—remain the same: system's inflexibility and resistance to change, isolation of learning from life, promotion of conformity and discouragement of creative thinking. What is at the centre of education is the child's *future*; its present is almost excluded.

We continue to swear by the basic values enshrined in the Constitution. During the past decades the constitutional framework has been further strengthened with more enabling provisions by way of amendments related to fundamental duties, fundamental right of education and empowerment of panchayats, concurrency of education and affirmative action to secure social justice through reservations. Enabling legislations relating to social and educational policies have been passed by States towards the realization of our social goals. If anything, we find ourselves more empowered than ever before, constitutionally, and in a better position, to secure economic and social justice for all.

## Notes

1. All further references of Naik are to this book unless otherwise indicated.
2. These are referred to in section IV
3. About Naik's book Malcom Adiseshiah in his *Foreword* wrote: "This rather unusual analysis is frank to the point of certain leaders finding it fearsome. In some respects the review amounts to a confession in the form of *mea culpa*".

## References

Adiseshiah, Malcom S., (1982). Foreword in J.P. Naik's *The Education Commission and After*, Allied Publishers.

Anuradha De and others, (2002). Private Schools and Universal Elementary Education, *India Education Report*, R. Govinda (ed.), New Delhi: Oxford University Press.

Gunnar Myrdal, (1970). *The Challenge of World Poverty*, Penguin.

Hirst, P.H., (1974). *Knowledge and Curriculum*, Routledge and Kegan Paul

Imtiaz Ahmad, (July 1969) Secularism and Communalism in Special No, *Seminar*,

Imtiaz Ahmed (1970). Indianization, in *Seminar*, No. 137.

Jagdeep S. Chhokar, (June 27 2006). Education is not just about jobs, in *The New Indian Express*.

Jean Dreze, (2002). Education and Development: An Unfinished Discovery in *Issues in Primary Education*, Ed. CIL, GOI, MHRD, New Delhi.

Jayaram, (May 2001). Helping students understand the place of studying Computer Science, *Journal of the Krishnamurty Schools (JKS)*, No. 5

Kumaraswamy, (May 2001). Does Information Technology Herald a Learning Revolution? JKS, No 5

Mark Lee, (May 2001). Computers, Internet and Schools—Are we connected to reality? *JKS, No 5*

Malavika Karlekar, (1975). Higher Education and the Scheduled Castes, *Journal of Higher Education*, Vol. 1, No. 2, p. 184.

Naik, J.P. (1982). *The Education Commission and After*, Allied Publishers.

Naik, J.P. (1975). *Equality, Quality and Quantity*, New Delhi: Allied Publishers.

Naik, J.P. (1975). *Policy and Performance in Indian Education-1947-74*, New Delhi: Orient Longman.

Naravane, V.S., (1964). *Modern Indian Thought—a philosophical survey*, Bombay: Asia Publishing House.

Peters, R.S. (1969). *Perspectives on Plowden*, London: RKP.

Plowden Report, (1967). *Children and their Primary Schools*
Pratibha, Dixit (Nov. 1, 1969). A Comment, *Economic and Political Weekly.*
Radhakrishnan, S. (1959). *An Idealist View of Life*, London: Allen and Unwin.
Renuka, Narayanan. The point of education, in *The New Indian Express.*
Shekhar Gupta, (June 24, 2006). Centre-right? That's all right, in *The New Indian Express.*
Shukla, S. (1975). Of Equality and Higher Learning, *Journal of Higher Education,* Vol. 1, No. 2, p. 152.
Salamathulla, (2004). Basic Education, *Encyclopaedia of Indian Education*, Ed. Rajput, J.S., NCERT.
Sadgopal, Anil (Feb. 6, 2004). Learning about barriers, in *The New Indian Express.*
Seshadri, C. (1981). The Concept of Moral Education: Indian and Western—a comparative study, in *Comparative Education,* Vol. 17, No. 3.
Seshadri, C. (2002). Do Aims of Education Matter? In *Issues in Primary Education* Vol. IV, No. 2 and 3, New Delhi: Ed. CIL, GOI, MHRD.
Seshadri, C. (1978). Moral Education in India, *Journal of Moral Education,* Vol. 8, No. 1.
Seshadri, C. (1988). The Academic Discipline and Value Orientation—An Epistemological Exploration, *Perspectives in Education,* Vol. 4, No. 1.
Seshadri, C. (1978). Education, Equality and Culture: An Analysis, *Journal of Higher Education,* Vol. 3, No. 3.
Sreekantaradhya, B.S. (2004). Globalization and Education in *Encyclopedia of Indian Education,* Vol. I.
Yadav, R.K. (1983-85). A Study of Recommendations on Teachers by Education Commissions in the post independence India, prepared for National Commission on Teachers, mimeo.

### Government of India, Ministry of Human Resource Development, New Delhi

*Challenge of Education—a policy perspective,* 1985.
Draft National Policy on Education, 1979.
*Education and National Development*, Report of the Education Commission 1964-66.
*Issues in Primary Education* Vol. IV, No. 2 and 3, June-December 2002.
*Learning without burden*, Report of the National Advisory Committee, 1993.
National Policy on Education-1986.
Report of Core Group on Value Orientation of Education, Planning Commission, 1992.
Report of the CABE Committee on Policy, 1992.
Report of the Committee on Emotional Integration, 1962.
Report of the Committee on Religious and Moral Education, 1959.
Report of the Review Committee on The Curriculum for the Ten Year School, 1977.
Report of the Secondary Education Commission, 1953.
Report of the University Education Commission, 1950.
Report of the Working Group to Review Teachers Training Programme (in the light of the need for value orientation), 1983.
The Teacher and Society, Report of the National Commission on Teachers-I and II, 1983-85.

*Towards an Enlightened and Humane Society*, National Policy on Education-1986—A Review, 1990.

### NCERT, New Delhi

*Common School System—Retrospect and Prospect*, 1999.
Gore, M.S. (1970). *et al.*, Ed. *Papers in the Sociology of Education in India.*
National Curriculum for Elementary and Secondary Education—A Framework, 1988.
National Curriculum Framework 2005.
National Curriculum Framework for School Education, 2000.
National Focus Group on Aims of Education, Position Paper.
National Focus Group on Peace Education, Position Paper.
National Focus Group on Work and Education, Position paper.
The Curriculum for the Ten-Year School—A Framework, 1975.

2

# Revisiting the Education Commission: Perspectives, Goals and Values

M. ANANDAKRISHNAN

## Introduction

Immediately after Independence there have been several Commissions and Committees of the Government of India to identify major issues concerning the structure and functions of the educational system. Notable among them are the University Education Commission (1948-49) and the Secondary Education Commission (1952-53). While steps were taken to implement the recommendations of these Commissions, the constitution of the Education Commission (1964-66), under the chairmanship of Prof. D.S. Kothari, was meant to take a comprehensive view of the entire education system to help initiate a fresh and determined effort for the development of education at all stages and in all aspects in an integrated manner.

The initiative to constitute such a commission reflects the bold political will of the leadership to consider education as the core of the national development goals. The fact that this initiative was taken at a time when industrial production was low, agricultural output was poor and monetary resources were negligible, deserves admiration. Perhaps the implicit assumption was that educational development in the right direction would spur developments in all other sectors.

While submitting the Report of the Education Commission to the then Education Minister, Shri M.C. Chagla on June 29, 1966, the Chairman of the Commission pointed out: "*Education has always been important but perhaps never more so in man's history than today. In a science-based world, education and research are crucial to the entire developmental process of a country, its welfare, progress and security. It is characteristic of a world permeated by science that in some essential ways the future shape of things is unpredictable. This emphasizes all the more the need for an educational policy which contains a built-in flexibility so that it can adjust to changing circumstances. It underscores the importance of experimentation and innovation. If I may say so, the single most important thing needed now is to get out of the rigidity of the present system. In the rapidly changing world of today, one thing is certain: yesterday's educational system will not meet today's, and even less so, the need of tomorrow."*

## National Policy on Education—1968

This prophetic statement is equally and perhaps more relevant today in the context of enormous changes that have taken place in the society and the economy during the past five decades. The National Policy on Education adopted by the Government of India Resolution on the Report of the Education Commission acknowledges that:

> *A radical reconstruction of education on the broad lines recommended by the Education Commission is essential for economic and cultural development of the country, for national integration and for realizing the ideal of a socialist pattern of society. This will involve a transformation of the system to relate it more closely to the life of the people; a continuous effort to expand educational opportunity; a sustained and intensive effort to raise the quality of education at all stages; an emphasis on the development of science and technology; and the cultivation of moral and social values.*

The Resolution spells out the following principles among others:

(1) Free and Compulsory Education for all children up to the age of 14;
(2) Improve the Status, Emolument and Education of Teachers;
(3) Development of Languages;
(4) Equalization of Educational Opportunity.

It also proposed that facilities for secondary education as well as technical and vocational education should be extended expeditiously. On University education, the resolution recommended that the number of students admitted should be commensurate with available facilities and staff; considerable care should be exercised in establishing new universities; and substantial support should be provided for research in universities.

### *The Premises*

The Education Commission probed the dynamics of the Indian education system at that time, examined in depth the influence of various currents and cross-currents and evolved a holistic educational policy framework and directions for the future. It was, undoubtedly, the most comprehensive and progressive document on education in the history of India. Therefore, at this stage, it will be helpful to revisit the work of the Commission, not so much to apportion blames or credit for acts of omissions and commissions, but to evolve a new policy framework for the future.

This is a formidable task, considering the enormous changes that have taken place in the country since the sixties. The philosophical foundation of the Commission enunciated during the period of great nationalistic spirit would be helpful in evolving the new policy framework. Education was a state subject at that time. Now that it has become a concurrent subject, the objectives of the Centre and the States would be similar, but the precise prescriptions may vary in view of the rapidly increasing size, greater demand for access, affordability and equity, availability of new technological pedagogic innovations, international influences and new spheres of knowledge and skills.

### Key Recommendations

One of the key recommendations of the Commission was to have a broadly uniform educational structure in all parts of the country with the ultimate objective of adopting the 10+2+3 pattern and to increase the investment in education so as to reach a level of expenditure of six per cent of the national income as early as possible. Though the educational structure has been broadly achieved, the recommended level of investment is yet to be realized. The principal objectives of the Commission were:

1. To reevaluate the role of education in the total programme of national development;
2. To identify the changes needed in the existing system of education; and,
3. To implement these programmes with determination and rigour.

The Commission laid particular emphasis on directing the educational efforts to attain self-sufficiency in food. Apparently the food situation in the 60s prompted the Commission to emphasize the role of education in improving agriculture and enhancing food production. In the present context this approach needs to be further elaborated in terms of the National Development Goals in several other sectors such as transportation, housing, energy, minerals and so on. In other words the perspectives of education at all levels must be to establish direct linkages with various development sectors.

The Commission emphasized the role of education in achieving rapid rate of economic growth and full employment. This message is equally valid today considering the fact that economic growth contributes to educational development and educational development in turn will accelerate economic growth. At the same time, the need to distribute income more equitably to benefit the deprived sections of the population and to control the growth of population through reduction in the birth rate were highlighted. The issue of economic equity is yet to fully materialize as also the educational equity. The decadal growth rate of population is significantly lower in those States, which have higher literacy level, Correlation Co-efficient: –0.098 (Table 2.1).

**Table 2.1: Decadal Population Growth Rate vs. Literacy Rate**

| *State/ UT Code* | *India/State/Union Territory* | *Decadal Growth Rate (1991-2001)* | *Literacy Rate 2001* | | |
|---|---|---|---|---|---|
| | | | *Persons* | *Male* | *Female* |
| 1. | Andaman & Nicobar Islands | 26.94 | 81.3 | 86.3 | 75.2 |
| 2. | Andhra Pradesh | 13.86 | 60.5 | 70.3 | 50.4 |
| 3. | Arunachal Pradesh | 26.21 | 54.3 | 63.8 | 43.5 |
| 4. | Assam | 18.85 | 63.3 | 71.3 | 54.6 |
| 5. | Bihar | 28.43 | 47.0 | 59.7 | 33.1 |
| 6. | Chandigarh | 40.33 | 81.9 | 86.1 | 76.5 |
| 7. | Chhatisgarh | 18.06 | 64.7 | 77.4 | 51.9 |
| 8. | Dadra & Nagar Haveli | 59.20 | 57.6 | 71.2 | 40.2 |
| 9. | Daman & Diu | 55.59 | 78.2 | 86.8 | 65.6 |
| 10. | Delhi | 46.31 | 81.7 | 87.3 | 74.7 |
| 11. | Gujarat | 22.48 | 69.1 | 79.7 | 57.8 |
| 12. | Goa | 14.89 | 82.0 | 88.4 | 75.4 |
| 13. | Haryana | 28.06 | 67.9 | 78.5 | 55.7 |
| 14. | Himachal Pradesh | 17.53 | 76.5 | 85.3 | 67.4 |
| 15. | Jammu & Kashmir | 29.04 | 55.5 | 66.6 | 43.0 |
| 16. | Jharkhand | 23.19 | 53.6 | 67.3 | 38.9 |
| 17. | Karnataka | 17.25 | 66.6 | 76.1 | 56.9 |
| 18. | Kerala | 9.42 | 90.9 | 94.2 | 87.7 |
| 19. | Lakshadweep | 17.19 | 86.7 | 92.5 | 80.5 |
| 20. | Madhya Pradesh | 24.34 | 63.7 | 76.1 | 50.3 |
| 21. | Maharashtra | 22.57 | 76.9 | 86.0 | 67.0 |
| 22. | Manipur | 30.02 | 70.5 | 80.3 | 60.5 |
| 23. | Meghalaya | 29.94 | 62.6 | 65.4 | 59.6 |
| 24. | Mizoram | 29.18 | 88.8 | 90.7 | 86.7 |
| 25. | Nagaland | 64.41 | 66.6 | 71.2 | 61.5 |
| 26. | Orissa | 15.94 | 63.1 | 75.3 | 50.5 |
| 27. | Pondicherry | 20.56 | 81.2 | 88.6 | 73.9 |
| 28. | Punjab | 19.76 | 69.7 | 75.2 | 63.4 |
| 29. | Rajasthan | 28.33 | 60.4 | 75.7 | 43.9 |
| 30. | Sikkim | 32.98 | 68.8 | 76.0 | 60.4 |
| 31. | Tamil Nadu | 11.19 | 73.5 | 82.4 | 64.4 |
| 32. | Tripura | 15.74 | 73.2 | 81.0 | 64.9 |
| 33. | Uttar Pradesh | 25.80 | 56.3 | 68.8 | 42.2 |
| 34. | Uttaranchal | 19.20 | 71.6 | 83.3 | 59.6 |
| 35. | West Bengal | 17.84 | 68.6 | 77.0 | 59.6 |
| | INDIA | 21.34 | 64.8 | 75.3 | 53.7 |

The Commission envisaged the role of education in achieving social and national integration in the context of a hierarchical and stratified Indian society. The Commission also stressed that education can play a key role in strengthening the political democracy.

## Policy Issues

The evolution of policy regimes is influenced by a variety of forces operating from within and outside the country at a given point of time. Such forces include the power centers, power structure, governance system, degree of sensitivity towards public interest as opposed to private interest, the extent of public awareness and alertness on the societal evolutionary process, prevailing value system and religious dogmas, and so on. The history of the evolution of Indian education from the time of monarchies to democracies demonstrates these influences. Though the present system of education has been largely inherited from the colonial period, the remnants of habits and attitudes from the historical period are still present to a significant extent.

In this context it is relevant to note that in spite of India enjoying high reputation in science from ancient times, and that it was more advanced than Arabia or Europe, the momentum could not be maintained in subsequent periods for reasons such as stratification of society, dominance of caste system, depriving education of a large section of people, superstitions and taboos, and complacency, among others.

The educational attainments of a large section of the population were not very high. Educational institutions in relation to the size of the population then were too few. The scientific and technological institutions were still dependent on foreign connections. The opportunities to upgrade skill levels were limited. Educational technologies were not available. The elitist attitude towards education was dominant. However, the desire to promote an egalitarian society was prominent.

## Policy Directions

- There is a policy vacuum relating to education, especially higher education. The developments in the country in post-reform period are poorly reflected in the national initiatives in education. There are dim prospects of rigorous policy dialogues. This would require a foresighted statesmanship on the part of those at the helm of affairs of education in India.
- In general, people are aware of the economic and social gains of the visionary initiatives for education. This has the potential to pull millions of people out of poverty and to provide opportunity for larger sections of the population in the mainstream economy and to gain credibility of the Indian education system globally. The hope created by the Kothari Commission has been frustrated by short term pressures, thereby ignoring the need to obtain maximum returns from our educational enterprises.
- There is an unmistakable trend of demand oriented growth caused by the tremendous desire on the part of all the sections of society to obtain education as a means of upward social mobility and economic security. However, the actual supply side of the educational system is heavily distorted and unbalanced. This needs to be corrected from the long-term interest of the society. Lots of hopes were generated

when the government announced the possibility of increased allocation for education to the extent of six per cent of the GDP, which is yet to materialize. The issue is not the availability of funds but the government's commitment to education as a national policy.

- The rationale for new directions should be articulated along with the modalities for action. The guiding principles to be enunciated will relate to such factors as access, affordability, excellence, competence, knowledge base, skill base, international standards and so on.
- The systemic lacunae of the current education system are indicated in the near defunct status of the regulatory system for education. There is ample evidence to show that the national move to bring education to the center of development agenda is gaining ground. This needs to be consolidated in the near future.

## Goals, Objectives and Values

### *National Objectives*

The starting point of the Commission's Report was to state explicitly and unambiguously the national objectives of education are as follows:

- To relate education to life, needs and aspirations of the people;
- To make education a powerful instrument of social, economic and cultural transformation;
- To increase productivity;
- To achieve social and national integration;
- To accelerate the process of modernization; and
- To cultivate social, moral and spiritual values.

Each one of these objectives is as relevant today, and perhaps, more relevant than in the sixties. In revisiting the Commission premises, it becomes necessary to underscore those recommendations, which could have saved the education system from the aimless drift and sense of crisis being witnessed in the country. The general public is often confused by expressions of pride and euphoria regarding the size, growth rate and brand names of Indian education system at the one end, and by perceptions of deep crisis voiced by eminent persons in high authority at the other extreme. This calls for a holistic analysis of the true state of education in India along with possible directions for the future.

### *Life, Needs and Aspirations*

The Commission highlighted the aspects of life, needs and aspirations of the people in terms of basic needs of food security, housing, water, clothing and minimum levels of decent quality of life through employment opportunities.

A re-examination of these aspects would primarily involve designing an education system along the guiding principles enunciated in the National

Curriculum Framework (2005). These would include new approaches to education based on:

- Connecting knowledge to life outside the school;
- Ensuring that learning is shifted away from rote methods;
- Enriching the curriculum to provide for overall development of children rather than remaining text book centric;
- Making examinations more flexible and integrated with class room life; and
- Nurturing an over riding identity informed by caring concerns within the democratic polity of the country.

Concomitantly, educational objectives should deal with problems that stalk rural schools and the underprivileged sections; high drop-out rates in rural schools, slow learners and children who leave school for extended periods. The fact that the life around rural children is very different from that of urban areas, poses interesting challenges to the design of context-oriented learning. The attitude of 'one size fits all' and compartmentalized learning of subjects needs to be eliminated.

The growing aspirations of the people, especially the first generation learners and underprivileged sections, would bring up the issues of access, equity, affordability and supply levels matching the rising demand. Keeping these issues in view, the Commission made far reaching recommendations on fee structure. It recommended: *"...the country should gradually work towards a stage when all education would be tuition free"*. It gave high priority to free education at primary stage and to the abolition of fees at the secondary stage intended mainly for the under privileged groups. Though the Commission did not advocate the immediate general abolition of fees in higher education, it suggested *"...this should be the ultimate goal of education policy"*.

The present situation where the education system, particularly higher education, is highly dominated by private institutions, the ideals of tuition-free education have vanished. On the contrary, commercialization of education has taken a deep root thereby reducing the goals of equity and affordability. This aspect should be discussed as key objectives. In this context it is relevant to recall the Commission's observation:

> *Quantitatively, education can be organized to promote social justice or to retard it. History shows numerous instances where small social groups and elites have used education as a prerogative of their rule and as a tool for maintaining their hegemony and perpetuating the values upon which it has rested. On the other hand, there are cases in which a social cultural revolution has been brought about in a system where equality of educational opportunity is provided and education is deliberately used to develop more and more potential talent and to harness it to the solution of national problems.*

### *Common School System*

The Education Commission emphasized that it is the responsibility of the education system to bring different social classes and groups together and promote the emergence of an egalitarian and integrated society. The schools managed by governments and local bodies are generally of inferior quality than the private schools. Since the private schools charge high fees at the secondary stage, these are accessible only to the rich children thereby contributing to class segregation. A large pool of children is left out of opportunity for quality education. By segregating their children, the privileged parents prevent them from sharing the life and experiences of children of the poor and coming into contact with the realities of life.

In order to eliminate these weaknesses and to make the education system a powerful instrument of national development and social and national integration, the Commission suggested a Common School System of public education which will be open to all children irrespective of class, creed, community, religion, economic conditions or social status. The access to good education will not depend on wealth or class but on talent. No tuition fee will be charged in the common schools.

### *Medium of Instruction in Schools and Colleges*

The medium of instruction should enable students to acquire knowledge with felicity and to express themselves with quality and to think with precision and vigour. The Commission therefore, proposed the development of modern Indian languages to enable them to become the medium of instruction in schools and colleges. However, the progress in this respect has been very slow. Unfortunately, there is a perception that the English medium schools are better in quality than the indigenous language schools. To a major extent this is a myth in as much as most of the teachers in these schools and colleges do not have sufficient English language skill to articulate the concepts. This inevitably leads to rote learning from the prescribed textbooks.

### *Knowledge Society*

The Commission pointed out that in a modern society the stock of knowledge is far greater and the pace of its growth infinitely quicker. One of the main tasks of education in the modern society is to keep pace with the advances in knowledge. Knowledge is not something that should be received passively but should be discovered actively. Therefore, a new approach with the objectives and methods of education and changes in the training of teachers would be an essential precondition for the development of a knowledge society.

### *Affiliation System*

One of the major drawbacks of Indian higher education system is the practice of affiliation of colleges to universities. In spite of recommendations by several committees that the affiliation system should be done away with, it continues to persist, rather on a magnified scale. Some universities have as many as 500 colleges affiliated to them. Consequently, the university becomes an examination body and not a source of inspiration for knowledge creation and innovation. The colleges tend to blindly follow the syllabi handed over to them based on the textbooks prescribed for this purpose and the students are driven to prepare themselves for passing the examination and not for acquiring knowledge, skill and experience. There is very little freedom to experiment with new ideas and new approaches to teaching and learning.

There is an immediate need to evolve a system, which overcomes the evils of the affiliation of colleges. There have been suggestions of converting some of the better institutions into autonomous colleges. Some scholars have proposed establishment of clusters of colleges, which can follow innovative educational practices. This is also linked to the evaluation methods and standards including the proposal for credit system, continuous internal evaluation, internal examination, transparency in evaluation and making examination a learning experience. It is necessary to evolve new standards for evaluation so that our degrees and diplomas become internationally comparable.

### *The Synergy*

The Commission proposed that universities and colleges should not remain in isolation from the education system at the school level. It suggested that each college can be functionally related to a number of secondary schools in the neighbourhood and provide extension services and guidance to them to improve their standards. This has rarely happened and it is high time that the nation considers these suggestions very seriously. Similarly, the Commission suggested that the universities could conduct special courses for school teachers. The UGC has been supporting academic staff colleges in selected universities and this programme needs to be reviewed and strengthened. As suggested by the Commission, some of the universities can adopt, on an experimental basis, secondary and primary schools to evolve improved techniques and standards. Some of the universities and colleges can add to the quality of school education by participating in efforts to improve the contents of textbooks and selecting talented students from the school to develop knowledge through exposure to laboratory facilities in their colleges.

### *Adult and Continuing Education*

Some of the key suggestions relating to Adult and Continuing Education made by the Commission have been implemented to a reasonable extent. These are:

1. Enable those who have not completed a stage of education to complete it;
2. Help such persons to have further education with or without formally enrolling in an institution;

3. Enable the workers to acquire knowledge, ability and vocational skills in order to be better and efficient workers and improve their chances of earning more; and,
4. Help to refresh knowledge of educated persons and enable them to keep pace with new knowledge in the field of their interest.

## Instrument of Transformation

The Commission has elaborated the role of education as an Instrument of Change in the following words: "*If the 'change on a grand scale' is to be achieved without violent revolution (and even for that it would be necessary), there is one instrument, and one instrument only, that can be used: EDUCATION.*" Its suggestions relate to the stock and attributes of the educated human resources, adoption of science and technology and development of physical resources.

In the changed context of the Indian economy, the need to assign a central role to education in relation to all the development sectors becomes necessary. Unfortunately, education has been totally de-linked from all other national endeavours. Barring a negligible area in the agricultural sector, the link of the education system with other sectors such as manufacturing, defense, transportation, financial systems, etc., is highly tenuous and haphazard.

## Education and Economic Growth

The economic growth in India has created a high demand for educated persons at all levels with appropriate knowledge, skill and experience. With 62 per cent of India's population in working age group, the demand for educational opportunities will increase in the next three decades. This feature combined with the growing services sector within the country and abroad would require highly qualified human resource. There is a need to organize the education system not only in terms of increased enrolment but also endowed with high quality comparable to the best in the world. The economic growth performance in the past and the projection for 2006-07 is shown in *Table 2.2*.

The overall growth in 2006-07 is projected to be in the range of 7.8-8.0 per cent. In the past, the education system was not particularly linked to the economic and social developments in the country. It remained largely in the periphery unconcerned with the changes in the economy and the society. In recent years, there is considerable attention to reforming the education system in a manner that it can play a pivotal role in the development of the nation. An analysis of enrolment in higher education suggests that there is broadly a positive correlation between enrolment in education and per capita GDP. The enrolment levels in the elementary and higher education stage against the Net State Domestic Product (NSDP) shown in *Tables 2.3, 2.4 and Figures 2.1, 2.2 and 2.3* indicate a high degree of correlation between the two factors.

**Table 2.2: Economic Growth Performance**

| | *2003-04* | *2004-05* | *2005-06* | *2006-07* |
|---|---|---|---|---|
| 1. Agriculture & allied activities | 10.0 | 0.7 | 3.9 | 1.5 |
| 2. Mining and Quarrying | 5.3 | 5.8 | 0.9 | 7.0 |
| 3. Manufacturing | 7.1 | 8.1 | 9.0 | 9.5 |
| 4. Electricity Gas & Water Supply | 4.8 | 4.3 | 5.3 | 5.5 |
| 5. Construction | 10.9 | 12.5 | 12.1 | 12.5 |
| 6. Trade, Hotels, Transport, Storage and Communications | 12.0 | 10.6 | 11.5 | 10.5 |
| 7. Finance, Insurance, Real Estate & Business Services | 4.5 | 9.2 | 9.7 | 9.5 |
| 8. Community & Personal Services | 5.4 | 9.2 | 7.8 | 7.5 |
| 9. Gross Domestic Product (Factor Cost, Constant prices) | 8.5 | 7.5 | 8.4 | 7.9 |
| Industry (2+3+4+5) | 7.6 | 8.6 | 8.7 | 9.7 |
| *Services (6+7+8)* | 8.2 | 9.9 | 10.0 | 9.5 |
| *Non-Agriculture (9-1)* | 8.0 | 9.5 | 9.6 | 9.6 |

*Above Figures indicate percentage change over previous years*

Taking the school enrolment per million population as an indicator, *Table* 2.3 shows the Per Capita NSDP against enrolment levels as well as the population below poverty line, indicating the disparities among different States.

**Table 2.3: Disparities among States in NSDP, BPL and School Enrolment**

| *States* | *Per Capita NSDP (Rs) (2002-03)* | *School Enrolment (000) (2004)* | *% Population Below Poverty Line* |
|---|---|---|---|
| Andhra Pradesh | 18661 | 148.7 | 15.8 |
| Arunachal Pradesh | 15616 | 191.3 | — |
| Assam | 11755 | 152.2 | 36.1 |
| Bihar | 6015 | 154.9 | 42.6 |
| Chandigarh | 52795 | 115.3 | — |
| Chhattisgarh | 11893 | 185.9 | — |
| Delhi | 47417 | 147.8 | 8.2 |
| Gujarat | 22047 | 134.6 | 14.1 |
| Haryana | 26632 | 103.2 | 8.7 |
| Himachal Pradesh | 22576 | 179.3 | 7.6 |
| Jharkhand | 9955 | 141.8 | — |
| Karnataka | 18521 | 149.5 | 20.0 |
| Kerala | 21853 | 93.2 | 12.7 |
| Madhya Pradesh | 11438 | 201.8 | 37.4 |
| Maharashtra | 26386 | 120.1 | 25.0 |
| Meghalaya | 15983 | 207.7 | — |
| Orissa | 10340 | 158.0 | 47.2 |
| Pondicherry | 38162 | 128.7 | — |
| Punjab | 25853 | 110.2 | 6.2 |
| Rajasthan | 12753 | 176.3 | 15.3 |
| Sikkim | 20456 | 213.5 | 36.6 |
| Tamil Nadu | 21433 | 156.8 | 21.1 |
| Uttar Pradesh | 10289 | 163.0 | 31.2 |
| West Bengal | 18756 | 160.5 | 22.0 |

Figure 2.1 shows a positive correlation between these NSDP and School Enrolment with a correlation ratio of 0.458. *Figure 2* shows a positive correlation between BPL and enrolment with a coefficient of correlation of 0.482.

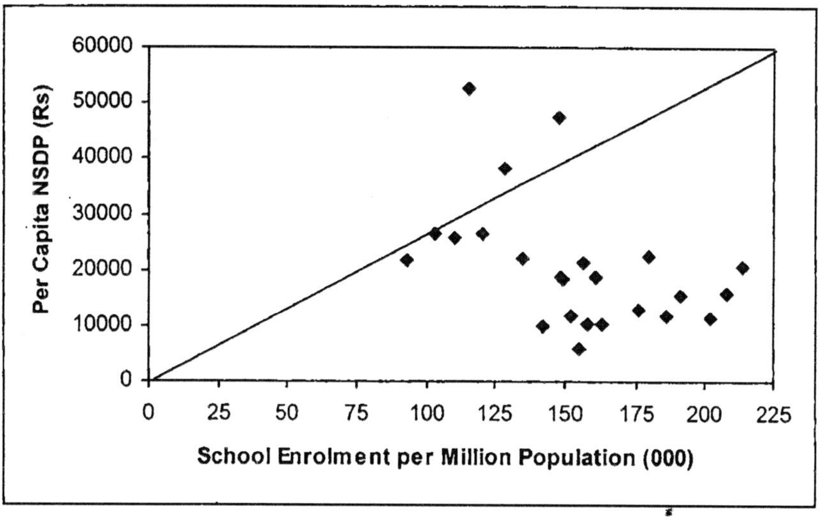


**Figure 2.1: Correlation between NSDP and School Enrolment**

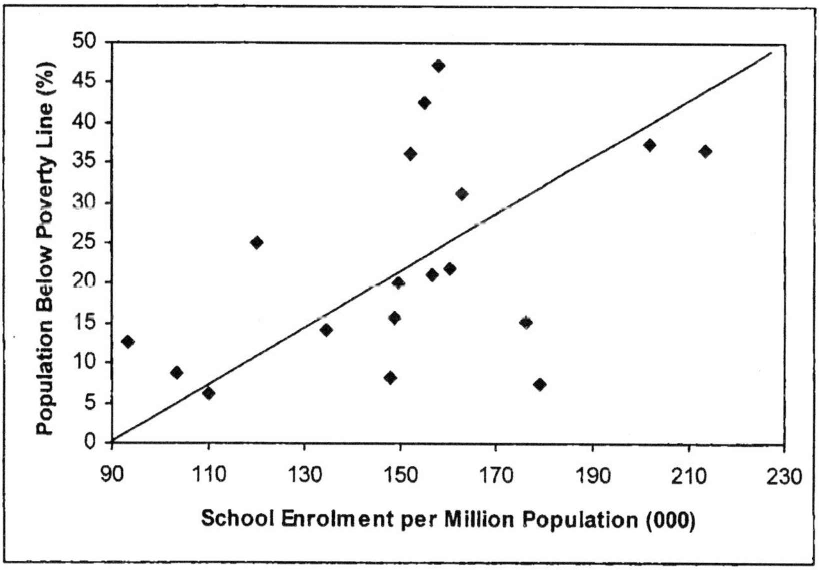


**Figure 2.2: Correlation between BPL and School Enrolment**

Similar correlation is seen in the case of higher education as shown in *Table 2.4 and Figure 2.3* with a correlation coefficient of 0.566 between Gross Enrolment Ratio (GER) and the NSDP.

**Table 2.4: NSDP and GER in Higher Education**

| *S. No.* | *State/Union Territory* | *Per Capita Net State Domestic Product at Current Prices (2002-03)* | *Gross Enrolment Ratio in Higher Education in % (2002-03)* |
|---|---|---|---|
| 1 | Andhra Pradesh | 18661 | 9.51 |
| 2 | Arunachal Pradesh | 15616 | 6.37 |
| 3 | Assam | 11755 | 8.67 |
| 4 | Bihar | 6015 | 7.3 |
| 5 | Jharkhand | 9955 | 7.27 |
| 6 | Goa | NA | 13.47 |
| 7 | Gujarat | 22047 | 9.65 |
| 8 | Haryana | 26632 | 10.56 |
| 9 | Himachal Pradesh | 22576 | 12.76 |
| 10 | Jammu & Kashmir | NA | 4.95 |
| 11 | Karnataka | 18521 | 8.12 |
| 12 | Kerala | 21853 | 9.92 |
| 13 | Madhya Pradesh | 11438 | 7.66 |
| 14 | Chhattisgarh | 11893 | 7.77 |
| 15 | Maharashtra | 26386 | 12:3 |
| 16 | Manipur | 12230 | 13.19 |
| 17 | Meghalaya | 15983 | 10.94 |
| 18 | Mizoram | NA | 9.51 |
| 19 | Nagaland | NA | 4.33 |
| 20 | Orissa | 10340 | 8.71 |
| 21 | Punjab | 25855 | 8.53 |
| 22 | Rajasthan | 12753 | 8.77 |
| 23 | Sikkim | 20456 | 6.29 |
| 24 | Tamil Nadu | 21433 | 10.91 |
| 25 | Tripura | NA | 5.84 |
| 26 | Uttar Pradesh | 10289 | 7.03 |
| 27 | Uttaranchal | NA | 12.25 |
| 28 | West Bengal | 18756 | 8.21 |
| 29 | A & N Islands | NA | 0 |
| 30 | Chandigarh | 52795 | 28.68 |
| 31 | Delhi | 47477 | 10.94 |
| 32 | Pondicherry | 38162 | 17.88 |

*Sources*: *Economic Survey 2004-05* and *CABE Committee on Higher Education Financing 2005.*

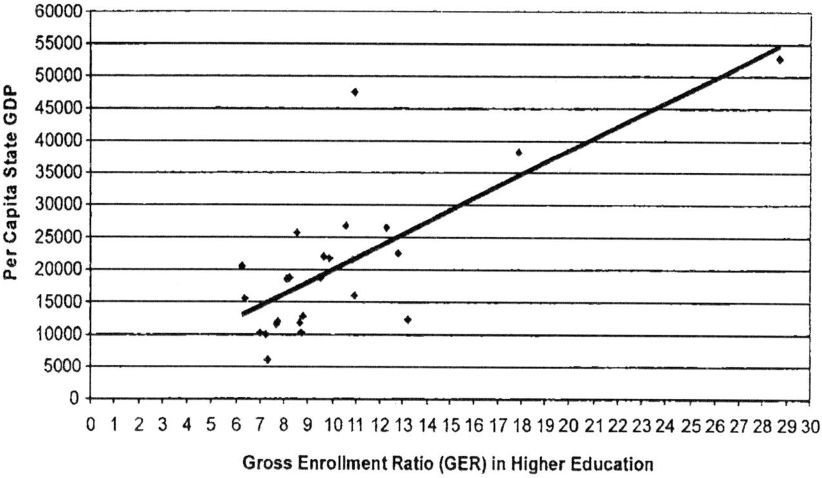


*Source*: Based on Table 2.4.

**Figure 2.3: NSDP vs. GER in Higher Education**

## Increasing Productivity

The Commission has dealt with education and productivity and offered several suggestions such as:

- Making science a basic component of education and culture;
- Making work-experience an integral part of general education;
- Vocational education at the secondary level; and
- Improvement of scientific and technological education and research at the university stage with special emphasis on agriculture and allied sciences.

Our record in implementing these suggestions is tardy, distorted and inadequate. The imbalances in the availability of skill development facilities are evident. The design and manufacturing skills and service-oriented skills for current conventional demand have been neglected in favour of a few services such as information technology and hotel management. All evidences point towards decline in quality and quantity of research even in prestigious institutions. The nature of research is largely disconnected with national priorities. The attraction to science, technology, arts and humanities is sharply declining in favour of commerce, management and selected technologies. These trends require a deeper examination to eliminate current distortions and provide scope for a balanced skill regime.

## Social and National Integration

The Commission lays out the dimensions of social and national integration for creating a strong, united country. These include collective self-confidence, equality of opportunity, regional balance, good governance and understanding ways of life of different sections of the nation. The suggested approaches to achieve these objectives include the Common School System of public education, social and national service as part of education, developing modern Indian languages as medium of instruction and promoting national consciousness. The degree to which these objectives have been realized and the reasons for shortfalls require detailed analysis.

## Modernization

The concept of linking education with modernization is dealt with in the Commission's report, highlighting the key features that characterize a modern society. These include, the capacity to absorb and assimilate vast amount of knowledge involving new ways of teaching and learning beyond "learning by heart", the role of education in rapid social change, awakening curiosity, habits of self study and capacity for independent thinking and judgment. These characteristics of educational processes are even more important in the present situation with advances in information and communication technologies, explosion of diverse forms of information, different approaches to transform information into knowledge and a variety of pedagogic methods.

## Attributes of Knowledge Society

Establishing a knowledge-based society in India is perceived as the foremost challenge in the immediate future. 'Knowledge' will not only be the driver of the Indian economy but also the source for attaining satisfactory quality of life and living conditions of every society. The social goal of the knowledge society is to attain "increased knowledge of the social, biological, cultural, economic and physical determinants of the well-being in order to build a society in which we Indians can enjoy health and independence and have a sense of belonging, identity and partnership".

No doubt that these expectations can be fully realized with a strong and dynamic higher education system, capable of supporting economic and social innovations and provide the basis for self-confidence and reduce the need for external dependency. While ushering in such a society, it is necessary to ensure that justice and human values prevail. For such a system of higher education to flourish, it is imperative that proper foundation is laid at the early stages of education, as a continuous chain from primary to post graduate level. A vibrant knowledge society will possess two main attributes: one, its goals of education will be unambiguously spelt out and carried forward; and two, it will include all sections of the society to participate in its development and operation.

## Aims of Education

The primary aims of education in a knowledge society should be to reach out to the learners at all levels of education in a manner that they derive meaning and substance from the educational process and relate them to creating a sustainable society. One of the immediate goals in the light of the prevailing approaches to education in India is to increase the context-oriented knowledge. No doubt, the contents of basic textbooks are the same for learners in any part of the world. Highlighting the meaning of the basic knowledge in the specific context of the day-to-day life of the learners will help them appreciate the value of the basic knowledge, enable them to retain the knowledge and create the desire to learn more. In the existing education system, since the content is contextually disconnected, students merely study the subjects for examination purpose and nothing more. This calls for drastic changes in the approach of the curriculum designers, text-book writers and teachers on how they visualize the process of context-oriented learning. It should be possible in a knowledge society to devise the learning process in tune with the physical, cultural, economic, political, spiritual and social experiences.

Consequently, the student would have many questions to raise, many occasions to think and speak out, embark on some investigations on their own and find room for sharing and integrating their life's experiences with the text-book knowledge. The learning experience will thus be free from fear and stress and become a source of enjoyment and satisfaction. Another important goal of education is the introduction of healthy social values resulting in appreciation of the principles of democracy, human rights, social justice and equity.

A knowledge society shall not be interpreted as consisting of great scholars and intellectuals only. The education system should provide substantial and deliberate scope for work-related experience in terms of various skills and healthy attitude towards skill development. At the same time, the educational experiences should include ability to appreciate beauty and art and facilitate creative expressions.

## Value System

The aspects relating to social, moral and spiritual values as necessary components of the education system are covered in the Commission's report with many valuable suggestions. Starting from the philosophical and practical aspects outlined in the report of the University Education Commission (1948) and CABE Committee (1959), the Commission makes recommendations on the need to understand and appreciate the values advocated by different religions, different traditions and cultures, secularism and tolerance. The Commission emphasized 'education about religions' and not `religious education'. The events of the past few decades within and outside India have made this aspect even more relevant today than in the Sixties. The form in which this could be achieved at the school and university levels needs to be explored.

## Growth Strategies

***The Structure:*** The Commission specifically categorizes the education system into three stages: the elementary, the secondary and the tertiary stage. The Commission visualized a flexible education structure covering:

- The pre-school stage of 1-3 years;
- The primary stage of 7 or 8 years divided into two sub-stages;
- The lower primary stage of 4 or 5 years and a higher primary stage of 3 years;
- The lower secondary or high school stage of 3 or 2 years in general education or of 1-3 years in vocational education;
- The higher secondary stage of 2 years of general education or 1-3 years of vocational education;
- The higher education stage having a course of 3 years or more for the first degree followed by courses of varying duration for the 2-year or research degrees.

The pattern of education in India follows the above recommendations with the elementary education from grades 1-8, consisting of primary stage of classes 1-5, the upper primary stage of classes 6-8, with variation in some states. The secondary education consists of the high school stage in classes 9-10 and senior secondary stage of classes 11-12. The higher education system consists of 3-year degree programmes in some disciplines and 4 or 5-year programmes in professional disciplines. While some of the schools offer vocational streams at the senior secondary stage there are also large number of polytechnics offering 3-year diploma after class 10.

What is neglected, however, is the suggestion of the Commission that at the elementary stage effort should be made to bring the schools closer to the community, with accent on serving the community in suitable ways. While, the secondary school should carefully develop planned programmes for promoting good school-community relations and suitable forms of service to the community, it should be obligatory for college students before getting the first degree to put in at least 60 days of national service, except in cases where institutions adopt the National Service Schemes (NSS) or National Cadet Corps (NCC). In its reflections on the growth strategy, the Commission was of the view that education should be properly organized both qualitatively and quantitatively.

While it advocated universal education up to the age of 14, as mandated by Article 45 of the Constitution, the Commission proposed that the growth of secondary schools and higher educational systems should be more directly related to the absorptive capacity of the economy and stressed the need for high quality of education at all stages. The Commission cautioned that excessive production of secondary school or college level graduates may accentuate the problem of unemployment. Poor quality of education can also render the children unemployed, which in turn could create social tension and retard economic growth.

## Growth Rate of Education

In the present context, it is essential to determine the desirable rate of growth at the secondary stage and tertiary stage. While some scholars argue that every student should be compulsorily provided with education up to 12th grade or alternately provided with sufficient opportunity to pursue skill oriented courses after 8th grade for at least 4 years. This issue requires careful consideration in the light of the economic growth trends in the country and the financial implications of expanding the secondary school system.

The expansion strategy for higher education needs to be clearly spelled out. There have been suggestions that about 15 per cent of the eligible age group should get higher education by the year 2012 and growing further to 25 per cent in 2020 and 50 per cent by 2030. The growth strategy should, therefore, be determined at the national level, after taking into account the growing demand for higher education, the capacity of the economy to absorb the graduates and cost implications.

## Discipline wise Distribution

The growth strategy for higher education should also indicate the desirable distribution of various disciplines like humanities and social sciences, commerce and management, basic sciences and professional disciplines such as agriculture, medicine, technology and law. Out of an estimated enrolment of 10.41 million students in higher education in India, about 2.5 million graduate each year. The estimated pool of graduates in 2003-04 is shown in *Table* 2.5.

The discipline wise enrolment in higher education in India reveal that of the total enrolment, about 45 per cent of the students are in arts; about 20 per cent in science; 18 per cent in commerce, and about 17 per cent in professional courses. Any redistribution of the disciplinary programmes within the overall higher educational system should be based on a careful assessment of the future manpower needs so that the initiatives to start new institutions and the increase in intake capacity can be properly guided.

**Table 2.5: Graduates Pool in India (2003-04)**

| | *Engineering Degree Holders* | *Engineering Diploma Holders* | *Arts Degree Holders* | *Science Degree Holders* | *Commerce Degree Holders* | *Total Graduates* |
|---|---|---|---|---|---|---|
| Stock (on 2003) | 1,200,000 | 1,750,000 | 11,500,000 | 4,985,000 | 5,933,000 | 21,986,000 |
| Out-turn (in 2004, estimate) | 155,000 | 130,000 | 1,150,000 | 540,000 | 480,000 | 2,460,000 |

*Source*: Institute of Applied Manpower Research and the Ministry of Human Resource Development, GOI.

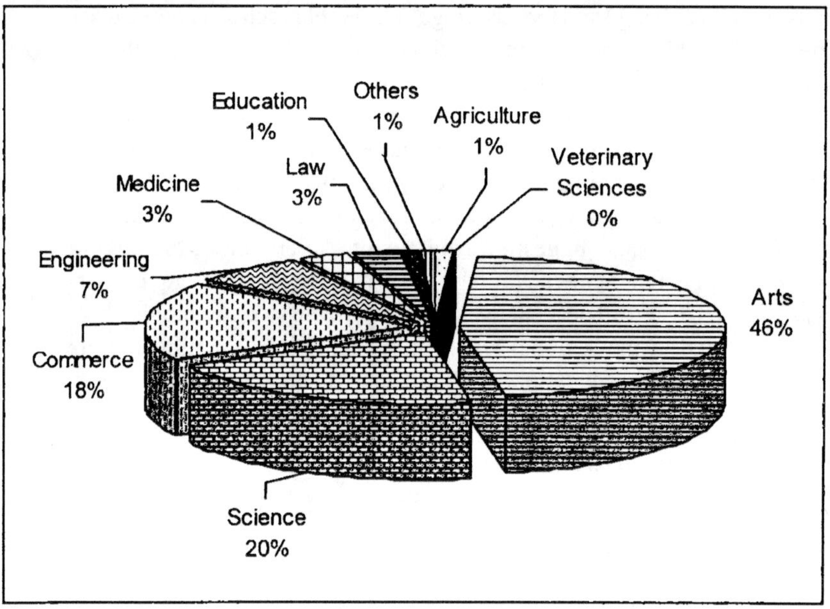


*Source*: University Grants Commission.

**Figure 2.4: Subject- wise Enrollments 2004-05**

## Distance Mode Education

In achieving the desirable access to educational facilities at the secondary stage or tertiary stage, the inclusion of distance learning programmes should be carefully done to avoid misleading inflation in numbers. In fact, it would be necessary to define the objectives and goals of the distance education programmes, which have proliferated in the country in an unplanned manner. One policy suggestion could be that distance education programme should be available only as a further education measure and not as a basic diploma or degree.

## Elementary Education

With the enactment of the Universal Elementary Education Act (UEE), the governments at the Centre and the States have the responsibility of ensuring education to all children in the age group of 6 to 14 years. The Sarva Shiksha Abhiyan (SSA) schemes have been launched throughout the country to achieve the target of UEE. The objectives of SSA are:

- All children should be in school, Education Guarantee Centre, Alternate School, or 'Back-to-School' camp by 2003;
- All children should complete five years of primary schooling by 2007;
- All children should complete eight years of elementary schooling by 2010;
- Focus should be on elementary education of satisfactory quality with emphasis on education for life;
- All gender and social category gaps should be bridged at primary stage by 2007 and at elementary education level by 2010; and,
- Should achieve universal retention by 2010.

The efforts relating to SSA are joint endeavors by the Central and State Governments, local bodies and the community. Besides attaining the quantitative targets, qualitative improvement in the elementary school environment should also take place. There are considerable challenges in fulfilling this responsibility in view of the vast differentes in the present status of school education in different parts of the country. The recent countrywide data on elementary education collected and compiled by the National University of Educational Planning and Administration (NUEPA) is available in their publications. The data relate to 931,471 schools from over 539 districts across 25 States and Union Territories (UTs) in India. The data show that there has been a significant growth in elementary education in recent years with a majority of the schools located in rural areas and managed by government (Table 2.6).

**Table 2.6: Growth of Elementary Schools in India**

| *Year* | *2003* | *2004* | *2005* |
|---|---|---|---|
| Total | 85360 | 931471 | 1037813 |
| Rural Schools | 742633 | 811520 | 901824 |
| % Rural | 87.00 | 87.12 | 86.90 |
| % Govt. Managed | — | — | 84.85 |
| % Private Managed | — | — | 15.15 |

Most of these schools, especially in rural areas, are government managed. Of the privately managed schools about one-third are aided by governments.

The primary schools are nearly 2.5 to 3 times the upper primary schools *(Table 2.7).*

**Table 2.7: Ratio of Primary to Upper Primary Schools**

| | *All Areas* | *Rural Areas* | *Urban Areas* |
|---|---|---|---|
| Govt. Managed | 3.26 | 3.38 | 2.24 |
| Pvt. Managed | 1.26 | 1.27 | 1.25 |
| All Schools | 2.68 | 2.93 | 1.63 |

In rural areas, the primary school-upper primary school ratio is 3.38: 1. This ratio is better for urban areas: for 2.24 primary schools one upper primary school.

## Enrolment Disparities

The Commission draws particular attention to the regional imbalances in enrolment, which still persists. The Gross and Net Enrolment Ratios (GER and NER) at primary and upper primary levels and enrolment of children per million population reveal large variation among the States.

There has been a steady growth in total enrolment of children of the eligible age groups. The enrolment rate has been increasing for both boys and girls but the gap still remains (Table 2.8).

**Table 2.8: Growth in Elementary School Enrolment**

| *Year* | *Primary (I-V)* | | | *Upper Primary (VI-VIII)* | | | *Elementary (I-VIII)* | | |
|---|---|---|---|---|---|---|---|---|---|
| | *Boys* | *Girls* | *Total* | *Boys* | *Girls* | *Total* | *Boys* | *Girls* | *Total* |
| 1950-51 | 60.6 | 24.8 | 42.6 | 20.6 | 4.6 | 12.7 | 46.4 | 17.7 | 32.1 |
| 1960-61 | 82.6 | 41.4 | 62.4 | 33.2 | 11.3 | 22.5 | 65.2 | 30.9 | 48.7 |
| 1970-71 | 95.5 | 60.5 | 78.6 | 46.5 | 20.8 | 33.4 | 75.5 | 44.4 | 61.9 |
| 1980-81 | 95.8 | 64.1 | 80.5 | 54.3 | 28.6 | 41.9 | 82.2 | 52.1 | 67.5 |
| 1990-91 | 114.0 | 85.5 | 100.1 | 76.6 | 47.0 | 62.1 | 100.0 | 70.8 | 86.0 |
| 1991-92 | 112.8 | 86.9 | 100.2 | 75.1 | 49.6 | 61.4 | 101.2 | 73.2 | 87.7 |
| 1992-93 | 95.0 | 73.5 | 84.6 | 72.5 | 48.9 | 67.5 | 87.7 | 65.7 | 77.2 |
| 1993-94 | 90.0 | 73.1 | 81.9 | 62.1 | 45.4 | 54.2 | 80.2 | 63.7 | 72.3 |
| 1994-95 | 96.6 | 78.2 | 87.7 | 68.9 | 50.0 | 60.0 | 87.2 | 68.8 | 78.4 |
| 1995-96 | 97.1 | 79.4 | 88.6 | 67.8 | 49.8 | 59.3 | 86.9 | 69.4 | 78.5 |
| 1996-97 | 97.0 | 80.1 | 88.8 | 65.8 | 49.2 | 58.0 | 85.9 | 69.4 | 78.0 |
| 1997-98 | 99.3 | 82.2 | 91.1 | 66.3 | 49.7 | 58.5 | 87.4 | 70.7 | 79.4 |
| 1998-99 | 100.9 | 82.9 | 92.1 | 65.3 | 49.1 | 57.6 | 87.6 | 70.6 | 79.4 |
| 1999-2000 | 104.1 | 85.2 | 94.9 | 67.2 | 49.7 | 58.8 | 90.1 | 72.0 | 81.3 |
| 2000-2001 | 104.9 | 85.9 | 95.7 | 66.7 | 49.9 | 58.6 | 90.3 | 72.4 | 81.6 |
| 2001-2002 | 105.3 | 86.9 | 96.3 | 67.8 | 52.1 | 60.2 | 90.7 | 73.6 | 82.4 |

## Drop-out Rates

The average national drop-out ratios at different levels of schooling are shown in *Table* 2.9. Though it is decreasing progressively, the rate is significantly high and is a matter of serious concern.

**Table 2.9: Dropout Rates at Primary, Elementary and Secondary Stages**

| | *1960-61* | *1970-71* | *1980-81* | *1990-91* | *1992-93* | *1999-00* | *2001-02* |
|---|---|---|---|---|---|---|---|
| Classes I-V | 64.9 | 67 | 58.7 | 42.6 | 45 | 40.3 | 39 |
| Classes I-VIII | 78.3 | 77.9 | 72.7 | 60.9 | 61.1 | 54.5 | 54.6 |
| Classes I-X | NA | NA | 82.5 | 71.3 | 72.9 | 68.3 | 66 |

## GER of Scheduled Caste and Schedule Tribe

The Gross Enrolment Ratio of the Scheduled Castes and Scheduled Tribes in elementary school in the 6-14 age group among the boys and girls shows that girls belonging to SC and ST communities are particularly vulnerable. Their GER is much lower than that of the boys.

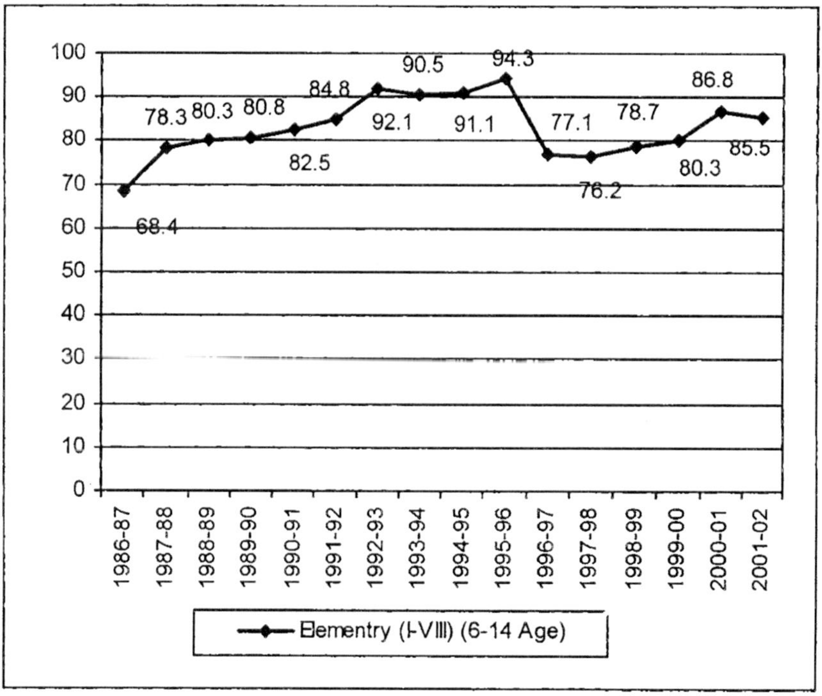


**Figure 2.5(a): GER of Scheduled Caste Students**

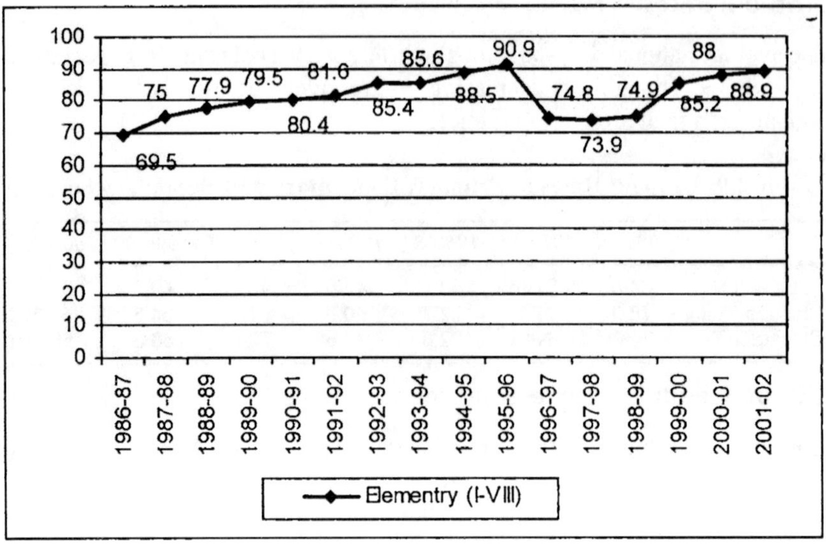


**Figure 2.5(b): GER of Scheduled Tribe Students**

## The Learning Environment

The learning environment in a significant proportion of these schools, in terms of adequacy of physical infrastructure and facilities and availability of teachers, requires considerable improvement (Table 2.10).

**Table 2.10: Variation in Facilities among Elementary Schools, 2005**

| | *All Areas* | *Rural Areas* | *Urban Areas* | *Govt. Managed* | *Pvt. Managed* |
|---|---|---|---|---|---|
| Number without Building | 41075 | 37795 | 3179 | 40062 | 1079 |
| % with Single Teacher | 13.36 | 14.66 | 4.41 | 15.13 | 3.45 |
| % without Drinking Water | 15.6 | 16.55 | 9.82 | 21.43 | 5.36 |
| % with Common Toilet | 46.82 | 44.82 | 64.44 | 42.82 | 69.23 |
| % without Black Board | 5.00 | 4.98 | 4.91 | | |
| Number with Computers | 93249 | 60023 | 33226 | 45245 | 48004 |
| % with Computers | 8.99 | 6.66 | 26.41 | 5.14 | 30.52 |
| Ave. Enrolment per class | 150 | 140 | 239 | 137 | 223 |
| % Girls Enrolment | 46.99 | 46.79 | 47.84 | 47.76 | 44.55 |
| % enrolment in Govt. Schools to Total enrolment | 76.3 | 83.16 | 41.48 | | |
| % enrolment in Rural Areas to Total enrolment | | | | 90.19 | 57.93 |
| % Survival Rate in Grade 5. | 67 | 64 | 64 | 58 | — |
| Primary: Under-aged | 8.46 | 7.95 | 11.22 | | |
| Primary-Over-aged | 5.80 | 5.72 | 6.22 | | |
| Upper Primary Under-aged | 11.11 | 10.46 | 13.55 | | |
| Upper primary Over-aged | 8.65 | 8.71 | 8.44 | | |

Considering the fact that the number of children in the age-group of 6-11 is 120.94 million and those in the age group of 11-14 is 73 million, it is observed that several thousands of students are deprived of the basic minimum facilities. This is particularly more severe in some states than others.

The enormous challenge that is involved in implementing Universal Elementary Education can be understood from the NUEPA report already cited earlier. The available data shows that there is a wide gap in the basic infrastructure facilities in most of the States and wide variations in the availability of these facilities. Not surprisingly, the drop-out rates are still high. Since the implementation of the UEE is a joint effort of the Central Government, State Governments, the local bodies and the community, a careful structured implementation programme with adequate financial resources and policy instruments will be essential to deal with this malady.

## Some Critical Issues

A review of various national level discussions on factors that affect the educational system leads to a set of issues that are critical for assessment of the current trends and future directions. These issues relate to policy, governance, resources, curriculum and syllabi structure, social issues such as access, affordability; regulatory issues, their adequacy and distortions; interference factors such as political, administrative, commercial, and others.

### *Development Directions for Education*

Education is increasingly viewed as an instrument of upward social mobility and economic security. Larger number of young students, including first generation learners, are seeking opportunities in higher education. Concomitant with the growth in numbers, there are also major changes in the disciplinary knowledge base and new combinations of disciplines. The physical migration of knowledge seekers, across the country and abroad, is steadily increasing. The presence of foreign higher educational institutions in India is rapidly growing. The scope for open and distance learning through conventional modes is considerably enhanced by the new technologies for e-learning and virtual classes. The flexibility in the configuration of courses and institutions is seamlessly available to the learners.

Added to these changes in the academic domain, there are several major socio-economic changes affecting the education sector. These include global economic integration, national economic reforms, changing demographic pattern, increased school enrolment and reducing drop-out rates, social norms favouring women and weaker sections, increasing environmental consciousness, changing family finances, demands of labour market, and so on. The strategy for development of Education Sector would have to take into account these trends in determining future initiatives. There are several aspects to be considered in determining future directions for higher education in India:

- Provisions for anticipated growth in enrolment;
- Reconfiguration of disciplinary intake capacities;
- Satisfying the demand for access, affordability, and social equity;
- Ensuring academic standards and functional quality;
- Making higher education endeavour financially viable and administratively efficient; and
- Developing a transparent and predictable policy framework for financing higher education.

The issues relating to equity cannot be viewed in isolation since all of the above aspects are interrelated and influence the equity processes.

### *Professional Education*

There is considerable need for alternate pathways for obtaining higher educational qualifications. Adoption of credit system will facilitate flexibility in obtaining advanced qualifications. In the case of professional degree programmes in higher education a three-track approach may be considered.

One track will enable students to progressively advance from certificate to diploma to bachelor's degree up to Ph.D. and research degrees, essentially producing human resources, which are skill oriented in design, development, manufacturing and maintenance of quality.

The second track would be for those who graduate from higher secondary schools to move on towards degree, post-graduate and research qualifications. They would obtain interdisciplinary knowledge specialized in some core subjects. Their analytical capability and knowledge base will be in demand in corporate bodies of major industries as well as for teaching and research career.

The third track could be for those with bachelor's degree in science to move towards bachelor's degree in professional subjects and further towards post-graduate and research qualifications. This would facilitate students coming out of the high schools to consider science degree as an option to progress towards professional degrees. They will be particularly suitable for research career in modern corporate bodies, universities and national laboratories.

### *Educational Equity*

The predominant theme running through the Commission's Report is the need to provide for access, affordability and equity. A sustainable knowledge society can be fostered only if the generation, transmission and diffusion of knowledge are pervasive across all sections of the society, irrespective of race, religion, caste, creed and income status. The education system in a knowledge society should eliminate the discrimination between the few who can afford access to knowledge and those who cannot. This process of inclusion can enlarge the knowledge base of the society by several orders of magnitude.

The University Grants Commission (UGC) highlights this concern as follows:

> *It is true that enhancing social access to higher education is still important in the country. But, the major challenge before the Indian higher education system is to bring equity in quality of education across the length and breadth of the country. This is more close to the hearts of students in rural, semi urban and urban areas, because they also wish to be able to participate in the new economic revolution. Several social, economic and political reasons seem to act as constraints to access and equity in higher education in India. Poverty leads to high drop-out rates even at primary, middle and secondary school levels. Lower status of women, lack of easy access, lack of implementation of existing programmes, inadequate utilization of resources, absence of political will and inadequacies in coordinated action across all equity fronts within institutions seem to be the other reason. Financial constraints also often form a significant factor in advancing inequity (Ref. 8).*

Without these measures the knowledge and skills will be confined to the privileged few leading to considerable disparities in the impact of developmental efforts. Referring to these challenges, the Prime Minister of India, Dr. Man Mohan Singh, while conferring the Shanti Swarup Bhatnagar Awards on September 26, 2006, states:

> *On the supply side, we have to enhance the supply of skilled scientists and technologists. This needs to be done through a judicious balancing of 'expansion', 'inclusion' and 'excellence'. On the demand side, we have to promote technology-led accelerated inclusive growth.*

## Constitutional Protection for Social Justice in Education

The Constitution of India contains several provisions emphasizing the principles of equality of status and opportunity to all the people of India. Article 14 stipulates that "the State shall not deny any person equality before the law or the equal protection of the laws within the territory of India". Article 15 prohibits "discrimination on grounds of religion, race, caste, sex or place of birth". At the same time clause (4) of Article 15 states: "Nothing in this Article or in Clause (2) of Article 29 shall prevent the State from making any special provision for the advancement of any socially and educationally backward classes of citizens or for the Scheduled Castes and Scheduled Tribes." Article 29(2) relating to protection of interests of minorities states: "No citizen shall be denied admission into any educational institution maintained by the State or receiving aid out of State funds on grounds only of religion, race, caste, language or any of them". Article 30(1) states that "all minorities whether based on religion or language shall have the right to establish and administer educational institutions of their choice."

Part IV of the Constitution containing the Directive Principles of State Policy, in Article 46, lays down that the State shall promote with special care the educational and economic interests of the weaker sections of the people, and, in particular of the Scheduled Castes and the Scheduled Tribes, and shall protect them from social injustice.

Article 19 relating to Protection of certain rights regarding freedom of speech etc., bestows in clause (1), sub-clause (8) the freedom "to practice any profession or to carry on any occupation, trade or business". Based on this article, the privately funded professional institutions represented to the Supreme Court that the State does not have the right to insist on admission of weaker sections of the people in their institutions and their contention was upheld. Therefore, the Parliament of India passed an amendment (104th Amendment) to Article 15 of the Constitution introducing a new clause (5) which states: "Nothing in this article or in sub-clause (8) of clause (1) of article 19 shall prevent the state from making special provisions by law, for advancement of any socially and educationally backward classes of citizens or for the Scheduled Castes and Scheduled Tribes in so far as their admissions to educational institutions other than minority institutions referred to in clause (1) of article 30 is concerned".

A Bill to give effect to Amendment 93 (Bill No. 76 of 2006) was introduced in the Parliament in August 2006. This Bill defines the expression "Other Backward Classes" (OBCs) so as to mean the class or classes of citizens who are socially and educationally backward and are so determined by the Central Government. This bill also empowers the Central Government to increase the number of seats in a branch of study or faculty.

### *Manifestations of Inequities*

The principles of equality of rights in the Constitution are intended to ensure dignity of every individual and not just the privileged classes; to accommodate political and cultural diversity; to assure social justice; and to impose limitations on any inequitable distribution of resources.

In certain walks of life it will not be possible to ensure absolute equality, however much one may wish. Equality in the strict sense of the term, meaning equal distribution of rights and resources with equal outcome will remain a utopian concept. In such situations, attempts are to be made to provide better opportunities, which can presumably reduce the degree of inequality and over a period of time reduce the gap to insignificance. This is the basis for the equity initiatives, such as reservation for disadvantaged groups, relaxation in admission criteria for some sections, subsidy by way of scholarships, etc. The nature of equity interventions depends on the sector of interest and the character of inequality. "Equity is a powerful and complex social theme. As a criteria for or commentary on public action, it is ideological and political, procedural and substantive. It offers, apparently, both resource for and an escape from the messy and conflict-ridden business of public allocation. The complexity of the idea cannot be reduced, but it can be ordered and explained."

Various efforts have been suggested and implemented to create the necessary conditions for equity in education. The type of interventions will vary from time to time based on the national policy priority areas. It will necessarily be political in character and hence will depend on the ideologies behind the dominant political system in power. The equity interventions are intended for compensating the built-in inequalities associated with mal-distribution of economic power, ownership of means of production, degree of social prejudices, and extent of willingness of majority to accommodate the interests of the minorities and degree of social sensitivity for the welfare of the disadvantaged.

## Opposition to Equity Efforts

The problem of inequities grows more acute with the lopsided growth in educational institutions. This calls for strategies for investment in education, catering to the needs of rural population, weaker and disadvantaged sections and an affordable higher education with potential for economic opportunities. With nearly 40 per cent of students passing out of higher secondary schools being first generation learners, special support for this population in counseling and guidance will be necessary. With reduced government support and greater proliferation of private institutions, the educational opportunities tend to move far away from the affordable range of nearly 40 per cent of the aspiring students coming from families below poverty line and low income groups.

Every political intervention introduces differentiation rather than undifferentiated equality. There is no escape from this dilemma. Some experts advocate the non-institutional model of market forces, individual preferences and reliance on judicial redresses on account of the potential for political mischief and bureaucratic inefficiencies of the interventionist approach to equity.

Some opposition is based on Benefit-Cost issues. Many argue that increased social expenditure intended for equity has not been accompanied by proportional reductions in social inequalities. Some groups advocate abandoning the concepts of degree of inequality so as to encourage efficiency of individual contributions to economic growth. They suggest that reward should be in proportion to his/her economic effectiveness. Some others are concerned with specification of equity needs by special groups such as the bureaucracy, professional groups and industrial organizations, which may lead to imposition of hidden values different from the real needs of the disadvantaged.

### *Educational Equity Efforts in India*

By and large the major thrust of the Indian educational equity efforts relates to reservation for admission in educational institutions for specified classes of people. Historically, this has been far more vigorous in the Southern States of India, such as Andhra Pradesh, Karnataka, Kerala and Tamil Nadu and virtually non-existent in most of the Northern States. The North Eastern States have reservation policies based on specified Tribes.

Reservation in education and public service began in the Madras Presidency, (now sub-divided in the four Southern States) since 1831. Over the next few decades the provisions for reservation were progressively redefined and modified, correcting anomalies and rationalizing equity measures. The policy of reservation for the down trodden communities in the Madras Presidency, viz., Backward Classes (BC), Scheduled Castes (SC) and Scheduled Tribes (ST) in admission into educational institutions and in appointments to the public service was started in 1921.

After Independence, the extent of reservation in educational institutions has undergone changes reaching different levels in different Southern States at present. The reservation policy of Tamil Nadu Government provides for 69 per cent reservation in all government and aided institutions, distributed as follows: Backward Class (BC) –30 per cent, Most Backward Class (MBC) – 20 per cent, Scheduled Class (SC) –18 per cent, and Scheduled Tribes (ST) – one per cent. In Karnataka State, the Governments' policies provide for 50 per cent reservation consisting of 18 per cent for SCs and STs and 32 per cent for Other Backward Classes (OBCs). The Kerala Government policy mandates reservation of eight per cent for SCs, two per cent for STs and 25 per cent for OBCs.

The experiences of the Southern States, which have adopted the reservation policy for admission of SC, ST and OBCs to educational institutions over several decades prove beyond doubt that the policy has helped a large section of the population access to higher and professional education, and that the policy has in no way diluted the educational standards. The achievements of OBCs are comparable to and even better than the Open Category students, and the policy has not created any serious tension in these States.

During 1990-91, the Mandal Commission recommended reservation of jobs in Central Government and public sector institutions to the extent of 49.5 per cent consisting of 17.5 per cent for SCs, five per cent for STs and 27 per cent for OBCs. There was considerable agitation against this policy in most of Northern India, but the Southern States did not oppose it. This policy could not be extended for admissions to educational institutions under the Central Government.

During 2006, with the 104th Amendment to the Constitution, the Central Government announced reservation of 27 per cent of seats for OBCs in Central educational institutions besides the existing 17.5 per cent for SCs and five per cent for STs. Due to extensive agitations against this policy, the Government announced that the number of seats currently available in the Open Category (OC) will be protected by increasing the in-take capacities in these institutions by 27 per cent, thus resulting in a total of 54 per cent increase. The process of implementation of this policy is currently under way.

### *Financial Commitments*

It is a well-known fact that government funding for education has been on a steep decline in real terms. Though there are nominally higher allocations for education year after year in the Government budgets, they are nowhere near the real needs to meet the inflation: to fill up vacant positions, to provide minimally decent infrastructure, not to speak of starting new institutions.

### Policy Options

- The educational institutions under the responsibility of the Government should conform to all norms for quality education.
- It should be mandatory for government educational institutions to ensure the following quality norms:
  - (i) The Student-Teacher ratio should be strictly followed. The practice of ad hoc or daily-wage teachers should be banned. There should not be more than 15 per cent vacant positions of teachers. The performance and accountability of teachers should be monitored. The appointment of teachers should be merit based and through transparent means.
  - (ii) The built up space should be adequate for the enrolled strength of students, and the number of teachers as per defined norms.
  - (iii) The institutional amenities such as library, computer center, toilets for boys and girls, laboratories, etc., should be according to prescribed norms.
- Government institutions, not conforming to such norms should be de-recognized; or de-affiliated by the appropriate regulating authorities such as UGC, AICTE, MCI, NCTE, DCI, etc., without any delay. In the case of schools, if the concerned School Boards do not take action to enforce quality norms, community/social interest groups should take initiative.
- Government institutions, capable of mobilizing extra-budgetary funds, should be allowed to use them for their own development and the Government should not take away such funds (as it is done now, thereby removing all incentives to raise additional resources).

- Self-financing courses should not be allowed in Government and Government aided institutions.
- The proportion of research funding is a tiny fraction of the overall expenditure of most Government funded institutions. There should be a fixed proportion of funds for research and development in higher education institutions including a large number of doctoral research fellowships.
- The States should try to seek sufficient allocation from Central Funds.
- For every two private institutions permitted to be opened, the State or the Centre should start one government-funded institution to prevent disproportionate dominance of private educational institutions.
- An effort should be made by the Government to float educational bonds to fulfill their constitutional and social obligations. Educational development funds needs to be created.

## Conclusion

The education system in India is beset with problems of inequalities and disparities. While some of the states are near the goal of UEE, others are lagging behind. At one end, there is a great deal of pride and euphoria about the size and growth rate of the educational system. On the other extreme, there is a perception of deep crisis voiced by persons of high authority, eminent scientists and educationists, as also the media. The public is often confused by these contradictory signals and suggestions from different directions. The various national seminars and conferences highlight one or the other kind of perception in a fragmented manner. Hence the need for a holistic analysis of the status of education in India, and the directions for the future.

The proposed national level discussions on factors that affect the educational system could lead to issues that are critical for assessment of the current trends and directions for the future. These issues relate to policy,, governance, resource, structural issues on the curriculum and syllabi, social issues such as access, affordability, etc., regulatory issues and their adequacy and distortions; interference factors such as political, administrative, commercial, and, several other factors.

- There is a policy vacuum relating to higher education. The developments in the country in post reform period are poorly reflected in the national initiatives in education.
- In general, people are not unaware of the economic and social gains of the visionary initiatives for education. This has a potential to pull millions of people out of poverty and to provide opportunity for larger sections of the population in the mainstream economy

> and help the Indian education system gain credibility globally. Often, hopes created by eminent education commissions and competent committees are frustrated by vested interest groups, thereby ignoring the need to obtain maximum returns from our educational enterprises.

The rationale for new directions should be articulated along with the modalities for action. The guiding principles to be enunciated should be based on factors such as access, affordability, excellence, competence, knowledge base, skill base, international standards, etc.

The lacunae of the current education system are best explained by the near defunct status of the regulatory system for education. There is ample evidence to show that the national move to bring education to the center of development agenda is gaining ground. This needs to be capitalized.

Education helps to build national human resources. Educational opportunities should be available to all those who can benefit through a system of social justice and fair access. The measures for inclusion are in the overall national interest. It is necessary to recognize and foster potential wherever it is found. And, it should not be viewed as a charity from those with entrenched privileges. Concomitantly, effort to promote educational equity with a new curriculum framework, which is relevant, flexible and context-oriented to attract and retain the underprivileged students, is to be taken up seriously. It is also necessary to demonstrate that equity measures can be undertaken, while preserving high quality and academic excellence.

Keeping the social and economic imperatives in view, extensive support is growing for national level consensus for including large sections of underprivileged population into the mainstream development domains, particularly education. In order to overcome the apprehensions and resistance from the existing privileged sections about the intervention effects, there is a need to evolve policy dialogue with different stakeholders and progressive policy changes. Undoubtedly, implementation of social justice measures will require mobilization of adequate financial and human resources from the public as well as private sectors. As demonstrated by the experiences in States like Tamil Nadu, Karnataka, Andhra Pradesh and Kerala, the inclusion policies have helped to raise the aspirations of new generations of underprivileged sections of population, whose educational achievements have matched with those of the privileged sections. By their inclusion, the educational institutions did not have to lower their standards, quality and status.

There is an unmistakable trend of demand-oriented growth caused by the tremendous desire on the part of all the sections of society to obtain education as a means of upward social mobility and economic security. However, the actual supply side of the educational system is heavily distorted and unbalanced. These need to be corrected in the long-term interest of the society. Lots of hopes were generated when the government announced the possibility of increased allocation for education to the extent of 6 per cent of GDP, which has not so far materialized. The issue is not so much related to the increased availability of funds but a reflection of the government's commitment to education as a national policy.

## References


Economic Advisory Council to the Prime Minister (August 2006). *Economic Outlook for 2006-07,*. New Delhi, P. 46.

Agarwal, Pawan (2006). *Higher Education In India: Need for a Strategic Paradigm Shift and Framework for Action*, New Delhi, Indian Council for Research on International Economic Relations.

Anandakrishnan, M. (2004). Equity, Quantity and Quality in Higher Education, in *Issues in Higher Education*, Hyderabad, Vol. II, p. 18-35. ICFAI, University Press.

Anandakrishnan, M. (2006). *Reservation Policy and Academic Performance: A Tamil Nadu Case Study,* New Delhi, Report submitted to the Oversight Committee of Government of India (Unpublished).

Centre for Management Development (2006). *Reservation for Socially and Economically Backward Classes in the Professional Courses in Kerala,* New Delhi, Report submitted to the Oversight Committee of Government of India (Unpublished).

Government of Andhra Pradesh (2006). *A Case Study on the Impact of Reservation Implemented in AP on the Educational Progress of Backward Classes,* New Delhi:, Report submitted to the Oversight Committee of Government of India (Unpublished).

Krishnamurthy, K.V. (2005). *History of Science*, Tiruchirapalli: Bharathidasan University, India, p. 190.

NCERT (2005). *National Curriculum Framework-2005*, New Delhi: National Council of Educational Research and Training, p. 140.

NUEPA (2005). *Elementary Education in India—Where Do We Stand?: State Report Cards,* New Delhi: NUEPA, p. 41.

NUEPA (2006). *Elementary Education in India: Progress Towards UEE. Analytical Report 2004-05,* New Delhi: NUEPA, p. 373.

Schaffer, Bernard and Lamb, G. (1981) *Can Equity be Organized?* Paris: UNESCO.

Shetty, N.R. (2006). *Implementation of Reservation Policy in Higher Educational Institutions in Karnataka,* New Delhi: An Interim Study submitted to the Oversight Committee of Government of India (Unpublished).

Tilak, Jandhyala B.G. (2005). Higher Education in Trishanku. *Economic and Political weekly,* (Sept. 10)

UGC (2003). *Higher Education in India: Issues, Concerns and New Directions*. New Delhi.

Venkatasubramanian, K. (2003). *An Approach paper on India's Development as Knowledge Society,* New Delhi: Planning Commission of India.

# 3

# The Education Commission's Perspectives on Society, Education and Development

M.S. YADAV

## Introduction

The Government of India assigned the task of reconstruction of the country's education to the Education Commission, in 1964. This task of reconstruction of education in India as a whole and across all stages and forms of education may be better understood and appreciated when placed in:

(i) The context of education and society of that period.
(ii) The context of education before and after independence.

Also, the socio-economic and political conditions in relation to the life of the people and their aspirations at that time may have to be examined. The role of education is basically linked to these conditions as it has to respond to challenges of social life and contribute to its progress.

The section that follows attempts to briefly describe the initiatives taken to improve education, especially in the context of socio-economic factors and the system of governance during the years just before and after independence. Education is expected to be in sharper focus on the individual and collective aspirations and lasting cultural ethos and values of the society, continually, and evolve in the process.

PART I: CONTEXT

## Genesis, Constitution and Terms of Reference of the EC

It may be of interest to look at the genesis of the Education Commission. Since the Despatch of the Court of Directors of the East India Company, popularly known as Wood's Education Despatch of July 19, 1854 and prior to the setting up of the Education Commission, 1964, five commissions were constituted. These are: Indian Education Commission (1882), Indian Universities Commission (1902), Calcutta University Commission (1917),

University Education Commission (1948) and the Secondary Education Commission (1952).

Of these Commissions, three dealt with university education, one with school education and one with secondary education. These commissions dealt with different aspects of education, but none of them examined the education system in India in a comprehensive manner.

Meanwhile, specific problems of education were dealt with by a number of committees appointed by the Central and State Governments and the Central Advisory Board of Education.

At the time of the appointment of the EC there was a general feeling in the country that the approach to the reconstruction of education had been rather piecemeal and not holistic, and this was echoed in the EC's inaugural session.

The Education Commission was appointed by the Government of India through its Resolution of July 14, 1964. The Resolution emphasized the new era of "national development" ushered in after the attainment of Independence. It clearly stated the basic premises for this endeavour, the significant ones being: secular democracy; modernization of agriculture and industrial sectors to eliminate poverty; adoption of science and technology and their harmony with traditional spiritual values; acceptance of the socialistic pattern of 'society', which will secure equitable distribution of wealth and equality of opportunity for all in education.

The Resolution placed greater emphasis on "educational development" and connected it with the realization that 'education', especially in science and technology is the most powerful instrument of social transformation and economic progress. It further stated that the attempt to create a new social order based on freedom, equality and justice can only succeed if the traditional "educational system" was revolutionized, both in content and extent.

It may be relevant to look at education from the people's perspective. During the first half of the 20th century, the people of India had become extremely dissatisfied with the system of education created by the British rulers. This dissatisfaction was vented through the Indian National Congress, which was then spearheading the struggle for freedom. In 1906, the INC adopted a resolution that "the time has arrived for the people all over the country earnestly to...organize a system of education—literary, scientific and technical—suited to the requirements of the country, on national lines and under national control, and directed towards the realization of the national destiny."[1] When the Congress had the opportunity of influencing and controlling education in 1938, it considered it essential "to build up national education on a new foundation and on a nation-wide scale."[2]

The demand for a national system of education became an integral part of the freedom struggle. M.K. Gandhi devised the Basic Education system to concretize this demand. Several institutions with Basic Education approach were established all over the country, like Gujarat Vidyapeeth, Kashi Vidyapeeth, Tilak Maharashtra Vidyapeeth and Jamia Millia Islamia. These innovative institutions, which experimented with national education as a concept and process, could not become very successful for several reasons.[3]

Thus, at the time of independence, there was no alternative system of education—tried, tested and accepted—for adoption as a national system. This presented a serious challenge for initiating the process of educational development, in consonance with the goals of education.

The Resolution under which the Education Commission was appointed clearly reflects two premises which relate to the nature of education and its functional aspect:

(i) The first concerns membership of the Commission. Of the 17 members that constituted the Commission; a sizeable number of them were from other countries, namely, UK, USA, USSR, France, and Japan. It may be mentioned here that in the pre-Independence period non-Indian members on the Commissions were taken exclusively from England. While in post-independence period, a few experts from the USA were also included in the University Education Commission and the Secondary Education Commission.

The Education Commission was intended to view education in international context while dealing with the substance of education and its processes. After the Commission was set up there had been criticism regarding its membership. The question as to why its membership was not confined to Indian nationals only was replied by the Union Minister of Education, M.C. Chagla, at the Inaugural Function of the Commission on October 2, 1964, in the following words:

*I think we should benefit by the advice and opinion of persons who come from different countries. They can tell us what their system of education is, how it compares with ours, what suggestions they have to make and so on. The decision is ultimately ours*[4]

(ii) The second premise refers to the field of educational development, as various parts of the educational system strongly interact with and influence one another. For instance, educational stages from the primary to the university are interlinked among themselves and their development is considerably influenced by their interdependence. Similarly, various systemic components of education at each stage like teacher education, examinations, administration etc., have vital dependence among themselves. This integrated process of education can be effective in attaining the goals of education.

These premises provided the broad framework of educational development for the Education Commission. More specifically the task for the Commission was operationalised by the Government of India in the following words:

> *The Commission will advise Government on the national pattern of education and on general principles and policies for the development of education at all stages and in all aspects. It need not, however, examine the problems of medical or legal education, but such aspects of these problems as are necessary for its comprehensive enquiry may be looked into.*[5]

## Planned Development

Immediately after independence, for the enforcement of the Constitution, planned development in the country was initiated. Planning was intended to raise the standard of living of the people and open opportunities for a richer and more varied life.

### *First Five Year Plan*

The Plan was launched in 1951. The main objectives of the plan were articulated as under:

> *While in the initial stage the accent of endeavour must be on increased production... our planning even in the initial stages should not be confused to stimulating economic activity within the existing social and economic framework. That framework itself has to be remolded so as to secure progressively for all members of the community full employment, education, security against sickness and other disabilities, and adequate income.*[6]

The Plan supported the following:

- A few experimental basic schools should be opened in the urban areas in order to adopt the "basic education" to urban needs.
- At least one Rural University should be established by the Central Government; and it should be located in a place where the earlier stages of basic education have been fully worked out.
- Adult education was viewed more broadly to include in addition to literacy, health matters, proper use of leisure, and citizenship. A new term "social education" was coined to signify the widened view.
- Some manual work should be encouraged as a daily routine at some stage during the course of education. This may extend from six months to a year. This period should be spent in manual activity related to areas of development, like community projects, irrigation works,

roads, improvement of slums and sanitation projects as social service. A beginning could be made with small groups (for instance, students taking the Master's degree) for a period varying from three to six months.

While assessing education in general, the Plan document observes that, by and large, teaching continues on the old lines and practically the entire task of remodeling the system still remains to be done.[7]

### *Social Welfare*

This is another area of development that was emphasized by the Plan. Some extracts from this plan bring out the context and, partly, the nature of programmes related to social welfare as a concept and its concretization while pursuing educational reconstruction. *See* Box 1.

**Box 1**

> Though the Constitution assures all citizens social justice in the abstract, it can only be realized fully, in practice, if people supplement the efforts of the State by willing co-operation. A good standard of life implies something more than the satisfaction of basic needs. It implies responsibility on the part of the State for creating a social environment in which citizens enjoy mental and physical health and derive pleasure from social and family life...[8]

In this connection several programmes were included in the Plan and financial allocations made for their implementation like:

- *Training and Research:* Towards this, rural schools for social work were to be established. It was proposed that a large number of voluntary workers be recruited and given training in rudiments of social work; and, knowledge of social, economic and administrative problems of national development were to be generated through research and investigation.
- *Social Legislation:* Its relevance and contribution to progressive social change was brought out in the Plan as in Box 2.

**Box 2**

> One of the important methods of bringing about progressive social change is social legislation. Since Independence, a good deal of social legislation of basic importance has been enacted, but existing legislation requires to be scrutinized with a view to ascertaining its adequacy and the modifications that may be necessary. Adequate measures for enforcement, backed by enlightened public opinion, are essential for any piece of social legislation to be effective.[9]

- *Community Approach in Social Welfare:* The Plan* emphasized the approach in which the local communities accept responsibility for solving their own problems. In this connection, it articulated associate ideas and brought out differences in programmes of community welfare in rural and urban areas. See Box 3

**Box 3**

Community Welfare Programmes embody four inter-linked ideas: (i) self-help and mutual service; (ii) maximum use and development of local resources through organized community life; (iii) economic betterment and cultural development through social participation in co-operative effort; and (iv) achievement of community objectives with minimum assistance from the State.

The aim is to transform not only technical environment in the villages but also social and economic relations and attitudes within the village community.

Urban life tends to shift the emphasis from the community to the individual with all the consequences that it implies. There is, therefore, considerable need to establish community centres through which local urban groups can survey their own urgent social and economic needs and seek solution through co-operative effort.[10]

### Community Development and Rural Extension

The Community Development Programmes were launched in 1952 as part of a major effort towards rural development through Extension Centres. The establishment of this organization provided an impetus to all rural work, and in particular, to the programme for increased agricultural production.

The extension organization functioned in interlinked layers, namely, Project Area, Development Blocks and Villages. The main fields of activity in the community projects were agriculture and related matters, communication, education, health, supplementary employment, housing, training and social welfare.

### Second Five Year Plan

A few points relevant to the present theme that emerge from the Second Plan are as follows:

- The Plan sought to rebuild rural India, to lay the foundations of industrial progress, and to secure to the greatest extent feasible opportunities for weaker and under-privileged sections of people and balanced development of all parts of the country.

- It emphasized reorientation of the system of education on 'basic' lines. The plan proposed large scale expansion of Basic Schools in the country. It also charged the newly established 'National Institute of Basic Education' with the responsibilities of production of literature for basic institutions and undertaking research to study problems affecting basic education.
- For the secondary stage of education, the recommendations made by the Secondary Education Commission formed the basis of development. Thus, the plan emphasized the implementation of multipurpose schools and junior technical schools.
- The Second Plan recognized that, despite the advance made during the First Plan, the requirements of engineering and technological personnel will be on a scale exceeding the capacity of existing institutions. Accordingly, the plan made several provisions for development of technical and management education in the country.
- The educational reforms in the area of social education initiated during the First Plan were strengthened further during the Second Plan. Consequently, the Ministry of Education proposed to establish a fundamental education centre.
- The Plan reiterated the phrase "socialist pattern of society" and treated the realization of social values as the basic objective.
- Rapid industrialization, with particular emphasis on the development of basic and heavy industries, was chosen as one of the objectives of the Second Plan.

### *Public Discourse on Education*

After Independence in 1947 and the Constitution of India was enforced with effect from January 26, 1950, the 'vision' of national development and progressive society got reflected in concrete terms through the Directive Principles and the Statutes enunciated in the Constitution.

This raised the people's expectations for a better and happy life, and their desire to witness greater social cohesiveness in the society. The problems of development for the nation as a whole were far too complex to be solved within a span of a few years. Also, the strategies, availability of resources and even the basic approach to conceptualize the substantive measures of development, became matters of public debate. The attainment of independence and consequent change of governance system appeared to people in general to be less effective and even less responsive to crucial problems of socio-economic and political development in general, and education in particular.

In order to give an idea of the problems and challenges faced in "educational reconstruction" and the nature of discourse in education in the country, views of important personalities drawn from different sources are mentioned. These views reflect the variety in ideas, and occasional controversies, and also reflect the approach to educational planning and reconstructing Indian education.

While highlighting obvious defects in the education system, Maulana Abul Kalam Azad*[11] expressed his views in October 1953 as under:

> ...we should so organize our system of education that the majority of our people, having passed through the secondary stage, are able to engage themselves in the various professions, trades, industries, etc. and only a small number adequate to the needs of society go on to the universities for higher education.[12]

Zakir Husain*[13] viewed future school education as under:

> This 'general culture' will not in the future educational system of the country enjoy the false prestige which is enjoyed by it today.... Our educational institutions of the future will have nothing to do with the inflated valuation of information nor with the naive over-estimation of an impossible 'general culture' which characterizes our present educational tradition (October 1953).[14]

Gandhi's views on education was as follows:

- Man is neither the intellect nor the gross animal body, nor the heart and soul alone. A proper and harmonious co-ordination of all the three is required for making the whole man and constitutes the true science of education.
- I hold that the highest development of mind and soul is possible under craft education. Only every handicraft has to be taught not merely mechanically as is done today but scientifically, that is, the child should know the why and therefore of every process.[15]

Jawaharlal Nehru touched upon the subject of education not as a theory but on its functionality in the building up of a new social order. He declared: "No social order can change without the help of an organized educational system",[16] and added, "It (education) has opened the doors and windows of mind to new ideas and dynamic thoughts."[17] While emphasizing the aims of education, he made it clear that neither he liked the divorce from the past nor the denial of the "new urges and creative tendencies".[18] He said: "We cannot afford to leave those ideals, which this country adopted some thousands of years ago,"[19] but emphasized, "It is an insult to talk of culture to people who have nothing to eat".[20]

It was India's way in the past to welcome and absorb other cultures. That is much more necessary today, for we march to the one world of tomorrow, where national cultures will be intermingled with international culture of human race.[21]

His vision of India included:

> A society which looks back for inspiration but forges ahead with firm determination to attain high ideals, shifting and improving her strengths, and is at the same time forever watchful of contemporary trends.[22]

While moving a resolution on basic education at the Avadi Session of the Indian National Congress in 1955, Nehru articulated its fundamental tenets:

> ...Since basic education uses the medium of productive activity and correlates academic subjects to different crafts, and to the social environment, it is eminently suitable for the needs and conditions of India.... Far reaching changes in the existing educational system are absolutely essential for achieving the national aims and social objectives of free India, and in particular to train the right type of personnel for the speedy execution of developmental plans.[23]

B.R. Ambedkar was passionately concerned about the pathetic conditions under which the 'untouchables' were living in the society then. He recognised that the main cause of their misery was the appalling poverty, which he attributed to their poor economic and educational status, and customs and traditions. Therefore, to improve their financial status he wanted reforms in their customs and traditions *inter alia*. Towards this cause he formulated an agenda of 'socialization'.

His main thesis to achieve this goal was two fold. The first was to educate the 'untouchables' about their own conditions and create awareness to improve their status. For this he formulated three fundamental action oriented processes. "Educate (make aware), agitate and organize".[24] The second was to establish institutions for providing education to the 'untouchables' with boarding facilities and the third, developing appropriate inputs for effecting socialization and also looking after the interests of the 'untouchables'.

He started many such institutions, particularly in Maharashtra. One of them is the Bahiskrit Hitakarni Sabha (BHS), established in 1924. In the appeal published by the BHS, it had exposed the injustice shown to the 'untouchables' and it declared that the main agenda was to eradicate poverty and frustration that impeded their progress. The objectives of the BHS were directed at socialization of 'untouchables' as well as *swarns*. The endeavour was mainly to prepare untouchables for social action and consequently, social progress.

To conclude, these observations mainly reflect:

- the purposive dimension of education, related to socio-cultural aspects of Indian society and national development, as visualized during the freedom struggle for a new and free India;
- the experiential dimension of the endeavour of reconstruction of education in the post-independence period, its contribution to the process of overall development, and its emergence as a sub-sector of national development.

During the 'freedom struggle' the need for organizing a system of education—literary, scientific and technical—for both boys and girls suited to the requirements of the country was earnestly felt. In 1906, the National Congress Committee adopted a resolution about the nature and organization of such a system of education; it should be on 'national lines' and under 'national control' and directed towards the realization of the 'national destiny' (p. 3).

Thus, the demand for a national system of education became an integral part of the agenda of freedom struggle. In other words the task of educational reconstruction in the country got included in the 'political process' to intensify the movement of freedom struggle.

In 1937, Gandhi devised a new scheme, Basic Education—popularly known as the Wardha Scheme. Later, in 1938, the Congress Party considered it essential to build national education on a new foundation and on a nation-wide scale.

Alongside, several institutions like Gujarat Vidyapith, Kashi Vidyapith and Jamia Millia Islamia were established on the lines of Basic Education (pp. 3-4).

After Independence, Basic Education was accepted as the national system of education; it was implemented through the first three Five Year Plans.

- Though there was considerable experimentation in education during freedom struggle there was no single model of education which could be accepted on conceptual adequacy and feasibility for the country as a whole.
- The very model of Basic Education was viewed differently by people in general and by those who mattered in education and politics.

It is clear from the discussion and from relevant quotes that the national system of Basic Education had full political support and, therefore, included in the Five Year Plans. Also, the conceptual soundness of the system appeared doubtful when assessed against the expectations in terms of its contribution to national development and the goal of creating a progressive India as visualized through the ideals of 'freedom struggle'.

The Education Commission, therefore, faced the challenge of devising an appropriate model for establishing the national system of education covering all stages. It may be remarked here that the purpose of establishing a national system of education was not accomplished fully by the two commissions set up after independence—the University Education Commission and the Secondary Education Commission—because they did not examine the education system as a whole.

Related to the national system of education and its effective reconstruction, the organizational perspective was also considered relevant. And, therefore, the Education Commission was specifically asked to suggest the pattern of education at the national level.

The Resolution, under which the Education Commission was appointed, clearly emphasized the new era of national development and the relevance of educational development therein; education was recognized as the most powerful instrument of social transformation and economic progress.

The perspective of education in the light of the basic premises provided to the Commission included the following: secular democracy; modernization of agriculture and industrial sectors to eliminate poverty; adoption of science and technology and their harmonization with traditional spiritual values; etc.

The Resolution also stated that the attempt to create a social order based on freedom, equality and justice can only succeed if the traditional educational system was revolutionized both in content and extent (p. 5).

The very composition of the Commission suggested that it was intended to view education in an international context while dealing with both its substance and process (p. 4).

The field of educational development includes apparently discrete parts of the educational system, which interact with and influence one another. This obtains across stages, primary to university; and, within a stage, among varied sub-systems, namely, teacher education, examination, administration and organization.

Recognition of this interaction and linkage among these sub-systems and the need to integrate them served as a perspective to reconstruct education.

In post-independence period development was conceptualized with a progressive outlook. For example, the First Five Plan and also the Second Plan explicitly stated that our planning even in the initial stages should not be confined to stimulating economic activity within the existing social and economic framework; but that the framework itself should be remoulded. This led to launching newer programmes like rural community development, agriculture extension, social education, establishment of newer institutions—rural university, community approach to social welfare, and amendment to the Constitution—to render them suitable to support programmes related to social justice.

The Second Plan reiterated the socialist pattern of society and treated the realization of social values as its basic objective. For this purpose new institutions like National Culture for Fundamental Education were created.

The emphasis on the development of 'basic' and 'heavy' industries was chosen as one of the objectives of the Second Plan (see p. 9).

The ideals with which the struggle for freedom were fought and pursued appeared prominently in the general public discourse. The major goal of the freedom struggle was to achieve 'Independence' for creating a free India, new India and developed India. Other considerations like caste, religion, language, state or region, etc., did not seem to matter at all during that period. Even later, when the Constitution of India was being created by the Constituent Assembly, similar ideals and ethos prevailed. The Constitution of India reflects the vision of a new Indian Society and the approach to national development to create such a society. It is in this sense the Constitution of India may be viewed as a source of general philosophy of socio-economic and political development.

It may be relevant to mention here that the Constitution of India is not merely an instrument to usher in a system of political governance. Of course, it does this largely to provide directions through statutes to all the three wings of governance—legislature, executive and judiciary. But it also plays a certain proactive role through the provisions under Directive Principles and Schedule-9. For example, Directive Principle-45 not only encourages the legislative wing to provide free and compulsory education but also prevents it from acting against this Directive Principle. Similarly, the provision in Schedule-9 supports the political process to take progressive measures, legitimately, without risking the strictly judgmental view of the judiciary.

When the Education Commission was appointed these functional perspectives to guide and support the developmental activities and programmes were available not only in abstract form but also with concrete experience in educational and developmental operations.

When the Education Commission began its work, the Constitution of India had been functioning for about fifteen years. The first three Five Year Plans of development had been experienced in terms of their formulation and implementation throughout the country.

These operational experiences helped in understanding developmental problems in terms of their complexity, inter-linkages and overlap across various departments, need for co-ordination among concerned programmes and the departments and most importantly, community co-operation and participation in the implementation process.

The social assessment of such development programmes has helped in gaining insights and developing skills and required competence among personnel engaged in the developmental activities. These experiences enhanced the repertoire of those concerned with implementation of developmental programmes in the country. Also, the people in general in the community accumulated their own stock of information about implementation of developmental programmes. This helped in generation of public discourse, both imperceptibly and consciously, on the process, nature and problems of development. The democratic system of governance, which provided scope for free expressions by individuals and the media, helped in highlighting such discourse. An observant mind could draw perceptual knowledge about the development process and its complexity from this discourse. It brought out clearly a more practical and life related perspective about programmes of education, development and social aspects of community involvement.

For the Education Commission, these experiences and the perceptual knowledge readily available provided the perspective to examine the tasks assigned to it. It was aimed at understanding the problems of educational development empirically, by conducting observation-based survey of the education field. As the message of the President of India to the Commission on the inaugural function said, the Commission was to "survey all aspects of education... and make recommendations to improve educational system at all levels."[25]

The Education Commission was entrusted with the task of making recommendations for reconstruction of the education system at all levels in the country. Since education is intrinsically related to society and national development, the following observations are made on the correlation between education and the society and national development.

## Education

- Education is a socially devised process for the benefit of the people, individually and also collectively. Thus, education has a "social purpose". It derives its strength in terms of its content and sustenance from the "social purpose".
- The "social purpose" entails visualization of the kind of people the society would like to have and in turn the kind of society it would like to sustain and evolve. To meet such a social purpose, education is a continual process; and it evolves through time.
- Education is based on both programme and activity. These are varied and apparently discrete, yet, they create a process of education.

It often makes use of current ideas in the social sciences to generate its programmes, activities, and process. These ideas are helpful to understand the educational tasks and process in conceptual terms.

Education also uses ideas, techniques and even theories from other areas of knowledge and studies. This perspective is more utility-oriented.

However, the education process and system are not mere collection of such discrete understanding, creation of programmes and activities and their improvement, individually. It is a complex mix of capabilities and resources;

these are utilized to create a composite process of education, mainly through insightful understanding of the seemingly discrete components of education. Education is, thus, inter-disciplinary.

For running a system of education, an organization of its own is required, which is expected to facilitate creation of the education process appropriately and effectively. Numerous human resources and their mobilization are required in education. Education is thus a human endeavour with its unique ways of handling and solving problems. This points to the organizational dimension of the perspective of education.

Education is thus a composite process with its own "perspective", or rather, perspectives brought together with conceptual connectivities among them.

## Society

The society here is viewed in the context of education and its reconstruction. Therefore, the main parameters to describe the society are two-fold:

- The society as envisioned for free India with democratic polity as the main guide to describe its profile. Other dimensions of such a society as described in the Constitution of India are: secular democracy, equality, equity, social justice, social cohesiveness, harmonizing with traditional spiritual values, socialistic pattern of society, etc.
- To usher in the ethos of such a society, considerable social transformation is to be brought about. For this purpose, "socialization" to promote appropriate social practices and perceptual modification in the behaviour of people towards certain traditional religions, practices and customs, traditions and values are to be adopted.

The social transformation is expected to reflect the role, which education can perform. Therefore, in sociological terms, education has to, in a consciously designed way, work for such a socialization; this is generally called "secondary socialization". Towards this purpose, appropriate educational inputs will have to be provided through curricular arrangements. In that sense, sociological perspective is quite significant in the process of educational reconstruction; for which the Education Commission was to make recommendations.

## National Development

National development in India, as in other nations, is determined by certain characteristics of the society. In India, these characteristics can be seen in terms of the diversities in language, religion, caste as well as social, cultural and economic stratifications.

- After independence, organized efforts were made through planned development such as Five Year Plans and several other schemes, programmes and establishment of institutions, to bring about a major change in education, both in its conceptualization and utilization in everyday life. These included: introduction of vocational courses, expanding agricultural courses, extension programmes to educate farmers for the adoption of innovations and awareness of technical knowledge, rural development and extension programmes for social and community development. Alongside, newer institutions were established in 1950s and 1960s.
- It may be remarked here that the view of national development and the role of education to promote it represents a paradigm shift in perspective. Earlier, up to the end of the 19th century education was having an academic orientation. Education at school stage was largely in abstraction and symbols and therefore memory was an important attribute. Also, since school education was mainly preparatory for higher education, life related courses like agriculture, technical and professional, technological and management programmes were not very much in vogue.

The 20th century India promoted the courses connected more directly to life situations for economic and social amelioration of life in general. Additionally, after Independence, the emphasis was on social transformation and social justice measures and related studies and programmes.

Therefore, national development since Independence has been viewed in a much wider context covering all dimensions and aspects of life. In the first three Five Year Plans, planned efforts had been made to actualize comprehensive development. And, national development covered: economic, social, political, social justice, equality of opportunity, social cohesion, cultural diversification, its retention and promotion, etc. Educational programmes had to be organized or reconstructed in such a way that they contribute towards national development. This provides a "developmental perspective" to education.

This perspective does not confine to instituting newer courses but, more significantly, it amounts to seeking knowledge and its significance in the context of its relevance to life and society. It takes knowledge to life either through technology or other measures to bring about social and cultural changes in people's life and social cohesion.

Thus, contribution to national development seems to have become the destination for knowledge and education to arrive at and a criterion to assess their relevance and worth.

# PART II: EDUCATIONAL RECONSTRUCTION IN RESPECT OF SOCIETY AND NATIONAL DEVELOPMENT—APPROACH AND RECOMMENDATION

## Introduction

As mentioned in the earlier section, the Education Commission was appointed to advise the Government on the national pattern of education and on the general principles and policies for the development of education at all stages and in all aspects. The Commission was appointed at an initial phase of development of Indian society after Independence, when people's life aspirations were crystal clear and their expectations from the government of free India well reflected in public discourse.

By early 1960s even the dissatisfaction of people in general had started surfacing as the outcomes of development measures undertaken by the government did not seem to match their aspirations and expectations.

The task of educational reconstruction assigned to the Commission, therefore, was a great challenge, intellectually as well as in action related aspects. The Commission formulated its own approach to accomplish the task. One significant parameter of their approach was to relate education with the Indian society and its progress through national development. The relationship of education with society and national development thus identified was treated as basic and fundamental to derive all principles and policies for the development of a national education system. This section, in fact, this paper as a whole, deals with objectives of education in this context and the general approach and action related measures towards educational development.

## Approach

Education, by its very meaning and process, is vital and relevant to India's progress and development—economic, cultural and spiritual. The Commission did recognize the hazards they were likely to face in making recommendations for reconstructing education such as:

- The recommendations may not be sufficiently radical; especially so, as the Commission chose to create a system of education that is flexible.
- Resources could be a problem; especially when long-term plans and long-term projections face uncertainties.
- The democratic polity, wherein people are to be trusted and their opinions respected, may pose its own problems. Similarly, multi-party system for political governance as obtained in the country presents its own challenges, especially for development pursuits

towards planning and implementing programmes of social, economic and cultural advancement.

The Commission asserted the goal of education in the following words:

> ...education, science-based and in coherence with Indian culture and values, can alone provide the function—as also the instrument—for nation's progress, security and welfare.[26]

While articulating national development, the Commission took a wider view covering all aspects of life such as the following:

> Self-sufficiency in food not merely as a desirable goal but a condition for survival. Towards this, the Commission emphasized the rapid rate of economic growth; equitable distribution of income; control of growth in population.

It needs to be noted here that these problems were highlighted by the Commission in the context of contemporary problems. At that time, import of food items was a great problem; Green Revolution had not taken place yet; social sensitivity to equity and equality measures were facing operational problems. The first amendment to the Constitution was enforced in 1958 to facilitate reservation policy implementation in respect of government jobs for backward classes.

An important role for education was visualized towards social and national integration in the country:

> These were viewed in the context of hierarchical, stratified nature of Indian society and its being deficient in vertical mobility as related to castes, religions, economic conditions, social status, etc.
>
> In this connection the Commission specially highlighted the erosion of "old values" which needs to be replaced by "newer sense of public responsibility", e.g. social disorganization due to corruption in public life, communal tension, students' unrest etc., which were on the rise in the 1960s.

Political development and education were viewed as being closely linked. In this connection the role of education was highlighted to stress political awareness among the people:

- Specific programmes to create educated electorate and a dedicated and competent leadership.
- Cultivation of essential values like self-control, tolerance, mutual goodwill and consideration for others, awakened sense of rights.
- For defence purpose, the need for creation of a secular, united and strong democratic state.

Appropriate inputs in the process of education were to be provided in the existing programmes and courses of studies. Also, the newer courses of studies and their organizational support structures were articulated by the Commission. These were primarily to render "development orientation" to education at all stages.

Alongside, the Commission did stress the complexity of the political scenario existing at that time, like the multi-party system and decentralization of political governance, federal structure of the nation state, multi-religious and mixed society consisting of highly sophisticated groups and the primitive ones, concurrently and spatially.

This context of multiplicity in Indian society, in terms of varied dimensions—collective, individual and group based—makes educational development more complex and presents a formidable challenge for reorganizing education to enhance its contribution towards creation of a progressive society and national development. The Commission emphasizes the need for a clear focus on these problems and recommends deeper understanding of them through conscious educational efforts. All such efforts are expected to contribute towards strengthening "India's faith in democratic socialism".

The analysis of national objectives and the perusal of their implications suggest the need for the cooperation and assistance of the "richer industrialized nations", who accept India's paradigm of "democratic socialism" and sympathize with her struggle to create a "new social order".[27]

## Education and National Development

The Commission felt that the system of education inherited was meant to fulfill the needs of an imperial administration within the limitations set by a feudal and traditional society, and would need "radical changes" if it were to meet the purpose of a "modern democratic" and "socialistic society". These changes would be mainly in three aspects:

- Internal transformation so as to relate education to the life, needs and aspirations of the nation;
- Qualitative improvement so that the standards achieved are adequate, kept continually rising and, at least in a few sectors, become internationally comparable; and,
- Expansion of educational facilities, broadly on the basis of man-power needs, and with an emphasis on equalization of educational opportunities.

The Commission considered that an endeavour to transform education is basic and urgent for "social and national development". The goal of such transformation in education should be to relate it to the life, needs and aspirations of the people and thereby make it a powerful instrument of social, economic and cultural transformation necessary for the realization of our national goals. Towards this, the Commission believed that it could be achieved if education:

- — Is related to productivity;
- — Strengthens social and national integration; consolidates democracy as a form of government and helps the country to adopt it as a way of life;
- — Hastens the process of modernization; and,
- — Strives to build character by cultivating social, moral and spiritual values.

Further, as an integral part of its approach to education, the Commission recognized that all these aspects are interrelated. Thus, they all operate through a complex process to bring about "social change" and thereby, progress in society. In such a situation, the endeavour to transform education cannot be viewed in isolation and that not a single aspect of those mentioned above can be achieved without striving for all.[28]

It may be relevant here to observe the relationship between education and national development. The Commission considers the goals of national development as being supreme for the society. Also, the Commission believes that education has to help the society in achieving this goal. And, for that purpose, education is considered as "an instrument" to transform the society. The directions of this transformation through education are not only linked to the goals of national development, but the latter also determines the purposive and developmental dimensions of education.

However, it is to be recognized that though national development and its goals is linked to improvement in individual's life and social progress, this view presents a limited role for education. On the one hand, education is instrumental for national economic development, at the same time; it is society specific, it relates to individual's life and aspirations and is thus highly personalized. And, that is determined by the individual himself or herself not only for its substance but also for its treatment.

It may thus be noted that the goals of national development are largely the goals of education. However, the content of such an education system, and even its organization, are managed by individuals. In that sense, this educational effort is not determined or organized by the government or even autonomous and sponsored organizations, though both of these may support, facilitate and sustain such a system of education in the societal context. This individual effort for one's own education is personalized; it is intended for one's own enrichment and advancement and self-fulfillment in life. For such an education system, the individual may not even exercise his/her right to education, as he/she may like to chose its content and acquire it in his/her chosen way. Education, in that sense, goes beyond the premises set by the government or its sponsored institutional structures. This may happen particularly about those components of education, which are intended to build the character of individuals. Towards this, the striving for development of attitudinal orientation and value inculcation will be mainly through an individualized process by evoking and activating individual rationality. Such value orientation, attempted through education, will aim at the development of attributes like social cohesion, national integration and national consciousness. These components as reflected in the individual behaviour and shared by members of the society, largely, will reflect the cultural dimension at the national level in the society.

In the context of wider meaning of education, the Commission argued that the national system of education is the only instrument that can reach all the people. Also, the Commission seeks support for the idea of the national system, empirically, as a tried and tested experience of other countries in their struggle for development. Significantly, the main argument of the Commission to devise the national system of education is indicative of the importance it attaches to the "social purposes" of education. At the same time, the Commission adds that this emphasis on the "social purpose" or the need to use it as a tool for the realization of national aspirations or for meeting national challenges does not imply any "underestimation of values for the individual". In a democracy, the individual is an end in himself and the primary purpose of education is to provide him the widest opportunity to develop his potentialities to the full.[29] The Commission emphasized the social perspective for creating an appropriate path to achieve this goal of education.

## Aims and Objectives of Education at Operational Level

Education is essentially a programme-based and activity-oriented process. It seeks to realize the goals that are derived from the collective 'vision' of the society, and the kind of people such a society would like to include. Such a vision and its perspectives at the societal level—macro level—have been discussed in the preceding parts of Section II.

The Commission has chosen "national development" and "social transformation" through education as the key concepts, which represent the main approach to reconstruct and reorganize the national system of education.

Education is expected to provide opportunities to individuals to help them develop along the lines set by broader goals of national development and social progress. In that sense education deals with the goals or aims that are determined already. However, for the realization of goals determined at macro-level, a well organized system of education is required, which can offer opportunities for individual development and social progress. The 'process' for this purpose has to operate in a more concrete form as derived from the vision or goal—in both abstract and philosophical forms. In this context, the following observations are made on the aims and objectives of education at operational level and also their connectivity with the macro level:

1. Though education is conceptualized as a composite process, it consists of several discrete components, namely, curriculum development, textbook preparation, teacher preparation, examination mechanisms, organizational structures and their administration, etc. For organizational convenience and also for reasons of academic efficiency and authenticity, separate instructional structures for the said components are in existence. Each component has to have its own objectives with a focus on its functioning and contribution. The contribution of each component has to be such that it gets integrated with the process of education, which, in composite form, facilitates the realization of goals or aims of education at the national level in macro form.
2. Aims and objectives of education are identified to primarily improve or reconstruct educational system in the light of the vision of society and quality of individuals. In case of the Commission, this vision has mainly been derived from the operationalisation of national development and progressive society. This vision is largely based on the general philosophy of development—social, economic and political development, and a democratic polity based on secularism, equality, equity and social justice. The major sources for a model of reconstruction of education, as identified by the Commission, are the ideals of life that surfaced during the freedom struggle, before Independence, and the Indian Constitution enforced in 1950. It may, however, be noted here that the Constitution has remained more or less stable in its fundamental structure; yet, to give more focused attention to certain aspects of national development, social sensitivity and educational response to the development measures, a few amendments in the Constitution and changes in educational perspective have taken place. For example; the First Amendment to the Constitution in 1958 and inclusion of schedule IX in the Constitution to facilitate implementation of measures of social justice; inclusion of education in the concurrent list of subjects in the Constitution, in 1976; specification of terms—secularism and socialistic pattern of development—in 1976; decentralization as a system of political governance in 1990; and education up to the age of 14 years as a fundamental right in 2004, etc. Similarly, in the field of education also a few changes have taken place; consequently, noticeable shifts in the perspective of education and corresponding

changes in the content of education and its utilization have been recommended by the Commission. For example:

- The Commission included in the national system of education, the concept and approach, based on work-experience and vocationalisation, in place of 'Basic Education' at all levels.[30]
- The Common School System of public education be adopted as a national goal, and implemented effectively in 20 years. [31]
- Science education should be an integral part of school education and ultimately become a part of all courses at the university stage also.[32]
- Social and national service should be made obligatory for all students at all stages. These programmes should be organized concurrently with academic studies in schools and colleges.[33]
- Every educational institution should try to develop a programme of social and community service of its own.[34]
- The development of a proper language policy can assist in social and national integration. Evolution of a policy is imperative for education, cultural and political reasons.[35]

3. The Commission specifies some special responsibilities to the university education as its objectives, which are described below:

   - The universities must learn to strive to serve as the "conscience of the nation", as assessors of the way of life. Such involvement is vital since universities are pre-eminently the forum for a critical assessment of society—sympathetic, objective.
   - In order to foster a "unity of outlook and faith" between the masses and the intelligentsia, the universities must develop the programmes of adult education in a big way.
   - The universities must strive to assist schools in their attempts at qualitative self-improvement.

These responsibilities are specially mentioned as they relate to the major perspective the Commission accepted for relating education in concrete terms to national development and social transformation of Indian society. The Commission's main expectation from universities had been that they would ensure "that every student who passes out of an Indian university takes with him some understanding of India's cultural heritage, its past achievements ...nd triumphs in the field of art, philosophy, science and so on.... This could, ...haps, best be done at the first degree stage where such a study could form ...f a programme of liberal education".[36]

... the basis of the citations from the Commission's report, it may be ...o make the following observations:

> National development and societal aspects keep changing. In that process, the perspective and emphasis on them shift continually. Consequently, national development and social transformation, evolve as parametric considerations for education. The shifts in these parameters, with respect to developmental perspective and the approach adopted, have an impact on education—its perspective and organization. Thus, education also evolves through time. In other words, national development, social condition and education are interlinked, and influence each other in a bi-directional manner.

This phenomenon of development, on these three key processes in society, renders the objectives or goals of education more dynamic due to the continual influence of the other two key processes. Therefore, educational objectives and goals need to be revisited periodically, rather continually.

## To Sum Up

The Commission concluded its articulation on "Education and National Objectives" by expressing the "challenge" which India faced in post-Independence period and the "faith" the country had on its people to overcome the challenge. They called it a new renaissance in the making.

While giving an account of the nature of the challenges in different aspects of the development of society, the Commission also cited great strides that had been made after Independence in industrialization, modernization of agriculture and providing better health and life to the people. The most powerful tool in the process of modernization is education based on science and technology, the Commission emphasized.

Also, the Commission asks whether India can contribute to the scientific achievements of the West. This great challenge offers a unique opportunity to the men and women of India and especially to the young people, who are the makers of the future. In this context, the Commission quotes what Nehru said in 1959:

> 'Can we combine the progress of science and technology with this progress of the mind and spirit also? We cannot be untrue to science because that represents the basic fact of life today. Still less, can we be untrue to those essential principles for which India has stood in the past throughout the ages. Let us then pursue our path to industrial progress with all our strength and vigour and, at the same time, remember that material riches without toleration and compassion and wisdom may well turn to dust and ashes.'[37]

# PART III: SHIFTS IN PERSPECTIVES OF EDUCATION VIS-A-VIS NATIONAL DEVELOPMENT AND SOCIAL TRANSFORMATION

## Introduction

The Education Commission brought national development and social transformation to the main focus for the purpose of reconstructing education at all levels and in all aspects. This has resulted in a new paradigm for seeking more comprehensive perspective of education as a process. Consequently, education has been conceptualized as a composite area of study towards which varied components of knowledge and the attributes of supportive systems like teacher education contribute.

In terms of content of education, the subject areas and other curricular activities provided at different stages of schooling—from nursery to university—constitute education as a system. Earlier, the schooling emphasized mainly the academic form of knowledge and abstract symbols; memory was an important factor. Such abstract theorization has been considered as foundational to indirectly influence the individual behaviour and other life activities. Of late, there has been a shift in this perspective of education, especially when it is to be related to national development and act as an instrument towards social change. Now, all the schooling pursuits—academic, technical and professional—have to seek their relevance in terms of the utility they have for life and society. In that sense, converting all knowledge into technology and life related abilities for amelioration in the society have become the goals of education. Also, these goals point towards the destination that all 'knowledge' has to arrive at.

It is in this perspective of education that the following observations are made:

### *Knowledge in Education*

1. Earlier, knowledge was imparted more for academic purpose. Even when technology developed it was considered more as an application of fundamental or basic knowledge. Similarly, society, human behaviour and human action were sought to be understood with the help of concepts, ideas and theories of social sciences in a more generalized manner.

However, the endeavour of national development and the efforts to bring about social change must use knowledge in such a way that its processing and final utilization are not mere applications of discrete knowledge components. This utilization is primarily in a development context, towards which a composite form of varied knowledge components is required. Such knowledge is composite and integrated in terms of its nature and inter-disciplinary in its structural form. The treatment of knowledge in this perspective is the domain of education as a system.

2. Knowledge in education is programme-related, activity-based and process-oriented. Also, it is multi-disciplinary and at differential levels, in an epistemological sense. Therefore, its form can be in terms of utilization of ideas and theories of varied disciplines, based on their respective perspectives. Such knowledge can be in the form of awareness, perceptions, insights and experiential understanding, etc. For the purpose of education, these disciplinary knowledge (s) have the inherent potential to contribute towards shaping education in the context of national development and social transformation. These knowledge components are to be considered as intellectual inputs and organized into a composite and integrated form. Also, while converting these inputs into an integrated form, the education perspective would be the major consideration to render the "composite knowledge" into appropriate and situation specific knowledge of education.

It may be relevant to observe here that the processing of knowledge of varied disciplines in this manner brings to surface the "education component" of the respective discipline. This knowledge is primarily "educational and pedagogic" in nature. In this sense, each discipline or area of study, at any level, has two major types of knowledge, namely, "disciplinary knowledge" which has been generated with respective perspective; and the "educational/ pedagogy knowledge", for the identification and development of which the perspective of education is the basis. Thus, each disciplinary area of study has these pursuits of knowing and practicing disciplinary knowledge and educational/pedagogical knowledge. Absence of this distinction in the nature of knowledge may lead to confusion, and even controversy at times, as it happened when NCF (2005) was debated in early 2005.[37]

3. The kind of knowledge identification and utilization as articulated above and also any other research in education based on this model helps understanding the process of education both at the pedagogical level and at macro-level.

This perspective of educational research is relevant especially for "developmental research"; the outcomes of such research will help in enriching the process of education, including professional reorientation of personnel in education. The present research in education leaves much to be desired in this direction. The systemic reforms like teacher education and examination and assessment require this kind of research, urgently. Reviews of educational research substantiate the felt need for such research.

The approach to the national development and social transformation is derived from the general philosophy of socio-economic and political development, with a system of democratic secular polity and values like equality, equity and social justice. In this connection it may be mentioned that this general philosophy is not based on a single "school of thought". Consequently, the approach, to national development and evolving a progressive and modern society as identified by the Education Commission, is not derived from just a single perspective. It draws from several philosophical orientations, consciously put in a coherent and composite model. And education as a system is shaped to serve these objectives.

Accordingly, the goals of education are visualized at macro-level, and realized through micro-level process of education with consciously provided inputs. This is organizationally achieved through creation of teaching-learning situations in schooling, with the help of appropriate curricular inputs and their transaction duly supported by other systems of education, like teacher education and examination and assessment.

Knowledge components, required to understand the process of education for the country as a whole, are identified and generated at macro-level; while situation specific approach at micro-level is followed for knowledge required for developing effective and efficient teaching-learning process. The former is largely derived from the conceptualization of liberal arts and the latter is mainly the pedagogical knowledge as discussed earlier. However, the pedagogical knowledge must fit into the larger framework of knowledge and objectives determined at macro-level. Against these parametric considerations the following observations may be relevant:

- The knowledge base in education is characterized by multiple-orientations. To put them in a composite and coherent framework is a complex task. Therefore, the linear models of analysis and arriving at conceptualization of educational process are not adequate. For this reason, the behaviorist approach to understand educational process needs to be revisited; its place in the pursuits of knowing and understanding in education may be slightly shifted.
- While education process is complex, it does not mean that theory based formulations in education cannot be arrived at rationally and empirically. In that sense to maintain that education has no 'theory' is an over-assertion. Of late, one notices a tendency to conceptualize education by going straight to 'practice' and bypass theoretical route. These issues would be more appropriately dealt with by re-examining epistemological basis of knowledge in education. And, that would perhaps, smoothen the path of conceptualization of education.
- There is a large variety of concepts used in the discourse on education. Many of them can be interpreted in different ways, highlighting certain notions attached to them and preferred by the one who uses them. For example; concepts related to religion, ancient culture, traditional values, nature of knowledge and practice-related concepts like teacher's role, teaching, secularism, social justice, social action, equality, equity, talent, equality of education, and effectiveness of education, seem to prompt people including teachers and other

personnel in education to articulate them differently and sometimes even in a contradictory manner. This leads to vagueness and absence of specificity in their meanings. Moreover, as education evolves over a period, concepts tend to lose older semantics associated with them and gain newer ones. For example; social justice, social action, role of NGOs in education, privatization in education etc., need to be re-assessed urgently in the context of social sensitivity and purposive dimensions of education. And this must be done continually, particularly because education as a process is not stable like other disciplines of natural sciences. In fact, education brings about changes in society and undergoes change on its own in process and substance. Therefore, the entire basis of conceptualization of education and the evolving perspectives must be subjected to social assessment continually and the concepts reformulated, if considered necessary.

- The values emphasized by the Education Commission are in the perspective of national development and social transformation. Such value inculcation through education has been subsequently included as an integral part of the National Policy on Education—1968 and later in NPE (1986 & Revised in 1992). These values are secularism, equality, equity, social justice, fraternity, scientific temper, objectivity, tolerance for other's viewpoints, social cohesion, plurality of culture, etc. At the same time, there are some other values also which flow from the past as our cultural heritage imbibed and preserved, mainly through socialization. Some of these values are obedience, religious faith, social adherence to caste system and religious classification of the society, non-violence, peace, tolerance, *Vasudhaiva Kutumbakam*, etc.

A close scrutiny of values emphasized by the Commission clearly shows that some of the traditional values in Indian society are given new names as per the changed scenario. Further, quite a few values are not only common to the cultural heritage and the modern Indian society, as visualized by the Commission, but also form the part of NPE (1986 & 1992). Moreover, the Commission emphasized that there should be a synthesis of the past cultural heritage and spiritual values and the values of the society built into a secular and modern polity.

To achieve such a synthesis, it is necessary to recognize the values commonly shared with the traditional Indian society and the need for a change in values required to bring about harmony in 'socialization' and the social dimensions of the national development. Wherever the behaviour of people is markedly different from what is accepted as part of national development, it may call for an exercise to identify "alternative values" that need to be inculcated through conscious efforts. For example, creating relevant literature for this purpose and making it available to all the people. Some efforts have been initiated already in this regard.

Education has become too complex and "widespread a process" due to the interlinked usage of varied knowledge components for meeting the goals of an envisioned "society",. It involves varied knowledge components appropriately processed to create educational results; and also requires the support of allied systems, like teacher education and other development sectors. For this reason, education process and its quality are to be viewed in terms of the attributes of a much larger set of institutional structures. In that sense, education is a much larger human endeavour, which cannot be left to be taken care of only by teacher education institutions and the departments of education in universities. Therefore, education is not a self-contained and limited domain of pursuits of "learning and actions" restricted to one or a few institutions created for the purpose. It is a much larger institutional and societal endeavour.

Moreover, education is a fragile institution without any defence and protection provided in the general sense. It is created by the society for achieving a socially devised 'purpose'. It is more a matter of faith and conviction plus the zeal to actualize them.

Some organizational changes and new institutional structures were recommended by the Education Commission. For example; "common school" and use of regional languages and their development were strongly recommended.

The Common School System is becoming an uphill task for implementation. Reasons for non-implementation of the system do not seem to be related to the "political will" or other intentional reasons. Certain basic questions related to "educational reality" as obtained in the country seem to be at its root. For example, the existing schools are so different in the quality of performance and organization that the whole idea of "common school" cannot move any further.

Similarly, the use of regional languages in varied situations of education and work has been carried out in a limited manner. For instance, one can appear in the all India services examination through the medium of regional languages. However, these efforts do not seem to have helped in according equal status to regional languages in comparison to English. Such problems are generally perceived as rooted in much larger social stereotypes and other social and economic factors.

Education faces these challenges in its pursuit of giving a direction to national development and social transformation. These problems of education must be understood in terms of their origin in social structures and sensitivity towards them. This pursuit must aim at the conceptual understanding of these challenges. That would hopefully lead us to more meaningful conceptualization of education as an endeavour at a much larger level. Such an understanding spread out at all levels would prepare us better to enhance the process of reconstruction of education. Those in education—academics and professionals—must undertake the responsibility of involving experts and practitioners engaged in varied fields of national development and social change to enrich the discourse on education. This pursuit may help in sharply focusing on the educational reconstruction, for which the comprehensive conceptualization based on theoretical considerations and practice related principles must be of paramount significance.

Lastly, education is a human endeavour, pursued through socially organized opportunities for learning and understanding about the natural and social environment and also about life. The life-related understanding involves one's own view about life, living and behaving, which is knowledge-cum-value guided. This is essentially a process of individual development, which is personalized in nature. The individual development is the goal of education, ultimately. It is through individual development that goals of national development and social transformation of the society are identified and pursued. Educational opportunities, although addressed to national development and largely provided by the State, are basically utilized and exploited for individual enrichment. The ultimate goal of education must be to encourage the individual to strive for what he/she can develop into and provide opportunities for learning and self-development. This needs to be offered through both organized educational system and the self-efforts made by the individual to acquire self-preferred learning from resources available in the society. The latter is conceptualized and imbibed by the individual himself/herself. That is real education and development.

## Acknowledgements

The author expresses his gratitude to:

1. Prof. S.B. Menon, Central Institute of Education, University of Delhi, with whom preliminary discussion was held about the nature and scope of the paper.
2. Dr. Varada M. Nikalje, Department of Languages, NCERT, New Delhi, for participating in continuous interaction on various issues related to the theme while the paper was being drafted; and also for the editorial assistance provided by her.

## Notes

1. Indian Institute of Applied Political Research, (1978). *The Surat Imbroglio Vol. 5, 1906-1910. The Encyclopaedia of the Indian National Congress*, Ed. A. M. Zaidi,, New Delhi: S. Chand and Co. Ltd., 1978, p. 15.
2. Indian Institute of Applied Political Research, (1980). *Combating an unwanted Constitution Vol. 11, 1936-38. The Encyclopaedia of the Indian National Congress*, Ed. A. M. Zaidi, New Delhi: S. Chand and Co. Ltd., 1980, pp. 431-32.

3. Yadav M. S. and Nikalje, Varada, *National Curriculum Frameworks for School Education: A Review*, 2006 (yet to be published).
4. Chagla M. N., Inaugural Address (2nd October 1964) *Inaugural Function of Education Commission*, Ministry of Education, Govt. of India, 1964, pp. 13-14.
5. Resolution No. F.413 (3) 64-E.1 of the Government of India, Ministry of Education, dated July, 14, 1964.
6. First Five Year Plan, Ministry of Information and Broadcasting, New Delhi, 1953, p. 11.
7. *Ibid.*, p. 220.
8. *Ibid.*, p. 239.
9. *Ibid.*, p. 240.

   * Five year plan is drafted by the Planning Commission. The plan-frame and other related documents are then considered by the National Development Council. After the approval by the Council, the plans are presented to the Government for submission to Parliament for reconsideration and final sanction.
10. Ibid., p. 242.
11. India's first Minister for Education.
12. Govt. of India, (1956). *The Future of Education in India*, Publications Division, Ministry of Information and Broadcasting,, 1956, p. 7.
13. Vice-Chancellor, AMU, and President of India 1967-69.
14. Govt. of India, (1956). *The Future of Education in India*, Publications Division, Ministry of Information and Broadcasting,, 1956, p. 21.
15. Ibid., pp. 75-6.
16. Nehru, Jawaharlal, (1964). *Glimpses of World History*, New Delhi: Asra, 1964, p.536.
17. Nehru, Jawaharlal, (1956). *Discovery of India*, London: Meridian Books, p. 312.
18. Singh, R. P., (1966). *Nehru on Education*, Jullundur: Sterling Publishers, p. 18.
19. Sharma, H. D. (1962). *Nehru Aur Nai Peeree*, N. D. Sehgal and Sons, 1962, p. 211-2, quoted in Singh, R.P. *Nehru on Education*, Jullundur: Sterling Publishers,1966, p. 15.
20. Nehru, Jawaharlal (1956). *Discovery of India,* London: Meridian Books Ltd., 1956, p. 526.
21. *Ibid.*, p. 522-3.
22. Indian Institute of Applied Political Research, (1981). Socialistic Pattern of Society" Vol. 15: 1955-57, *The Encyclopaedia of the Indian National Congress*, Ed. A. M. Zaidi, New Delhi:, S. Chand and Co. Ltd., 1981, p. 63.
23. Kaushik, P. K. (1992). Ambedkar: Prophet of Self-Help and Saviour of Untouchables,, *Political Thinkers of Modern India*, Vol. 16, Ed. Verinder Grover, New Delhi: Deep and Deep Publications, 1992, p. 252.
24. NCERT, (1970). Message from the President, *Inaugural function of Education Commission*, New Delhi: Ministry of Education, Govt. of India,1964, p. i 'Foreword', *Report of the Education Commission* Vol. 1, 1970, p. ix.
25. NCERT, (1970). *'Foreword', Report of the Education Commission,* Vol. I, New Delhi, p. ix.
26. NCERT, (1970). *Report of the Education Commission 1964-66* Vol. 1, p. 7.

27. *Ibid.*, p. 11.
28. *Ibid.*, p. 8.
29. Pts. 1.25-1.33, *Ibid.*, pp. 13-16.
30. Pts. 1.36-1.38, *Ibid.*, pp., 17-19.
31. Pts. 1.23-1.24, *Ibid.*, pp. 12-13.
32. Pt. 1.40, *Ibid.*, p. 20.
33. Pt. 1.45, *Ibid.*, p. 21.
34. Pt. 1.49, *Ibid.*, p. 23.
35. Pt. 11.09, *Report of the Education Commission, 1964-66*, Ministry of Education, Govt. of India, p. 277.
36. Nehru, Jawaharlal, (1962). India and the World, *Azad Memorial Lectures, 1959*, New Delhi: Indian Council for Cultural Relations.
37. Safdar Hashmi Memorial Trust (SAHMAT), (2005). *Debating education: A critical appraisal of National Curriculum Framework 2005*, New Delhi.

# 4

# Education Commission and After: A Segregated School System

ARJUN DEV

## Introduction

Professor D.S. Kothari submitted the Report of the Education Commission, titled 'Education and National Development', to the Minister of Education, Government of India, on June 29, 1966. Perhaps the most significant feature of the Report was its "emphasis on the social purposes of education, on the need to use it as a tool for the realization of national aspirations or for meeting national challenges" (Para 1.14). It rejected as 'naïve belief' the view that "*all* education is necessarily good, both for the individual and for society, and that it will necessarily lead to progress". "Quantitatively," it stated, "education can be organized to promote social justice or retard it. History shows numerous instances where small social groups and elites have used education as a prerogative of their rule and as a tool for maintaining their hegemony and perpetuating the values upon which it rested. On the other hand, there are cases in which a social and cultural revolution has been brought about in a system where equality of opportunity is provided and education is deliberately used to develop more and more potential talent and to harness it to the solution of national problems" (Para 1.16). It further stated: "Judged from this point of view, it becomes evident that the present system of education, designed to meet the needs of an imperial administration within the limitations set by a feudal and traditional society, will need radical changes if it is to meet the purposes of a modern democratic and socialistic society—changes in objectives, in content, in teaching methods, in programmes, in the size and composition of the student body, in the selection and professional preparation of teachers, and in organization. In fact, what is needed is a revolution in education which in turn will set in motion the much desired social, economic and Cultural Revolution" (Para 1.17).

## Social and National Integration

One of the major 'National Objectives' that the Report dealt with was the promotion of 'social and national integration'. Social and national integration was a major problem which, according to the Report, would have to be tackled 'on various fronts, including education'. It was in the context of this objective that the concept of *a Common School System of public instruction* was articulated in the Report. The concept of Common School System, and of the nighbourhood school, which was viewed as an integral part of the Common School System, and various related issues were explained in detail in Paragraphs 1.36, 1.37, 1.38, 10.09, 10.10, 10.11, 10.12, 10.13, 10.14, 10.15, 10.16, 10.17, 10.18, and 10.19. The most significant part of the Report in some of these Paragraphs related to the question of *social segregation*. They also included recommendations with regard to the place of private schools.

The Paragraphs of the Report dealing with the concept of the Common School System are reproduced below:

1.36 *The Common School.* In a situation of the type we have in India, it is the responsibility of the educational system to bring the different social classes and groups together and thus promote the emergence of an egalitarian and integrated society. But at present instead of doing so, education itself is tending to increase social segregation and to perpetuate and widen class distinctions. At the primary stage, the free schools to which the masses send their children are maintained by the government and local authorities and are generally of poor quality. Some of the private schools are definitely better; but since many of them charge high fees, they are availed of only by the middle and the higher classes. At the secondary stage, a large proportion of the good schools are private but many of them also charge high fees which are normally beyond the means of any but the top ten per cent of the people, though some of the middle class parents make great sacrifices to send their children to them. There is thus segregation in education itself—the minority of private, fee-charging, better schools meeting the needs of the upper classes and the vast bulk of free, publicly maintained, but poor schools being utilized by the rest. What is worse, this segregation is increasing and tending to widen the gulf between the classes and the masses.

1.37 This is one of the major weaknesses of the existing educational system. Good education, instead of being available to all children, or at least to all the able children from every stratum of society, is available only to a small minority which is usually selected not on the basis of talent but on the basis of its capacity to pay fees. The identification and development of the total national pool of ability is greatly hampered. The position is thus undemocratic and inconsistent with the ideal of an egalitarian society. The children of the masses are compelled to receive sub-standard education and, as the programme of scholarships is not very large, sometimes even the ablest among them are unable to find access to such good schools as exist, while the economically privileged parents are able to 'buy' good education for their children. This is bad not only for the children of the poor but also for the children from the rich and privileged groups. It gives them a short-term advantage in so far as it enables them to perpetuate and consolidate their position. But it must be realized that, in the long run, their self-interest lies in identifying themselves with the masses. By segregating their children, such privileged parents prevent them from sharing the life and experiences of the children of the poor and coming into contact with the realities of life. In addition to weakening social cohesion, they also render the education of their own children anaemic and incomplete.

1.38 If these evils are to be eliminated and the educational system is to become a powerful instrument of national development in general, and social and national integration in particular, we must move towards the goal of a Common School System of public education:

- Which will be open to all children, irrespective of caste, creed, community, religion, economic conditions or social status;
- Where access to good education will depend not on wealth or class but on talent;
- Which will maintain adequate standards in all schools and provide at least a reasonable proportion of quality institutions;
- In which no tuition fee will be charged; and
- Which would meet the needs of the average parent so that he would not ordinarily feel the need to send his children to expensive schools outside the system.

The Report mentioned that "such an educational system" had been built up in the USSR and, in different forms and to varying degrees, in some other countries. Referring to England, it said, "The traditional English system has been different and has allowed good education, under private management, to be largely reserved for those who have the capacity to pay the necessary fees. But recently, the so-called Public Schools have come in for strong criticism in England itself and it is not unlikely that a radical change may be initiated to make them more democratic." In this context, the Report mentioned that "a somewhat similar system was transplanted in India by British administrators and *we have clung to it so long because it happened to be in tune with the traditional hierarchical structure of our society.*" But it clearly and unambiguously stated that "Whatever its past history may be, *such a system has no valid place in the new democratic and socialistic society we desire to create.*" [Emphasis added]

The Report in its Para 10.19 on the concept of 'neighbourhood school' reads as follows:

We drew attention earlier to the social segregation that now takes place in our primary and secondary schools and pointed out that such segregation should be eliminated if education is to be made a powerful instrument of national development in general, and social and national integration in particular. From this point of view, we recommend the ultimate adoption of the 'neighbourhood school concept' first at the lower primary stage and then at the higher primary. The neighbourhood school concept implies that each school should be attended by *all* children in the neighbourhood irrespective of caste, creed, community, religion, economic condition or social status, so that there would be no segregation in schools. Apart from social and national integration, two other arguments can be advanced in support of the proposal. In the first place, the neighbourhood school will provide 'good' education to children because sharing life with the common people is, in our opinion, an essential ingredient of good education. Secondly, the establishment of such schools will compel the rich, privileged and powerful classes to take an interest in the system of public education and thereby bring about its early improvement.

The Report in Para 10.20 stated that the "neighbourhood school concept should be adopted as a long-term goal, to be reached in a well-planned programme spread over the next 20 years."

The establishment of a Common School System—*an integrated desegregated school system of public education*—has been among the most ignored and the most flouted recommendations of the Education Commission. The entire course of educational development in India during the past 40 years has been in the direction of perpetuating, consolidating and further spreading a highly segregated system of school education. It can be described as a system of *apartheid* in education based on class, social status and wealth, both white and not-so-white. All the ills that the Education Commission had mentioned in its critique of the segregated system of school education have aggravated over the years. The desegregated character of a not insignificant number of schools that existed in the 1950s and in the early 1960s when the Education Commission prepared its Report has been eroded if not become entirely extinct. This phenomenon is as true for the school systems created, justifiably or otherwise, by the Union Government or others. There is not even a pretence here of the "separate but equal" doctrine which was advanced on behalf of the racially segregated school systems in some countries.

## Education Commission and After

J.P. Naik, who had served as Member-Secretary of the Education Commission and had played a leading role in preparing its Report, published *The Education Commission and After* in 1982.[1] The book, written in 1979, examined the Report of the Education Commission and the steps taken to give effect to its recommendations during the preceding 12 years.[2] Malcom S. Adiseshiah, in his Foreword to the book, described it as an "extraordinary work which is as illuminating for its informativeness as for the deep perception it exhibits of the meshing process of educational, economic and political decision-making."[3] The book "examines the manner in which the recommendations of the Education Commission were implemented" and makes "an evaluation of the recommendations themselves". The process of discussion of the Report after its submission to the Minister of Education, its consideration by a Committee of Members of Parliament and, finally, the drafting of the Resolution issued by the Government of India on the Report of the Education Commission, which was the first statement on the National Policy on Education, described in the book is highly instructive. It also illustrates the seriousness with which issues of education are deliberated and decisions taken.[4] The Statement on National Policy on Education issued in 1968 is described by Naik as "far from satisfactory, mainly because of the political and economic circumstances of the period and the violent eruption of the language controversy." "It should not be forgotten", he states, "that it was finalized by a weak Central Government, which was more anxious to avoid controversies than to bring about radical educational changes".[5]

Naik has discussed in much detail the controversies within the Education Commission, in the Committee of Members of Parliament and within the government when the 1968 Statement on National Policy on Education was being drafted on the neighbourhood school concept, which, according to him, formed the essence of the Common School System. A minority within the Commission strongly favoured the adoption, immediately, of the neighbourhood school concept as the first major step to create the Common School System all over the country. What was, however, adopted in Paras 10.19 and 10.20 of the Report was the majority view, which favoured it to be phased over a period of 20 years. When the Statement on the National Policy on Education was being drafted, it was decided "that there need be no reference at all to the controversial concept of the neighbourhood school and that even the time-limit of 20 years mentioned by the Commission for realizing the goal of the Common School System... should not be mentioned." "Consequently, we had a non-controversial but ineffective and colourless statement which said: "to promote social cohesion and national integration, the Common School concept as recommended by the Education Commission should be adopted" and that "efforts should be made to improve the standard of education in general schools.... As an immediate action programme, it was also decided that the public schools and other special schools were required to reserve a percentage of their available seats to talented but economically handicapped children and provide them with adequate scholarships. To make the decision more palatable, no *specific* minimum percentage was laid down; and in keeping with the policy of avoiding controversial issues, nothing has been done to implement this decision which is of real significance. For all practical purposes, therefore, this proposal has remained a dead letter for the last 12 years".[6]

J.P. Naik's account, mainly that of an insider but for that reason not uncritical even of his own role, covered the first 12 'After' years. It may be useful to recall the concluding statement from his 'Overview':

> It would, therefore, be incorrect to describe the existing educational system as an instrument for educating the people; the evidence... clearly shows that it is more appropriately designed for *not* educating them. In fact, the primary objective of the system is not to spread education among the people, but to function as an efficient and merciless mechanism to *select* individuals who should continue to remain in the privileged sector or enter it afresh. It does not discharge even this task impartially and... functions in such a biased fashion that those who are already in the privileged sector find it easier to continue therein while the under-privileged find that the access to the privileged sector through the portals of education is becoming more restricted (and) increasingly dependent on chance rather than on merit. The main achievement of the system, therefore, is to condemn the bulk of the children of the common people as drop-outs and failures and to consign them to a life of drudgery and poverty which has hardly any parallel in the contemporary world or even in our own earlier history.[7]

## Education for Equality

The early 1980s saw much debate and discussion, including the release of what many viewed as a truly radical document, *Challenge of Education: A Policy Perspective*, which culminated in the adoption of the National Policy on Education, 1986. This was a lot more elaborate statement of policy than the 1968 statement, most of it rhetoric with even a whole chapter on Education for Equality. Education had by then become a concurrent subject, which meant that a statement on Education Policy adopted by Parliament would be expected to be more effective. However, on the question of the Common School System, there was little in the new Policy that was different from the 1968 Policy. The sole reference to the Common School System appears in Para 3.2 of the New Policy, which stated, "The concept of a National System of Education implies that, up to a given level, all students, irrespective of caste, creed, location or sex, have access to education of a comparable quality. To achieve this, the Government will initiate appropriately funded programmes. Effective measures will be taken in the direction of the Common School System recommended in the 1968 Policy." Any reference to the concept of neighbourhood school was again conspicuous by its absence in this Para or anywhere else in the new Policy. It was obviously considered irrelevant to the "effective measures" that the Government thought it would take "in the direction of the Common

School System". It was perhaps not due to an oversight that in the statement about access to education of a comparable quality irrespective of caste, creed, etc., the words 'economic conditions or social status', which were a part of the Education Commission's explanation of the meaning of Common School System, were excluded. And, unlike the 1968 Policy, the adoption of the 1986 Policy was followed by the adoption of two Programmes of Action [in 1986 and in 1992, the latter after a perfunctory revision of the Policy] to give effect to the Policy but neither of these Programmes of Action had anything to say on the 'effective steps' that were proposed to be taken 'in the direction of the Common School System'. It was clear that promoting *social integration* or even mitigating the segregated character of the system of school education was not on the agenda even as a formal, though not-to-be-taken-seriously, gesture.

The segregated system of school education has thus remained intact; it has, in fact, proliferated and prospered. It was commonly described as a dual system but, as A.R. Kamat pointed out: "Actually the system is not merely dual, it has several hierarchical channels of education." He spoke of a "four-fold hierarchy, a *chaturvarnya* in education, *a la* the four-class hierarchy in government services."[8] The actual hierarchy is manifold, with the state providing new channels with Non-Formal Education Centres [Alternative Schooling], schools with para-teachers and various others at one end of the hierarchy and various types of 'public schools' [and even Kendriya Vidyalayas (KVs) and Navodaya Vidyalayas (NVs)] at the other end.

The reasons for the continuing and aggravating segregation have been gone into by a small number of scholars and, to a significant extent, by J.P. Naik himself. Kamat questioned the basic assumption made by the Education Commission [and of many other pure-education wallahs and social scientists of the late 1940s, 1950s] regarding "education being the main instrument of social change [meaning radical social transformation]".[9] He disagreed with the view "that education is determined completely by social factors and has, therefore, no role in social change, at most, it follows social change" and described it as the position of 'mechanical' Marxists. He summed up his own position in the following words: "If social change is meant to connote fundamental structural changes in society, it is clear... that the socio-economic factors and its executive arm, the political factor—and not education—have primary importance in the process of social change. They are, by and large, the real prime movers.... Education, no doubt, can help the process of social change as a necessary and vitally important collateral factor.... Moreover, in a rapidly-changing situation (e.g., in a post-revolutionary period) when fundamental structural changes are rapidly taking place, education can undoubtedly operate as a powerful weapon to demolish the old cultural and ideological superstructure, and to build in its place an altogether new and appropriate structure in harmony with the new-born society."[10] Malcom S.

Adiseshiah, in his Foreword to *The Education Commission and After*, referred to the 'unequal struggle between education and political economy' and stated: "Consider, for instance the reaction to the proposals for establishing neighbourhood schools, abolishing public schools and evolving a common school system, or for that matter recommendations on the selective development of educational institutions and the priority to elementary and adult education as a first essential step in the educational transformation. All of these were envisaged as vital aspects of the much-needed educational revolution in the country, but became eventually either non-issues or non-starters. *The basic truth that a democratic and egalitarian educational system is impossible in an in-egalitarian and unjust society has come to the surface time and again.*" [emphasis added][11]

J.P. Naik himself critiqued the Education Commission's work on broadly similar lines. In a section dealing with Education and Society, he stated, "The view of the Commission was that a radical restructuring of education (or the creation of a national system of education as indicated by it) will set in motion corresponding socio-economic changes and that education is the instrument for the peaceful transformation of society." The Commission also believed that "the most effective way of breaking the vicious circle in which we find ourselves is to begin educational reconstruction in a big way.... As a matter of hindsight, I find that this view is not theoretically correct. *It also ignores the basic fact that the existing power structure will do its damnedest to see that no radical reconstruction of education contrary to its interests takes place.* I have also realized to my regret that such a view does an actual disservice to the cause because people in responsible positions avoid recourse to direct action for social transformation (which may be coercive) on the ground that the same results can be obtained peacefully through education. All things considered, I believe that we must now abandon the role of primacy in social transformation, which we have been traditionally ascribing to education for years. It is a hangover of the pre-independence struggle for national education and has outlived its utility" (emphasis added)[12]. It is interesting that the person who is believed to have played a leading role in drafting the Report of the Education Commission came to the conclusion that the 'power structure' would not permit education to serve the social purposes that the Commission had ascribed to it. It was a critique of the Commission but, equally or more, a condemnation of the prevailing power structure. Kamat referred to *The Education Commission and After* as reflective of "the penitent mood in which J.P. Naik reappraises his [and his colleagues'] effort".[13]

J.P. Naik was wary of the role of the political parties and wrote, "No political party in the country is committed to a radical reconstruction of education and for the creation of a national system of education". He quoted the view of the Education Commission—"The responsibility for creating a national system of education is that of the Governments, Central and States", and added: "We should also add that it is the basic responsibility of the political parties that make these governments. If they will not accept it, no one else can or will."[14] Referring to the differing opinions on the Common School System and the neighbourhood schools when the 1968 Policy was being drafted, as well as on the issue of public schools, he wrote, "The battle is essentially political and will have to be decided politically."[15]

## The Continuing Debate

The political battle had been lost both in 1968, and, as mentioned earlier, in 1986 as well as during the course of subsequent developments. J.P. Naik wanted to 'keep the debate going' and it has gone on—through the media, forums of concerned citizens, Public Interest Litigation (PIL) cases relating to the rampant violation of contractual obligations on the part of various 'public-progressive' schools, and the now aborted Right to Education Bill. There was also a CABE Committee on Girls' Education and the Common School System. There was no debate on why there was only one Committee to go into two very distinct areas of concern. The Report of this Committee on the Common School System part of its work has, for reasons unknown, chosen to remain more or less completely silent on the experience of 39 years—it was finalized during the 39th anniversary of the Report of the Education Commission—of the flouting of the recommendation of the Common School System and the neighbourhood school system. In some of its facts, the Report is highly selective. In its Para 5.7, for example, it states: "When recently some state governments took the simple decision to enforce the admission of children from deprived families in private schools enjoying considerable government subsidies..., there was an uproar against the move." It, however, forgets to mention that this 'simple decision' should have been taken decades ago and that, when it was taken, it was at the direction of the judiciary. The statement made in Para 5.7.3 [iii] that "at least since 1968...not only the Union Cabinet but also the principal opposition parties in Parliament were invariably found supporting the main recommendations of the Education Commission Report" is simply not true. The Report, however, has made many significant recommendations. It was submitted in June 2005 but nothing is known of the view that the authorities—and the power structure—have taken of these recommendations and the step they propose taking, in the words of the 1986 Policy, 'in the direction of the Common School System'. Given the past record of the state and its power structure in this matter, there may not be sufficient ground for great optimism. It may not be inappropriate to consider linking the issue of Common School System with 'direct action for social transformation' and to treat the battle for it as 'essentially political' which 'will have to be decided politically'.

## Notes

1. Naik, J. P., *The Education Commission and After*, Allied Publishers, New Delhi, 1982.
2. *Ibid.* p. ix.
3. *Ibid.*, p. v.
4. *Ibid.*, pp. 41-42 [*See* for discussion on universal elementary education].
5. *Ibid.*, p. 43.
6. *Ibid.*,p. 79.
7. *Ibid.*, pp. 170-71.
8. Kamat, A.R., *Education and Social Change in India*, Somaiya Publications, Bombay, 1985, p. 132.
9. *Ibid.*, p. 3.
10. *Ibid.*, pp. 14-15.
11. Naik, op. cit., pp. vi-vii.
12. *Ibid.*, p. 57.
13. Kamat, op. cit., p. 4.
14. Naik, op. cit., p. 44.
15. *Ibid.*, p. 80.

# Part II

# Equality and Social Justice

# 5

# Literacy and Elementary Education: Regional Imbalances and Social Inequities

R. GOVINDA

## Introduction

Inspiration for writing this paper came from a re-reading of the Tagore Memorial Lectures delivered by J.P. Naik at the University of Poona in August 1975, nearly ten years after his monumental contribution to the preparation of the Education Commission 1964-66.[1] The lectures undoubtedly broke new grounds in contemporary understanding of school education, both conceptually and operationally. Perhaps, the best and the first of its kind exposition on the 'common school system' in the Indian context was presented. It was critical for a proper understanding of the neighbourhood school approach envisaged by the Education Commission earlier. The lectures also articulated the need for interpreting quality as organically linked to equity. Juxtaposing the discourses on the subject onto the Indian stratified and hierarchical social structure, Naik expounded the futility and inappropriateness of viewing 'quality' in the traditional framework of 'merit', which is heavily loaded in favour of the privileged sections of the society. While Naik sounded optimistic about the actions initiated by the State for improving the educational conditions of Scheduled Castes and Scheduled Tribes, he amply cautioned that there was still a long way to go for overcoming the historically inherited inequalities among different social groups in India. Naik traced many of the persisting inequalities in education in different parts of the country and among different social sections to the faulty policies pursued by the British. At the same time, tracking the progress made during the post-independence period, Naik expressed deep displeasure with the laid back approach of the leadership and argued that the traditional school-bound approach might not prove adequate to move in a speedy manner towards the goal of universal elementary education envisioned by the Constitution. Naik emphatically pleaded for plurality of perspective in the delivery mechanisms as well as the structure and contents of the school system if the demands of quantity, quality and equality are to be effectively met.

## Twin Problems of Regional Imbalances and Social Inequities in Education

Uneven spread of education reflected in persisting regional imbalances and social inequities is a historical legacy inherited from the British past or even beyond. During the colonial period, some princely states such as Travancore and Baroda moved ahead with a forward looking leadership; Baroda introduced compulsory education more than 100 years ago, in 1893. Also, better attention was bestowed on some parts by the British rulers and progress was achieved due to a combination of Government attention and private efforts, which included missionaries and a number of indigenous charitable organizations invariably driven by a nationalistic spirit. While these efforts by the Government of the day coupled with private efforts attempted to compliment each other, they were never comprehensive enough, thus leading to a skewed development of education in the country. The system remained elitist, despite efforts by the nationalist leadership, accessible only to the upper segments of the society. In fact, British rulers openly advocated such a policy of elitism through the principle of downward filtration and, therefore, the ensuing imbalances and inequities were not viewed as serious anomaly.

The advent of Independence and the Indian Constitution laying the foundations for an egalitarian society based on principles of equity and social justice made educational provision an obligation of the State. Consequently, the State took upon itself the responsibility of overcoming imbalances and inequities through a planned development of the sector. With nearly six decades of independence and having completed ten cycles of five-year development planning how far have we succeeded in building mass education system with an even spread across the country and among all sections of the society? And, if we are still in the process of building such a system, who and where are the educationally deprived? What has been the response of the State to achieve better balance and equity in education development? These were indeed some of the critical questions addressed by the Education Commission, forty years ago. The Commission made far reaching recommendations to rectify the inherited inequities and anomalies. The present paper revisits some of these questions and examines the ways in which the State has responded to them in recent years. Even recently, the persisting problem of imbalances and inequities was amply recognized by the Planning Commission: "Regional, social and gender variations in literacy continue to remain serious areas of concern. There are at least seven major states with more than 15 million illiterates each, accounting for nearly two-thirds of total illiterates in the country. Though the gender gap has narrowed since 1991, it is still big. The literacy rates for SCs (54.69%) and STs (47.10%) are far below the national average."[2]

The paper is based on an analysis of existing macro-level data bases including 2001 Census and periodic NSSO survey findings to explore the current status with respect to the spread of literacy and education attainment levels in different parts of the country. The major focus of analysis is to look at the persisting inter-state disparities and review the state of education development among different social groups. The paper also examines the policies and programmes promoted at the national level to overcome such disparities and present some proposals.

## Mapping Literacy Status across Indian States[3]

Independent India began its educational journey with a serious handicap as only around 18 per cent adults possessed basic literacy skills. The situation has vastly changed as successive generation got the opportunity to pursue school education. Thus, examining literacy status across the country indirectly reflects on the efficiency and effectiveness of the school system that has grown multi-fold during the last six decades.

Over the last five decades, there has been an impressive growth in literacy in India. In 1901, a little over five per cent of Indian population was literate, which increased to around 16 per cent in 1950, a mere increase of 11 percentage points in the literacy rate during the first half of the century. In the post-independence period, the decadal growth in literacy has shown a substantial progress—from 18.35 per cent (5+ age group population) in 1951 to 65.38 per cent (7+ age group population) in 2001. The female literacy rate was just 8.9 per cent in 1951, which went up to 54.2 per cent in 2001. In 2001, almost two-thirds of India's population (65.38 per cent), and around three-fourths of males (75.85 per cent) and more than half of females (54.16 per cent) were literate.

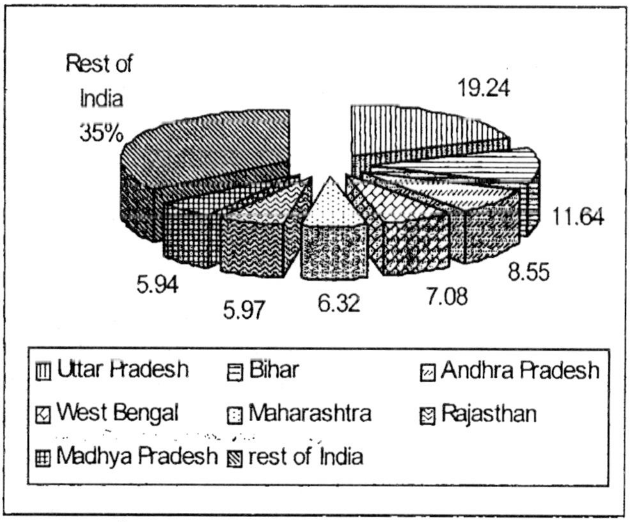


**Chart 5.1: Share of Illiterates (Persons) in India 2001**

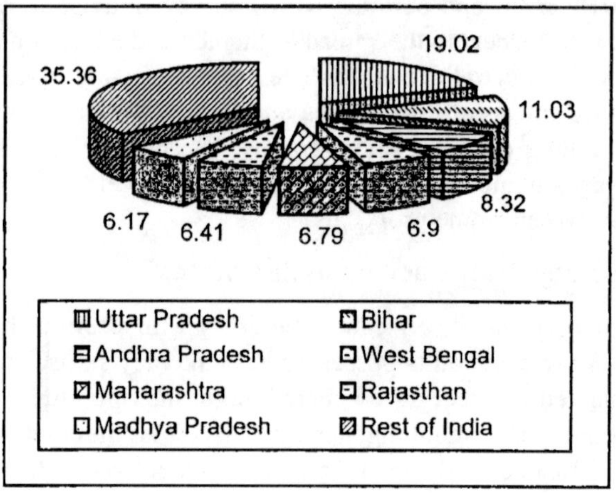


**Chart 5.2: Share of Female Illiterates to total Female Illiterates in India 2001**

However, average figures do not reveal the real picture of progress and problems. There are huge variations in literacy rates across states in India. According to 2001 census, Kerala remains on the top with a literacy rate of 90.9 per cent, while Bihar is at the bottom with a literacy rate of 47.5 per cent. States/UTs having literacy below the national average are Assam, Madhya Pradesh, Orissa, Meghalaya, Andhra Pradesh, Rajasthan, Dadra and Nagar Haveli, Uttar Pradesh, Arunachal Pradesh, Jammu and Kashmir, Jharkhand and Bihar. States having female literacy rate below the national average include Chhatisgarh, Andhra Pradesh, Orissa, Madhya Pradesh, Rajasthan, Arunachal Pradesh, Dadra and Nagar Haveli, Uttar Pradesh, Jammu and Kashmir, Jharkhand and Bihar.

Charts 5.1 and 5.2 give a picture of the disparities among different states with respect to literacy levels. Seven states seem to carry the burden of two thirds of the illiterate population. In fact 60 per cent of the illiterate population is accounted for by the States of UP, Bihar, West Bengal, Rajasthan, Madhya Pradesh and Andhra Pradesh which had been identified as educationally backward nearly three decades ago.

Regional variations in literacy rate become more pronounced when analysis is done at the district level. According to 2001 census, around one-fifth of the 591 districts[4] (i.e. 81 districts) have literacy rate equal to or less than 50 per cent; 21.3 per cent of the districts have literacy rate in the range of 50-60 per cent, much below the national average. Most of the low literacy districts (26 districts having literacy rate less than 40 per cent) are located in the educationally backward states such as Bihar (11 districts; 42.3 per cent), Jharkhand (3 districts; 11.5 per cent), Orissa (4 districts; 15.4 per cent), and

Uttar Pradesh (5 districts; 19.2 per cent). Most of the high literacy districts (46 districts having literacy rate = 80-90 per cent) are found in Kerala (6 districts; 13.0 per cent), Maharashtra (9 districts; 19.6 per cent), and Delhi (6 districts; 13.0 per cent). Districts having more than 90 per cent literacy rate are found in Kerala (8 districts; 61.5 per cent), Mizoram (4 districts; 30.8 per cent) and Pondichery (1 district; 7.7 per cent).

In terms of absolute number of illiterates in 2001, the top 100 districts are found in 11 states — Andhra Pradesh, Bihar, Gujarat, Jharkhand, Karnataka, Maharashtra, Orissa, Rajasthan, Tamil Nadu, Uttar Pradesh and West Bengal (see Chart 5.7). These districts are home to 120.03 million illiterates (around 40 per cent of illiterates of the country). Among these 100 districts, female literacy rate is more than 70 per cent (maximum 77.86 per cent) in 12 districts in Bihar (7 districts) and Uttar Pradesh (5 districts)—Araria (Bihar), Bahraich (UP), Purnia (Bihar), Katihar (Bihar), Purba Champaran (Bihar), Budaun (UP), Paschim Champaran (Bihar), Sitamari (Bihar), Madhubani (Bihar), Gonda (UP), Rampur (UP), and Siddharthnagar (UP).

Sixty-seven districts in the country spread over nine states are having million plus illiterates. These districts are home to 88.51 million illiterates, which is 29.5 per cent of the total illiterates in the country. These districts are located in Andhra Pradesh (14), Bihar (15), Gujarat (2), Karnataka (2), Maharashtra (3), Rajasthan (1), Tamil Nadu (1), Uttar Pradesh (20), and West Bengal (9). The top 10 districts in terms of absolute number of illiterates are found in 4 states—Bihar (3 districts), West Bengal (5 districts), Uttar Pradesh (1 district), and Andhra Pradesh (1 district). These are Murshidabad (WB), Medinapur (WB), Purba Champaran (Bihar), South 24 Parganas (WB), North 24 Parganas (WB), Bardhaman (WB), Madhubani (Bihar), Moradabad (Uttar Pradesh), Mahbubnagar (Andhra Pradesh), and Muzaffarpur (Bihar). These 10 districts have 17.85 million illiterates accounting for around six per cent of illiterates in the country.

More than half of the population is illiterate in 81 districts located in 15 states. Most of these districts are located in Bihar (around 28 per cent) and Uttar Pradesh (around 22 per cent). Around one-fifth of the illiterates (61 million; 20.32 per cent) live in these 81 districts. Female illiteracy rate is more than 50 per cent (maximum 81.51 per cent) in 253 districts mostly located in Andhra Pradesh, Arunachal Pradesh, Bihar, J and K, Jharkhand, Madhya Pradesh, Orissa, Rajasthan, and Uttar Pradesh (see Chart 5.14). These districts have 104.62 million female illiterates, which accounts for 54.51 per cent of female illiterates in the country. In 17 districts, more than three-fourth of the females are illiterates. These districts are again located in Bihar (7), Chhatisgarh (1), Jharkhand (2), Orissa (4), and Uttar Pradesh (3). These districts are Kishanganj (Bihar), Shravasti (UP), Pakaur (Jharkhand), Dantewada (Chhatisgarh), Nabarangapur (Orissa), Supaul (Bihar), Malkangiri

(Orissa), Balrampur (UP), Araria (Bihar), Madhepura (Bihar), Garhwa (Jharkhand), Bahraich (UP), Purnia (Bihar), Katihar (Bihar), Rayagada (Orissa), Purba Champaran (Bihar), and Koraput (Orissa).

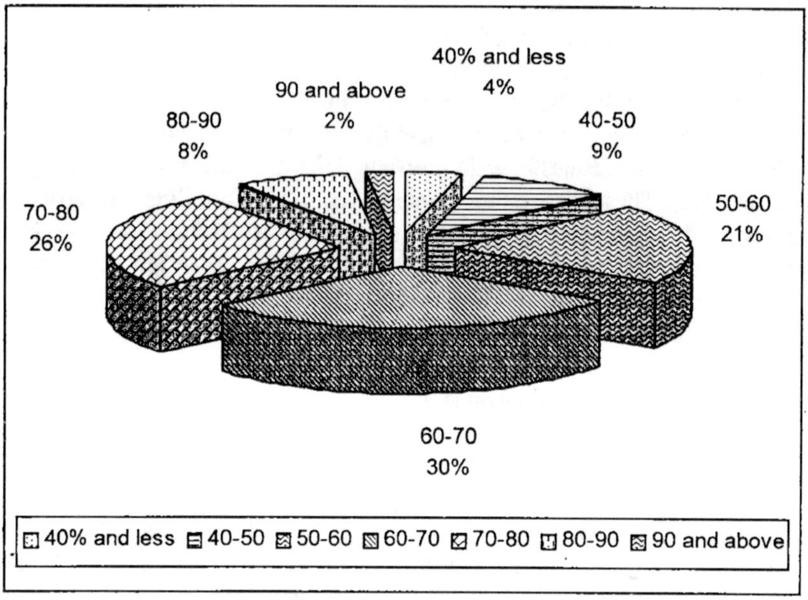


**Chart 5.3: Distribution of Districts According to Range of Literacy Rate (Persons) 2001**

The variation in the literacy rate across social groups and household type is also very high. In terms of social status, the population can be grouped into four categories—i.e. Scheduled Castes (SC), Scheduled Tribes (ST), Other Backward Class (OBC), and others. The SC and ST population are generally disadvantaged in most of the states in India. According to the 2001 Census, India has 16.2 per cent and 8.2 per cent of SC and ST population respectively. The greatest concentration of population of SCs is in Andhra Pradesh, Tamil Nadu, Bihar, West Bengal, Uttar Pradesh, Uttaranchal, Punjab, Rajasthan, Himachal Pradesh, Maharashtra, Karnataka, and Orissa. Besides the northeastern states, STs are found in greater numbers in Orissa, Maharashtra, Madhya Pradesh, Jharkhand, Chhattisgarh, Gujarat and Rajasthan. It may be noted that the educational status of ST households is relatively better in most of the northeastern states.

Analysis of Census 2001 and NSS data reveals that the seven states having around 65 per cent of illiterates have high concentration of SCs and STs, and the illiteracy rates of agricultural and casual labour households are relatively very high. Besides, in most of the sates, where female illiteracy rate is high, the percentage share of females in total agricultural labourers is also high. However, there are a few states where high female illiteracy rate is accompanied by low share of female agricultural labourers, primarily because women are engaged in other household based paid activities or other commercial activities, particularly in Rajasthan and northeastern states.

District level analysis also shows that the correlation coefficients among the number of illiterates, SC and ST population and the number of agricultural labourers are extremely high, positive and significant. A correlation coefficient of 0.750 (significant at 0.01 level) supports the fact that irrespective of the social characteristics, low economic status of the households (agricultural labourers as a proxy variable) contributes to high illiteracy rate. This finding is further supported by the findings of the NSS 55th round that the level of illiteracy and the Monthly Per Capita Consumer Expenditure (MPCE[5]) of households are inversely related to each other.

**Table 5.1: Correlations among Illiterates, SC and ST Population, and Agricultural Labour in India, 2001 (Based on District Level Records, N=591)**

| | *Number of Illiterates (Persons)* | *SC Population (Persons)* | *ST Population (Persons)* | *Estimated Number of Agricultural Labourers* |
|---|---|---|---|---|
| Number of illiterates (persons) 2001 | 1.000 | 0.711** | 0.142** | 0.750** |
| SC population (persons) 2001 | | 1.000 | – 0.097* | 0.524** |
| ST population (persons) 2001 | | | 1.000 | 0.212** |
| Estimated number of agricultural labourers 2001 | | | | 1.000 |

** Correlation is significant at the 0.01 level (2-tailed).
* Correlation is significant at the 0.05 level (2-tailed).

As per NSS, 55th round, the educational attainment and economic status of households are directly related to each other. Illiteracy rate is relatively high among members of households having low MPCE, both in rural and urban areas. Compared to urban areas, the literacy rate increases at a relatively slower rate with the increase in the MPCE of rural households. In fact, the illiteracy rate declines very sharply with the increase in the MPCE of the urban households. Compared to rural areas, the percentage share of secondary school graduates and above increases at a faster rate with the increased MPCE of the urban households. In other words, MPCE as a variable directly explains the economic characteristics of the household, and now, it is evident that poverty is the most important factor explaining the low literacy level of rural households. Cultural factors also contribute to the low literacy status of households, particularly in the Hindi heartland of India. It is also argued that, in this region of the country, mainly covering Uttar Pradesh, Bihar, Rajasthan and Madhya Pradesh, much weaker process of emergence of sub-nationalism and a virtual failure to give rise to a middle class, which in most other parts of the country have spearheaded the social reforms, have created a value system that perhaps does not give adequate recognition to education as a critical individual endowment.[6]

## Progress of Elementary Education across States[7]

The Indian scenario is too complex and varied to be effectively captured through aggregate national figures. On the one hand, there is Kerala with practically every child attending primary school, and every school having at least five teachers and five classrooms. At the other end of the spectrum, there is Bihar where only one out of two children in the relevant age group is in the school. Towards the end of the 1990s, it was estimated that three-fourth of the out-of-school children lived in six states of the country, namely, Andhra Pradesh, Bihar, Madhya Pradesh, Rajasthan, Uttar Pradesh and West Bengal. Gender disparity was as high as 42 percentage points for enrolment rates in Bihar and 31 percentage points in Uttar Pradesh but was only three percentage points for Kerala and 5 percentage points in Punjab.[8] Has the situation significantly changed? Chart 5.6.

Estimates derived from the 7th All India Education Survey reveal a very similar story in 2002-03. Nearly 69 per cent of out-of-primary school children are concentrated in seven states, namely, Andhra Pradesh, Bihar, Jharkhand, Madhya Pradesh, Rajasthan, Uttar Pradesh and West Bengal. Bihar and Uttar Pradesh alone account for 33.87 per cent of out-of-school children at the primary stage. Surprisingly, with respect to girls' education, some of the states like Gujarat and Haryana have regressed in recent years falling below the national average. Thus, the problem of UEE continues to be one of inter-state disparities.

It should be mentioned that, way back in 1978 while preparing the Sixth Five-Year Plan, the Planning Commission identified these states, along with a couple of others, as educationally backward states. To find the same cluster of states appearing as low UPE states after implementing development plans for nearly 25 years and going through at least four full cycle Five-Year Plans raises serious questions on the strategy being adopted for overcoming inter-state disparities in the country. At the upper primary stage, even relatively better performing states such as Karnataka and Maharashtra show serious problems with a large proportion of children remaining outside the fold of schooling. That they have persisted in spite of five decades of development planning shows that the strategies adopted for education development have not adequately dealt with the issue. There is undoubtedly an urgent need to

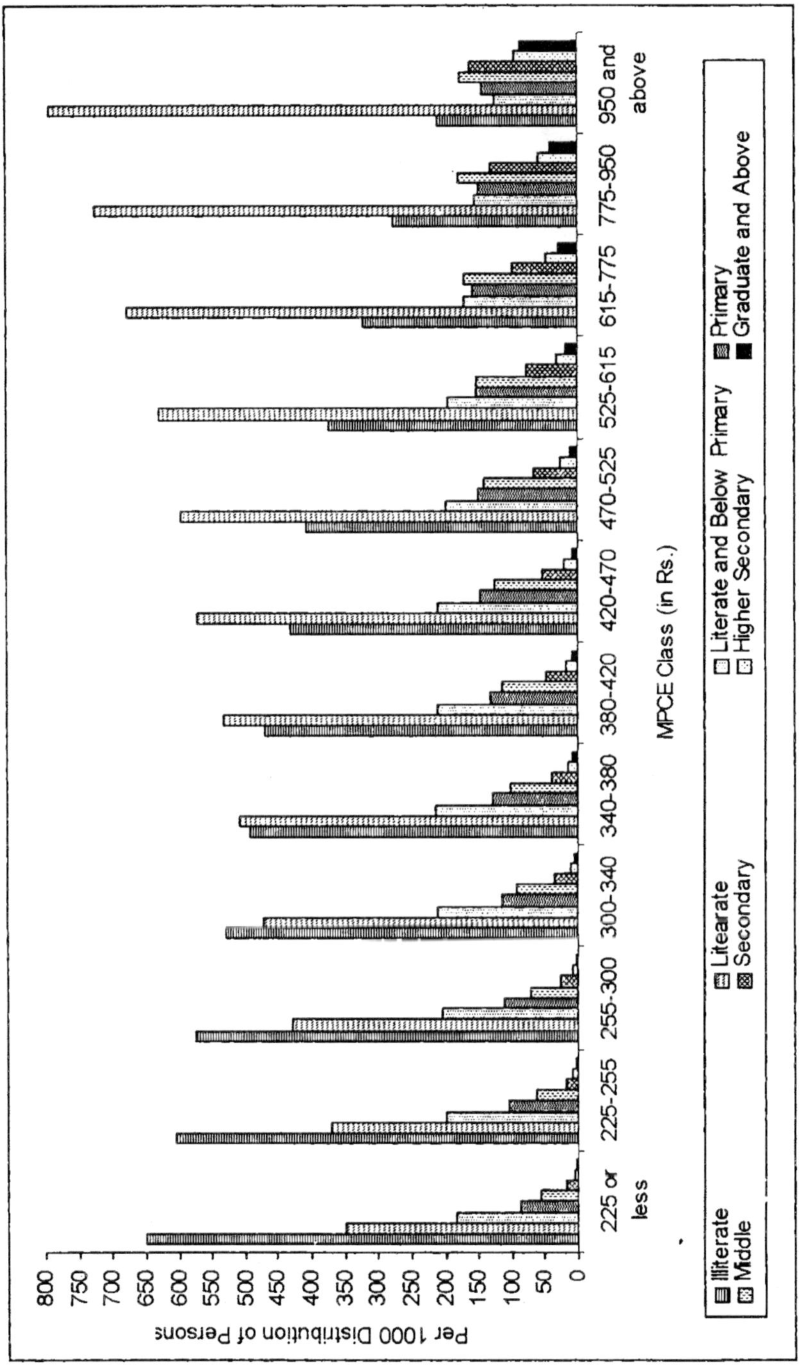


**Chart 5.4: Per 1000 distribution of 7+ Age Group Population by Educational Level and MPEC Class in Rural India, 1999-2000**

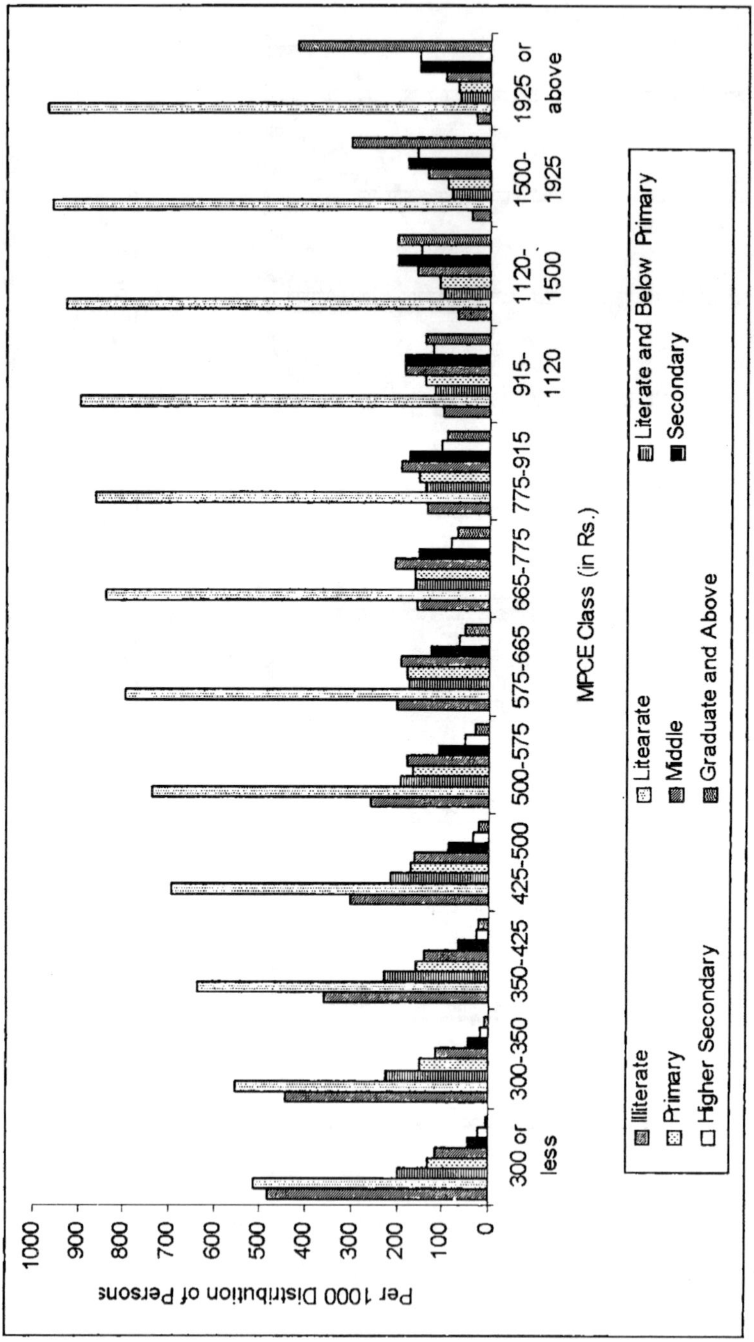


**Chart 5.5: Per 1000 distribution of 7+ Population by Educational Level and MPEC Class in Rural India, 1999-2000**

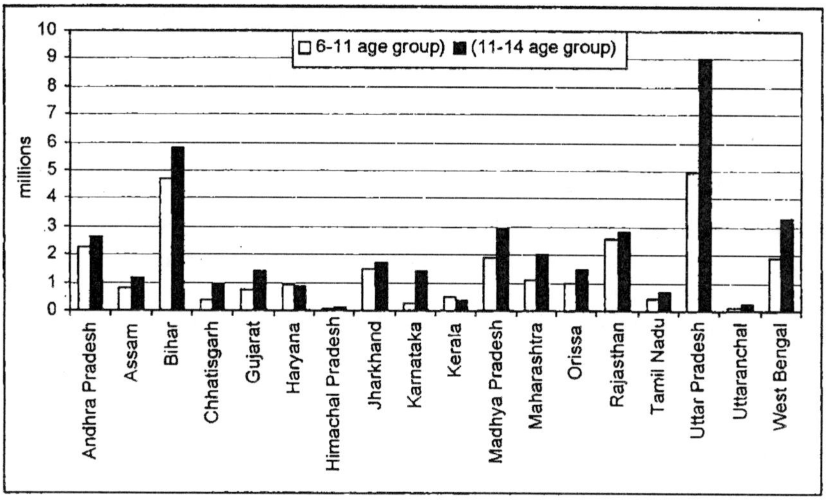


**Chart 5.6: Out-of-school Children**

treat these states on priority basis and enhance the funding for them in a focused manner, as without making a significant impact on the status of elementary education in these states, it is impossible to show substantial progress towards UEE in the country as a whole.

The Census of India reported similar findings. In 2001, out of 15.8 million out-of-school children in the age group of 11-13 in the country, more than 40 per cent were found in Uttar Pradesh and Bihar. Nine states namely, Uttar Pradesh (and Uttaranchal), Bihar (and Jharkhand), Madhya Pradesh (and Chhattisgarh), West Bengal, Rajasthan and Andhra Pradesh accounted for more than 70 per cent of the country's out-of-school children in the age group of 11-13 in 2001. During the period 1991-2001, all major states, except Bihar and Assam, had contributed positively towards reduction in the number of out-of-school children in the age group of 11-13 in the country. During 1991-2001, at the all India level, the coverage of the out-of-school children in the age group of 11-13 had improved by 13.1 percentage points. During the same period reduction in the number of out-of-school children was significant as compared to other states in Rajasthan, Uttar Pradesh, Madhya Pradesh and Andhra Pradesh. Assam was the worst performer in reducing the number of out-of-school children in the age group of 11-13.

Based on the Census of India 1991 and 2001 data, attempt has also been made to find out the performance of major states in reducing the out-of-school children (OSC) by social category and gender. In 2001, about 70 per cent of the total OSC from all communities in the age group of 6-10 in the country was concentrated in five states namely Uttar Pradesh, Bihar, Madhya Pradesh, West Bengal and Rajasthan. These five states were also home to around 76 per cent of the country's Scheduled Caste OSC in the age group of 6-10. Madhya Pradesh, Bihar, Orissa, Rajasthan and Gujarat accounted for around 68 per cent of the Scheduled Tribe OSC in the age group of 6-10 in the country in 2001. More or less similar trends in the concentration of OSC (11-13 age group) by social category were found in the country in 2001.

### School Attendance Rates

School attendance rate (SAR) using data from C-series tables of the Census of India, 1991 and 2001 were computed to compare the performance of major states in terms of participation of children (6-10 and 11-13 age groups) in school education in the 1990s. Even though the estimated school attendance rates (SARs) do not strictly correspond to primary and upper primary levels, these rates help us assess the progress in states in terms of coverage of school age children, and also the increase/decrease in the number of out-of-school children in the relevant age groups. In the absence of alternative database, the Census of India perhaps provides the most comprehensive information on school participation by age, sex, place of residence (rural/urban) and social category (SCs/STs). To make the data comparable between 1991 and 2001, data of the newly created states of Jharkhand, Chhattisgarh and Uttaranchal have been added to Bihar, Madhya Pradesh and Uttar Pradesh respectively.

At the all India level, the school attendance rate (SAR) of children in the 6-10 age group increased by 17.6 per cent from 51.17 per cent in 1991 to 68.77 per cent in 2001 (see Table 5.2). In the major states, excluding Kerala, the SAR of 6-10 age group children ranged between 11.11 per cent in Bihar to 31.43 per cent in Rajasthan during the same period. Educationally backward states such as Rajasthan, Andhra Pradesh, Uttar Pradesh, West Bengal and Madhya Pradesh had performed relatively much better in terms of increase in the SAR of 6-10 age group children in the 1990s. Bihar, Orissa and Assam were poor performers in this regard.

The SAR of children in the age group of 11-13 increased by 13.1 percentage points over the 1991 status from 63.8 per cent to 76.9 per cent in 2001. It ranged from 59.1 per cent in Bihar to 97.83 per cent in Kerala. Among the educationally backward states, the performance of Rajasthan was the highest (more than 21 percentage point increase) in raising the SAR of 11-13 age group children during the 1990s. The performance of Uttar Pradesh, Madhya Pradesh and Andhra Pradesh was also relatively high in increasing SAR during the same period. Among the cluster of states having more or less the same level of SAR of 11-13 age group children in 1991 such as Orissa (59.4 per cent), Madhya Pradesh (58.9 per cent) Andhra Pradesh (57.6 per cent), Bihar (51.6 per cent), Rajasthan (53.1 per cent) and Uttar Pradesh (52.6 per cent), the performance of Bihar and Orissa was poor, and Assam and West Bengal also did not do very well in raising SAR during the period 1991-2001 (see Table 5.10).

**Table 5.2: Out-of-School Children (OSC) at Primary and Upper Primary Levels across Major States in India, 1993 and 2002**

| States | OSC, 6th AIES, 1993 (In Millions) | | OSC, 7th AIES, 2002 (In Millions) | | % Share to the Relevant Age Group Population at the Elementary Level In the State | | %Share to the Country Total | | | |
|---|---|---|---|---|---|---|---|---|---|---|
| | | | | | | | OSC, 1993 | | OSC, 2002 | |
| | Primary (6-10) | Upper Primary (11-13) | Primary (6-10) | Upper Primary (11-13) | OSC, 1993 (6-13) | OSC, 2002 (6-13) | 6 to 10 | 11-13 | 6 to 10 | 11-13 |
| Andhra Pradesh | 3.02 | 2.05 | 1.83 | 2.45 | 42.53 | 33.56 | 7.85 | 10.42 | 7.85 | 6.32 |
| Assam | 0.72 | 0.62 | 0.67 | 1.10 | 28.13 | 33.72 | 1.86 | 3.15 | 2.82 | 2.74 |
| Bihar $ | 5.02 | 4.49 | 4.41 | 5.70 | 47.19 | 51.61 | 13.03 | 22.79 | 22.19 | 18.02 |
| Gujarat | 1.28 | 0.37 | 0.29 | 1.22 | 22.18 | 22.69 | 3.34 | 1.86 | 2.51 | 3.37 |
| Haryana | 0.71 | 0.47 | 0.76 | 0.65 | 34.24 | 40.46 | 1.84 | 2.39 | 3.28 | 2.09 |
| Himachal Pradesh | 0.09 | 0.06 | 0.01 | 0.01 | 16.02 | 18.90 | 0.24 | 0.29 | 0.28 | 0.30 |
| J & K | 0.53 | 0.27 | 0.41 | 0.39 | 48.09 | 40.61 | 1.39 | 1.36 | 1.64 | 1.07 |
| Karnataka | 1.22 | 0.63 | – 0.18 | 1.27 | 22.36 | 17.22 | 3.16 | 3.22 | 0.94 | 3.40 |
| Kerala | 0.46 | 0.10 | 0.43 | 0.32 | 12.46 | 19.24 | 1.19 | 0.48 | 1.69 | 0.87 |
| Madhya Pradesh* | 1.96 | 1.58 | 0.90 | 2.08 | 28.47 | 34.21 | 5.09 | 8.00 | 7.88 | 9.28 |
| Maharashtra | 2.86 | 1.26 | 0.31 | 1.52 | 27.23 | 17.42 | 7.42 | 6.41 | 3.89 | 4.84 |
| Orissa | 0.98 | 0.99 | 0.83 | 1.46 | 32.37 | 34.17 | 2.54 | 5.01 | 3.35 | 3.58 |
| Punjab | 0.64 | 0.35 | 1.07 | 0.86 | 27.52 | 46.91 | 1.67 | 1.80 | 4.14 | 2.31 |
| Rajasthan | 2.83 | 1.35 | 1.79 | 2.38 | 45.71 | 41.68 | 7.33 | 6.87 | 8.96 | 6.78 |
| Tamil Nadu | 1.38 | 0.49 | 0.22 | 0.42 | 18.66 | 11.65 | 3.59 | 2.46 | 1.40 | 1.63 |
| Uttar Pradesh* | 10.33 | 5.74 | 4.50 | 8.65 | 53.42 | 36.26 | 26.82 | 29.13 | 20.70 | 22.55 |
| West Bengal | 3.71 | 1.06 | 1.31 | 2.96 | 42.59 | 32.87 | 9.62 | 5.36 | 6.66 | 7.90 |
| All India** | 38.52 | 19.70 | 21.68 | 36.77 | 36.27 | 33.08 | 100.00 | 100.00 | 100.00 | 100.00 |

*Source*: Estimated by authors based on *Sixth and Seventh All India Educational Survey* (AIES) data, NCERT, 1993, and 2002, New Delhi.

*Note*: The number of OSC at primary and upper primary levels for 2002 has been estimated by the author using enrolment and projected child population data of the 7th AIES, 2002. To find out the enrolment in the relevant age group (net enrolment) at primary and upper primary levels, enrolment data of the 7th AIES have been adjusted by applying the share of under and over-aged children in the total enrolment as reported for the same year in DISE data. For the states of Arunachal Pradesh, Punjab and J&K, national average has been used for under and over age children, as no information was available from DISE 2003.

* To make the data of 1991 and 2001 comparable, Jharkhand has been included in Bihar, Chhattisgarh in Madhya Pradesh, and Uttaranchal in Uttar Pradesh in the census year 2001.

** Includes all 35 states and UTs.

**Table 5.3: School Attendance Rate (SAR) of Children in 6-10 and 11-13**

| State | SAR (Rural + Urban), 2001 | | | | | | SAR (Rural + Urban), 1991 | | | | | |
|---|---|---|---|---|---|---|---|---|---|---|---|---|
| | All Communities | | SC | | ST | | All Communities | | SC* | | ST** | |
| | 6-10 | 11-13 | 6-10 | 11-13 | 6-10 | 11-13 | 6-10 | 11-13 | 6-10 | 11-13 | 6-10 | 11-13 |
| Andhra Pradesh | 81.28 | 75.78 | 31.32 | 73.43 | 68.26 | 59.32 | 53.01 | 57.60 | 42.88 | 49.50 | 28.34 | 31.56 |
| Assam | 61.01 | 70.25 | 58.45 | 74.30 | 66.39 | 76.67 | 45.98 | 64.57 | 53.12 | 68.72 | 46.60 | 64.07 |
| **Bihar*** ** | 45.40 | 59.10 | 31.93 | 42.98 | 41.75 | 52.92 | 34.29 | 51.58 | 17.76 | 29.82 | 25.02 | 37.96 |
| Gujarat | 76.08 | 79.45 | 31.94 | 85.00 | 62.54 | 64.51 | 62.26 | 71.02 | 69.72 | 78.63 | 50.22 | 56.90 |
| Haryana | 75.49 | 85.89 | 58.31 | 77.74 | 0.00 | 0.00 | 62.17 | 75.76 | 48.62 | 61.77 | NA | NA |
| Himachal Pradesh | 89.19 | 95.51 | 37.42 | 94.17 | 85.89 | 92.20 | 75.50 | 87.09 | 68.35 | 80.99 | 64.47 | 74.81 |
| J & K | 61.22 | 73.42 | 71.59 | 80.44 | 43.61 | 55.21 | NA | NA | NA | NA | NA | NA |
| Karnataka | 77.23 | 78.95 | 72.11 | 71.58 | 67.37 | 65.27 | 61.89 | 65.72 | 49.63 | 54.36 | 47.57 | 49.77 |
| Kerala | 92.98 | 97.83 | 92.84 | 96.85 | 81.27 | 83.23 | 91.22 | 94.54 | 90.02 | 92.41 | 90.02 | 92.41 |
| **Madhya Pradesh*** ** | 70.20 | 77.28 | 70.78 | 78.73 | 55.04 | 60.07 | 47.37 | 58.96 | 40.69 | 52.91 | 27.47 | 35.65 |
| Maharashtra | 84.67 | 89.87 | 34.96 | 89.70 | 73.00 | 75.97 | 69.09 | 77.71 | 63.17 | 75.42 | 43.44 | 53.33 |
| Orissa | 68.75 | 72.91 | 57.24 | 68.30 | 49.73 | 51.79 | 54.35 | 59.43 | 42.15 | 40.83 | 30.43 | 26.92 |
| Punjab | 78.40 | 85.75 | 71.11 | 77.30 | 0.00 | 0.00 | 65.92 | 76.43 | 53.64 | 60.97 | NA | NA |
| Rajasthan | 70.30 | 74.29 | 54.59 | 67.38 | 59.33 | 61.80 | 38.87 | 53.14 | 28.03 | 41.42 | 21.27 | 33.73 |
| Tamil Nadu | 89.44 | 87.57 | 39.16 | 86.74 | 68.39 | 62.65 | 77.36 | 74.36 | 71.83 | 68.25 | 46.57 | 45.38 |
| **Uttar Pradesh*** ** | 60.85 | 72.30 | 30.54 | 70.49 | 67.78 | 76.72 | 36.71 | 52.60 | 28.12 | 40.71 | 39.79 | 52.14 |
| West Bengal | 69.21 | 75.92 | 38.79 | 72.36 | 55.83 | 60.14 | 45.86 | 63.13 | 31.40 | 43.76 | 24.05 | 33.29 |
| **All India** | **68.77** | **76.90** | **65.78** | **72.98** | **58.36** | **63.53** | **51.17** | **63.80** | **NA** | **NA** | **NA** | **NA** |

*Source*: Govinda, R., K. Biswal and Geetha Rani (2006).

*Notes*: * India total includes only 16 states; ** India total includes only 14 states.

*** Bihar includes Jharkhand, Madhya Pradesh, includes Chhattisgarh, and Uttar Pradesh includes Uttaranchal for 2001 data.

Besides SARs of children (6-10 and 11-13 age groups) from all communities, it may be useful to examine the progress in states in terms of coverage of children in the relevant age group from socially backward communities, and separately for boys and girls in rural and urban areas. Trends in the reduction of spatial, social and gender differentials in SARs along with trends in the total attendance rates would provide a better understanding of a state's performance in the coverage of school age children during 1991-2001.

It may be noted that most of the educationally backward states are also relatively bigger in size in terms of number of child population in the age group of 6-14. According to the Census of India 2001, four major sates, namely Uttar Pradesh (+ Uttaranchal), Bihar (+ Jharkhand), Maharashtra, and Madhya Pradesh (+ Chhattisgarh) account for 48.44 per cent of the total 6-14 age group child population in the country. Add three more states—West Bengal, Andhra Pradesh and Rajasthan, the share of the child population of seven states in the country total goes up to around 69 per cent. Except Maharashtra, all others in this group of states are educationally backward states. In fact, six major educationally backward states (plus Chhattisgarh, Jharkhand and Uttaranchal)—Uttar Pradesh, Bihar, Madhya Pradesh, West Bengal, Andhra Pradesh and Rajasthan—account for 60.5 per cent in the country total of 6-14 age group child population. Bihar and Uttar Pradesh (before bifurcation) account for 31.6 per cent of child population (6-14 age group) in the country (See Chart 5.7).

Concentration of SC population adds further complexity to the problem of size of these six educationally backward states. These six states account for 66.4 per cent of the total SC children (6-14 age group) in the country. These states along with Tamil Nadu have 72.1 per cent of the SC child population in the country. Almost 47 per cent of SC children (6-14 age group) live in Uttar Pradesh (+Uttaranchal), Bihar (+Jharkhand) and West Bengal. Similarly, the share of these six states in the total ST child population (6-14 age group) in the country is 68.5 per cent. In fact, more than half (51.56 per cent) of the ST child population lives in four states, (seven states including Uttaranchal, Jharkhand and Chhattisgarh) i.e. Uttar Pradesh, Bihar, West Bengal and Madhya Pradesh. It is important to keep in mind that better performance of these six sates (nine after bifurcation) would have a huge implication for reducing regional disparity. Our analysis of educational development, therefore, largely focuses on these educationally backward states.

Analysis of the data in major states reveals that, during the period 1991-2001, in most of the educationally backward states, except Bihar, SAR of SC children (6-10 age group) increased substantially, more than 30 percentage points over the base year. It may be noted that, except Andhra Pradesh and Madhya Pradesh, the size of the SAR of SC children (6-10 age group) was pretty low in 1991 in all other major educationally backward states. In the SC

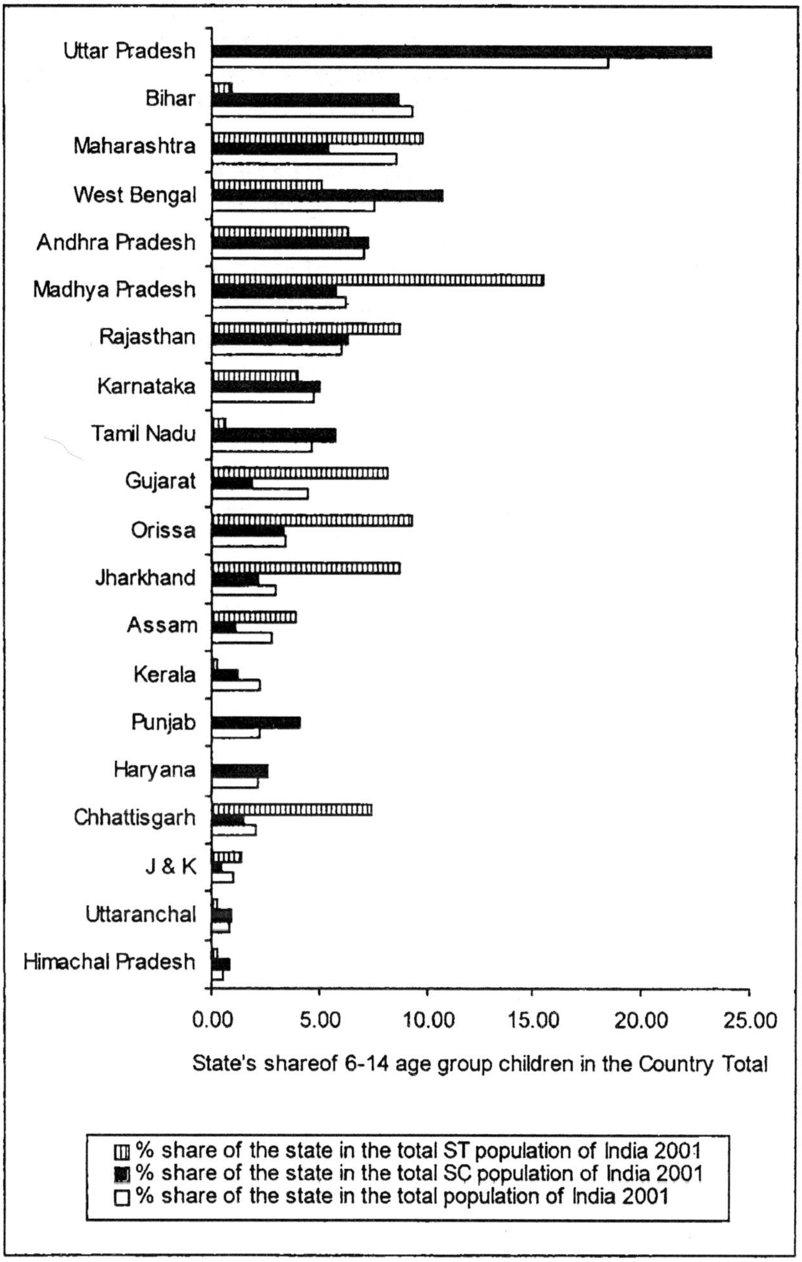


**Chart 5.7: Share of Major States in the Total Population of India (6-14 Age Group) by Social Category in 2001**

*Source*: Estimated using data from Census of India 2001.

concentrated states, the SAR of SC children (6-10 age group) in 2001 ranged between 31.4 per cent in Bihar and 89.16 per cent in Tamil Nadu. Similar trend is found in the case of SAR of 11-13 age group SC children in the major states during 1991-2001. Five states namely; Uttar Pradesh, West Bengal, Orissa, Rajasthan, Madhya Pradesh and Andhra Pradesh, four of them having a substantial size of the SC population, had registered more than 23 percentage point increase in the SAR of SC children (11-13 age group) during the same period.

During 1991-2001, most of the educationally backward states registered impressive increase in the SARs of ST children. Increase in the SAR of 6-10 age group ST children in Andhra Pradesh, West Bengal, Maharashtra, Uttar Pradesh ands Madhya Pradesh was more than 27 percentage points, and it ranged from 39 percentage points in Rajasthan to 12.32 percentage points in Gujarat. It may be noted that there was a decline in the attendance rate of ST children (6-10 age group) during the 1990s by around nine percentage points. Among the educationally backward states having more or less the same rate of school participation (between 21-28 per cent) in 1991, the performance of Andhra Pradesh, Rajasthan and West Bengal was very impressive, more than 31 percentage points increase in the attendance rate during 1991-2001. Bihar clearly stood out as a poor performer in raising the school participation rate of ST children. More or less similar trend is found in the progress in the participation of 11-13 age group ST children in school education across major states in the country. Seven states—Rajasthan, Andhra Pradesh, West Bengal, Orissa, Uttar Pradesh, Madhya Pradesh and Maharashtra—registered an increase of more than 22 percentage points in the SAR of 11-13 age group ST children.

Increase in the SAR of children was relatively more in rural India, and also high for girls during 1991-2001. However, the increase in the SAR of rural girls (6-10 age group) was most impressive in Rajasthan (more than 41 percentage points) and Andhra Pradesh (around 39 percentage points) during this period. Uttar Pradesh, Madhya Pradesh and West Bengal had also done reasonably well in raising the participation rate of girls in school education in rural areas (more than 28 percentage points increase for 6-10 age group girls) during the same period. Similarly, the increase in the school participation rate of urban girls (6-10 age group) was also relatively high in Rajasthan and Uttar Pradesh. Similar trends in the school participation rate of 11-13 age group children are found across major states during the same period.

Progress in the school participation rate of rural girls is perhaps one of the best proxy indicators of improvements in access to schooling. Analysis of data reveals wide variations in the SAR of rural girls across states in India. During the period 1991-2001, the increase in the SAR of rural SC girls (6-10 age group) was very impressive in Andhra Pradesh (48.75 percentage points), Rajasthan (45.1 percentage points) Uttar Pradesh (40.89 percentage points),

West Bengal (39.44 percentage points), and Madhya Pradesh (38.66 percentage points). It may be noted that these states have the largest concentration of SC population in the country. Bihar having substantial number of SC population was a clear laggard in raising the SAR of rural SC girls during the same period. The increase in the SAR of rural girls was just 14.55 percentage points during this period. The performance of other states having sizable SC population—Maharashtra, Tamil Nadu, Orissa, Punjab, Haryana, Karnataka—was also visible in raising the SAR of rural SC girls. Similar pattern in the increase in the SAR of rural girls in the age group of 11-13 is found across major states in India. In the SC concentrated educationally backward states, it ranged from 16.6 percentage points in Bihar to 43 percentage points in Uttar Pradesh.

The gender disparity in SAR of SC children (6-10 age group) in major states, excluding Kerala, ranged from 0.99 percentage points in Tamil Nadu to 15.51 percentage points in Rajasthan in 2001. The gender difference in the SAR of SC children in the age group 11-13 ranged from 2.62 percentage points in Tamil Nadu to 28.11 percentage points in Rajasthan in 2001. During 1991-2001, the decline in the gender difference in the SAR of SC children (both in 6-10 and 11-13 age groups) was relatively more in Uttar Pradesh, Tamil Nadu, Maharashtra, Madhya Pradesh, Karnataka and Andhra Pradesh.

So far as SAR of rural ST girls (6-10 and 11-13 age groups) are concerned, it increased substantially in all the ST concentrated states during 1991-2001 ranging from 44.4 percentage points in Andhra Pradesh to 15.79 percentage points in Gujarat.

The gender difference in the SAR of ST children was also high in these states in 2001. The gender difference in the SAR of ST children (6-10 age group) was highest in Rajasthan (19.82 percentage points) followed by Orissa (13.51 percentage points), J & K (12.37 percentage points), Bihar (10.94 percentage points) and Andhra Pradesh (10.76 percentage points). However, the gender difference in the SAR of ST children in the age group 11-13 was relatively high in most of these states. Gender difference in the SAR of ST children in the age group 11-13 was very high in Rajasthan, Andhra Pradesh, Orissa and J & K (around or more than 20 percentage points) in 2001. It was more than 15 percentage points in West Bengal, Madhya Pradesh and Bihar. During 1991-2001, the highest reduction in the gender difference in SAR of ST children (6-10 age group) was in Uttar Pradesh (including Uttaranchal), followed by Himachal Pradesh and Karnataka. Similarly, progress towards narrowing down the gender difference in the SAR of ST children in age group 11-13 was substantial in Uttar Pradesh, Himachal Pradesh, Rajasthan, Maharashtra, Karnataka and Gujarat. Orissa, Andhra Pradesh and West Bengal were poor performers in reducing difference in the SAR of ST children in the age group 11-13 during the same period.

## Dropout and Transition Rates

Mere school attendance rate does not provide information about what happens to children after they are enrolled? How many of them continue in the system? What proportion of them drops out of the school? The dropout rate is one of the process indicators that, to a large extent, indicate the holding power of the school, after accounting for the socio-economic and household related characteristics of students. Although, on the basis of available secondary data mostly collected from schools, we cannot definitely talk about as to what proportion of the dropouts are 'push outs' or 'pull outs'. Variations in the dropout rates across similar settings generally provide some indications of varying quality of schools.

**Table 5.4: Dropout Rates at Primary and Elementary Levels of Education across Major States in India**

| *States* | *Classes (I-V)* | | | *Classes (1-VIII)* | | |
|---|---|---|---|---|---|---|
| | *1991-92* | *1998-99* | *2003-04* | *1991-92* | *1998-99* | *2003-04* |
| Andhra Pradesh | 53.0 | 43.6 | 42.6 | 70.93 | 73.3 | 59.8 |
| Assam | 57.0 | 50.5 | 53.2 | 70.73 | 68.82 | 70.8 |
| Bihar | 64.4 | 58.8 | 59.0 | 79.38 | 77.06 | 78.0 |
| Gujarat | 43.6 | 29.0 | 26.0 | 59.5 | 60.3 | 46.9 |
| Haryana | 18.1 | 12.2 | 13.3 | 39.95 | 23.08 | 21.3 |
| Himachal Pradesh | 28.9 | 24.1 | 17.0 | 29.62 | 18.06 | 14.3 |
| Jammu & Kashmir | 49.0 | 27.0 | 36.7 | 53.35 | 32.55 | 47.5 |
| Karnataka | 43.9 | 33.9 | 9.8 | 64.05 | 57.82 | 50.6 |
| Kerala | –1.9 | 0.0 | 0.0 | 3.28 | 0.0 | – 9.5 |
| Madhya Pradesh | 35.5 | 24.6 | 23.8 | 57.78 | 48.64 | 46.8 |
| Maharashtra | 31.7 | 18.6 | 13.1 | 52.85 | 39.18 | 33.3 |
| Orissa | 47.2 | 47.8 | 38.2 | 65.84 | 64.77 | 61.7 |
| Punjab | 30.3 | 21.8 | 22.0 | 40.13 | 27.91 | 35.2 |
| Rajasthan | 61.6 | 59.8 | 57.9 | 69.45 | 59.54 | 68.5 |
| Tamil Nadu | 19.3 | 36.5 | 3.2 | 41.67 | 35.23 | 25.2 |
| Uttar Pradesh | 34.8 | 49.6 | 13.5 | 59.07 | 50.46 | 42.8 |
| West Bengal | 39.4 | 58.0 | 33.5 | 51.19 | 74.2 | 63.8 |
| **All India** | **42.0** | **41.5** | **31.5** | **58.67** | **56.31** | **52.3** |

*Source*: *Education in India*, Vol(s), 1991-92, 1998-99 and Selected Educational Statistics, 2003-04.

At the national level, dropout rate at the primary level (I-V) was 42 per cent in 1991-92, which came down to 31.5 per cent in 2003-04. During the same period, dropout rate at the elementary level declined from 58.67 per cent to 52.3 per cent. It may be noted that in 1991-92, the dropout rate in Uttar Pradesh, Madhya Pradesh and West Bengal at the primary level was below the national average, and that of Gujarat, Karnataka and Andhra Pradesh much above the national average. On the basis of the dropout rate at the primary level, clear clusters of major states, excluding Kerala, emerge; i.e., (i) Haryana and Tamil Nadu (18-20 per cent); (ii) Himachal Pradesh, Punjab, Maharashtra (28-32 per cent); (iii) Uttar Pradesh, Madhya Pradesh and West Bengal (34-40 per cent); (iv) Gujarat and Karnataka (43-44 per cent); (v) Orissa, J & K and Andhra Pradesh (47-53 per cent); (vi) Assam, Rajasthan and Bihar (57-65 per cent).

In cluster I, while Tamil Nadu was successful in reducing the dropout rate at the primary level to 3.2 per cent in 2003-04, Haryana registered an increase in the dropout rate, particularly during 1998-2003. In cluster II, while the performance of Himachal Pradesh and Maharashtra was much higher in reducing the primary level dropout rate, Punjab's performance was relatively poor, where the dropout rate increased by 0.2 per cent during the same period. In cluster III, Uttar Pradesh was the best performing state in terms of decline in the dropout rate at the primary level; it came down from 34.8 per cent to 13.5 per cent during 1991-2003. Though the decline in the dropout rate in Madhya Pradesh was relatively less, its performance was consistent during this period. West Bengal lagged behind others in this group of states. In cluster IV, both the states have performed consistently, but the decline in the primary level dropout rate was more pronounced in Karnataka than Gujarat, particularly during 1998-2003. In cluster V, Orissa has performed relatively better in bringing down the primary level dropout rate, and J&K was a poor performer. In fact, all the states in this cluster have relatively performed poorly in reducing the dropout rate at the primary level. States in cluster VI are the worst performers. Even with a very high dropout rate in the base year (1991-92), Assam, Rajasthan and Bihar could reduce the dropout rate only marginally (3-6 percentage points) during 1991-2003. To make the situation further worse, during 1998-2003, primary level dropout rate in Assam and Bihar increased by 2.7 and 0.2 percentage points.

Another important process indicator is the transition rate from one level to the next level of education. It provides an idea about the dropout rate at the stage transition level, an equally important indicator of the efficiency of the education system. At the all India level, the transition rate from primary to upper primary level was 89.4 per cent in 1991-92, which declined by 3.42 percentage points to 85.95 per cent in 1998-99.

The variation in transition across the states is indicative of the level of functioning of the school system. Indirectly, it is also an indicator of the quality of the system as transition between cycles is decided based on centralized exams in most states. It is of course necessary to note that the practices vary widely across different states as no common policy is adopted for conducting examinations and promoting students to the next level of schooling.

**Table 5.5: Transition Rates from Primary to Upper Primary and from Upper Primary to Secondary in Major States in India, 1991-1998**

| *State* | *Primary to Upper Primary* | | | *Upper Primary to Secondary* | | |
|---|---|---|---|---|---|---|
| | 1991-92* | 1995-96 | 1998-99 | 1991-92* | 1995-96 | 1998-99 |
| Andhra Pradesh | 87.51 | 78.5 | 81.62 | 98.43 | 91.7 | 91.6 |
| Assam | 78.57 | 79.1 | 77.57 | 77.53 | 85.7 | 83.8 |
| Bihar | 77.37 | 75.9 | 76.37 | 80.20 | 79.9 | 83.45 |
| Gujarat | 71.31 | 66.8 | 73.85 | 81.67 | 81.1 | 80.26 |
| H.P. | 92.59 | 86.0 | 92.18 | 82.88 | 62.7 | 74.17 |
| Haryana | 80.00 | 80.9 | 97.41 | 72.90 | 49.4 | 73.93 |
| J & K | 132.99 | 98.0 | 99.59 | 101.32 | 91.7 | 90.4 |
| Karnataka | 93.04 | 92.9 | 99.78 | 86.83 | 95.5 | 90.2 |
| Kerala | 90.24 | 93.0 | 93.42 | 83.19 | 83 | 84.54 |
| M.P. | 77.77 | 85.3 | 75.67 | 60.89 | 74.6 | 60.73 |
| Maharashtra | 90.01 | 86.2 | 89.71 | 91.64 | 86.2 | 88.9 |
| Orissa | 86.23 | 92.9 | 97.99 | 85.58 | 85.6 | 83.5 |
| Punjab | 94.03 | 95.8 | 96.3 | 87.50 | 79.3 | 83.6 |
| Rajasthan | 95.34 | 101.5 | 97.11 | 91.38 | 79.9 | 62.9 |
| Tamil Nadu | 81.62 | 80.8 | 79.67 | 66.03 | 59.3 | 53.74 |
| Uttar Pradesh | 87.47 | 86.6 | 87.81 | 70.15 | 73.5 | 95.5 |
| West Bengal | 131.57 | 80.6 | 88.35 | 62.11 | 83.4 | 75.6 |
| **All India** | **89.40** | **84.4** | **85.98** | **77.93** | **78.7** | **72.3** |

*Source*: Calculated based on data from Education in India, vol.(s), various issues.
*Note*: * Calculated based on data from Education in India, vol.(s), 1990-91 and 1991-92.

## Age Specific Educational Attainment Rates

Analysis of Census of India (2001) data on the educational attainment by age group in major states also provides an indication of the efficiency of the education system both in terms of coverage of the relevant age group of children and timely grade promotion through a particular level of school education. It is perhaps the best outcome indicator of the education system, where wastage is reduced to zero when children of all relevant age groups complete a particular level of school education in time. Analysis of the educational attainment of children of 11 years (who should have completed primary level of education if they entered grade I at the age of 6 years) reveals that, at the all India level, 50.29 per cent of children of 11 years are primary level graduates (see Table 5.12). Surprisingly, only 22.99 per cent of 11-year old girls are primary level graduates in India. Among the major states, the primary school graduation rate[9] of 11-year old children varies from 32.8 per cent in Bihar to 78.1 per cent in Tamil Nadu. In Bihar, only around 13 girls out of one hundred 11-year old girls complete primary education in time. The primary level graduation rate of 11-year old children in West Bengal, Rajasthan,

Madhya Pradesh, Uttar Pradesh, Haryana, Punjab, J&K and Assam is below the national average.

**Table 5.6: Educational Attainment of Population by Age Group in Major States, 2001**

*(In Percentage)*

| *State* | *Primary Level Graduates (Population-11 Years of Age)* | | *Middle Level Graduates ((Population-14 Years of Age)* | | *Secondary Level Graduates (Population-16 Years of Age)* | | *Higher Secondary Level Graduates (Population-18 Years of Age)* | |
|---|---|---|---|---|---|---|---|---|
| | *Total* | *Girls* | *Total* | *Girls* | *Total* | *Girls* | *Total* | *Girls* |
| Andhra Pradesh | 65.66 | 30.31 | 48.25 | 21.01 | 36.15 | 16.07 | 18.79 | 7.93 |
| Assam | 48.16 | 23.40 | 36.82 | 18.05 | 21.41 | 10.45 | 6.34 | 2.89 |
| Bihar | 32.80 | 12.99 | 27.98 | 10.50 | 19.10 | 7.07 | 9.84 | 2.88 |
| Gujarat | 57.96 | 25.53 | 43.07 | 18.30 | 29.85 | 13.39 | 15.03 | 6.89 |
| Haryana | 40.32 | 18.13 | 34.35 | 15.81 | 28.98 | 13.31 | 17.80 | 7.94 |
| Himachal Pradesh | 53.33 | 25.32 | 41.08 | 19.88 | 30.79 | 15.28 | 19.06 | 9.49 |
| J & K | 46.62 | 20.83 | 36.30 | 16.03 | 24.93 | 10.93 | 13.81 | 5.87 |
| Karnataka | 58.12 | 28.28 | 41.03 | 19.18 | 29.61 | 14.27 | 14.20 | 6.58 |
| Kerala | 74.30 | 37.98 | 68.17 | 36.42 | 46.52 | 26.61 | 24.22 | 14.95 |
| Madhya Pradesh | 38.84 | 16.93 | 24.44 | 10.45 | 16.22 | 7.00 | 9.66 | 4.09 |
| Maharashtra | 65.30 | 31.04 | 48.88 | 22.62 | 36.70 | 16.71 | 20.61 | 9.12 |
| Orissa | 59.13 | 26.72 | 44.73 | 20.15 | 26.88 | 12.54 | 15.10 | 6.14 |
| Punjab | 44.68 | 21.16 | 37.85 | 18.62 | 30.63 | 15.98 | 19.14 | 10.13 |
| Rajasthan | 36.61 | 14.27 | 25.59 | 9.35 | 17.24 | 6.31 | 10.55 | 3.62 |
| Tamil Nadu | 78.10 | 38.09 | 59.13 | 29.62 | 39.16 | 19.74 | 18.79 | 9.85 |
| Uttar Pradesh | 39.11 | 16.36 | 31.57 | 12.90 | 21.60 | 8.97 | 13.56 | 5.96 |
| West Bengal | 36.23 | 16.94 | 22.52 | 10.37 | 13.50 | 5.98 | 6.78 | 2.73 |
| **India** | **50.29** | **22.99** | **36.92** | **16.50** | **25.68** | **11.65** | **14.10** | **6.26** |

*Source*: Estimated by Author Using C-series Data of the Census of India 2001.

At the all India level, the educational attainment of 36.92 per cent of 14-year old children is middle school certificate, but only 16.50 per cent of 14-year old girls completed the same level of education. Wide variations exist across major states in the educational attainment of 14-year old children. The percentage of 14-year old children completing middle level education varies from 22.52 per cent (10.37 per cent for girls) in West Bengal to 68.17 per cent (36.42 per cent for girls) in Kerala (see Table 5.12). The gender gap in the educational attainment is very high in almost all the states. However, the percentage of 14-year old children attaining middle level of education is relatively higher in Kerala, Tamil Nadu, Maharashtra, Andhra Pradesh, Orissa, Gujarat, Himachal Pradesh and Karnataka (more than 41 per cent). The educational attainment of 14-year old children is very low in Madhya Pradesh, West Bengal, Rajasthan and Bihar (between 22 per cent and 27 per cent).

The educational attainment of 16-year old children is further low at the national level. Only 25.68 per cent of children have completed secondary level of education at the age of 16 years in India. And, in the case of 16-year old girls it is only 11.65 per cent (see Table 5.12). Extreme variations in the educational attainment of 16-year old children exist across major states. While at the national level 13.5 per cent of 16-year old children (5.98 per cent for girls) have completed secondary level of education, the percentage of these children attaining secondary level of education is as high as 46.42 (26.61 per cent for girls) in Kerala. More or less similar trend as that of 14-year old children is also found in case of the educational attainment of 16-year old children across major states in India. The percentage of children completing secondary level of education is relatively low in West Bengal, Madhya Pradesh, Rajasthan, Bihar, Assam and Uttar Pradesh (between 13 per cent and 22 per cent) (See Chart 5.7).

The educational attainment (senior secondary level) of children of 18 years is further low at the all India level; 14.1 per cent for the total population and only 6.26 per cent for girls. It varies from an abysmally low of 6.34 per cent (2.89 per cent for girls) to a high of 24.22 per cent (14.95 per cent for girls) in Kerala. Children completing senior secondary level of education is 10 per cent or below in Assam, West Bengal, Madhya Pradesh, Bihar and Rajasthan. The percentage of children completing senior secondary level of education at the age of 18 years is above the national average in Kerala, Maharashtra, Punjab, Himachal Pradesh, Tamil Nadu, Andhra Pradesh, Haryana, Orissa, Gujarat and Karnataka. It follows from the above analysis that the efficiency of the school system in terms of coverage of the school age children is low in educationally backward states as well as in educationally advanced states, in terms of children completing particular level of school education in time (i.e. at the appropriate age). It indicates either a low stage transition rate or a high repletion rate or both in these states.

## Imbalances and Inequities in Teacher Provision

Studies have also shown significant variation in provision of infrastructure facilities and other development inputs for schooling across different states. Most important among them is the provision of teachers. This seems to suffer from two problems: One, the actual availability of teachers per specified number of students, generally referred to as Pupil-Teacher Ratio (Chart 5.8). The second problem is that of ensuring a reasonable number of teachers are available in every school in order to efficiently carry out teaching-learning process.

There is a general euphoria in recent years over the enormous increase in enrolment of children in primary schools. Are we recruiting adequate number of teachers to teach them? In fact, in general, state governments are slow in recruiting teachers even against the existing positions. Almost all states have backlog of vacant posts of teachers. Consequently, notwithstanding the

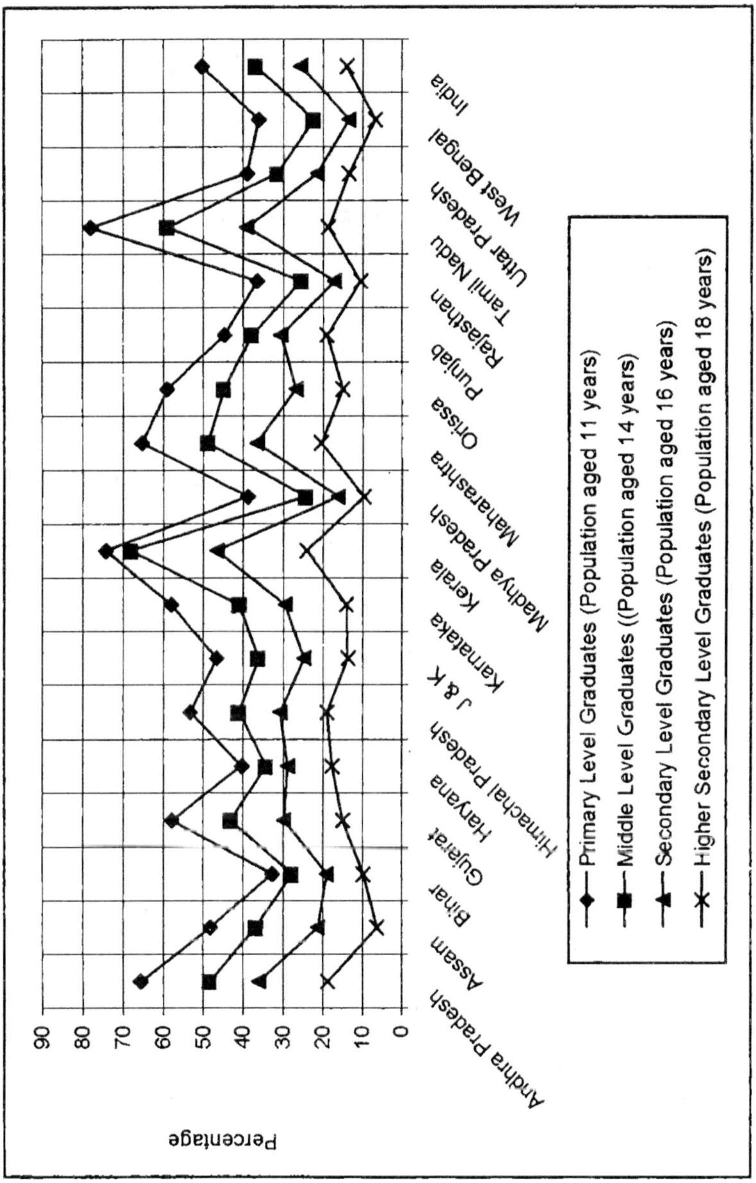


**Chart 5.7: Educational Attainment of Population by Age Group in Major States, 2001**

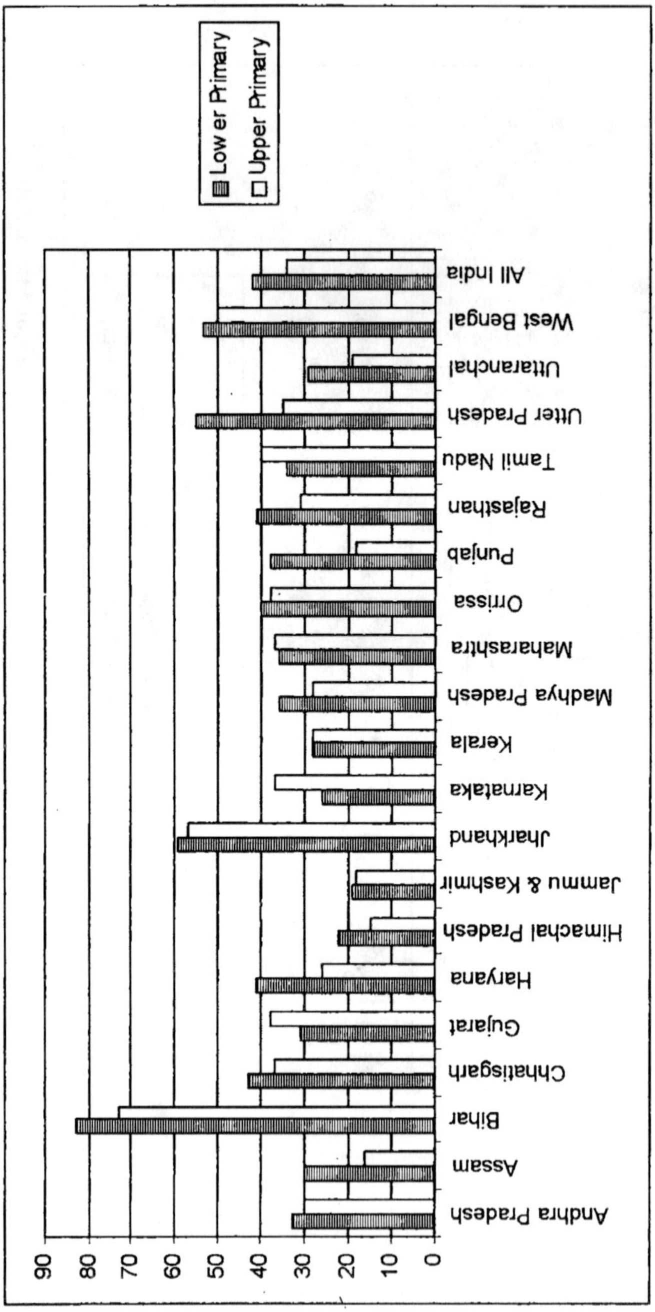


**Chart 5.8: Pupil-Teacher Ratio in Major States**

*Source*: All India Education Survey, NCERT, 2003.

recruitment of teachers on contract basis, teacher-pupil ratio is far above the norm of 1:40 in some of the states, pushing even the national average to 1:42. In particular, the situation requires immediate attention in four states, namely, Bihar, Jharkhand, Uttar Pradesh and West Bengal. In fact, the situation in Bihar is really alarming as teachers are recruited in the states for several years now without any professional training in pedagogy.

Apart from the fact that teachers have to deal with crowded classes in these states, they have also to contend with very minimal infrastructure and academic facilities in a large number of schools. Around three out of four primary schools in the country involve multi-grade teaching requiring the teachers to be innovative in simultaneously teaching students of several grades. As already noted earlier, a substantial proportion of schools do not have even a proper building, leave alone other facilities. This complex situation in which the teachers have to work gets further compounded when one considers the figures for single teacher schools.

Primary schools functioning with just one teacher can be found in both rural and urban India. Tamil Nadu is the only major state, which does not have a single teacher primary school. Relatively, single teacher primary schools are in rural areas. According to the Seventh AIES, single teacher rural primary schools ranged between 0.63 per cent in Kerala and 32.75 per cent in Jharkhand. The largest number of urban single teacher primary schools is also found in Jharkhand. The states like Andhra Pradesh, Chhattisgarh, Jharkhand, Karnataka, Madhya Pradesh, Maharashtra, Punjab, and Uttaranchal have more than 15 per cent single teacher primary schools in rural areas; it is more than one-fifth in Jharkhand, Karnataka and Maharashtra.

On the whole, it is found that nearly one out of every six primary schools in the country is a single teacher school. This is quite surprising since the OBB Scheme was launched more than ten years ago with the main aim of eliminating single teacher schools. To expect that UEE will be achieved just by appointing a community teacher invariably without professional training to teach in so called schools, which have neither physical infrastructure nor academic facilities, is far fetched. One could agree that state governments may operate at times under exigencies and expediency is understandable. But it is difficult to conceive that long-term national plans are implemented through such ad hoc unsustainable measures. In this context, the proposal under SSA, to provide one teacher for every class in every school, simultaneously, opening schools in small habitations even with 25-30 children in the age range of 6-11, stands no logic and requires serious rethinking.

It is not only geographical imbalances in teacher allocation, but also poor quality of teachers at elementary level is a major issue. In the 1990s, as a teacher diversification strategy, more and more states have gone for deployment of para-teachers (*Shiksha Karmis, Shiksha Mitras, Gurujis,* and other types

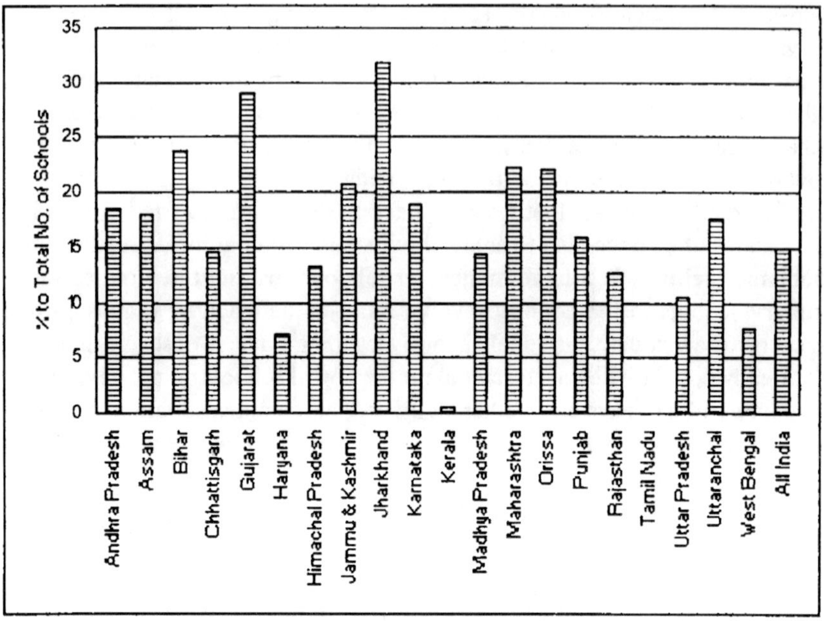


**Chart 5.9: Single Teacher School in Major States**

of temporary teachers) mostly at the primary level to meet the additional teacher requirements due to increase in enrolment. In some states like Uttaranchal, even para-teachers are appointed against the vacancy of regular full-time teachers. The relative share of primary and upper-primary para-teachers is high in Gujarat, Andhra Pradesh, Himachal Pradesh, Uttar Pradesh, Uttaranchal and Maharashtra. Increasingly, more para-teachers are being appointed in rural primary and upper primary schools. In Gujarat, for example, more than 43 per cent of rural primary teachers and 31 per cent of rural upper primary teachers are temporary teachers. These teachers are generally less qualified; most of them have no pre-service training; and they are paid abysmally low salaries. Deployment of para-teachers at primary and upper primary schools has definite implications for the quality of primary/elementary education being imparted in these states. On the other hand, deployment of para-teachers has been the easiest method of meeting the increasing requirement of additional primary and upper primary teachers in major states.

Further, in almost all states, trained teachers with higher qualifications are generally concentrated in urban areas. Several factors, including political and bureaucratic interventions, lack of qualified teachers in backward and remote areas, lack of proper database on the status of teachers at the school level, low motivation of urban teachers to serve in rural areas, etc., come in the way of rational deployment of teachers. Transfer of teachers is highly influenced by political interventions, and more influential teachers, particularly female teachers, are more likely to be found working in urban schools and schools located in areas well connected with road or rail transport network. Lack of basic facilities, viz., and residential facility in remote rural areas also acts as a de-motivating factor for female teachers to serve in rural areas.

Even where teacher availability is ensured, poor monitoring and sub-optimal use of teachers is another serious concern in most of the states. Teacher absenteeism is a serious issue in many states. Even if teachers attend schools, their presence in the classroom is often significantly lower than the school attendance rate. This happens because teachers are often engaged in non-teaching activities. According to a recent study[10] on teacher absence in 20 sates of India, nearly one-fourth of teachers remain absent from government primary schools on a typical school day. Absence rates range from around 15 per cent in Maharashtra to 38 per cent in Bihar and 42 per cent in Jharkhand. The absence rate is more than 30 per cent in Chhattisgarh, Uttaranchal, Assam, Punjab, Bihar and Jharkhand.

## Bridging the Public-Private Divide

As noted earlier, participation of private providers without State support has been a historical phenomenon. However, the situation drastically got transformed after Independence with State becoming the major provider either directly or indirectly through programmes of grants-in-aid. While this situation continued for the major part of the last 60 years, the recent past has witnessed an unusual growth of private self-financing schools. The situation is particularly serious in urban areas but is fast spreading to rural areas also. Should this alarm us? Why should this add to imbalances and inequities? The reason for alarm is because such expansion of the private sector (a) is accompanied by fast decline in the quality of the Government schools; (b) is directly creating a social divide between the rich and the poor, directly contravening the constitutional commitments of social justice and equity; and (c) is significantly affecting the livelihood of the poor people, who are compelled to sacrifice their daily needs to pay for the school fees. As Mehrotra[11] points out, the share of private unaided schools in enrolment in urban areas, in descending order, is: Uttar Pradesh 33.5 per cent, Rajasthan 32.4 per cent, Bihar 28 per cent, Madhya Pradesh 19.33 per cent, Assam 17.6 per cent, Andhra Pradesh 17 per cent, and West Bengal three per cent, all of which are educationally as well as economically under developed. Generally, private self-financing schools have expanded particularly in those states of India that have the most dysfunctional government school system. Analysis of national level data (NSSO 52nd Round, 1995-1996) showed that the latter states also tend to be the ones with the lowest per capita income in the country, showing the willingness of even poor parents to pay for schooling (even though the ability may be lacking); in other words, demand for schooling remains high. Private schooling is also gender-biased (against girls, who are a larger share of the children out of school), and does not help to redress the bias against the lower castes. The lower castes, which have much lower enrolment rates than the upper castes generally, are less likely to be enrolled in fee-paying schools than the upper castes.

## Conclusions and Propositions

The analysis presented above clearly indicates that an egalitarian system of education that provides equitable access to quality education for all irrespective of caste, class and gender has remained a dream even after five decades of planned development. Rather the system is deeply entrenched in policies and practices that militate against efforts to overcome imbalances and inequities. Disparities in educational provision as well as outcomes—geographical, interstate, intra-state and between gender and social groups have remained unbridged despite making substantive overall progress in literacy and elementary education. A few states continue to have large concentration of illiterates and out of school children. The finding is not new and is, in fact, similar to what many other researchers have found. The situation becomes accentuated as one moves from urban to rural areas and focuses on SCs and STs, and in particular on girls. "In rural areas, between one fifth and one third of all girls in five states (Bihar, Madhya Pradesh, Rajasthan, and Uttar Pradesh) have never been enrolled in state schools. The states like Bihar and Uttar Pradesh have a high incidence of never-enrolled children even in urban areas. Unlike the progress in enrolment during the last two decades, the trends in retention and quality are not very encouraging. Drop out in both rural and urban areas is higher at the upper primary (classes 6-8) than primary level (classes 1-5). That means, older children are not remaining in school. Analysis by states shows that the problem of dropouts is particularly high in the rural areas of four States: Andhra Pradesh, Assam, Rajasthan, and even the educationally advanced State of Tamil Nadu."[12] Mehrotra goes on to add: "... what hits home repeatedly is that girls, and Scheduled Caste (i.e. the erstwhile untouchables) and Scheduled Tribe children are the ones being left behind—especially in rural areas. Regardless of the progress in enrolment for all categories of children, there is often a triple burden borne by certain groups of children: if you are a girl, plus if you are a dalit (i.e. Scheduled Caste), plus if you live in rural areas, the likelihood of your being never-enrolled or of dropping out early is greater. And this is more likely if you live in Bihar, Uttar Pradesh, Rajasthan or Madhya Pradesh. The expansion of schooling facilities within a reachable distance and teacher supply are insufficient and incapable of meeting the growing demand for education. While 90 per cent of the population in rural areas might have gained access to schooling, nearly 10-15 per cent of the Scheduled Tribe (ST) and Scheduled Caste (SC) groups in rural areas are still deprived of schools (given that in many states they continue to live in segregated hamlets). Moreover, the proportion of the population from backward caste groups not served within the habitation exceeds 50 per cent in states such as Madhya Pradesh and Uttar Pradesh. The lack of upper primary schools is even more dramatic, with one fourth to one half of the STs without a school within the habitation. Among the eight states (surveyed) the number of villages without schools ranges from 2000 in Tamil Nadu to more than 39,000 in Uttar Pradesh."

A pertinent question is 'why and how have some states done better than others?' It is difficult to find a categorical answer. Economic prosperity cannot definitely explain the phenomenon. A State like Kerala which cannot boast of high economic growth has continued to perform extra-ordinarily in terms of human development indicators; Gujarat which has had consistently high economic growth rate fails to enter the 'high' bracket. Per capita expenditure on education may partially explain but not fully. It is perhaps a combination of factors—historical, social, demographic and economic, that is influencing the pattern of education growth and development in different states. Yet, the fact that the same states have continued to appear at the bottom of the pile in terms of literacy and elementary education progress and that the efforts have failed to benefit the marginalized groups despite explicit directive from the Constitution for affirmative action points to the need for changing the strategies and programmes.

**Table 5.7: Human Development Index: Comparison across States**[13]

| |
|---|
| **High** |
| Goa, Kerala, Maharashtra, Mizoram |
| **High Middle** |
| Gujarat, Manipur, Nagaland, Punjab, Sikkim, Tamil Nadu |
| **Middle** |
| Andhra Pradesh, Arunachal Pradesh, Haryana<br>Himachal Pradesh, Meghalaya, Karnataka<br>Tripura, West Bengal, Uttaranchal |
| **Lower Middle** |
| Assam, Chattisgarh, J & K, Jharkhand, Rajasthan |
| **Low** |
| Bihar, Madhya Pradesh, Orissa, Uttar Pradesh |

It is clear that merely doing more of the same is not likely to serve any purpose. The task is enormous, but there is no excuse for the failure to change course in spite of five decades of planned development. The onus is on the

State to adopt pro-poor policies and programmes that can make a difference to the lives of the people who have remained on the fringes without benefiting from the education development programmes launched by the State. The following paragraphs illustrate some of these measures that could possibly make a difference and address the twin problems of regional imbalances and social inequities. Many of these directly or indirectly suggest the shifting the emphasis as well as strategies adopted under the Sarva Shiksha Abhiyan (SSA). Some of the measures are directly within the purview of the education sector while some others need closer coordinated action in a multi-sectoral fashion.

## Prepare Focused Action Plans for Educationally Backward States

Historically, school education has been a State subject. The 1970s marked a major change in this regard with school education becoming a concurrent subject. Following this the Central Government included elementary education under the Minimum Needs Programme and identified nine Educationally Backward States for special provisions. This was a conscious decision based on an objective analysis of the state of progress of UEE and the magnitude of the task remaining in different states. Yet it is the National Policy on Education-1986 accompanied by the Programme of Action that dramatically changed the scene. From the late 1980s, the country saw a large number of Centrally Sponsored Schemes being launched significantly shifting the locus of planning and action from the state level to the Central level.

The situation got further transformed with the advent of the DPEP, and more recently the SSA, which are managed at the Central level. Interestingly, the programme adopts a more decentralized planning approach but effectively undermines the active involvement of the state governments. More importantly, the SSA does not significantly differentiate between districts in different states. Norm based funding according to district level plans is made available to all the states irrespective of the overall state of elementary education and literacy in different states and without building adequate interface with and appreciation of state government-sponsored indigenous initiatives. Is this an appropriate arrangement to overcome regional imbalances? The question demands careful examination and revision of the existing programme implementation framework of the SSA.

Emphasis has to be on adopting measures that are locally relevant and provides adequate scope for adopting plural strategies. It is important to recognize that what works with the tribal population in Andhra Pradesh may not work in the North East. In this context moving from state level planning to district level planning for education development has helped identify variations in the conditions characterizing sub-regions even within a state and adjust the developmental inputs accordingly. The strategy is based on the assumption that the district plans are prepared through a participatory process involving district personnel. It is also envisaged that the district plan will be prepared after micro-level diagnosis of every village and community. However, such participatory planning is yet to materialize in most places. Consequently, the plans have tended to be typecast in standard formats designed centrally and scrutinized at the national level for final approval and release of funds, and lack sensitivity to local variations in the strategies to be adopted. While recent policy pronouncements including the Tenth Plan document reiterate the need for carrying out such habitation-level planning under the SSA framework, no concrete action plan has been worked out for ensuring such processes in all districts. Experiences from successful initiatives in the country demonstrate that such an approach could go a long way in addressing issues of imbalances and inequities at the grassroots level in a sustained fashion through socially sensitive participatory processes.

### Who should Design Programmes-the Centre or the State? Let the States take the Lead

A direct corollary of the above proposition is the need to revisit the approach being currently adopted for designing and monitoring the implementation of development programmes in education. A pertinent question is: "Should the state governments be encouraged to draw up their own programmes and strategies as part of the Five-Year Plan cycle and the Centre should only extend assistance, if needed at all?" Or, is it more desirable to present a total and probably common package drawn up at the national level to all states with some option for choosing the relevant components from the package? The SSA seems to have pre-decided the path by binding the country as well as the states to go with the large basket of programmes as the route to progress towards UEE.

Considering that education is under the Concurrent List, appropriateness of a proactive approach by the Centre in designing development activities cannot be questioned. However, if past experience of implementing centrally-sponsored schemes is any indication, there is a danger that, after initial enthusiasm, state governments may seek financial resources under SSA but loose interest in and ownership for actions in the field; the proactive approach of the Centre could be taken by many states as a license for them to be inactive. In particular, one finds a gradual decline in state-initiated action plans for literacy and elementary education in the educationally backward states, further exacerbating the problems of imbalances and inequities.

If the SSA should not degenerate into such a level, it is imperative that the programme is frequently refurbished with new ideas and innovative strategies, which are locally derived. It is important to recognize that there is no pan-Indian solution for the problem of UEE. The real test of the SSA would be its adaptability to the changing contexts of different states and its ability to enthuse the state governments to continuously innovate the strategies for demanding central assistance. This would also imply that the norms for support under the SSA should have the flexibility to accommodate new initiatives at district and sub-district levels. Also, these should carry full endorsement of the state government authorities. At present, the District Education Plans are prepared largely keeping in view the prescribed national norms rather than local necessities; the activities are viewed as project activities under the SSA (similar to the perception under the DPEP). This perception has to change. The dichotomy between project activities and components of regular programme of the state government has to disappear. Probably, there is greater need to decentralize the designing of inputs to the SSA depending on the needs of individual states and greater level of involvement of state level professionals in the review and revision of programmes. The monolithic view of the SSA needs to be replaced by a truly pluralistic perspective as an all encompassing and also largely accommodative programme. Under such an arrangement, the Central interventions should be essentially focused on the states that have remained educationally backward, a principle propounded during the 1980s. The states which have made progress should formulate their own state-specific programme. Even within a state it is those blocks and districts with high concentration of marginalized groups such as SCs, STs and minorities should receive special attention.

## The Key for Overcoming Social Inequities Lies in Fairness of Provision

Information on the size and human resources available in primary schools indicate that one-fourth of the number of primary schools are very small with only one teacher and/or one classroom and generally located in small habitations. Increase in such small schools in recent years has been the result of modifying traditional distance and population norms and opening schools in small habitations which has no doubt yielded positive results by bringing in more children to school. *But who goes to such schools?* The answer is quite obvious—it is the children of the poor and the marginalized who are enrolled in such schools. Field observations have also showed that if proper care is not taken, this may lead to legitimization of social divisions through schooling, as often such small habitations are inhabited by marginalized groups living on the fringes of the main village with a full fledged school. An insightful analysis of the efforts made under a major externally funded project on primary education in India, researchers found that a virtual *hierarchy of access* is emerging in terms of nature of primary school provision corresponding to the marginalized status of the children, in particular affecting the education of the girl-child.[14] As a matter of fact, children of the poor by definition are handicapped by poor levels of endowment in their homes. *Fairness of provision demands that the poor have access, at the least, to equally endowed schools as provided for the not-so-poor, and are, perhaps, given even better provisions in order to compensate for the poor endowments at home.*[15]

Some may argue that quantitative expansion is likely to affect the nature of provision and bring in some amount of inequity of provision as an inevitable consequence similar to the equity-efficiency trade-off alluded to in economic analysis. But accepting such an argument in the provision of basic education is self-defeating when examined how this leads to further inequity rather than breaking the vicious cycle of poverty. Serious differences in educational opportunities affect learning and the opportunities in later life that are related to learning, such as wages, employment probabilities, and poverty. The issue is equitable opportunities to learn such as provision of textbooks, qualified teachers and so on; desisting from actions that are likely to create differences in learning opportunities. Policy makers do not generally see the downstream and intergenerational costs of seriously unequal learning opportunities. Markets do not solve fairness problems. These problems are the natural responsibility of the public sector and have to be integrated into public education debate and policy. If the governments do not adopt preventive and equilibrating strategies, the consequences of aberrations in provision may overtake the scene before we realise the need to develop a solution.[16] Creation of such small schools also raises the question of their long-term viability, as such schools are also invariably under-equipped and fail to improve in terms of quality.

## Strengthen Quality Monitoring to Avoid Silent Eexclusion of the Poor within the School

It is clear from various studies that the marginalized groups whether it is SCs, STs, Muslim minorities or girls in general continue to depend on Government schools for their education. Unfortunately, recent surveys of learner achievement[17] reveal that attendance in Government school does not guarantee even basic literacy and numeracy skills, and therefore, many children in these schools suffer a process of silent exclusion from learning even while being present in the school. This situation has to change. *Main focus of action will have to be on improving the functioning of schools and enhancing the quality of their outcomes*. In fact, in the existing framework two components are specially focused on individual schools, namely, school specific grants provided to each school following the pattern of the DPEP and offering individual teacher grant. However, these components have remained unexamined and isolated from the overall concern for improving quality of every school in a holistic manner. Neither has there been any assessment on the impact of such grants in cumulatively transforming the school nor in classroom teaching of teachers. It is worthwhile, that these interlinked investments in schools are viewed from a long-term perspective of improving the quality of every school. *The goal has to be that all schools change—change for better*, and this is needed especially for the schools that serve the poor and the marginalized.

Global experience shows that overall improvement in quality of education can be achieved more effectively if schools are holistically targeted for improvement in terms of their management and performance. In other words, such support to schools has to be designed internally for each school and the initiative should be at the local level.[18] Financial support to schools should be linked to preparation of holistic plans for school improvement. This could be effectively implemented making use of the process of political and administrative decentralisation unfolding in many states. PRIs and other grassroots level bodies such as School Management Committees and VECs could be involved in preparing such plans and receiving funds for elementary education. Individually viewed, the funds transferred through this process to the school level may not be very large. However, cumulatively they are to be the means of transforming the existing schools into qualitatively superior schools.

Towards this end, *institutional arrangements have also to be made at the system level for regular overseeing of school functioning.* Quality improvement in schools cannot be achieved only through input provision. It also demands a regular system for overseeing and monitoring. In most of the States the internal monitoring mechanisms have collapsed. Also international experience has demonstrated the value of *establishing independent organization for quality assessment and monitoring of schools* whose role will be to function as social watch on the functioning of all schools—public and private. Schools that cater to the marginalized groups and those located in remote locations have to receive priority attention in such exercises.

## Re-examine the Role of Private Providers

The Tenth Five Year Plan document referred to creating Public-Private partnership in implementing programme of elementary education. However, no attempt has been made to define the nature of such relationship and consequently, giving rise to controversies on privatization and reduction of government responsibility. This has also led to rhetorical and ideological debates occupying extreme positions in favour of or against private schools. For instance Mehrotra[19] argues for 'nationalisation' of all private schools. He further argues that stricter regulation framework not subsidy is required for private schools. Whatever the position one takes, the current *laissez-faire* approach of the Government is likely to result in increased social inequity.

At the same time it is quite unlikely that the Government will take the extreme step of taking over the control of all private unaided schools. Therefore, the goal has to be one of giving a clear shape to the involvement of private providers in the Plan framework. It cannot be defined in terms of privatization. The constitutional commitment for free and compulsory education entitles everyone, rich or poor, to benefit from the State support. The move in this regard should be to give shape to a common school system as envisaged by the Education Commission that provides quality education for all irrespective of class and caste distinctions. Many observers have pointed out that the existing understanding of the producer-provider framework in elementary education needs to be reexamined. There is no reason why non-profit private providers (NGOs) could not be encouraged to participate in the process of both producing and providing elementary education. This would require identifying specific areas where such involvement would bring value addition. Teacher education could be one such important area. NGOs could also be invited to take up implementation of formal sector activities. In fact, non-profit organizations set up by several corporate entities have already demonstrated the value of getting them associated in such activities.

## Halting the Intergenerational Spiral: Focus on Out-of-school Youth and Adolescents

Considering that a large number of children drop out without completing even the primary cycle of schooling, and that most of these belong to marginalized social groups, it is time that much greater attention is paid to programmes of out of school youth and adults. This is an important area, particularly in India, which hosts one third of all illiterates in the world. In fact, the low level of literacy and life skills is a major factor contributing to the perpetuation of poverty in an intergenerational framework. Functioning of adult education programmes, however, have been uneven and their potential impact on household poverty has not been fully explored, particularly in South Asia. In contrast, the East Asian countries seem to have benefited from non-formal adult education programmes. The difference seems to lie in the nature of programmes offered. Programmes that are limited in scope, focusing on removal of illiteracy as the main goal have not proved to be of much help.

On the other hand, programmes with direct link to the economic life of the people have been quite successful. In such programmes, literacy acquisition by the adults has invariably followed their involvement in skill acquisition programmes directly related to their life. One of the main outcomes of such programmes impinging on their quality of life is the creation of durable economic assets. The Grameen Bank in Bangladesh, along with Bangladesh Rural Advance Committee, and the Self Employed Women's Association of Ahmedabad in India are shining examples of economic empowerment and education going hand in hand. In recent years such activities have also been initiated as part of the government sponsored programme of continuing education under the auspices of the National Literacy Mission in India.

An important dimension of such livelihood-oriented education programmes should not be lost sight of. With no production assets, credit is a fundamental instrument for escape from poverty for the working poor. Therefore, many of these successful experiences have focused on making the credit market work for the poor. This also indicates that mere basic education through schooling may not fully meet the requirements of the poor, even if the primary education is completed. It is necessary to reclaim more active space for adult education which seems to have become a low priority area in recent years. A common feature of the successful experiences is also their emphasis on creating local neighbourhood networks. The value of such neighbourhood networks commonly referred to as Community Based Organizations (CBOs), go beyond the economic advantages that accrue. Utilizing local information and local networks can thus be a more effective substitute for state agencies in delivery of services including credit and education.[20]

## Educational Needs of the Poor Require Multi-Sectoral Strategies

The discussion above reveals that the illiterate and those excluded from elementary education are essentially the poor whether they belong to SC or ST or are simply landless peasantry dependent on agricultural labour. Yet, the issue is not necessarily one of lack of demand. Increased enrollment in primary schools in recent years clearly indicates to high awareness of the value of education among the poor. Thus merely measuring progress in terms of number of children enrolled, classrooms added, schools opened, teacher appointed or the money spent does not help. The State has to view the needs of the poor in a more comprehensive manner. Efforts to strengthen the human resources of poor must recognize that, unlike the non-poor, the absolute poor are trapped in a situation in which economic growth and social development are interdependent. The strong interrelationship between economic growth and social development highlights the vicious circle wherein low growth spawns low growth and poverty breeds poverty. Poor parents cannot provide their children the opportunities for better health and education needed to improve their lot. Because the poor lack the economic capabilities and social characteristics necessary to emerge from poverty, the legacy of poverty is often passed from one generation to the next.[21] This squarely requires the State to be proactive and bring legislations and initiate programmes in a convergent fashion. It is necessary to address fundamental issues and adopt structural reform measures for ensuring that poor benefit from the facilities created by the State. For instance, Pal and Ghosh, based on their analysis of state-level data for the period 1960-92, attribute the continuance of disparities in health and education to elite dominance that discriminates against women and low-caste people and systematically under-invest in mass education. They suggest that higher share of land held by the top five per cent of the population (a) lowers spending on education as well as total developmental spending; (b) increases total non-developmental spending; (c) greater proportion of minority representations (female and low-caste members) in the ruling government however fails to have any perceptible impact on both development (including education) and non-development spending; and (d) while under investment in education by the elite is supported by the lack of demand for education from the poorer population (who are often the marginalised people) greater initiatives of the State to enact land reform legislations enhance the spending on education.[22] As Sainath observes, the peculiar links between land, labour, credit and market have trapped the poor into perpetual penury and dependence.[23]

In the current Indian context implications of these observations for education sector programmes are very significant. (a) Off-setting household costs through measures that support the families beyond basic schooling facilities. For instance, the National Nutritious Meal Programme could go a long way if effectively implemented and expanded to cover the poor in a focused manner. Direct transfer of resources to families like the Girls' Stipend Programme in Bangladesh needs serious consideration. (b) The SSA should design special need-based packages for operation in backward districts in coordination with the Districts where the National Rural Employment Guarantee Programme is in operation.

## Re-examine the Framework of Centre-State Partnership in Financing

The idea of Centre-State partnership in implementing developmental programmes through sharing of finances is a positive step towards gradual take over of all activities by the state government. During the Ninth Plan period, no uniform principle was adopted for all programmes, while the DPEP was made operational with the formula of 85:15 for sharing finances between the Centre and the state governments. However, integration of all national programmes for elementary education under the umbrella of the SSA irrespective of whether the funds are drawn from national or international sources also brought in new norms of sharing between the centre and the state as proposed under the SSA. Following the SSA guidelines, the Tenth Plan initiatives operate under the formula of 75:25 between the Centre and the state governments. This is expected to be moved to a 50:50 formula during the Eleventh Plan.

How is the approach for sharing working? There is no systematic assessment made of the impact of the funding formula on implementation of the programme in different states. It should be noted that the situation with respect to internal finances of the state governments varies widely. A common point made is that a uniform formula is not helpful for promoting faster progress in educationally backward states, which are also poor in their economic status. There is a danger that some of the state governments may stop evolving any new development initiatives for elementary education and would begin to depend solely on centrally-sponsored programmes as they are required to squeeze their finances to meet their share for the SSA. The fall out of such a phenomenon is that it would further increase disparities in education development among different states.

It is urgent that a careful analysis of the impact of the current formula for sharing of resources on progress towards UEE is taken up so that an appropriate strategy can be formulated in preparation for the Eleventh Plan. The capacity of state governments have to be examined not only in relation to current level of expectation, which is quite modest, as the total allocation towards elementary education during the first two years of the Tenth Plan period has been only one-tenth of the total requirement of funds, if the goals of UEE is to be reached by 2010. Will the capacity of the state governments increase so dramatically to raise resources multi-fold for elementary education in the coming years?

Recent analyses of financing of elementary education have raised several issues on state initiated spending on elementary education development. In the final analysis, progress in school education will almost entirely depend on the state governments. While central support to elementary education development has consistently increased, it is unclear how different state governments are investing their resources for the development of the sector. In fact, recent steps taken by several states in virtually dismantling the professional cadre of teachers by appointing para-teachers, essentially as a cost saving measure, raises serious questions on the wisdom of investing plan funds without adequate commitment from the state governments. One gets the impression that fighting hard to ward off current deficit is driving some of the states to completely depend on Central grants for even minimal expansion of the system to accommodate the growing demand for elementary education.

There is a necessity to conduct a detailed analysis of state expenditure on elementary education, differentiated from the 25 per cent offered as the complementary funding for the Central grants received under the SSA. How much investment is being made by individual state governments towards building a sustainable system of elementary education in terms of infrastructure development and maintenance, teachers and teaching learning material and so on? It is important to note that, with increased demographic pressure, the demand for school places would also increase. How are the states prepared financially to face the situation? What level of contribution would be required from the Centre in each state if a sustainable system of elementary education has to emerge?

## Development cannot be Anchored to ad hoc Measures

There have been several Schemes to offset existing regional imbalances and disparities among different social groups. In fact, the current programmes in many states also would have components that focus on this issue. But most of these have been either short term measures abandoned after the project period or have become too routinised and become victims of bureaucratic inefficiency. What is required is sustained action leading to cumulative change in the ground reality. Plan inputs should add value to the existing system in a cumulative fashion and incrementally transform the system over a period of time in the desired direction. As plan implementation progresses one should be able to clearly perceive the improvement in the system. *Ad hoc* measures cannot drive long-term progress. But, unfortunately, contingency measures seem to dominate Plan proposals distorting not only the trajectory of progress but also the whole process of planning and budgeting.

Appointment of para-teachers in several states using the Tenth Plan funds is one such short-term strategy adopted essentially as a cost saving measure by many state governments. These teachers are recruited often without ensuring the accepted norms of qualification and on short-term contracts with lower levels of salary as compared to regular teachers. In several states, thousands of para-teachers have been appointed through the SSA funds. Further, such teachers are also being appointed in several states against the posts of regular teachers. These developments have begun to distort the field situation in several ways. First, it hides the real magnitude of the problem to be addressed in the long run, in financial terms. Second, it distorts the shape of the budget by projecting teacher salary which should in the normal course be part of the recurring expenditure as plan expenditure, unlikely to be absorbed as non-plan component as they are on contract basis. Third, this places the evolution and strengthening of a professional community of teachers in serious jeopardy. Needless to emphasize that development of a professional cadre of teachers is at the core of development of a sustainable school system. Therefore, any measure that obstructs the process of developing a professional cadre of teachers cannot be supported through plan proposals. In fact, it needs to be explored if such measures have brought down the non-plan expenditure of the state, particularly towards teacher salary, which traditionally accounted for most of the expenditure on education.

Some states like Madhya Pradesh have changed the recruitment rules of teachers through decentralization and consequently brought down the actual salary level of the teachers. It is not clear if the salary paid to teachers through PR bodies is shown as recurring non-plan expenditure incurred through the state treasury or is accounted as part of the block grant given to the PR bodies. There should be no objection to decentralising the teacher cadre to district or sub-district level. But that should not negatively impact the growth and development of a teacher cadre. It should be noted that such short-term measures would not help in solving the problem. It may only lead to legal complications and burden the state finances doubly at a later stage creating more serious shortfalls. Further, in many of these educationally backward states, the demand for school places and consequently for teachers would increase substantially due to the population growth (unlike several of the southern states).

In conclusion, it appears that the governments are heavily preoccupied with reporting the progress in terms of expansion of the schooling facilities and coverage of children in the relevant age group. This supply-oriented approach to development of elementary education, to a large extent, has resulted in inadequate attention towards critical issues of regional imbalances and social inequity. Attention has been missing on the marginalized areas and social groups. Acting in their favour is not only desirable but would also make a significant difference in quantitative progress. Improving the schools catering to the marginalized and the poor is again a neglected area. What is the extent of efforts made recently to improve management of schools and teaching-learning processes in the classroom? Are the schools functioning better now compared to the past? What efforts have been made to make functional decentralization a reality, particularly in educationally backward states? Have any improvements in the utilization of resources at the sub-district and school levels taken place? What state specific interventions have been taken to improve internal efficiency of elementary education? Developmental efforts during the coming years need to focus more on these aspects, rather than on quantitative indicators. Even from cursory observations, it is clear that states which have addressed such issues in the last decade have registered greater progress than those which have invested their attention mainly on improving quantitative targets by utilizing resources provided by the Centre. The two have to go hand in hand; quantitative progress without attending to processes and outcomes would only lead to unviable and unproductive structures in the long run, eventually burdening the poor and increasing inequalities.

## Notes

1. J.P. Naik (1975)..
2. *Mid-Term Appraisal of 10th Five Year Plan (2002-2007)*, Government of India, June 2005.
3. See R. Govinda and K. Biswal (2005). for a more comprehensive analysis of the issue.
4. Census of India, 2001 has been conducted in 591 districts out of the total 593 districts.

5. MPCE is defined in NSS, 55th round as the per capita consumer expenditure in the last 30 days of the survey. MPCE = (Household's last 30 days total consumer expenditure/Household size). In the NSS, 55th round, the MPCE classes have been assigned to households based on the data with reference period of "365 days" for items of education, medical expenses (institutional, clothing, footwear, and durable goods and of "last 30 days" for the rest of the items. NSSO, Report No. 473, p. 11, 2001.
6. For a detailed discussion, see Gupta, Shaibal (2000).
7. See for a more detailed analysis R. Govinda and K. Biswal (2006) and R. Govinda, K. Biswal and Geeta Rani, *Progress of Elementary Education across Indian States: Delineating Drivers of Change and Progress*, CREATE Project, University of Sussex and NUEPA, New Delhi (Forthcoming).
8. See M. Haq and K. Haq (1998)..
9. The primary level graduation rate here is loosely defined as the proportion of 11-year old children who have successfully completed the primary level of education.
10. Kremer et al. 2004. The study is based on a nationally representative survey of 3750 primary schools in India. Ten districts in each state and 10 Primary sampling units within each district have been selected in the study using geographically stratified random sampling. The study considers a 'teacher to be absent' if the investigator cannot find the teacher while looking for him/her in the school during the regular working hours of the school, excluding cases where the school was closed due to official or scheduled holiday, extreme weather, construction or repair of the school building and official school function such as examinations, picnics, sports days, etc. Teachers in the study include part-time and voluntary teachers. The survey focused on government primary schools but also covered rural private schools and private aided schools, and the estimates of teacher absence are based on the 'direct physical verification of presence or lack thereof'. Over 16,500 teachers have been covered across the sample schools.
11. Santosh Mehrotra (2006).
12. Mehrotra *Ibid.*
13. Report of the 12th Finance Commission, Government of India. New Delhi.
14. European Commission, *Hierarchy of Access: Gender and Social Equity in Primary Education*, Research coordinated by Vimala Ramachandran, New Delhi, 2002.
15. More detailed discussion of the proposition can be found in R. Govinda (2003).
16. World Bank, *op. cit.*, pp. 22-23
17. See for instance the *Annual Survey of Education Report* by Pratham, New Delhi, 2006.
18. This is not an untested proposition. See for examples from within India, R. Govinda, "Raising quality through school improvement planning: Indian experiences". Paper presented at the International Conference on School Development Planning, Gansu, China, September 2004.
19. Mehrotra, *Ibid.*
20. Pranab Bardhan "Social Justice in the Global Economy" *Economic and Political Weekly*, February 3-10, 2001

21. *Report on the World Social Situation 1997*, United Nations, New York, 1997. p. 84
22. Sharmishta Pal and Sugata Ghosh, "*Elite Dominance and Under-investment in Mass Education: Disparity in the Social Development of the Indian States, 1960-92*" Department of Economics and Finance, Brunel University, West London, UK.
23. P. Sainath, (1996).

## References

Bardhan, Pranab (2001), Social Justice in the Global Economy, *Economic and Political Weekly,* February 3-10.

Census of India (2001), *Population Totals, Series 1, India, Paper 1, 2001*. New Delhi: Web edition.

European Commission (2002), *Hierarchy of Access: Gender and Social Equity in Primary Education*, New Delhi: Research coordinated by Vimala Ramachandran.

Government of India, *Report of the 12th Finance Commission*, New Delhi.

Govinda, R. (2003), Making Basic Education Work for the Poor, *IDS Bulletin*, April.

Govinda, R. (2004), *Raising quality through school improvement planning: Indian experiences*. Paper presented at the International Conference on School Development Planning, Gansu, China, September.

Govinda, R. and Biswal, K. (2005), *Mapping literacy in India: Who and Where are the Illiterates in India*, Paris: GMR Background Paper, UNESCO.

Govinda, R. and Biswal, K. (2006), *Elementary Education in India: Promise, Performance and Prospects*, New Delhi: Background Paper for the Mid-Term Assessment of 10th Five Year Plan, Human Development Centre, UNDP.

Govinda, R., Biswal, K. and Rani, Geetha (2006), *Progress of Elementary Education across Indian States: Delineating Drivers of Change and Progress*, New Delhi: CREATE Project, University of Sussex and NUEPA (Forthcoming).

Gupta, Shaibal (2000), Status *of Literacy in India*. Philadelphia: Asian Development research Institute, Paper presented at the Summer Literacy Training Programme (SLTP), 2000, International literacy Institute, University of Philadelphia, July 5-28.

Haq, M. and Haq, K. (1998), *Human Development in South Asia,* New Delhi: Oxford University Press.

Kremer, Michael, Karthik Muralidhran, Nazmul Chaudhury, Jeffery Hammer, Halsey Rodgers (2004) *Teacher Absence in India*. Working Paper, Department of Economics, Harvard University.

Mehrotra, Santosh (2006) Reforming elementary education in India: A menu of options, *International Journal of Educational Development,* 26: 261-277.

Ministry of Human Resource Development (various years), *Education in India, Vol.(s), 1991-92, 1998-9.* New Delhi: Government of India.

Ministry of Human Resource Development (various years), *Selected Educational Statistics,* New Delhi: Government of India.

Naik, J.P. (n.a.) *Equality, Quality and Quantity: The Elusive Triangle in Indian Education,* New Delhi: Allied Publishers.

National Sample Survey Organisation (2001), *Literacy and Level of Education India,*

*NSS, 55th Round (July-1999-June 2000)*. New Delhi: Report No. 473 (55/1.0/11), Ministry of Statistics and Programme Implementation, GOI.

NCERT, *Sixth and Seventh All India Educational Survey (AIES) data, 1993, and 2002*, New Delhi.

Pal, Sharmishta and Ghosh, Sugata (n.a.), *Elite Dominance and Under-investment in Mass Education: Disparity in the Social Development of the Indian States, 1960-92,* West London: Department of Economics and Finance, Brunel University, UK.

Planning Commission of India (2005, *Mid-Term Appraisal of 10th Five Year Plan (2002-2007)* New Delhi:, Government of India.

Pratham, (2006) *Annual Survey of Education Report*, New Delhi.

Sainath, P. (1996), *Everybody loves a good drought: Stories from India's Poorest Districts*, New Delhi: Penguin.

United Nations (1997) *Report on the World Social Situation 1997*, New York.

# 6

# Regional Imbalances in Educational Development

R.P. SINGH

## Introduction

In a number of ways, the Report of the Education Commission (1964-66) is unique. For instance, it was for the first time ever that an Education Commission in India acknowledged that Education had a direct bearing on national development. Education was seen as a composite whole—indivisible into problems or areas or stage-wise units. Additionally, successful models, both within and without the country, were not easy to adopt for implementation. Historically, at the time when the Education Commission was set up, the Nation had only recently thrown out from its soil the Colonial Rule *per se*—the British, French and the Portuguese, all put together. The country was trying to redefine its cultural and social identity alongside educational development. It was a tough job, not because of the paucity of funds alone, but because the nation was suffering from lack of social cohesiveness and embedded regional imbalances.

The Commission had taken care to see that an unequal society like that of India must address the problem of inequality in a manner that meets the norms of advanced societies. In a modern world, where science and technology rule the roost, India was yet to register its presence. Education was, therefore, logically considered to be the principal effort that the nation had to make.

If it has been difficult to reconcile varying levels and types of social goals, the economic scenario too was arguably disturbing. Free India was basically a poor economy and its education a sadly neglected area of politico-social endeavor. Development needs high levels of intellectual competence including mass literacy, social cohesiveness, thriving economy and a general agreement on goals and means, wherein the absence of even a single factor is capable of frustrating all efforts.

Great nations have to evolve effective mechanisms for sustained growth and achievement in designated sectors. The basis for all development has to be the economy of a nation. In our case, a philosophy for economic development, besides a variety of roles that needed well-thought out working definitions and suitable blueprints for the same, had as yet to be evolved. The Report of the Commission acknowledges two diverse approaches to the definition of the role of local authorities vis-à-vis primary education. The B.G. Kher Committee rejected the British Indians' view that the charge of primary education should be handed over to the local authority, as this would benefit all in learning democratic governance. The other view was advanced by the Balwantrai Mehta Committee report, which said that unless "a representative and vigorous democratic institution" was created at an appropriate level to take charge of all development work in the rural areas "and invested with adequate powers and appropriate finances", local interest and local initiative was hard to develop. The reorganization of the States became difficult because of these divergent views. They created problems because a cohesive, unified, democratic and secular State had to evolve and grow on the foundations of princely states, on the one hand, and the British Dominion on the other. Small French and Portuguese colonial pockets too needed a policy to integrate. The nation was lucky in its leadership. They knew precisely what was needed.

Indians are a racially mixed people and in terms of religion there is hardly any religion in the world that does not have its adherents in its population. Hinduism *per se* is not a religion but it is commonly regarded as such. If we have no social homogeneity because of our history, there is no common law either that applies to all equally. Most of our problems could be traced back to history. Broadly speaking, we have problems related to languages, cultures, tribes and non-tribes, castes and racial stocks. Even within a single category, for instance, tribes—we have vast differences in educational development and mass literacy. Mizos are a tribe yet they are highly literate and culturally as advanced as any other non-tribe and even vie with Kerala in terms of its rate of literacy. The same cannot be said of others. The problem of education, therefore, is of generalization. The spread of literacy or education is highly correlated with castes and communities. Differing segments of a single population group or category like caste for instance, demand individual attention.

The more Indians try to do away with caste in the name of socio-economic cohesion and advancement, the more it gets entrenched either because of ritualistic compulsions or political horse-play. It is a matter of surprise that a number of States continue to run separate SC/ST schools. There are people who have started questioning this reality.

If one looked at the educational tables presented by Adam in his surveys conducted during Warren Hastings's time, since they are the first-time documented pointers to the precise nature of relationship of education with caste, one would notice the differing ratios of prevalence of education in different caste groups and their motivations for studying in the Madrasahs (institutions of higher learning).

Ideally, it should no longer be acceptable that educational advancement or lack of it be related to caste, but the fact is if one went by the annual examination results at all levels and the rate of economic success in all spheres of life in India, one would find a positive correlation between the two. One must delve deeper into the dark recesses of Indian society to find the nuggets of truth. Any plan that does not take into account the socially embedded considerations or ignores this social reality is unlikely to succeed.

We must also remember that poverty, though very significant, alone is not the major factor in the denial of education. Similarly, the highly educated and also rich castes and communities too have their black sheep. It is not caste alone or the generally touted poverty factor that usually gets accused for keeping a community educationally backward. But by and large, the provision of opportunities has the potential to turn the tables in this regard.

Meanwhile, no one could deny that Muslims are an educationally backward community. Based on the Census Report, Prakash Patra wrote in the Hindustan Times (Aug. 22, 2006): "One of the Census findings is that a larger number of Muslim children in the age group of 9-13 are out of school compared to SC/ST children. Also, at the higher end, as poverty increases, the percentage of Muslim graduates and post-graduates falls at a faster rate than for any other community. One argument could be that while policies like reservation in higher education and jobs give SC/ST families a motivation to keep their children in schools which does not exist for Muslims. But it cannot be denied that it is the linkage of education with possible jobs that propels even poor families to spend scarce resources on sending their children to private schools when government schools aren't available or don't function." The author, therefore, pleads that if Muslims are to be prevented from going into the huddle and fall into the spell of their conservative leaders, the State should take some affirmative action quickly.

## Theories and Models

For educational progress in India, we could consider either adopting a model that is readily available somewhere in the world, or, evolve one that suits our conditions. In either case it is not possible to think of a single model that could have been successful in our case. Still, we might like to consider a couple of models that have already succeeded in varying degrees. It would be very difficult to affirm with any degree of certainty that great powers must necessarily be highly educated as well. Historically at least, it would not be possible to support this view. Most of the countries that are today regarded as highly advanced were initially not very literate nations For instance, England at its peak in colonial prowess was not a very literate nation (see, *Education in an Imperial Colony*, (1979) Singh, R.P.; National Publishing House, pp. 10-25; Delhi) and neither was the USSR or China when they went in for a political change. Chile and Japan, although geographically so distant, were the only two nations that were highly literate nations at the end of the 19th century. Japan's self-sacrificing aristocracy was responsible for bringing in the Emperor to Tokyo from Kyoto and had asked the latter to govern the Nation once again. In fact, the Japanese Edict on Education in 1868 brought about a sea change in the education scenario in that country. And by the turn of the century Japan could even defeat Russia. Nations rise above narrow considerations and become great powers. It is true that national literacy rates and school teachers do not always have a positive correlation. Majority of the social and political changes that should normally be associated with formal education or teachers are, sadly enough, not linked with either schools or school teachers. Education, one should realize, is a response to either a social or political necessity. In our case neither politics nor the society itself ever realized that the support to education or its spread would be a harbinger of progress. Despite all the laws and express desires of a few, India continues to remain an educationally backward country.

Education is indeed an instrument of social change but that does not mean that mere formal schooling was ever positively correlated with social change. As we look around, we notice that most of the changes even in school practices such as curricula, methods of teaching, or teaching aids have not been teacher-dependent. Business acumen, technological innovations and/or even political parties, either singly or jointly, could easily take credit for changes in the classroom practices. The arrival of ICT for instance, cannot be attributed directly to school requirements or to any given teacher or be traced back to anything being done in the classrooms for its development either; but the creation of 'a virtual class' is definitely the outcome of ICT. Similarly, schools do not contribute to the formation of a polity or the development of a political ideology but the latter do help create conditions under which education may or may not flourish.

Religions are a potent factor in the spread of literacy but they never pretend to have anything to do with classroom practices. Still, they continue to wield enormous influence on the spread of education—an education whose models excelled in the past. Their founders had proved to be the greatest teachers of all times. Religious education freezes timeframe.

We have some secular models too that have proved to be the biggest influences in the spread of literacy. Consider, for instance, the fact that in the USSR it was the Communist Party cadres that made the nation literate and even helped evolve scripts in many cases. Similarly, in China it was the Red Army that brought about changes in its national literacy scenario. Che Guevara was no practicing teacher and neither is Fidel Castro, but their writings and efforts have to be gone into depths for appreciating the real reasons behind their concern for mass literacy. Yet all these factors, if seen against the light of the present discussion, seem to have contributed much more than any classroom practice or a practicing teacher. In other words, *educational efforts or the rates of literacy are basically a function either of a progressive religion, or, of an emerging political ideology and in some cases even of the technological innovation or business acumen.* Education, in such situations, appears to be an extension of religious and political thought and in most cases merely an implementation of a Party Manifesto or even the promotion of a religious philosophy. We see nothing of the sort emerging in this country.

The major political party—the Indian National Congress, (which has ruled the country in the initial years for several decades)—could never think beyond Mahatma Gandhi's Basic Education, which to be truthful lacked national support, and its own cadres never desired to implement it seriously either.

It is essential that we understand clearly that mere provision of schools would not bring about mass literacy. Literacy must either be linked with some political or social philosophy or let it get hitched on to some other bandwagon on its own; but in case it is left to fend for itself for support it would end up nowhere near the target.

It is rather naïve to think that mere provision of money for more schools would prove to be sufficient for spreading mass literacy. Such an approach smacks of believing that spread of either literacy or education is dependent on the budgetary provision. The fact is that if one were to go into the figures of the children, who either do not go to school at all or drop out of the school at the first occasion offered, they would invariably be either SC/ST or from lower castes or may be from the minority community, which in any case is educationally backward for historical reasons or they would be street children, whose irresponsible parents have left them to fend for themselves. Others would in any case learn enough to manage their professional occupations and become socially useful.

Similarly, in urban areas it is the children of the slum dwellers, girls, ghettoized religious populations, street children or the orphans who would opt out of schools on the first available opportunity. It is untrue that there are no schools for them but they have no motivation for remaining in the school. Twenty seven per cent of our population is very poor. In their case the children have only one choice—either they go to school or earn to survive. In their case schooling means remaining hungry. An excellent paper (Now for a No-Work Policy) on the subject by Reva Nayyar (HT, Aug. 06, 2006), pleads for a change in a policy that forces poverty-stricken children to make a choice to be either at school and die hungry or work to survive. In our enthusiasm, we are likely to overlook the pitiable condition of these poor hapless children.

While in rural areas, mid-day meal might be one temptation, in urban areas even this singular attraction does not prove to be enough to continue attending classes. In my opinion, we are surely mistaken to hold the view that mere provision of more schools would resolve this basic major problem. *Flexible educational policies for different groups and sections of our children must address their need-based requirements.* We must also not forget that gender bias drives away half of this country's population from the facilities that the other half gets without much effort or ado. This gender bias is not always impacted by the family's education or its affluence, or else Haryana and Punjab would be the most literate States.

We must evolve some model, which comprises features that satisfy the entire population of our nation. Even in the most advanced countries we have a segment of population that either does not go to school at all or continues to attend classes with no educational motive. This section of population remains as illiterate as ever. That is why the Americans wish to find out *Why Johnny Can't Read?* It is in these countries that literacy and attendance in a school do not have a positive correlation. Mere attendance of a school does not ensure literacy. And this happens even after the most stringent of laws introduced by some nations. We generally hold the view that education is a tool for progress. It is an instrument of advancement. It helps one to excel and realize one's potential. All these benefits imagined of education have middle class origins. Beyond this class it is difficult to defend any such thesis.

At least for once we must make an effort to approach the question of inequality and regional imbalances in education from an entirely different point of view, and refrain from thinking that mere allocation of more money or opening of more schools would help us resolve our educational problems.

When we talk of regional imbalances, we must first analyze our society and the political system it has given itself. No educational system can rise above these two major considerations. If Indian society lacks social cohesiveness, it is because historically it has developed and grown as highly fragmented, self-contained autonomous units. Politically too, we are a nation in the making. There are considerable numbers of people, who refuse to accept that they are part and parcel of this Indian Nation and that they have any stakes in it. Our major political parties also have no Grand National dreams or ideas beyond winning elections.

The imbalances that we are talking about today arise from the nature of our society/polity and no matter how much we condemn the reality as it exists, we cannot wish it away. The inherent contradictions in our society are today getting reflected in our education, polity and the economy. It is these contradictions that are responsible for the imbalances that we witness all around ourselves. If we do not accept this scenario then all discussions on the subject would become either irrelevant or futile.

Therefore, let us analyze our social system first against the well-known parameters. The Education Commission too was aware of these parameters. In the end, this Commission also made recommendations on these very lines, only they refused to be drawn into a purely academic discussion. The following pages present the Commission's views on the matter.

## The Education Commission (1964-66) on Regional Imbalances

Education had developed unevenly, both in British India and the princely states. The Education Commission (1964-66) Report presents a case for reducing the existing imbalances that have historically been around both in our society and education. The Commission's Report highlighted the existing problem in their own way.

The Report of the Commission provided data on the basis of a survey they carried out. In the language of the Commission, imbalances existed in terms of State's income, rate of literacy, enrolment and gender bias, etc. For instance, the Report recorded, "the State income per head is lowest in Bihar (Rs. 220.7) and the highest in Maharashtra (Rs. 468.5). The percentage of money allocation for education is lowest in Orissa (1.5) and the highest in Kerala (3.6). Illiteracy is lowest in Kerala, both among men and women (450 and 611 respectively per 1000 population), and highest in Jammu & Kashmir (830 and 957 respectively).

At the lower primary level, the enrolment of boys and girls is the highest in Kerala and the lowest in Rajasthan. These figures are: 115.4 per cent and 100 per cent respectively for boys and girls of the corresponding age group; and 64 per cent for boys and 16.3 per cent for school-going age group of girls in Rajasthan. At the higher primary level, Kerala again leads the pack with Orissa appearing on the bottom of the list.

Assam is first in the enrolment of boys (25.5) and Kerala in the enrolment of girls (13.6) at the secondary stage. At the higher education levels Bengal leads the pack by enrolling 49 per 1000 population and Orissa comes last with an enrolment of 8 only.

The differences as they appeared at the district levels were far greater than at the State level. The most striking conclusions that emerged are as follows:

*Lower Primary Stage (Classes I-V)*: At the lower primary stage the target to be reached is an enrolment of 142 per thousand. As against this, there is a wide spectrum of achievement. At the State level, in case of total enrolment it ranges from 55 in Rajasthan to 140 in Kerala while in the case of girls it ranges from 23 in Rajasthan to 130 in Kerala. The mean enrolment of all children for all States was 74 with a standard deviation of 24.6. The mean for girls was 46.7 with a standard deviation of 23.8.

*Higher Primary Stage (Classes VI-VIII)*: At the higher primary level, the picture is similar, although the task that remains to be done is greater. At the State level, the highest total enrolment was 41 per 1000 in Kerala and lowest 5 per 1000 in Orissa. In respect of girls, the highest enrolment was 35 in Kerala and the lowest 1 per 1000 was in Orissa, 2 per 1000 in Bihar and it was 3 per 1000 in M.P., Rajasthan and UP. The mean and standard deviation for all States were 13.7 and 7.3 in the case of girls. The variations between the districts were far wider than imagined.

*Secondary Education Stage (Classes IX-XI)*: Kerala again stands at number one in matters of enrolment of 11 per 1000 of population for total enrolment and of 8 per thousand of population for girls, while Orissa stands last with an enrolment of 2 per thousand for all children and a negligible enrolment for girls. The mean enrolment for all States was 6.29 for total (with a standard deviation of 3.5) and that for girls was 2.21(with a standard deviation of 2.8). At the district level, the differences are even greater. For instance, while in Kalahandi in Orissa; Bastar & Sidhi in M.P.; and Laddak in J&K was 1 per thousand and in Greater Bombay it was 23, Dehradun 21, Kanya Kumari in Tamil Nadu was 20, etc.

*Educational Expenditure*: With regard to total expenditure per capita, Kerala spends the highest (11.2) and Orissa spends the lowest with (2.8) per thousand. In terms of districts, Poona spends the highest Rs. 16.2 followed by Thiruvananthapuram Rs. 15.6 per head and the lowest was Rs. 1.1 Kalahandi in Orissa followed close behind by Mahendragarh in Punjab Rs. 1.2.

On the strength of the data presented, the inevitable recommendation by the Commission was the introduction of a program that would reduce these imbalances. More money for schools in the eyes of the Commission meant higher enrolment. The assumption behind this recommendation is that if more schools get opened the greater would be the enrolment.

We will examine this assumption in some detail in the later paragraphs. In the meantime, we shall present the plan of action as proposed by the Commission to meet this deficiency. The suggested lines were:

(a) These recommendations should be read with the proviso that total elimination of these differences in educational development is neither possible nor desirable. In the larger interest of the country each region should be free to strive its best and to develop at its own pace.

This will necessarily lead to some inequalities but what is needed is a balancing factor, a deliberate and sustained effort to assist the less advanced areas to come up to at least certain minimum levels so that the gap between them and the advanced areas would be reduced to the minimum. This is the policy of equalization under which each area is assisted, subject to the condition that it makes a given effort to come up to certain minimum levels prescribed. Our grant-in-aid in education will have to be broadly based on this principle of equalization.

(b) The district should be adopted as the basic unit for educational planning and development. The Commission discussed the plan of action under chapter XVIII in part III under *Implementation* titled *Educational Planning and Administration* in which the various roles of private and public agencies have been discussed in detail.

(c) At the State level, there should be a deliberate policy of equalization of educational development in the different districts and the necessary administrative and financial measures to this end should be taken.

(d) At the national level, it should be regarded as the responsibility of the Government of India to secure equalization of educational development in different States. The necessary programs for this, including special assistance to the less advanced States, should be developed.

## Education of the Girls

The Commission realized that education of the girls was imperative if the nation was ever to achieve the goal of modernization. It stated, "for full development of our human resources, the improvements of homes, and for moulding the character of children during the most impressionable years of infancy, the education of women is of even greater importance than that of men." The growth of women's education in the country is comparable to snails pace. In 1901 the Report records that only 0.8 per cent women were literate. The number of girls enrolled for every 100 boys was only 12 at the primary and 4 at the secondary stage. The total enrollment in higher education was only 264 (which included 76 girls reading in medical colleges and 11 in colleges of education). The comparative figures of progress in the field since 1950-51 to 1960-61 and 1965-66 (estimated) show a phenomenal upward trend (Table 6.1).

The Commission's Report recorded an interesting phenomenon: The rate of expansion of education of girls was found to be much faster than that of boys. Consequently, the gap between the enrolments of the two was steadily narrowing. At the lower primary stage, the number of the girls enrolled per 100 boys had gone up from 12 in 1901 to 39 in 1960 and 55 in 1965. At the secondary stage, the corresponding figures were 4 in 1901, 15 in 1950 and 26 in 1965. And, in the higher education stage, the enrolment had gone up from a meager 264 in 1901 to 40,000 in 1950 and to 240,000 in 1965. Education in mixed schools had come to be accepted by the year 1965. Still, several measures had to be taken to improve the situation. There was still considerable resistance to girls' education in rural areas and also in urban pockets.

**Table 6.1: Participation of Girls in School, General Tertiary and Professional Education**

| *Sl. No.* | | *1950-51* | *1960-61* | *1965-66 (Estimated)* |
|---|---|---|---|---|
| 1. | Enrolment of Girls in classes 1-V Total enrolment (in 000's) | 5,385.0 | 11,401.0 | 18,145.000 |
| 2. | Number of girls for every 100 boys enrolled | 39.0 | 48.0 | 55.000 |
| 3. | Percentage of girls in schools for boys | 74.8 | 82.1 | 85.000 |
| 4. | Enrolment of Girls in Classes VI-VIII | | | |
| | Total enrolment (in 000) | 534.0 | 1,630.0 | 2,839.000 |
| | Number of girls for every 100 boys enrolled | 21.0 | 32.0 | 35.000 |
| | Percentages of girls in schools for boys | 26.7 | 68.9 | 78.000 |
| 5. | Enrolment of Girls in Classes IX-XI | | | |
| | Total enrolment in (000's) | 163.0 | 541.0 | 1.069 |
| | Number of girls for every 100 boys enrolled | 15.0 | 23.0 | 26.000 |
| | Percentage of girls in boys' schools | 21.0 | 36.4 | 40.000 |
| 6. | Enrolment of Girls at the University (General Level) | | | |
| | Total enrolment (1000's) | 40.0 | 150.0 | 271.000 |
| | Number of girls for every 100 boys enrolled | 14.0 | 23.0 | 24.000 |
| | Percentages of girls in boys 'institutions | 56.0 | 50.2 | 48.200 |
| | Enrolment of girls in Vocational Course (School standard Total enrolment in (000's) | 41.0 | 86.0 | 120.000 |
| | Number of girls for every 100 boys enrolled | 28.0 | 25.0 | 23.000 |
| 7. | Enrolment of Girls in Professional Course (Collegiate Standard) | | | |
| | Total enrolment in (000's) | 5.0 | 26.0 | 50.000 |
| | Number of girls for every 100 boys enrolled | 5.0 | 11.0 | 14.000 |

*Source*: Report of the Commission, various Years.

In the opinion of the Commission the development of girls' education will have to take two forms. The *first* was to emphasize the 'special' programs as recommended by the National Commission for Women's Education headed by Durgabai Deshmukh. And the *second* was to consider the development of their education as an integral part of the progress of general education *per se*.

1. The education of women should be regarded as a major program for some years to come and a bold and determined effort should be made to face the difficulties involved in closing the gap between the education of boys and girls.

2. Special schemes should be prepared for this purpose and adequate funds allocated.
3. Both at the central and the State levels special mechanism will have to be put in place so that the efforts are not slackened in any manner. Both officials and non-officials should be included in the planning and execution of the program.

The Commission had noted that, "these special programs, by their very nature, are temporary and will have to be pursued only till the gap between the education of the boys and girls is almost bridged. But they should not be made an excuse for neglecting the second aspect of the strategy, viz., giving adequate attention to the education of girls at all stages and in all sectors." It further stated: "In fact, if this had been done right from the beginning, the need for special programs would hardly have arisen." The Report records their opinion according to which "a stage had been reached when intensive effort should be made to develop this aspect of the strategy so that the need for special programs will disappear in the course of a few years."

The Report went into the role of women, both inside and outside home. While she has been blessed to be the homemaker by Mother Nature, she also has to perform yet another role and i.e. of following a suitable career. It is for the performance of these roles that she must receive education. The Census of 1961 shows that there were more than a million young women, below the age of 24 and with a minimum qualification of matriculation, leading the life of home makers. This number, it stipulated, was likely to increase. It is these women, below the age of 24, who have to be enabled to find opportunities of part-time employment. Additionally, efforts should be made to encourage some of them to participate in all types of nation-building activities.

Side by side, the Report recommended that opportunities for full-time employment have also to be found/created. With the rise in the age of marriage, full-time employment has to be found for all young unmarried women. And, for married women, when their children reach the school-going age and when they are free from household chores, they have to be offered suitable full-time jobs, just as in several other countries. Teaching, nursing and social service are well-recognized areas where women can play a useful role. Opportunities for women will have to be expanded in these fields and new avenues covering almost all walks of life, will have to be opened out to them. The Commission was careful to acknowledge and record that while making these recommendations for the education and employment of women, their recommendations for men need not be overlooked since both may be seen in perspective.

## Education of Scheduled Tribes

For reasons hidden in antiquity and discussed for centuries without end, numerous sections of Indian society have existed on the social periphery.

Special attention has to be paid to raise their lot like in many other countries, (for instance in Japan). The earlier indigenous efforts, like that of Lord Buddha or centuries later by some saint poets, could only touch upon the fringes of the problem. The time has come when this problem should be dealt with at the roots through education. The Commission, therefore, logically enough thought of addressing this problem. It is necessary, the Report said, to pay special attention to the education of the children from the backward classes, which include the Scheduled Castes, the Scheduled Tribes, de-notified communities and a few nomadic and semi-nomadic groups.

The Commission made the following recommendations to address the problem:

1. In view of the decrease in the incidence and prevalence of untouchability, there was some improvement in the situation. For its early resolution, the Commission advised the continuation of the existing programs intended to impart education to the Scheduled Castes.
2. With regard to de-notified communities and a few nomadic and semi-nomadic groups the problem did not appear to be easy to resolve. Still one must acknowledge the reality and try reorganizing their economy and their way of life. The recommendation in this regard was quite revolutionary in nature. While reorganizing their economy and their way of life would take time, efforts have to be made to provide marketing, credit, health and educational facilities in a mobile form where there are sizable nomadic groups. Similar facilities are required for communities that migrate from their homes for several months in a year.
3. The problem of the de-notified communities is small in magnitude but extremely difficult. Patience is the key to the resolution of their problem. Provision of hostels for the children of these communities, where proper atmosphere can be offered to study was considered the best solution.
4. After having identified the habitation pattern of the tribals both within non-tribal areas and the accessible and non-accessible forests, the Commission stated that the problem of the education of the tribes living in 'small pockets' with the non-tribes was rather simple. A little extra attention to their special requirements was enough to help them acquire education. But the situation becomes uniquely challenging in the predominantly tribal areas because it presented an ideal opportunity for an integrated development. These are the areas where three things are needed on a priority basis. Firstly, develop communications system; secondly, transform their agriculture system; and thirdly, offer education that is related to their economic and social development.

## Primary Education

On the basis of the data made available by the U.N. Dhebar Commission on Scheduled Areas and Scheduled Tribes, the Commission stated that if the proportion of the ST population was 20 per cent, and if their educational progress were the same as that of the general population, one would expect that the enrolment percentage of the tribal students would also be identical. But then this is not so. In Assam, it was found that the enrolment of tribal children was higher than that of the non-tribal. But by and large, lower percentage in school enrolment of the tribal children goes to establish that they are educationally quite backward.

The Report records that special efforts are needed to improve the situation. Other than Assam, the percentage of school going population to their total population is very low. Perhaps, the only other exceptions are Gujarat and Bihar. But in these states also, the percentage of the population to school going number fail to match. The establishment of Ashram schools was recommended for the sparsely populated areas. Elsewhere, it was expected that "to attract children to schools and to hold them, the working programs have to harmonize with the environment. Vacations and holidays should coincide with agricultural and forest operations and social festivities. These measures are needed for the rural population as a whole. But they are of special significance for the tribal people.

Moreover, the introduction of work experience and an emphasis on art education should attract tribal children, as would the teaching of folk songs, stories and riddles, which are so popular with them. Tribal games, archery as well as music and dance should be introduced as extra-curricular activities.

## Secondary Education

Far greater attention has to be paid to the development of higher primary and secondary education. For this a program of hostels is very essential. Brighter children should be identified from lower primary stage and admitted to hostels. Careful arrangements should be made to give personal guidance to these children, besides coaching them, so that their performance may become comparable with the performance of the non-tribal children. Ashram schools scheme was hugely appreciated.

Tribal children find it difficult to get admission in good higher primary and secondary schools. The Report says the Department of Education should assist them in securing such admissions, even if it means offering some inducements in the bargain to the schools for the purpose. Since these special efforts amount to providing coaching to these children for admission, necessary provision for this also has to be made. It was discovered that these children prefer vocational courses. "Special vocational schools should also be organized for the grown-up children, who leave school at the end of the lower primary stage."

## Higher Education

It is necessary to streamline the administration of the scholarships program instituted by the Government of India. The Commission made the following recommendations in this regard:

1. The administration of scholarships and other aids need to be decentralized. Heads of the institutions should be authorized to grant these scholarships. Necessary funds for the purpose should be given to these institutions in advance. This could easily be calculated on the basis of the previous years' expenditure allowing a margin of increase.
2. The scope of the program should be expanded to include, not only the provision of funds but also the provision of necessary additional facilities. Monitoring the progress, planning their careers and ensuring placement in appropriate institutions would then become imperative. The staff necessary for this purpose should be made available.
3. The scope of scholarships should cover all courses available to those who leave secondary school. But special preference should be given to those in vocational and technical courses, including those at industrial training institutes.

The Report laid emphasis on "the basic issue in the development of tribal life and education, which is to provide leadership of the right type." This would loom large for a long time to come. This leadership, at least for the time being, has to come from the non-tribal population—officials and non-officials. But the ultimate solution lies in the emergence of indigenous tribal leadership. The very purpose of this education should be the achievement of that goal.

The Report advocates adoption of unorthodox methods for developing indigenous leadership such as setting aside rules when absolutely necessary for help in admissions, training or recruitment.

The Commission desired that transfer rules, postings and creation of sub-cadres in tribal service be suitably modified to improve the lot of the tribal people. There are officers who are not familiar with the tribal language. They may be encouraged to learn it. Not many sincere non-tribal persons can be found who wish to live in tribal areas and work for their betterment. But if such people can be identified they may be encouraged to do so.

To be able to do justice to the tasks and problems of tribal education, it is important that the Ministry of Education at the Center and the Departments of Education in the States, which have sizable tribal population, should be equipped with special sections or units whose specific task may be to address the problems faced by the tribals in regard to their education. The Commission also recorded an immense lacuna in the data about the tribal people and the tribal areas. This data was to be collected and authentic information provided.

## The Ground Reality—An Analysis

The presence of imbalance in the provision of education is almost universal. The societies that claim to have resolved this particular issue are not always truthful. Imbalances are endemic, simply because equality among humans is an ideal construct and not a reality. Ideally, we all try to achieve this goal but seldom, if at all, do we arrive at it.

In the past 40 years or so after the Commission's Report, numerous changes have occurred. We have, since 1968, yet another Policy on Education. The National Policy on Education (1986, and revised 1992) envisaged free and compulsory education to all children in 6-14 age group. Through the 86th amendment of the Constitution of India, the Government. has made free and compulsory education to all children in the age group of 6-14 a fundamental right.

Sarva Shiksha Abhiyan (Education for All) is a program of the Government. of India to provide education to all children including children with disabilities. Under this program, new schools have been opened in school-less habitations and the existing school infrastructure has been improved by providing additional classrooms, toilets, drinking water, maintenance grant and barrier free access. Additional teachers, organization of teacher training program, intensive monitoring and special focus on education of children with special needs, made the program more effective. Decentralized planning is one of the specific features of this program.

## The Caste and Literacy—Education of the Dalits

Pretensions apart, the factual position on untouchability came out in a Report based on a survey of 565 villages in 11 States by a group called Aman Biradari. It hardly needs any emphasis that untouchability has a direct bearing on one's literacy/education. The convener of the group, Harsh Mander, whose other associates are: Ghanshyam Shah, Sukhdeo Thorat, Satish Deshpande and Amita Baviskar, reported a brief summary of their findings in the Hindustan Times on August 15, 2006.

"Children in the rural areas learn early the rules of the caste, even as their country races into the 21st century". It was found that 38 per cent of the Dalit children in government schools are made to sit separately. 20 per cent of the Dalit children are not allowed to drink water from the same source as others. A 'shocking' 27 per cent Dalits are prevented from entering Police Stations and 28.7 per cent are prevented from ration shops. 33 per cent health and social workers refuse to go to Dalit homes and 23.5 per cent do not get their letters delivered at their residence. Segregated sitting for Dalits was found in 29.5 per cent Panchayats. And, in 14.4 per cent villages they were not allowed even entrance to a Panchayat building.

The conclusion is rather obvious. Despite being charged with a constitutional mandate to promote social justice, various local institutions of the Indian State have still to go a long way to ameliorate the situation.

Dalit settlements are more often segregated from the main village. Such traditions are repeated even by government departments, just as in Indira Avaas Vikaas Yojana. The NGOs too do not lag behind in this practice. In the post-earthquake (2001) rehabilitation programme in Gujarat, the NGOs followed the government norms i.e. segregation of the Dalits from non-Dalits.

The research also found that the landless Dalits are disproportionately poor and discrimination in labor and consumer markets condemns them to lower wages with harder work, uncertain employment and restrictions on their access to natural resources as well as markets for their products. Even more than in secular and religious public spaces, the practice of untouchability prevails most in upper-caste rural homes, in what people regard to be the private sphere.

The study concludes on a rather highly disappointing note: "With untouchability thus persisting unashamedly in state institutions like schools and police stations, in public spaces like temples and shops, in farms and markets, and in homes and hearts, the Dalit still lives in India waiting hopelessly and sometimes in anger for the long-betrayed dawn of equality."

Here are a few tables that explain the reality in very vivid terms.

**Table 6.2: Literacy Rates of SCs/STs (7+ Age Group) 2001 Census**

*(in Percentages)*

| | *Total* | *SC* | *ST* |
|---|---|---|---|
| Total | 64.8 | 54.7 | 47.1 |
| Male | 75.3 | 66.6 | 59.2 |
| Female | 53.7 | 41.9 | 34.8 |
| Gender Gap | 21.6 | 24.7 | 24.4 |

**Table 6.3: Dropout Rates of the SCs and STs at Primary, Elementary and Secondary Stages (1990-2004)**

| *Year* | *Primary (I-V)* | | *Elementary (I-VIII)* | | *Secondary (1-X)* | |
|---|---|---|---|---|---|---|
| | *Boys* | *Girls* | *Boys* | *Girls* | *Boys* | *Girls* |
| 1990-91 | 60.3 | 66.1 | 75.7 | 82.2 | 83.3 | 85.0 |
| 1995-96 | 55.0 | 58.9 | 62.3 | 71.2 | — | — |
| 2001-02 | 51.0 | 54.1 | 67.3 | 72.7 | 79.9 | 82.9 |
| 2003-04 | 49.1 | 48.7 | 69.0 | 71.4 | 77.9 | 81.2 |

*Source*: Educational Statistics at a Glance 2003-4, GoI, MHRD, May 2006.

**Table 6.4: Gender Parity Index for the Elementary Stage for SCs & STs.**

| *Year* | *Primary School (I-V)* | *Upper Primary School (V-VIII)* | *Elementary School (I-VIII)* | *Primary ST (I-V)* | *Upper Primary ST (V-VIII)* | *Elementary ST (1-8)* |
|---|---|---|---|---|---|---|
| 1986-87 | 0.62 | 0.50 | 0.60 | 0.61 | 0.48 | 0.59 |
| 1990-91 | 0.69 | 0.52 | 0.63 | 0.65 | 0.50 | 0.60 |
| 1995-96 | 0. 78 | 0.62 | 0.72 | 0.70 | 0.70 | 0.71 |
| 2000-01 | 0.80 | 0.70 | 0.78 | 0.73 | 0.73 | 0.73 |
| 2003-04 | 0.89 | 0.80 | 0.87 | O.93 | 0.79 | 0.90 |

## Girls' Education

The country has 593 districts, 5470 sub-districts, 5161 towns and 6,38,588 villages. As per Census of India, 2001, the total population of India was 10,027,015,247 with 531,277,078 males and 495,738,169 females. The literacy rate of the country stands at 65.38 per cent. *The difference between the male and female literacy rate comes to 21.69 per cent.* The education of the girls in India has its own story to tell. Despite all the laws and statutory provisions that a civil society should have in place, the ratios of birth and education for the girls and boys continues to be skewed. Right from the stage of conception, the girl child faces hurdles in her life. The imbalance in the education of the girls is not limited to her education, the male child preference in many communities across the country, makes her birth itself a question mark. The Government has tried to ameliorate the condition by enacting laws which make prevention of the birth of a girl child a punishable offence. Her education is facilitated with plenty of incentives through a variety of means such as, no tuition fees, award of scholarships, etc. Still a lot needs to be done.

## The Disabled Children

The National Sample Survey Organization through its 58th round of survey, conducted in 2002, has shown that the total number of persons with disability in the country was 1.85 crore, which constituted 1.8 per cent of the total estimated population. About 10.63 per cent of them suffered from more than one type of disabilities. A break up for the population with disability (disability wise) is shown in Table 6.5.

The survey also revealed that for every one lakh persons in India, there were 1755, who were either mentally or physically disabled. Among the rural residents, the prevalence of disability was 1.85 per cent as against 1.50 per cent for the urban population. The prevalence of disability was also found to be marginally higher among males than females. The number of intellectually disabled (mentally retarded) persons per one lakh population comes to 115 male and 72 females while these numbers for mentally ill are 122 and 86

**Table 6.5: Estimated Number of Disabled Persons**

| *Type of Disability* | *Rural* | | | *Urban* | | | *Rural+ Urban* |
|---|---|---|---|---|---|---|---|
| | *Male* | *Female* | *Persons* | *Male* | *Female* | *Persons* | |
| (1) | (2) | (3) | (4) | (5) | (6) | (7) | (8) |
| Any Disability | 83.102 | 57.748 | 140.850 | 25.811 | 18.249 | 44.060 | 184.91 |
| Mental Retardation | 4.34 | 2.561 | 6.995 | 1.824 | 1.128 | 2.951 | 9.946 |
| Mental Illness | 5.022 | 3.377 | 8.399 | 1.623 | 0.988 | 2.611 | 11.01 |
| Blindness | 7.494 | 8.536 | 16.030 | 1.793 | 2.311 | 4.104 | 20.13 |
| Low Vision | 2.982 | 3.563 | 6.545 | 0.711 | 0.877 | 1.588 | 8.133 |
| Hearing Disability | 12.516 | 11.171 | 23.687 | 3.617 | 3.313 | 6.930 | 30.67 |
| Speech Disability | 9.495 | 6.532 | 16.027 | 3.416 | 2.102 | 5.518 | 21.545 |
| Loco motor Disability | 49.987 | 29.839 | 79.826 | 16.352 | 10.162 | 26.514 | 106.44 |

respectively. The survey also found that about 84 per cent of the mentally retarded persons were born with the disability. So far as marital status is concerned, results showed that at the All India level, out of 1000 disabled males living in rural areas 471 never got married and this number for urban was 484. Amongst the females, the number of never married females for rural and urban areas, were 376 and 415 respectively. In the case of mentally retarded persons, it was found that most of them have to lead an unmarried life. The percentage of illiterate disabled persons (age 5 years and above) was found to be 55 per cent (59 per cent in rural areas and 40 per cent in urban areas). However, the highest percentage of illiterate disabled persons belonged to mentally retarded group (87 per cent) followed by visually disabled persons (74-77 per cent). The literacy figures of mentally disabled persons (mentally retarded and mentally ill persons) per 1000 disabled persons of five years plus were as follows:

**Table 6.6: Literacy Figures of Mentally Retarded/Ill**

| | *Mentally Retarded* | *Mentally ill* |
|---|---|---|
| Not literate | 866 | 591 |
| Up to Primary level | 106 | 215 |
| Up to Middle level | 24 | 102 |
| Secondary to above | 3 | 89 |

*Source*: NSSO Survey, 2002, India.

The Government of India has opened two types of schools to cater to the educational requirements of children with mental retardation. Though special schools have been opened for all categories of disabilities, the number of such schools for mentally retarded is the largest. The total number of special schools working in the country for persons with mental retardation as on April, 30, 2001 was 1062 with an enrolment of 21,952 males and 12,129 females.

## Home-Based Program and Self Help Groups

Home-based programs for the disabled have come into existence in India at places where service programs are not available at district, sub-district and rural levels, and also for children, whose disability is more severe or they are too young. In both center-based and home-based programs, parents are trained to train their children at home and make required interventions. Self-help groups help parents of children to help themselves and to improve the programs for parents in the task of bringing up a child with retardation. Parent's participation and cooperation in training and management of the child have produced positive results.

## Sarva Shiksha Abhiyan

Under the Sarva Shiksha Abhiyan (SSA) scheme, an additional sum of Rs. 1200 per year, per child with disability is also made available by the Government. This amount can be utilized for various activities including early detection, formal and functional assessment, providing aids and appliances, support services like special equipment, reading material, physio-therapy for children with physical or multiple handicaps, occupational therapy for children with physical handicaps and mental retardation, etc., parental counseling, awareness building, material development, resource support and harnessing support from NGOs. (Draft National Policy for Persons with Disabilities, MSJ&E, 2005).

Under this scheme, the first step towards providing education to children with disabilities is to identify them. Till date, the categories of children identified and enrolled in schools are as follows:

**Table 6.7: Category-wise Children Identified and Enrolled**

| *Category* | *Children Identified* | | | *Children Enrolled* | | |
|---|---|---|---|---|---|---|
| | *Total* | *Male* | *Female* | *Total* | *Male* | *Female* |
| Visual Handicap | 3,11,174 | 13,1958 | 14028 | 252176 | 118536 | 104248 |
| Hearing Handicap | 356550 | 161588 | 17840 | 254893 | 16508 | 93949 |
| Orthopedic impairment | 599398 | 292282 | 87893 | 50917 | 276808 | 179922 |
| Mental Retardation | 285414 | 133571 | 996724 | 16266 | 104129 | 67609 |
| Mentally Deficient | 30663 | 12225 | 10977 | 15108 | 8435 | 6673 |
| Learning Disabled | 184322 | 102980 | 70039 | 157303 | 85806 | 67703 |
| Others | 131333 | 71745 | 49323 | 50785 | 27641 | 22979 |

*Note*: Regarding identification: Only 14 states have provided gender wise data, only 8 states given category wise data and 13 states provided total figure. Children with Mental Retardation stand at 2.85 lakh (0.285 million). Regarding enrolment: 14 states have provided category wise, gender wise data, 5 states have provided category wise break up, 8 states have not provided any data and 8 states have provided total figures.

Children with mental retardation stand at 1.96 lakh (0.19 million). Out of 11,17,944 schools covered under the scheme, 2,22,689 schools have now barrier free access, which comes to 19.92 per cent (source: DISE data 2003-04). Besides this 43.86 per cent teachers have been benefited by Mass Teacher Training, while 13.02 per cent teachers have received 3-5 days training in inclusive education. Out of 20,60,756 children with special needs identified, which constitutes 1.02 per cent of the child population, 15,85,916 children (76.96 per cent) are enrolled in schools, while 46,591 are enrolled under Education Guarantee Scheme and 9,594 are being provided home based education. The number of NGOs involved in this program is 470. Out of 3,36,371 children requiring aid and appliances, 2,94,881 have been provided with these facilities. A total of 28,97,875 Village Education Committee members and 89,176 parents have also been benefited through an orientation program. A total of 56,174 master trainers trained under the program are equipped with competence to improve the overall teaching-learning process in the classroom, influencing the life of children with disabilities.

## National Policy for Persons with Disabilities

A comprehensive National Policy for Persons with Disabilities is also being prepared by the Ministry of Social Justice and Empowerment, Government of India, which has taken care of all the aspects of persons with disabilities, including education, rehabilitation and employment. It has recognized that a large percentage of persons with disabilities (55 per cent) are still illiterate and that there is a need for mainstreaming the persons with disabilities in the general education system through Inclusive Education. Under the Sarva Shiksha Abhiyan, the Government. of India has set up the goal of providing eight years of elementary schooling to all children including children with disabilities. Various learning options like open learning system and open schools, alternative schooling, distance education and learning, special schools wherever necessary, home-based education, itinerant teacher model, remedial teaching, part time classes, community based rehabilitation (CBR) and vocational education and cooperative program available to other children, are also available to children with disabilities, including children with intellectual disabilities. Government of India also provides scholarships to students with disabilities for pursuing studies at post-doctoral level.

The Draft National Policy for Persons with Disabilities of the Ministry of Social Justice and Empowerment, Govt. of India, has also dealt with the employment aspect. The Ministry of Labor and Employment is the main Ministry dealing with employment issues. This policy envisages that persons with disabilities shall be provided equal opportunities for productive and gainful employment and the Government will ensure three per cent reservation for persons with disabilities against identified posts, which is the statutory requirement. It also envisages employment of these persons in private sector by developing appropriate skill for their employability and enhancing opportunities of self-employment.

## Disability Laws

Equality, dignity, autonomy and liberty, which are the basis of International Human Rights law, are reflected in true sense in the Constitution of India. During the 1970s a group of persons with disabilities started a sustained movement demanding protection and recognition of their human rights. The Government recognized the need for such a legislation and that is how the Persons with Disabilities (Equal Opportunities, Protection of Rights and Full Participation) Act came into existence in 1995. Other disability laws with focus on intellectual disabilities include, National Trust for Welfare of Persons with Autism, Cerebral Palsy, Mental Retardation and Multiple Disabilities, Act (1999), Mental Health Act (1987) and Rehabilitation Council of India, Act (1992).

About teacher preparation, supply and recruitment policies, etc., the situation has not improved even a bit over the years. The Report had recorded, "Nothing is more important than securing a sufficient supply of high quality recruits to the teaching profession, providing them with the best possible professional preparation and creating satisfactory conditions of work in which they can be fully effective." Unless meaningful transformation is brought to teacher education, nothing tangible can be expected to happen in school education. The statutory bodies must note the issue with utmost seriousness.

One can conclude that the ideal set by the Commission is nowhere near achievement. The figures for Delhi are even more depressing. Each year, the performance of MCD run schools is assessed and the usual ceremonial praise lavished. Similarly, the annual results announced by the CBSE put a question mark on the quality of teaching in the Government-supported secondary schools. The question remains: Who should do What, How and When?

# 7

# National Commitment to Education of the Dalits: A Critical Commentary on the Report of the Education Commission

PADMA VELASKAR

## Introduction

The dalits of India have come a long way educationally, from the caste-based exclusion they experienced in pre-colonial caste-patriarchal society. Thirty one million dalit children are currently enrolled in elementary schools, four million at the secondary and higher secondary stage and over a million in colleges across the country. The educational achievements of dalits in certain regions like Kerala, Maharashtra and Tamil Nadu are quite spectacular, at times, even better than the progress of the other sections of the society. At the same time, however, the larger scenario is rather dismal. There are striking regional disparities in dalit educational progress, substantial gender disparities within dalits and large gaps in rates of educational survival, attendance and scholastic achievement between dalits and non-dalits. Moreover, dalit educational participation declines and gaps widen as we move up from the primary to higher education stage.

Clearly, educational inequality continues to affect large sections of dalits even as the pursuit of modern secular education continues to be a central plank in dalit people's struggle for freedom from social oppression and attainment of dignity, equality and social justice. On its part, the post-colonial state, in fulfillment of its constitutional obligations of providing equality of opportunity and "upliftment" of its "weaker" sections, adopted policies of educational expansion and positive discrimination that specifically targeted dalits.

What went wrong with the state's educational action in favour of dalits? A look back into history is always useful to understand the current situation better, especially the causal elements. After sixty years of official educational policy and action, and forty years after the submission of its report, this is indeed an opportune time to reflect on the Report of the Education Commission 1964-66 (EC/ECR). Charged with the monumental responsibility of creating a national system of education, the EC went on to produce the most comprehensive educational policy perspective documents written in Independent India. What was the ideology of development and equality that underlay the EC's perspectives on education of the dalits? Today, under the impact of a "structurally adjusting" education and an apparently worsening situation of opportunities, is there any scope for envisioning greater educational equality for historically oppressed sections, such as dalits? What would be the ideal kind of reforms towards this goal? In the context of the continuing search for explanations and guiding principles towards the achievement of egalitarian goals in the future, it would indeed be pertinent to critically re-examine the egalitarian ideology and policy perspectives that emanated from the ECR.

Almost all aspects of the educational policy and programmes of action contained in the ECR have implications for dalits. It is not possible within the confines of this paper to consider all of them. This paper examines the EC's concern regarding education of the dalits, policy directives relevant for their educational progress and their underlying assumptions. The paper critically surveys the EC's social philosophy, in particular, the translation of the constitutional ideals of equality and social justice, its articulation of the assumed role of education in egalitarian social transformation and its specific agenda for education of dalits. It is also important to undertake a gender analysis and explore the vision for women's education, with the objective of considering separately the situation of dalit women. This is important because dalit women are generally subsumed under the categories of 'dalit' or 'woman', without taking cognizance of their special location at the intersection of caste, class and patriarchy. This intersection is reflected in the sharp gender disparity that exists within the dalit population and between dalit and non-dalit women.

Part I of the paper presents a selective narration of relevant portions from the text of the ECR that cover its ideological orientations, approach to educational expansion, egalitarian agenda, including its most celebrated strategy, the Common School System, and finally, its notions of curriculum and concerns regarding teachers. Part II, critically evaluates the recommendations of the EC in key areas that have significant relevance to dalits from their own perspectives.

## Part-I: The EC Ideology of Change and Development, Role of Education in Egalitarian Transformation and Agenda for Dalits

The EC defined, enhancing economic growth, achieving self-reliance in food and full employment, as the basic economic goals of national development. The building of a science and technology based production system and a prosperous society was a central idea in its vision of modern economic development. It runs as a recurrent theme in the introductory chapter of the

ECR. Social and national integration of a hierarchical and culturally plural society and people constituted the second major developmental goal. The third goal of political development required the strengthening of democracy and the establishing of freedom and equality and rights for the people.

Education was conceived as a powerful instrument of achieving these national development goals. The "educational revolution" envisaged by the EC constituted a proper qualitative and quantitative reorganization of the nation's school and college systems towards these goals. Education had a paramount role in the development of human resources, in the arena of science and technology and in developing new ways of life, thought and work for the people. Science was emphasized as a basic component of education and culture. The EC adopted and developed a human capital approach to education, entrusting it with bringing change in knowledge, skills, interests and values of people towards development. It emphasized as crucial, the education-productivity-income link, if India were to change from a society of a privileged few to one in which the masses benefited.

The "social purpose" of education was defined as the realization of national aspirations. While "values for the individual" would be important, "social reorganization and social perspectives" were to be emphasized. One of the important principles was "socialistic pattern" of society, which could be achieved by "the dedication of all to wider loyalties of national development in all its parameters" (GOI, 1966, 4). In stating its position on education's role in social justice, the EC criticized the elitist, unequal and hegemonic education systems of the past, and advocated a "social and cultural revolution in education", where equality of educational opportunity would be provided and education would be deliberately used to "develop more and more potential talent which would be harnessed to the solution of national problems" (GOI, 1966, 5). The relation between education and life needs and aspirations of common people is spelt out by linking them with the national development goals.

The education-productivity link revolves around participation in productive work in school—as a method of integrating work and education and of eroding the mental/manual labour distinction—and vocationalizing education with a view to diverting youth to different walks of life, especially agricultural and technological innovation. The university system has to be geared to the production of competent professional manpower.

The conceptualization of education as an instrument of social and national integration demanded that education be organized in a manner that would curb widening gulfs between classes, between rural and urban regions and would also stem sectarian processes. A Common School System of public education, compulsory national and social service, participation in programmes of community development, promotion of modern Indian languages, community living, promoting national consciousness and democratic values, were defined as key educational strategies for bringing about integration and solidarity. Education's role in modernizing society, which means a society that increasingly adopted science-based technology, lay in gearing itself to meet the challenges of knowledge explosion and the rapid pace of advance. Education should focus on producing educated and skilled citizens. The EC believed that this could be achieved through prioritization of science, technical and vocational education and research. A radical change in quality and standards is crucial and to achieve this a few major universities of international standards must be established.

Addressing the question of values, the EC held the view that technological modernity in the production process had important implications for social and cultural life. For the future of society and of the common good, individuals need to make right choices. It was unequivocal in its commitment to strengthening and deepening the sense of social responsibility and to keener appreciation of moral and spiritual values. The EC recognized that merely imparting knowledge without essential values may be dangerous. It was aware of the serious social and ethical conflicts in western societies that stemmed out of the failure to balance scientific knowledge and skills with *"the values and insights associated with ethics and religion at its best, viz., a search for the knowledge of the self, of the meaning of life, of the relationship of man to other human beings and to the ultimate reality" (GOI, 1966, 4).*

Thus EC stressed the importance of giving proper value-orientation to the educational system. *"What we would like to emphasize is the need to pay attention to the inculcation of right values" (GOI, 1966, 19).* Explaining what this meant in the Indian context, it said:

> In the attempt to inculcate values through education, we should draw freely upon our own traditions as well as the traditions of other countries and cultures of the world. There are strands within Indian thought itself which can lead to the new outlook appropriate for a modern society and which can prepare the people for a willing acceptance of life with all its joys and sorrows, its challenges and triumphs. In them, too, we can find inspiration for social service and faith in the future. Mahatma Gandhi, for instance, and some other great leaders of thought, discovered the inspiration for their idealism and their passionate striving for social justice and social reconstruction largely from these sources. It is such re-interpretations and re-evaluations of the past that are now most needed. It is, however, specially important in the world of today that this effort should not be restricted to the national sources only. It would be necessary to draw upon liberalizing forces that have arisen in the western nations and which have emphasized, among other things, the dignity of the individual, equality and social justice, e.g. the French Revolution, the concept of the welfare state, the philosophy of Marx and the rise

> of socialism. A major weakness of the Indian, and particularly of the Hindu society, in the past, has been a lack of equality and social justice. These balancing influences have, therefore, a great significance. Similar assimilations of whatever is significant should also be discriminatingly made from other important nations and cultures such as Chinese, Japanese or Islamic (GOI, 1966, 20).

## Towards Equalization of Educational Opportunity

This brings us to the EC's own treatment of equality of opportunity in education. According to the EC, an important social objective of education is to equalize opportunity, enabling the backward or under-privileged classes and individuals to use education as a lever for the improvement of their condition. To quote:

> Every society that values social justice and is anxious to improve the lot of the common man and cultivate all available talent must ensure progressive equality of opportunity to all sections of the population. This is the only guarantee for the building up of an egalitarian and human society in which the exploitation of the weak will be minimized (GOI, 1966, 108).

In analyzing the sources of educational inequality, the EC drew attention to the following socio-economic and educational factors: the absence of facilities, the need to address regional imbalances and economic imbalances (through scholarships), poverty, differences in standards of educational institutions, inegalitarian methods of selection in admissions and scholarship disbursement and differences in home environment that create differences in opportunity for rural and urban, and poor and rich children. In this context, the EC while suggesting that the problem is *fundamentally* of living standards, advocates that "something can be done" by paying special attention to children from underprivileged homes and providing day study centres and boarding houses at school.

The EC then highlights two forms of educational inequality peculiar to India: (1) gender disparity, and (2) disparity between the advanced classes and the SC/ST. It advocates the need to identify factors, which tend to create significant forms of inequality and adopt measures to eliminate them. It begins with identification of economic obstacles, as one of the most crucial of these factors, and makes a strong case for abolishing tuition fees at the elementary school level. Tuition fees are seen as an anti-egalitarian regressive force, which burden the poor and are, therefore, undesirable. It recommends a gradual move to abolish fees at all levels, beginning with the primary but continuing up to lower secondary in government and aided schools. Girls and poorer classes should be totally exempted. The EC also aspires to achieving the goal of free higher education but advocates, for the time being, a liberal provision of free studentships to the needy and deserving. It is concerned about increasing costs (on textbooks, co-curricular activities) and the heavy expenditure incurred by parents. It recommends efforts towards reduction of these costs and a large scale programme of text book provision at the primary, secondary and university stages. The programme of scholarships is to be reoriented and expanded to cover all stages of education, so that no "promising child" is prevented from continuing school education due to poverty. The EC expresses concern about those who go to "weak" schools and display inferior level of achievements "for no fault of theirs". As a measure to enhance quality, the opening of one good secondary school in each community development block is recommended. Access is to be based on talent, which is to be identified through properly devised testing. Special enrichment programmes are to be developed in "math, verbal, artistic and experimental skills which together constitute "talent". Merit-based national scholarships are needed for providing "equal opportunity" for all talented children.

*Education of SC and ST:* Specifically, on the issue of education of the Scheduled Castes, the EC's brief statement is as follows:

> In so far as the Scheduled Castes are concerned, the problem has become a little easier because of the diminution in the rigour of untouchability. For its early solution, however, we recommend that the existing programmes for the education of the Scheduled Castes should continue and be expanded (GOI, 1966, 139).

The Scheduled Tribes are dealt with in much greater detail with special concern for neglected groups like nomadic and semi nomadic tribes and de-notified tribes. The EC feels that the problem is simpler in the case of tribals living in "small pockets" or are mixed with the general population. The predominantly tribal areas, however, pose challenges of developing communications, transforming/modifying shifting cultivation systems to developed agricultural economy, and developing a system of education that will respond both to the "national goal of economic and social development and to economic and cultural needs of the people". It suggests intensive efforts to provide effective education through strategies of parental education, girls' education (commenting that women have good status in tribal life), teaching material preparation in tribal languages, and restructuring provision of facilities to suit tribal life. At the secondary stage of education, emphasis is placed on picking up "brighter" children and providing them all support to further their educational advance. Special efforts at vocationalization, special attention to tribal students in higher education and to institutions working for tribal welfare, tribal leadership development, devising of context specific strategies and setting up of special units for tribal education in States constitute the range of policy directives that figure in the ECR.

*Education of Girls*: According to the EC, the significance of the education of girls cannot be over-emphasized. For "full development of our human resources, the improvement of homes, and for moulding the character of children during the most impressionable years of childhood, the education of women is of even greater importance than that of men..." It moves on to stress the importance of women's education for reduction in birth rate and the roles women *have* to play in the home and beyond. Indian women and men are to engage in equal partnership to fight hunger, poverty, ignorance and ill-health. The EC is also appreciative of women now adopting careers of their own and sharing, equally with men, the responsibility for societal development. The two-pronged strategy for women's education incorporates a special effort to close the gender gap. Attention is to be given to the education of girls at all stages and in all sections. The EC was of the view that differentiation of curriculum may be essential in the transitional phase to equal opportunity, wherein psychological differences and sex role divisions will have to be accepted. However, steps are to be taken so as not to intensify or perpetuate sex differences. Maths and science are to be taught to girls, along with other subjects like Home Science, which are 'popular' with girls, with a view to prepare women teachers of Maths and Science. The Commission also expressed its concern about the problem faced by women in carrying out the dual role of home-making and career. Women required special support to enable them to participate in programmes of national reconstruction. It recommends opportunities for part-time employment and involvement in all types of nation-building activities on an honorary basis. Simultaneously, it recognizes the need, given the rising age of marriage, for opportunities for full-time employment of unmarried women. The EC adds: "Married women, once their children reach a school-going age, would also have a great deal of time on their hands and will desire to spend it usefully in full-time employment." Teaching, nursing and social service are singled out as fields specially suited for them, where opportunities will have to be expanded. Several new avenues such as nutrition, dietetics, administration and institutional management would have to be opened to women.

## Common School System: Aims and Ethos

The EC's philosophy of egalitarianism was best reflected in its advocacy of a Common School System that would encompass both primary and secondary education. The objective is to bring together social classes and groups to promote egalitarianism, integration and social cohesion in the larger interest of national integration and national development. The EC lamented that the present education system tended to increase social segregation and widen class distinctions. Segregated schooling was a major weakness of the system, inconsistent with the ideals of a democratic and egalitarian society. A Common

School System, that provided good quality education was essential for effective equal opportunity to all children irrespective of caste, creed, community, religion, economic condition and social status. A key concern was that the total "national pool of ability" was left untapped by a segregated system in which the masses of children were receiving substandard education. The EC also saw in the common school an opportunity for rich children to share and learn about the poor and enrich their education.

It was envisaged that all existing schools receiving government aid would be brought within the ambit of the new system with a view to evolve a system of uniform quality. Teacher-related reform, a decentralized system of administration and regulative mechanisms to set quality standards for the small number of private schools were suggested to create a properly functioning public education system. It was recommended that the concept of neighbourhood school be adopted as the long term goal.

### *Approach to Educational Expansion*

The EC is committed to universalisation of elementary education which includes a focus on stopping wastage and stagnation, and enhancing quality. Having identified the basic educational flaw to be the lack of proper articulation between education and life, as well as the poor capacity of schools to engage its students, the EC recommended a nationwide programme of school improvement along with quantitative expansion of lower and upper primary schools. Enabling access within walking distance, especially to girls and tribals, is of crucial importance along with devising special interventions. It advocated a restricted secondary school expansion emphasizing the need to focus on quality and standards. The best students from the upper primary should continue in secondary schools through a process of self selection and external evaluation.

### *Curriculum and Teachers*

The teaching-learning process is at the heart of education and both curriculum and teachers are integral to it. The EC spells out in considerable detail what it considers the vital core content of education at each stage. For the first seven years of schooling, the EC recommends an undifferentiated course of general education for all. Those (approximately 20 percent) who continue their studies after Class VII are to be provided with full-time or part-time vocational education. The remaining 80 per cent of pupils are to continue to receive general education for a further period of three years without any diversification of studies, but with provision of courses at two levels, and of options in creative activities and different types of work-experience. Thus for the vast majority of pupils there would be a single curricular stream from Class I to Class X, ending with the first external or public examination. There would be no "streaming" or specialization in this general course.

The standard of attainment at the end of each stage requires to be clearly indicated in terms of the knowledge, skills, abilities and attitudes to be developed with reference to the overall objectives of school education. A very simple curriculum is envisaged for lower primary class with a reduced load of formal subjects and which includes the informal study of environment. Only language and elementary mathematics are to be specially emphasized since they are the basic tools of learning. At the upper primary stage, a broader and deeper curriculum will include a second language, either Hindi or English as link languages. Mathematics and science are to receive greater stress than before. The strong commitment to science education is a recurrent theme. Social studies may continue as an integrated course "if competent teachers and the requisite facilities are available, otherwise the study of history, geography and civics should be taken up as separate disciplines". Arts and crafts will figure as part of work experience, along with physical education, games and social service, education in moral and spiritual values and respect for all religions. The subjects will be continued at the secondary stage and with the increasing maturity of the students, their study having to gain in rigour and depth. Competence in science subject is particularly important in view of the phenomenal advances made in recent years in scientific knowledge. History, geography and civics and "present-day problems" are to be taught separately, "with any such correlation as is natural and necessary". Work experience is to be organized on a farm, workshop or any other production unit.

The post-schooling phase will involve the formation of special interests and abilities of the student. With a good system of guidance and counseling, "he can be helped in the choice of his future career and educational course". An extensive and varied programme of vocational education is to be provided at this stage. In the light of the proposed enrolment policies, 50 per cent of those wishing to continue their studies are expected to take up full-time or part-time vocational courses and 50 per cent will go for courses of general education, which will be more diversified to provide opportunities. Elective subjects are to be reduced to arts and sciences, without maintaining a sharp distinction between the two.

Language learning incorporates a three languages formula to include: (1) The mother-tongue or the regional language, (2) The official language of the Union or the associate official language of the Union as it exists; and (3) A modern Indian or foreign language not covered under (1) and (2) and other than that used as the medium of instruction. A strong foundation in the English language is emphasized, which is to be laid from school stage at Class V. But the EC recognized that it may not happen before Class VIII in rural areas.

Along with English and Science, the EC emphasized Mathematics, in the context of its critical role in the growth of the physical sciences, biological sciences and the advent of automation and cybernetics, which marks the beginning of the new scientific-industrial revolution. Proper foundations in the knowledge of the subject should be laid at schools. The EC declares that "an effective programme of social studies is essential in India for the development of good citizenship and emotional integration. The aim of teaching social studies is to help the student to acquire knowledge of their environment, an understanding of human relationships and certain attitudes and values, which are vital for intelligent participation in the affairs of the community, the State, the nation and the world. At the higher secondary stage, the EC recommends specialized study of the social sciences, history, geography, civics, economics and sociology. It also adds that something of the scientific spirit and methods of the social sciences should permeate the teaching of social studies and of history, geography and civics even at the lower stage. The natural and social sciences should also relate to and benefit from each other.

Work experience, involving participation in forms of productive work under conditions approximating the real life situations is regarded as an integral part of education at all stages. In this connection, the EC recommends a basic shift in the Gandhian programme of Basic Education from indigenous activities of the village-based economy to fulfilling the needs of a modernizing society. In the EC's words, "work-experience must be forward-looking in keeping with the character of the new social order", and its effective value is seen as largely proportional to the extent it is imbued with the spirit of modernization.

Overall, curriculum must aim at social and national integration, raising the standards of living and inculcating a deep sense of values and obligations of citizenship, mutual understanding and respect. The general emphasis is on the application of reason and free enquiry, the development of analytical skills, ability to apply them to problems of material environment and social living and to promote a spirit of enquiry and experimentation. It is the belief of the Commission that "commitment of man to free enquiry and to the quest for truth loosens bonds of dogmatism and is a powerful dispeller of fear and superstition, fatalism and passive resignation".

*Teachers and Teaching*: The EC's main concerns are the status, salary and civic rights of teachers. Women teachers for rural and tribal areas are recommended. A sound programme of professional teacher education is also advocated. Development of education as a social science and as a separate academic discipline and improvement of quality of teacher education are strategies for long-term professional development of school teaching.

The subject of "education of the backward child" features once again in the chapter on teaching methods, guidance and evaluation. The concern is about under-achievement due to emotional conflict, lack of motivation, poor study habits, cultural deprivation and economic handicaps. The first step towards a solution is to observe, quiz and test the child to diagnose the cause of failure. The second is to initiate a remedial programme to be conducted individually or in groups, aimed at correction and improvement of academic achievement, assessed in terms of the child's earlier performance. This is expected to re-establish in the "backward child, his confidence in himself and in his ability to succeed and creating for him new interest and motivation in his studies" (GOI, 1966, 242).

## Part II: A National Commitment to Education of the Dalits?

### *A Critique of the ECR*

The ECR is rooted in liberal ideology, which was historically constituted in India as Nehruvian modernity. This in turn shaped a development model of a Western science and technology based industrial and agrarian society. The values of liberty, equality, fraternity and justice were enshrined in the Constitution. As we have seen, the Commission whole-heartedly supported the programme of economic and technological nationalism and was of the firm view that the educational system was to be dedicated to its production and sustenance. The agenda was shaped by a world in which there was escalating competition between countries for nuclear power and technological superiority. Thus, the EC endorsed the state programme of capitalistic development and echoed the broadly consensual views of the dominant intellectual, business, bureaucratic and political elites of the times.

An unproblematic positive relation was held to exist between educational advance and modernization. Liberalism was the dominant ideology as evident in assertion of individual rights and duties, values of universalism, achievement orientation, and in the economic approach to education as an investment in human capital. In the matter of social development, one notes, along with the liberal value system, an unmistakable allegiance to Gandhian values and a somewhat awkward and partial attempt to synthesize the two philosophies. In the section on 'Social, Moral and Spiritual Values' we would expect to see a categoric espousal of constitutional values. The EC starts by emphasizing the need to inculcate necessary moral and spiritual values and self-discipline but fights shy of explicitly naming the values.

Of the vast array of social purposes assigned to education, those concerning equality and social justice are most relevant to dalits. The EC's vision for social transformation gave primacy to the goal of social and national integration, which was conceptualized as "harmonious bringing together" of a socio-economic unequal and culturally plural people. The dismantling of invidious and unjust inequalities is not strongly voiced. Why did an agency of the state, which had the power and legitimacy to articulate a vision of education as an instrument of desirable cultural (value) change, not do so, especially when society was deeply infused with castist, communal and patriarchal values?

The notion of equality of opportunity, which was adopted was that of a meritocracy. The EC is an unrelenting advocate of meritocracy, as is evident at numerous places, where it recommends the special nurture of talent, special opportunities for the "meritorious" and selectivity of admissions to secondary and higher education. As conceptualized by Michael Young, IQ + effort = merit. The notion legitimizes the categorization of children by intelligence type. In a meritocracy, the chief goal of education is to train and select the most talented people for important, technical jobs. As in the West, the drive for educational efficiency was considered congruent with equality of educational opportunity (Karabel and Halsey, 1977). The EC uses this to legitimize selective expansion at the secondary level and the tracking of children into 'academic' and 'vocational' types. It thus rationalizes the imparting of limited education to some and more education to others. Thus the conflict between equality/social justice on the one hand, and individualism and meritocracy on the other gets settled in favour of the latter. The ideal of equal opportunity assumes an open society and universalistic values, a minimum economic well being, equal citizenship and equal rights for its society's members. These were deeply problematic assumptions to make for India, which was barely emerging out of a feudal mode and a colonial encounter. It was due to this reason that a synthesis of meritarian and compensatory principles was sought in the Constitution. In this context, theories of democratic socialism would have been of greater relevance to envision equality. From the perspective of dalits, the Phule-Ambedkarian and other dalit subaltern ideologies on the power of education as an instrument of social transformation held the most promise. They espoused ideals of critical rational thinking and valued re-socialization into a new humanistic culture based on self respect, self assertion, freedom and equality.

The EC lacked a theory of society and social transformation. It did not make an expanded critique of hierarchical social structure, nor did it squarely confront the social reality of caste. A class centric analysis of the educational situation of underprivileged sections is underlined by the view that the main contradiction lies between the rich and poor and the educated and uneducated. Caste and patriarchy are not acknowledged as historical systems of oppressive social inequality nor are their very real consequences recognized. As was the case with race in the U.S., caste was reduced to class (McArthy, 1988). Even as it passes strictures against the undemocratic institution of caste and castigates its extending influence on polity, the EC does not dissect caste as a system of social subordination nor condemns its historical injustices on dalits. Its position seems to fit into that post colonial position on Indian society, which refuses to attribute to caste any significance and is able to uphold the legal-political principle of the modern state (Chatterjee, 1993).

Only one paragraph is devoted to articulating the significance of education for the Scheduled Castes in an entire volume of nearly 700 pages. The issues of tribals and girls are dealt with in more detail at various points. This is commendable but it is strange and shocking that the social and educational problems of dalits are not given comparable attention. The ECR does not identify the sources of their oppression in the systems of caste and untouchabilty. The interchangeable use of the terms, "poorer classes", "backward classes", "backward children", "underprivileged children" and Scheduled Castes, camouflages the real and specific identity of the multiple groups being encompassed and referred to. The state's social policies and practices were predicated upon specificities of backwardness of the groups. In the case of the dalits, their social disabilities arise not merely from poverty but basically from the stigma of pollution and social oppression. The state's official approach is not reflected in the ECR and a clear agenda for education of dalits is conspicuous by its absence. Dalits are subsumed under the "poor masses". The EC seems to believe that general pro-poor ameliorative measures under educational policy are enough. In its disapproval of caste politics, the EC did not distinguish between different kinds of politics and hence did not recognize the contribution of dalit liberation movements and their self defined educational agenda.

Within this perspective, the EC's egalitarian strategy hinged on the Common School System. The recommendation was truly path breaking and the EC passionately advocated its implementation. It was a bold and laudable policy initiative, its working out inspired by systems of comprehensive schooling established in some of the Western countries. In hindsight, it appears idealistic and ambitious given the power of ascriptive forces during the time. The EC does not give due recognition to the fact that the Western systems of common schooling had evolved in the context of strong indigenous egalitarianism. Even in the U.S., where egalitarianism was a home grown ideology, supportive programmes like federally funded compensatory education programmes were carefully designed and extensively implemented to assist in the learning process of disadvantaged minorities and blacks. Even then desired goals were not achieved and a more radical notion of "equality of results" had to be conceived.

The Common School System was not rejected but took pride of place in the first education policy document of 1968. It is also a part of the 1986 policy. But untill now, not a finger has been lifted to see the progression of this idea into reality. This situation actually brings to light the deep-rootedness of hierarchical ideology in Indian social life and the recent history of discriminatory and exclusionary social practices in the colonial education system. The common school strategy ignores and underestimates the tremendous social resistance to social mixing that is characteristic of Indian society. Social relations continue to be based, to a greater or lesser extent, on endogamy, commensality, and residential segregation; and ideologies of superior and inferior statuses and differential social worth are commonly upheld. Despite the societal wrath faced by dalits in accessing education in colonial times, no programme for ending caste discrimination in school is conceptualized despite the grand array of other programmatic recommendations. What was needed was an anticipation of the brakes that would be put on equalizing processes. A well thought out strategy of strengthening the government schooling system (which by default functions as a Common School System in many parts of rural India) would have perhaps served the egalitarian goals better. Abolishing fees at this level was essential. In addition, the recommendation for liberal provision of scholarships was meant to support education of the poor. A comprehensive package of investments in classroom and curriculum practice at the elementary level was also needed.

Perhaps, nothing else helped dalit educational advance more concretely than the provisions such as scholarships and hostels, made by the Department of Social Welfare, They proved to be the supportive bulwark for self motivated dalit families, which sought to educate their children to pursue school and college education. Reservation in higher education and white collar jobs have served as a key motivating factor. The EC did not advocate any separate measures or assume any special responsibility for dalits even in the educational domain, except remedial programmes to be carried out by individual schools. All special provisions and measures of redressal were entrusted to welfare. It is almost as if the responsibility for the marginalized sections lay exclusively with that Department.

Gender relations are constructed in an embarrassingly patriarchal manner in the ECR, even for those times. The first phase of the women's movement had put equal education for women firmly on the agenda for women's emancipation. The First Plan had stated that the general purpose and objective of women's education cannot be different from men. However, the ECR legitimized as normal and natural notions of different spheres for men and women. On the basis of these gender stereotypes, it took a limited view of girls' interests and capacities and sanctioned the exclusion of girls from full educational participation. It upheld the conservative view in which the main objective of education was not to benefit the girls themselves but society and the patriarchal home. It lent official support to the unwritten societal policy and practice of less and separate education for girls and undermined the women's movements' concerns about discriminatory education of girls. Nehruvian modernity had had no qualms about valorizing the traditional Hindu cultural ideals of womanhood (Forbes, 1998). Women were homogenized and the lives of masses of peasant, low caste, dalit, tribal women, who worked in farm and public labour did not enter the world view of the dominant classes. Dalit women are affected by their social locations, experiences and identities as both dalits and as women. Gender disparities in educational participation among dalits can only be explained with reference to patriarchal practices in labour and family This compounds experience of castism and influence educational policies and processes. When it came to both caste and gender, the contradiction in the EC policy between idealized notions of "equal opportunity" and "differential opportunity" was stark.

Despite a lot of attention being paid to women, one continually gets a sense due to the strong gendered ideology that permeates the discourse of the ECR, that the prime target of the goal of modernization through education is the higher caste male, whose intellectual superiority is unchallenged. The perceived link between women's education and national development—makes the EC refrain from pressing for gender equality as a valuable social goal in its own right. As it has been pointed out, "equality should not be termed as a means of social efficiency, then we can risk losing it entirely. If equality can be subsumed it can also be eliminated when it does not facilitate economic goals" (Apple 1979). This is rapidly happening at present.

Curriculum was seen as value neutral, equal and in a de-contextualised manner. In the context of modernizing goals and the desire to overturn colonial design, the EC privileged knowledge of Western hard sciences, technology, the dominant regional language and the English language, in the selection and structuring of knowledge for the school curriculum. Consensus was assumed. There was a compulsion to retain some of the colonial character of the curriculum. The EC, in fact, promulgates a modern ideology of hierarchical knowledge giving top priority to knowledge of science and technology and lower priority to social sciences. Ruling ideas were thus the ideas of the ruling classes which were defined as befitting educational transmission.

The entire approach to selection and transmission of values is problematic. The cultural tussle between competing and contrasting visions and ideologies of western and Nehruvian modernity and Gandhian thought (which are privileged in the ECR) is not sorted out, leaving a lot of ambiguities and convoluted statements of value positions. From the point of view of dalits the cultural emphasis on scientific rationality and free enquiry was welcome. However, a lot of space was left open in the curriculum for it to serve as mediator of ideological dominance and hegemony by cultural elites. The curriculum of social sciences, and humanities in particular, give ample scope for cultural domination. Given the cultural majoritarian Brahmanical Hindu dominance, the curriculam was dominated by specific forms of mental capacities and pedagogies, so called "pure" language forms and other cultural forms, literature, history as well as their religion-cultural practices, symbols and modes of life. It was not recognized that curricular change supposedly aimed at indigenization can have a distorting influence.

There is absence of subaltern groups, culture and ideologies in the recommended curriculum. The historical significance of structural oppressions of caste, gender, tribe and religion is made invisible in a school curriculum in which the dominant discourse was of a cultural majoritarian nationhood. The dominant construction of knowledge was evident in the absence of "lesser" dialects, cultures, traditions, and in the absence of knowledge, skills and cognitive capacities rooted in productive processes of lower and dalit castes and their socio-cultural habitat (NCERT 2005). Rather, schools were to provide linguistic and social competencies that would facilitate their "equal integration" in dominant society. However, in viewing teachers and bureaucrats as purely occupational, and not sociological, categories, the EC did not apprehend the education system as a site of caste prejudice and discrimination.

A cultural document of this magnitude and significance should have been a more explicit harbinger of a change-oriented value framework. It needed to define for debate and dialogue, areas of worthwhile knowledge and values for a newly independent nation. The ideology of modernization and of liberal and democratic socialist values and indigenous philosophies worthy of nurturance and preservation were all competing for attention. The issue requires serious thinking and development of theories that are vibrant expressions of critical multiculturalism and would create a new moral order for Indian society. Today, dalits challenge high caste epistemology and knowledge. However, their issues have remained peripheral and their representation weak in the "national" curriculum (*Ibid* 2005).

The manner in which the devaluation of manual labour is sought to be reversed would remain superficial and notional, as long as its structural basis in the system of caste-untouchability and in the gender division of labour is not problematised. Work experience was the strategy chosen to reduce the unfair distinction between manual and intellectual labour. Work experience was intended to overcome the cultural denigration of manual work with an emphasis on setting right the imbalance in elite privilege and its parasitical nature. The route chosen is primarily ideological. Technology based productive/farm work is to enhance the value and worth of labour. There is a rather facile substitution of "over academic" nature of curricula with "manual work" or "work experience". The focus is on the peasant as a symbol of toiling people. An inadequate understanding of the relationship between culture and work speaks nothing of caste-based menial, occupational patterns and of work characterized as derogatory and polluting. Concepts of dignity of labour failed to take into account demeaning caste occupation links.

The EC perceives a role for education in reproduction of gender-based division of labour, by assuming a natural link between women and domesticity. For dalit women, the new role model is the upper caste/class woman, and the path suggested is that of emulation of her dual roles. In reality, education facilitates entry into caste/gender segregated labour market.

To sum up, the EC gave more emphasis on modern economic development and less on social transformation. The fundamental conflict of interest between rapid modernization and egalitarianism in a resource-poor country went unacknowledged. Justice and equality are underplayed and development, integration and modernization over-emphasized in the ECR. There is no critical appraisal of Indian society and no specific agenda to use schools as avenues to challenge caste-occupation links or hierarchical ideology. No policies are suggested for eliminating caste discrimination in schools or constructing new social relations through schooling. There is a refusal to acknowledge the material and cultural reality of the dalits. The EC displayed the problematic tendency to construct the nation as an imagined homogeneous cultural community, through the adoption of discourses of nationalism, integration and development of all. It failed to differentiate, except very mechanically, a population that is highly differentiated in terms of its existential and ideological reality. Equality of opportunity thus remains a decontextualized and a historical notion in the ECR. Instead of the dominant discourse of national integration, a clear articulation of caste and gender egalitarianism and the scope for egalitarian action, however limited in practical terms, may have served the goals better. For the dalits, the ECR is a disappointing treatise on social justice and attainment of dignity and a new identity through education. The clash of priorities has become even more strident today, and the state commitment to egalitarianism within or outside of education is almost nonexistent.

## References


Aloysius, G. (1997) *Nationalism without a Nation in India.* Delhi: Oxford University Press.

Apple, Michael (1979) *Ideology and Curriculum.* London: Routledge & Kegan Paul.

Beteille, A. (2000) The Scheduled Castes: An Inter-Regional Perspective, in A. Beteille (ed.), *Journal of Indian School of Political Economy*, 12 (3 and 4): 367-80.

Byres, T.J., (ed.) (1998) *The State, Development Planning and Liberalisation in India.* New Delhi: Oxford University Press.

Chatterjee, P. (1993) *The Nation and its Fragments: Colonial and Post Colonial Histories*, Princeton: Princeton University Press.

Forbes, G. (1998) *Women in Modern India*. Cambridge: Cambridge University.

Gore, M.S. (1993) *The Social Context of an Ideology: Ambedkar's Political and Social Thought*. New Delhi: Sage Publications India Pvt. Ltd.

Government of India (1966) *Report of the Education Commission 1964-66: Education and National Development.* Delhi: Government of India.

Ilaiah, K. (1996) *Why I am not a Hindu: A Sudra Critique of Hindutva Philosophy, Culture and Political Economy*. Kolkata: Samya.

Karabel, J. and A.H. Halsey (1977) *Power and Ideology in Education.* Oxford: Oxford University Press.

Kaviraj, S. (2000) Democracy and Social Inequality in Frankel, F.R. and Others (eds.),

*Transforming India: Social and Political Dynamics of Democracy* pp. 89-119. New Delhi: Oxford University Press.

Kumar, Krishna (1991) *The Political Agenda of Education: A Study of Colonialist and Nationalist Ideas.* New Delhi: Sage Publications.

Kumar, K. (1996) Agricultural Modernisation and Education Contours of a Point of Departure. *Economic and Political Weekly*, Vol. 31(36), pp. 2367-2373.

McCarthy, Cameron (1988) Rethinking Liberal and Radical Perspectives on Racial Inequality in Schooling: Making the Case for Non-synchrony, in *Harvard Educational Review,* Vol. 58, No. 3, Aug. pp. 265-279.

NCERT, (2005) *Position Paper of National Focus Group on Problems of Scheduled Caste and Scheduled Tribe Children*. New Delhi: NCERT.

Naik, J.P. (1997) *The Education Commission and After.* New Delhi: A.P.H. Publishing Corporation.

Ogbu, J.U. (1978) *Minority Education and Caste: The American System in Cross-Cultural Perspective.* New York: Academic Press, Inc.

Sharma, B.D. (1994) *Dalits Betrayed.* New Delhi: Har-Anand Publications.

Shukla, S. (1997) Nationalist Educational Thought Continuity and Change. *Economic and Political Weekly*, Vol. 32, No. 29, pp. 1825-1831.

Velaskar, P. (1998) Ideology, Education and the Political Struggle for Liberation: Change and Challenge Among Maharashtra Dalits, in S. Shukla and R. Kaul (eds), *Education, Development and Underdevelopment.* New Delhi: Sage, pp. 210-40.

# 8

# Inclusion in Indian Education Policies: Revisiting Equality in the Kothari Commission Report

MADAN MOHAN JHA

## Introduction

The term "Inclusion" is an international buzzword in education and Indian education is no exception. This is ordinarily construed as bringing children with disabilities into mainstream schools[1] . However, internationally it endorses the concept of giving equal opportunity to *all* children in mainstream schools. The term was formally introduced at the UNESCO World Conference on Special Needs Education held in Spain (Salamanca) in 1994. Giving a sort of definition of inclusive schools, its Framework for Action (p. 11-12) stated:

> These inclusive schools...must recognize and respond to the diverse needs of their students, accommodating both different styles of learning and ensuring quality education to all, through appropriate curricula, organizational arrangements, teaching strategies, resource use and partnerships with their communities.

The conference further asked the nations to adopt, as a matter of law or policy, the principles of *inclusive education,* enrolling all children in regular schools unless there are compelling reasons for doing otherwise (UNESCO, 1994, Statement, p. ix). A plethora of literature has emerged recently, which looks at inclusive education as a systemic issue and expects schools to respond to diverse needs of child population, not confining to only children with special needs or those with disabilities. This calls for a total reform in schooling as argued by Ferguson (1996), Udavi-Solner (1996), Thomas *et al.* (1998), Ainscow, (1999) and Mittler (2000). In the heart of inclusion lies equal opportunity in education. The purpose of this paper is to revisit the Kothari Commission and examine the issue of equality as addressed in the report and ask the *key question:*

> How did the Education Commission Report, if at all, address the question of equality and inclusion in the Indian school system?

Analyzing a document written 40 years ago has to be done with some caution. The context and developments have to be taken into account. Hence, for a comparative study, while focusing on the EC (1964-66), the paper examines what had been stated 20 years earlier, when the post-war education development report was written by John Sargent in 1944, and how the policy developed later in the shape of the National Policies on Education in 1968 and 1986.

There is one more caveat. One chapter of the EC Report, titled[1] *Towards Equalization of Educational Opportunity* has been examined deeply with passing references to the connections elsewhere. Besides, the paper may be read keeping in view the author's 'bias' constructed due to the prevailing state of affairs in school education in the country that did not exist when the Report had been written. Unfortunately, the authors of the Report could not visualize the same. The question is, if they had been able to do so, would the EC Report have been different?

## Structure of the Paper

The paper begins with a description of the theoretical framework for analysis: Right Based Approach (RBA) against the Need Based Approach (NBA). After examining the issues of equality and inclusion in the context of RBA, the following major policy documents have been examined:

1. Post-war Education Development Report: or the Central Advisory Board of Education (CABE) Report of 1944—also known as the Sargent Report.
2. Education Commission (1964-66) Report (EC Report)—popularly known as the Kothari Commission Report (KCR).
3. National Policy on Education (NPE) 1986 (modified in 1992).

Notwithstanding the approach adopted in the policy documents, there has been a parallel build up for the RBA in the country, with the help of civil society, largely due to court interpretations and landmark judgments relating to education. After tracing these developments centered on the RBA, the paper examines the institutional framework, if any, suggested in the aforementioned policy documents. It concludes with the observation that while the school policy documents lay more emphasis on the programmes and projects as per the NBA, a slow but steady movement for systemic reforms in education backed by democratic movements and judicial pronouncements is building up.

## Framework for Analysis: RBA vs. NBA

The theoretical framework adopted by the author for analysis is the Right Based Approach (RBA) as against the Need Based Approach (NBA). Under NBA, the state decides children's need. It becomes the provider and children the receivers. There is a hierarchy in the relationship, more of bureaucracy and less of democracy. Under the RBA, the relationship that develops is out of demand and response, demand from the children and the parents and response from the state. It is built up around a dialogue that brings in more of equality. The outcome is more of democracy and less of bureaucracy.

While the NBA draws from the theme of help and benevolence to meet the "special needs" of different groups of children, the RBA is built up around entitlement, equality and social justice. The implications are a cry for a change in societal and institutional policies and attitudes. A sociological perspective provides a theoretical background to the rights discourse for marginalized groups to enable them to challenge the charity and benevolent approach against discrimination and segregation (Allan, 1999; Armstrong *et al.*, 2000; Lindsay, 2003). The 1980s and the 1990s saw a series of United Nations conventions and declarations that gave impetus to the rights discourse.

The RBA is an important political issue and as Fulcher (1999: 30) observes, "its themes are equality of citizenship and its strategy is one of confrontation and demand", unlike the NBA where marginalized children would become "grateful recipients" of the services, and "the issue of who benefits from these services is rarely made clear" (*Ibid*).

The RBA in the modern Western conception may be traced to the English Magna Carta, the US Declaration of Independence and the French Declaration of the Rights of Man and the Citizen. In the wake of the Holocaust, on December 10, 1948, the UN General Assembly proclaimed a Universal Declaration of Human Rights (UDHR), which included the right to "life, liberty and security of person", "freedom of movement", "nationality", "freedom of thought, conscience and religion", "freedom of peaceful association and assembly", and "freedom to take part in the government". The Indian concept of rights developed, during the freedom movement, with a demand for self-governance and total independence from the colonial rule. Education cuts across all the elements listed in the UDHR and becomes integral to achieving the goals of the declaration.

The following paragraphs examine how the issue of equality and inclusion has been examined in the three policy documents under the RBA or the NBA.

## Post-War Education Development Report (1944)

None of the documents, being discussed in the paper, has used the term "inclusion" or "inclusive education". It is understandable as the term got into educational vocabulary in the late 1980's and more liberally since the Salamanca Statement (UNESCO, 1994). Thomas and Vaughnan (2004: 89) trace the first use of the word inclusion in favour of integration by a group of people "concerned about the slow progress of integration" in the Canadian city of Toronto in July 1988, when they "came up with the concept of *inclusion* to describe better formally, the process of placing children and adults with disabilities or learning difficulties in the mainstream" (emphasis original).

Nevertheless, the Sargent Report is examined from the perspective of education for *all* children whether in a holistic sense or in a segregated or compartmentalized mode. In particular, how did it advocate education for children with disabilities since the term "inclusion" owes its origin to the disability movement? I have argued elsewhere that while inclusion in western countries may mean bringing children with disabilities from special schools to mainstream schools, since education in these countries is already inclusive of girls, the disadvantaged and ethnic groups, it would mean much more in the Indian context, where children are segregated into different types of schools. PROBE report has examined categories of schools. "In India, education has been largely an instrument for differentiation by separating children according to social classes" (Weiner, 1991: 6).

### *Basic Education: An Organic Whole*

The idea of giving eight years of education envisaged in the Constitution was diluted by programmes like the District Primary Education Programme (DPEP), which was designed only for five years of schooling. Notably, the Sargent Report was emphatic on keeping eight years of education as "organic whole". It stated:

Basic education from 6-14 is an organic whole and will lose much of its value, if not so treated; in any case an education, which lasts five years and ends about the age of eleven, cannot be regarded as an adequate preparation either for life or for livelihood (p. 3).

### *Education for All*

The report did advocate *education for all* or EFA now being attributed to the Jomtian Conference and linked the EFA goal with democracy, though the country was yet to become a democratic republic. It argued against divisive education. Quoting from the report:

The primary requisite for any system of public education for a democracy is that it should provide for *all* its members, and not for a few only, at least such training as may be necessary to make them reasonably good citizens (p. 7).

### *Education for the Disadvantaged*

The socially and economically disadvantaged community, for example, Scheduled Castes and Scheduled Tribes had not been identified and 'labeled' at that time. However, the report was conscious of the prevailing caste division in the country. It recognized the prevalence of the "communal and caste divisions" in "political and social life of India". It also realized that these divisions may "complicate the solution of purely educational problem".

However, the report addressed the issue of equality in a systemic sense when it argued:

> *A national system of education... will aim at satisfying impartially the needs of everybody. It is certainly intended that the educational provision contemplated in this report will cater* equally for all, *irrespective of the community or caste to which they may belong (emphasis added).*

### Education of Girls

The report adopted similar approach to education for girls and women. It realized that "in any modern community it [was] even more important for mothers to be educated than the fathers", and therefore, recommended that "whatever [was] needed for boys and men, will be required for girls and women".

### Education for Children with Disabilities

'The report seems to have been influenced by the developments in England at that time. The 1944 Education Act in England had made it mandatory for the local education authorities to provide "special educational treatment" to all those with disabilities of body and mind in special schools or elsewhere. The English Act was a major effort to move the disabled children from medical domination and give them special education in ordinary schools (Tomlinson, 1982; Barton and Tomlinson, 1984). Similarly, the Sargent Report recommended a "national scheme of education" for all children with considerations to be given to those...classed as "handicapped".

The report recommended for special schools, when "the nature and defect [of children] made it necessary"; otherwise, it stated, "wherever possible, handicapped children should not be segregated from normal children". The report made two other major recommendations. First, it recommended making education of the disabled "an essential part of a national system of education [to] be administered by the Education Department", and secondly, it wanted ten percent of the total expenditure on basic and high schools to be set aside for education of the "handicapped" (*Ibid*).

The report can be said to be progressive of its time in that it argued for integrated education and for making education of children with disabilities a part of the "national system of education" under the education ministry. This part of the recommendation is yet to be realized as the subject of "special education" comes within the purview of the Ministry of Social Justice and Empowerment. According to a UNESCO report, ninety five percent of the countries have removed systemic segregation of special education (UNESCO, 1995).

## Education Commission (1964-66)

The Education Commission Report does not mention "inclusion" or "rights" anywhere while there is a whole chapter (VI) titled "Towards Equalization of Educational Opportunity". Conceptual back up for equalization of educational opportunity is derived from deprivation and need of children. The opening sentence of the chapter says:

> One of the important social objectives of education is to equalize educational opportunity, enabling the backward or under-privileged classes and individuals to use education as a lever for improvement of *their* condition (emphasis added) (p. 108).

The subsequent paragraphs refer to the "ways" in which "the inequalities in educational opportunities arise" and go on to suggest remedies to overcome them. First, it identifies unavailability of schools in the neighborhood as a major factor for creating inequality in educational opportunity. To "overcome" this, the report recommends "the widest dispersal of educational institutions", "institution of an adequate scholarship programme", providing hostel facilities and transport arrangements. While nothing much seems to have been said about hostel and transport facilities[2], sufficient space (nine pages) has been devoted on scholarships. As regards the need for "the widest dispersal of educational institutions", a very elaborate exercise (ten pages) has been done on "regional imbalances". When it comes to the recommendations, it says: "A total elimination of these differences in educational development is neither possible nor desirable" (p. 135).

The report contains rhetoric of "equalization" and responsibility of the State to "make a deliberate policy of equalization of educational development in the different districts" but there is very little on "how" the same could be done. There is a recommendation for district based planning for removing unequal development of educational facilities, and the Chapter VI refers to another Chapter XVIII for a detailed proposal. One turns to the chapter referred to in the hope of some "techniques" and proposals on removing the imbalances but the opening section of this chapter says:

There has been an over-emphasis on achievement of targets in enrolments and expenditure. It is true that expansion was badly needed and expansion will have to continue. But an *over emphasis* on this aspect leads to the neglect of the still more important aspect of quality (p. 443). (emphasis added).

While the EC underplays the "over emphasis" on the "expansion" and stresses on the "aspect of quality", the Sargent Report talked about a "system of public education" in "a democracy" that would "provide for *all* its members, and not for a few only".

Secondly, poverty has been blamed for the cause of inequality as a result of which, the report says, poor children are not able to access education even if it is available in the neighbourhood. The solution has been suggested by way of "progressively" abolishing fees, and making provision for free books, stationary and "even school meals and uniforms". In addition, "a large programme of scholarship" has been recommended. As stated earlier, the programme for scholarship has been discussed at length in the report. The report has given adequate consideration to fees but its abolition even at the primary stage[3] has remained confined only to "tuition fees". It says:

> Even though 'compulsory' part of the [constitutional] directive may take about 20 years for realization, the 'free' part of it should be implemented without delay...all tuition fee at primary stage should be abolished as early as possible and preferably before the end of the Fourth Five-Year Plan (p. 111).

As regards universalisation of primary education, the EC recommendation is contrary to the "organic whole" approach of the Sargent Report. The EC recommended:

The constitutional directive of providing free and compulsory education...should be fulfilled in all parts of the country through the development of the following programmes:

1. Five years of good and effective education should be provided to all children by 1975-76.
2. Seven years of such education should be provided by 1985-86" (p. 632).

Thus for all those who would have completed five years of education before 1975-76, there was no guarantee that they would get enrolled in grade six for additional three years of schooling. Many parents may not send their children for a few years of education if they do not have facilities for higher grades of schooling. Thus, dropout was in-built in the education system and it was designed to fail.

The reason for reducing the eight years of education to seven years remains unexplained. It is also a reminder to those who critique the international agencies and the programmes launched with their support (e.g. DPEP, BEP) for diluting the agenda of the "organic whole" approach of the Sargent Report, subsequently mandated by the Constitution (see Sadgopal, 2003) for taking up only five years of basic education. The EC had already made up the ground for them.

Apart from abolition of tuition fees at the primary stage, the EC recommended distribution of free textbooks. The other hidden costs required to be compensated by the state for equalization of opportunity, though referred to in the EC, do not find a place in the list of recommendations.

The third factor outlined in the EC Report that creates inequality is the differences in the standards of schools and colleges. It realizes that when admissions are made on the basis of marks, the students attending ill-equipped schools, for example, those in rural areas are put into disadvantage. It does not, however, give any specific alternative, except making a rhetorical suggestion, "to evolve more reliable and egalitarian methods of selection, whether for admission to institutions or for award of scholarships" (p. 109).

Fourth, "home environments" have been regarded for contributing to "gross inequalities", and suggests a non-educational solution, "general improvement in the standard of living of the population". On the educational side, the Report refers to the "provision of day-study centres or boarding houses".

The EC identified "two other forms of educational inequality" which it says is "peculiar to the Indian situation": "disparity between boys and girls" and "the educational development between the advanced classes and the backward ones—the Schedules Castes and the Schedules Tribes".

Before outlining the policies on reducing inequality in the next twenty years, the EC made a prophetic statement of despair:

> Like all ideals in life, perfect equality of educational opportunity is probably unattainable...the essence of the problem is not attainment of goal, but an impassioned faith and earnest striving...there should be a continuous attempt to identify factors which tend to create significant forms of inequality and identify measures either to eliminate them altogether or at least reduce them to the minimum (p. 109).

### *Education of Girls*

The EC has adopted a feminine, stereotyped and discriminatory approach to address the issue of inequality in the case of education of girls. For example, it says, the "significance of the education of girls" is for "improvement of homes, and for moulding the character of children". Furthermore, "the education of women can assist greatly in reduction in fertility rate". However, to be true to the EC, it notes that women are now adopting a career of their own and sharing equally with men the responsibility for the development of society in all its aspects (p. 135). While arguing for special programmes for women's education it recommended giving "attention to education of girls at all stages and in all sectors as an integral part of the general programmes for the expansion and improvement of education" (p. 138).

### *Education of the Disadvantaged*

While referring to the education of children from "backward classes", EC has listed only two groups: Scheduled Castes and Scheduled Tribes.

The Scheduled Castes have been disposed of in one small paragraph by making a statement but without giving any evidence: "the problem [of reducing inequality with regard to the Scheduled Castes] has become a little easier because of the diminution of the rigor of untouchability". The report, nevertheless, recommended that "existing programmes for the education of the Scheduled Castes should continue and be expanded" (p. 139).

While the education of the Scheduled Tribes has been discussed in the KCR under the heading "the problem", there is no heading of "recommendations" as in other cases. The chapter ends with a proclamation:

> "The education of the backward classes in general and of the tribal people in particular is a major programme of equalization and of social and national integration" (p. 143).

### *Education of Children with Disabilities*

The EC observed that "the education of the handicapped children should be an inseparable part of the general education system"; that "the methods employed to teach the child and the means used to acquire information" should not "influence the content or goals of education" (p. 123). It also noted that the constitutional directive on compulsory education under Article 45 included handicapped children as well. The initial premise seems to be drawn from the inclusive approach built up on the RBA. However, the contradiction in the approach can be easily noticed as it called for "their education" to be "organized not merely on humanitarian grounds, but also on grounds of utility" (*Ibid*). Such an ambivalent approach can be seen in other parts of the report also. For example, it recommended that only 10 per cent of the children should be covered by 1986; and that the disabled children might "find it psychologically disturbing to be placed in an ordinary school" (*Ibid*).

Drawing upon the report, the 1968 national policy made a commitment to make "attempts" "...to develop integrated programmes enabling the handicapped children to study in regular schools" (MHRD, 1998). After eight years of the policy announcement, the central government launched a programme named 'Integrated Education for the Disabled Children' (IEDC) in 1974 (MHRD, 1992).

In yet another section of the Report on "teaching methods, guidance and evaluation", it defined educational "backwardness" as due to two overlapping reasons: first, "mental handicap or low intelligence, arising from hereditary or congenital factors or disease or injury; and secondly, underachievement ...due to...emotional conflict...cultural deprivation and economic handicaps" (p. 242). The NBA, therefore, is very much evident in the EC Report. It further divided "mentally handicapped" into four groups of "the idiots, the imbeciles, the educable mentally handicapped morons and the dull or slow learners", the terms having been discontinued in England since 1945 (see Tomlinson, 1982). It observed that these children "are unable to profit from normal education. The result is wastage of educational facilities and of human resources, neither of which a developing country can afford" (p. 242).

Thus, the EC, otherwise very popular and most frequently referred to for any progressive ideas in post-Independent educational development, took special education in the country twenty years backwards, undid what the Sargent Report had achieved and set up the tone of a discourse on "their" education which is still reverberating in Indian policies.

## National Policy on Education 1986/1992

The NPE 1986/92 has a chapter on "education for equality". It does not refer to "rights" and is based largely on the NBA. It declares:

> The new policy will lay special emphasis on the removal of disparities and to equalise educational opportunity by attending to the specific *needs* of those who have been denied so far (MHRD, 1998: 7) (emphasis added).

With these introductory remarks, the policy goes on listing the 'needs' of different groups of recipients: women, Scheduled Castes, Scheduled Tribes, educationally backward sections and areas, minorities and the handicapped.

"Education for women's equality" section is full of rhetoric: "Education will be used as an agent of basic change in the status of women...the policy of nondiscrimination will be pursued vigorously to eliminate sex stereotyping."

For other sections, however, actionable steps have been suggested, for example, scholarships, hostels, location of school buildings, etc.

Minorities have figured in for the first time in the policy document. As in the case of women, rhetoric has been used in the case of minorities also: "Some minority groups are educationally deprived or backward. Greater attention will be paid to the education of these groups in the interests of equality and social justice...all possible measures will be taken to promote an integration based on appreciation of common goals and ideals, in conformity [with] the core curriculum."

Listing of programmes and incentives, however, have been done in the Programme of Action 1986/92. The education of children with disabilities has been examined especially because in a segregated education system 'they' are the most marginalized and vulnerable group. This is the only group which had been extensively dealt in both the Sargent and Kothari Commission Reports.

### *Education of Children with Disabilities*

The policy states: "wherever it is feasible, the education of children with motor handicaps and other mild handicaps will be common with that of others". Further, the policy encourages "voluntary effort for the education of the disabled" and opening of special schools with hostels for "severely handicapped children". It recommends the "reorientation" of the teacher training programme, particularly for the primary teachers, and arrangements to be made for the vocational training to the "disabled".

The policy did not address any substantive or systemic issues to achieve its stated objective of "education for equality". This is reflected later in the review report of the Ramamurti Committee (MHRD, 1990) and the comments of Jangira (1997). The committee observed that education for the "handicapped" is being regarded as a "social welfare" activity; "special schools have been treated in isolation from other educational institutions" and the IEDC scheme is run as "mini special schools" (MHRD, 1990: 85). The modified policy in 1992 did *not* take any note of the observations and recommendations of the review committee and the policy on education for the "handicapped" remained unchanged. Jangira (1997: 496) finds the policy "hesitant in full commitment to universalisation of elementary education for this group of children" and it also remained "silent on the department of education assuming full responsibility for education of children with disabilities".

Thus, though the 1986/92 policies were not as pessimistic as the 1966 commission report, the education of the children with disabilities continued to remain on the fringe, isolated from the mainstream education.

## Institutional Framework for Realisation of RBA

School provides an institutional framework for realization of the right to education. The school, as an institution, is the product of the industrial era. While the need for mass education to respond to the industrial era remained confined to basic literacy and numeracy for the masses, schooling for enhancing life chances remained confined to a select few even in the West. For example, in England until the 1960's children were sorted and selected at the age of eleven.

India had "indigenous schools" spread over thousands of villages in the nineteenth century that produced "professionals" required during that period (DiBona, 1983). However, locally relevant education was meant for the masses in Pathashalas; the select few belonging mainly to the Brahmins went in for scholarly Sanskrit education in the Gurukuls. A great debate in Indian education began at that time between the occidentals, supporting a Western style education and the orientalists, favouring an education system based on Indian values and cultures. The debate ended with the famous minute of Macaulay on February 2, 1835 intending to create "a class of persons, Indian in blood and colour, but English in tastes, in opinions, in morals and in intellect" (cited in Fagg, 2002: 19). Over the years, the system became "hierarchical and elitist, top heavy with higher education at the expense of primary education" (Steele and Taylor, 1994 cited in Fagg, 2002: 34).

I would argue that two major institutional frameworks in the background of the RBA was Gandhi's Basic Education (1937) and the Common School System (CSS) recommended in the EC Report.

## Gandhi's Basic Education

Gandhi's Basic Education was the first official policy and a home grown model of schooling in India aimed "to change the established [hierarchical] structure of opportunities for education" (Kumar, 1994: 508). Talk of "basic education" and what comes to mind? It was "contemporary not modern, ideal not practical, and it might have achieved limited success but ultimately failed" (Jha, 2002 a). Fagg (2002) has contested these perceptions in his study based on the primary sources on Basic Education; he says that the education system unveiled by Gandhi in 1937 influenced government policy for the next thirty years until the KCR replaced it by "work education" as a subject for study in Indian schools.

The EC, however, came up with yet another institutional framework and called it the Common School System (CSS) discussed in the following section.

## The CSS in EC Report

The EC coined the term 'Common School System' for the first time. While in England, the "comprehensive struggles" had a larger objective of ending "two nations in education" divided by grammar and secondary modern schooling (Tomlinson, 2001: 14), in India the Common School System was part of a report to improve school administration and remove the 'caste' system in school management and reduce the bureaucratic control.

There is one section in Chapter X on "school education, administration and supervision" that suggests the *right based approach*. For equal opportunity, the CSS introduced the concept of neighbourhood schools. The report said, "each school should be attended by *all* children in the neighbourhood irrespective of caste, creed, community, religion, economic condition or social status, so that there would be no segregation in schools" (p. 257, emphasis original). If the report were to be written today one would have expected terms like disability and special needs to be included in the "all". Arguing for the neighbourhood school, the EC advanced two arguments:

[First], a neighbourhood school will provide 'good' education to children because sharing life with common people is...an essential ingredient of good education. Secondly, the establishment of such schools will compel rich, privileged and powerful classes to take an interest in the system of public education and thereby bring about its early improvement (p. 257).

The developments in school education during the post-Kothari period demonstrate that the "rich, privileged and powerful classes" did not "take an interest in the system of public education" to bring about any improvement in it. The growth of private schools at the cost of public education (or government schools) in recent years confirms the theory given by Archer (1979): "education has the characteristics it does because of the goals pursued by those who control it" (p. 2).

The 1968 National Policy on Education accepted the EC Report that targeted the implementation of the neighbourhood school concept within twenty years. After about twenty years in 1986 the new policy maintained the rhetoric of the CSS but abandoned it in reality, as would be evident from the discussion in the following paragraphs.

## CSS in the NPE 1986/92

The NPE 1992 is a modified version of the original policy announced in 1986. Though the CSS was introduced in the EC Report as a part of school management, the 1968 national policy treated it as "education for equality". The 1986 policy, however, shifted the CSS from the "education for equality" chapter to the "national system of education". It stated:

> The concept of a National System of Education implies that up to a given level, all students, irrespective of caste, creed, location or sex, have access to education of comparable quality (MHRD, 1998: 5).

The EC, however, had recommended the neighbourhood school concept for all children irrespective of caste, creed, community, religion, *economic conditions and social status* (p. 257). The 1986 policy dropped the phrase "economic conditions and social status".

Further, the 1986 policy also assured to take "effective measures" to implement the CSS. The Programme of Action 1992, meant to implement the policy, made *no mention* of the Common School System (MHRD, 1996). Thus, dilution of the commitment on "education for equality" coincided with the direction in the Indian economy towards privatization, and at the international level, with the rhetoric of "education for all" from the Jomtien Conference of 1990.

In 1990, the government set up the Ramamurti Committee (1990)[4] to review the 1986 policy. The committee outlined the reasons for the CSS not gaining the ground: low investment in government schools because elites and privileged class were not sending their children, lack of political will, craze for English medium (private) schools, and growth of institutions like central schools for specified categories of children. The committee expanded and extended the scope of the CSS as a "first step in securing equity and social justice". It recommended that the CSS be extended to private schools and selection of children by these schools even at the primary stage be dispensed with. These recommendations, based upon the RBA, had potential to change the face of school education system in the country and remove increasing disparities in the access to the school. But none of them were incorporated in the modified policy of 1992.

The CABE committee on policy (MHRD, 1992) while reviewing the Ramamurti Committee report expected the "privileged schools" to accept "social responsibility by sharing their facilities and resources with other institutions and facilitating access to children of the disadvantaged groups" (MHRD, 1992: 16). There is a "fall out of this policy—private schools running 'centres' for the 'underprivileged' in the afternoon", thereby "doing excellence in the forenoon and equity in the afternoon"[5] (Jha, 2004). Skrtic (1991:233) had argued, "the successful schools in the post-industrial era will be the ones that achieve excellence and equity simultaneously—indeed one that recognizes equity as the way to excellence".

## Advocacy for the RBA Outside Policy

Though the policies have sidelined the systemic issues under the RBA and have concentrated on educational programmes and projects in a differentiated manner, there has been a series of developments—pre-and post-Independence—outside the policies, which have adopted the RBA towards education.

The first attempt to regard elementary education as a matter of right, though obliquely, was made way back in 1909 when Gokhale introduced a Bill under the Indian Council Act of 1909 to make it compulsory under the state funding. However, the Bill fell through by a large majority. While addressing the legislatures, Gokhale made an emotional observation that the issue would keep coming again and again until all children realized their right to free and compulsory education.

In 1950, the country got its own Constitution, which provided Fundamental Rights to equality, to freedom, against exploitation, to freedom of religion, to constitutional remedies and cultural and educational rights. However, the right to free and compulsory education was retained in Part IV of the Constitution that incorporated Directive Principles of State Policy. Article 45 of the Constitution read:

> The state shall endeavour to provide, within a period of ten years from the commencement of this Constitution, for free and compulsory education for all children until they complete the age of fourteen years.

The distinction between Fundamental Rights and Directive Principles of State Policy is well settled under the Indian Constitution. While the former is absolute and legally enforceable the latter is a policy directive to the state.

The 1980s and the 1990s saw liberal interpretations of Article 21 of the Indian Constitution by the Indian judiciary that extended right to life and security to a series of issues required for enhancing life chances for common people. More importantly, it declared the right to basic education 'fundamental' as defined under Chapter III of the Constitution. The court ruled that Article 45 of the Directive Principles of State Policy must be read in harmonious conjunction with Article 21, since the right to life and personal liberty loses its meaning if a child is deprived of elementary education (Unnikrishnan v. State of AP., A. 1993 SC. 217). In addition to making the right to free and compulsory education as good as a fundamental right, the Unnikrishnan judgment ruled against commercialization of education also; economic and financial constrains could be a ground for restricting the state from making provisions of post-basic and higher education, but *not* for elementary education.

The Unnikrishnan judgment activated several civil society groups to demand incorporation of right to education as a Fundamental Right in Part III of the Constitution. The government finally agreed to bring a new FR marked 21A in December 2002, which reads:

> The State shall provide free and compulsory education to all children of the age 6 to 14 years in such manner as the state may, by *law*, determine.[6]

Notably, the amendment was rightly introduced after Article 21, keeping in view the spirit of interpretation of this article by the Supreme Court of India.

Many activists have criticized the amendment for two reasons. First, it is argued that 21A gives power to the state to decide 'manner' for providing 'free and compulsory education'. Secondly, it restricts the 'right' to the age group 6-14, unlike the original Article 45 of the Directive Principle of State Policy, which referred to 'all children until they complete age 14' (see Sadgopal, 2003, 2004).

Many legal luminaries and educationists in the country, however, have emphasized the wide ramifications of right to education. For example, Justice J.S. Verma, former Chief Justice of India and also former Chairman of the National Human Rights Commission, observes that providing free elementary education is an "essential sovereign function" of the welfare state[7].

Justice (Retd.) V.R. Krishna Iyer wrote recently: "Education is a cardinal component of human dignity and, therefore, the basic structure of the Constitution...the right to education derives an ideational activism, which judicial construction cannot...jettison based on the subconscious impact of the dubious mantra of privatization (*The Hindu*, 26 November, 2005, p. 11).

The expert group set up by the Government of India after the Unnikrishan judgment chose the Right Based Approach to elementary education. As the report said:

> From being an incremental developmental goal in the process of education for all, UEE [Universalisation of Elementary Education] has, in consequence of the [Unnikrishnan] judgment, now become a justiciable entitlement of every Indian child... entitlements sanctioned by the Constitution cannot be deferred by the State at its convenience. The State has to make the necessary reallocation of resources, by superseding other important claims, if necessary, in a manner that the justiciable entitlement can become a reality.

As regards the criticism on restrictive age group of 6-14 in Article 21A, it is argued that since Article 21 has *not* been amended, the scope of Unnikrishnan judgment remains intact, with a possibility of modification through Article 21A by reinforcing the right of children in the age group of 6-14 years. To clarify the point further it may be noted that education of children below six years of age qualifies to be accepted as a fundamental right, notwithstanding Article 21A.

As regards the perception that introduction of the phrase "in such manner as the state may, by *law,* determine", would give unfettered power to the government to control or dilute the scope of elementary education for all children, it is argued that Article 13 (2) bars the state from taking away or abridging any right contained in Part III of the Constitution. Furthermore, the Supreme Court in the same judgment ruled that, after the age of fourteen years, the Fundamental Right to education continues to exist but is "subject to limits of economic capacity and development of the State" as per Article 41. In other words, even finances cannot be made an excuse for not providing free and elementary education to all children. This aspect comes into picture only when we go beyond the ambit of fundamental rights. The essential sovereign duty of the state is to secure "equality of status and opportunity"; "the dignity of individual" and social justice laid down in the preamble of the Constitution, is likewise not limited by the financial capacity of the state[8].

By implication, legislative operationalisation of Article 21A does not give a free hand to the state, and it is fair to expect that the law made in this regard would only extend the right further rather than restrict it.

The introduction of a new Article 21A in the Constitution provides a renewed opportunity to reduce the increasing inequality in education at the elementary level and achieve the goals of justice—social, economic and political—as pledged in the preamble. However, the import of this new fundamental right is yet to sink in the minds of policymakers and academics, or appear on the agenda of genuine social and political activists. Firstly, it is a new right yet to be demanded from and enforced by the state. Secondly, while the original fundamental rights affect most of us on a day-to-day basis and they have become integral to our milieu, the right to "free and compulsory education" does not affect us, as all those who matter can afford to pay for private education for their children. Hence the fundamental right to free education of children of ages 6-14 as given by Article 21A since December 2002, is yet to acquire the stature of other fundamental rights.

No wonder, those who drafted the recent report of the CABE (Central Advisory Board of Education) committee on the free and compulsory education bill argued: "Right to education which Article 21A seeks to confer is different from other fundamental rights...while the earlier fundamental rights had no or insignificant financial implications for the state, the Right to Education has major financial implications... ." It is argued that such artificial classification and hierarchy in fundamental rights is the product of the gaps in the class characteristics of those who control education and those who are being deprived of the equal opportunity.

Also, who can deny that the state is not spending huge amounts on police and higher judiciary to protect citizens' right to life and liberty, and equality before law? Therefore, the argument of "financial implications" and treating this right as lower in status to other rights is flawed. Thus, I would argue that as police is largely to guarantee the fundamental right on protection of life, and judiciary is meant to secure justice and equality before law, schools and teachers need to be regarded as a guarantee of right to elementary education. This guarantee seems possible only within the framework of common schools. Extension of this argument would mean less and less scope for fee charging private schools, as all children including those who opt for private schools have right for free education. It is argued that many parents go to private schools because of the absence or deficient functioning of the government schools in the neighbourhood.

## Growth of Exclusive Schools

The non-inclusive characteristics of the policies with the need-based approach have resulted in proliferation of exclusive private schools. Educational institutions in India need to be "not-for-profit" for the purpose of recognition and affiliation from the government and government bodies. However, there is no law that would ban opening of institutions, which intend to remain "unrecognized", or run like a private sector company for educational training and preparing learning materials, including text books. This explains the mushrooming of teaching shops and coaching centres in the country.

Article 19 of the Indian Constitution guarantees the right "to practice any profession, or to carry on any occupation, trade or business". In a recent court verdict[9], this provision was interpreted liberally to allow "all citizens to establish educational institutions of their *choice*" (Kumar, 2003: 5164, emphasis added). The judgment, according to Kumar (2003) provides "liberal scope of private initiative" *(Ibid)* in education, including opening of schools. The question of choice is in direct conflict with the equity issue as the choice is not uniformly available to the heterogeneous Indian society with heterogeneity and gaps being reflected in a variety of aspects such as: social, economic, gender and "special needs". Private schools are contributing to the social and economic divide by "perpetuating inequalities" in education (Panchmukhi, 1983; Tilak and Sudarshan 2001). According to Sadgopal (2000) it is a consequence of the policy failure on the part of the state.

The equity issue has acquired more importance since the insertion of "right to education" as a Fundamental Right in the Constitution and the onus on the state to provide "free and compulsory education" under Article 21A. It is argued that in the light of this article, any school following the state curriculum and public examination cannot charge fees from the 6-14 age group children. This restriction would apply to the private schools also as they function, in this regard, as an *instrumentality* of the state[10]. The Supreme Court of India in earlier verdicts has observed that any agency discharging state function as its "instrumentality" is bound by the constitutional provision.

## Conclusion

It is thus seen that while there is a strong foundation for rights and equity in the Constitution, at least at the elementary stage, there is very little appreciation in the policy making to address this question. The approach of the policies is not in principle with the rights perspective and inclusiveness; it has fragmented programmes and projects that treat children into different groups as objects. The decisions are passed on to those who have power and control over destiny of "others".

## Notes

1. Human Resource Development Minister, while announcing the policy on inclusive education in the parliament, stated: "The need for inclusive education arises precisely because it is now well understood that most children with disabilities can, with motivation and effort on the part of teaching institutions, become an integral part of those institutions".
2. However, there is a reference to schools in rural areas, which provided cycles to students coming from a distance, and a passing recommendation has been made to extend this facility.
3. Primary in the KCR refers to seven or eight years of schooling (p. 29).

4. The Congress government in 1986 had announced the NPE. In 1990, the non-congress government set up the Ramamurti Committee to review the policy, but by the time the committee submitted its report, the Congress came back to power in 1992.
5. Many urban private schools in Delhi run learning centres in the afternoon for the disadvantaged as a charity.
6. The Constitution (86th Amendment) Act 2002 (emphasis original).
7. Observation made at the national convention on the Right to Education Bill 2005 organised by the People's Campaign for the Common School System in New Delhi on December 9, 2005.
8. Observed by Justice Verma at the above convention.
9. Supreme Court: TMA Pai Foundation vs State of Karnataka (2002).
10. A submission was made on behalf of the Public Study Group—a Delhi based group of academics and activists before the CABE meeting on July 14, 2005 to reconsider a draft bill on the 'right to education' on this ground. The bill is under consultation at the time of writing.

## References

Ainscow, M. (1999) *Understanding the Development of Inclusive Schools*. London: Falmer.

Allan, J. (1999) *Actively Seeking Inclusion: Pupils with Special Needs in Mainstream Schools*. London: Falmer.

Archer, M.S. (1979) *Social Origins of Educational Systems*. London: Sage.

Armstrong, D., Armstrong, F., and Barton, L. (2000) Introduction: what is this book about? In Armstrong, F., Armstrong, D. and Barton, L. (eds.), *Inclusive Education: Policy, Contexts and Comparative Perspectives*. London: Fulton.

DiBona, J. (ed) (1983) *One Teacher, One School: The Adams Report on Indigenous Education in 19th Century India.* New Delhi: Biblia Index.

Fagg, H. (2002) *Back to Sources: A Study of Gandhi's Basic Education*. New Delhi: National Book Trust.

Ferguson, D.L. (1996) Is it inclusion yet? bursting the bubbles. In Berres, M.S., Ferguson, D.L., Knowblock, P. and Woods, C. (eds.) *Creating Tomorrow's Schools Today*. New York: Teachers' College, Columbia University.

Fulcher, G. (1999) *Disabling Policies? A Comparative Approach to Education Policy and Disability.* Sheffield: Philip Armstrong

Jangira, N.K. (1997) Special education,. In *Fifth Survey of Educational Research 1988: Trend Report*, Vol. 1, New Delhi: NCERT.

Jha, M.M. (2004) Too many nations in education. In *The Indian Express*, New Delhi: November 4.

Kumar, K. (2003) Judicial ambivalence and new politics of education. In *Economic and Political Weekly*, 6, December, 5163-5166.

Lindsay, G. (2003) Inclusive education: a critical perspective. In *British Journal of Special Education*, 30(1) 3-12.

Mittler, P. (2000) *Working Towards Inclusive Education: Social Context*. London: Fulton.

Ministry of Human Resource Development (MHRD) (1990) *Towards an Enlightened and Humane Society: NPE 1986—A Review*. New Delhi: Government of India.

Ministry of Human Resource Development (MHRD) (1992) *Report of the CABE Committee on Policy*. New Delhi: Government of India.

Ministry of Human Resource Development (MHRD) (1992a) *Scheme of Integrated Education for the Disabled Children.* New Delhi: Government of India.

Ministry of Human Resource Development (MHRD) (1996) *National Policy of Education 1986: Programme of Action 1992*. New Delhi: Government of India.

Ministry of Human Resource Development (MHRD) (1998) *National Policy on Education (As modified in 1992) with National Policy on Education, 1968*. New Delhi: Government of India.

Panchmukhi, P.R. (1983) India: a century of effort. In Simmons, J. (ed) *Better Schools: International Lessons from Reform*. New York: Praeger.

Sadgoplal, A. (2000) *Siksha mein Badlaw ka Sawal: Samajik Anubhawon se Niti Tak (A Question of Educational Change: From Social Experiences to the Policy)* Delhi: Granth Silpi.

Sadgoplal, A. (2003) Exclusion and inequality in education: the state policy and globalization. In *Contemporary India*, Journal of the Nehru Memorial Museum and Library, 2 (3).

Sadgopal, A. (2004) *Globalization and Education: Defining the Indian Crisis.* New Delhi: Zakir Husain College.

Skrtic, T.M. (1991) *Behind Special Education: A Critical Analysis of Professional Culture and School Organisation.* Denver: Love Publishing.

Thomas, G. and Vaughan, M. (2004), *Inclusive Education: Readings and Reflections*. Berkshire: Open University Press.

Thomas, G., Walker, D. and Webb, J. (1998) *The Making of the Inclusive School.* London: Routledge.

Tilak, B.G. and Sudarshan, R.M. (2001) *Private Schooling in Rural India.* New Delhi: National Council of Applied Economic Research.

Udvari-Solner, A. (1996) Theoretical influences on the establishment of inclusive practices. In *Cambridge Journal of Education*, 26 (1) 101-119.

UNESCO (1994) *The Salamanca Statement and Framework for Action on Special Needs Education.* Paris: UNESCO

UNESCO (1995) *Review of Present Situations in Special Needs Education*. Paris: UNESCO

Weiner, M. (1991) *The Child and the State in India.* New Jersey: Princeton University Press.

# 9

# The Education Commission's Vision on Inclusive Education: Beginning of a Long Journey

SUDESH MUKHOPADHYAY

## Introduction

The Education Commission's Vision on Inclusive Education can be interpreted in two ways—it can be what Nobel Laureate Herbert Simon observed in 1981, "*Each of us sits in a long dark hall within a circle of light cast by a small lamp. The lamplight penetrates a few feet up and down the hall, then rapidly attenuates, diluted by the vast darkness of future and past that surrounds it*" (p. 178). The second way is to look at it with the eyes of Miyamoto Musashi, who observed that *the journey of a thousand miles begins with one step*[1]. My analysis tends to capture both the views. Some important developments in the early years of Independent India made the Education Commision a landmark commission and its vision on inclusive education as the foundation stone of the recent developments. These developments, on the one hand give a context to what this Commission thought, visualised and dreamt. They also give a context to the recommendations made that, today, may appear as light cast by a small lamp. The vision for inclusion may have been limited due to vast darkness of future and past that surrounded it but looking back after forty years, it proves to be that first important step on the long journey.

## Contexts of Inclusion in the1960s

India has its own history, traditions and practices that evolved over centuries. India has been an inclusive society. From the eighteenth century onwards, considerable awareness started building up in many Western countries about the pragmatism of imparting regular education and training to the blind and the deaf. India also witnessed some developments on this account, but more attention was paid to persons with visual impairments. Miles (2001) has prepared the Datelines for Education & Welfare of Blind People in South Asia. A few examples have been cited in the Table 9.1. It is noteworthy that inclusion was part of the society even in those times. Secondly, development also included enabling conditions and the role of NGOs always remained central to these developments.

**Table 9.1: Datelines for Education and Welfare of Blind People in India**

| | |
|---|---|
| 1891 | Mr. Suvisashamuttu, a blind young man taught by Jane Askwith, starts teaching sighted children at Ootacamund. |
| 1901 | Report by S.V. Ramaswami Iyengar on ophthalmic study of 4,300 schoolboys in various parts of India, among whom 48% have impaired vision. |
| 1923 | First All-India Conference of Workers for the Blind & Deaf is held at Bombay. |
| 1943 | Uniform Indian Braille code devised by expert committee. |
| 1952 | National Association for the Blind established in India. |

*Source*: Miles, M. (2001).

It is difficult to draw any concrete conclusions about the systemic provisions before the British period as India has many sub-systems. However, it must be squarely accepted that social security systems, well organized and widespread in the developed countries, remained very rudimentary in India and many developing nations. Till recently, India had no organized social security against such needs as unemployment, destitution, disability and old age. Social security measures are a post-independence phenomenon in India, where traditionally the joint-family system has taken care of the unemployed youth, the elderly person and the disabled, and continues to do so (Narasimhan and Mukherjee 1990). But the middle of ninteenth century witnessed many activities across the globe that may have been the result and necessity of the post-war reconstruction processes.

In 1945 the League of Nations adopted the Universal Declaration of Human Rights. In the field of education, Article 26 of the Declaration proclaims the right of every citizen to an appropriate education, regardless of gender, race, colour and religion. This right is also enshrined in the constitutions of all independent nations. The question is: To what extent are national governments guaranteeing the right of "every" citizen to an "appropriate" education as we approach the new millennium? What measures are in place at the national and local levels to address imbalances in education? (Kisanji 1999) The call for inclusive education is the outcome of a complex set of discourses about equality of education, driven by changing demographics, ideologies, and perceptions of groups as well as by social issues. The legal beginnings of inclusion began when educational institutions responded to the Civil Right's Movement in the 1950s and 1960s, a time of reform and the public joining forces to gain identity and respect. The landmark case, Brown vs. the Board of Education of Topeka, Kansas, entailed that "separate was not equal". This set a legal precedent in establishing education as a right that must be available to all on equal terms (Winzer and Kas 2000: 28). For India, this came only in 2005 through the 93rd Constitutional Amendment.

The concepts of social inclusion and exclusion are used in many debates on injustice and inequality. These concepts have found their way into the mainstream discussions of education policy through the influence and experience of the disabled people's movements and "special needs schools". ...Yet there are a number of concerns about the efforts to increase social inclusion. Social inclusion and exclusion are thought of in various ways reflecting the different experiences and local contexts out of which a demand for more inclusion stems and resulting in a different set of policy approaches and priorities. Since the 1950s there has been increasing dissatisfaction amongst educators in many countries with the practice of "special education" which separates so-called "disabled" or "different" children from the rest of the society and educates them in different schools. Special education is seen as simply reinforcing problematic inequalities and exclusion. When thinking about social inclusion in education and developing policy to aid it, it is necessary to consider the highly complex ways in which race, class, gender and other categories intersect and inter-relate to produce unique individual and group experiences (Sayed 2005).

In the history of education, the growth of the facilities for the handicapped is linked with the education provision for normal children. The trend has been to make adequate provisions for the normal children first and then provisions for the handicapped children or for the deprived ones (Mukhopdhyay 1984). This statement holds true for the developments in nearly all countries. The state of facilities provided depends upon the attitude of the society at large towards the handicapped children. In ancient Indian literature, one does come across examples like *Surdas,* whose poetry is still held in high esteem. It can be inferred that he must have been able to write or was "educated" enough and facilitated by the oral tradition of learning. It can further be implied that, may be, the society was not alien to handicaps. Yet it is difficult to comment, especially in the absence of appropriate evidence. Though India claims to have deep-rooted traditions of education, the documented history can be traced to the British period, especially the year 1813, when education was made the responsibility of the "employer" or "ruler". This period runs parallel to the movement in the West for mass education. In the context of present writing, it will not be appropriate to trace the general history of education in India, yet it needs to be emphasized that the priority in development was not mass education but getting suitably qualified people to run the ruling machinery.

The first official attempt to analyze the problem of educating the "handicapped" was made in the report of the Central Advisory Board of Education (CABE) in 1944 (Sargent 1968). The report recommended special schools when "the nature and defect [of children] made it necessary"; otherwise, it recommended that "wherever possible, handicapped children should not be segregated from normal children" (CABE 1944). The report made two other major recommendations. *First, it asked for making education of the disabled "an essential part of a national system of education [to] be administered by the Education Department", and secondly, it wanted ten per cent of the total expenditure on basic and high schools to be set aside for education of the "handicapped".* The report was progressive of its time. Though it was under the influence of defects-in-children theory, it argued for integrated education and for making the education of children with disabilities a part of the "national system of education under the education ministry, an objective yet to be realized" (Jha 2004).

The Secondary Education Commission, also known as the Mudaliar Commission, submitted its report in the year 1952-53 (GOI 1953). This Commission made specific recommendations for schools for the handicapped.

**Box 9.1**
**Provisions under the Secondary Education Commission, 1952-53**

There should be a few schools in each State for such children where methods especially suited to their needs may be adopted. This is also necessary in the interest of the smooth progress of normal children.

We also note with pleasure that Government of India has taken special steps to evolve a common Braille Code for use in all schools of the blind. These schools must, of necessity, be residential where the pupils can be kept for a number of years till they are fit to take up some useful occupation. The number of such schools needs to be considerably increased if they are to cater to this unfortunate class of children.

The commission also referred to open-air special schools for children suffering from Tuberculosis or grave physical deformity where side-by-side medical treatment can also be provided.

Compared to the reporting of the Sargent Plan (1944) it is clear that during this period of about 10 years, the country embarked on the establishment of special schools for handicapped children. This need was extended to children suffering from contagious diseases like T.B. and Leprosy, which are usually not mentioned in the Western literature. Compared to the provision for normal children, the provision for handicapped children was far behind the requirement. This can be explained by referring to Five Year Plans[2].

- First Five Year Plan, 1951, emphasised the need for detection and prevention of the incidences of handicapping conditions; however, the initiative and work was left to voluntary efforts.
- Second Five Year Plan, 1956, provided for additional facilities, such as model schools for blind children, deaf children and women's section in training schools for the adult blind, and provision for scholarship, etc. The Government started taking some steps for the education and training of handicapped persons, though the voluntary organisations continued to occupy an important place.

- The Third Five Year Plan, 1961, covered education of the handicapped under "Education" and recommended: "The National Centre for the Blind will be strengthened and a National Braille Library started; A training centre for the adult deaf and a school for the mentally deficient children will be established; The Scheme of Scholarship under which assistance is given to higher education, technical and professional education to the handicapped children will be further extended; Emphasis will be laid on the development of services for the handicapped through voluntary agencies and on the provision of special employment exchanges for the physically handicapped" (p. 598).

If one looks at the development in the pre-Kothari commission period, it is easy to discern that though socially an inclusive society, India had not given much thought to the systemic interventions and provisions. Secondly, emotional and sympathy orientation was much stronger than the political or human resource approach. *India was yet nowhere near the human right orientation. But before one takes any logical stand on the issue, it is also important to understand the education levels in general and the challenges that were faced by the largest (but just a 15-year old) democracy. Table 9.2 speaks volumes on the issue:*

**Table 9.2: Literacy Rates in India**

| Year | Persons | Males | Females |
|---|---|---|---|
| 1901 | 5.35 | 9.83 | 0.60 |
| 1911 | 5.92 | 10.56 | 1.05 |
| 1921 | 7.16 | 12.21 | 1.81 |
| 1931 | 9.50 | 15.59 | 2.93 |
| 1941 | 16.10 | 24.90 | 7.30 |
| 1951 | 16.67 | 24.95 | 7.93 |
| 1961 | 24.02 | 34.44 | 12.95 |
| 1971 | 29.45 | 39.45 | 18.69 |
| 1981 | 36.23 | 46.89 | 24.89 |
| 1991 | 52.21 | 64.13 | 39.29 |
| 2001 | 65.38 | 75.85 | 54.16 |

*Source*: MHRD Reports.

As can be seen Independent India started with a literacy rate of 16.67, with huge gap between male and female literacy rates. Secondly, in ten years these rates improved by about 5 per cent points only. Significant jump has been observed only in the 1991 census, practically after 25 years of the Education Commission. This also indicates the many challenges that the Commission had to address. As observed by Moonis Raja and Aggarwal (1986), "Low literacy in the country are the result of uneven spread of schooling facilities, particularly the gross neglect of rural areas in this respect." The First Plan also was conscious of this and focused on equitable distribution of educational opportunities. The Second Plan focussed on raising the levels of literacy and the Third Plan worked towards pooling of resources to correct regional disparities. The Fourth moved on to still complex issues.

## Inclusive Education under the Education Commission (1964-66)

*The Fourth Plan started in the year 1966. The Kothari Commission submitted its report during this plan. The facilities for handicapped were referred to as the rehabilitation of the handicapped persons under* Social Welfare. *The Fourth Plan read:*

> Besides developing existing institutions such as the Model School for Blind Children, the workshop for the manufacture of Braille appliances and the Central Braille Press at Dehradun, some new institutions were also established including the National Library for the Blind, Training Centre for the Adult Deaf and Model School for Mentally deficient children. Eight special employment exchanges were established for physically handicapped persons. Scholarships were provided for general as well as technical and professional education.

Thus the Fourth Plan further increased and consolidated the facilities for handicapped persons but in terms of magnitude the coverage was meagre. India had educational facilities for only one per cent of the total number of blind and deaf children in the country. The Education Commission Report (1964-66) reviewed the total education system of the nation in the light of national objectives. Later on, the country formulated its First National Policy Resolution on Education (1968) on the recommendations of the Education Commission. Another National Policy was prepared in 1979 but it remained at the draft stage and with slight additions, the policy of 1968 contiued as the National Policy. Much of the work after the Fifth Plan and in the Sixth Plan is guided by the recommendations of the Education Commission.

### *Commission's Views*

The Education Commission viewed the need for education of the handicapped children not merely on humanitarian grounds but also on grounds of utility. It observed, *"Proper education generally enables a handicapped child to overcome largely his (or her) handicap and makes him into a useful citizen. Social Justice also demands it: it has to be remembered that the Constitution Directive on Compulsory education includes handicapped children as well"*.

If one looks at this statement not as an isolated observation of a learned person chairing a commission, but also as the prediction of a visionary, then this single statement unfolds the developments of today. For example, India has taken a position to have Education as a Fundamental Right and amended the Constitution in 2001[3]. It is also interesting to note that some of the observations of the Commission on universalisation of elementary education also have made an impact especially on the 0-6-year age group that is very crucial for any intervention for children and persons with disabilities. Now (2001) it is left to the state government to "endeavor" to provide this essential component, which for these children, as per Kothari Commission, would have been a priority under the Constitutional Directives. Hence, though the Commission did not use explicitely the Right's perspective it was interwoven.

May be some of these decisions are affected more by financial and logistic complusions than spirit of social justice. According to Advani (1964)[4], "The existing compulsory education laws declare that a physical or mental handicap may be regarded as a 'reasonable excuse' for non-attendance and provide for the exemption of handicapped children from compulsory attendance at schools. This is obviously a negative decision which seeks to avoid difficulties that would be created if handicapped children began to attend schools." Perhaps, the reference was being made to the financial implications of the task ahead as well as the increased magnitude of all those factors that have been in the way of enforcing compulsory primary education for non-handicapped children.

The Education Commission commented on the scope and size of the programme. It referred to the provision as special education and described it as follows:

> *The primary task of education for a handicapped child is to prepare him for adjustment to a socio-cultural environment designed to meet the needs of the normal. It is essential, therefore, that the education of handicapped children should be an inseparable part of the general educational system. The differences lie in the methods employed to teach the child and the means the child uses to acquire information. These differences in methodology do not influence the content or the goals of education* (p. 123).

The Commission estimated the number of the handicapped children to be 2.5 million. Category-wise breakup is as under:

| *Category* | *Estimated number of Children* |
|---|---|
| The Blind | 4,00,000 |
| The Deaf | 3,00,000 |
| The Orthopaedically Handicapped | 4,00,000 |
| The Mentally Retarded | 14,00,000 |
| Total | 25,00,000 |

Two things are important here—to understand why this otherwise forward looking commission listed only these four categories and how were these numbers estimated? The Report as such does not give much information. But it is to be noted that eduation of the handicapped (the term used by the Commission) was with the Ministry of Social Welfare and had a system in place to medically assess them for this categorisation. This is also the time when, internationally, WHO definitions were being followed for persons with disabilities. India picked up only four visible/observable catogories of disabiling conditions, as against WHO's 11 categories, including chronically ill children. In this sense, the limitation of definition and decision to cover only a few categories, was reinforced by the Commission. The issue of categories, certification of disability and the resultant impact on the magnitude remains a critical and unresolved issue till date.

## Issue of Definitions

The Education Commission mentioned that the determination of the size of the handicapped population has eluded educators, planners and social workers not only in this country but also in many of the economically advanced countries. For estimating the number of the blind, the Education Commission has quoted figure of four lakhs as suggested by the Ministry of Health; this was also the estimate given by the Royal Commonwealth Society for the Blind, London. Simultaneously, the estimation for the deaf is based on a few sample surveys; it estimates the total deaf population to be about 1.5 millions and school-age number to be 3 lakhs. For the orthopaedically handicapped and the mentally retarded the figures are based on inadequate sample surveys.

Thus it can be seen that the Commission did not have access to a sound basis for estimating the numbers for which the educational policy or programmes could be drawn. One could say that this situation of defining the disability, selecting the categories of children that such programmes may serve and estimating the numbers with confidence is a persistent issue even today. *However, all plans need some sort of targeting and in this sense the Commission drew its plan of action that were limited by two considerations namely, teachers and financial resources*. It observed, "*a reasonable target will, therefore, be to provide, by 1986, education for about 15 per cent of the blind, deaf and orthopaedically handicapped children and to about five per cent of the mentally retarded ones—this will mean the provision of educational facilities for about 10 per cent of the total number of handicapped children. As a part of the programme, it should be possible to have at least one good institution for the education of handicapped children in each district.*"

The Commission has included the issue of the education of the handicapped under the chapter on Equal Opportunities—this itself is the most important step as disability is seen as a disadvantage that can be addressed through positive discrimination, just as other disadvantages. Medical model of the disability was the order of the day; hence the Commission was also restrained by the circumstances. This is a live issue and the National Policy on Education 1986 took it further. Internationally also, we are moving towards a social model of disability.

Today, world has moved much ahead. One of the recent publications by OECD (2004) has used three categories: A, B and C for categorizing disabling conditions.

*Category A*: Refers to educational needs of students, where there is substantial normative agreement such as blind and partially sighted, deaf and partially hearing, severe and profound mental handicap and multiple handicaps. *These conditions affect students from all social classes and occupations* (emphasis added). Typically, adequate measuring instruments and agreed criteria are available. These are considered in medical terms to be organic disorders attributable to organic pathologies (e.g. in relation to sensory, motor or neurological defects).

*Category B*: Refers to educational needs of students who have difficulties in learning, which do not appear to be directly or primarily attributable to factors, which would lead to categorization as A or C.

*Category C*: Refers to educational needs of students, which are considered to arise primarily from socio-economic, cultural and/or linguistic factors. There is some form of disadvantage or atypical background for which education seeks to compensate.

The definition of special educational needs (SEN) as given in the International Standard Classification of Education (ISCED-97) manual and the derived resources definition have, in practice, presented problems for some countries. Specifically, for example, the special education needs of the association of students from ethnic minorities clashes with some national policy frameworks and national understanding of the concept of SEN. This also makes one think of reinterpreting the Salamanca statement, which in a way is the basis of all developments in inclusive education for the last 15 years or so. According to the OECD survey (a comparison has been made on the conceptualization, legal framework and practice of inclusion across many countries), the basic issue raised is of defining the groups, which are to be covered under the term inclusion. The overall policy framework flows from this very definition in the context of a given nation. *Hence the issue is how one defines inclusion in international context and also creates a space for the conceptualization of this very important term, which is likely to shape and mould the education policy parameters in many countries.* There are not many straightforward answers, but I personally feel that the OECD definitions can be reviewed for implications in various countries especially those not covered by OECD.

The Commission recommended Integrated Education and also estimated the facilities required for each area of disability.

*The Blind*: The country had 115 schools providing education to about one per cent of the blind child population. Most of these institutions provided primary education coupled with training in a few simple handicrafts. Music occupied an important place in the curriculum. The institutions are being run by voluntary agencies but assisted by State Governments. The Central Government has set up a comprehensive National Centre for the Blind at Dehra Dun. This centre includes a Central Braille Press, which publishes textbooks and other reading material in Braille. There are three centres for training of teachers of the blind sponsored by the Government and they can train between 30 and 40 teachers, annually. In addition, the governments of two States (Tamil Nadu and Andhra Pradesh) conduct courses for training teachers when needed.

*The Deaf*: The number of schools is about 70. These provide primary education with some pre-vocational training in engineering and non-engineering occupations. About half a dozen centres for the training of teachers are in function with an annual output of 50 to 60 teachers.

*The Orthopaedically Handicapped*: These children often attend ordinary schools. There are about 25 institutions with an enrolment of 1,000 students. Since these children do not present any special problems, it is not considered necessary to have specially trained teachers.

*The Mentally Retarded*: This category has received very little attention. There are only 27 schools with an enrolment of 2000. Government of India runs only one school. Two teacher training centres are in operation with a turnover of 20 teachers annually.

There is no provision for other handicaps and provision for one per cent of the handicapped children leaves much to be done.

However, when it came to making suggestions on the programmes, the Commission recommended special as well as integrated education. It was of the view that special education programmes have developed in this country to some extent as compared to mainstream programmes, but the Commission was fully aware of the developments in other countries and made a case for promoting integrated education in the near future. Taking an overall view of the problem, the Commission felt that experimentation with the integrated programmes is urgently required and every attempt should be made to bring in as many children into integrated programmes as possible. The Commission was quite considerate in recommending special services, though on pilot basis, for additional categories of children with peculiar education needs as partially sighted, speech handicapped, the aphasic, the brain injured and the emotionally disturbed. However, in view of the limited facilities available for these categories, the Commission recommended that the next two plans should set up a few centers on a pilot basis and the problem should be reviewed after ten years.

It is interesting to note that it has taken practically 30 years for the PWD Act (1995) to really make a case for many such children, who are not covered under IED Scheme till date. It is only now (due to the PWD Act and the National Trust Act (1999) that many of these children have got some sort of right to opportunities for education. *One should give credit to the Commission that though it could not see well into the future, it did lay the foundation on which the future could be built.*

However, in terms of implementing the programmes, the Commission focused mainly on preparation of teachers in the ratio of 10:1 and also recommended coordination and networking across other agencies like Ministry of Education, Central Social Welfare Board, Voluntary organizations and Ministry of Health. *It identified NCERT to have a cell for the Study of Handicapped Children and recommended that its principal function should be to keep in touch with the research that is being done in the country and outside and to provide materials for the use of teachers.* The Commission analysed the problem in terms of requirement for additional teachers and finances. The target was fixed for provision to 10 per cent by the end of 1986. The Commission recommended two programmes—special and integrated. In addition, it also expressed the need for services for additional categories like the partially sighted, speech handicapped, aphasic, brain injured and emotionally disturbed.

It was in the light of the above-mentioned recommendations, that the schemes for the education of the handicapped children were initiated and provision made in the Sixth Five Year Plan.

## Impact on Post-1968 Developments

The impact of the Kothari Commission is being traced till the National Policy on Education, 1986 with the assumption that post-1986 developments are likely to be the results of reflections and directions of NPE 1986.

The Education Commission recommendations were so comprehensive and forward looking that CABE proposed these to be adopted in the National Policy Resolution of 1968. Accordingly, CABE prepared the draft that was later on rectified as the National Policy Resolution. It goes to the credit of the Commission that the coming years witnessed many developments; important for inclusive education is the proposal for establishing special education cell at NCERT (Box 9.2). It is a different matter that this could really be implemented only in 1983—in the International Decade of the Disabed Children. The reason for this delay is not a lack of vision—rather it shows the poor preparedness of the system and lack of awareness on the part of the policy planners and implementors. Another significant reason is the location of education, rehabilitation and all other HRD related plans and actions in the Department of Social Welfare.

**Box 9.2**

A Silver lining was that the NCERT got the Special Education Cell in its Deprtment of Teacher Education in 1983. The NCERT took sometime to prepare itself for this role as manpower with the appropriate skills and competence and commitment to education of the disabled children was not readily available. Some incubation period was a must. The NCERT responded to the challenge and contributed to this need through a number of strategies such as identifying and training manpower from within, creating posts, developing training modules, materials and starting extension and research activities. A partnership with NGOs and the Social Welfare Ministry also started.

Hence, all the recommendations by the Kothari Commission, seen in this context, appeared something like encroaching into another department, a case of overstepping. This separation still continues, though more networking is visible in this millennium as compared to the past fifty years of Independence. One must give credit to the Commission for putting India on the map of inclusion and giving a base on which future policies could be anchored.

The Fifth Plan (1974-79) initiated action for streamlining the working of the four National Institutions for the Blind, the Deaf, the Mentally Retarded and the Orthopaedically Handicapped (under the Ministry of Social Welfare) and for suitable expansion and improvement of their activities. The institutions for the blind and the deaf were proposed to be reorganised for diversifying their training and other programmes. The Model School in the Institute for Mentally Retarded was to be upgraded to provide additional services. Other important schemes for the welfare of the handicapped like scholarships, sheltered workshops assistance to voluntary organizations and special employment exchanges were to receive greater attention. Soon after the presentation of the Fifth Plan, the Ministry of Social Welfare came out with a scheme for Integrated Education for the Disabled Children (IEDC).

The IEDC scheme was shifted to the Ministry of Education in 1983, during the Sixth Five Year Plan (1980-85). The scheme of integrated education was to be revised and expanded so that varying needs of different types of handicapped children might be met effectively. The Plan emphasized the need to prevent accidents and incidents leading to handicaps. It stressed the provision for pre-and post-natal care and immunization, legal framework for the prevention and treatment of accidents and opportunities for integrated education, vocational training and economic rehabilitation for integration of the disabled in the mainstream of socio-economic life.

Special schools were discouraged except for severely handicapped, who could not be educated along with normal children. The scheme of scholarships, both at the Centre and the States, would be expanded to offer financial support to the students pursuing educational and vocational pursuits. The existing facilities for the production of textbooks and literature would be augmented to meet the requirements of expanded educational facilities. Similarly, the plan also provided for vocational rehabilitation centres, and proper aids and appliances. *As can be seen, the IEDC scheme in its conceptualisation reflects many ideas of the Commission. Since, on timeline, the Commission came earlier one can appreciate this development as an extension of the views expressed by the Kothari Commission.*

**Box 9.3**

**Scheme of Integrated Education of Disabled Children (1974)[5]**

India witnessed phenomenal expansion of educational facilities for all but disabled children could not get the share which they deserved. To cover maximum number of children under the provision of equality of opportunities, it is proposed to recommend the placement of disabled children in ordinary schools. It is referred to as 'integrated education'.

Integrated education is not seen as a replacement for special education. Special Schools will continue to play their vital role as institutions offering compensatory teaching and special educational treatment to disabled children and centres of research. The parallel development of special schools and integrated programme should be seen as a part of a planned effort to develop educational services for disabled children. The scheme aims at placing the disabled children in ordinary schools with the help of special teachers, aids and other resources. The scheme is to be implemented by the state governments and all other central and autonomous bodies working in the area of school education. The role of voluntary and cooperative agencies is also very important.

Since the magnitude of the task is enormous, it is planned to make provision for integrated education for (i) the blind and partially sighted, (ii) the deaf and partially hearing, (iii) the orthopaedically handicapped and neurologically handicapped, and (iv) multiple-handicapped children in a phased programme on a selective basis. Pre-school training and parental counseling can be a part of the schools implementing the scheme. The Central Government sponsored the scheme during the Fifth Plan period.

It is important that children stay with their families and attend ordinary schools. A teacher-pupil ratio of 1.8 or 10 has been envisaged. An attendant will be provided for severe cases. Salary and special pay will be paid by Central Government to the teachers working under this scheme.

(*Contd.*)

(*Contd.*)

Teachers of disabled children will possess the same qualifications as those of ordinary schools. In addition, it would be desirable that they have a recognized diploma or certificate in teaching of children of particular disability. For fulfilling immediate need, short-term courses will be organized for the in-service training of teachers.

Each State shall appoint a co-ordinator for the programme to undertake psychological assessment of children and monitor their progress on a regular basis. The team shall consist of specialists like pediatrician, ophthalmologist, ENT surgeons, orthopedic surgeon, psychologists and special teachers.

For integration to be workable, it will be necessary to modify the existing architectural facilities. Special allowances will be provided to disabled children for equipment, books and stationery, transport, readers and escorts depending upon the nature of the disability.

However, critics can also take up a position that the Commission should have expanded its vision in line with other developments abroad as it did, for example, in Vocational Education. In that case, the history of inclusion would have been different! To some extent this concern is important and cannot be overlooked.

For example, the Seventh Plan period (1985-90) did not witness any dynamic developments in inclusive education, "*Not much could be observed for the education of children and persons with disabilities in the Section on Education, Culture and Sports in the 7th Plan. It also implies that in spite of the Scheme on Integrated Education of the Disabled (1983) being shifted to the Education Department of the MHRD, the Plans as such did not adequately record developments in this evolving approach to services for the education of children and persons with disabilities*" (Mukhopadhyay 2006).

## National Policy on Education 1986 and Programme of Action (POA)

National Policy on Education was formulated in 1986 following, for the first time, large scale consultation process across the country. The current reference is to the National Policy on Education *(with modifications undertaken in 1992)*. The NPE recognized that the National Policy of 1968 marked a significant step in the history of education in post-Independence India. It aimed to promote national progress, a sense of common citizenship and culture, and strengthen *national* integration. It laid stress on the need for a radical reconstruction of the education system, to improve its quality at all stages, and gave much greater attention to science and technology, the cultivation of moral values and a closer relation between education and the life of the people. *It also acknowledged that since the adoption of the 1968 Policy, there has been considerable expansion in educational facilities all over the country at all levels. More than 90 per cent of the country's rural habitations now have schooling facilities within a radius of one kilometre. There has been sizeable augmentation of facilities at other stages also. While these achievements are impressive by themselves, the general formulations incorporated in the 1968 Policy did not, however, get translated into a detailed strategy of implementation, accompanied by the assignment of specific responsibilities and financial and organisational support. As a result, problems of access, quality, quantity, utility and financial outlay, accumulated over the years, have now assumed such massive proportions that they must be tackled with the utmost urgency.*

Speaking on the education of the handicapped, NPE 1986 (as modified in 1992) laid down the following objectives:

"The objective should be to integrate the physically and mentally handicapped with the general community as equal partners, to prepare them for normal growth and to enable them to face life with courage and confidence. The following measures will be taken in this regard:

(i) Wherever it is feasible, the education of children with motor handicaps and other mild handicaps will be common with that of others;
(ii) Special schools with hostels will be provided, as far as possible at district headquarters, for the severely handicapped children;
(iii) Adequate arrangements will be made to give vocational training to the disabled;
(iv) Training programmes for teachers will be reoriented, in particular for teachers of primary classes, to deal with the special difficulties of the handicapped children;
(v) Voluntary effort for the education of the disabled will be encouraged in every possible manner."

The POA (1992) estimated that there were 12.59 million children with disabilities and considered the same categories of the disabilities as was stipulated by the Kothari Commission in 1966. However, the passage of time and developments were visible in the strategies—IEDC continued to be the centrally sponsored scheme but more emphasis was placed on early intervention and need for field demonstration. This took forms like: Project Integrated Education of the Disabled (PIED) by the NCERT with UNICEF support, and innovative teacher training methodologies like multi-category training and resource centres in DIETs. Coordination with the schemes in the MHRD, such as Operation Black Board, and with other ministries (special schools and District Rehabilitation Centres of the Social Welfare and Vocational Rehabilitation Centres of the Ministry of Labour) emerged. Some focus on training of educational administrators as well as resource teachers was also created. *One can say the seeds planted by the Kothari Commission were showing some significant off-shoots; but as one looks back from the year 2006, it was still in the budding stáge.*

**Box 9.4**
**Project Integrated Education of the Disabled Children (PIED)**

The PIED was the first systematic programme conceptualized and implemented by the NCERT in the country to facilitate inclusion of children with disabilities by strengthening the general system of education. The programme was fully assisted by the UNICEF, during the period 1987-1994, and many states continued the work even after the withdrawal of support by the UNICEF. The project covered Delhi, Haryana, Maharashtra, Mizoram, Orissa, Madhya Pradesh, Nagaland, Rajasthan, Tamil Nadu, and Baroda Municipal Corporation. The enrolment of children under the PIED reveals that, 41.9 per cent were physically disabled; 20.5 per cent were hearing impaired; 13.5 per cent were mentally retarded; 12.6 per cent were visually impaired and 11.5 per cent were persons with learning disabilities. Though the PIED was implemented only in ten representative blocks in India, the lessons of the project have been absorbed in the subsequent schemes such as the revised IED scheme.

Action points emerging from the NPE were visible in the five year plans. Like in the Seventh Plan, the Eighth Plan (1992-97) also paid attention to the persons with disabilities as part of the Section on Social Welfare. Most of the schemes started in the Seventh Plan were continued and extended. Landmark developments were witnessed in the Social Welfare sector under the Ministry of Social Justice and Empowerment—the establishment of the Rehabilitation Council of India in 1986 through an Act of Parliament, and the PWD Act of 1995. *It is interesting to note that IEDC Scheme, which found mention till the Seventh Plan practically, has no mention either in the Welfare Department or in the education sector during the Eighth Plan. While it is a fact that under the DPEP and other programmes, this component was duly addressed and is also presently being addressed, the specific allocation under the IEDC Scheme could not be discerned from the plan document.*

## Ninth Five Year Plan and Beyond

The turning point is the Ninth Five Year Plan (1997-2002), which reported the progress on Integrated Education for the Disabled. After the enactment of the Persons with Disabilities Act (1995), the education of the disabled up to the age of 18 has become a legal obligation. The proposed action plan included revision of curricula involving the NCERT, NCTE and SCERTs. It also refers to restructuring the scheme of Vocationalization of Education at 10+ Stage so as to provide employability to this target group. The strategy was to have an Empowered Committee, representing government and non-government partners, and to promote vocational courses having strong linkages with industrial units. The third proposed strategy was to make Distance Education broad-based with wider responsibilities to National and State Open Schools. A composite Area Approach was to be adopted and additional blocks were to be covered under IED. Some other noteworthy points of this Plan are:

- Major reporting has been done under the Section on Social Welfare. Referring to the NSSO Surveys of 1981 and 1991, it recorded 163.62 lakhs persons with disabilities in 1991. Another critical observation was reference to the exclusion of persons with mental disabilities from the NSSO Surveys but having a different Sample Survey 1991 on Persons with Delayed Mental Development. About three per cent of the child population (1-14 years) was estimated to have mental retardation; one per cent was suffering from various forms of mental disorders and ten to fifteen per cent were suffering from various mental health problems.
- The Plan strategy involved empowering the persons with disabilities and reforming the social deviants and caring for those with other disadvantages. It also took note of the rural, urban deviate and proposed a comprehensive rehabilitation of persons with disabilities as the major effort. Community Based Rehabilitation was recommended as one of the important approaches. The mainstreaming of the persons with disabilities was to be achieved through integrated schools by extending special incentives like free books, uniforms, transport, aids and appliances, etc. IEDC was to be extended further during the Ninth Five Year Plan.

*The Ninth Plan period also witnessed some important Acts and Commitments; the new millennium started on a positive note creating emphasis on the responsiveness of the system and the society.*

- Government of India launched Sarva Shiksha Abhiyan with commitment to Education for All towards the end of the IX Plan. Statutory Acts of Rehabilitation Council of India (1992), National Council of Teacher Education (1993), Persons with Disabilities (Equal Opportunities, Protection of Rights and Full Participation) Act of 1995 and the National Trust for the Welfare of Persons with Autism, Cerebral Palsy, Mental Retardation and Multiple Disabilities Act, 1999, gave impetus to the education of children and persons with disabilities. The 86th Constitutional Amendment Act 2002, provided for free and compulsory education for all children in the age group of 6-14 years as a Fundamental Right under Article 21A of the Constitution. Efforts were made to define disabilities and plan for provisions for the life-cycle of a person with disability. Census survey 2001 enumerated persons with disabilities. All these paved the way for planned provisions, enactments and base for monitoring to be accountable—a change from charity to Rights-Based-Approach.

**Box 9.5**
**Disabilities Presently Covered by Acts**

According to *The Persons with Disabilities (Equal Opportunities, Protection of Rights and Full Participation) Act of 1995,* "Person with disability" is defined as a person suffering from not less than forty per cent of any disability as certified by a medical authority. Broadly, the following seven types of disabilities have been defined and included in the Act.

- Blindness
- Low vision
- Leprosy-cured
- Hearing impairment
- Locomotor disability
- Mental Retardation
- Mental illness

In addition to the above, the *National Trust for the Welfare of Persons with Autism, Cerebral Palsy, Mental Retardation and Multiple Disabilities Act, 1999,* has defined and enlisted the following disabilities:

- Autism
- Cerebral Palsy
- Mental Retardation
- Multiple Disabilities

## Implications for Contemporary Developments

The Kothari Commission had basically madc three important recommendations that influenced the future of inclusion in this country both as part of the Policy Statement, Programme of Action as well as starting other activities, which can be counted as policy implementation processes. These refer to:

- Promoting inclusion as an approach;
- Creating a need to estimate the numbers of children to be served and also the related issue of definitions of children with special needs;
- Preparing ground for a centrally sponsored scheme on inclusion; and lastly,
- Earmarking the need for capacity building both for the institutions with inclusive orientation and the need based special schools.

One can see the impact of these four important seed-actions in the near future. Though this is a fact, as shown by the analysis of five year plans and the programmes promoted under them, the translation of vision into action has been hindered by the systems' preparedness. I think this is where the role of the Programme of Action (1986, 1992) is very important, as by this time the policy makers recognized the need to have an accompanying plan of action; vision by itself being not enough.

The Kothari Commission recommended inclusion for educating the children and youths with disabilities as one of the accepted approaches using the term "Integrated", which was an internationally accepted nomenclature at that time. One also needs to take into account the other developments in education of 1990s like Education for All programme and Salamanca Statement and Framework for Action on Special Needs for Education (1990-94). These forums, where India is also a signatory, emphasized the access to quality education for all and endorsed the need for policy shift to promote inclusion in education. India witnessed a number of developments during this period. The enactment of Persons with Disabilities (Equal Opportunities, Protection of Rights and Participation) Act, 1995 was one of the most important empowering developments. This Act made provision of free education in an appropriate environment for all children with disabilities up to the age of 18 years, a statutory responsibility on the part of agencies. This Act also endorsed the inclusion of learners with disabilities in general schools.

Two other important things happened, practically after a gap of about ten years since the POA 1992. One is the 86th Amendment of the Constitution of India (2002), making education a fundamental right, and the second was the Biwako Millennium Framework for Action (2002), an international commitment on the inclusion of children and youth for personal, social and vocational development, with a clause for adequate legislation and national data collection on children with disabilities (0-16 years). This also made for the first time a case for women with disabilities. This period also witnessed Sarva Shiksha Abhiyan. The Minister for Human Resource Development gave an important commitment in Parliament in March 2005, which led to the development of National Action Plan for Inclusion of Education of Children and Youth with Disabilities (MHRD 2005). *A recommendation of the Kothari Commission, which hardly occupies three to four pages of the enormous report, thus resulted in a National Action Plan for Inclusion after 40 years.*

The second impact has been with reference to the issue *of estimating the numbers* and the achievements. This is an issue, not resolved to the satisfaction of the persons with disabilities, the policy planners, administrators and NGOs till date. We are still debating how to have a definition which will give a more reliable estimate of people, who need to be served through the policies of the government. The PWD Act is the legal reference point for this definition but it left out some disabilities, which now have been added through the National Trust Act of 1999. And today, we talk about ten disabilities as compared to the four, which were initially mentioned by the Kothari Commission. These are: blindness, low vision, leprosy-cured, hearing impairments, locomotive disabilities, mental retardation, mental illness, autistic, cerebral palsy and multi-disability. Issues are still raised about the definitions of these disabilities. Besides the issue of definitions, an equally important issue is who and how these numbers will be estimated?

Currently, there are two mechanisms: the Census and the National Sample Survey. In education, we also have DISE. Reports of NSSO 2002 survey on persons with disabilities and Census 2001 are now available[6].

According to NSSO 2002, the estimated number of persons with disabilities in the country is 1.85 crore, which constitutes 1.8 per cent of the population. According to Census 2001 there are 2.19 crore persons with disabilities in the country, which constitute 2.19 per cent of the population. Considering that one source of data is a sample survey and the other is through census, the variation, which is not very large, should be accepted. Thus, one could believe that the persons with disabilities may be approximately 2 per cent of the population. However, a difficulty is experienced when the comparison is made in the estimated numbers from the NSSO and figures from the Census by the type of disability. Comparative figures from the two sources of data are presented in Table 9.3:

**Table 9.3: Persons with Disabilities (in lakhs)**

| *Disability* | *NSSO, 2002* | *Census, 2001* |
|---|---|---|
| Locomotor | 106.34 | 61.05 |
| Visual | 28.26 | 106.35 |
| Hearing | 30.62 | 12.62 |
| Speech | 21.55 | 16.41 |
| Mental | 20.96 | 22.64 |

The difference is attributed to the different definitions used by the NSSO and the Census. The NSSO estimates have been comparatively consistent over the years. The NSSO 2002 brings out comparative figures of the prevalence of disability across earlier rounds. These are presented (Table 9.4) along with proportion of persons with disabilities from the Census, 2001.

The percentage of persons with disabilities from the Census is higher than the prevalence rate from the NSSO Surveys. The NSSO figures indicate a decline in prevalence of disability, probably due to the aggressive campaigns for prevention like the Pulse Polio Programme.

**Table 9.4: Prevalence Rates of Disability and Proportion of Persons with Disabilities**

*(Per Lakh Population)*

| | *NSSO-36th Round, 1981* | *NSSO-47th Round, 1991* | *NSSO-58th Round, 2002* | *Census, 2001* |
|---|---|---|---|---|
| **Rural** | | | | |
| Male | 2045 | 2277 | 2118 | 2453 |
| Female | 1632 | 1694 | 1556 | 1950 |
| Persons | 1844 | 1995 | 1846 | 2210 |
| **Urban** | | | | |
| Male | 1532 | 1774 | 1670 | 2164 |
| Female | 1297 | 1361 | 1311 | 1686 |
| Persons | 1420 | 1579 | 1499 | 1933 |

*Source*: NSSO 36th, 47th and 58th Round and Census, 2001.

The Tenth Five Year Plan (2002-2007) has a special section on *Other Special Groups,* and re-affirms the earlier commitment of making disabled persons active, self-reliant and productive contributors to the national economy, through the process of empowerment. The PWD Act of 1995 has already generated a lot of awareness among the disabled about their rights, besides raising their expectations towards a better future. The state will need to gear itself up to fulfill these expectations through workable policies and programmes.

The Tenth Plan commitment is, therefore, to create an enabling environment, wherein persons with disabilities can exercise their rights, enjoying equal opportunities and full participation. It also reports the progress made under the PWD Act (pp. 484-485). The IEDC Scheme has reported school facilities for 1,00,000 children in 22,000 schools; three per cent reservation in Kendriya Vidyalayas; Restructuring of Curriculum by the NCERT to suit the needs of children with disabilities; special schemes for teacher preparation by RCI and UGC and up-gradation of 50 polytechnics to impart vocational courses to 5,000 and diploma to 1,250 disabled students.

Present efforts, though noteworthy, are still inadequate. Since the initiation of the National Institute of Open Schooling, the cumulative enrolment of the learners has gone up from 49,000 to 7,23,346 during the period 1989-1990 to 2001-2002. But there is no significant improvement in the enrolment of children with disabilities. In the year 2001-2002, about 1,816 children were registered under the category of the disabilities out of the total enrolment of 1,93,000, which is approximately one percent of the total enrolment in the same year. As the technology is growing fast, the concept of distance education is becoming popular and the enrolment in the National Institute of Open Schooling is likely to grow in future.

In India, there are more than 3,500 NGOs serving people with disabilities. Services provided to persons with disabilities by NGOs include clinical, rehabilitation, educational and referral services. Some of the NGOs provide all types of services under one roof. While regular education shows a steady gradual growth over the years, a rapid increase in special schools has been reported during the last three decades. Reasons for this may be the establishment of National Institutes for training special educators and providing technical assistance for the establishment of special schools by NGOs. Streamlining teacher training through the regulations by Rehabilitation Council of India (RCI), financial assistance for establishment of special schools by the Ministry of Social Justice and Empowerment and general increase in the awareness about disabilities among public can be the other contributing factors.

**Table 9.5: Growth of Institutions (Regular and Special Schools)**

| | *1961* | *1971* | *1981* | *1991* | *2001* |
|---|---|---|---|---|---|
| General schools | 399228 | 539911 | 674345 | 808064 | 956519 |
| Mental Retardation | 39 | 120 | 125 | 650 | 1000 |
| Blind | 40 | 110 | 268 | 440 | 960 |
| Visually impaired | 45 | 80 | 114 | 500 | 700 |
| Locomotor | 40 | 90 | 140 | 424 | 900 |
| Hearing Impairment | 164 | 400 | 647 | 2014 | 3560 |

*Source*: NIMH, 2004.

Special schools for children with disabilities receive financial assistance from the Ministry of Social Justice and Empowerment. The integrated educational programmes are carried out with funding from the Ministry of Human Resource Development. Special education is yet to get exclusive funding from government to meet the actual demand. Through Assistance to Disabled Persons for Purchase/Fitting of Aids/Appliances (ADIP) Scheme initiated by the Ministry of Social Justice and Empowerment, children in need receive aids and appliances and educational material such as Braille slates, tape recorder and assistive devices. Travel concession and scholarships are provided to students with disabilities.

Ministries other than Education have undertaken various efforts in response to the growing manpower created by education. The Ministry of Social Justice and Empowerment (MSJE) supports approximately 190 NGOs in running vocational training programs for persons with disabilities. Special Employment Exchanges have been established in certain state capitals, and special cells in other employment exchanges have been set up to register physically handicapped persons seeking jobs and to arrange for their placement in suitable assignments both in the public and private sectors. In fact, 11,400 people have been placed through 40 Special Employment Exchanges from

1992 to 2000. Three per cent of jobs in respect of identified posts are reserved in government organizations for people with disabilities, of these, one per cent each is designated for people with visual, hearing and locomotor disabilities. Many state government departments dealing with disability have placement officers, whose primary function is to enable employment of persons with disabilities. The Ministry of Labour has set up Vocational Rehabilitation Centres (VRCs), whose main function is to assess the vocational needs of physically handicapped persons and to render all assistance for their rehabilitation. The VRCs also arrange for their training in industries as apprentices and in formal training institutions. In addition to assisting them in improving their skills, the VRCs also assist them in their placement in industries.

While voluntary enterprise is substantial and has shown the way and complements government efforts, government should play a pro-active role to launch new suitable programmes and implement and monitor with responsiveness and accountability. Disabled children also are a part of the National Plan of Action for Children-2005 launched by the Department of Women and Child Development under MHRD, and a National Policy for Persons with Disabilities has also been put forward by the Ministry of Social Justice and Empowerment. The Education Commission talked about networking across all these agencies and this still needs to be resolved so that no child or person with disabilities is left un-served or under-served.

The third important issue initiated by the Commission relates to the estimation of facilities required for each area of disability. This also brings up other significant issues like barrier-free environment, disability certificates, social security, etc. Through Sarva Siksha Abhiyan and other programmes, the Government has made a commitment to serve every child and accordingly work is in progress. However, it is expected that if the National Action Plan on Disabilities is actualized then we have moved a step forward in the stipulated direction.

The last and the most important aspect is capacity building. This is an area where the Kothari Commission recommended a special cell in the NCERT. The last 40 years have witnessed many more partners including the Rehabilitation Council of India, NCTE, NUEPA, and a host of NGOs, but we are still to have a master plan for generating the necessary manpower resources; and we need to work for it. A related but little thought of issue is the availability of resource materials for children and persons with disabilities. We have as of now 17 VRCs and about 14 Braille presses. Alimco provides the aids and equipments and the four national institutes under social welfare have also been roped in, but still the logistics and mechanisms are nowhere near the services required. This is quite evident from the literacy data (first-time reporting on disabled persons) of Census 2001.

As per Census 2001, the literacy level of the disabled population is only 49 per cent. Literacy rates for the disabled female population are around 37 per cent as compared to the national average of over 54 per cent for the female population. Literacy rates for the disabled male population are 58.14 per cent as compared to 75.85 per cent for males.

As can be seen, even the disparities between males and females with disabilities and also between rural and urban locations are quite glaring. Variations across the disabilities are also noteworthy. The Census has also provided information on literacy rates among a cross section of the disabled population. According to the Census, approximately 40 per cent of the Total Disabled Scheduled Caste population and 33 per cent of the Total Disabled Scheduled Tribe population are literate. Literacy rates are lower among females with disabilities from the Scheduled Castes and Scheduled Tribes. About one-third of the disabled SC females and one-fifth of the ST females are literate. The Census has been able to show that a vast expansion of services is required for the disabled in education, rehabilitation and employment. Proper strategies are needed to target disadvantaged sections of the population.

**Table 9.6: Census 2001: Literacy Rates of Disabled Indians**

| *Disability* | *Residence* | *Persons* | *Male* | *Female* |
|---|---|---|---|---|
| **Disabilities Total** | Total | 49.31 | 58.15 | 37.32 |
| | Rural | 44.40 | 54.11 | 31.31 |
| | Urban | 63.87 | 70.05 | 55.36 |
| **Seeing Disability** | Total | 49.85 | 59.56 | 38.50 |
| | Rural | 43.56 | 54.18 | 31.28 |
| | Urban | 67.77 | 74.61 | 59.53 |
| **Speech Disability** | Total | 36.23 | 41.91 | 28.57 |
| | Rural | 31.38 | 37.30 | 23.41 |
| | Urban | 51.41 | 56.33 | 44.75 |
| **Hearing Disability** | Total | 43.17 | 55.73 | 28.79 |
| | Rural | 39.31 | 52.20 | 24.38 |
| | Urban | 59.72 | 71.24 | 47.11 |
| **Movement Disability** | Total | 57.37 | 65.44 | 43.08 |
| | Rural | 53.74 | 62.52 | 38.17 |
| | Urban | 69.04 | 74.80 | 58.18 |
| **Mental Disability** | Total | 37.89 | 43.68 | 29.27 |
| | Rural | 34.72 | 41.17 | 25.21 |
| | Urban | 45.44 | 49.55 | 39.15 |

## Summing-Up

The 1968 Policy Resolution, based on the Kothari Commission recommendations, indicated that facilities for education of the physically and mentally handicapped would need to be expanded. For this expansion, it also mentioned the establishing of one good institution in each of the districts. One can see the manifestation of this idea in some concrete decisions taken in the POA 1986, and also in the Eighth Plan targets, which emerged from the POA 1992. For example, special schools with hostels at district headquarters for the severely handicapped were to be planned as per the 1986 and 1992 POAs. However, though, NGOs have established many such facilities, government-run facilities are not visible to the required extent. Another factor, which also has not found a suitable place, relates to the arrangements for vocational education for the disabled children proposed by the NPE-1986 as well as 1992.

Only the recommendation on integrated programmes that started as a notion by the Kothari Commission, has occupied the center-stage. As already mentioned this component has been submerged by the larger framework of the SSA. Also, pending further decisions on Universal Secondary Education (USE), a separate scheme for Inclusion in Education For Secondary Schools is taking shape and pending with the Planning Commission. It may become a reality in the Eleventh Plan.

The Kothari Commission showed a way for coordination of activities under different agencies but this notion has taken variable forms in the follow-up actions through policies and programmes. For example, today, the ADIP Scheme of the Social Welfare Ministry has become one of the large coordinating programmes for provision of aids and equipments under the SSA. The removal of architectural barriers has also taken many shapes, including rethinking about the school buildings and the funding of infrastructure modifications under large programmes like the SSA. The Kothari Commission indicated the need for having some measures for estimating the number of children, who will be served under integrating programmes, but till date the database continuous to be poor. This idea was further taken up by the POA 1986, but except for information flowing from the latest Census 2001 and some efforts by the NSSO and information now made available by the District Information System for Education (DISE) and household surveys under the SSA, it is still difficult to say with confidence as to how many numbers we are talking about.

Manpower development for implementing programmes of integrated education is through training in special education and rehabilitation by National Institutes and NGOs. Initially, as envisioned by the Commission, a well-thought out strategy for manpower development, is now required to implement the policies for the PWD. A much wider and integrated approach in training, coupled with involvement of various agencies and universities is required to provide for large number of professionals to serve in the area of education and rehabilitation of the disabled.

As described before, although there are several schemes for promoting employment of the handicapped, there is, however, no comprehensive programme for the economic rehabilitation of all handicapped persons seeking employment. No doubt, the present schemes do provide jobs for a large number of the handicapped individuals, but their overall impact on their economic rehabilitation remains insignificant with an employment rate at 34 per cent. In India, medical and health services are provided free by the State and handicapped individuals are also eligible for these benefits. However, facilities for rehabilitation services in the health set-up are non-existent and, therefore, there is no security for the disabled. Employees in the organized sectors of the economy have extensive social security benefits, but very few handicapped employees belong to these outfits. By and large, the disabled population does not have easy and significant access to organized sectors; therefore, in actual practice, they do not get security in the event of unemployment or other similar contingencies (National Trust 2004).

## A Vision for the Future

Inclusive educational policies are presently undergoing a change in nature and prospects to better serve the children and youth at a much higher speed than ever before. Let us think for a while about the vision D.S. Kothari would have had if he were to now frame policies for the education of the disabled in the present context. Compared to the time of the Kothari Commission, when visibility of children with disabilities was rather poor, today, when education has become a fundamental right and efforts are being made to provide education to all, how would he visualize a school which caters to "All Children"?

Would that mean planning and allocating specific and more finances for programmes for the disabled or that the existing institutions, systems and processes should undergo change to automatically incorporate "needs of the disabled"? Could "inclusive education" be extended to serve the special needs of children from poor and SC/ST backgrounds? Would he think that all special needs of children can be served under a single umbrella education system which, instead of having separate programmes for different focus groups, becomes a convergent but responsive "inclusive education" programme?

Considering education of the disabled as a human resource development issue, the Commission recommended "integrated education". Now, enabled by the IEDC Scheme and IED component in the SSA, when there are a large number of children with disabilities in primary schools, what does one visualize for their future? A policy maker would consider the concerns of any parent or any child with disability. What are the opportunities and supports that my child would get to complete secondary education and move on further to higher education/vocational training to get suitable employment opportunities? Now that the National Plan of Action on Children and Youth with Disabilities is being drafted, one can hope a lot from it. But the issue still remains as to whether secondary schools, colleges and universities have a place for children with disabilities? A change in notions of "normal child" is required to see whether our systems are accessible to all children. Can we think of a system in school, colleges and other places, which automatically becomes activated once a child or a person with disability becomes a part of it and provide support services? Another issue is that most of the children and youth with disabilities have different educational needs and different abilities. Can guidance and counselling services as well as placement services in higher education acquire meaningful place in educational institutions?

An estimate of number of persons with disabilities is critical for planning the services. A natural corollary of this is the issue of defining disabilities and the level of impairment. Rather than having special disability surveys, disability should be made part of every survey done by the government, education or any other agency. Another step would be to network with other sectors like health. For example, hospitals, PHCs or representatives from various developmental programmes can provide data about the disabled population they serve.

Emanating from the above vision is the issue of systems of teacher education and training. The Kothari Commission visualized a capacity building cell at the NCERT in the context of the 1960s. Every teacher today needs to teach children from diverse backgrounds and with different abilities; how far our teacher training programmes have been successful in preparing teachers for this role? A national policy on manpower for education is required.

Kothari would have faced many more such questions but he would have gone for overhauling the system around a philosophy and commitment to Rights of people and calling upon the system to be responsive and accountable. Lack of funds would not be used as an excuse as was done in 1964, as observed by another crusader of education of the disabled, Lal Advani. We will not go for inequitable education and grouse that standards are falling.

## Notes

1. Miyamoto Musashi (1584-June 13 *(Japanese Calendar May 19)*, 1645), was a famous Japanese swordsman. He is the founder of the Hyoho Niten Ichi-ryu, or Niten Ryu style of swordsmanship and wrote *Go Rin No Sho, The Book of Five Rings*, a book on strategy, tactics, and philosophy that is still studied today. http://en.wikipedia.org/wiki/Miyamoto_Musashi

2. Some of the portions are from the other writings of the author, especially from 'Education of Children with Disabilities in India'. In Mukhopadhyay, M. (ed.) 2006, Understanding Indian Education, New Delhi: Shipra.
3. CABE has endorsed a Draft Bill on Compulsory Primary Education and is now available at the website of MHRD, September 2005. Constitutional Amendment was enacted in 2001.
4. Lal Advani has contributed significantly to the education of persons with disabilities. Himself a blind person, he occupied many senior positions in the Government of India. He expired in 2004.
5. This Scheme was transferred to Department Of Education in 1983, was *modified* in 1992 and still continues. Till July 2006, MHRD had two Departments-Department of Elementary Education and Literacy and Department of Secondary and Higher Education. This Scheme is located in the Department of Secondary and Higher Education. However, IEDC/IED Component of Sarva Shiksha Abhiyan (SSA) is in the Department of Elementary Education and Literacy. Now this Department is named as Department of School Education and scheme has received EFC recommendation. May be 11th Plan will see a scheme on Inclusive Education in Secondary education.
6. This information has been taken from the *Newsletter, Vol. 3, December 2004* of the National Trust for the Welfare of Persons with Autism, Cerebral Palsy, Mental Retardation and Multiple Disabilities, Govt. Of India, Ministry of Social Justice & Empowerment.

## References

Advani, L. (1964) Education of the Handicapped, in *The Indian Year Book of Education: Second Year Book (Elementary Education)*. New Delhi: NCERT.

GOI (2002) *86th Amendment of the Constitution of India.*

Jha, M.M. (2004) From Special to Inclusive Education: International Perspectives and Indian Policies. Paper presented at the National Seminar on Planning and Management of Inclusive Education. New Delhi: NUEPA.

Kisanji Joseph (1999) Historical and Theoretical Basis of Inclusive Education. Keynote address for the Workshop on Inclusive Education in Namibia: The Challenge for Teacher Education, 24-25 March 1999, Rossing Foundation, Khomasdal, Windhoek, Namibia.

Miles, M. (2001) Historical Bibliography on Educational & Social Responses to Disabilities & Childhood in Some Middle Eastern & South Asian Countries from Antiquity to the 1950s, Version 4.0, July 2001.

Moonis Raza and Aggarwal, Y. (1986) An Analysis of the Equities in the Levels of Literacy in India, In Malhotra, P.L. (*et al.*) (Ed.), *School Education in India: Present Status and Future Needs*. New Delhi: NCERT.

Mukhopadhyay, Sudesh (1984) Developments in Special Education in Great Britain and India: Implications for Teacher Training. *Report for the Associateship of University of London Institute of Education 1983-84.*

Mukhopadhyay, Sudesh (2006) Education of Children with Disabilities in India. In Mukhopadhyay, M. (ed.) 2006, *Understanding Indian Education,* New Delhi: Shipra, (forthcoming).

Narasimhan, M.C. and Mukherjee, A.K. (1990) *Disability: A Continuing Challenge.* Wiley Eastern Ltd.

NIMH (2004) *Status of Educational Services for Children with Disabilities in India.* Hyderabad.

OECD (2004) *Classifying Educational Programmes: Manual for ISCED-97 implementation in OECD Countries, 1999 Edition.*

Pandey, R.S., Advani, L. (1995) *Perspectives in Disability and Rehabilitation.* New Delhi: Vikas Publishing House Pvt. Ltd.

*Sargent, J. (1968) Society, School and Progress in India* Oxford: Pergamon.

*Sayed* Yusuf (2005) *One size fits all? Approaches to Inclusive Education.* Copyright © 2005 id 21.

Simon, H. (1981) *The Sciences Of The Artificial (2nd ed.).* Cambridge, MA: Massachusetts Institute of Technology Press.

UNESCO (2002) *Biwako Millennium Framework for Action.*

Winzer, Margaret A. & Mazurek, Kas (2000) *Special Education in the 21st Century.* Washington, DC: Gallaudet University Press. http://tiger.towson.edu/users/bwitko1/paper1.htm

Reports of the Government of India.

Report of the Post-War Educational Development in India 1944, CABE, 1947.

First Five Year Plan: Review; 1951-56.

The Secondary Education Commission, 1952-53.

Second Five Year Plan, 1956.

Third Five-Year Plan, 1961-66.

Report of the Indian Education Commission 1964-66.

National Policy Resolution, 1968.

Fourth Five Year Plan, 1969-74.

Fifth Five Year Plan, 1974-79.

Draft National Policy on Education, 1979.

Sixth Five Year Plan, 1980-85.

Seventh Five Year Plan, 1985-90.

National Policy on Education, 1986 and Programme of Action, 1986

Towards an Enlightened and Humane Society, NPE, 1986-A Review, 1990. (Also Known as Acharya Ramamurti Committee Report)

National Policy on Education, 1986 (as modified in 1992) and Programme of Action, 1992.

Eighth Five Year Plan, 1992-97.

Ninth Five Year Plan, 1997-2002.

Tenth Five Year Plan, 2002-2007.

# 10

# Gender and Inclusive Education at All Levels

ANITA GHAI

## Introduction

> "The destiny of India is now being shaped in her classrooms. This, we believe, is no mere rhetoric.... On the quality and number of persons coming out of our schools and colleges will depend our success in the great enterprise of national reconstruction, the principal objective of which is to raise the standard of living of our people.... The task is neither unique nor quite new. But its magnitude, gravity and urgency have increased immensely."
>
> (1.01 and 1.02, *Report of the Education Commission*).

The opening statement of the Report of the Education Commission (REC), 1964-66, (also referred to as the Kothari Commission) builds a fantasy in which all children—regardless of their class, caste, residence, ability, disability and gender—will be given education by the State. The report intended to provide direction to the State to formulate plans that would make education not a privilege accorded to "some", but a basic right for "all". This year—also Professor Kothari's centenary year, and almost fifty three years after the report first saw the light of the day—is an apt time to introspect and reflect on the ramifications of the report for the present status of Indian education.

Much water has flowed under the bridge since the Report first saw the light of day. Education still continues to fight many battles of access, affordability and exclusion. In this paper, I endeavour to look at girls' education in particular, and inclusive education in general, at all levels. At the outset, I would like to situate the discussion about both gender and inclusive education in the context of the educational system as a whole. The nature of schooling, the kind of education children have a right to, role of State and State-run institutions are all issues of critical significance.

Since the publication of the report, it has become customary to discuss issues of gender and inclusion under the broader umbrella of equity issues in education. Though different in scope, both themes are interrelated, as neither can be understood without reference to the larger discourses within which they are situated. While the cultures of normativeness and patriarchy might appear different, the roots of oppression are quite similar. Consequently, neither gender nor inclusion can be comprehended without the social, cultural, economic and political matrix within which they function. It is interesting that the two issues have been clubbed together. While it might be a pragmatic strategy, I wonder whether there is a subtle nuance that needs to be noted.[1] I have deliberately dealt with the two issues separately to underscore the fact that the dynamics of the exclusionary pressures are quite similar for both girls and the disabled.

## Putting Gender Issues on the Educational Landscape: A Glimpse into the Policy

The Constitution of India has underscored the need to create a gender-sensitive society, which is not possible without a gender-sensitive educational system. Throughout Indian history, gender has been an important principle of stratification, but the manner in which this layering of society manifests itself culturally varies—both over time and among social classes. It is in the non-recognition of society as "gendered" that democracy fails most evidently.

Gender, by definition, is not restricted to girls alone as boys are also recipients of gendered constructions. By and large, patriarchy rests on specific notions of masculinity and femininity, which are socially constructed. However, as power is vested more in men than women, discussions of gender do get limited to a discourse on women. Constitutionally, Article 14, Article 15 and Article 15(3) empower the State to make special provisions for women and children. There have been innumerable reports and reviews regarding the status of women and its bearing on education.[2] The Kothari Commission report, in fact, acknowledges the contributions made by several committees (6.55, EC Report).

## The Education Commission Report (1964-66)

The Kothari Commission was indeed sensitive to equity issues in education and had foreseen that there would be imbalances that would call for correction. The section on education of girls starts by reiterating: "The significance of the education of girls cannot be overemphasised. For full development of our human resources, the improvement of homes, and for moulding the character of children during the most impressionable years of infancy, the education of women is of even greater importance than that of men" (6.53, EC Report). Education was thus understood as serving an instrumental function. The report recognised the fact that there might be changes with the passage of time and "modern women" would want a career as well as children. The report recommended that there should be special schemes, and attention should be given to the education of girls at all stages and in all sectors as a part of the general education programme (6.56, EC Report). It lamented that the education of women in India was not moving fast enough and noted that had attention been given to the education of girls right from the beginning, there would have been no need for special programmes. But it did not make any in-depth analysis of the reasons that were responsible for the existing state of affairs.

Besides, the dominant construction that gets reflected is that of wives, mothers and housewives, by and large reinforcing the dominant paradigm, which, to quote T. Saraswathi, viewed women in a linear way. For instance, Saraswathi (1999, p. 214) says, "Females in all social classes are groomed to become good wives and mothers. Even the increasing career option of the middle class girls is subsumed under the primary goal of marriage and motherhood, leading to consensus rather than conflict in parent-child relationships. In a culture in which chastity is cherished as more precious than life itself, girls are over-socialised from childhood to accept their subservient role in a patriarchal set-up."

The Kothari Commission report reflected this paradigm. Though there is recognition that "in the modern world, the role of women goes much beyond the home and bringing up of children", it is clear that the report does not take into cognisance the issues of patriarchy or neglect of their role as social producers. For instance, the Commission reinforced these beliefs by asserting: "The education of women can assist greatly in reducing the fertility rate" (6.53, REC). The message was that women should be taught because it will be useful. The recognition of women's agency is barely reflected. Thus, the need to educate women was felt because they could be seen as means to serve certain ends.

However, an interrogation of the social construction inherent in the perceived gender differences was not deemed important. Such approaches do not consider the identity of girls as a desired objective in its own right. They just stick to the instrumental function, without changing the status of girls in society. The possibility that they may aspire to earn independently and to pursue careers equally is, therefore, not engaged with. Girls are objectified with their own needs prioritised only in passing. As Chanana (2006, p. 215) points out, "a notable refrain in the policy documents is that the education of girls should be relevant and should prepare them for life. Nowhere is it mentioned that education should prepare all children for life. What should one infer from this differentiation in policy perspective? Is it not obvious that while there is need for differentiation through affirmative action at the implementation level, there is need to have a common conceptual framework?"

## The National Policy on Education (NPE), 1986, and Later Developments

It was the National Policy on Education (NPE), 1986, which, in principle, challenged the patriarchal social order and demanded gender parity. The policy's introductory statement was very powerful indeed in its impact. It stated: "Education will be used as an agent of basic change in the status of woman. In order to neutralise the accumulated distortions of the past, there will be a well-conceived edge in favour of women. The National Education System will play a positive, interventionist role in the empowerment of women.... This will be an act of faith and social engineering" (4.2, NPE). Thus, the goal of NPE was to achieve true emancipation of women and equality between the sexes via education.

However, this pious intent becomes questionable when the policy contradicts itself by saying: "The growth of our population needs to be brought down significantly over the coming decades. The largest single factor that could help achieve this is the spread of literacy and education among women" (1.13, NPE). This only helps to reinforce the causal link between female schooling, female autonomy and low fertility. Both at national and international levels, policies to foster women's education often have the ulterior goal of controlling population growth through reducing fertility. This instrumentality is common to many development policies (Menon, 2004) and (Swaminathan, 2002).

The NPE also recognised that it wasn't the infrastructure alone that was responsible for pushing girls out of education. For any meaningful change in this situation, "the empowerment of women is possibly the most critical precondition for the participation of girls and women in the educational process". The Programme of Action (POA, 1992), in the section "Education for Women's Equality", (Chapter XII, pp. 105-107) reiterated this conviction. The POA states, "Education for Women's Equality is a vital component of the overall strategy of securing equity and social justice in education". While the policy believed that "concerted efforts are made to reach out to the girl child", the solutions were cast in the form of alternative schooling and providing "educational opportunities through Non-Formal Education (NFE)". Moreover, there was a provision of afternoon centres for girls. This indicated that while there was a lot of noise about gender stereotyping as an important factor in education, the policy makers were not in a mood to challenge the gender stereotype of the role that girls play in domestic chores and sibling care. This was a ratification of both child labour and patriarchy (Sadgopal, 2006).

The POA (1986) went on to add, "keeping in view the importance of enrolment of girls, and also the fact that NFE has the potentiality of developing into a major programme of women's development, wherever possible, women will be appointed as instructors." The question then is: if girls are pushed to non-formal schooling, how would equality be achieved at higher and technical stages?

Research attests to the fact that an increasing proportion of boys go to the private or tuition-aided government schools, whereas girls, particularly from lower castes and tribal communities, are being enrolled in alternative schools (Ramachandran, 2002, 2004). A NUEPA report (2004) shows that it is the girls who are being drawn into the sub-standard schooling of Education Guarantee Scheme (EGS), and this can be viewed as feminisation of non-formal education. Manjrekar (2003, p. 4,582) points to the dichotomy that has been set up between boys—superior/private, and girls—inferior/government, and its tragic consequences for the self-esteem and identity of girls. She speaks of girls "who with considerable anguish question, but also resign themselves to, this divide which casts them as educationally less deserving than their brothers".

Ramachandran reports that "despite the rapid growth of private and aided schools in many areas of the country, it has been noted that the proportion of girls is higher in government schools as compared to private schools" (2004, p. 78). NFE thus represents an inclusion politics that "reaffirms" a hegemonic core, to which the margins are added without any significant destabilisation of the core (Dhaliwal, 1996). It also continues to valorise the very centre that is problematic to begin with. Thus, without challenging the hegemonic core of patriarchy, it is not possible to give girls what is their fundamental right.

A serious engagement with the issue was reflected in the recommendations of the Acharya Ramamurti Committee (1990), which stated that "the evaluation of policy in relation to women's education needs to be made in the larger context of the socio-cultural reality in which women live; and the educational situation that is sought to be addressed and subsequently redressed". However, its recommendations were largely ignored. Consequently, despite several schemes and policies, inclusion of a large section of girl children into the 'system' of formal education has not been achieved. It is hardly surprising that such exclusion occurs in a context where there is an obvious absence of social sensitivity towards the needs of women, leaving them most vulnerable to poverty and abuse. It is clear that unless the entire range of social, cultural and economic factors that have inhibited women's access to education is addressed, the issue will remain unsolved.

The Kothari Commission Report did point to this imbalance and recommended that effort and research should be undertaken to improve the future. Several researchers, such as Ramachandran (2004), have hailed the massive, World Bank-sponsored District Primary Education Programme (DPEP) launched in the nineties as a programme that focused on gender in an effective way. The real picture seems to be different, though. Introduction of measures such as Education Guarantee Scheme (EGS) in the DPEP have added to the woes of girls. The Sarva Shiksha Abhiyan (SSA), which followed the DPEP, was thought to be a panacea though it has limited financial provisions for girls' education in the form of free textbooks and innovations at district levels.

Yet another programme, entitled National Programme for Education of Girls at Elementary Level (NPEGEL), has been formulated to provide additional support for education of underprivileged/disadvantaged girls at the elementary level. The NPEGEL is a part of the SSA and will be implemented under its umbrella, but as a distinct and separate gender component plan of the SSA. The thrust still remained on designing special schemes and programmes that tinker with the system but are not adequate. It has become clear that such pro-poor, pro-women or "pro-excluded" programmes had only a temporary and limited impact.

On the other hand, the programmes that did work were stripped of their significance. Mahila Samakhya is one such example. Launched in 1988, it was a concrete programme for the education and empowerment of women in rural areas, particularly of women from socially and economically marginalised groups. It initiated a process, which created a space for the most disadvantaged rural women to collectively seek empowerment on their own terms according to their varying place-specific realities (Agarwal 1994; Nagar 2000, 2004). Yet, as many experts have indicated, the programme remained marginal throughout the nineties. "For every 100 rupees allocated for elementary education in the Union Budget, hardly 25 paise were given to it. In due course, even this minuscule programme, operating barely in a few dozen blocks seems to have lost its basic direction, the notable exceptions that continue to be informed by the original vision notwithstanding" (Sadgopal, 2005, p. 90).

That such programmes can be instrumental in creating dilemmas becomes clear from an insightful comment by Shivani, a woman activist from Tehri Garhwal. Says Shivani: "There is no doubt that Mahila Samakhya transformed many of us from overworked domestic creatures into fiery feminists.... But when we started searching and addressing the most profound and hidden causes of our oppressions, it removed the support from under us.... What was the use of lighting the fire in our hearts, then? Just to cause more burnout and bitterness?....What do we do with the band-aid feminism that is happy when we label our feudal men as our enemies, but terribly unhappy when we critique the government, take issue with water privatisation policies, or challenge the community forestry schemes of the World Bank?" (Shivani interviewed by Richa in Tehri Garhwal, May 1999) I think this is a telling comment on the frustration experienced by women when they realised that genuine empowerment depends on the extent to which government policies allow for it.

## Interrogating the Dynamics of Exclusion

Both chronologically and philosophically, the policy documents had pre-empted the World Education Forum in Dakar in 2000. They had already drawn attention to the fact that gender discrimination continued to permeate education systems and to the need for reforms. In this sense, the policies were ahead of the International Conference on Women at Beijing in 1995 as well, which identified 12 critical areas—including women's access to non-discriminatory education and training—for action. Yet again, September 2000 saw the adoption of the UN Millennium Declaration, committing nations to stronger global efforts towards promoting gender equality and empowering women.

However, despite the deadlines and the directives of national and international measures, the truth is that the gender disparities in education continue to be more a rule than an exception. Time and again, there have been pointers that girls' education was impacted by both school-level as well as system-level barriers. On the one hand, the social classification of attributes and qualities into 'masculine' and 'feminine' are reflected in the realm of culture. On the other, the material basis and unequal power that underlie social relations between men and women influence the allocation of resources, roles and entitlements at the level of individual households, thereby influencing decision-making in relation to the education of children. Other dimensions of social structure in India, such as caste and community status, are also constitutive of gender dynamics and influence the nature of participation in educational institutions.

While these factors have been highlighted many times, it is still useful to list them to get an insight into the oppressive practices that have besieged educational provisions for girls. For instance, access to primary education continues to be a matter of serious concern, especially among girls from economically and socially powerless groups. 'Accessibility' is the measure or condition of things and services that can readily be reached or used (at the physical, visual, auditory and/or cognitive levels) by people.

Traditionally, the issue of access has been addressed from two distinct perspectives: one that relates to affordability or cost of access, and the second, in opposition to culturally constructed norms that cause barriers to accessing public goods and services. The first factor concerns the non-availability of school. Due to the typical geophysical features, many habitations have no schools that are easily accessible. For instance, the National Focus Group[3] on gender indicates that "rural residence has emerged as a very acute handicap." This is a result of the failure of policies, due to which there are far fewer schools and educational facilities for the poor living in rural areas and in the slums of cities and metros. Even if enrolment was to be taken as a reliable index, it is clear that the total number of girls enrolled is much below the mark. While it is true that there has been an increase in the number of girls going to schools as well as colleges, the percentage enrolled at all levels still falls below 50 per cent.

**Table 10.1: Percentage of Girls Enrolment to the Total Enrolment by Stages**

| *Year* | *Primary I-V* | *Middle VI-VIII* | *Sec./Hr. Sec/ Intermediate (IX-XII)* | *Hr. Education (Degree& above level)* |
|---|---|---|---|---|
| 1950-51 | 28.1 | 16.1 | 13.3 | 10.0 |
| 1955-56 | 30.5 | 20.8 | 15.4 | 14.6 |
| 1960-61 | 32.6 | 23.9 | 20.5 | 16.0 |
| 1965-66 | 36.2 | 26.7 | 22.0 | 20.4 |
| 1970-71 | 37.4 | 29.3 | 25.0 | 20.0 |
| 1975-76 | 38.1 | 31.3 | 26.9 | 23.2 |
| 1980-81 | 38.6 | 32.9 | 29.6 | 26.7 |
| 1985-86 | 40.3 | 35.6 | 30.3 | 33.0 |
| 1990-91 | 41.5 | 36.7 | 32.9 | 33.3 |
| 1991-92 | 41.9 | 38.2 | 33.8 | 32.3 |
| 1992-93 | 42.6 | 38.8 | 33.9 | 33.2 |
| 1993-94 | 42.7 | 39.1 | 34.3 | 33.5 |
| 1994-95 | 42.9 | 39.3 | 35.9 | 34.0 |
| 1995-96 | 43.1 | 39.5 | 36.1 | 36.0 |
| 1996-97 | 43.2 | 39.9 | 36.4 | 36.7 |
| 1997-98 | 43.5 | 40.3 | 36.6 | 37.5 |
| 1998-99* | 43.5 | 40.5 | 37.8 | 38.1 |
| 1999-2000* | 43.6 | 40.4 | 38.9 | 38.7 |
| 2000-2001* | 43.7 | 40.9 | 38.6 | 39.4 |
| 2001-2002* | 44.1 | 41.8 | 39.5 | 39.9 |
| 2002-2003* | 46.8 | 43.9 | 41.3 | 40.1 |
| 2003-2004* | 46.7 | 44.0 | 41.1 | 39.7 |

* Provisional, Selected Educational Statistics, (2003-2004) MHRD, Department of Education, Government of India.

A large number of girls are still out of school and college, because access to education continues to be difficult. The gender parity index shows that whereas it has increased from 0.041 in 1950-51 to 0.095 in 2003-04 for primary, 0.22 to 0.86 in 1950-51 to 0.086 in 2003-04 for upper primary and 0.038 in 1950-51 to 0.093 in 2003-04 for elementary, the rates of dropout have decreased with the gap widening as girls reach the secondary school. Girls experience difficulties in mobility from primary to secondary and secondary to higher education stage. It is also important to note that certain marginalised girls, such as disabled, tribal or dalit girls, do not find mention in the collected statistics. Educational statistics also reveal disparities in school enrolment rates between girls and boys that sharpen at higher stages of education. As Leela Visaria and Vimla Ramchandran (2004, p. 43) point out, "For girls, along with cost of education, their usefulness and help for the work at home were given as reasons for their non-attendance." Very often, the dropout rates among girl children are a result of availability of educational facilities, their coverage and quality. For instance, lack of infrastructure, such as toilets, is a major factor in keeping the girls away from school. As Madan (2004; p. 148) says, "Most schools have few classrooms and too many students resulting in multi-grade situations both in academic and physical terms. Toilets and drinking water facilities are lacking. Often, in some schools, the backyard is used as an open toilet."

Another factor concerns the home environment of children. Geeta Nambisan (2004) points out, "Girls are at a disadvantage in comparison with boys, not merely in relation to their chances of school entry and retention but in the kind of academic environments provided by the home as well. For instance, boys tend to have an advantage over their female siblings in terms of resources invested in their education, time made available for studies within the home, academic support (such as tuition or private coaching) and other educational experiences provided to children." Reviewing available data, Mukhopadhyay (1994, p. 108-9) comments, "Even the well-off, education-oriented families...view educational achievement, especially in scientific fields, differently for girls than boys, and are less inclined to invest family resources in the academic success of daughters than sons."

While some of these issues might appear reconcilable, a more serious issue is that of safety. There is enough evidence to suggest that insecurity/sexual harassment faced by girls in school/college premises and on the way to school/college is considerable. Though safety issues concern both young boys and girls, a family will very often let the son travel miles to go to the high-school or college, but not be as comfortable letting the daughter travel alone. Concerns for inadequate safety in schools are justified as it is not uncommon to find caretakers in school involved in cases of molestation and rape.

Further, as pointed out by the Acharya Ramamurti Committee, access acquires a different orientation when we look at the connections between access to water, fuel and fodder and the schooling of girls. It is difficult to understand how women are expected to be "included" when they (only girls, and not boys) walk long distances to collect fuel, fodder and water; when their sources of revenue, which are linked with natural resources are destroyed; when their rights to these resources are not recognised.[5] Finally, sibling care has been one of the major reasons for low-enrolment and high dropout rate among girls. Early childhood care and education (ECCE) is far from being integrated into the policy planning though its significance has been realised. The major provider of ECCE is the Integrated Child Development Services (ICDS). The observation of the Acharya Ramamurti Committee, that ICDS had come to acquire rigidity, bureaucratisation, low performance, lack of community participation, insensitivity to local needs, patterns and socio-cultural conditions, is worth remembering. To be truly effective, they would need to be invigorated.

Even if girls reach school, they are confronted with skewed educational content that reiterates the prejudices they must contend with in society. Whether it is the classroom practices, representation in texts and curricula, expectations of teachers, choice of subjects, availability of women teachers, gender bias runs through it all (Nambisan, 2001; Bhog 2002, 2005; Chanana, 2006). For instance, the divisions of work in school, teachers' comments—(girls) should not laugh loudly or whistle—and constant reminders about their 'eventual roles' is definitely cause for concern. Since the school reproduces the cultural structures of domination and patriarchy, it discourages the active participation of girls in classroom activities. Biases in curriculum framework have been identified as critical in casting girls as suited for traditional roles (Bhog, 2005). When curricular choices are made after secondary school, girls tend to cluster in what are perceived as the more 'feminine' arts and humanities courses, while a relatively larger proportion of boys are found in 'career-oriented' science, commerce and, more recently, computer courses. These subject choices reflect gender inequality in education and constrain future options and life chances of girls.

Psychological discourse informs us that the formation of gender identity begins very early in the family as children internalise what are seen as culturally appropriate qualities and attitudes associated with being 'masculine' and 'feminine'. Though there are variations among different social groups, the preference for son and the notion of the daughter as 'parai' (other) are prevalent. However, my submission is that psychological analysis alone is insufficient. Issues of access and ongoing practices highlight two aspects—the socio-cultural issues and economics that dictate the position of women in the society. It is obvious that suggestions such as provision of special support services, setting of deadlines and effective monitoring are important, but do they complete the story?

Another factor that is often used as a defence for inferior provision refers to *budgetary allocations, the expenditure incurred as well as the intent of the policies/schemes/programmes*. There are major gaps between the women-related policy statements of the government and the resources committed for their implementation. For instance, even in the case of Education for All, the total fund requirement for the three major programmes of girls education in the Tenth Five-year Plan was Rs 41,080 million (Table 9.6, POA of EFA). The distribution is as follows:

**Table 10.2: Estimated Fund Requirements for Major Programmes of Girls Education During the Tenth Five-year Plan Period**

| *Scheme* | *Centre* | *State* | *Total* |
|---|---|---|---|
| Free education for girls | 1125 | 375 | 1500 |
| Mahila Samakhya | 250 | 0 | 250 |
| KGSV | 1200 | 0 | 1200 |
| Secondary Education | 1158 | 0 | 1158 |
| | 3733 | 375 | 4108 |

Thus, of a total fund requirement of Rs 9,52,770 for implementing the National Plan of Action for EFA (Table 9.12), a meagre Rs. 41,080 was allocated for girls. This allocation pattern can be traced to the fact that EFA accepts non-formalisation of girls' education. Unless gender budgeting becomes a part of the fiscal policies, the difference between intent and action will not become perceptible.[6]

A significant lacuna within the educational establishment is to ignore the centrality of gender and Its intersections with class, caste, disability and rural-urban divide. While POA 1986 and 1992 have chapters on these categories of intersections, gender concerns are not included within their ambit. The Acharya Ramamurti Committee recognised this issue (4.1.2). The CABE committee as well as the National Focus Group on gender issues in education reflect this fragmentation by making issues related to gender an exclusive concern of one committee. All issues need to be understood in a gender-sensitive context.

As I have argued elsewhere, a significant question for me is whether it is enough to establish an hierarchy of oppression (Ghai, 2003)—women are more oppressed than men, lower caste women are more oppressed than high caste women, the SC/ST are more vulnerable and so on. While it is generally agreed that all human beings suffer when they are located in terms of fixed categories, it is nonetheless a gross oversimplification to say that all women are oppressed equally and in similar ways. Feminists have recognised this problem in their questioning of the ways in which identity politics employs a language of authentic subjective experience. Such scaling can be not only devastating but discordant and disengaging. As Menon (2004) points out, "We must go much further than saying that 'women' mobilise as upper caste/ dalit and so on. Rather we need to come to the more complex recognition that under different circumstances and given different kinds of political mobilisation, 'people' identify and come together as dalits, Muslims, working class or, much less often, as women." Padmini Swaminathan (2002) also says that the slogans of autonomy and empowerment are narrowed down to certain decontextualised categories of literacy, etc., without considering the multiple variables that constitute the paradigm of "empowerment". The dynamics of how education can lead to women's autonomy is rarely specified.

Also, though existing social and cultural biases are impediments to girls' education, it is difficult to map a one-to-one relationship between these biases and either girls' education or women's empowerment. An economically advanced state like Punjab, which has a female literacy of 63.5 per cent, and a metropolitan city like Delhi, with a female literacy of 75 per cent, have sex ratios of 874 and 821 respectively. These statistics raise a question about the kind of education imparted to students. The question that remains is whether increased access to education would be instrumental in improving women's status. It is obvious that there is a lot of gap between what is taught and the demands of reality. If all investments in education are guided by profitability, the objectives such as realisation of personhood become problematic. Thus the conviction of the Jomtien-Dakar Framework of EFA, postulating a correlation between literacy and indicators such as infant mortality rate, is really an illusion. The correlation was much more between economic levels and social indicators (Sadgopal, 2004).

## Confronting Globalisation

When the Kothari Commission was making its recommendations, it would not have visualised an India that would embrace globalisation. The availability of labour sans boundaries and the building of a truly united world is a long-desired ideal. Globalisation has been promoted as the "gateway to heaven" in terms of opportunities, offering immense possibilities in enhancing trade, communication, cultural interaction and travel. However, even its staunchest supporters would agree that globalisation has a selective and uneven nature. As Alison Symington (2002, p. 3) puts it, "Its impacts are felt in innumerable ways by various groups of people in different regions of the world; the processes of globalisation are exacerbating existing inequalities and at the same time they produce all new divisions and asymmetries." While it may take different forms, the dominant pattern is that of neo-liberal capitalist ideals. Structural adjustment policies—which aim to balance budgets and increase competitiveness through trade and price liberalisation—include reduction of the public-sector expenditure and growth of the private sector. This has resulted in a recasting of citizens as consumers. The locus of control shifts from the public domain of politics to an individualised and privatised world of economic cost-and-benefit analysis.

The paradigm of profit, thus becomes all-important and pervades all aspects of life. It also restricts the use of State revenue towards welfare activities. Governments, therefore, find themselves unable to finance education. The pious intent of governments comes under a lot of doubt. For instance, in the National Policy on Education, 1986, it was stated that "the investment on education be gradually increased to reach a level of 6 per cent of the National Income as early as possible" (Para 11.4). However, will a deregulated market economy fulfil the promise? Now, with the government's increasing dependence on external sources for financing a priority sector such as elementary education, the picture is extremely dismal. Regardless of the initial reluctance to accept external funding in the education sector, the government changed its stand drastically in the last fifteen years. Obviously, this leads to denial of access to education of a vast segment of the population who live on the margins of society. In fact, their struggles have demonstrated that the right to education, rather than being a universal right, represents "a terrain of struggle over forms of knowledge, social practices, and values that constitute the critical elements of tradition" (Giroux, 1988, p. 5). While every child is affected in such attempts, the worst affected are the so-called vulnerable groups that were in any case marginalised in the education process.

Increasingly, it has become clear that globalisation as an economic force subordinates and marginalises women further. In fact, there is exploitation of pre-existing gender hierarchies to re-inscribe patriarchal norms and practices, thereby exacerbating the contours of women's subordination. Thus, neo-liberalism increasingly threatens women's hard-won rights, particularly the right to education, to gainful employment and to health. Neo-liberalism, likewise, results in the weakening of people's democratic gains as states continue to give political concessions in the pursuit of more foreign investment. Today, globalisation is being led by a few hundred multinational corporations that have economies larger than many national economies. Rarely do women play any role in their decision-making, but often women are their victims. In the developing world, there is growing poverty; the gap between the rich and poor continues to increase. Most of the poor are women as they are the primary victims of exploitation and marginalisation.

In such a context, educating and training women and girls, especially in non-traditional work, is the key to their economic development. It is not surprising that in the face of an acute shortage of gainful employment opportunities, millions of women opt for migrant work, particularly in areas that make them more vulnerable to emotional, psychological, physical and sexual violence. Salaries are still often determined by gender, rather than the skills required for the job resulting in unequal pay for equal work. The cutting of government subsidies and social welfare provisions has hit women the hardest, making it more difficult for them to escape poverty. The provision of education, housing, healthcare and childcare would certainly lessen the economic burden on women and assist in their economic independence.

I am sure that the Kothari Commission would not have imagined that education would feature under the umbrella of General Agreement on Trade in Services (GATS). But since education is now construed as a service industry, there is every possibility that countries with different academic needs and resources will be forced to conform to systems inevitably designed to serve the interest of corporate educational providers, thereby breeding inequality and dependence. This commodification of education can further marginalise the weaker sections, including girls. In a socio-cultural landscape where investments in girls' education are always secondary, girls will end up getting poor quality higher education.

Another insidious way in which globalisation affects women is what is referred to as "State-organised feminism", which is replacing feminist politics on the ground. Empowerment of women is a slogan much in use by government agencies (Menon, 2004). The programmes of the government, however, aim at empowering women only to the extent of harnessing women's contribution to growth—a goal that the government is under considerable external pressure to attain. While the government spiel in the language of rights might appear enticing, it can never be enough, because it discourages ordinary women from taking the initiative. In the long run, cultural norms cannot be challenged without collective action rooted in awareness of ground-level realities. It is worthwhile to remember that co-option by the State can kill activism of the highest order. In Wallach's (1991, p. 41) words, "Feminists and all those committed to emancipatory theorising must challenge the dominant, oppressive and repressive cultures of these institutions by creating a space and culture, a holding environment, in which we can come to terms with our social realities and their representations. The ongoing process of creating a holding environment for ourselves and each other, a social, intellectual space for political, intellectual sociability, for reflecting on our given 'realities', strengthens and empowers us to address and challenge the oppressive and repressive nature of those realities and the representations of those realities."

## Inclusive Education

In educational discourse, "inclusive education" has been a buzz word. The philosophy behind inclusive schools is that all children have the right to be educated with their peers in regular classrooms in neighbourhood schools. The concept of "inclusive education" advocates intrinsic respect for difference, thereby celebrating diversity rather than creating labels that delimit human potential. The philosophical underpinnings of inclusive education are rooted in the purpose of education itself, which was underlined by the Kothari Commission as: "In our opinion, therefore, no reform is more urgent than to transform education, to endeavour to relate it to life, needs and aspirations of the people and thereby make it a powerful instrument of social, cultural transformation necessary for realisation of our national goals" (1.20).

Despite recognising the transformative potential of education as well as the inherent hierarchies of the Indian society, an analysis of the education of 'handicapped' persons by the Kothari Commission is at best conventional and conservative. While on the one hand, it speaks of social justice as well as constitutional commitment, it looks at disability as an individual problem. The report says, "Their [handicapped] education has to be organised not merely on humanitarian ground, but also on grounds of utility. Proper education generally enables a handicapped child to overcome his (or her) handicap, and makes him also a useful citizen" (6.42). The instrumentalist underpinning of this argument is too clear. It runs counter to the Commission's understanding of education as an inalienable right of every citizen. The recommendations thus, wittingly or unwittingly, ratify the assumption that disability is a self-evident condition of bodily inadequacy and private misfortune. While the report does articulate "the need for the education of handicapped children as being an inseparable part of the general educational system, the primary task is to prepare him [handicapped] for adjustment to a socio-cultural environment designed to meet the needs of the 'normal'. However, it does not question the fact that a society is characterised by hegemony of the normative. It recommends both the 'special' and integrated education for the 'handicapped'.

For me, it implies the division of students into standard and non-standard populations. It is a ranked notion of ability that disrupts the notion of true diversity. The binary of regular/special reflects at a deeper level a paradigm of 'normal' or 'regular'. Thus the construction of 'what is normal' would decide the meaning of the special. Therefore, when the Kothari Commission mentions the necessity of setting up "one good institution for the education of handicapped children in each district", it keeps the binary of regular/special alive, thereby belying the recommendation that, "it is essential that the education of the handicapped children should be inseparable part of the general education system" (6.46). While the report did consider, "the several advantages....[such as] reduction of costs and promoting mutual understanding between handicapped and non-handicapped children," it highlighted the disadvantage that "many handicapped children find it psychologically disturbing to be placed in an ordinary school" (6.47). Though skeptical, the report still recommended integration.

It was this skepticism that every policy thereafter has continued to reflect by non-engagement with understanding of disability. The policies have thus adopted a very casual attitude towards the issues of the disabled children, painting a picture that it is absolutely impossible to include the disabled children in the same class as every other child. It is worth noticing that the intent of the Kothari Commission was to cover only ten per cent of the total number of handicapped children. In retrospect, the Commission was ratifying the dominant Indian cultural ethos that seal the fate of the disabled with labels such as 'langra' (crippled), 'andha' or 'surdas' (blind), 'behra' (deaf) and 'pagal' (mad).[7] Disability thus epitomises 'failure', and is conceived of as a personal tragedy. Destiny is seen as the culprit, and disabled people are accorded the victim status with a clear enunciation that posits disability as a retribution for past *karmas* (actions) from which there can be no reprieve. It seems that such an understanding of disability is at the root of low expectations from disabled students. To quote William Rhodes (1995), "the metaphor of illness (e.g., diagnosis, treatment) was codified and imported directly into school system.... The imported medical metaphor of illness constructed differences in learning styles as "pathology", "handicaps" and "deficiency" (p. 459). So the Kothari Commission became a forerunner of policy stipulations that assume the ideology of pathology as the only way to read the lives of disabled children. It is interesting to note that while, on the face of it, the Commission is keen on rehabilitating the "handicapped", the confidence that the goal can be accomplished is not evident.

Thereafter, the NPE 1968 recommended that "educational facilities for the physically and mentally handicapped children should be expanded and attempts should be made to develop integrated programmes enabling handicapped children to study in regular schools." This report was followed by the UNESCO initiatives on whose recommendations the then Department of Social Welfare launched the Centrally Sponsored Scheme of Integrated Education for Disabled Children (IEDC), in 1974. The scheme was meant for four categories of students, viz., blind and partially sighted children, deaf and partially hearing children, orthopaedically and neurologically handicapped children and children with multiple handicaps (Ministry of Social Welfare). The implementation of this scheme was transferred to the Department of Education in 1982. Under the scheme, 100 per cent financial assistance is admissible for the education of disabled children studying in common schools by way of supply of aids/equipments; allowances for books, uniforms, transport, readers in respect of blind children, escorts in respect of severely orthopaedically handicapped and employment of helpers/attendants. The scheme also provided for meeting the cost of salary of special teachers, setting up of resource rooms, carrying out assessment of disabled children, training of special teachers, removal of architectural barriers in schools and production of instructional material.

Now, if the scheme was so comprehensive, why is it that education of disabled remains a neglected area? In my view, IEDC became a prototype of the "scheme/project" approach, which clearly stated that education of the 'disabled' needs to be viewed only as a 'project' or 'scheme' rather than as a *responsibility of the education/school system.* This scheme-based approach also negates the possibility of looking at the issue of education of the disabled as an opportunity for undertaking systemic reforms in the formal education system. Despite constant pointers (Ghai, 2001; Jha, 2006) the discrimination has been perpetuated by having two separate systems. Whereas the general educational needs come under the purview of the Ministry of Human Resource Development, the responsibility for special education is discharged by the Ministry of Social Justice and Empowerment, thereby sandwiching the disabled children between the two ministries. As the PSG[8] input to the CABE Committee indicates, "The education of children with disabilities (treated as special education) continues to remain outside the HRD Ministry. This is in contrast with other countries in the world, which have transferred special education to the respective education departments or ministries" (Ghai, 1999). The location of education of the disabled in the welfare department actually kept the charitable mode alive (Jha, 2006; Ghai, 2001). That there was scope for dilution was indicated by the use of both "common school terminology" and special school. It might be useful to ask why the scheme failed. The IEDC was extended to two more categories, namely, children with learning disabilities and children with severe disabilities. At this stage, the scheme became the Project Integrated Education for the Disabled (PIED), a joint NCERT effort. This was deemed necessary for strengthening the implementation of the IEDC scheme. That the impact of these schemes was barely perceptible is clear from estimates, which reveal that only seven per cent of the disabled children are being educated (Ghai, 2001b).

The National Policy on Education (NPE), 1986 (with modifications in 1992) continued to use the language of integration by stating that the physically and mentally disabled will be educated with the general community as equal partners to prepare them for normal growth and to enable them to face life with courage and confidence. However, the effect was diluted by its use of the terms such as *wherever it is feasible* and *as far as possible*. It also provided room for dilution by resorting to vocational training as well as by emphasising the *special difficulties* of disabled children. In a certain sense, the State was already in the process of abdicating responsibility by encouraging voluntary effort for the education of the disabled (4.9, p. 14).

While it did advocate that education of children with mild and moderate disabilities be given space in general schools, the children under integration were still constructed as "problems", thereby making a mockery of the supposed mainstreaming. This represents what is called an add-on approach, in that the child is simply added to the programme. Scholars such as Ferguson (1995) would call this as being "in but not of the class" (p. 284). The disabled child is really not a functional member of the class or an active participant in its activities. Thus, it is not the system that gets transformed; rather, it is left to the disabled child to adjust. This amounts to an "integration" that is more a token rather than a realistic inclusion in the classroom, curriculum or wider school activities.

This approach is reflected in the educational statistics provided by the MHRD. A comparatively saner voice did get verbalised in the form of recommendations made by the Acharya Ramamurti Review Committee. Though the committee suggested some good measures, such as providing support to the families of disabled children, it did not take a firm stand on inclusive education. While acknowledging that the educational system for the "handicapped" should be flexible, it continued to advocate a range of educational provisions—special schools for those who cannot be educated in general schools, special classes in general schools, educational packages for hearing-impaired children, integrated education for the disabled of the type already in existence. Thus, despite its critical outlook and emphasis on the Kothari Commission's recommendation of a common school, it fragmented education for the disabled in terms of formal, non-formal, open schools, home based schools, vocational centres, etc. It advocated that "sustained researches should be undertaken to determine the needs of the physically handicapped and produce technological aids capable of helping in overcoming handicaps." It also suggested that the Indian Institutes of Technology and other technological institutions in the area of higher education should be given specific responsibilities for undertaking these researches. Even with all these recommendations, the focus remained very narrow. One only wishes that the esteemed committee could have understood disability as a social category requiring serious academic engagement and research (4.3.6).

Even as the Ramamurti Committee stressed that sensitisation of general public is important, it continued to locate the problems of the disabled in individual impairments. Policy documents are totally oblivious of the paradigm shift in understanding of impairment and disability. In POA 1992, the Government admitted: "The evaluation of special schools and the scheme of IEDC have revealed some grey areas. General education system is not yet mobilised for the education of the handicapped, either at Central or state level. Inputs from different schemes like CBR, DRC, ECCE, non-formal education, adult education, etc., are not being brought together for the education of the physically handicapped...The goal of UEE for this disadvantaged group would remain an unachievable dream unless concerted and urgent measures are taken" (4.19, POA, 1992, p. 17). Thus, one can see that there was acceptance of the fact that it would be difficult for the State to progress with respect to education of the disabled. More problematic were the 'pragmatic' principles which stated that "a child with disability, who can be educated in general school, should be educated in general school and not in a special school" (4.2.1 POA 1992 p. 18). It is being assumed that assessment practices are apolitical. The suggested upshot of this evolutionary construction, incidental or assured, is that we have advanced toward the zenith of best practices in education, both scientifically and morally. Thus all that is left is the issue of finding the best match.

Such a narrative, however, does not take into account the historical predicament of school segregation. There was no re-structuring of programmes that could disrupt and disengage the course of human stratification, which is deeply entrenched in the education policy. It is particularly instructive to note this in a narrative that casts the DPEP as an extremely successful project (Ramachandran, 2004). Many scholars, such as Vandana Madan (2004), Vani Periodi (2004) and others, lament the absence of a meaningful discourse on disability. Most educational provisions for disabled children remain exclusionary, commanding low priority as a whole. As a result, rather than equipping disabled children and young people with the opportunities to live a full and active adult life, it largely conditions them to accepting a much devalued social role and in so doing, condemns them to a lifetime of dependence.

The need to educate the disabled was yet again articulated in the Persons with Disabilities Act (Equal Opportunities, Protection of Rights and Full Participation), 1995, better known as PWD Act. According to the Act, the Central and state governments and local authorities are legally bound to provide access to free education to all the disabled children until the age of 18 years within integrated school settings. The Act envisages a comprehensive education scheme to provide transport facilities, remove architectural barriers, supply free books, uniforms and other materials, grant scholarships, restructure curriculum and modify the examination system for the benefit of children with special needs. But it is also quick to point out that this can be accomplished as and when resources permit. However, even a cursory glance at the suggestions in the Act, such as part-time classes, non-formal education, open schools and open universities for children with special needs belie the thrust on inclusion.

Yet another programme that was introduced by the Government of India was the Sarva Shiksha Abhiyan. It stated: "The thrust of the SSA will be on providing integrated and inclusive education to all children with special needs in general schools. It will also support a wide range of approaches, options and strategies.... This includes education through open learning system and open schools, non-formal and alternative schooling, distance education and learning, special schools, wherever necessary, home-based education, itinerant teacher model, remedial teaching, part-time classes, community-based rehabilitation (CBR) and vocational education, and cooperative programmes." Thus, it was not systemic reforms that the SSA was looking for. Indeed, it negates inclusion by promoting parallel streams in education for children with disabilities. The ratification of the National Mission of the Sarva Shiksha Abhiyan by the disability sector reflects the fact that serious educational realities have not been negotiated.

Within the stipulations made, there are contradictions. While there is a directive that, as far as possible, every child with special needs should be placed in regular schools with needed support services, it also says that, wherever necessary, special schools may be strengthened to obtain their resource support in convergence with departments and agencies working in the field of education and welfare of the students with disabilities. There is absolutely no discourse on the meaning of "as far as possible" and "wherever necessary". Similarly, though the support services listed are indeed impressive, with a grant of Rs 1,200 per disabled child, these stipulations are nothing more than rhetorical statements. While it is true that almost half the children in the age group of 5-14 are out of school (Sadgopal, 2000, p. 251), the dream that there will be space for children with disabilities (especially if segregated schooling is being advocated for them) is really far-fetched.

## International Pressures

The policy stipulations discussed above are to be understood in the context of international discourse, which is articulated in various programmes and statements, such as the UN World Programme of Action Concerning Disabled Persons (1983), the UN Convention on the Rights of the Child (adopted in 1989 and ratified by over 190 countries, including India), the World Declaration on Education For All (1990), the Standard Rules on Equalisation of Opportunities for Persons with Disabilities (adopted in 1993), and the UNESCO Salamanca Statement and Framework for Action (1994). The Salamanca Statement proclaimed that every child has a fundamental right to education and children with special needs must have access to regular schools, which should accommodate them within *child*-centred pedagogy. The World Summit for Social Development (1995) and the UNDP's Inter-regional Programme for Disabled People (1995) echoed similar sentiments. While India has been a signatory to most of these agreements, reflection on the need to restructure the disability discourse has been absent from wider educational discourse. More recently, the UN has ratified a convention that will govern the rights of disabled people. It is interesting that various policies, starting from the Education Commission's Report, indicate that a different curriculum would be needed for disabled children. It is worth noting that, despite these nods of recognition, no premier institute of education has actually engaged itself with either curriculum or pedagogy issues in the context of disabled children. Peter Clough (1988, p. 66) argues that, "if curriculum could have been placed at the centre of special needs inquiry, then the special needs provision will necessarily move nearer to the centre of curriculum issues, no longer marginalised but the very touchstone and proving point of coherent, sensitive and moral curriculum planning for all." The obsession with the tag 'special' person leads to a focus on disconnected planning, such as task analyses, behaviour modification, and training in specific (even, limited) skills. It does not engage with the 'whole' person.

My contention is that whether it is disability or some other form of marginalisation, the significant question is how we accommodate this difference. In other words, difference has to be re-theorised. In the specific historical context of neo-liberalism, which attaches value to individualism and not inter-dependence, the disabled person is perceived as having a deficit. As Susan Peters puts it, "the disabled students are relegated to a silent and silenced world, where they become what they are perceived as being: incapable, illiterate, dysfunctional and non-productive members of school and society" (Peters 1999, p. 104). In a globalised economy, such commitments will remain more an exercise in rhetoric rather than real change. This becomes even more significant when one realises that the Government of India had reconstituted the Central Advisory Board of Education (CABE) in its Resolution dated

July 6, 2004. Though initially not considered within its frame of reference, the government did include inclusive education at the behest of the Public Study Group. Taking a cue from the disability movement's slogan of "Nothing for us without us", the government nominated two disability activists to the CABE. However, before the CABE submitted its report, the HRD Minister announced an action plan which stated: "It should and will be our objective to make mainstream education not just available but accessible, affordable and appropriate for students with disabilities." But in reality no financial allocation was made. As Alur (2006) pointed out, "...unfortunately the Ministry of HRD seems to have not been able to put their act together and has put this on the back-burner, forgetting the commitment made by their Minister in Parliament, it has not worked out the financial allocation needed. No policy can be operationalised without fiscal support and it is likely that the Minister's Statement in Parliament will remain a policy without teeth...just a statement of pious intent." The all-important question that begs an answer is whether the State, which is abdicating its responsibility, is serious about such committees. It is quite telling that the justification of the government's action plan is vested in the literacy figures obtained for the disabled, rather than the absolute number of the disabled being educated. It notes that compared to a national level literacy figure of around 65 per cent, the percentage of literate disabled population is only 49 per cent. According to the National Sample Survey Organisation (NSSO), 2002, of the literate disabled population, only nine per cent completed secondary (and above) education. The question that begs an answer is whether the government wants to provide formal education or just literacy skills. The focus on "social training", "general life skills" and specialist disability skills work against the disabled, resulting in lack of formal qualifications, higher unemployment and social isolation.

A report in *The Times of India*[9] dated April 20, 2006 indicates that *out of the total of 44,000 available* seats in the University of Delhi, 1,320 seats are reserved for the "*physically disadvantaged*".[10] However, in 2001, only 250 such disabled students gained admission under this quota. What could be the reason? Is it because none of the disabled students qualify or is it because of the structural amnesia and attitudinal conservatism that inflict our society? If this is the situation when higher education is financed by the State, one can well imagine what would happen if the resources were to get transferred to the private sector as suggested by the Ambani Birla Report (2000). One can see the sinister control of the disabled in this. By keeping them as vulnerable will only help them feed into the corporate world, which is reluctant to consider providing facilities[11] for the disabled.

Perhaps it is important to understand the assumptions that render the education of disabled a difficult endeavour. Policy is guided by the medical constructions that encourage cure/overcoming theories. A paradigmatic shift in disability and related issues came in the form of recognition that social oppression transforms 'impairment' into 'disability'. As a pioneer in disability studies, Mike Oliver (1992, p. 101), comments, "Disability cannot be abstracted from the social world which produces it; it does not exist outside the social [and economic] structures in which it is located and independent of meanings given to it. In other words, disability is socially produced." The responsibility for turning the impairment into disability lies with the economic system. Capitalism requires that greater value is placed upon individuals, who make a productive contribution to the market economy. This image of not being able to contribute to production has serious implications on all walks of life, including education, which is seen more in instrumentalist terms rather than genuine empowerment.[12]

Consequently, training offered to the disabled often has little or no meaning outside the special school classroom. As the national focus group on work and education[13] points out, "With these so-called vocational skills that we impart, the disabled will never be able to catch up with their peers or transfer the skills taught in school to the real world, because society has no jobs for them. Thus, we deny most of the disabled a real chance of becoming gainfully employed and living a healthy life." A move away from construction of deficiency mandates that we provide skills that focus on full and equal citizenship rather than a bare minimum. To construct disability as a limiting condition that marks the end of human agency is tantamount to doing injustice to humanity.

A more serious danger arises when inclusion is presented as a means of alleviating oppression and subordination. Thus, disabled children and adults, who are defined by reference to their lack of power—which is seen as a natural outcome of their generalised low position within the hegemony of normality—often have to learn to live with the benevolence of the State and the civil society. Consequently, when the State backs out, their condition becomes worse because of the sudden withdrawal of resources. The only hope that disabled people have then is to coexist, but only if there is no conflict potential in terms of resources. The alteration of built environment, translation of study material into sign language and Braille, or providing computer technology for the visually impaired has severe resource implications for the State and are, therefore, high on conflict potential. This kind of inclusion then becomes a meaningless and often an accidental by-product, albeit one which has tremendous ideological potential.

It is interesting to note that the Kothari Commission had felt that the progress in providing educational facilities to handicapped children will be limited by two main considerations; teachers and financial resources. The latter can be understood in a context where the stipulated six per cent of the GDP was never really spent on education. The former problem of not finding teachers, however, reflects a mindset that does not visualise the role of a teacher as a keen facilitator. Teachers, who have absolutely no difficulty in acknowledging oppression on the basis of class, caste or gender, would still be resistant to admitting a disabled child to their class. This, in my belief, is a political and not a resource issue. A teacher is not someone who can only bring to situation theories and concepts learned in teacher training courses. S/he is the 'vicarious consciousness' (Bruner, 1985), sharing the burden of learning with the student and reducing the complexity of the task to be mastered, in order to allow the learner to concentrate on critical features. The understanding that education provides the means through which disabled people are eventually able to participate in the production of a body of knowledge that reflects their own experiences, interests and ways of knowing does not get reflected in such discourses.

As Jenny Corbett and Roger Slee (2000, p. 136) comment: "Inclusive education is a distinctly political 'in your face' activity that proceeds from larger political, as opposed to technical, questions about the nature of society and the status afforded to people in varying forms and structures of social organisation. A political movement in the first instance, inclusion is about establishing access for all people. It is not conditional, nor does it speak about partial inclusion. Its impetus emanates from the recipients of professional services, rather than from being orchestrated by professionals themselves."

The twin pressures of globalisation and disability are much more difficult for girls. It does not require any creative effort to realise that the world that we live in is gendered and that education is seen as a central factor that effects socio-economic change. While some of the boundaries are being blurred, the space that the girl child occupies in the educational system is at best marginal. As I argue elsewhere, penetrating resistance that disabled women confront in a society where the dominant norm that operates is that of a perfect/unimpaired body is a very difficult endeavour (Ghai, 2003). The recognition that disability as an identity category has to be understood as plural in nature (including factors such as caste, class, religion, urban/rural divide and, most importantly, gender) is missing from educational research and analysis.

## The Way Forward: A Common School System

One of the most important recommendations of the Kothari Commission was the establishment of a 'Common School System' across the country, which would provide the bedrock for social justice, national integration and educational equality through a common admission policy, tuition-free school education, parity among teachers, besides equality in access and retention. In fact, subsequent policies in 1986 and 1992 also reiterated the Commission's recommendations. The report recognised the responsibility of the education system to bring different social classes and groups together and promote an egalitarian and integrated society. It also took note of the poor quality of government schools and lamented the fact that education tended to "increase social segregation and to perpetuate and widen class distinctions". Common school was thus seen not as a choice but as an imperative. The "internal transformation of education" so as to relate it to the life, needs and aspirations of the nation and the values enshrined in our constitution towards the development of a pluralist open society and a State that is secular, democratic and socialist in nature, are goals that cannot be fulfilled without a firm political conviction. If the furore caused by the recent order of taking the poor children into public schools[14] is any indication, it is not difficult to see that in a divided society, inclusive school will remain a pipedream, more by design than by default.

## Understanding Diversity

Diversity thus is not just a reality to be tolerated, accepted and accommodated; it is a reality to be treasured. For me, inclusion, therefore, does not speak only to disabled children. It is a term that sets out to undo the harm of a divided society. However, more as a rule than an exception, inclusion has come to denote the attempts to end the discrimination against all marginalised people. I do not think that inclusion of either girls or disabled children can be achieved until we get rid of all other places to which we plan to send children and youth when the system stops responding. Therefore, schools will not change until policy removes the alternatives. The suggested alternatives of non-formal education, minimum levels of learning and multi-grade teaching do not spell hope either for girls or the disabled. When education is implicated in a process of reducing 'the human' to capital, those who are not seen as fulfilling this are marginalised. In resisting the social drives incorporated within capitalist education and training, we simultaneously resist the reduction of our personhoods to a form of capital. The only alternative that we need urgently is a shift to an alternative view of education.

## Creation of a Discursive Place

My submission is that education has to be seen as a discursive space in which people can formulate, consider and debate the issues of the day. There must be 'public discourse' that interrogates issues transcending the narrow-minded concerns of the powerful groups, with the aim being other than the promotion of governmental aims. For education to offer a potential site for developing a 'civil society' with intrinsic respect for difference, it has to be forever open to change. As a result, the implications for the reduction of inequalities do not point to a single direction of change. Guaranteeing equality of access to and participation in 'mainstream' education requires a change in the system. However, that will come only if we question what children should learn, what kind of society we ought to visualise, and finally who the 'we' is who should debate and take the discourse further.

## Role of Society

The recognition that educational issues of girls and the disabled cannot be resolved without working at societal structures is urgently required. If both disabled and women have to claim space, voice and power, they need to disrupt the hegemonic discourses of patriarchy as well as normality. The knowledge generated by women studies and disability studies do need to become the bedrock of any educational planning. Developing a political analysis of marginalisation, influencing public opinion and evolving policies that do not have spaces, which are to be filled or have been left unsaid, will definitely go a long way in reaching the unreached.

## Hope against Hope

Justice will accrue to both gender concerns and disability only if we accept the philosophical underpinnings of inclusion. I am convinced that presence or participation, though important, is not enough to address the deep structural inequalities, which any marginalised group experiences. Simply removing barriers is not going to work as new and more subtle barriers may emerge. What we need to address is inclusion into 'what' rather than 'how'. Answers to these questions cannot come until we ask more fundamental questions such as: what is education all about. We have to guard against the cynic in us getting the better of us. While hope might be an accomplished liar, hope is all we have. As the genius Paulo Freire (1998, p. 69-70) says, "It needs to be clear that the absence of hope is not the 'normal' way to be human. It is a distortion.... For this reason, as human beings, one of our struggles should be to diminish the objective reasons for that hopelessness that immobilises us." Hope, according to him, is an ontological need. Says Freire (1998, p. 115), "I don't believe that women and men of the world are independent of their political positions yet conscious of their dignity, as men and women will not want to reflect on the sense of foreboding that is now universal in this perverse era of neo-liberal philosophy. A foreboding that one day will lead to a new rebellion where the critical word, the humanist philosophy, the commitment to solidarity...and the proclamation of a world worthy of human habitation will be instruments of change and transformation."

## Notes

1. As I have written elsewhere, historically, the belief that being a woman is the biggest disability has been quite widespread. A look at the socio-cultural meaning ascribed to female bodies and those assigned to disabled bodies is quite illuminating. Both are excluded from full participation in public and economic

spheres and are conceived in opposition to a norm that is assumed to possess natural superiority. Such comparisons can be both emancipatory and oppressive. If the objective of invoking such comparisons is to understand different people's life experiences and grasp their authenticity, the potential is immense. However, if the underlying realities of the categories serve only at a metaphorical level, it can lead to a total erasure of the category, which is being invoked. One is, therefore, compelled to focus on what gets "valorised" and "suppressed" in the process. A shift from the theoretical/metaphorical to the material is essential to render visible the "culture constructions" that have supported the currently flawed conceptualisations of disability and womanhood (See Ghai, 2003).

2. Report of the Durgabai Deshmukh Committee on Education of Women (1959), Hansa Mehta Committee on Differentiation of Curricula (1964), the Report of the Committee on Status of Women (CSWI) Towards Equality, 1974. The UN Development Decade (1975-85) saw growth of institutional mechanisms such as the Department of Women and Child Development. The National Perspective Plan for Women (1988-2000) chalked out the national gender agenda with a focus on disadvantaged women. Also, the National Policy on Women's Empowerment was issued in 2001.
3. Twenty one focus groups were formed to undertake an evaluation of the major areas of the curriculum as well as significant areas of national concern. The focus group on gender issues in education was chaired by Dr. Sharmila Rege, Women's Studies Centre, University of Pune.
4. See Bina Agarwal's seminal work *A field of ones own: Gender and Land Rights in South Asia* (1994, Cambridge University Press), She focuses on facets of gender inequality that have received relatively little attention, such as inequality in command over property, in social norms and perceptions, and in emerging community institutions for environmental governance.
5. I feel that an emphasis on what the financial provisions hide is warranted. The real question is whether we really want to 'educate' girls.
6. While language is often thought to be for communication, its role in generating discourse about social reality is often undermined. As a fellow disability activist Colin Barnes says, "The first and most important thing to remember about discussions of language and disability is that they arise because disabled people experience discrimination daily and are denied the same rights and opportunities as the rest of the population."
7. Public Study Group on CABE committees was formed in September 2004. PSG appreciated the reconstitution of CABE and responded to many areas of educational policy making. The funding for PSG came from the Council for Social Development, New Delhi.
8. I often wonder about the efficacy of higher education provisions that remain disassociated from the provisions at the school level. Once again, it highlights a fragmented approach to education. The Kothari Commission (1964-66) said that energising school education is possible if higher education and school education come together.
9. A research study by National Centre for Promotion of Employment for Disabled People (N.C.P.E.D.P.) reported that of a total of 119 respondent Universities, only 1,635 students with disabilities are enrolled. Considering that there is three

per cent reservation, the figure of 0.1 per cent is abysmally low. It is worth noting that many reputed universities, such as Delhi University, All India Institute of Medical Sciences, Indira Gandhi National Open University, Jamia Millia Islamia University (all of these in New Delhi), Bangalore University (Karnataka), University of Calcutta (West Bengal), University of Calicut (Kerala) amongst others did not respond to the survey. Details of the research study available at http://www.ncpedp.org.

10. Delhi University has initiated a multi-purpose Resource Centre with a variety of study materials in Braille format and special studios, which will transform text messages in audio cassettes. Braille production, talking book production and electronic text production will be the three focus points for the Centre.
11. It is not as if the disabled had a carefree life before capitalism, they however, did have spaces in family -based work as well as local units that would absorb them in a dignified way. However a shift came with capitalism as both the social organisation and concept of human labor changed (Stewart and Russell, 2001). With increasing assembly lines as well as precise mechanisation of factory work the disabled workers were not seen as capable of keeping pace with the factory based system of production. In a capitalist society, disability becomes a marker through which people were categorised as belonging to either the work-based or needs-based system of distribution. In such a categorisation, disabled people are excluded from the wage-labour system as they do not fulfill the demands of the capitalist society. This tendency gains impetus resulting in increasing marginalization of the disabled, thereby having a direct impact on the educational system, which becomes a collaborator in keeping the disabled unskilled, further adding to their anguish.
12. The focus group on work and education was chaired by Prof. Anil Sadgopal, a senior Fellow, Nehru Memorial Museum and Library, New Delhi. The reports can be accessed from the NCERT web site.
13. According to Prof. Sadgopal, "The Central Advisory Board of Education constituted the Kapil Sibal Committee two years ago to draft the required legislation. Apart from suffering from several lacunae, the Committee's draft Bill attempted to promote the falsehood that provision of 25 per cent free seats in private unaided schools to poor children from the neighborhood was equivalent to moving towards a Common School System.... This deliberate confusion helped divert the debate away from the issue of Fundamental Rights to that of the discomfort (and loss of profit) the '25 per cent idea' would cause to the powerful private school lobby and the global market forces" (The article entitled "Centre's Move Places Education at Risk" was published in *The Hindu* on September 26, 2006).

## References

Agarwal, Bina. (1994) *A Field of One's Own*, Cambridge: Cambridge University Press.

Alur, Mithu. (2006) Education for the disabled: Wither budgetary support? In *India Infoline News Service*. Feb. 24.

Barnes C. (1993) Political Correctness, Language and Rights. *Rights Not Charity,* Vol. 1

Bhog, Dipta. (2002) Gender and Curriculum, *Economic and Political Weekly*, Review of WS, Apr 27.

Bhog, Dipta. (2005) Looking beyond schooling for girls: The gender question in education. In A myth or reality in Rajni Kumar, Anil Sethi & Shalini Sikka (Eds.) *School, Society, Nation: Popular Essays in Education,* New Delhi: Orient Longman.

Bruner, J.S. (1985) Vygotsky: A historical and conceptual perspective, in: J.V. Wertsch (Ed) *Culture, Communication & Cognition: Vygotskian Perspectives,* Cambridge: Cambridge University Press.

Chanana, Karuna. (2006) Educate girls, prepare them for life. In Ravi Kumar, (Ed), *The Crisis of Elementary Education in India,* New Delhi: Sage.

Clough, Peter. (1996) Bridging the gap between 'mainstream' and 'special'. A curricular problem, *Journal of Curriculum Studies*, 20(40), 327-338.

Corbett, Jenny & Slee, R. (2000) An international conversation on inclusive education. In F. Armstrong, D. Armstrong, & L. Burton (Eds.) *Inclusive education: Policy, Context and Comparative Perspectives.* England: Davis Fulton Publishers.

Dhaliwal, A. (1996) Can the subaltern vote?: Radical democracy, discourses of representation and rights, and questions of race. In David Trend (Ed.) *Radical Democracy: Identity and Citizenship.* New York: Routledge.

Freire, Paolo. (1998) *Pedagogy of Freedom.* New York: Rowman & Littlefield Publishers Inc.

Ghai, Anita. (2001) Marginalisation and disability: experiences from the Third World. In M Priestley (Ed.) *Disability and the Life Course: Global Perspectives,* Cambridge: 26-37. Cambridge University Press.

Ghai, Anita (2002) *Disabled Women: An Excluded Agenda of Indian Feminism.* Hypatia 17: 49-66.

Ghai, Anita. (1999) Education of disabled: An excluded agenda. Paper presented at a Conference on Education in South Asian Context: Issues and challenges. November 14-18.

Ghai, Anita. (2003) *(Dis)Embodied Form: Issues of Disabled Women.* New Delhi: Har-Anand Publishers.

Ghai, Anita. (2005) Inclusive education: A myth or reality. In Rajni Kumar, Anil Sethi & Shalini Sikka (Eds.) *School, Society, Nation: Popular Essays in Education* New Delhi: Orient Longman.

Ghai, Anita (2006) *Education in a Globalising Era: Implications for Disabled Girls, Social Change,* (In Press).

Giroux, H.A. (1988) *Schooling and the Struggle for Public Life: Critical Pedagogy in the Modern Age.* Minneapolis, MN: University of Minnesota Press.

Government of India (GOI) (1966) Education and National Development: Report of the Education Commission 1964-66. New Delhi: Ministry of Education, Government of India.

GOI (1986) National Policy on Education, 1986, and Programme of Action, 1986. New Delhi: Department of Education, Ministry of Human Resource Development, Government of India.

GOI. (1990) Towards an Enlightened and Humane Society: Report of the Committee for Review of National Policy on Education, 1986 (National Policy on Education Review Committee Report [NPERC] or Acharya Ramamurti Committee Report). New Delhi: Department of Education, Ministry of Human Resource Development.

GOI. (1992) *National Policy on Education, 1986 (as modified in 1992) with National Policy on Education, 1968.* New Delhi: Department of Education, Ministry of Human Resource Development.

GOI. (1992) *Programme of Action, 1992*, New Delhi: Department of Education, Ministry of Human Resource Development.

GOI. (1993) *Education For All: The Indian Scene,* New Delhi: Department of Education, Ministry of Human Resource Development.

GOI. (1995) *District Primary Education Programme: Guidelines.* New Delhi: Department of Education, Ministry of Human Resource Development.

GOI. (1998) DPEP Moves On: Towards Universalising Basic Education, New Delhi, Department of Education, Ministry of Human Resource Development.

GOI. (2000) A Policy Framework for Reforms in Education. (Mukesh Ambani and Kumaramangalam Birla). New Delhi: Prime Minister's Council on Trade and Industry, Government of India.

Government of India, Sarva Shiksha Abhiyan: A Programme for Universal Elementary Education: Framework for Implementation. Dept. of Elementary Education and Literacy, New Delhi: Ministry of Human Resource and Development.

Jha, M.M. (2006). Inclusive education in the context of common schools: A question of equity, social justice. In Ravi Kumar, (Ed), *The Crisis of Elementary Education in India,* New Delhi: Sage.

Kumar, K., Priyam, M., Saxena, S., (2001) Looking beyond the smoke screen: DPEP and Primary education in India. *Economic and Political Weekly,* 34(7), 560-568.

Kumar, Krishna; Priyam, Manisha; and Saxena, Sadhna. (2001) Looking beyond the Smokescreen: DPEP and Primary education in India, *Economic and Political Weekly.* Feb 17.

Madan, Vandana. (2004) Inside the classroom: Content analysis of classroom practices in eight states. In V. Ramachandran, *Gender and Social Equity in Education: Hierarchies of Access.* New Delhi: Sage.

Manjrekar, Nandini. (2003) Contemporary Challenges to Women's Education: towards an elusive goal, *Economic and Political Weekly* 38(4), pp. 4577-4582.

Mukhopadhyay, C.C. (1992) Family Structure and Indian Women's Participation in Science and Engineering, in Carol C. Mukhopadhyay and Susan Seymour (ed.) (1994) *Women, Education, and Family Structure in India.* Colorado: Westview Press, pp. 103-135.

Menon, Nivedita (2004) *Recovering Subversion: Feminist Politics beyond the Law.* Permanent Black, Delhi.

Nagar Richa and. Swarr Amanda L. 2004. Organizing from the Margins: Grappling with 'Empowerment' in India and South Africa. In eds. Lise Nelson and Joni Seagar, (eds.) *A Companion to Feminist Geography.* London: Blackwell, pp. 291-304.

Nagar, Richa, (2000) Mujhe Jawab Do [Answer Me]: Feminist Grassroots Activism and Social Spaces in Chitrakoot (India), *Gender, Place and Culture* 7(4): 341-362.

Nambissan, B. Geetha (2004) Integrating gender concerns. Paper presented in a seminar on Are we learning: Improving the quality of elementary education. http://www.indiaseminar.com/2004/536/536%20geetha%20b.%20nambissan.htm.

Oliver, M. (1992). *Changing the social relations of research production, Disability, Handicap &. Society,* 7, pp. 101-114.

Periodi, Vani (2004) Second generation issues in equity and education: learning from Kolar district, Karnataka. In V. Ramachandran, *Gender and Social Equity in Education: Hierarchies of Access.* New Delhi: Sage.

Peters, Susan (1999) Transforming disability identity through critical literacy and the cultural politics of language. In M. Corker & S. French (Eds), *Disability Discourse* (pp. 103-115). Buckingham and Philadelphia: Open University Press.

Ramachandran, Vimla (2002) *Gender and Social Equity in Primary Education: Hierarchies of Access.* New Delhi: The European Commission.

Rhodes, W.C. (1995) Liberatory pedagogy and special education. *Journal of Learning Disabilities, 28,* 458-462.

Sadgopal, Anil. (2006) Dilution, distortion and diversion: A post-Jomtien reflection on the education policy. In Ravi Kumar, (Ed), *The Crisis of Elementary Education in India,* New Delhi: Sage.

Sadgopal, Anil (2005) Globalisation: Deconstructing its knowledge. In Rajni Kumar, Anil Sethi & Shalini Sikka (Eds.) *School, Society, Nation: Popular Essays in Education,* New Delhi: Orient Longman.

Sadgopal, Anil. (2004) Globalisation and Education: Defining the Indian Crisis. (XVI Zakir Husain Memorial Lecture). New Delhi: Zakir Husain College, University of Delhi.

Sadgopal, Anil (2000) *Shiksha Ka Sawal.* Granth Shilpi. India Pvt. Ltd.

Saraswathi, T.S. (1999) Adult-child continuity in India: Is adolescence a myth or an emerging reality. In Saraswathi, T.S. (Ed). *Culture, Socialisation & Human Development: Theory Research and Applications in India.* New Delhi: Sage.

Stewart, J & Russell, M. (2001) Disablement. Prison and Historical Segregation. *Monthly Review,* 53(3), 61-75.

Symington, Alison (2002) Re-inventing Globalization for Women's Rights and Development. Conference report of 9th International Forum on the theme of "Reinventing Globalization" was held in Guadalajara, Mexico, October 3-6.

Swaminathan, Padmini (2002) The Violence of Gender-Based Development: Going Beyond Social And Demographic Indicators, in Kapadia, Karin (ed.) *The Violence of Development: The Politics of Identity, Gender and Social Inequalities in India,* Zed Books: London & New York.

*Times Of India* (2006), Right to information, April 20th, 2006.

Visaria, L & Ramachandran, Vimla (2004) What DPEP and other data sources reveal. In V. Ramachandran, *Gender and Social Equity in Education: Hierarchies of Access.* New Delhi: Sage.

Wallach, Balogh R. (1991) Learning from Feminism: Social Theory and Intellectual Vitality, in Lemert C (ed). *Intellectuals and Politics: Social Theory in a Changing World.* London, Sage Publications.

# Part III

# Curriculum, Pedagogy and Knowledge

# 11

# Deciphering Policy Discourse on Place of Work in Curriculum

ANIL SADGOPAL

*Our education has got to be revolutionized. The brain must be educated through the hand. If I were a poet, I could write poetry on the possibilities of the five fingers. Why should you think that the mind is everything and the hands and feet nothing? Those who do not train their hands, who go through the ordinary rut of education, lack 'music' in their life. All their faculties are not trained. Mere book knowledge does not interest the child so as to hold his attention fully. The brain gets weary of mere words, and the child's mind begins to wander. The hand does the things it ought not to do, the eye sees the things it ought not to see, the ear hears the things it ought not to hear, and they do not do, see or hear, respectively what they ought to. They are not taught to make the right choice and so their education often proves their ruin. An education which does not teach us to discriminate between good and bad, to assimilate the one and eschew the other is a misnomer.*

—Mahatma Gandhi
Discussion with Teacher Trainees, *Harijan*,
18 February, 1939[1]

## Introduction

In 1906, the Indian National Congress, then spearheading the Indian freedom struggle against the British empire, resolved that the time had arrived "for the people all over the country to take up the question of national education for boys and girls, and organise a system of education, literary, scientific and technical, suited to the requirements of the country, on national lines, and under national control, and directed towards the realization of the national destiny." According to J.P. Naik (1979), Member-Secretary of the Education Commission (1964-66), this movement for a national system of education took two distinct forms during the freedom struggle:

> "(1)...to attempt a conceptual clarification of the objectives, content, organisation and other related aspects of the national education system; and (2) to try out some experiments outside the official system based on this vision of national education."

Amongst several concerns that provided the framework for "conceptual clarification", a major concern was regarding the tendency of the colonial system of education to reinforce the fragmentation of the society into (a) the so-called "educated" people, who not only denigrate productive manual work but also lack the necessary skills for the same and often have a parasitic relationship with the society; and (b) the vast majority of the people who work with their hands and produce wealth but are deprived of the benefits of formal education. The nationalist movement was committed to creating a system of education that will not promote this dichotomy between work and education and thus transform the paradigm in which colonial education was rooted. The pre-independence period was witness to a host of experiments outside the official framework to gain experience in building an alternative system. The present Jadavpur University and the institutions set up by Tagore, viz., Sriniketan, Shantiniketan and Vishva Bharati were amongst the trailblazers in this respect. Inspired by the non-cooperation movement (1921), thousands of young people quit schools and colleges of the colonial model in their search for alternatives. In response to this national call, institutions like the Gujarat Vidyapeeth, Tilak Maharashtra Vidyapeeth, Kashi Vidyapeeth and Jamia Millia Islamia were set-up, where new ideas in education were experimented.

## Genesis of the Idea

The National Education Conference held at Wardha, Maharashtra, in October 1937 under the leadership of Mahatma Gandhi represented a sort of culmination of this nation-wide debate on "conceptual clarification" of the alternative educational paradigm that ought to shape the national system of education for Independent India. Apart from the educationists and workers then engaged in this endeavour, the Conference was also attended by the Ministers of Education of the seven newly elected provincial governments. The Conference deliberated upon Gandhiji's proposal of Basic Education that would make productive work the pedagogic basis of learning in schools. Learning through a co-operative process and making schools self-reliant through the income of the productive work were amongst the key features of the original proposal. While addressing the Conference, Mahatma Gandhi stated:

> What I am going to place before you today is *not about a vocation* that is going to be imparted alongside education. Now, I wish to

> say that whatever is taught to children, *all of it should be taught necessarily through the medium of a trade or a handicraft.* You may argue that, during the middle age, children were taught only trades (crafts) in our country. While I agree with this contention, but the proposition of imparting the whole of education through the medium of trades (crafts) was not considered in those days. A trade (craft) was taught only from the standpoint of a trade (craft). We aim at *developing the intellect also with the aid of a trade or a handicraft*.... Therefore, it is my submission that, instead of merely teaching a trade or a handicraft, we may as well educate the children entirely through them. Look at *takli* (spindle) itself, for instance. The lesson of this *takli* will be the first lesson of our students through which they would be able to learn a substantial part of the history of cotton, Lancashire and the British empire.... How does this *takli* work? What is its utility? And what are the strengths that lie within it? Thus the child learns all this in the midst of play. Through this he also acquires some knowledge of mathematics. When he is asked to count the number of cotton threads on *takli* and he is asked to report how many did he spin, it becomes possible to acquaint him step by step with a good deal of mathematical knowledge through this process. And the beauty is that none of this becomes even a slight burden on his mind. The learner does not even become aware that he is learning. While playing around and singing, he keeps on turning his *takli* and from this itself he learns a great deal. [emphasis added][2]

The Wardha Conference constituted a committee under the chairpersonship of Dr. Zakir Husain to evolve a curriculum of Basic Education (*Nai Talim*) on the basis of the principle of placing productive work in the form of a trade or craft at the centre of the educational process, the latter being selected keeping in mind the socio-cultural milieu of the children (Hindustani Talimi Sangh, 1957). While accepting the Zakir Husain Committeee Report (1939), the Indian National Congress, at its meeting held at Haripura (Gujarat) the same year, resolved to build up a national system of education on the basis of three principles, viz., (1) all children should receive "free and compulsory" education for a minimum of seven years[3]; (2) the medium of education should be the mother tongue; and (3) this education be provided through the medium of some productive trade or handicraft and, to the extent possible, all other activities be built around this central craft, the latter being chosen in accordance with the conditions in which the child is placed. The Congress further resolved to constitute a body called, Hindustani Talimi Sangh, to promote this national system and also authorized Dr. Zakir Husain and Shri Aryanayakam to prepare a concrete programme of such education under the guidance of Mahatma Gandhi. Backed by such a clear-headed call for reorganising the nation's system of education, the seven provincial governments started setting up teacher training centres and opening schools to promote the Gandhian pedagogy of integrating the "world of work" with the "world of knowledge". Of course, all this early enthusiasm, though lukewarm, came to an abrupt end with the onset of the Quit India Movement.

Recognising this spirit of the national movement, the Report of CABE (Govt. of India, 1944) observed:

> Basic (Primary and Middle) education, envisaged by the Central Advisory Board, embodies many of the educational ideas contained in the original Wardha scheme, though it differs from it in certain important particulars. The main principle of *'learning through activity'* has been endorsed by educationists all over the world. At the lower stages the activity will take many forms, *leading gradually up to a basic craft or crafts suited to local conditions*. So far as possible *the whole of the curriculum will be harmonized with this general conception*. The *three R's by themselves can no longer be regarded as an adequate equipment for efficient citizenship*. The Board, however, is unable to endorse the view that education at any stage and particularly in the lowest stages can or should be expected to pay for itself through the sale of articles produced by the pupils. The most which can be expected in this respect is that sales should cover the cost of the additional materials and equipment required for practical work. [emphasis added][4]

Admittedly, there is evidence of some confusion in the above CABE Report that is reflected in its reference to "learning through activity". When the pedagogic concept of "learning through productive work" or "learning through craft" is replaced by "learning through activity", it would normally imply "work without its context of orientation towards production". The notion of "decontextualised activity" is definitely not productive work. Perhaps this is the reason why the CABE Report talks of activity taking many forms at the lower stages, "leading gradually up to a basic craft or crafts", instead of "learning through craft or crafts". However, this ambiguity, at least to some extent, is taken care of when one reads the same report on its computation of costs involved in teacher education for Basic Education, as elaborated below.

While formulating a plan of teacher education and working out the costs involved for the same for fulfilling the programme of "free and compulsory" elementary education, CABE (1944) recognized the significance of the new curricular principles in the following words:

> An all-round improvement in the standard of teaching is all the more necessary because *Basic Education in view of its emphasis on craft work and the correlation of other subjects therewith* demands a high level of teaching skill, if it is to be really successful. [emphasis added][5]

The complete set of recommendations of CABE (1944) with respect to incorporation of Basic Education's curricular and pedagogic ideas into the national system of education on the eve of India's independence are available (Government of India, 1944, Introduction & Chapter I; Chapter III; Chapter V).

## Education Commission's Approach

The Education Commission (1964-66) attempted to look at the issue of the relationship between the "world of work" and the "world of knowledge" as part of its perspective of viewing education as an instrument of social, economic and cultural transformation (see Chapter I of the Commission's Report). Its Report contended that an important dimension of the endeavour "to relate it [education] to the life, needs and aspirations of the people" is, among others, the relationship between *education and productivity* (Section 1.20). It was in this context that the Commission recommended that "work-experience should be introduced as an integral part of all education" and defined it as "participation in productive work in the school, in the home, in a workshop, on a farm, in a factory or in any other productive situation" (Section 1.25). While *clearly distinguishing between work-experience in education and vocationalisation of education (or, for that matter, vocational education)*, the Commission stated:

> Work-experience is thus *a method of integrating education with work. This is not only possible but essential in modern societies which adopt science-based technology*. In all traditional societies, an antithesis between education and work is usually postulated.... The need to provide some such corrective to the *over-academic nature of formal education* has been widely recognized...a revolutionary experiment was launched by Mahatma Gandhi in the form of basic education. The concept of work-experience is essentially similar. It may be described as *a redefinition of his educational thinking in terms of a society on the road to industrialization*.... In addition to being an effective educational tool, work-experience can, in our view, serve some other important purposes. It can help to make the distinction between intellectual and manual work less marked as also the social stratification based on it. It could make the entry of youth into the world of work and employment easier by enabling them to adjust themselves to it. It could contribute to the increase of national

> productivity both by helping students to develop insights into productive processes and the use of science, and by generating in them the habit of hard and responsible work. And it might help social and national integration by strengthening the links between the individual and the community and by creating bonds of understanding between the educated persons and the masses.[emphasis added][6]

In the chapter on 'School Curriculum' (Chapter VIII), the Report elaborates further on the concept of work-experience:

> We have recommended [earlier] that *work-experience*, which involves participation in some form of productive work under conditions approximating to those found in real life situations, should *be introduced as an integral part of education at all stages.* It will provide a *much-needed corrective to the extremely academic and bookish character of present school education*.... In the lower classes of the primary school, work-experience may begin as simple handwork, the objective being to train children to make use of their hands and thereby *help their intellectual and emotional growth.* In the senior classes, it may take the form of learning a craft which *develops technical thinking and creative capacities* in the pupils. Even here, however, some work-experience can be provided in real life situations, such as work on the farms at the time of harvesting or sowing or in a family production unit, and opportunities of this kind of activity should be utilized to the maximum extent possible.... At the higher secondary stage, where the students will be more mature, and their numbers will be comparatively smaller, work-experience should be made available in school workshops and also on farms and in industrial or commercial establishments. [emphasis added][7]

Comparing its proposal of work-experience with Basic Education, the Commission observed:

> We pointed out earlier that the concept of work-experience is closely related to the philosophy underlying basic education.... If in practice basic education has become largely frozen around certain crafts, there is no denying the fact that it always stressed the vital principle of relating education to productivity. What is now needed is *a reorientation of the basic education programme to the needs of a society that has to be transformed with the help of science and technology*. In other words, *work-experience must be forward looking in keeping with the character of the new social order* [emphasis added].[8]

The Education Commission's perspective on Mahatma Gandhi's proposal on Basic Education and its place in the school curriculum is elaborated in Sections 8.105-8.110. The Commission's views on the concept of work-experience and Basic Education call for three observations:

1. The rationale offered by the Commission for including work-experience as an integral part of all education in Section 1.27 needs a critical examination. The underlying premise seems to be that, as the traditional society undergoes "modernisation" in its techniques of production, the "traditional resistance of educated persons to engage themselves in productive work tends to disappear" and the "educated person thus becomes an important source of production and the uneducated person, an unproductive burden on society". The so-called "modernisation" that has taken place in India since independence, particularly under the more recent impact of globalization and market forces, has led to further "eliticization" and alienation of the upper and middle classes from the masses. In contrast, the "uneducated" sections of society continue to be engaged in productive tasks requiring a range of manual skills, though at less than even the minimum wages. Evidently, the employment opportunities for the masses in productive tasks have been steadily declining with the march of globalisation. Even then, there is adequate ground for questioning the validity of the Commission's premise. Although this debate is critical to the pedagogy of relating work with the learning process, it is not the focus of our present inquiry.
2. The Commission seems to have taken a rather limited view of the significance of placing productive work at the centre of the learning process. Although the original proposal of Basic Education emphasized the pedagogic dimension of relating work with knowledge, *Nai Talim* was much more than merely a pedagogic exercise. Fagg (2002) cites three commentators on Gandhiji's educational ideas as follows (pp. 15-16):

   [Craft work] incidentally makes the boy more 'peaceful' and assiduous; being productive work, it relates the boy's activity to his environment and the society in which he lives; and, lastly, by imparting instruction through some serious craft not only the boy's practical intelligence is trained but he gets the conception of labour as a moral force (N.R. Malkani, *Harijan* 5:332).

   A sharp intellect can be cultivated through other methods, but then it may not be socially developed. On the other hand, an intellect developed through the medium of socially useful manual labour must of necessity become an instrument of service. Mere intellectual training ordinarily makes a child individualistic. But education through work and activities brings him in contact with other children in cooperation with whom he has to work (Avinashilingam, 1964, 63).

From the beginning [Gandhi] had seen that the vigorous manual work to meet the needs of a family or community was the basis both of physical health and of an ethic of generous sharing and mutual respect (Sykes, 1988, 34).

Gandhi himself elaborates upon his conception of Basic Education, "as the spear-head of a silent social revolution fraught with the most far-reaching consequences". While planning the curriculum of today's schools, we need to be aware of the *ethical, political and social dimensions of pedagogic integration of work with the learning process*. Both Sykes (1988) and Fagg (2002) deal with these dimensions of *Nai Talim* extensively.[9]

3. The Commission appears to be rather hesitant in unambiguously acknowledging the pedagogic relationship between the "world of work" and the "world of knowledge" as an *essential (and also universal)* element of the curriculum. Its use of the phrase "*correlation* [emphasis added] of the curriculum with the productive activity and the physical and social environment" (Section 8.105), falls short of the holistic vision of learning that emerges when one reads Gandhiji's or Zakir Husain Committee's vivid descriptions of learning languages (with emphasis on articulation), mathematics, science, environment, history, geography or civics from *takli*, carpentry, farming or other contemporary tools of production (see Sykes, 1988, for a philosophical, socio-political and pedagogical treatment of this subject). We may consider the proposition that at least a part of the problem in the Commission's 'hesitant' conception of work-experience arises from the reduction of this revolutionary idea as a programme of *merely* "Education and Productivity", rather than viewing it as a programme of *reorientation of educational aims and curricular transformation*. This might also explain why the Commission, while being appropriately concerned about the rural-urban differences relating to work-experience, recommends introduction of "programmes oriented to industry and simple technology…in *a fair proportion* of rural schools" and "gardening in *as many urban schools as possible* and…experience in farm work to *at least a small proportion* of urban pupils" (Section 8.76) [emphasis added]. In spite of its otherwise sensible reference to "forward-looking type of work-experience for every child", the Commission contradicts itself by recommending that "a beginning should be made immediately *in selected schools*" and then steps be

taken to increase the facilities "*as rapidly as possible*" (Section 8.77) [emphasis added]. The Report does not tell us how this partial and gradual introduction will be reflected in the teacher education programmes, preparation of learning materials and the student evaluation and examination system. Nor does such a graded approach help build a vision of a common *curricular framework*[10], as its implementation is apparently made contingent upon the State's willingness to make adequate resources available, rather than a matter of national priority for curricular transformation in the *entire* school system. Also, there is plenty of evidence from the history of experiments in education in India, (including *Nai Talim* and Tagore's *Sriiniketan*) that tells us that any partial introduction of a new idea, howsoever beautiful it might be, in *selected* schools is never accepted by the parents as they feel insecure about their children's future who are bound to be alienated from the mainstream.[11] It would be worthwhile inquiring whether the nation's failure in making work-experience a pedagogic basis of learning in the school curriculum, almost four decades after the Commission's recommendations, is a consequence of this hesitant approach recommended by the Commission itself.

## Policy's Vision: From Hesitation to Confusion

The hesitation of the Commission in building a new curricular vision for the nation is reflected in the 'soft' policy measure included in the National Policy on Education-1968 [Section 4 (6)] as is cited below:

> The school and the community should be brought closer through suitable programmes of mutual service and support. Work-experience and national service, including participation in meaningful and challenging programmes of community service and national reconstruction, should accordingly become an integral part of education. Emphasis in these programmes should be on self-help, character formation and on developing a sense of social commitment.

The above statement is more like a normative expression than a declaration of a national resolve in the State policy. Further, the educational administrators, examination boards and the teachers cannot be faulted for having interpreted the ambiguous policy statement as a call for including work-experience and community service as co-curricular activities that can be dispensed with in order to complete the prescribed course. This is precisely what has been the case at the ground level. Now, look at the National Policy on Education-1986 as also at its modified version of 1992 wherein this lack of conviction grows into confusion:

> Work-experience, viewed as purposive and meaningful manual work, organised as an integral part of the learning process and resulting in either goods or services useful to the community, is considered as an essential component at all stages of education, to be provided through well-structured and graded programmes. It would comprise activities in accord with the interests, abilities and needs of students, the level of skills and knowledge to be upgraded with the stages of education. This experience would be helpful on his entry into the workforce. Pre-vocational programmes provided at the lower secondary stage will also facilitate the choice of the vocational course at the higher secondary stage. [12]

Let us recall here that the notion of work-experience was viewed in both Basic Education and Education Commission's Report as a universal pedagogic element in the curriculum aimed at social change. Instead of emphasizing this critical dimension of work-experience, the policy is more concerned with student's "entry into the workforce" and pre-vocational programmes to "facilitate the choice of the vocational course at the higher secondary stage". The underlying premise seems to be that work-experience is meant for building the workforce and vocational courses, rather than for providing a powerful medium for acquisition of socially relevant knowledge and building up creative and purposeful citizens. In this attempt at what amounts to "reductionism", the policy framework of work experience also ends up ignoring the relationship of this critical curricular dimension in enriching the social relevance of education and, thereby, also its quality.[13]

This concern is being articulated here precisely because the prevailing curricula in various school systems neither reflect Basic Education's vision of placing work at the center of curriculum as a pedagogic source of knowledge, skills and values nor the Education Commission's conception of work-experience. The radical vision today stands both marginalized and trivialized in practice. Ironically, the three curriculum frameworks designed by the NCERT successively in 1975, 1988 and 2000 give a place of prominence to work-related education.[14] Yet, the CBSE-affiliated schools, where the NCERT framework is implemented entirely, do not even feign to reflect the original vision. In the CBSE-affiliated schools, as in the State Board-affiliated schools, work experience/SUPW is viewed as marginalized elements of curriculum. Further, in popular perception as also in academic discourse, work-experience is often confused with vocational education[15], something which Gandhiji, as quoted above, warned us about in his address to the Wardha Conference in 1937.

## Community Work and Social Service

A commentary on the place of community work and social service in the school curriculum is in order at this juncture. This aspect of school curriculum had a significant place in the conceptualization of *Nai Talim* by the Zakir Husain Committee (1939) and was seen in relationship with work-centred education. The Education Commission (1964-66) wrote:

> The present educational system ...is also responsible for increasing the gulf between the educated and the uneducated classes, between the intelligentsia and the masses.... Our traditional 'elite' as a whole—with some noble exceptions—had no close ties with the masses, and the new 'elite' created by modern education also remained largely aloof from the people, except during the struggle for freedom under Mahatma Gandhi, when he was able to inspire large numbers of educated and even well-to-do persons to identify themselves with the interests of the masses and the country as a whole. But from the time the struggle for freedom came to an end with the attainment of Independence, they have again tended to move away from the people. This is a great danger and, with a view to meeting it, suitable programmes to help in the evolution of a well-knit and united nation have to be devised.... For this purpose, we recommend that some form of social and national service should be made obligatory for all students and should form an integral part of education at all stages. This can become an instrument to build character, improve discipline, inculcate a faith in the dignity of manual labour and develop a sense of social responsibility.[16]

The Ishwarbhai Patel Committee Report (1977) reviewed the NCERT's document entitled 'The Curriculum for the Ten-Year School—A Framework', published in 1975, and observed that the 10-year curriculum should be capable of (only a partial list is excerpted here):

- moulding the learner after the image of citizen as visualized in the Constitution;
- releasing learning from its bookishness and elitist character so as to relate it closely to socially productive manual work and the socio-economic situation of the country;
- emphasizing the qualities of simplicity, integrity, tolerance and cooperation in all aspects of life; and
- being available to every individual...in such a way that working and learning can always be combined.[17]

While discussing the place of "purposive, meaningful, manual work" in the curriculum and preferring to term it as Socially Useful Productive Work (SUPW), the Ishwarbhai Patel Committee observed:

> It will be recalled that programmes of Work Experience were introduced as a result of the recommendations of the Kothari Commission with the objectives of relating education to productivity. These programmes, however, *lacked the component of social usefulness and, in practice, were not even casually correlated to other subject areas*. The purpose of demarcating a distinct curricular area as Socially Useful Productive Work is *to emphasize the principle that education should be work-centred*.... The aim of this curricular area is *to provide children with opportunities of participating in social and economic activities inside and outside the classroom*, enabling them to understand scientific principles and processes involved in different types of work and in the setting in which they are found in the physical and social environment.... The *component of Social Service in the curriculum is allied to Socially Useful Productive Work*...[it] *must not be confined to the four walls of the school, nor can they be provided by the teacher only*. Programmes should, therefore, be so planned and implemented that the local community, community development organisations, and governmental agencies participate in them and cooperate with the school [emphasis added][18].

The above mentioned relationship between work-centred education, on the one hand, and community work and social service, on the other, as conceived by the Ishwarbhai Patel Committee, laid the basis for it to propose the following six "work situations" in which SUPW needs to be conducted: health and hygiene;

(i) food;
(ii) shelter;
(iii) clothing;
(iv) culture and recreation; and,
(v) community work and social service.

The following set of observations are aimed at providing a framework in which one can see why even Ishwarbhai Patel Committee's proposal on SUPW could not be translated into practice:

1. The placement of "culture and recreation" and "community work and social service" in the same category as the other four work situations (which are pre-dominantly centred around productive work)

is probably itself a source of distortion of SUPW in schools, the essential linkage of these two parts of SUPW notwithstanding. This has given the school managements and the teachers an *alibi* to prefer "culture and recreation" and "community work and social service" over productive works and thus continue the *status quo*.

2. The notion of community work and social service, as it is perceived in Indian society, as also in the school system, is basically bourgeois and patronizing in character. This misconception has been the basis of planning a range of programmes, where the children neither learn anything useful nor have the satisfaction of having done any creative work. Essentially, these programmes, including NSS, have been directionless. What is required instead is a curricular design of community work where the objective is to acquire knowledge—in science, social sciences, mathematics, languages and especially about the society as a whole—and learn to work with people and be sensitive to their problems, rather than *solving* people's problems or *teaching* them something; such an attitude can be quite presumptuous on the part of the school system. The pedagogy of "learning from the people" can be the most rewarding experience for students, teachers and the entire school. This particular observation applies to the notion of social service as envisaged by the Education Commission as well (see GoI, 1971, Sections 1.39-1.48; Sections 8.79-8.87).
3. The school system is ill-designed to undertake purposive, meaningful and productive work and community activities. Its design of curriculum focused on learning from textbooks, fragmented view of knowledge, fixed timetables and periods, evaluation parameters, examination system, value framework and lack of respect for the sources of knowledge outside the classroom,[19] are amongst the factors that become obstacles in the path of transformation. Changes are required, therefore, it is necessary to bring about epistemic, pedagogic and structural reconstruction of the whole school system, at the policy level.
4. A general misconception about the system needs to be flagged. When a programme or a new idea fails in education, the usual diagnosis is to blame its lackadaisical implementation. This diagnosis is based on the premise that the theoretical design of the programme, the structures of the school system and the broader policies are flawless. This premise is to be questioned before further progress can be made. For more than a century, commissions and committees are recommending certain changes and the policies are made to fulfill the recommendations. The persistence of failure must make us sit up and ask ourselves whether something is not wrong at a more fundamental level. There are studies now available showing that,

> more often than not, the policies and the programme designs themselves are flawed and the failure is a result of *"reasonably efficient and faithful implementation of flawed policies"* (Sadgopal 2003, 2004). This observation is being made in the hope that it might help us in understanding why otherwise apparently sensible ideas have not worked in our country.

The concept of SUPW, as proposed by the Ishwarbhai Patel Committee, was fully endorsed by the National Review Committee on Higher Secondary Education with Special Reference to Vocationalisation (Adiseshiah Committee, 1978) for the +2 stage. In spite of this conceptual clarity, the dimensions of social relevance and work-centeredness of the education system remained weak. While getting ready for the formulation of a new education policy in 1985, the Government of India issued its perspective document on policy entitled, 'The Challenge of Education—A Policy Perspective', which observes:

> A great deal has already been said about the gap between education and educational institutions on the one hand, and society on the other. Taking educational institutions as entities by themselves, it is observed that these are generally oblivious of and unconcerned with the problems, potentials and characteristics of their environment. This has resulted in lack of orientation and dysfunction of research and educational content, lack of support from the environment and the isolation of the teachers and students from the realities of life and the world of work. On the other hand, the community around these institutions is also a great loser since it is denied the opportunity of enriching itself and finding solutions to its problems through the intervention and support of a technically knowledgeable and mentally and physically agile group of people. Lack of social relevance has serious consequences for the students emerging from educational institutions. They are unable to acquire insights and skills relevant either to socio-cultural processes, or to the world of employment and work.[20]

Probing the causes of this lack of social relevance, the policy document further commented:

> Socially Useful Productive Programmes, National Service Scheme (N.S.S.) and other similar initiatives have not yielded the desired results, largely because the character of examinations determines the curricular content and methodologies of education and also circumscribes the attitude of students. Over the years, the examinations have become memory-based, highly routinized and unconcerned with the evaluation of the total personality, attitudes

> and values, and unable [?] to the mental ability and physical dexterity of students. [21]

It is evident that the policy makers seemed to know the alarming impact of the examination system on the relevance and quality of education. The consequent 1986 policy reflected this concern and resolved "to recast the examination system so as to ensure a method of assessment that is a valid and reliable measure of student development and a powerful instrument for improving teaching and learning" (NPE-1986, Sections 8.23). Yet, the colonial character of the examination system hardly changed; it may have become worse. The policy perspective document of 1985 made the following perceptive but apparently helpless observations:

> Lack of relevance of educational content to life situations is one of the reasons for the majority of the people, including some of the intellectuals, having apathetic attitude to education. This is why the educational processes are not getting much support from opinion leaders, planners, farmers, industrialists and, what is worse, even from the intended beneficiaries.... Initially, up to the early sixties, great expectation that people had from education found expression in their active contribution in the form of physical, material and financial resources to construct and equip school buildings and social education centres, etc...[but] the system as a whole failed to re-evaluate and re-orient either its objectives or its methods of functioning. It moved away from direct contact and involvement with society and opted for wholesale bureaucratization to secure certain privileges and escape not only from the arbitrariness of the management but also from accountability to the community.[22]

In spite of a Programme of Action (1986), approved by the Parliament, that had detailed chapters on each of the above mentioned concerns, the system did not respond. In 1990, while undertaking a comprehensive review of the 1986 policy, the Acharya Ramamurti Report observed:

> The Education Commission, 1964-66, identified work experience and social service as essential elements of purposeful education.... Work experience which is to develop creative skills, however, has *degenerated into trivial activities, most often extra-curricular, the social dimension essential for the concept missing altogether*.... The problem faced by school education in today's context is *near exclusive emphasis on knowledge through theory alone*. Even when theory is taught, its teaching remains barren and partial, due to the *pedagogic constraint of divorcing knowledge from practice*. The accent is to be on *integration of theoretical knowledge with skills, attitudes,*

> *productive work, social responsibility, and creativity*. Education is to be linked with the emerging problems of the world of work. For this purpose, the method of project work should be an integral feature of the educational process. [emphasis added][23]

The Acharya Ramamurti Review Committee recommended a range of modifications that were required in the Policy and the Programme of Action in order to break the isolation of the education system from its political, socio-cultural and economic contexts, especially relating to infrastructural, accountability and pedagogic issues. These modifications were necessary for being able to meaningfully integrate social service in the school curriculum, as recommended by the Education Commission (see Govt. of India, 1977, Sections 1.39-1.48; Sections 8.79-8.87). Most of these modifications as proposed by the Acharya Ramamurti Committee were not accepted when the Policy was modified by the Parliament in 1992. The consequence of this rigidity in policy making (see GoI, 1992a for evidence of rigidity) is the continuing gap between the "world of work" and the world of knowledge" and lack of social relevance in the school curriculum.

## Concluding Observations

The above analysis of policy discourse on the place of productive and community work in curriculum and its relationship with knowledge laid the basis for NCERT's National Focus Group on 'Work and Education' to present a radical vision for incorporating this Gandhian concept in the school curriculum from pre-school to senior secondary stage (NCERT, 2005b). This was done while keeping in mind the contemporary challenges faced by India in the context of globalisation as well as the distortions that are likely to be caused to the concept itself due to class, caste, religious, cultural, gender and disability dimensions, each of these having serious epistemic and curricular implications (NCERT, 2005b, Section 3). The proposal aims at institutionalizing the role of productive and community work as a medium of knowledge acquisition, developing values and skill formation in school curriculum. The task of translating this vision into practice is premised on the essentiality of *linking curricular reforms with appropriate policy-level reforms leading to structural changes* in the school system. It may be contended that when curricular reforms are introduced in a multi-layered schools system, the disparity in quality is likely to increase, rather than decrease. This is precisely why a policy resolve to build a Common School System (which includes private unaided schools) functioning through neighbourhood schools, along with contingent reforms in evaluation and assessment system, is almost a pre-condition for realizing the vision (see NCERT, 2005b, Sections 4, 7-9). Herein lies the essence of the policy discourse analysis undertaken in this paper.

## Notes

1. The Collected Works of Mahatma Gandhi, Vol. 68, pp. 372-73.
2. Excerpted from the address by Mahatma Gandhi at the Wardha Education Conference, October 22, 1937. *Translated from Hindi, Hindustani Talimi Sangh,* 1957, pp. vii-viii.
3. Later, this commitment to provide Elementary Education to all children in Independent India was extended to eight years as recommended by CABE in 1944 and incorporated by the Constitution in the original Article 45 for all children up to the age of 14 years. It incorporates primary stage of five years (6-11 age group) and upper primary or middle stage (11-14 age group). This commitment continues to be reflected in the new Article 21A, introduced through 86th Constitutional Amendment in December 2002, in its reference to 6-14 age group. Yet, there are several states which have failed to upgrade their Elementary Education programme from seven to eight years duration, with their primary stage ending at grade IV instead of grade V and the upper primary stage at grade VII instead of grade VIII. This failure, with adverse implications for access to Elementary Education, can be partly attributed to the ambiguous position taken by the Report of the Education Commission itself with respect to the duration of Elementary Education.
4. Report by the CABE, Govt. of India, January 1944 Chapter 1, Section 3.
5. Report by the CABE, January 1944, Chapter 1, Section 4.
6. Report of the Education Commission (1964-66), Sections 1.27-1.29.
7. Report of the Education Commission (1964-66), Section 8.72-8.73.
8. Report of the Education Commission (1964-66), Sections 8.75.
9. Both of these studies attempt a critical view and philosophical elaboration of the Gandhian conception of education.
10. It is imperative that we distinguish curriculum framework from curriculum and syllabus and not use them as synonyms. The latter two can be regional and/or state-specific as long as they broadly follow the national curriculum framework, as also specified in 1986 policy (NPE-1986, Sections 3.2-3.4); there is full provision of flexibility in curricula and syllabi provided a "common core" is retained (NPE-1986, Section 3.4). The policy further provides for contextual textbooks and other learning materials as well as plural learning processes that would reflect the rich geo-cultural diversity of the country. In light of this policy framework, it would be worthwhile to investigate how and why the curricula, syllabi, textbooks and the learning process have come to acquire rigidity and are, by and large, alienated from local socio-economic and cultural milieu. *Why indeed does NCERT publish textbooks at all when these can't be contextual?* A similar argument would apply to SCERTs as well. The pre-dominant influence of the evaluation parameters and the examination system in enforcing rigidity and promoting uniformity, *in violation of the curricular principles as well as the policy framework*, also need to be studied. In this context, the Acharya Ramamurti Committee Report (GoI, 1990, Chapter 12) and the Yash Pal Committee Report (GoI, 1993) will be particularly helpful.
11. The most recent example of this phenomenon is the well-known Hoshangabad Science Teaching Programme (HSTP), which won nation-wide recognition for

making the entire science curriculum activity-based, inquiry-oriented and contextual at upper primary level. It was implemented in more than 1,000 schools (mostly government and government-aided) of 14 districts of Madhya Pradesh during 1972-2002 with full involvement of the government system. Yet, it never became the policy of the state government to teach science in a scientific manner through contextual activities and experiments in the *entire* state school system. The result of this half-hearted approach eventually created conditions for destabilization of the programme and gave the state government an opportunity to take the retrogressive step of closing it in July 2002. The result: these 1,000 schools with more than one lakh students reverted to learning science by rote like the rest of the schools in the country. This experience is clear evidence of *lack of conviction and clarity at the level of policy making.*

12. National Policy on Education-1986 (As modified in 1992), Section 8.14.
13. It may be noted here that there is an increasing tendency in the academic discourse to de-link the issue of the quality of education from that of its social relevance. This tendency has begun to impact upon field practice, planning and research especially since the following two policy changes were made viz. (a) the entry of international funding of primary education in India from 1993-94 onwards; and (b) the relatively more recent phenomenon of the government giving space to the private corporations and their Foundations/Trusts (particularly those related to ICT industry) and NGOs in *defining and determining the pedagogic quality of education* in the name of public-private partnership (see Sarva Shiksha Abhiyan framework, GoI, 2002 and Education For All, GoI 2003). The issue of the relationship between the "world of work" and the "world of knowledge" in the emerging discourse stands either marginalized or trivialized as one of *merely* training students in vocational skills and preparation of work force for the market. It must be clarified that, while the objective of skill development is integral to education, the holistic purpose of education related to social relevance and pedagogic quality of education can't be allowed to become subservient to market. Unless checked consciously, this tendency will have an adverse impact, as brought out in several studies and NSS surveys, on the national goal of universalizing education as no child will devote 8 or 10 years of her life in an educational programme, which lacks both relevance and pedagogic quality.
14. A careful and critical comparison needs to be made of the philosophical and pedagogic place of work in the curriculum as conceptualized by NCERT in its three successive curriculum frameworks viz. in 1975, 1988 and 2000. This study will also reveal how NCERT's vision was being influenced by the changing political conditions and the shift in the economic paradigm since the onset of the recent phase of globalization and the impact of the neo-liberal ideology on educational thinking in India.
15. A new vision of vocational education, as distinguished from work-centred education, was evolved by NCERT's National Focus Group on 'Work and Education' (NCERT, 2005b) and incorporated in the National Curricular Framework-2005 (NCERT, 2005a).
16. Report of the Education Commission (1964-66), Sections 1.39-1.40
17. Report of the Review Committee on "The Curriculum for the Ten-Year School" (1977), Chapter 2, p. 6.

18. Report of the Review Committee on "The Curriculum for the Ten-Year School" (1977), Chapter 3, pp. 10-11.
19. The National Curricular Framework—2005 (NCF-2005) has made an important contribution to curricular discourse by emphasizing the role of the sources of knowledge *existing outside the school.* The significance of this contribution, however, is limited by reluctance of NCF-2005 to address the issue of the inevitable linkage between curricular reforms and structural reforms in the school system.
20. The Challenge of Education—A Policy Perspective', GoI, 1985. Sections 4.94-4.95.
21. The Challenge of Education—A Policy Perspective', GoI, 1985. Sections 4.96 & 4.98.
22. The Challenge of Education—A Policy Perspective', GoI, 1985 Section 4.99.
23. Committee for Review of National Policy on Education, 1986 (1990) Sections 8.6.0 & 8.8.3.

## References

Fagg, Henry (2002). *Back to the Sources: A Study of Gandhi's Basic Education*, New Delhi: National Book Trust.

Gandhi, M.K. (1953). *Towards New Education*, Ahmedabad: Navajivan Publishing House.

Govt. of India (1944). *Post-War Educational Development in India: Report by the Central Advisory Board of Education*, Bureau of Education, India, (January).

Govt. of India (1971). *Education and National Development: Report of the Education Commission 1964-66*, New Delhi: NCERT.

Govt. of India (1968). *National Policy on Education-1968*,, New Delhi: Ministry of Education.

Govt. of India (1977). *Report of the Review Committee on 'The Curriculum for the Ten-Year School* (Ishwarbhai Patel Committee), New Delhi: Ministry of Education and Social Welfare.

Govt. of India (1978). *Report of the National Review Committee on Higher Secondary Education with Special Reference to Vocationalisation* (Adiseshiah Committee), New Delhi: Ministry of Education and Social Welfare.

Govt. of India (1986). *National Policy on Education-1986 and Programme of Action-1986*, New Delhi: Ministry of Human Resource Development.

Govt. of India (1990). *Towards an Enlightened and Humane Society: Report of the Committee for Review of National Policy on Education, 1986* (Acharya Ramamurti Committee), New Delhi: Ministry of Human Resource Development, (December).

Govt. of India (1992a). *Report of the CABE Committee on Policy*, New Delhi: Ministry of Human Resource Development, (January).

Govt. of India (1992b). *National Policy on Education-1986 (As modified in 1992)*, New Delhi: Ministry of Human Resource Development.

Govt. of India (1993). *Learning Without Burden: Report of the National Advisory Committee*, New Delhi: Ministry of Human Resource Development.

Govt. of India (2002). *Sarva Shiksha Abhiyan*, New Delhi: Ministry of Human Resource Development.

Govt. of India (2003). *Education For All: National Plan of Action*, New Delhi: Ministry of Human Resource Development, (June).

Hindustani Talimi Sangh (1957). *Aath Salon ka Sampoorna Shikshakram*, Sewagram, Wardha: Maharashtra.

Hindustani Talimi Sangh (1946). *Samagra Nai Taleem: Sewagram Rashtriya Shiksha Sammelan, January 1945 ka Vivaran*, Sewagram, Wardha: Maharashtra.

Naik, J.P. (1979). *The Education Commission and After*, New Delhi: A.P.H. Publishing Corporation.

NCERT (1975). *The Curriculum for the Ten-Year School—A Framework*, New Delhi.

NCERT (1988). *National Curriculum for Elementary and Secondary Education—A Framework*, New Delhi.

NCERT (2000). *National Curriculum Framework for School Education*, New Delhi.

NCERT (2005a). *National Curriculum Framework*, New Delhi.

NCERT (2005b). National Focus Group Position Paper on 'Work and Education', New Delhi.

National Council for Teacher Education (1998). *Gandhi on Education*, New Delhi.

Sadgopal, Anil (2003). Exclusion and Inequality in Education: The State Policy and Globalisation,, *Contemporary India*, Journal of the Nehru Memorial Museum and Library, July-September, pp. 1-36.

Sadgopal, Anil (2004). Globalisation: Demystifying its Knowledge Agenda for India's Education Policy, 2004 Durgabai Deshmukh Memorial Lecture, Council for Social Development and India International Centre, (15 July).

Sykes, Marjorie (1988). *Foundations of Living*, Parisar, Pune.

# 12

# Teacher Education: How far have We Traversed the Path Envisioned by the Education Commission (1964-66)

M.A. KHADER

## Introduction

Teacher education has always been a disputed territory; its true landscape is quickly forgotten as soon as it is drawn by the Commissions or policy makers. Whether they are teacher educators, university academics, administrators or civil society groups, each draws its own images of the landscape. At the same time, all are equally concerned about the prevailing images of teacher education programmes—their structures, content and process of operationalization. Though islands of change are visible, the domination of the landscape by the one-year programme of study prevents the winds of change from blowing across. All arguments in the debate unfold the change perspective. But the needed change is seldom effected, neither in outer forms (courses continue to carry such titles as "Psychological Foundations of Education", and "Philosophical and Sociological Foundations of Education") nor in substantive content, underscoring the continued hegemony of the colonial past. The prevailing reality reflects the "thought" process of key players in teacher education. In fact, actions reflect thought. This is the setting that prompts me to revisit the report of the Education Commission 1964-66.

## The Commission's Road Map

It is forty years since the EC report established itself as a document for actions. During this time we have seen several initiatives in quality education. Yet, we have to traverse miles to complete the critical path drawn by the Commission. The opening statement of the report states that "the destiny of India is now being shaped in her classrooms". In the same vein, chapter three begins with: "Of all the different factors which influence the quality of education and its contribution to national development, the quality, competence and character of teachers are undoubtedly the most significant." The Commission, with profound insight, maps the connectivity between quality education and national development. Recognition of the primacy of the teacher in actualizing this connectivity sets the tone of the Commission's vision. The connectivity has wider social, political and economic meanings in the context of our multicultural society, made up of numerous regional and local cultures. All groups have equal rights to co-exist and flourish and the education system needs to respond to the inherent cultural pluralism.

The constitutional vision of India as a secular, egalitarian and pluralistic society, founded on the values of equality and social justice implies that the education system should provide for nurturing independence of thought and action, sensitivity to others, participation in the democratic process, the idea of living together and the ability to contribute to economic processes and social change (NCERT, 2005). It means education has to serve as a means of strengthening the democratic way of life in our society. Creation of a citizenry conscious of their rights and duties and commitment to the principles embodied in our Constitution becomes an essentiality. The Commission's vision gives meaning to the role of teacher in this context. The teacher becomes the agent of "connectivity between quality education and national development".

Perception of education as a common good (Tyack, 2004) is yet another dimension that is deeply embedded in this vision. Like air or water, education is essential and benefits all, not just those who use it always. The notion of education as a common good, contrasts sharply with market-oriented conceptions of education as a consumer good that yields its primary rewards to the individual who purchases it. The idea of common good is intrinsically linked to and springs from the complex issues of diversity. Diversity has several layers of meaning. Though certain notions such as ethnicity, race, class, religion and gender have received more attention, differences stemming from language, caste, rural background and the kind of work people perform and their thought patterns have deeper meanings, but are often glossed over. Widening the frame of diversity for the inclusion of different groups provides a lens to see deeper meanings. For instance, like race, ethnicity and gender, caste or rural background can be seen as the most intractable marker serving as a means to stereotype and relegate lower caste or minority or rural children to the bottom of the educational heap. In fact, diversity is a strength rather than a problem for national unity. When children of different socio-economic and cultural backgrounds study together, the classroom ethos gets enriched (NCERT, 2005). The vision, thus, has wider and deeper consequences for the teacher and teacher development programmes.

For actualizing the vision, the Commission unfolds road maps for promoting teacher status and development of quality teacher education programmes. Updating remuneration of teachers assumes primary concern. A study of the remuneration of teachers in States and Union territories helped the Commission to discern the substantial differences in remuneration that prevailed across States/UTs. Even within a State/UT differences in the remuneration of teachers working under different managements was found glaring. Based on the principles of parity, the Commission recommends the same remuneration for teachers of the same category working under different managements. Further, specification of scales of pay for teachers of primary, secondary and higher secondary stages, illustrates concern for the formation of a cadre of teachers. Recognition of stage specific qualification of teachers as a key component of recruitment is a move to ensure quality. Provision of higher pay or advance increment when trained speaks of the weightage placed on professional training. Stress placed on retirement benefits, retirement at the age of sixty years and the provision of pension marks the Commission's effort to look beyond teachers' welfare, focusing on the concern for building a cadre of teachers. Minimum facilities in the classroom, teaching aids, library and laboratory facilities and manageable pupil-teacher ratio become essential conditions of work. The Commission's recommendation of a school system that encourages initiative, experimentation, creativity and research and programmes for teachers' professional growth, outlines a shift towards an enabling system that promotes and sustains professional development of teachers. While highlighting the need for employment of women teachers in increasing proportion, the Commission underscores the need to secure good teachers for the tribal areas. Increase in the number of national awards, obviously paves the way, for the creation of more space for the recognition of those who excel in their professional roles. Whether it is remuneration, qualification, retirement benefits, minimum facilities, creation of an enabling system or national awards, a visible factor that threads them together is teacher professionalism. This perspective gains more ground and becomes sharper as one moves to the road map for improving the quality of teacher education.

The Commission critically examines the functioning of training institutions and their professional education programmes and calls for breaking the isolation of these institutions from the university system, from schools and from one another. The suggestion to bring education into the mainstream of university academic life and recognize education as a social science or an independent discipline provides larger space for intense academic engagement. Involvement of university system opens up multiple options for enriching educational studies. For instance, under-graduate and post-graduate courses of study in education, professional education programmes from pre-primary to secondary under the university system and inter-disciplinary studies in education are visualized as specific forms of action.

Active interactions between teacher training institutions and schools, breaking their isolation, paves the way for generating mutually enriching professional experience based on field reality. While arguing for strengthening the linkage among various types of training institutions, the commission recognizes the need for upgrading training institutions for pre-primary and primary teachers to the collegiate standard. The idea of comprehensive colleges of education, which prepare teachers for various stages of schooling, marks a new initiative for reform.

The concern for improving the quality of teacher education is quite visible across the text of the report. Re-orientation of subject knowledge in course content and its implementation in collaboration with university departments give a new meaning to the teacher education programme. The importance attached to reformulation of course components to address the emerging professional needs of teacher trainees, obviously, reflects the concern for quality. This demands that teacher educators need to shift out of their comfort zones of generalities to the specifics of subjects or themes. It is crucial, in this context, that training institutions usher in strategies of active pedagogy and evaluation reforms in their institutional practices. Though the commission finds meaning in strengthening the one-year course of study, its concern for providing space for integrated programmes of teacher preparation is quite visible. Pointing out that the prevailing curricula at different stages have grown out of the traditional perspective, the commission pleads for their revision in the light of the need for preparing teachers in effective performance of their roles in an evolving system of education. The content that is presented under theory should be of direct relevance to the task that a teacher is expected to perform in the school. The relationship among different subjects should be discerned and they should be taught in an integrated manner. Practice-teaching is an area that needs improvement. The commission conceives it in two stages. Stage-1 envisages orientation of trainees to the entire school situation and initiation into the process of teaching. Stage-2 provides trainees actual school situations, where they engage in continuous teaching for a specified period of at least eight weeks. The emphasis placed on developing problem solving abilities, whether it is the course content or practice, teaching is quite visible. Such abilities should first be developed among the trainees by the teacher educators. Whether it is primary or secondary stage teacher education programmes need to focus on experience based training to address stage specific teaching and learning problems. While underscoring the rationale for restructuring the M.Ed. course of study, the commission outlines the need for developing undergraduate and postgraduate courses in education.

Improving the quality of training institutions is yet another area that has been probed in detail. The secondary level training institutions should be manned by staff, who possess a double Master's degree—in an academic subject and in education. A fair proportion should have a doctorate degree. However, considering the need for specialists in related disciplines (e.g.

educational psychology or sociology or science or mathematics), it is desirable to appoint specialists in such areas even if they do not have professional training. The commission is critical of the practice of interchanging training staff and inspecting officers and insists on selection of competent persons for the faculty of training institutions. Salary scales should be the same as those of the academic staff of arts and science colleges.

When it turns to primary level teacher training institutions, the commission observes that the majority of training staff is selected from the teachers of secondary schools and they are inadequately trained to perform the new roles assigned to them. It is of the view that the staff, besides the B.Ed. degree, should hold a master's degree either in education or in an academic subject. However, they should be adequately trained for their work through special orientation or induction courses including experience of primary school. They are entitled to receive the same scales of salary as lecturers in arts and science colleges.

The Commission's recommendation that all training institutions should have an attached demonstration or experimental school and the suggestion that tuition fees in such institutions should be done away with, show concern for professional development and social justice. Systematic and well planned programme of in-service education is recognized as a major input for professional development of teacher educators and teachers. The commission also pinpoints the need for professional preparation of teachers in higher education. It recommends the setting up of a standing committee for teacher education at the national level for ensuring standards in teacher education. All these different recommendations manifest the Commission's deep concern for enhancing quality of teachers at all levels to realize the national goals of development.

## The Road Traversed

Of the various recommendations of the Commission, those bearing on teachers' remuneration, status and welfare, received the most attention. The relevance and significance of these recommendations were explained by J.P. Naik (who was Member Secretary of the EC) as follows:

> *It will be readily seen that the main objective of the Commission was to ensure that existing discrimination against teachers in the public services is done away with, that teachers get an adequate remuneration so that a reasonable proportion of the best talent available is attracted to the profession, and that the existing wide differences in the remuneration of different categories of teachers are removed so that teachers of all types and at all stages of education become a unified and cohesive profession. It was these recommendations that made*

*Mr. M.C. Chagla describe the* Report of the Commission as the Magna Carta of teachers (Naik, 1982, pp. 92-93).

Naik points out that the Commission's recommendations on remuneration of teachers were implemented over a period of time. Though the Commission provided a rallying point, a variety of factors played in the implementation of these recommendations almost *in toto*. The efforts of the Central and State Governments for improving the remuneration of teachers of all categories are quite visible. Organized agitation by teachers in all parts of the country and at all levels acted as a catalyst. Obviously, the agitation set in motion by the teachers acquired certain degree of political influence. The combined effect of all these factors led to substantial improvement in the remuneration of teachers of all categories, at all levels and in all parts of the country. Today, teachers have category-wise scales of pay and enjoy periodic revision. The main contention is on the scales of pay provided for different categories and the differences that exist across the scales. Prevailing pattern of pay scales in some states cited below illustrate this contention (Table 11.1).

**Table 11.1: Pay Scales of Teachers in a Few States**

| *State* | *Pay Scales of Teachers* | | |
|---|---|---|---|
| | *Primary* | *Secondary* | *Senior Secondary/ Junior College* |
| Haryana | 4500-7000 | 5500-9000 | 6500-10500 |
| Himachal Pradesh | 4550-7000 | 5480-8925 | 6400-10640 |
| Kerala [a] | 6680-10790 | 8390-13270 | 11070-18450 (s) |
| Orissa | 3600-5600 [b]<br>4000-6000 [c] | 5000-8000 | 6500-10500 |
| Punjab | 4550-7220 | 5480-8925 | 6400-10640 |
| Rajasthan | 4500-7000 | 5500-9000 | 6500-10500 |

*Note*: [a] Revised scales based on Pay Commission 2005; [b] Scale of pay of matric (class X) trained primary teachers; [c] Scale of pay of +2 trained primary teachers; j = scale of junior teachers; s = scale of senior teachers.

Instances cited above are few but it does not mean that the picture in the rest of the States is quite different. What it speaks is that teachers today enjoy category specific scales with provision for senior scales, periodic revision and avenue for promotion. This has been made possible by the continuous efforts of teachers, political interventions and government level decisions. It points to the existence of a cadre of professionally qualified teachers. However, certain recent initiatives, rather than strengthening the cadre of teachers, have shaken the very foundation of the idea of cadre.

## The Issue of "Para Teachers"

There is a growing tendency in recent times for the engagement of "para teachers" against regular vacancies. This tendency is gaining wider acceptance among States across the country (Dayaram, 2000). Para teachers differ in designation, salary, qualification, duration and recruitment. They are engaged in varying contexts, such as to respond to teacher shortage or teacher absenteeism or teacher requirement in remote areas etc. The para teacher approach for ensuring teacher supply is a departure from the national policy; the context that provides for such an approach needs critical reflection.

Following the launch of DPEP and, subsequently, Sarva Shiksha Abhiyan (SSA), the number of schools and enrolment of children have multiplied in striking rate and this has resulted in increase in the demand for additional teachers. Appointment of additional teachers on regular basis naturally entails States to substantially increase financial allocation. Instead, the States preferred to address this issue by choosing a route of financial convenience, of engaging teachers on contract basis. The issue of para teachers thus stems from the States' perception of fund shortage. Deployment of para teachers as a cost-saving device would systematically erode the development of a cadre of professionally qualified teachers (Govinda and Josephine, 2005). Increasing tendency of the States to choose this route is well sheltered by the recommendations of the National Committee of State Education Ministers (GoI, 1999). Responding to the urgency of teacher shortage in the context of elementary education being made a fundamental right, the national committee called for appropriate modification in the national policy. With many States experimenting with para teachers, the Committee considered the para teacher approach as appropriate for ensuring teacher supply within a short time. In fact, the practice of employing para teachers can be traced to the 1980s, to the "volunteer teacher" scheme of Himachal Pradesh and the Shiksha Karmi Project of Rajasthan. The practice of engaging contract teachers gained momentum during the implementation of the DPEP. Today, para teachers exist in several states and their number continues to multiply. The recommendation of the national committee has become a convenient tool for States for charting their own courses for the recruitment of para teachers. In certain States, para teacher has become the legitimate route for becoming a regular teacher. The following text illustrates the practice that is set in motion in Orissa:

> *Engagement of new Shiksha Sahayaks (SS) will be made by Zilla Parishads as per requirement under the programme of elementary education and Sarva Shiksha Abhiyan (SSA)...70 per cent of the vacant posts in each education district will be for candidates having matric/+2 with C.T. qualification and 30 per cent for candidates having BA/B.Sc. and B.Com. with B.Ed. qualification. The candidates*

*shall not be below 18 years and above 42 years of age.... The SS will get remuneration of Rs. 2000/- per month. The engagement would be on the basis of annual contract.... After every 3 years of satisfactory engagement, a junior teacher will be granted an increase in remuneration of Rs. 500. The junior teachers after completion of 5 years of continuous satisfactory engagement...will be eligible for appointment as regular primary school teachers...subject to the fulfilment of following conditions:*

- The Junior teachers must have rendered at least 5 years of service as such, satisfactorily with unblemished record.
- They must have ensured 90 per cent attendance of children in their respective schools in all classes.
- They must have been given positive certificate by the VEC about regular attendance and satisfactory teaching. They must have ensured Minimum Level of Learning (MLL) for the students as prescribed by the competent authority.
- They must have reduced the dropout of children in the schools to below 10 per cent.

  The Junior Teachers of Zilla Parishads on rendering satisfactory service as reviewed every 3 years can continue in service but not beyond 58 years of age.

*Source*: Resolution No. 11676/SME Dt. 31-5-2006, Department of School and Mass Education, Government of Orissa.

The text narrates selection, placement, remuneration and the tasks to be performed by the Shiksha Sahayaks. It also speaks of the complex path (woven on exploitative service conditions) they have to traverse for reaching the terrain of regular teachers. They need to perform the work of regular teachers but without the benefits accorded to regular teachers. Evidences point out that they are subject to non-payment of honorarium on time or lack of provision for casual, medical and maternity leave (Pandey, Rani and Kumar, 2003). It is natural for them to form collectives and raise collective voice against the prevailing practice. Obviously, it would place the schooling system in peril and quality would become a casualty. This is a reality and it is not specific to Orissa alone. There are states, which practically avoid recruitment of regular teachers and, instead, opt for teachers on contract. The fact that teacher is an essential conduit for ensuring quality can neither be ignored nor brushed aside. The critical issue is that when the States formulate a policy, which culminates in differential treatment of teachers, how can teachers become partners in providing quality education? How do they respond to issues of inequality in school practices when they are themselves victims of differential treatment? The para teacher issue calls for serious debate and intense reflection on the part of academics and various levels of stakeholders and viable solutions are to be found that would strengthen and sustain the cadre of professionally trained teachers.

## New Structures

Quality is the focal point of the EC recommendations, whether they are on teaching or teacher education. It is significant, in this context, to recall the effort of the Committee of Members of Parliament in transforming the Commission's recommendations into policy statements (National Policy on Education-1968). The Committee while turning down specifics of several recommendations identified 16 programmes for action (Naik, 1982). They cover Indian languages as media of education, neighbourhood school system, 10+2+3 pattern, teacher status, teacher education, work experience, science education, development of essential student services, post-graduate education and research, education of girls and marginalized groups, spread of literacy, recruitment policies of government, admissions to higher education, district as a unit for planning, administration and development of education, curricula and examination reform, agricultural research and education, and facilities for part-time education. In particular, the significance attached to teacher status, teacher education, recruitment policy, curricula and examination reform and district as a unit for planning, administration and development is quite visible and they find place in the National Policy. The Policy reaffirms the Commission's thrust placed on quality in teaching and teacher education. However, these points remained as mere policy statements and failed to get transformed into actions. The Committee's selective approach in dealing with the recommendations cast a shadow on the initial fervour for moving forward. In fact, without political will, radical reconstruction of education cannot be attained. When quality education for the nation's children assumes primacy convergence of minds, breaking the boundaries of region and political affiliations becomes essential for policy makers.

Around twenty years later the new National Policy on Education (NPE) 1986 (modified in 1992), reaffirmed the Commission's vision on quality in school system and teacher education. Its recommendations on the national system of education, common educational structure, education of girls and marginalized groups, to cite a few, form the markers of this perception. Other recommendations included: objectivity in recruitment of teachers, pay and service conditions, grievance removal mechanism and role of teacher associations. Further, greater meaning has been given to "overhauling" of the system of teacher education, the process perspective of teaching and learning and forging connectivity between pre-service and in-service education. While the Commission points out the need for improving the quality of training institutions and setting up a mechanism for ensuring quality control, the NPE went further ahead and defined it in terms of establishment of district institute of education and training, upgrading of secondary teacher training colleges and the National Council of Teacher Education. The quality perspective conceived by the Commission gained further impetus in the NPE. With the onset of the NPE, the nation witnessed a striking shift from thrust on quantitative expansion towards quality, during the latter half of the eighties.

The nineties witnessed unprecedented developments ushering in mechanisms for ensuring quality in teacher training. Creation of structures like District Institutes of Education and Training (DIET), Institutes of Advanced Studies in Education (IASE) and Colleges of Teacher Education (CTE) mark a departure from the past towards quality. The establishment of Block Resource Centres (BRC) and Cluster Resource Centres (CRC) under the District Primary Education Programme advanced the cause of decentralization of training at the elementary stage. The National Council of Teacher Education (NCTE) was institutionalized as a statutory authority in 1995 for achieving planned and coordinated development and ensuring standards in teacher education system. The Programme of Mass Orientation of School Teachers (PMOST) and later, the Special Orientation of Primary Teachers (SOPT), opened space for large scale training of teachers in the in-service sector. It is true that all these started taking shape as a follow up of the NPE but their seeds had been sown much earlier by the Commission. The seeds started germinating later in the protective terrain mapped by the NPE, 1986.[1]

The new structures signal construction of the path for strengthening and setting standards of quality in teacher education programmes and institutions. The way they function indicates whether they perform their roles meaningfully. The DIETs were set up as pace setting institutions with multiple functions covering pre-service and in-service training, curriculum and material development, planning and management, and research and extension. Till November 2005, a total of 556 DIETs and District Resource Centres (DRCs) had been sanctioned and by December that year, 58 new such institutions were added to the list (MHRD 2006). Though some of them have yet to take concrete shape, substantial numbers are in functional form. Professionally, DIET faculty members are trained to teach at secondary school (B.Ed.) level. Rarely, do they possess any experience in primary or elementary stage of education. Most DIETs are primarily engaged in pre-service training; in-service training is yet to become a common feature. Even if in-service programmes are at a low key, a critical look at them unfolds two fault-lines; the eagerness to complete more number of programmes (reflecting importance attached to quantity) and gradual routinization of the programmes. Also, it is not unusual for DIETs and non-DIET training institutions in many states to offer the same pre-service course. But the critical question is: Are the DIETs more effective than the non-DIET training institutions? With a few exceptions, quite often, it would be difficult to find a satisfactory answer. A critical analysis of the pre-service course would reveal that the course content is either packed with knowledge that is divorced from the realities of school practices or lacks the essential pedagogic components for addressing specific learning problems of children. Pre-service training blissfully continues with its traditional academic style of functioning in splendid isolation (Seshadri, 2002). The DIET's engagement in research and creating a data system at the district level for planning and management of intervention strategies are yet to become realities. In certain states, DIETs are not fully staffed and frequent posting of secondary school teachers to the vacant positions on "adjustment" has set erosion in their academic functioning. This points to the prevailing nature of systemic failure. In fact, there exists a mismatch between teacher training programmes and the realities of school practices. Reformulation of teacher education curricula is yet another dimension that seeks immediate attention.

The images of Colleges of Teacher Education (CTEs) and Institutes of Advanced Studies in Education (IASEs) are not all that attractive. A total of 104 CTEs and 31 IASEs were sanctioned up to November 2005 and 11 new CTEs and 4 new IASEs were added to the list by December 2005 (MHRD, 2006). Though the progress is slow more and more institutional settings are being created. It is logical to enquire into the way they function. Evidences emerging from a study (Pandey, Yadva and Rani, 2004) provide insights into their functional form. Based on a sample drawn from different states the study points out that a good number of CTEs face faculty shortage. This is often addressed by positioning faculty members on ad hoc or part-time basis on consolidated pay. Though these institutions are preoccupied with pre-service and in-service education of teachers more time is invested on pre-service training. However, quality of these forms of teacher training needs a critical look. Research, development and innovative activities are yet to take concrete shape. Library facility appears to be a weak link. Availability of fund on time is a matter of major concern.

The picture of IASEs is in no way different. A recently concluded study (Bhardwaj and Arora, 2006) tells that for IASEs, pre-service and in-service training of teachers forms the major area of activities. There is a felt need among the participants for context specific, need based and innovative programmes. Research appears to be a weak spot in the functioning of IASEs. Availability of fund on time remains a problem as in the past. These evidences question the capacity of both CTEs and IASEs in performing the mandated roles. There is no guarantee that quality concerns can be effectively addressed by meeting faculty shortage through ad hoc or part time arrangement. Many of the IASEs fail to provide quality in their professional training programmes. Both IASEs and CTEs under the same university offer the same B.Ed. programme of study. The course content and the way pre-service teacher-training programme is carried out needs to be critically studied to unearth the fault-lines. It appears that in-service teacher training programmes are constructed based on teacher educators' perception centered around what they know rather than focusing on the professional needs of teachers or participants. What is critical for ensuring professionalism in teacher education, is the curriculum and its transaction by the teacher educators. Mere creation of new structures without evolving mechanisms for capacity building of functionaries does not advance the cause of quality.

## Issues

Whether it is DIET, CTE or IASE, they are created with a vision. But are they capable of realizing the vision? A sizeable number among them are incapacitated by faculty shortage and delayed fund flow. Formulation of a need based capacity development programme for strengthening these structures is essential to set the wheels in motion. This needs to be designed with space for growth-oriented inputs and feedback mechanisms. In the absence of such mechanisms mere creation of structures does not yield the desired results. Also, the teacher training curriculum that is being practiced in these institutions needs to be critically examined, for the programme content and the manner in which teacher educators impart training are the pathways for exploring the quality of training. A critical analysis of B.Ed. syllabi of 12 universities of eastern region (Khader, 2004), unfolds that the course contents are woven around traditional forms of knowledge and do not reflect any connectivity with school practices. As an instance, the core paper on educational psychology is constructed around meaning, growth and development, individual differences, learning, personality, educational statistics and such components. Each topic is treated as if it is a course in psychology. Personality, for example, is elaborated in terms of concept, structure, type, traits, etc. How does such knowledge matter for a teacher in school situations? Other papers dealing with the perspectives on philosophy and sociology and methods of teaching are in no way different. A comparison reveals that the course contents do not differ much from those prevailed in the forties. Titles of papers in several universities continue to be "philosophical and sociological foundations of education" and "psychological foundations of education". Even the title of primary stage teacher training institutions continues to be "secondary teacher training schools". Curricula restructuring in teacher education is not a regular feature and the attempts often end up in tinkering. The prevailing trend reflects the past focused on traditional and rigid knowledge base with no space for new perspectives. This trend reflects the mindset of teacher educators and the policy practitioners.

Equally crucial for ensuring quality is the professional practice of teacher educators. When there is a change in the course structure and the nature of inputs, a corresponding shift in training practices is expected. However, teacher educators continue to remain good at imparting knowledge centered conventional approach (Khader and Das, 2003). For example, while dealing with discovery learning, enquiry or problem solving, they often fail to illustrate or demonstrate how they are to be conducted. Instead, they deliver discourses on them. This is not to suggest that theory is not essential; it is to draw attention to the importance of showing how theory works in concrete situations especially in a professional development programme. If teacher educators are to be effective in supporting the transformation of teachers they too must undergo shifts in their knowledge, belief and habits of practice that are akin to transformation than to tinkering around the edges of their practice (Stein, Smith and Silver, 1999). They need to know how teachers learn within organizations and through interactions with others. They need not only to access a variety of strategies but also to have the ability to gauge which strategy will be the most effective with a given set of teachers in a given setting. Obviously, teacher educators need to shift out of their comfort zones and fine tune their mindset and practice and set in motion the change process for professional development. The Education Commission, forty years ago, placed highest importance to the qualitative improvement of teacher education and training institutions and it gains greater meaning and validity even today.

## National Council of Teacher Education (NCTE)

The NCTE is a major manifestation of the Commission's recommendation for the maintenance of norms and standards in the teacher education system. Though the Government of India constituted the NCTE as a non-statutory body in the early seventies to advise the Government on matters relating to teacher education it took a concrete shape only in 1995 as a statutory authority through an Act of Parliament for achieving planned and coordinated development of teacher education throughout the country. This initiative for the regulation and maintenance of norms and standards in teacher education is a turning point in the quality reform of teacher education. It is now mandatory for teacher education institutions to seek the recognition of the NCTE. The norms and standards cover course duration, size of intake, entry qualification, teaching days, curriculum transaction, qualification of teaching staff, terms and conditions of service, infrastructural facilities and financial management. The NCTE conducts periodic review on the basis of feedback from the field and accords recognition to institutions through its regional centres. Such initiatives have paved the way for exercising control over the functioning of teacher education institutions. However, non-observance of norms not only by individual institutions but also by states, adds to the prevailing complexity. Instances of non-observance of norms related to staff strength, duration of training, student strength, facilities and practice of placement of teachers trained at the secondary level in primary schools are common. This casts a shadow on the NCTE's functioning. What is more alarming is the uncontrolled growth of teacher training institutions within a short span of 5 years. (Table 11.2). The number has more than doubled during 2000-2005. Reduction in number in certain States (e.g. Assam and Bihar) is mainly due to withdrawal of recognition. Whether it is non-observance of norms or growth of institutions, the overarching influence of number driven approach in the functioning of the NCTE is glaring. This is a major concern that seeks attention.

A major activity of the NCTE is the development of curriculum framework for teacher education programmes for different levels of schooling.

The latter part of the seventies witnessed development of the *Teacher education curriculum: a framework* (NCERT, 1978). The document outlines stage specific—pre-school, primary, secondary, higher secondary and collegiate stages of teacher education curricula. The curriculum across stages is structured on three broad components—pedagogical theory, working with the community and content-cum-methodology and practice teaching with varying content, treatment and sub-components. At the pre-school stage, methodology and practice teaching forms the third component, while it is content-cum-methodology and practice teaching for the remaining stages. The weightage for the three components, respectively, is 20 per cent, 20 per cent and 60 per cent from pre-school to secondary stage. However, it is 30 per cent, 20 per cent and 50 per cent at the higher secondary and collegiate stages. A significant feature of the framework is conceptualization of *Teacher and education in the emerging Indian society,* replacing philosophical and sociological foundations of education and space provided for core training and skill development programme.

The NPE (1986) thrust on content and process of school education provided the conceptual frame for the formulation of *National curriculum for teacher education—a framework* (NCERT 1988). The framework focuses on the development of teacher education programme for transforming teachers as facilitators of learning, effective communicators, and designers and users of learning resources. The curriculum is structured around foundation courses, stage relevant specialization and field-work. Interestingly, the framework articulates alternative integrated teacher education models for pre-primary (two year), primary (three year), secondary (four year) and higher secondary (three year) stages. The framework favours an eclectic approach to respond to multiplicity of theoretical perspectives derived from various disciplines that are cognate to education (NCTE, 1998a). The process of evolving a teacher education curriculum based on innovative practices and teacher educator's own experience and reflection is the key feature of this framework.

The *Curriculum framework for quality teacher education* formulated by the NCTE in the late nineties covers the entire spectrum of teacher education programmes (NCTE, 1998). By providing adequate space for flexibility and innovation, the document supports curriculum framework for early childhood, primary, elementary, secondary and senior secondary stages. The senior secondary stage covers both academic and vocational streams. Besides, the framework covers curriculum for preparation of teachers of alternative systems and students with special needs and physical education. Further, it provides space for in-service education and the education of teacher educators. The framework is structured around theory and practicum. With varying stage specific academic inputs, the framework assigns weightage of 40 per cent to theory and 20 per cent each to pedagogical analysis, practice teaching and other practical work for various stages. However, the distribution for theory and practice at pre-primary stage is 30 per cent and 70 per cent respectively. It is significant to note that the framework, in tune with the 1978 and 1988 frameworks re-conceptualizes core papers. It suggests *Emerging Indian society* in place of *philosophical and sociological foundations of education/teacher and education in the emerging Indian society*. The change perspective is also seen in educational psychology/ psychological foundations of education in terms of *Psychology of teaching and learning*. The change perspective also covers status, problems and issues in education specific to stages, pedagogical analysis, work education, and action research. The importance attached to pedagogical analysis of school subjects as an essential component of practice teaching and the mode of transacting the teacher education curriculum marks the shift to quality in teacher education. Further, the document focuses on structural reform by suggesting 2-year models of teacher training from pre-primary to senior secondary and 4-year integrated courses from pre-primary to elementary stages with options for either 4-year or 5-year programme at secondary stage.

However, a critical look at the academic functioning of teacher education system raises serious questions on the implementation of these frameworks. Though certain efforts on the implementation of the change perspective, articulated in the 1978 framework could be seen, they failed to make substantial changes at the operational level (NCTE 1998a). What needs to be probed is the manner in which these courses are implemented by the teacher education system. The fact that still there are universities, which continue with philosophical and sociological foundations of education or psychological foundations of education, without reformulation of curricula in tune with the change perspective, tells that the 1978 framework did not take roots. In the case of 1988 framework no attempt was made to implement the same. Except for a few instances, the seeds of 1998 framework are yet to germinate. On the initiative of the NCTE and in collaboration with the NCERT, a two-year secondary teacher education curriculum was formulated and introduced in the four Regional Institutes of Education. Gujarat Vidyapeeth also joined the group in offering the two-year course. Beyond this, no significant change is visible in curricular reform.

**Table 11.2: Teacher Education Institutions**

| Sl. No. | States/UTs | Teacher Training Schools | Teacher Training Colleges | **As on 31.3.2000 | As on 31.3.2001 | As on 31.3.2002 | As on 31.3.2003 | As on 31.3.2004 | As on 31.3.2005 |
|---|---|---|---|---|---|---|---|---|---|
| | | *As on 30.09.1992 | | | | | | | |
| 1. | Total Institutions | 1328 | 557 | 2052 | 2172 | 2265 | 2650 | 3197 | 4550 |
| 2. | Arunachal Pradesh | — | — | 2 | 2 | 2 | 2 | 2 | 3 |
| 3. | Assam | 33 | 9 | 42 | 46 | 31 | 34 | 28 | 39 |
| 4. | Bihar | 95 | 15 | 20 | 18 | 6 | 26 | 28 | 30 |
| 5. | Jammu & Kashmir | 14 | 4 | — | — | — | — | — | — |
| 6. | Jharkhand | Included in Bihar | | | | 7 | 15 | 20 | 27 |
| 7. | Manipur | 2 | 3 | 4 | 3 | 3 | 4 | 6 | 6 |
| 8. | Meghalaya | 10 | 1 | 8 | 7 | 7 | 8 | 10 | 10 |
| 9. | Mizoram | 2 | 1 | 1 | 3 | 4 | 4 | 4 | 4 |
| 10. | Nagaland | 4 | 1 | 6 | 6 | 6 | 7 | 7 | 7 |
| 11. | Orissa | 71 | 11 | 84 | 82 | 87 | 85 | 85 | 87 |
| 12. | Sikkim | 1 | — | 2 | 2 | 2 | 2 | 4 | 4 |
| 13. | Tripura | 2 | 1 | 5 | 4 | 5 | 5 | 5 | 7 |
| 14. | West Bengal | 58 | 43 | 25 | 29 | 32 | 38 | 43 | 47 |
| 15. | Chandigarh | — | — | 4 | 5 | 5 | 5 | 6 | 7 |
| 16. | Delhi | 20 | — | 33 | 40 | 40 | 44 | 53 | 67 |
| 17. | Haryana | 7 | 17 | 60 | 63 | 63 | 69 | 71 | 87 |
| 18. | Himachal Pradesh | 6 | 2 | 18 | 19 | 19 | 25 | 45 | 47 |
| 19. | Punjab | 18 | 19 | 36 | 36 | 37 | 40 | 49 | 68 |
| 20. | Rajasthan | 41 | 33 | 95 | 103 | 104 | 112 | 123 | 129 |
| 21. | Uttar Pradesh | 121 | 13 | 220 | 253 | 253 | 341 | 446 | 651 |

(*Contd.*)

| Sl. No. | States/UTs | Teacher Training Schools | Teacher Training Colleges | **As on 31.3.2000 | As on 31.3.2001 | As on 31.3.2002 | As on 31.3.2003 | As on 31.3.2004 | As on 31.3.2005 |
|---|---|---|---|---|---|---|---|---|---|
| | | *As on 30.09.1992 | | | | | | | |
| 22. | Uttaranchal | Included in UP | | | | | | 11 | 14 |
| 23. | Andaman & Nichobar Islands | 1 | 1 | 2 | 2 | 2 | 2 | 2 | 2 |
| 24. | Andhra Pradesh | 25 | 49 | 125 | 155 | 178 | 261 | 393 | 414 |
| 25. | Karnataka | 128 | 64 | 270 | 271 | 274 | 280 | 280 | 771 |
| 26. | Kerala | 101 | 12 | 140 | 142 | 155 | 165 | 171 | 319 |
| 27. | Pondicherry | — | 1 | 4 | 5 | 6 | 7 | 7 | 13 |
| 28. | Tamil Nadu | 170 | 21 | 103 | 111 | 111 | 111 | 156 | 325 |
| 29. | Chhatisgarh | Included in MP | | | | 27 | 35 | 41 | 50 |
| 30. | Daman & Diu | — | — | 2 | 1 | 2 | 2 | 2 | 2 |
| 31. | Goa | 1 | 1 | 4 | 4 | 3 | 4 | 3 | 6 |
| 32. | Gujarat | 79 | 41 | 139 | 142 | 168 | 246 | 338 | 442 |
| 33. | Madhya Pracesh | 52 | 20 | 118 | 117 | 98 | 118 | 166 | 220 |
| 34. | Maharashtra | 266 | 174 | 480 | 501 | 528 | 553 | 592 | 645 |

[Institutions include those offering Pre-primary, Elementary, B. El. Ed., Secondary (B. Ed) face to face, Secondary (B. Ed)—Distance Mode, (M. Ed) face to face, (M. Ed)—Distance Mode, C.P.Ed., B.P.Ed., M.P.Ed. etc. in the area of teacher education]

*Source:* * Selected Educational Statistics (1992-93), MHRD (GOI), New Delhi, 1993.

** Annual Report, 2000-2001, 2001-2002, 2002-2003, 2003-2004, 2004-2005, NCTE, New Delhi.

However, in these islands of change, sustainability of the two-year teacher education programme is at stake. Further, the way the course is practiced or implemented is another dimension that seeks attention. Research evidences are to be sought on the validity of teacher education curriculum by relating it to teacher's performance and children's learning in classroom situations (Ministry of Education, 1985). Obviously, criticality of teacher educator's performance at the operational level of the course has greater meaning (Khader and Das, 2003). It appears that a data based approach in the implementation of teacher education curriculum is not the agenda of curriculum designers or managers. The emerging concern is that curriculum framework suggests change perspective in the course structure and its practices but the winds of change rarely blow across.

In 2003, the NCTE circulated two approach papers on curriculum renewal, one for elementary stage and the other for secondary stage (NCTE, 2003a and 2003b). The paper dealing with elementary stage outlines a teacher education curriculum structured on general education courses, pedagogic courses, school experience programme, practical work and post-coursework six-month internship. At the secondary stage, the paper maps the curricular components covering theory courses—contemporary and emerging Indian society, teaching/learning process, evaluation, curriculum development and action research, pedagogic courses, optional courses, practice teaching, co-curricular activities, practicals and post-coursework six months internship. Though these papers are yet to transform into curriculum framework the suggested curricular components reflect the path sketched for the development of professionalism in teacher education programmes. Obviously, the critical point is the transformation of these ideas into course details and their operationalization in the teacher education system.

The recent initiative of the NCTE in collaboration with the NCERT in formulating a draft curriculum framework for teacher education, depicts its renewed and continued effort for improving the teacher education system (NCTE, 2006). The draft framework, set against the *National Curriculum Framework-2005* perspectives of pedagogic and professional concerns of the child and the teacher, builds up the rationale for redesigning teacher education programme. It seeks to reformulate the education of teachers for their professional development that enables them to evolve pedagogic approaches and create a learning environment conducive to addressing the needs of learners. The design focuses on creation of reflective teachers through the process of weaving theoretical knowledge across disciplines with the student teachers' own experiential realities and the learners' social milieu. The critical components of teacher education curriculum consists of childhood, child development and learning, teacher and learner in society, aims of educating children and adults, knowledge and curriculum, developing self and aspirations as a teacher, human rights and rights of the child, adolescence education, and environmental education, teacher-child engagement, learning to integrate ideas, experiences and professional skills, learning to assess and evaluate, and establishing teacher learning centres. The draft document also articulates the ideas for continuous professional development of teachers in the in-service sector and systemic reform in teacher education. Focusing on systemic change, the document suggests alternative models of pre-service teacher education; one year B.Ed. with 5/6 months school attachment, four year integrated interdisciplinary programme for different stages of school education and five years integrated undergraduate and post-graduate programmes. Specifics post-graduate courses in teacher education and post-graduate diploma/certificate courses are also indicated.

In short, the draft framework visualizes continuous reflective engagement of student teachers through the process of connecting knowledge with their own experiential realities. It signals the pathway for professional development. It is an insightful and challenging idea but raises several concerns. The prevailing theoretical knowledge that forms the base of on-going teacher education courses does not fit into the suggested perspective. Formulation of theoretical knowledge from multidisciplinary perspective becomes a necessity and it needs to be evolved for structuring the course content and details. Evolving the methodology for weaving the theoretical knowledge with the student teacher's experiential realities is yet another challenging task. The ground reality is that teacher education institutions across the country are at different levels of quality for providing professionalism in teacher training. Most of them need to be empowered for operationalising the suggested curriculum in its intended form. Creation of texts and sub-texts of course components and well informed teacher educators as change agents, emerge as a critical concern in this context. Teacher education system needs to evolve programmes that help prospective teachers to understand deeply learning, social and cultural contexts and be able to enact these understandings in complex classrooms, serving increasingly diverse students. If prospective teachers are to succeed in this task teacher educators need to design programmes that transform the settings in which novices learn to teach and later become teachers (Darling-Hammond, 2006). Yet another dimension is the suggestion for development of integrated courses. It resonates with the views of the EC 1964-66, the National Commission on Teachers-I, 1983-85 and the curriculum frameworks for teacher education, 1988, 1998 and 2006. In fact, the four-year integrated model of teacher education at secondary stage prevailing since the mid sixties is confined to the Regional Institutes of Education of the NCERT. The four-year integrated course in elementary teacher education (B.,El.Ed) developed by the University of Delhi, a recent development, makes a departure from the trend prevailing across the country.

Likewise, the effort of the University of Pondicherry to introduce four year integrated course for secondary stage in three of its colleges and similar initiative of the University of Mysore in two of its colleges signal the meaning in such courses. These are islands of change reflecting the willingness to choose alternative path in teacher education but the winds of change have failed to blow across the country. Lack of collective conscious effort, on the part of the teacher education institutions and teacher educators, has foiled the change perspective. Mere adding up of three-year content and one-year pedagogy components does not create an integrated course. Though the integrated course at secondary stage has been in practice for a pretty long period the teacher educators are yet to evolve a model curriculum for development of professionalism in teaching. The task ahead for the NCTE is quite challenging and complex and the issues involved are multiple.

## Issues

The NCTE, during its ten years of existence, has been successful in bringing various teacher training institutions under its fold. At the same time, it is disquieting that there are instances of non-observance of norms and standards by teacher education institutions and states as well. What is alarming is the multiplication of teacher training institutions in recent times. It does not mean that new institutions should not be opened. Rather, the nature of teacher education programme and the new institution's capacity for providing quality education should form the focal points for consideration. An increase in the number of teacher training institutions for the spread of conventional programmes does not yield the desired result.

Setting up new institutions, focusing on integrated models of teacher training for different stages, is an alternative path for effecting change. This, obviously, calls for formulation of stage specific integrated courses and also opens up the issues related to curriculum formulation and its management. Analysis of various teacher education curriculum frameworks (1978 to 2006-draft version), indicates the gradual shift from conceptual level to professionalism. This shift is mirrored in new concepts of teacher and teaching and new ways of conceiving and organizing teacher education curriculum as already described. However, experiences show that systematic efforts for transforming the curriculum frameworks, constructed at regular intervals, into realities did not take place. Though a few efforts are visible, they did not make substantial impact at the operational level of the curriculum. It speaks of the strength of the NCTE in ushering in and regulating quality in teacher education. Quality does not confine merely to norms and standards of structural dimensions of the institution. Functional aspect of the institution has greater meaning. What matters is the formulation of state-of-the-art curriculum for teacher education and its implementation. The initiative rests with the NCTE.

The prevailing trend reflects the NCTE's pre-occupation with number-driven approach and it needs to move out of its comfort zone, if ensuring quality is its primary concern. The NCTE alone cannot be held responsible for the prevailing trend, the system of governance in the country; and the teacher educators are equal partners in this.

## The Road Ahead

The existing weakness in teacher education can be traced at two levels; one at the level of knowledge base of teacher education and the other at the transactional level. The contention is that there exist adequate structures in teacher education system but they need to be empowered for meaningful performance of their professional role on priority. The Commission's recommendations on improving the quality of teacher education programmes and institutions acquire great significance in this context. Forging linkage between teacher education institutions and the university system opens a new path for enhancing quality. The linkage indicates the transformative role of higher education institutions; it implies that higher education should interact with basic education in a manner that the interconnections lead to societal change (Karuna Chanana, 2004). The Commission's reflections on the connectivity between education and society (chapter 1 of its report) provide a framework work for a re-look at teacher education programmes. The National Curriculum Framework (NCF) 2005, reaffirms this connectivity and outlines the crucial role of education in enabling social transformation. Redesigning of teacher education from the NCF perspective implies planned engagement with the social context of learning and learners, issues of knowledge, learner diversity and the process of learning. Teacher education programmes, pre-service or in-service, need to be redesigned to engage teachers with the larger socio-political context in which education is situated, with children in real contexts, enabling critical questioning of their own assumptions and beliefs about knowledge, learner and learning and their position in society vis-à-vis gender, caste, class, equity and justice (Batra, 2006). The draft curriculum framework for teacher education (2006) articulates a frame for construction of teacher education curriculum, based on this perspective. It essentially means weaving theoretical knowledge across multiple disciplines for generating a knowledge base for teacher education. Two possibilities are available in this situation; one, university scholars' engagement in intellectual enquiry in the area of education or teacher education and the other, their participation along with teacher educators and teachers in the process of redesigning teacher education curriculum.

Intellectual engagement of scholars from different disciplines cognate to education not only enriches knowledge but also contributes to the development of education as a discipline. Scholars in sociology of education, for instance, explored the ways in which the organization of school curriculum and knowledge itself worked to sort students. Their works offer a way to explain how social reproduction enacted at the daily routine of school practice and also offer teachers and others a space for intervention in these processes (Weis, Mc Carthy and Dimitriadis, 2006). The way curricular knowledge is structured tells the functioning of school—schools do not merely process people, they also process knowledge; they enhance and give legitimacy to a particular type of cultural resources, which are related to unequal economic forms. Such developments in the domain of knowledge are critical for professional development of teachers. Developments in sociology of education further point out the need for reformulation of the treatment of the idea of inequality or equality in teacher education. For instance, Flecha (1999) points out that modernism presumes that different cultures or ethnic groups have unequal levels of intellectual, political and economic progress. The underlying assumption is that ethnicities or cultures are either superior or inferior. It means that minor ethnic groups are inferior to dominant ethnic groups and the former needs to imbibe the values or cultural patterns of the dominant groups. Post-modernism rejects the assumptions of modernism by stating that ethnicities or cultures are neither inferior nor superior; they are simply different. It implies that the cultural patterns and values of each ethnic group are equally important and each has equal rights. Flecha advances the dialogic perspective for creating conditions that allow people from different ethnicities to live together. Dialogic perspective focuses on the need for opening dialogue between different ethnic or cultural groups in order to establish common rules for living together in the same territory. The difference is simply a part of equality, the equal right of everybody to live differently. Such a treatment of the concept would help in seeing the interconnections of diverse social groups, school system, inequality, equality and living together, and sharpen the mindset of teachers in understanding the dynamics of society and the underlying rationale of the idea of living together and interpreting the school practices meaningfully.

Likewise, perspectives derived from critical theory have major consequences in school practices. Critical theory outlines how educational ideas, policies and practices shape human consciousness and how they are related to larger political and ideological perspectives and social realities. Understanding and analyzing the linkages between day-to-day practices in schools and larger domains and values that are linked to social and political realities, is central to the critical theory perspective on teacher education and teaching. Critical theory focuses on social dimensions and their consequences for educational practices, ideological meanings of texts and experiences, power relations in schools and other institutions and the need to integrate theory into practice in new ways (Beyer, 2001). Such an approach is vitally important to make sure whether and to what extent schools serve the learning needs of all children equally well, and whether they hear previously marginalized voices and empower all such children. Critical theorists often look into ways in which classrooms provide for mechanisms that goes against the interest of the students, who are marginalized. They also look at the ways in which teachers can develop activities and modes of interaction that work for social justice and toward social change.

Developments in psychology are equally important. Woolfolk Hoy's (2000) analysis of the texts in educational psychology in teacher education courses in USA unfolds the change perspective since 1926. Hoy's evidences show that the content during the period 1926-1956 focused on tests and measurement, psychology of school subjects, learning, teaching methods, brain physiology and heredity and instincts. Elimination of "faculty psychology" and "formal discipline" was the noticeable change during the period. However, during the period 1956-1975 the contents were centered round learning (behaviourism), tests and measurement, development, motivation, and social and emotional issues. The noticeable change here is, less emphasis on school subjects and brain physiology, but more focus on personality, counseling and development. During the period 1975-1983 further shifts were visible. Content emphasis was on learning, development, individual differences, motivation, and tests and grading. The shift could be observed from "mental health", "personality adjustment", social and emotional issues, and statistics, to "classroom management" and "exceptional children". From 1983 to the present, the content is spread around learning, development, individual and group differences, motivation and management, teaching methods and assessment. The focus is on diversity, constructivism and psychology of school subjects rather than on testing and intelligence.

Woolfolk Hoy's analysis illustrates the changes that took place in the content of educational psychology in tune with developments in the field and also the needs of teachers for addressing classroom realities. The current focus on individual and group differences, motivation and management, diversity, constructivism and psychology of school subjects demonstrates how the emerging ideas in educational psychology are used for the professional training of teachers.

When we examine the Indian scenario, we rarely find similar changes brought in the course content in tune with the changes taking place in the subject. Treatment of constructs or concepts, based on conventional ideas, does not enable the teacher to address learner and learning concerns adequately. For instance, the way individual difference is articulated around intelligence and aptitude indicates that it is meant to know more about intelligence and aptitude rather than individual difference. Discourses on individual difference mediated through diversity provide a meaningful lens for the teacher to look at the learner and learning. Works in the area of teacher cognition (schema) and teacher reflections on the learner and learning provide insightful ideas for the integration of pedagogic theory and classroom practice leading to integration within the teacher (Korthagen and Kessels, 1999). More instances can be unlocked from sociology, psychology and other disciplines cognate to education. The thrust of the argument here is that developments in these disciplines can be a rich source for the formulation of knowledge base of teacher education and education *per se*. What is strikingly visible today is the felt need for building a culture of intellectual inquiry in the field of education. Encouraging researches and dialogues involving scholars from related disciplines and education becomes essential for building such a culture in future.

The EC initiative for connecting teacher education institutions, university system and schools, which have been referred to earlier, is linked to building of such a culture of intellectual inquiry in education. It assumes significance in the context of redesigning teacher education curriculum and its operationalization. Two cases illustrate this point. The recently initiated University School Resource Network (USRN), a multidisciplinary project involving multilevel institutions, envisages forging academic connectivity between higher education and elementary education systems. The project is operationalized through a network of multilevel institutions consisting of the JNU, the Delhi University, the Institute of Home Economics, Gargi College, DIET Motibagh, Mirambika, Ankur and participating schools. The network visualizes to effect quality in curriculum practices and professional development in teaching and teacher training processes at elementary stage in terms of multiple inputs through collaboration and sharing. The inputs are woven around interventions on school practices and processes, mathematics, school health, material developments in EVS, science, social sciences and language, documentation of stories and story telling techniques and interventions in the DIET. Other inputs include: a regional resource centre with the support of a web-portal, institutionalizing new ideas and pedagogic approaches, teacher fellowships and teacher learning centre in the DIET. The process of intervention and development of inputs is planned through the involvement of teachers and students of teacher education courses (B.El.Ed and DIET). Another case is the Eklavya science and social science programme from Madhya Pradesh. Eklavya provided a curriculum and textbooks that seek major shift in the pedagogic approach of the teacher in providing for active participation of the learner in the construction of school knowledge. A significant aspect of this intervention is the removal of intellectual isolation of the school teacher by bringing together teachers from high schools, colleges and universities through intensive in-service training and continued academic and intellectual support. Inspired by this experience, similar initiatives have taken shape in the states of Gujarat and Rajasthan (Batra, 2006). Though these two cases are "islands" of initiatives, they demonstrate the change perspective and the willingness of the university system, teacher education institutions and schools to forge connectivity for strengthening teacher education. Such connectivity is essential in the context of redesigning teacher education curriculum. To begin with, such an approach can be adopted for designing integrated courses that provide the needed pathway for building a cadre of teachers. The immediate question is: what is the mechanism for institutionalizing such connectivity across the country? Probably, the NCTE, UGC, NCERT, NUEPA, and the system of governance need to open up and initiate a dialogue for evolving such a mechanism.

Though islands of change can be traced, majority of the teacher education institutions are far from these islands. Strategic initiatives in this context assume significance for moving forward. Recognition of the primacy of the teacher in actualizing the connectivity between quality education and national development, articulated by the Commission, forms the basic framework for such initiatives. Building up a cadre of teachers is a pre-requisite for ensuring quality, more so today, than ever before. The issues related to para teachers seek immediate attention and they need to be addressed through well planned administrative and academic initiatives. Administratively, the system should open up and consider deployment of the teachers, following the initial selection, on probation for a period of 3 to 4 years on consolidated pay and then on to the regular scale. At the academic level, initiatives are needed to take action on the suggestion on integrated teacher education courses. Such courses pave the way for building and strengthening the cadre of teachers. In each state, one DIET can be upgraded for offering integrated course in teacher education at the elementary stage. Setting up of an institution for offering graduate level integrated courses for different stages of schooling, and postgraduate programmes in teacher education in each state is an option worth considering. Products of such courses of studies would gradually take over as the faculty of stage specific teacher education programmes. This would pave the way for the wrap up of the on-going engagement of secondary level trained personnel teaching at the pre-school and elementary stage teacher education. It also opens the path for development of professionalism in teacher education and teaching. Success of integrated course depends considerably on redesigning of teacher education curriculum and its operationalisation. Redesigning the knowledge base of teacher education from interdisciplinary perspective becomes necessary. Formation of study groups of scholars and educational practitioners from different disciplines can be considered as a strategic initiative. The groups' continuous engagement in intellectual inquiry, not only provides for generating the knowledge base, but also facilitates in creating a culture of such inquiry. Critical study of the emerging perspectives from disciplines and interdisciplinary researches on teacher, learner, and teacher education curriculum and its management, assume the centre stage. Scholars' engagement in intellectual enquiry leading to creation of new perspectives definitely needs to be recognized and strengthened through an award system. Similarly, formation of projects like USRN is essential for curriculum design and its operationalization. Creating USRN-type web portals, to facilitate on-line interactions involving scholars, experts, teacher educators and the teacher community, is an alternative channel for nurturing professionalism. These initiatives are systemic in nature and do not find space in teacher education without initiating structural reform; and call for willingness of the system to absorb such changes. Equally, the NCTE needs to move out of its number driven approach and choose the path for initiating reform in teacher education. The various curriculum frameworks reflect a gradual shift towards professionalism in teacher education. Mere formulation of frameworks does not bring change; the NCTE needs to evolve strategies for implementation. Strategic initiative on the part of the NCTE for ensuring collective effort involving the UGC, NCERT, and NUEPA is essential for building a culture of intellectual inquiry in teacher education for realizing the Commission's vision.

## Summing Up

The Commission, forty years ago recognised the primacy of the teacher in actualizing the connectivity between quality education and national development. That sets the tone of its vision. Keeping in tune with the vision, the Commission draws a road map for improving teacher status and quality of teacher education and teacher training institutions. The attempt here is to connect the key features of the road map and later developments in the country. Apparently, there are not many direct linkages but a discerning eye captures a different image. Category-wise scales of pay are a significant marker. Though there may be multiple factors, the Commission's recommendations became a rallying point in this context. However, certain recent events have placed the cadre of teachers at risk and the emerging issues are multiple. The nineties witnessed unprecedented developments for ensuring quality in teacher education through a series of new structures. Though these developments can be treated as the NPE effect, it is significant that the quality perspective conceived by the Commission gains further impetus in the NPE. Mere creation of structures does not ensure change or quality. What matters is the capacity of these structures in performing their functions effectively. Despite formulation of a series of curriculum frameworks for teacher education they failed to take root across the country. Redesigning of teacher education curriculum and its implementation emerge as a major concern and opens up several issues related to quality. As mentioned earlier, the NCTE needs to move out of its number driven approach and seriously engage itself in initiating reform in teacher education curriculum. The NCTE, the system of governance and teacher educators are partners for the prevailing trend in teacher education. The road to future calls for building a culture of intellectual inquiry in teacher education involving scholars from multiple disciplines and the teacher community. This would set the stage for realizing the Commission's vision on quality teacher education. Strategic initiative on the part of the NCTE for organizing a collective thrust, involving the UGC, NCERT and NUEPA, opens the pathway for moving towards the vision.

## Notes

1. It can be seen that knowledge in any area is historically constructed and teacher education is no exception. Like other knowledge fields, teacher education, constructed historically, provides a body of knowledge indicating the development of a system of knowledge based on rationality and also the evolving nature of society. Wittgenstein (1953) provides a way of understanding historical change as multiple states developing across different institutions or fields at different times that came together. He likened historical change to a thread made up of many fibres. The strength of the thread does not reside in the fact that some fibres run its entire length but in fact that many fibres overlap.

## References

Batra, P. (2006). *Locating the agency of teachers in a changing Indian educational context*, London: Paper presented at the conference on preparing teachers for changing context, Institute of Education, (May 3-6.)

Beyer, L.E. (2001). The value of critical perspectives in teacher education. *Journal of Teacher Education*, 52(2): 151-163.

Bhardwaj, B.P. and Arora, R. (2006). *Appraisal of functioning and performance of Institutes of advanced Study in Education* (Study Report). New Delhi: NCERT

Darling-Hammond, L. (2006). Constructing 21st-century teacher education., *Journal of Teacher Education*, 57(3): 300-314.

Dayaram, (2000). *Para teachers in primary education: A status report*, New Delhi: Ed. CiL.

Flecha, R. (1999). Modern and post modern racism in Europe: Dialogic approach and antiracist pedagogies, *Harvard Educational Review*, 69: 50-171.

Govinda, R. and Josephine, Y. (2005). Para-teachers in India: A review, *Contemporary Education Dialogue*. 2(2): 193-224.

Karuna, Chanana (Ed.), (2004). *Transformative links between higher and basic education*. New Delhi: Sage.

Khader, M.A. and Das, P. (2003). Teacher educators initiate reforms in teaching, yet...*Journal of Indian Education*, 28(4): 5-16.

Khader, M.A. (2004). *Analysis of B.Ed. Curriculum (Secondary) of Eastern region (Study report)*, Bhubaneswar: Regional Institute of Education (NCERT).

Korthagen, F.A. and Kessels, J.P. A.M. (1999). Linking theory and practice: Changing the pedagogy of teacher education. *Educational Researcher*, 28(4):, 4-17.

Ministry of Education, (1966). *Report of the Education Commission (1964-66): Education and National Development.* New Delhi: Government of India.

Ministry of Education, (1985). *Report of the National Commission on Teachers-1 (1983-85).* New Delhi: Government of India.

Ministry of Human Resource Development, (2006). *Annual Report 2005-06.* New Delhi: Department of Education, Government of India, 98-99.

Naik, J.P. (1982). *The Education Commission and After.* New Delhi: Allied Publishers.

National Council of Educational Research and Training, (1978). *Teacher education curriculum: A framework, prepared for NCTE.* New Delhi.

National Council of Educational Research and Training. (1988). *National Curriculum for Teacher education: A framework.* New Delhi.

National Council of Educational Research and Training, (2005). *National Curriculum Framework 2005.* New Delhi.

National Council for Teacher Education, (1998). *Curriculum framework for quality teacher education.* New Delhi.

National Council for Teacher Education, (1998a). *Policy Perspectives in teacher education: critique and documentation.* New Delhi.

National Council of Teacher Education, (2003a). *Approach paper for elementary teacher education curriculum renewal.* New Delhi.

National Council of Teacher Education, (2003b). *Approach paper for secondary teacher education curriculum renewal.* New Delhi.

National Council of Teacher Education, (2006). *Curriculum framework for teacher education (Draft Document),* New Delhi.

Pandey, S., Rani, R. and Kumar, R.G. (2003). *Professional Support system and classroom performance of para teachers (Study Report).* New Delhi: NCERT.

Pandey, S., Yadav, D.D. and Rani, R. (2004). *Appraisal of the functioning and performance of colleges of teacher education (Study Report).* New Delhi: NCERT.

Seshadri, C. (2002). Educating the educators: Review of Primary teacher training. In Govinda, R., (Ed.) *India Education Report: A profile of basic education.* New Delhi: NUEPA, 202-217

Stein, M.K., Smith, M.S. and Silver, E.A. (1999). The development of professional developers: Learning to assist teachers in new settings in new ways. *Harvard Educational Review*, 69: 121-138.

Tyack, D. (2004). *Seeking common ground: Public Schools in a diverse society.* Cambridge, MA: Harvard University Press.

Weis, L., Mc Carthy, C. and Dimitriadis, G. (Eds.), (2006). *Ideology, curriculum and the new sociology of education: Revisiting the work of Michael Apple.* New York: Routledge.

Wittgenstein, L. (1953). *Philosophical investigation (3rd ed.)* New York. Macmillan.

Woolfolk Hoy, A. (2000). Educational psychology in teacher education. *Educational Psychologist*, 35(4): 257-270.

# 13

# Teacher Education: Vision of Kothari Commission and Its Realisation

MOHD. AKHTAR SIDDIQUI

## Introduction

The common aspirations of Indian people, after having achieved Independence, was to see the country progress in all spheres of life, for they rightly believed that their prosperity and security lay only in her economic, cultural and political development on the lines charted out in the Constitution of India. The national development for the tradition-bound Indian society depended on a pervasive social transformation of its people which could only be brought through the most powerful instrument of education.

This exactly was the vision of the Kothari Commission, which was appointed to prepare a blueprint of a national pattern of education. The EC firmly believed—and accordingly made all its recommendations—that it is the development of human resources involving changes in the knowledge, skills, interests and values of the people as a whole that will solve India's long pending problems of poverty, self sufficiency in food, full employment, social and national integration, etc., on the one hand, and ensure national economic and social development and prosperity of the masses, on the other. The Commission stressed that this direct link between education, the sole instrument of human resource development, and national development exists only when the national system of education is properly organized, both qualitatively and quantitatively, and is reflected in the quality and number of persons coming out of our schools and colleges.

In an attempt to effectively relate education to the life, needs and aspirations of the people and through it raise their productivity; modernize their outlook; and inculcate in them social, moral and spiritual values; and bring social and national integration in the society, it recommended all round changes and improvements in the entire system of education and presented a new educational pattern of 10+2+3 as a common ground for implementing various educational reforms and principles.

The Commission emphasized equality in access to education for all people without discrimination and making provision of a relevant curriculum for their suitable educational development. It repeatedly stressed that of all the factors, which influence the quality of education and its contribution to national development, the quality, competence and the character of teachers, are undoubtedly the most significant. Hence, a sound programme of professional education of teachers was considered as an essential condition for the qualitative improvement of education (p. 124). It was argued by the EC that "investment in teacher education can yield very rich dividends because the financial resources required are small when measured against the resulting improvements in the education of millions".

Though this pivotal role of teachers in national development and the need for their professional preparation was repeatedly stressed by the University Education Commission (1948), the Secondary Education Commission (1952-53) and the International Team on Teachers and Curricula in Secondary Schools (1954), yet, arrangements to meet this need could not be made in any large measure. As a result, even after about two decades of Independence, the Education Commission found the teacher education system suffering from several major weaknesses as mentioned below:

- Isolation of primary and secondary teacher training institutions (i) from mainstream of the academic life of the university (ii) from daily problems of the schools, and (iii) from one another;
- Quality of training institutions remains, with a few exceptions, either mediocre or poor.
- Competent staff/faculty is not attracted to teacher education.
- Vitality and realism are lacking in the curriculum and programme of work which continue to be largely traditional.
- Set pattern and rigid techniques are followed in practice teaching with a disregard for present day needs and objectives.

In order to remove each of these weaknesses and strengthen the teacher education system in the country, the Commission made several recommendations, which will be discussed in the section that follows.

## The Commission's Recommendations and their Implementation

### *Mainstreaming of Teacher Education*

Professional preparation of teachers for qualitative improvement in education, so that education brings development and change in Indian society, was the vision of the EC for which it had expressed its concern and suggested various initiatives to be taken at different levels. This section examins as to what extent and in what manner these suggestions have been taken to bring improvement and change in teacher education.

In order to make professional preparation of teachers effective, the EC considered it necessary to bring teacher education in the mainstream of academic life of universities as well as of the school system and in all areas of the educational developments. Modalities followed in each of these domains of mainstreaming are discussed here.

### *Removing Isolation from University Life*

Education, as distinguished from pedagogy, should be recognized as an independent academic discipline and introduced as an elective subject in courses for the first and second degrees and schools of education should be established in selected universities to develop programmes in teacher education and studies and research in education in collaboration with other university disciplines. This only will help break the isolation of teacher education from universities. The Commission stated, "In India, the general trend has been to identify education with pedagogy. It has been taught mostly in training institutions and is studied only by those who decide to enter teaching profession, after such a decision has been made. In the educationally advanced countries, however, education has developed considerably as a social science and a separate academic discipline. The realization that education is an instrument of change—social, political and economic—is having far-reaching implications, not only for education as an intellectual discipline of great scientific and philosophic import, but for other disciplines as well. It is also worth noting that philosophers and social scientists have begun to give special attention to education as an important part in their fields of study. We, therefore, recommend that in view of the increasing scope and importance, 'education' should be recognized as a social science or an independent discipline" (p. 125).

The National Policy on Education-1968 that largely followed the EC report sidelined this issue altogether. Later, the *Teacher Education Curriculum—A Framework* brought out by the NCERT in 1978 discussed this issue and re-emphasized that education should be offered as a subject of study for both horizontal and vertical mobility (p. 7). It was envisaged that if education is allowed to be pursued as an academic discipline, like other disciplines, right after Class X up to postgraduate level along with other disciplines under one roof and also as task-oriented training programme for becoming a teacher at a particular level, there is a strong possibility that education will grow as an important discipline. It was also envisaged in the Framework that teacher training institutions would prepare various task-oriented courses and the university departments of education would develop variety of education courses to be pursued as a discipline (p. 9).

In order to further the EC's resolve in this regard the NPE-1986 proposed that colleges of education and university departments of education will be networked and that university departments of education will be strengthened

(p. 26). But neither the NPE and POA-1986 nor POA-1992 talked about breaking the isolation of teacher education institutions from universities. Both these documents skipped the issue of development of education as a discipline or as a social science. As a result, the Ramamurthy Committee (1990) pointed out that teacher education programmes continue to exist in isolation of the academic life of the universities (p. 300), though it also did not clearly suggest as to how this isolation could be ended.

On the ground, it has been observed that a few colleges in some states, now offer education as an optional subject at undergraduate level and some university departments of education are now offering M.A. in Education. Some departments and centers of education in universities are also facilitating research in education. Still there is no such dedicated department of education in any university, which is entirely devoted to conducting research in foundation subjects of education in the Indian context. However, centers like, CASE at M.S. University, Baroda, Zakir Husain Centre for Educational Studies at JNU, New Delhi, are serving this cause to some extent. Education as a discipline, like other social sciences, is yet to gain general recognition. As long as this situation persists, teacher education will remain isolated from the mainstream of academic life of the universities.

Recently, it has been proposed to the Govt. of India that a full fledged university of education should be established in the XI Plan period for focused, all round development of this discipline. Acceptance of this proposition will only be a small step forward in recognizing the status of education as a discipline and will help in further promoting its cause. Whatever step taken so far in this direction is not going to change the state of general isolation of teacher education institutions from the university life across the country, unless universities in general admit education as a social science or as an independent discipline in its academic life.

### *Breaking Isolation from School Life*

For bringing teacher education institutions closer to the school life, realities and problems it was suggested by the EC that extension work should be made an integral part of the teacher education programme. Alumni associations of teacher training institutions should be formed to bring together faculty members and their old students, now school teachers, to discuss and plan curricula and other programmes. Also, periodic exchange of staff between cooperating schools and teacher education institutions should take place and due recognition to be given to cooperating schools by the Departments of Education in states for this act of cooperation.

In the sixties, the NCERT was able to organize extension service centres in about 50 per cent of the secondary teacher training institutions (KECR). In 1969, there were 159 extension service centers, which were meant for extending help to neighbouring schools and teachers in their academic pursuits (Siddiqui, 1991). Having recognized their significance for breaking the isolation between schools and training institutions, such extension education units were created in SCERTs and DIETs also. These units in many states now are not actively engaged in extension activities in the neighbouring schools. The concept of alumni association of pass outs of a teacher training institution has not got off the ground. The cooperating schools are neither recognized as such by the State Department of Education nor do they regularly interact with the teacher education institutions in their area. The only limited occasions, when the schools and institutions of teacher training come into contact and interact with each other, are during the practice teaching sessions in schools and at the time of organizing in-service training programmes for school teachers in teacher training institutions. Even on these occasions, the interaction remains highly formal and rigid. The idea of exchange of teachers between cooperating schools and concerned colleges of education for a specified period has not received recognition in the Indian situation as yet.

Interestingly, as was recommended by EC, the POA-1986 had specifically provided that a cadre of teacher educators will be created, an interchange will be organized between teaching and teacher education and a sufficient number of supernumerary/reserve positions will be created in schools to enable people from this cadre to go as teachers for 1-2 years every 4-5 years (p. 190). But nothing concrete has been done to implement these provisions so far. Hence, as observed by Ramamurthy Committee also much of isolation between teacher education and school life continues to persist (p. 300).

A campaign for the formation of alumni associations of "pass outs" of teacher training institutions with active involvement of the faculty may bear some fruit in this direction. For establishment and role of extension units in all teacher training institutions and for exchange of their faculty and school teachers some specific provision may have to be made in the NCTE norms for compliance by all teacher training institutions.

### Breaking Isolation From One Another

It was observed in the EC report that teacher education institutions offering teacher training programmes for different levels of teachers often remain isolated and hence do not benefit from each other's resources and experiences. The NPE, POA-1986 and the Centrally Sponsored Scheme for Teacher Education (1987) have tried to remove this isolation to some extent. After the implementation of the Scheme, 38 colleges of teacher education/departments of education in universities got upgraded to the status of Institutes of Advanced Studies in Education (IASE) from 1988 onwards. The IASEs are required to perform the function of comprehensive colleges of education and provide for pre-service/in-service teacher education for primary and secondary teachers and even for nursery teachers and teacher educators. But this has happened on a limited scale and only a few teacher education institutions have been able to break this isolation existing among them. Majority of them, around 3,000 teacher training institutions, still remains isolated from one another. A better and effective cooperation between the IASEs and SCERTs, which directly coordinate the activities of the DIETs, can further help in breaking this isolation. The IASEs acting as comprehensive colleges, as visualized by EC, should become nodal research and resource centers and common meeting places for faculty of the DIETs and CTEs on a continuing basis, provided the IASEs are evenly opened across the country in a planned manner. In the past, as many as nine IASEs were established by the MHRD in a single state. Out of them, three existed in one small district of that state. Besides, effective networking and extensive cooperation beyond in-service education should take place between the IASEs and rest of the teacher training institutions in a given area. At present this cooperation is confined to organization of some in-service training programmes by the IASEs for the faculty of the DIETs and SCERTs.

The EC's idea of State Boards of Teacher Education, which were supposed to be responsible for all functions related to teacher education at all levels and in all fields in each State has not seen the light of the day till now. The alternative structure of the SCERTs has been created in states, but it is responsible only for teacher education upto the upper primary level, though it also acts as a coordinating agency for in-service education of teachers for all levels of school education.

The Commission had also suggested that for removing existing separation among teacher education institutions, all these institutions should be upgraded to the collegiate standard in a phased manner, and to ultimately bring them under the supervision of the universities (p. 129). The secondary teacher education institutions are already working under the control of the universities. However, teacher education institutions for elementary and nursery education are still outside the ambit of university supervision. Upgrading the DIETs to collegiate level will surely improve the faculty status, their motivation, quality of teaching and examination standards. In XI Five Year Plan, this part of the Kothari Commission's recommendation may be taken into consideration.

The Commission had repeatedly visualized an important and active role of national organizations of teachers and teacher educators in improving the quality of teacher education. Although more than one such organizations exist at the national level, they are hardly found systematically cooperating and collaborating in achieving the goal of improvement of quality of teacher education.

### *Improving Quality of Teacher Education*

The EC while commenting on the quality of teacher education had observed that the "essence of a programme of teacher education is 'quality' and in its absence teacher education becomes not only a financial waste but a source of overall deterioration in educational standards" (p. 160). It further remarked that vitality and realism are lacking in the curricula and programmes of work continue to be largely traditional (p. 124). Even in a limited area, like methods of teaching, the teacher educator fails to impress upon the trainees about the usefulness and applicability of these methods, as he himself rarely uses any method other than the talk and chalk method. Set patterns of lesson planning and rigid techniques of teaching are followed in practice teaching regardless of the nature of subject matter and the objectives to be achieved in terms of behavioural changes. Evaluation procedures, especially those followed for assessing the competence of would-be teachers are, by and large, subjective and unscientific, seeking to find out mainly how successfully factual knowledge has been memorized. The Commission made several suggestions to improve the quality of teacher education which encompassed improvements in content courses, professional studies, methods of teaching and evaluation to be used, student-teaching, special courses and curricula for all levels of teacher education.

However, these suggestions failed to attract the attention of NPE-1968 and its declaration hardly spelled out any steps to be taken for the improvement in teacher education and its curriculum. The draft Education Policy Document of 1979 only mentioned "that the curriculum of teacher education at the elementary and secondary stages will suitably be changed in order to enable the teachers to play their proper role in reforming education", (Naik, 1982, p. 225) but this Draft Policy could never reach the stage of implementation. It was the NCTE's document, *Teacher Education Curriculum—A Framework* (1978), which for the first time, highlighted the teacher education related observations of the EC and spelled out detailed guidelines for curriculum change.

These observations were translated into a workable scheme of courses by the Framework (1978), which suggested two broad models of curriculum, one for pre-primary to secondary stage and the other for senior secondary and higher education. The models had three common components of: (i) Pedagogical Theory (ii) Working with Community and (iii) Content-cum-methodology of Teaching School Subjects and Practice Teaching. The weightage for these components in the first three stages of education, i.e., pre-primary, primary and secondary would be 20 per cent, 20 per cent and 60 per cent, respectively, and for higher secondary and higher education it was proposed to be 30 per cent, 20 per cent and 50 per cent, respectively. Many teacher education institutions followed this Framework and adopted its scheme during the course of revision of their teacher education curricula.

A closer look at the EC recommendations regarding teacher education curriculum vis-à-vis the provisions made in education policies and Teacher Education Curriculum Frameworks that followed these recommendations, till recently, reveals the following:

### Reorientation of Subject Knowledge

With a view to reorient subject knowledge of student teachers in the respective subjects, content-cum-methodology courses with emphasis on taking up remedial and enrichment teaching in important and new concepts were incorporated in the curriculum of the elementary and secondary teacher education. However, one is not sure, for want of research evidence, as to what extent this was effectively implemented in the teacher training institutions, particularly, at the level of transaction of curriculum. It very much depends on the method and competence of the teacher-educator on the subject and his own understanding of this approach.

However, for this reorientation of the subject knowledge, rarely any collaboration is found to have been made between teacher education institutions and university departments or liberal arts and science colleges in the concerned subjects, either in the form of involving their faculty or in using their laboratory and library facilities. Thus, the isolation between these two sets of institutions continues to exist. Nevertheless, due to the steady emphasis on in-service education of school teachers, refresher programmes in subject areas are being organized by the DIETs, CTEs, and IASEs, in which, subject experts from university departments and arts and science colleges are taking up teaching on remedial and enrichment of content, based on the relevant school curriculum. Thus, it has been observed that, at least in in-service teacher education, the teacher training institutions and university departments and colleges have come closer and teachers have started drawing benefit from this collaboration to whatever extent it is available. However, in pre-service teacher education, this does not seem to be true.

### Integrated versus Professional Courses

For arranging four-year or five-year integrated courses of general and professional education, as has been experimented in RIEs and a couple of other institutions at the secondary teacher education stage, the Commission itself was skeptical and had felt that it would be too heavy a proposition considering the very limited number of teachers (5 to 10 per cent of the requirement) that could be trained through this model (p. 133). It had suggested that we should better concentrate on improving the professional one-year course for secondary teachers following the first or second degree. If at all such integrated courses are to be organized then it should be done in the schools/departments of education in universities in collaboration with other departments. However, the Commission did appreciate the utility of such experiments of integration in an elastic and varied system. This kind of experiment in integrated course is being implemented, for the last few years, in eight colleges of arts and science affiliated to the Delhi University for preparing elementary school teachers wherein subject courses along with professional course are taught under one roof in close collaboration with the faculty members of relevant departments. The course, called Bachelor of Elementary Education (B.El.Ed.), is a four year programme after +2. The NCTE has already notified norms for recognition of this course. However, impact of this innovative programme is yet to be ascertained by an empirical research.

## Revitalization of Professional Studies

The low status of professional studies in teacher training institutions is due to the absence of adequate research on problems related to teacher's work in school, in the Indian context. It is also due to teacher educators' failure to deal with the specific classroom situations to be faced by the trainee teachers. The low status is also due to non-availability of textbooks and other materials on professional studies, which are written keeping the Indian conditions in view, in both English and the regional languages. This requires establishment of dedicated educational research centers or departments of educational research in universities which would entirely be devoted to pursue research in professional studies and in areas of foundations of education in the Indian context and—in the light of their researches—would guide the teacher education programmes, teacher educators and writers of textbooks in professional studies. Barring very few departments/centers of education in universities all the teacher education institutions still remain completely engaged in teacher training activities only, for they have neither resources nor time to attend to research activities in any area. In 1980, Jamia Millia Islamia had tried to initiate this kind of research by creating a dedicated department called Department of Foundations of Education to pioneer research in areas of foundations of education in Indian context. However, the innovative initiative could never take-off the ground due to the distorted research priorities of the department.

## Improved Methods of Teaching and Evaluation

The Commission had emphasized the use of such methods of teaching by teacher educators that would encourage participation and self study, and give opportunities to trainee-teachers to think, read, study and discuss. This would entail students to engage themselves actively in library work, project work, preparation of reviews and reports, etc. Teacher educators were also expected to resort to frequent use of emerging new technologies (pp. 134-135). The EC also recommended reform in the examination system in training institutions and implementation of the process of continuous and comprehensive evaluation with inbuilt component of internal assessment. Cumulative record of students was also suggested to be maintained for their consultation (for their training in keeping such records).

These recommendations of the EC were reflected in the Curriculum Framework (1978), which emphasized task orientation of teacher education to enable the teacher to handle variety of tasks inside and outside the classroom. Endorsing the views of the EC on evaluation, it argued that reliable and valid internal system of evaluation should be developed in which focus should change from "assessing" to "guiding" the trainee-teacher. For this, a sort of clinical approach with a warm and personal touch was suggested to be introduced in place of the so-called impersonal and objective normative approach of assessing personality. It also suggested that internal and external assessment must be shown separately and not added together to a single aggregate (pp. 15-16).

The NPE and POA-1986 and revised POA-1992 also dwelled on this important aspect of teacher education and emphasized introduction of continuous and comprehensive evaluation compulsorily. However, the Education Policy Review Committee (1990) reiterated the EC recommendations and the education policy provisions by stating that teacher training programme should cover concepts and methods relating to child centered approach, multi-grade teaching, continuous and comprehensive evaluation, adopting playway and activity based approach in primary education, etc. (pp. 302-303). These were endorsed in the report of the CABE Committee on Policy (1992) (p. 64).

Emphasis on varied and new methods of teaching and process oriented rather than only product oriented evaluation of the trainee-teacher (which primarily focuses on helping and guiding him continuously to develop into a sensitive, innovative, and competent teacher) is a major improvement in the area of teaching methodology in teacher education institutions.

However, as evident from the Curriculum Framework for Quality Teacher Education (CFQTE, 1998) the NCTE was not much satisfied with these recommendations of the EC and other committees and the consequent changes brought about in teaching and training methods in teacher education. It observed that "the changes at the level of teacher education have not adequately responded to the emerging realities at the school level, particularly after the introduction of the 10+2+3 pattern and other developments which, out of necessity, demand training of teachers in new pedagogy and innovative evaluation techniques. Instead of using a uniform methodology of teaching and learning, the Framework suggested that stage specific and culture specific pedagogical practices, transactional strategies and evaluation methods should be taught to the trainee teachers (pp. 14-17). The document observed that it is still not being taken care of in most of the teacher education institutions. It emphasized that for effective curricular transaction, interactive teaching, cooperative teaching-learning, self discovery approaches, etc., should be used and in the training process emphasis should be on development of competencies and skills, which would help in shaping the teacher for effective role play (p. 54).

## Turning Practice Teaching into an Effective Programme of Internship

Student-teaching is the core of any teacher training programme and, therefore, it must enable the trainee teacher to see for himself the principles and processes of teaching, learning, evaluation, etc. as learnt by him theoretically, in their full practical form. This real experience must enable him to develop all desired competencies in teaching to be used in varied conditions in his professional life.

The EC was of the opinion that student-teaching should be provided in two phases for its better impact on the trainee-teacher. The objective of the first phase should be to acquaint him with the entire school life through detailed observations and initiate him into actual teaching in which he may also begin his practice teaching by teaching individual children and then a small group of students. The second phase should enable him to do continuous teaching for at least eight weeks under actual school conditions by working as a teacher in a selected school (p. 136). Though the EC did not use the term internship for the second stage of student-teaching, the very fact that in this phase it wanted the trainee to teach like a teacher continuously for eight weeks suggests that it meant internship in the second phase of practice teaching.

The TECF (1978) (p. 39) recommended a task-oriented teacher education system, where teacher is to be readied for effective performance of his role; where practice teaching is made more realistic and suited to actual classroom situation by using a series of simulating and microteaching situations, before the trainee is sent for practice teaching. It did not specifically provide for internship as it was felt that internship programme has not really gone beyond practice teaching concept. However, on the lines of the EC, it emphasized pre-practice teaching activities, which will include systematic simulated teaching and observation of lessons by teacher educators and good teachers; actual practice teaching through block-teaching approach rather than delivering one lesson everyday; and post practice teaching follow-up by taking up related practical work in evaluation, etc. Since work experience and health education and recreational activities are included in the curriculum, practice teaching duration has to be substantially increased and at least 20 lessons should be taught at appropriate interval (p. 40).

The Chattopadhyay Commission (1983-85), also felt that internship would not only help develop teaching skills in related subjects it would also prepare the teacher for many other roles he is expected to play outside the classroom. This requires not only a sound programme of pre-internship simulated teaching but also cooperation between cooperating school, its principal and the cooperating teacher, under whose supervision the trainee-teacher will complete his internship. This aspect remains quite weak so far. In the name of internship only block practice teaching is organized, which is generally confined to classroom teaching experience. The Chattopadhyay Commission rightly observed that this recommendation of the EC given about twenty years ago has remained unattended so far (p. 52). It suggested internship in B.Ed. for at least six weeks to be preceded by a general orientation of one week (p. 53). The Ramamurthy Committee (1990) too was all for internship model of student teaching and had forwarded several detailed arguments as well as suggestions for its implementation against conventional practice teaching. This model of internship was recommended for all categories of school teachers (p. 308). However, CABE Committee on Policy (1992) was of the view that "at the moment there are no well documented experiences on the internship model and practical aspects for its adoption on a large scale and its comparative advantages need to be examined further". It suggested that an expert body of the NCTE should study the model in depth and guide teacher education institutions (p. 66).

However, the CFQTE (1998) found that changes in the pattern and practices of student-teaching have been only peripheral and the content-cum-methodology approach, wherever attempted, remained limited to the introduction of an additional component of content without fully achieving the objective of integration. The problem solving approach, discovery method, competency-based teaching-learning and application of educational technology, informatics, telematics, cybernetics, etc., have yet to make a discernible headway. It suggested provision of induction programme for proper exposure to school experiences followed by school based practice teaching for capacity building which should include practical work other than classroom instructions, like community experiences and activities related to personality and leadership development (pp. 54-55).

Though the EC and other committees and commissions, suggested the internship programme, it remained a weak and elusive step in teacher training programmes, particularly when we talk about its quality and duration. The NCF (2005) has reiterated the need for use of internship model in all pre-service teacher training programmes in order to sustain teacher engagement with children in school situations and experiences of teaching the children alongside regular teachers. This, it has rightly argued, will help teachers choose, design, organize and conduct meaningful classroom activities, critically reflect upon their own practices and develop strategies for evaluating children's learning for feedback into curriculum and pedagogy (p. 98).

### *Development of Special Courses*

The EC recommended development of new courses in order to meet special needs, e.g. training programme for headmasters and principals, special course for teacher educators of primary and secondary training institutions, courses for training teachers for two consecutive stages or in such a way that with some further orientation or training, they could also teach at a higher level.

Such courses have not generally been planned. Only some effort has been made to train teacher educators for elementary training institutions in the RIEs and Jamia Millia Islamia. Otherwise most of the teacher educators at all levels starting from pre-primary through senior secondary are being trained through a general M.Ed. programme. The need for special training for headmasters has also been felt on a peripheral scale. Jamia has only recently launched a diploma course in school management and a course on educational administration is already being offered for quite sometime.

However, besides these special courses for meeting the special needs of teachers and teacher educators, there are many other emerging areas, which perhaps were not found so urgent or distinct at the time when the Kothari Commission had surveyed the educational situation and need in the country, but now they also need to be addressed on a large scale. For example, courses for teaching handicapped children, with different forms of physical and mental challenges, a course for their teacher educators, courses in ICT application and integration in education, educational supervision and guidance, management information system in education, course for vocational education teachers and teacher educators, a training course for alternative and innovative education centers, etc. Endorsing this emerging need for special teacher education courses, the CFQTE (1998) rightly observed that global upsurge for universal education, knowledge explosion, and expectation and aspirations for better quality of life have led to the exploration of alternatives to the formal system, which includes non-formal education, adult education, distance education, etc. As democracy also envisages equality not only in terms of access but also in achievement and life chances, this calls for individual attention to child in the classroom for which teacher needs to be trained through alternative models of teacher preparation and also sensitized to the needs of children with special circumstances and difficulties (p. 92). Developing new teacher education courses should be a continuing exercise, which should be contingent upon the emerging needs of the society.

## Revision and Improvement of Curriculum

In view of the developments taking place in the society at national and international planes and in school education and in the light of the fundamental objectives of preparing teachers for their varied responsibilities it was felt necessary by the EC that curricula and programmes at all levels of teacher education must be revised. The TECF (1978) made first detailed attempt to implement this resolve of the Commission and came out with improved models of teacher education curricula for teachers of the preschool stage, primary stage, secondary stage and higher secondary and collegiate stages. The proposed curriculum framework had substantially departed from the earlier traditional teacher education curriculum in two ways. One, that it had separately visualized curriculum structure for different stages of education, and two, it had followed a semester approach in these curricula. The course structure was also changed in its orientation and approach. It assigned 20 per cent weightage to pedagogical theory, 20 per cent weightage to working with community and 60 per cent weightage to content-cum-methodology area, which included practice teaching and related practical work. Working with community, it was envisaged in the TECF, will provide actual life experiences to the trainee teacher and reinforce his theoretical learning, (p. 28). Similarly, it was felt that methods are meaningful when taught in relation to content. To achieve this end it was suggested that teaching skills may be developed in two groups, viz., core skills, which are indispensable for all types of teachers and specific skills necessary for teaching different subjects at different levels.

Contrary to the EC's recommendation for non-integrated teacher training programmes, the National Commission on Teachers (1983-85) was in favour of five-year integrated model of teacher training after +2 which should focus on both general education and professional education. However, it also suggested that until this model is implemented, attempts should be made to strengthen the existing one-year B.Ed. and two-year Diploma in elementary teacher education courses by revamping the current curricula and extending the working days to at least 220 in an academic year. The Commission (1983-85) also felt that methods of teaching or content-cum-methodology component in teacher training courses, remains the weakest link in the chain and that insufficient time and attention is being paid to practice teaching in schools. Training technologies in the training colleges have to be improved radically by using educational technology in training trainee-teachers and by training them in its use in schools. Though it commended the attempt made by the NCTE to strike a balance between educational theory and practice through its TECF (1978), yet it felt that in the light of experiences of teacher education institutions and the new demands on the teacher, this framework also needs revision. Hence, in 1998, the NCTE revised its earlier Curriculum Framework

(1978). The revised Framework was presented for all stages of education, which had three major components of theory, practice-teaching and practical work. In practice-teaching at primary and higher levels, the concept of pedagogical analysis of relevant school subjects was the new focus, besides practice teaching and observation of model lessons. Similarly, in practical work, aspects like school experience, inclusive of internship, work education, school community interaction, action research studies and organization of relevant educational activities, etc. were included. The teacher education curricula were revised in the light of this Framework, but it was felt that at the transactional level, teacher educators could not carry out pedagogical analysis of content and so they continued to follow the old approach of planning for teaching. In curriculum of secondary teacher education, some optional courses concerning current issues and concerns like vocational education, environmental education, computer education, etc., were incorporated.

The Yashpal Committee Report (1993), "Learning without burden", has noted that the emphasis in teacher education programmes should be on enabling trainees to acquire the ability for self learning and independent thinking. Despite all these concerns and recommendations, as rightly observed by the NCF (2005), "in reality teacher education programmes today train teachers to adjust to the needs of a system in which education is seen as the transmission of information. Attempts at curricular reform (at school level) have not been adequately supported with efforts at teacher-education..... Existing programmes do not address curricular design and issues of relations between school and society. There is little engagement with the numerous recent innovative educational experiments (p. 95). Hence, there is a need to come up with a fresh scheme of teacher education programmes, which can help in transacting the new school curricula in right perspective and enable teachers in responding to the children's needs and bring desired changes in them. This, however, would not be accomplished, as was cautioned by the Kothari Commission, by any initial teacher training, however complete it is. It observed that the more dynamic a vocation is, less the chances of giving a complete initial training. So, what is important in a teacher training programme, as stressed by Yashpal Committee (1993) also, is to develop in the student insight and understanding, the capacity to learn and resourcefulness (pp. 138-139). This, in other words, was also stressed by International Commission on Education (1996) when it observed that "initial education can be regarded as powerful if it has provided the impetus and foundation that will make it possible to continue to learn throughout life" (p. 88).

## Postgraduate Course in Education

The EC was also concerned about postgraduate courses in education for earning Master's degree in education, which are neither closely linked with professional needs at a higher level nor have the depth and intensity necessary for the study of education as a discipline (p. 139). Duration of M.Ed. Course and its curriculum both need a review. The EC recommended that its duration should be extended to three academic terms in order to allow students to undertake a deeper, scientific and academic study in some specific field, requiring special knowledge and initiative and should consist of core courses in foundations of education, courses in areas of specialization, study of methodology of research and a dissertation. These postgraduate courses have been reviewed and improved but the duration of these courses has remained unchanged. For M.Ed., it continues to be one-year and for M.A. in Education it is two years. Short duration of post graduate course in education deprives students of many learning activities and opportunities of professional development.

### Duration of Courses

The Kothari Commission was of the view that elementary teacher education programme should be of two-year duration and secondary teacher training of one-year. But in an academic year, in its view, there should be at least 230 working days in the one-year B.Ed. programme. For M.Ed., as stated earlier, it recommended 3 academic terms instead of existing one year.

The Curriculum Framework (1978) and the National Policy on Education and POA-1986 & 1992 have preferred the existing arrangement of two years' training after senior secondary school for elementary teachers and one year's training after graduation or post graduation for secondary school teachers. Extension in working days in an academic year from 180 days to 230 days for making better use of one-year duration was recommended by the Commission. However, for financial and practical reasons the Commission did not agree to the proposition of two-year B.Ed. programme (p. 132).

The idea of extension in working days in the academic year to 230 days was modified to 220 days on the recommendations of the National Commission on Teachers-I (1983-85) (p. 49). However, it did not find favour with teacher training institutions as well as the NCTE. The NCTE's norm for working days requires at least 180 teaching days which includes 30 days internship. Teacher education institutions have to adhere to these norms.

Though the EC was not in favour of a two year B.Ed. programme, the NCTE in its document, Curriculum Framework for Quality Teacher Education (1998) has proposed such a programme and has come out with guidelines for the same (p. 77). This two year B.Ed. model is under experiment in four RIEs and the Gujarat Vidyapeeth for the last few years. Quality of output of this model and its effectiveness are yet to be ascertained. It is argued that many features of the two-year B.Ed. can be condensed in the existing one-year programme with some extension in working days as was recommended by the EC. This has successfully been tried in Jamia Millia Islamia and the Kurukshetra University.

The Teacher Education Curriculum Framework (1978) had recommended replacement of existing annual system by semester system, where each semester should be of 120 working days in order to implement the task-oriented teacher training programme (p. 10). The idea of a semester system in first degree course in education is yet to catch up in teacher training institutions for its own practical reasons. Many universities have switched over from semestrial to the annual system.

The question of extension in duration of elementary or secondary teacher education programme to four/five or two years has financial, educational and administrative implications. Four-year integrated courses, where general education and professional education is integrated, can effectively be offered in general colleges and departments of education in universities rather than in colleges of education. This may also help in removing isolation between department of education or college of education and university's mainstream departments. But the two-year B.Ed. as suggested by the NCTE, as a way out between one-year and four-year models, may be organized in colleges of teacher education. It will require enhancement in faculty strength and infrastructural facilities in colleges of teacher education and the IASEs. For want of extra resources and investment there appears to be a general lack of enthusiasm for the two-year B.Ed., though, in principle, it is appreciated as it is expected to provide more space to trainee teachers to acquire competence in teaching.

### *Management of Teacher Education through State Boards*

The EC suggested setting up of State Boards of Teacher Education in each state which will conduct surveys of teacher education programmes and curricula and initiate necessary action for maintaining standards of teacher education in the states. These Boards have neither been set up nor did the subsequent committees or commissions care to discuss their need or formation. Instead, the SCERTs, as state-level structures have been created. These Councils have often remained confined to elementary teacher education though sometimes they also work for in-service education of secondary school teachers. After the establishment of the NCTE as the national statutory regulatory body, there does not seem to be any need and relevance of state-level Boards of Teacher Education. In fact, when the Kothari Commission recommended that all teacher training institutions should be given collegiate status and they all should ultimately be brought under the supervision and control of universities, it de-emphasized the need for creation of State Boards of Teacher Education.

### *Postgraduate Courses and Research in Education*

It was observed by the EC that existing postgraduate courses in education are not closely linked with professional needs at a higher level; nor do they have the depth and intensity necessary for the study of education as an academic discipline. They appear to have grown out of the B.Ed. courses without any clear idea of their purpose (p. 139). In view of the increasing demand for qualified teacher educators for rising number of elementary, secondary and other teacher education institutions, it is necessary that curricula of post graduate teacher education courses are revamped keeping in view of the stage-specific needs of teacher trainees, of the changes that are being introduced in school curriculum, of the teacher preparation programmes and of the new challenges that are being faced by school education.

The existing M.Ed. programmes, as rightly pointed out by the UGC's Review Committee on Education, lack effectiveness and thoughtful direction and are mostly ornamental except for service in a training college (p. 139). These courses are characterized by lack of perspective in terms of contents as well as qualifications and are generally academic in nature and not adequately professional in content (NCTE, 1998). For want of these needs the Revised POA-1992 resolved that existing programmes of teacher educators will be suitably modified. For improving the M.Ed. course, the Chattopadhyay Commission (1983-85) called for treating it as an extension of the period of professional preparation, which should contain a high degree of specialization and be geared to the preparation of teacher educators, curriculum consultants, inspectors, supervisors and educational administrators (p. 57). Similarly, the NCTE in its Curriculum Framework for Quality Teacher Education (1998), suggested organization of separate M.Ed. programmes for different categories/ areas to cater to the need of stage specific and category specific preparation of teacher educators, e.g., M.Ed. (Pre-Primary), M.Ed. (Elementary) M.Ed. (Secondary and Senior Secondary), M.Ed. (Special), M.Ed. (Distance), etc. To further enhance the quality of teacher educators the NPE & POA-1986 decided to create a separate cadre of teacher educators for appointment as staff in the SCERTs, CTEs and DIETs (p. 190).

The EC also discussed in detail the quality of research in education and felt that the development of educational research will go a long way in preparing persons competent to work at the postgraduate level. However, it also accepted that every postgraduate lecturer need not be a research worker. Already a lot of research studies in education have been accomplished. There is a need to focus research on needs and problems of schools, teachers and students.

### *Quality of Training Institutions*

In order to strengthen teacher training institutions of different levels the EC made stage specific recommendations. Many of these recommendations have since been incorporated in succeeding educational policy documents. The recommendations covered the faculty and physical resources and students entering in these institutions.

### *Secondary Teacher Training Institutions*

Teacher educators at this level are inadequately prepared. They should possess a double Master's degree in academic subject and education and a fair proportion (say 10 per cent) should also hold doctorate degrees. But in psychology, sociology, science or mathematics specialists without professional training may be appointed. The Commission recommended substantial increase in output of Ph.Ds, M.Eds. and MAs in Education. To improve the performance of working teacher—educators, organization of summer institutes for them was recommended (p. 141). So far as quality of students joining these institutions is concerned it leaves much to be desired. Secondary training institutions do not attract students holding good degrees and they come with deficiencies in subject knowledge which becomes a serious hurdle to progress when it is proposed to upgrade the curricula of secondary schools substantially. It was recommended that by offering scholarships in teacher training institutes and good salaries in schools, better qualified students should be attracted. Similarly, it was observed that facilities available in these institutions, including libraries, laboratories, audiovisual aids and workshops and craft rooms are far from satisfactory and the same should be improved through intensive efforts. Provision of hostel facility for at least half of the students was particularly recommended by the Commission.

### *Institutes for Primary Teachers*

The EC found the condition of primary teacher training institutes very depressing and their standards more unsatisfactory than secondary training institutes and hence suggested that a supreme effort be made to improve their condition. It was observed that their staff, generally taken from secondary schools, are trained for secondary stage. The Commission recommended that the staff of these institutes should possess a Master's degree either in education or in an academic subject and should be adequately trained for their work either through special orientation or induction training. Except in case of primary training institutions located in big cities, the condition of facilities in these institutions was found to be generally poor.

### Tuition Fee

The EC was of the view that tuition fees in all teachers training institutes should be abolished.

## Demonstration School

All training institutes should have a demonstration school or experimental school, which will be used for purposes of demonstration or special studies.

## Intake Capacity

Training facilities should be drastically enhanced to meet the demand for trained teachers. The EC recommended that the size of existing primary teacher training institutes should be raised to a minimum of 240 and that of secondary teachers' training institutions to 200, to optimally utilize the facilities. For new teacher training institutes, the minimum size should not be less than 400 students. In planning the location of teacher training institutions several factors should be considered and a certain proportion, especially those at the primary stage, should be located in rural areas.

From the facts presented earlier it may be clear that teacher education institutions at elementary and secondary levels did not receive any attention in the NPE-1968 that followed the EC Report. The CFTE (1978) also dealt with only curricular reforms in teacher education, without referring to the improvements needed in the physical and human resource conditions of these institutions. As a result, "a large number of the 1200 elementary teacher training institutions and 360 secondary teacher training institutions were found suffering from inadequate facilities—human, physical and academic, to provide good professional education" (POA-1986). To ensure that condition of these institutions necessarily improves the NPE-1986 envisaged a special Centrally Sponsored Scheme for Teacher Education, which was eventually launched in 1987 with arrangements of substantial funding for strengthening and establishment of elementary and secondary teacher education institutions, viz., DIETs in every district of the country and 250 CTEs and 50 IASEs in selected secondary teacher education institutions. As of date around 500 DIETs, 87 CTEs and 38 IASEs have been provided Central assistance for arranging sufficient facilities and faculty in these institutions.

The NCTE on its part ensured that teacher educators in secondary and elementary teacher training institutions possess minimum desired qualifications by making it mandatory that a secondary teacher educator must possess a double master's degree in school subject and professional education and, as required by the UGC, a Ph.D. degree or NET in education, as was recommended by the EC also. For the elementary teacher educator also, the essential qualifications include a master's degree in education or in a school subject with graduate degree in education with five years of school teaching experience. The EC's recommendation that the master degree holders in sociology, psychology, science or mathematics without any professional training may be appointed as secondary teacher educators, could not be accepted as trained educators in these subjects are now available. The EC's recommendation, for substantial increase in output in M.Ed. and M.A. and Ph.D. in Education, is being implemented at a slow pace, though the demand for these courses is steadily increasing due to continued establishment of new institutions of teacher education on a large scale. However, the faculty being appointed in elementary teacher education institutions still does not receive professional training in elementary education; most of them are trained for secondary education. There is a serious dearth of elementary teacher education courses at both first and second degree levels in education.

The Commission's recommendations for improvement in physical facilities are now a part of the NCTE's norms for infrastructure, etc., for a teacher education institution and these have to be essentially adhered to by all the teacher training institutions. However, the recommendations on compulsory provision of hostel facility in training institutions and provision of demonstration or experimental school attached with each of these institutions, though quite important, have not been generally implemented due to financial and administrative reasons. Since the submission of the EC Report, salaries and service conditions of teachers have received substantial boost on the recommendations of the NPE-1968 and the Chattopadhayay Commission (1983-85). This has, to an extent, helped in attracting better students to teacher training institutions, though for other reasons, still the best amongst them are not coming to training institutions.

The EC's recommendation of size of existing secondary or elementary teacher education institution of 200 and 240 students respectively for optimum utilization of its facilities has not fully been implemented. Most of the training institutions existing or new have an intake of 100 students only. The recommendation of fixing a minimum intake of 400 students in new teacher training institutions also has not been implemented. The NCTE's norms for intake of students have restricted it to units of 50 and 100 students for elementary and secondary training institutions, respectively in the beginning; this can later be enhanced to two or more units subject to satisfaction of norms for expansion. The Commission's recommendation for at least 230 working days for an institute in an academic year, has been found unfeasible by the NCTE, and it has restricted it to 180 teaching days, including 30 days of internship inclusive of preparation for the same (pp. 100 & 119). The Commission's view that expansion in training facility in each state should be based on a properly developed expansion strategy and on an institutional location plan has hardly received any attention. The exception is that in the case of elementary teacher training institutions, one state-run DIET is now essentially located in each district. In the absence of any development plan, an unbalanced increase in the number of teacher education institutions, especially at the hands of private investors, is taking place in many states on a large scale. It is true that there is still a huge unfulfilled demand for trained teachers. This should be met by establishing institutions on the basis of a perspective plan and institutional mapping exercise, so that the expansion is more evenly distributed and becomes beneficial for trainee teachers and schools as was argued by the EC.

### *In-service Education of School Teachers*

Continuing in-service education and training of school teachers as well as faculty members of training institutions is a need of paramount significance for improving the quality of school education, especially when the expansion in knowledge and changes in working conditions are taking place at an unprecedented fast pace. The EC visualized this need four decades ago; it has only become much more relevant and demanding now. For in-service education system to be effective, attention on three major dimensions was emphasized by the EC: (i) systematic follow up after every long term in-service education programme to gauge its impact on the ground; (ii) close coordination between school authorities and in-service education agencies; and (iii) continuing in-service education to be supported by research in education, where results of research flow down to schools and training institutes and problems of these institutions climb up to research institutions. It also suggested that in-service education of at least two to three months should be received by every teacher in a block of five years of service. For continuing professional development of school teachers, the EC also recommended establishment of school complexes as an innovative strategy.

Important work in the direction of in-service education had started in the country in the fifties with the establishment of Extension Service Centres and Units in teachers' colleges and with the setting up of State Institutes of Education, most of which later expanded to SCERTs for secondary and elementary school teachers. It was arranged by the NCERT and Continuing Education Centres were set up under its aegis for primary teacher educators and primary and secondary school teachers. Later, 1,800 school complexes were also set up in Bihar, Tamil Nadu, Haryana, Rajasthan and Maharashtra (National Commission on Teachers, p. 59). But, as observed by the Commission on Teachers-I, "in-service education neither became obligatory for every teacher for his professional growth nor a continual further learning could become a part of work ethos of teaching profession" (pp. 59-60). In-service teacher education is an integral and longest part of the teacher education continuum. The NPE-1986 had rightly observed that pre-service and in-service education components of teacher education are inseparable (p. 32). The Centrally Sponsored Scheme for Teacher Education-1987 provided a fillip to in-service education of teachers and teacher educators by funding the DIETs, SCERTs, CTEs and IASEs for different levels of teachers and teacher educators. However, the Scheme diluted the duration of in-service education and resolved that every teacher will be required to undergo a training of at least three weeks in every block of five years of his service. All these institutions actively organized in-service education programmes.

Despite these activities, the Education Policy Review Document (1990) found the same old weaknesses in in-service education programmes as were noticed by the EC. It stated that "in-service programmes are not effectively organized; there is poor coordination and monitoring of programmes, and research base for making them more effective is absent" (p. 301). A more balanced attention on pre-service and in-service training of teachers was stressed in the POA-1992 (p. 109). Despite many initiatives, particularly after 1987, the NCTE found the situation of in-service education in the country was not very encouraging. In its National Quality Teacher Education Framework (1998) it was observed that on an average 40 per cent of the teachers are provided in-service teacher education once over a period of five years, (p. 3) and that too is limited to a maximum duration of three weeks.

In such circumstances, organization of 2-3 months training for every working teacher over every block of five years of service, as recommended by the EC seems to be a remote possibility. The in-service programmes as being organized by the NCERT, SCERTs, CTEs and IASEs for teachers and teacher educators need a lot of fresh look, both at their content and strategy. For example, the innovative strategies of School Complexes and Teachers' Centres, which have already been tried successfully in the country, need to be popularized along with other strategies and agencies. Also, there is an urgent need to monitor the quality of these programmes and evaluate their impact. In recent years it has been noticed that the State Governments and SCERTs, in an attempt to meet the numerical and expenditure targets, are indulging in serious compromises with the quality of these programmes.

### *Professional Development of Teachers in Higher Education*

The Kothari Commission had rightly observed that in India there is no provision for the professional initiation of a university teacher, because such training is regarded as unnecessary. It stressed that there is a need for some orientation and training of university lecturers beyond any doubt and recommended that, to begin with, suitable arrangements of professional orientation of junior lecturers in higher education should be made by universities or a group of universities; regular orientation of newly appointed faculty be organized in every university and, wherever possible, in every college, and in bigger universities or group of universities these courses should be organized on a permanent basis by establishing staff colleges (p. 156). The professional orientation of higher education teachers could receive some attention only after the implementation of the NPE-1986, which envisaged establishment of

Academic Staff Colleges in different parts of the country to organize general professional orientation courses of four weeks duration for newly appointed lecturers, under direct funding from the UGC. These colleges began to organize orientation courses from 1987. Later, they were also assigned the responsibility of organizing subject-based refresher courses of three weeks duration for senior faculty in different disciplines. Theme-based seminars and workshops for the benefit of faculty members and academic administrators of higher education institutions are also organized by these staff colleges. With a view to further facilitate professional development of university teachers on a larger scale, the UGC has also extended support to universities to organize refresher courses in different disciplines in the concerned departments by allotting them Refresher Course Centres for specific subjects. However, so far no thought has been given to organization of full-fledged pre-service training institutes for college lecturers. The Kothari Commission, though it did not make any recommendation in this direction, did not totally rule out the possibility of this kind of an initiative.

### *Standards in Teacher Education*

The EC was concerned about the absence of any national or state level authority that could ensure standards in teacher education. Instead of suggesting for creation of a statutory body for this purpose, the Commission preferred to recommend that this task be done by a joint standing committee to be set up in the UGC with representatives of the NCERT, State Boards of Teacher Education and other organizations. The Committee should be concerned with all aspects and all levels of teacher education. Similarly, the EC recommended that State Boards of Teacher Education should be set up and they should be responsible for raising the standards of teacher education at the State level. The Government should provide funds to the UGC for improving teacher education in universities and through a centrally sponsored scheme the states should also be assisted to improve teacher education.

In response to these recommendations, the UGC formed a Standing Committee on Teacher Education, which got model teacher education curricula developed for both undergraduate and postgraduate courses in teacher education and the same were adopted by most of the teacher education departments in universities. For helping the universities to improve teacher education in their departments and in colleges and institutes of teacher education, as explained earlier, after 20 years of the EC Report, the Government launched the Scheme for Strengthening and Reorganizing of Teacher Education (1987), which was operationalized through the State Governments. The establishment of State Boards of Teacher Education, however, could not take place. The role and functions as visualized for these Boards have, however, been mainly taken up by the NCTE and its regional committees since 1995 and some functions by the SCERTs.

## Contemporary Issues and Future Challenges

As evident from the previous account, teacher education experienced some changes on the lines of the recommendations made by the EC, particularly after the implementation of the NPE 1986. Yet, these changes remained much below the expectations of the Commission. The teacher education system, as it exists today, is not robust enough to effectively face the challenges of our education system in the 21st century. Priority attention needs to be paid on making it more relevant to the emerging needs of changing socio-cultural context of Indian society.

## Professionalism in Teacher Education

Teacher education programmes at all levels need to be so remodeled that they reflect professionalism in the process of teaching and training. The essence and central concern of professional ideal is competence, which will ensure quality and character of teaching in our schools (Prakash, p. 344). Teacher education, revamped with this ideal in view, will "equip teachers with personal attributes of empathy, perception of the need-profile of learners from different educationally backward sections of society, and the capability to impart education in all aspects of cognitive and affective domains as well as psychomotor skills' (Ramamurthy, p. 302). It is only professionalized teacher education which will help realize the vision of the NCF 2005, which asserts that teacher education "must become more sensitive to the emerging demands of the school system and prepare the teacher to play the role of an encouraging, supportive, humane, facilitator in teaching-learning situations" (p. 95).

Professionalism in teacher education necessitates that teachers are subjected to a prolonged period of preparation and exposed to a sizeable body of specialized knowledge (Pandey, 1998, p. 407). This demands extension in duration of teacher education programmes and greater emphasis on well-organized internship in real school situations. Emphasis on professionalization also demands specialized focus on different levels and types of teacher education, like early childhood care and education, for +2 or higher secondary stage or for vocational stream teachers, etc., due to distinct differences in the nature of learners and curricula of these stages.

## Development of Education as a Discipline

Linked with the issue of professionalization of teacher education is the issue of developing and recognizing education as a discipline. Education is still predominantly perceived within the domain of teacher training and equated with pedagogy, which is expected to be located in training institutions. This restricted view of the rich area of study of education curbed its development in the past. Serious attempts by educational administrators in universities will have to be made to visibly correct this perception. Education should acquire the same place in teaching and research at undergraduate and postgraduate levels as other social sciences, and closer interdisciplinary interaction should be encouraged. Education should also be one of the subjects offered in senior level civil services examinations and an all-India service cadre of educators be created so that education acquires the status of a full-fledged independent area of study. Once education achieves this status, larger number of students with varied aims will take to the study of this discipline. It will then easily become a part of the mainstream life of the universities and its isolated and stagnant existence will be replaced by dynamic and interdisciplinary progress.

## Bridging Gap between School and Teacher Education Curricula

Teacher education at different levels remains weak for the fact that its programmes have little scope for studies in school subjects. Also, due to lack of researches on problems faced in schools, it keeps the teacher education programme and practices quite aloof from the school needs, which keep changing and are reflected in its updated curricula at different levels. Teacher education has to regularly attune itself to the demands of the school curriculum both in terms of knowledge and competence in subjects taught in schools as well as in their pedagogical orientations. For example, peace education, environmental education, sustainable development, HIV/AIDS education, being emphasized in the revised National Curriculum Framework for schools (2005), should be reflected in the updated teacher education curriculum. Similarly, the constructivist approach followed in the NCF (2005) and the shift in focus of pedagogic theory from pure disciplinary knowledge to the learner and his context (p. 97) need to be immediately reflected in teacher education programmes, so that the spirit and intent of the new curriculum framework is realized in schools.

### *Quality Control in Teacher Education*

The NCTE, as a statutory regulatory body, is responsible to ensure that teacher education institutions observe essential norms laid down for maintaining standards and quality of education. It has also taken the help of NAAC in order to get the quality standards of teacher education institutions assessed and accredited. However, it is common knowledge that quality standards especially relating to faculty and training processes are still not being sincerely maintained in teacher education institutions. There is a feeling that once the NAAC certification is granted, the institutions exploit it due to absence of any mechanism for follow up action by the NAAC or NCTE. Persistent follow up needs to be an on-going responsibility of the NAAC once it carries out initial assessment and accreditation of any teacher education institution.

The curricula of teacher education institutions have also to be updated and attuned with the emerging social, national and international issues. They will have to be more dynamic and responsive to the emerging demands of the society and school curriculum like multicultural education, human rights education, computer and ICT application in education, use of technology in the transaction of curriculum, etc. (Mukhopadhyay, p. 409).

## Need for Qualified Teacher Educators

A general deficiency, noticed in many teacher education institutions, relates to non-availability of suitably qualified teacher educators. This is seriously affecting the quality of teaching and training in these institutions. Due to dearth of institutions offering postgraduate programmes for teacher educators, the teacher education institutions are forced to appoint under-qualified or poor quality, unsuitable teacher educators. Therefore, arrangements need to be made to enhance capacity of institutions for preparing teacher educators for all levels and types of training institutions.

### *Globalization of Economies*

For meaningful survival of educational institutions in the 21st century globalized world, adequate preparations in terms of constant curriculum changes is indispensable at school, university and teacher education levels. This demands teachers to be so empowered that they continuously update the curriculum and are able to transact it in the changing perspectives of education. A teacher education institution needs to equip its prospective teachers with the ability to do careful future scanning (of the threats and opportunities in future) and to reach such valuable knowledge, which may work as base for constant curriculum change in a dynamic and vibrant socio-economic system.

Globalization of economic activities has a strong cultural dimension also. It increases multicultural orientation and richness of the ethos in society which essentially demands that its future citizens must have the capacity to live peacefully and in harmony with people from varied cultures. Teacher education system would have to equip the teachers with the ability to deal with multicultural realities in schools and classrooms and also with the competence to teach children to learn to live together with understanding and in harmony in multicultural settings.

### *Increasing Media Support Including New Technologies*

Fast pace developments in technology, particularly Information Communication Technology, is forcing its extensive use in training colleges and schools for improving the quality of teaching and learning. Teacher educators as well as prospective teachers need to be trained to use and integrate these technologies effectively in teaching and learning. They should be made aware of the sources from where to get the software and plan linkages with curriculum and also be so acquainted with every aspect of the hardware and that they be able to maintain them on their own for their unhindered use in classrooms. Teacher training programmes would have to be sufficiently redesigned to incorporate these technology related needs of educators and trainee teachers.

### Continuing Education of Teachers

The rapidly changing world has posed the challenge of making learning a life long process. More than any one else it is the knowledge worker, who is required to face this challenge most effectively as the quality of education being imparted by him will entirely depend on his following the principle of learning throughout life. This demands development of in-service teacher education in a manner that it allows frequent access to it by teachers and facilitates them in not only keeping themselves fully abreast of developments in their area of teaching but also in renewing their teaching skills based on developments taking place in information and communication technologies. For this purpose dedicated in-service education institutions have to be established, where round the year facilities and human resources are available not only for training of teachers but also for other services like guidance, research, resource support, etc. In India, so far, the INSET programmes, though distinctly emphasized after NPE-1986, have not really become avenues of need based continuous professional development of teachers.

Institutions like the IASEs, CTEs and DIETs as well as Teachers Centres and School Complexes with greater support and autonomy in their activities may become permanent centers of continuing education and resource support for teachers.

### Unregulated Expansion of Teacher Education

Excepting the centrally sponsored scheme of teacher education providing for establishment of a DIET in each district and 250 CTEs and 50 IASEs across all states, there is no other detailed plan in place for development of teacher education in the country. In the absence of any such plan, the mushroom growth of teacher education institutions, particularly in the private sector, is taking place. This is adversely affecting the quality of training. There is urgent need to prepare a detailed teacher education development plan, based on a survey of the need for trained teachers in different sectors at state and sub-state levels. The regulatory authority is also required to enforce more objective and stringent measures to maintain quality of teaching and training in these institutions on a continuing basis.

### Common School System

With a view to provide education of quality equitably to all children it is likely that in future a Common School System, in place of a multi-layered school system, will be introduced. A beginning in this direction has been made with the 86th Amendment to the Constitution, which has granted Right to Education, vide Article 21(A), to the children. Under the Common School System, children of varied backgrounds from the neighbourhood will attend the same school and will receive education of the same quality. Ensuring high quality of education in each neighbourhood school will be a challenge for teachers and administrators. It would need special orientation and preparation to understand the varied contexts, needs and aspirations of students and satisfy the same through reformulation of curriculum, syllabus and textbooks and remodeling of teaching strategies and methodologies.

## Conclusion

In the foregoing pages the vision of the Kothari Commission about teachers and their role in the process of educational and national development in the country has been discussed. The Commission had recommended several actions to translate its vision into reality. These proposed actions were also meant for removing various weaknesses that were present in the teacher education system of the country. During the last four decades, as explained earlier, many attempts have been made to implement these recommendations and bring improvements in the teacher education system. However, from the discussion presented here it is evident that teacher education is yet to receive the desired level of attention of educational administrators and others. The vision of the Commission and most of its propositions are still valid and relevant. Various socio-economic developments in the recent past have posed fresh challenges before the education system. A further reinforced and creatively reorganized teacher education would go a long way in helping the education system face these challenges effectively. Its success will lie in making itself continuously attuned to the changing needs and curricula of schools and other institutions as also to the demands made by the continuing economic and technological advances.

## References

Buch, M.B. and Palsane, M.N. (eds.), (1968). *Reading in Inservice Education*, Vallabh Vidyanagar, Sardar Patel University.

Goel, D.R. (ed.), (2006). *Quality Concerns in Teacher Education*, Vadodra: CASE, MS University.

Government of India, (1985). *The Teacher and Society, Report of the National Commission on Teachers*-I—1983-85, New Delhi: Govt. of India.

Government of India, (1990). *Towards an Enlightened and Humane Society. Report of the Committee for Review of National Policy on Education, 1986*, New Delhi: Governemt of India.

Kamat, A.R. (1989). *Perspectives for Educational Reform in India, Vol. I of Studies in Educational Reform in India*, P.R. Panchmukhi (ed.), Bombay: Himalaya Publishing House.

Ministry of Education, (1968). National Policy on Education-1968, New Delhi: Govt. of India.

Ministry of Education, (1979). *Draft National Policy of Education-1979,* New Delhi: Government of India.

Min. of Education, (1985). *Challenge of Education—a policy perspective*, New Delhi: Govt. of India.

MHRD, (1986). *National Policy on Education-1986*, New Delhi: MHRD, Govt. of India.

MHRD, (1986). *Programme of Action, NPE-1986*, New Delhi: MHRD, Govt. of India.

MHRD, (1992). *Programme of Action, 1992*, New Delhi: MHRD, Govt. of India.

MHRD, (1992). *Report of the CABE Committee on Policy*, New Delhi: MHRD, Govt. of India.

MHRD, (1998). *National Policy on Education-1986 (As modified in 1992) with* NPE-1968, New Delhi: Govt. of India.

Mukhopadhyay, M., *et al.* (eds.), (1998). *Education India: The Next Millennium*, Howrah: Institute of Education, Rural Studies and Development.

Naik, J.P. (1982). *The Education Commission and After*, New Delhi: Allied Publishers.

NCERT, (1966). *Education and National Development", Report of the Education Commission 1964-66*, New Delhi: NCERT.

NCERT, (1978). *Teacher Education Curriculum—A Framework*, New Delhi: NCERT.

NCTE, (1998). *Curriculum Framework for Quality Teacher Education*, New Delhi: NCTE.

NCTE, (2003). *Envisioning Teacher Education in the 10th Plan and Beyond*, New Delhi: NCTE.

NCTE, (2004). *Some Specific Issues and Concerns of Teacher Education*, New Delhi: NCTE.

NCTE, (2005). *NCTE Act, Rules and Regulations*, New Delhi: NCTE.

Pandey, Saroj (1998). *Teachers for the 21st Century: Redefining Professionalism for Global Perspective* in Mukhopadhyay, M. et al., (eds), Howrah.

Paliwal, M. R. (1985). *Teacher Education on the Move*, New Delhi: Uppal Publishing House.

Prakash, Ved (ed.), (1998). *Teacher Empowerment and School Effectiveness at Primary Stage*, New Delhi: NCERT.

Siddiqui, M.A. (1991). *Inservice Teacher Education*, New Delhi: Ashish Pubishers.

Singh, L.C. (ed.), (1990). *Teacher Education in India,* New Delhi: NCERT.

Thomas, Elwyn (2002). *Teacher Education—Dilemmas and Prospects*, London: Kogan Page.

UNESCO, (1996). *Report of the International Commission on Education in 21st Century*, Paris: UNESCO.

# 14

# Teacher Education in the Eyes of Education Commissions: Time We Made Incisive Decisions

A.K. SHARMA

## Introduction

"The status of the teacher reflects the socio-cultural ethos of the society; it is said that no people can rise above the level of the teachers", avers the National Policy on Education 1986 (revised in 1992). The Education Commission (1964-66) also rightly emphasized that "the destiny of the nation is being shaped in the classrooms". Such exhortations are an expression of the recognition of the important role played by the teachers as transmitters and as inspirers of man's eternal quest for knowledge, of himself, and of his external environment. If this role expectation is not to remain a mere rhetoric, but is to be taken as a goal to be constantly striven for, we have to address ourselves afresh to an examination of the issues related to the preparation of teachers as well as the theory and practice of teacher education, as has been undertaken in the historical past, as it is operative in the living present and as it is likely to emerge in the developing future.

## The 'Guru' or the Professional Teacher?

Not infrequently, nostalgic references are made to the 'guru' ideal in any discussion on the role of the teacher in the national context. The 'guru' ideal although archaic in its outer forms, in its essential spirit has some eternal message in that every teacher should: (i) constantly strive to develop himself/herself both as a person and as a teacher, (ii) have a commitment to the growth of his/her students, and (iii) exude a concern for the society. These are universal principles, which time and space do not pale, and teachers will do well to take these principles as constant reminder to them. It is good to keep alive the 'guru' ideal and at least use it as a symbol for inspiration, howsoever unreal, unrealizable and utopian the concept may be in the present context.

## Historical Landmarks in Indian Education

Major concerns and imperatives of Indian education have been discussed from time to time by various Commissions and Committees. It is relevant to refer to these documents for the perspectives of teacher education contained in their reports. Some of these landmarks are indicated below:

- University Education Commission (1948-49).
- The Secondary Education Commission (1952-53).
- Education Commission: (1964-66).
- UGC panel on Teacher Education (1970).
- Teacher Education Curriculum: A Framework (1978), NCTE.
- Working group to Review Teachers' Training Programme (in the Light of the Need for Value Orientation) (1983).
- National Commission on Teachers-1 (1983-85).
- National Policy on Education (1986 and revised in 1992) and its Programme of Action.
- The National Council for Teacher Education Act, 1993
- Curriculum Framework of Quality Teacher Education (1998), NCTE.
- National Curriculum Framework (1975, 1988, 2000, 2005)

A large number of pertinent concerns in teacher education have been debated from time to time. Some of them find implementation in varied forms but a good many of them seem to have defied intended solutions. Time has come when decisions have to be taken at national and sub-national levels by universities, state departments of education and teacher education institutions to come to grips with the problems so that what is needed for reorganizing and restructuring teacher education is in the direction of positive implementation.

## Professionalization of Teacher Education: A Priority

People in this country have been slow to recognize that Education is a profession for which intensive preparation is necessary, as it is for any other profession. This concern expressed in the report of the University Education Commission (1948-49) is alive in its relevance even today. But it cannot be lost sight of that as long as the conditions of service and salary are unattractive and the status of teacher remains low and unimportant, compared with other learned professions, there is no possibility of drawing a large number of really qualified, enthusiastic candidates to join the profession as their first choice. Under this reality, how does teacher education acquire a status commensurate with the professionalism associated with it?

A profession is characterized by features such as choosing the right clientele to nurture the demands of the profession, a minimum duration of professional training considered necessary for initial entry into the profession, a rigorous curriculum, which cannot normally be handled outside an institutional framework, commitment to continuous learning on the part of the teacher, and a code of professional ethics. These concerns have been synoptically outlined in the sections that follow.

## *Quality of Intake*

The professional status of a programme is linked with the quality of the intake that joins the profession and the rigour that characterizes the various aspects of the programme. Since becoming a teacher is generally the last resort of a person, it becomes important to ensure that the teacher training programme compensates for the mindset arising out of such social deficiencies. The quality of education largely depends upon the quality of teachers, which in turn, depends upon the quality of those, who join the profession at the time of initial training. Admission to institutions of teacher education should be carefully made to admit only those, who have the highest promise of becoming successful teachers. But how do we select such persons? Presently, "admission test" is conducted by the universities and other state level agencies to identify the candidates for admission. However, it is important to re-examine certain pertinent concerns.

- What elements which give a fairly good indication of the promise of a person to become a good teacher should comprise the admission test?
- What should be the nature of such a test? Should it consist of written test, test of aptitude, communication skills, performance in interview, etc?
- Should such tests be conducted at the state level by the university to which the teacher education institutions are affiliated?
- Could individual teacher education institutions be allowed to conduct such tests for admission to their respective institutions?

Almost every state is now conducting admission to the training institutions for all stages on the basis of a Common Entrance Test, the purpose obviously being to eliminate those who are unfit to be admitted to the teacher training programme. It requires serious debate as to whether such tests really identify the right talent for a teaching career. It has also come to notice that in some cases almost all who appear in the examination get admitted thus putting a question mark on the very purpose of conducting the admission test. This has happened in one state, may be because of proliferation of teacher education institutions, particularly at the secondary level.

## *The Duration of Teacher Preparation*

The question of duration becomes significant to define the professional nature of a programme. The exercise to determine the duration of professional training should involve:

- Spelling out the various tasks necessary for certification of a person to be entrusted with the education of children. Such an exercise which virtually amounts to preparing a profile of a teacher needs to be developed.
- The time required to accomplish the identified tasks.
- Inter-linkages between various stake holders to ensure commitment to the profession on the part of the prospective teacher.

The Secondary Education Commission suggested that for those who have taken the High or Higher Secondary School Leaving Certificate, the period of training should be two years. For Graduates, the SEC recommended that the training "may, for the present, be of one academic year but extended as a long term programme to two academic years". This concern also engaged the attention of the Education Commission (1964-66), which suggested that the duration of training at the primary stage be a minimum of two years. In respect of secondary education, the Commission did not find the two-year duration feasible from the financial and practical point of view. In fact, it suggested that it should be possible to make better use of the existing duration of one-year teacher preparation by extending the working days in an academic year from the existing level of 180-190 days to 230 days in all institutions without delay.

The Commission has also commented on the four-year integrated teacher education programmes being offered in the Regional Institutes of education of the NCERT since 1963. It felt that there is no evidence to show that the products of these integrated courses are better in anyway than teachers, who have first taken their degree and then completed their professional education. Moreover, these integrated courses, even when developed to their fullest potential, can only provide very small proportion of the total number of trained teachers required at the secondary level. The Commission was of the view that it will be wrong to place undue emphasis on such marginal experiments and that from the point of view of raising standards in teacher education it would be better to concentrate on improving the professional one-year course following the first or the second degree.

According to the Commission, if such integrated courses need to be supported, they should be organized in universities rather than in separate institutions set up for the purpose as is now being done. Such colleges necessarily prove to be expensive as they require staffing and equipment. This programme should be tried in universities having strong departments or schools of education, which should work in collaboration with departments in other subjects.

In the report of the National Commission on Teachers-I (1983-85), entitled, 'The Teacher and Society', it was suggested that each state may make a beginning by introducing at least one four-year integrated College of Education and the existing one-year B.Ed. course must be made effective by lengthening the time available and by revamping the current courses and curricula.

It is evident that except for a recent reiteration of extending the duration of one-year to two-year B.Ed., which too has remained confined only to the four RIEs, the educational system has not responded to enhance duration of teacher preparation for the secondary stage.

The Working Group to Review Teachers' Training Programme suggested that efforts should be initiated, without delay, to introduce two streams of teacher training programme: (i) five-year teacher-education programmes, after Senior Secondary, leading to Master's degree in education and (ii) two-year teacher-education programme, after the first three-year graduation of five-year post-graduation, leading to Master's degree in education. These programmes would be designed on the basis of the pedagogical ideas and value-oriented curricula suggested in the Report of the Working Group.

The very infrastructure of the RIEs—impressive campuses, workshops, science laboratories, libraries, multidisciplinary faculty to handle both subject specializations and related pedagogy was a strong pointer to professionalize the programmes of teacher education. It is rather unfortunate that such a vision of teacher education has till today remained confined only to the four RIEs although the experimentation with the model has proved its worth through the general quality of its products and their acceptability by educational institutions. It is not the concern here to bring out the trials and tribulations undergone by these innovations in teacher education. However, it needs to be pointed out that the focus of making the four-year programme resulting in a composite degree involving three-year of B.A./B.Sc and one-year of B. Ed. and seeking equivalence of the programme with these degrees of universities did result in some distortion of the professional nature of the programme. This issue requires a detailed discussion before a final judgment can be pronounced on the merit of these programmes.

The NCTE must give some fresh thought to this aspect and come out with an unequivocal pronouncement on the duration of teacher training. The NCTE needs to reconsider whether it can continue to accord its approval for both one-year and two-year B.Ed. programmes. If it means a policy change then it must unequivocally state that henceforth secondary teacher education shall be a two-year programme and the existing one-year institutions should convert them into two-year over a period of time, say three years. If it wishes to support longer duration teacher education programmes, it must initiate a serious discussion on such programmes, at the same time, outlining its curricular structure and organizational design. It has given special permission to some colleges of Delhi University to offer four-year Bachelor of Elementary Education (B.El.Ed) as an innovative model for elementary school teachers. The NCTE has also been approached by some institutions to offer five-year integrated programmes leading to Masters Degree in Teacher Education but no policy decisions have come up.

### *Teacher Education Curriculum*

The coursework of any teacher education programme generally comprises some core papers dealing with philosophical, sociological and psychological foundations of education apart from courses related to methods of teaching and some elective papers. The non-statutory NCTE was the first to evolve a document called, "Teacher Education Curriculum—A Framework", with the involvement of the UGC Panel on Teacher Education, to revamp teacher education pertaining to all stages of education. The unique features of this framework were the following:

- Teacher education was made task-oriented and less theoretical.
- The instructional time was apportioned to various tasks as follows:
  - Pedagogical theory including Teacher and Education in the Emerging Indian Society, Educational Psychology; special courses according to needs and facilities available, 20 per cent;
  - Content-cum-Methodology and Practice Teaching including related practical work, 60 per cent;
  - Working with the Community, 20 per cent;
  - Health and Physical Education to be made an integral component of teacher preparation;
  - Accumulating of credits leading to teacher education degrees/diplomas; and
  - Interaction with the university system to influence revamping of university curricula in tune with 'Teacher Education Curriculum: A Framework'.

### School Curriculum to Gel with Teacher Education Curriculum

School education can achieve its intended objectives only if there is corresponding reflection of the same concerns in the programme of teacher education, as teacher is the pivot on which the outcomes expected of any educational system can blossom. These concerns dominated the leaders of the nation through the establishment of various Commissions, Committees, Working Groups, etc., from time to time. The implication of establishing such Commissions was far-reaching as this was to provide the foundation on which the ultimate edifice of Indian education in the post-colonial era was to be developed and nurtured. This had also an in-built concern for modification of the programmes related to training of teachers to handle the onerous task of building a free nation. The National Curriculum Framework-2005 has made paradigm shifts for teacher education. A new National Curriculum Framework for Teacher Education needs to be urgently evolved, which should become the new basis of revamping teacher education programmes at various stages of school education in the country.

### Process/Pedagogy of Teacher Education: The Transactional Aspects

There are several concerns which need to be discussed in depth in order to formulate the processes and pedagogies of teacher education. Any attempt to develop teacher education curriculum, both in terms of content and methods, will require attention on several issues such as the ones listed below.

Presently, teacher education is stage-specific, for example, the pre-school, primary, elementary, secondary, etc. Considering the specific nature of learners in each of these stages, it is understandable to plan for stage-specific teacher education programmes. The present day realities are such that the system is utilizing the professional training in general for any level of school education. A case, therefore, may be made in favour of formulating a teacher education programme, which orients a prospective teacher to the pedagogical aspects of different stages. It is also significant to ensure that the demands on school curriculum are effectively matched with those of teacher education curriculum. For example, the emphasis on developing the courage to question, spirit of inquiry, objectivity, creativity, problem-solving skills, decision-making skills and aesthetic sensibility are critical concerns to be developed in the children. A teacher education programme must clearly focus on these in the theory and practice of teaching. Presently, these dimensions remain somewhat dormant.

The evolving concerns in teacher education also need to consciously take into account the ground realities of the education system in preparing teachers, who can effectively handle these realities. To mention a few, pedagogical training should deal with concerns such as the following:

- Handling large sized classes.
- Methodology of teaching in multi-grade settings.
- Implications of inclusive education to give practical shape to integration of physically and mentally challenged children in normal settings, also including other marginalized and socially disadvantaged.
- Perspectives related to gender equality including all forms of discrimination.
- Requirements of slow learners.
- Special concerns of gifted learners.

If integrated models of teacher education take some shape in future, it would be relevant, while designing such programmes, to point out the nature of integration; for example, how integration can be reflected in the design of a programme, and how integration takes place in the mind of the teacher.

### *School Practice/Internship in Teaching*

This is a significant aspect of teacher preparation but too little time is given to school practice and too little weight is given to practice in assessing students' performance. The University Education Commission (1948-49) felt that in a one-year course, not less than 12 weeks should be spent by the student in supervised practice (not expecting that the supervisor is present throughout the 12 weeks). Technically, the school practice should become the basis of development of theoretical perceptions about teacher education. Implications for increasing amount of school practice would mean using more schools; and schools do not generally like being used for practice. The training institution should not, therefore, admit a number greater than can be given proper school practice. Towards improving the situation, governments must come to the help of the universities and make it a condition of aid or even recognition to suitable schools that they shall play their proper part in the practical training of the recruits, whose services they subsequently intend to use. In fact, one of the conditions of grant of recognition by the NCTE to a training institution should be to ensure that the institution has the support of the schools for granting appropriate practice teaching facilities. The ideal situation should, however, be that a training institution should have its own laboratory in the form of a Demonstration School as an integral part of its infrastructure. Unfortunately, this has taken a peculiar turn in a recent development—schools are now seeking permission to run a training institution within the school on the plea that they can provide the required infrastructure of rooms. The intentions behind this appear to derive more from commercial considerations.

### *Training Methodologies vis-à-vis Teaching Methodologies*

In the teacher education curriculum, the methodology component occupies an important place. It is here that different approaches are taught to the trainees about the art of handling classroom dynamics. Experience tells us that this often turns out to be a routine drill and does not leave any scope for the student-teacher to design his/her perceptions about how learning can be imparted meaningfully. There is more emphasis on teaching but relatively much less on ensuring the intended learning. We need to learn from programmes offered by the management institutions where students are trained in their respective assignments through meaningful participative strategies. We need to spell out what goes into training methodologies apart from teaching methodologies as part of pedagogical orientation, particularly of teacher educators.

Teacher education programmes, in that case, should focus on self-directed learning and development of "learning to learn" skills. Specifically, this would mean that teacher training should stress:

- Training and perfecting of tools of acquiring knowledge viz., observation, inquiry, discovery, intuition, analytical reasoning, synthesizing, imagination, and creativity.
- Training in the location, selection and use of different learning resources viz., library, laboratory, educational media and materials, and expert teachers.
- Training in evaluating progress towards achieving learning goals and assessing the effects on their performance.
- Development of information processing skills rather than memorization of information.

## *Teacher Education in the Light of the Need for Value Orientation*

It has been felt that value orientation should be the central focus of education and that teacher should be given necessary training in effective methods of development of values in students. Towards this end, a Working Group was constituted by the Government of India in 1981, to review the teacher training programmes for promoting value education. The objective of the Working Group was to suggest necessary changes in the content and scope in the curriculum with special reference to development, among students and teachers, of the highest values of physical, emotional, mental, aesthetic, moral and spiritual culture as also of values, which are uniquely Indian and promote secularism, pride in heritage and composite culture. This was the first value-based focus on reviewing teacher education. This group deliberated on several aspects and worked out a detailed outline of the programme.

This model of teacher preparation did not get acceptance by the institutions as it was totally focused on preparing a teacher, who was more a symbol of value transmission than a communicator and a practitioner of handling various areas of school curriculum. What is perhaps needed now is to synthesize the concerns into a new blended curriculum.

## Professional Development of Teachers

The National Policy on Education (NPE) looked at the role of the teacher and expectation from teacher education in a holistic perspective. It mentioned that the government and the community should endeavour to create conditions which will help, motivate and inspire teachers on constructive and creative lines. Teachers should have the freedom to innovate, to devise appropriate methods of communication and activities relevant to the needs, capabilities and concerns of the community.

A significant recommendation of the NPE/PoA was the formulation of a centrally sponsored scheme on restructuring and reorganization of teacher education as a key step towards its "overhauling". Among the significant components of the scheme are:

- Making pre-service and in-service components of teacher education inseparable. This meant periodic and recurrent orientation of teachers not only in different subjects but also in relevant pedagogy.
- Mass Orientation of School Teachers to apprise teachers of the basic thrusts of the policy and role of teachers in achieving the policy goals.
- Establishment of DIETS with the expectation of operationalizing the following vision:
    - Designing convergence of formal, non-formal and adult education.
    - Planning and management perspectives to be incorporated into teacher education programmes.
    - DIET to be the nodal center for educational development of the district.
    - Identification of 'Lab Areas' for DIET's own learning to focus on a contextual curriculum.
    - Strengthening 250 Colleges of Teacher Education (CTEs) and upgrading 50 of them into Institutes of Advanced Studies in Education (IASEs) as technical resource support structures for secondary as well as elementary teacher education.
    - Strengthening State Councils of Educational Research and Training (SCERTs) to perform a networking role in establishing inter-linkages between teacher education institutions.
    - Strengthening university departments of education.

The beautiful vision of professional development of teachers as contained in the Centrally Sponsored Scheme of Teacher Education needs to be translated into action. A national evaluation found that the scheme was left high and dry. A well designed analysis of our failures to implement this scheme in the right perspective is immediately called for.

## Profile of Teacher Educators

One major area of weakness in existing teacher education programmes is the quality and experience of those who have the responsibility of training young entrants to the profession of teaching. These teachers are professionally known as teacher educators and identified as a class by themselves. A large majority of them may themselves have no direct experience of teaching school children. Since they have to instill the methods amongst the student teachers without themselves having the confidence of presenting a model lesson in a school context, they cannot create a convincing impression on the learners. It is felt that the issue should be discussed to define the profile of teacher educator and a scheme for their professional development prepared. Nothing will change significantly in the preparation of teachers if the corresponding changes are not visualized in the preparation of teacher educators.

## Professional Preparation of Teachers in Higher Education

The Education Commission observed that at present, there is no provision for the professional initiation of a university teacher. He/she receives no initiation into her/his duties and no orientation to profession. He/she even lacks at times the knowledge of the mechanics of his/her profession which involves curriculum planning, including aspects related to evaluation techniques. In this situation, the teacher is generally content to copy mechanically the methods and procedure adopted by his own teachers and inflict them on his/her students. By and large the tradition of giving lectures and dictating notes gets passed on from one generation of teachers to another. There is no intention of suggesting establishment of full-fledged training colleges for them. The institution of Academic Staff Colleges needs to be looked into and specialized training methodologies appropriate to higher education need to be developed. It is emphasized that such specialized training for teachers of higher education should not be a replica of the B.Ed. programme.

## Norms and Standards in Teacher Education

The Education Commission (1964-66) had deliberated on the aspect of maintenance of standards in teacher education and had suggested that the UGC in collaboration with the NCERT set up a joint Standing Committee on teacher education. The Committee was to be concerned with all aspects of teacher education, general and professional, at both under-graduate and post-graduate level. A lot of development has taken place since the recommendation of the Education Commission. A non-statutory NCTE was created by the Government of India, by a resolution in 1973, to influence quality teacher education in the country and to check the menace created by the proliferation of poorly planned correspondence courses in teacher education. In order to bring some order to the disturbing situations in the field of teacher education and the inadequacy of the non-statutory status of the NCTE existing at that time, the NPE recommended providing necessary resources and capabilities to the NCTE to maintain standards and norms in teacher education. In pursuance of this goal, the NCTE was set up by an Act of Parliament in 1993 and it commenced its statutory functioning with effect from 17th August, 1995. This was a landmark in the history of teacher education.

As events open themselves, the NCTE has evolved norms for various teacher education programmes but these norms have been ingeniously circumvented by the mushrooming growth of private teacher-training institutions, particularly at the secondary level. The disadvantages of correspondence education modality for teacher education led to huge enrolments by universities from which the revenues to the university system were substantial. The NCTE did succeed in controlling this menace but it had no way to check the aspirations of people to earn a degree in teacher education by whatever means. The aspiration, which led to the mushrooming of correspondence courses, provided the inputs to privately managed teacher education institutions, in a much more serious proportion. The NCTE has a lot to address itself to—generating process norms and developing monitoring strategies to ensure that teacher education institutions at least function with a modicum of the required sensitivities to the teaching profession. There is also need to take a fresh look into the existing norms for distance education and teacher education formulated by the NCTE (in collaboration with the UGC, Indira Gandhi National Open University and Distance Educational Council). Distance Education is a significant modality for in-service professional development of teachers and teacher educators and should be boldly developed. It enables a larger coverage of teachers in a shorter time, making available the best resource support from experienced professionals.

## Manpower Planning and Teacher Education

One of the provisions of the NCTE Act is "to coordinate and monitor teacher education and its development in the country. No survey of requirements of teachers for various levels and stages of school education has as yet appeared on our educational scene, except for the one conducted by the Institute of Applied Manpower Research in 1998. In the absence of such data there is no possibility of even making a suggestion to the state governments and other decision-making authorities to ensure whether new teacher education institutions are required, and if so, for what level and in what geographical areas so that there is no unwanted concentration of such institutions in areas where they are not needed. This aspect is very significant in view of the fact that many institutions, whose major areas of interest are in engineering, technology, medicine, offer B.Ed. courses in the same premises as they can afford to spare more rooms and infrastructure in accordance with the norms of the NCTE. The professional character of teacher education has been hit very hard by such a lackadaisical approach to give approvals for such institutions.

Linked with this is another unfortunate reality, that of institutions seeking recognition adopting devious means to satisfy the NCTE visiting committee. They not only hire equipment but also staff thus violating basic values, which teacher education institutions are expected to instill amongst those who have to shape the "destiny of the nation".

## Breaking the Isolation of Teacher Education

The Education Commission (1964-66) attached great importance to breaking the isolation of training institutions. This, in their opinion, was one reform that could achieve a breakthrough to vitalize teacher education and through it the process of learning and teaching in our classrooms. Teacher training institutions are isolated from university life, from schools and also from one another. The Commission recommended the following:

- Education should be brought into the mainstream of the academic life of the universities.
- Education should be recognized as a social science or an independent discipline and should be introduced as an elective subject at the under graduate and post graduate stages.
- Such a programme should be sponsored by the UGC in a few selected universities and develop speedily on a large scale. In each selected university, a department or institute preferably a school of education should be established to develop research and training programmes in collaboration with other programmes. The study of education itself will also begin to receive the enriching inter-disciplinary attention that is now lacking.
- An extension department should be established in each training institution—pre primary, primary or secondary—and should be regarded as an essential part of the programme and the responsibility of the training institution as a whole.
- Teacher education institutions should have effective Alumni Associations. A close link between old students and the staff has immense potentialities for making teacher education dynamic and progressive.
- Student teaching must be made into a comprehensive internship in which trainees are able to observe the entire work of the school and participate actively in all the important professional activities both in and out of the classroom.
- *The ultimate objective should be to bring all the teacher education institutions under the universities in such a manner that they continue to function in close collaboration with state education department and teachers organization.*
- Comprehensive colleges should be established, wherever possible, to prepare teachers for several stages of education and/or a number of special fields. What is now needed is a planned attempt to develop more institutions of this type and to add sections for training primary and/or pre-primary teachers to training colleges that prepare teachers for secondary schools only.

The above recommendations of the Education Commission (1964-66) are as valid today as they were at the time of their formulation. We have already lost considerable time, over the years, in implementing the recommendations. The UGC, NCTE and NCERT can probably take this as a priority agenda for implementation.

## Research in Teacher Education

A major weakness mainly responsible for the comparatively low status of professional studies in teacher education is the absence of adequate research on problems of education, including pedagogy under Indian conditions. The Educational Research and Innovations Committee (ERIC) of the NCERT is already seized of this inadequacy as is evident from the trend reports of researches documented in the various surveys of educational research. Substantial numbers of these researches are not directly linked with improving classroom practices and related pedagogical concerns.

There are some other concerns that dominate discussion in the field of teacher education and have implications for culture and values. There is a discussion on Indianization of teacher education. What does it actually mean? Do we need to derive from our ancient thought and also the wisdom of the Indian thinkers in education to formulate our curriculum? It is one thing to discuss Indian thinkers in education, it would be quite another to design teacher training pedagogies based on the thoughts of these thinkers. Are there indigenous pedagogies? If so, how do we reflect them in our teacher education programmes in today's context? Perhaps there is a need to study indigenous learning patterns in our own sub-cultures.

## Teachers for Vocationalization of Education

The vocationalization of education, particularly of higher secondary education, was recommended by the Education Commission (1964-66), but unfortunately this concern has not seen the light of effective implementation as was visualized. Vocational programmes, visualized by various Commissions and Committees, as part of school education, have not taken root. The traditional school system does not seem to be geared to offering vocational programmes and the situation is much worse when it comes to teacher preparation for vocational areas. In order to make a success in this area, we need to come out clearly on whether vocational education has to be a part of the school as visualized by the Commission or part of a system outside the school.

## References

University Education Commission (1948-49).

The Secondary Education Commission (1952-53).

The Education Commission: (1964-66).

Teacher Education Curriculum: A Framework (1978), NCTE

UGC panel on Teacher Education (1970).

The Working group to Review Teachers' Training Programme (in the Light of the Need for Value Orientation) (1983).

National Commission on Teachers-1 (1983-85).
National Policy on Education (1986/1992) and its Programme of Action.
The National Council for Teacher Education Act, 1993.
Curriculum Framework of Quality Teacher Education (1998), NCTE.
National Curriculum Framework (1975, 1988, 2000, 2005).
Multi-dimensional Role of Teachers: A paper prepared by Prof. C. Seshadri for the National Commission on Teachers-I.

# 15

# The Kothari Commission and Curricular Imperatives

VIJAYA S. VARMA

## Introduction

The history of modern Indian education is full of examples of governments setting up commissions, commissions submitting reports, and the reports gathering dust without much effort at implementing their recommendations. Pressures for reform, which had been quietened temporarily as a result of the report of the latest commission, start building up afresh. These pressures become more and more difficult to resist because people can see no evidence of any reform impacting the state of education. The government of the day then sets up yet another commission to take yet another comprehensive look into the state of Indian education. This new commission then dusts out the older reports, meets a cross-section of the "stake holders" in education, seeks some expert opinion, applies its own mind and prepares yet another report to add to the set, which already decorates the shelves of libraries and the mandarins of the Department of Education.

Given this situation, and the fact that I am dealing with the curricular implications of the recommendations of the Kothari Commission, the structure of this essay will consist of an overview of the Kothari Commission Report, focusing on its recommendations that relate to curricular issues. I shall then try and trace how these ideas have developed in time, focussing on the latest document in the series—the National Curriculum Framework prepared by the NCERT in 2005. This document is expected to guide the unfolding of new initiatives in school education, starting with the preparation of the new set of school textbooks. After a critique of some of these textbooks, I shall conclude with a description of what I consider to be a model of curriculum development that is worth emulating.

## The Kothari Commission Report

The Kothari Commission, originally known as the Education Commission, was set up by the Government of India in July 1964, with Professor D.S. Kothari as its Chairman, to advise it on the national pattern of education and on the general principles and policies that should govern the development of education at all stages and in all aspects. Significantly, the Commission chose to begin its work on the October 2, 1964—Mahatma Gandhi's birthday. In the Foreword to its Report, the Commission admits that, in the face of a task of such colossal magnitude and complexity, it was afraid that its recommendations would either turn out not to be sufficiently radical or they would go beyond the capacity and resources of the nation. It was conscious that educational plans are long-term plans and long-term projections of needs and resources are beset with uncertainties. It, therefore, advocated an in-built flexibility in the system to facilitate mid-stream adjustments to changing situations and requirements. The one thing it had no doubts about was that education, science-based and in coherence with Indian culture and values, could alone provide both the foundation and the instrument for the nation's progress, security and welfare.

The Commission believed that Indian education needed a drastic reconstruction, almost a revolution, and that tinkering with the existing situation, and moving forward with faltering steps and lack of conviction would only make things worse than before. To help it in its task, the Commission set up 12 Task Forces and seven Working Groups. It spent about 100 days in travelling across the country visiting universities, colleges, schools and holding discussions with teachers, educationists, administrators and students. It actually interviewed a great many people—almost 9,000 in all. It received over 2,400 notes and memoranda from across the country. It had the benefit of discussions with a number of internationally known consultants in education, in addition to having a number of international educators as its members. While taking stock of the prevailing condition of the educational scene, it recalled that the earlier University Education Commission set up in 1948 had laid great stress on the need for the improvement of the system as well as on the need to establish its connection with agriculture. It noted with concern that nothing significant had happened in the intervening years. Its apprehension that such could be the fate of most of its own recommendations proved to be a self-fulfilling prophecy.

The programmes of education reconstruction, proposed in the Kothari Commission Report, fall into three broad categories:

- a transformation of the system so as to make it relevant to the life, needs and aspirations of the nation;
- an improvement in the quality of education so that the standards achieved are high, keep improving continually and, at least in some sectors, become comparable to the best world-wide; and,
- an expansion of facilities broadly on the basis of manpower needs and with a stress on equality of opportunity for all.

The Commission strongly believed that the destiny of India could only be shaped in its classrooms. It was convinced that in a world, based on science and technology, it was education that determined the level of prosperity, welfare and security of any nation. Success in the great enterprise of national reconstruction, whose principal objective was to raise the standard of living of the people, depended on the quality and number of persons coming out of schools and colleges. In this context, the Commission felt an urgent need to:

- re-evaluate the role of education in the total programme of national development;
- identify the changes required in the existing system, and prepare a programme of reform based on these changes; and
- implement such a programme with determination and vigour.

The Commission believed that to accelerate the pace of national development, there was need for a well-defined, bold and imaginative educational policy and determined and vigorous action to vitalise, improve and expand education.

In 1966, when the Commission submitted its report, the population of India stood at 500 million, about half of which was under the age of 18 years. The total number of educational institutions in the country then was around 500,000. The number of teachers was in excess of two million and the total student population stood at about 70 million. Today, the total population has more than doubled, the number of schools is of the order of a million, the number of teachers has gone up to 5.5 million and the total population of children in schools stands at 203 million. According to government statistics, 82 per cent of our children today have a primary school within one kilometre, and 75 per cent have an upper primary school within three kilometre of their homes. Yet 37 per cent of the population is illiterate, 53 per cent of our children drop out at the elementary stage and 75 per cent of our schools are multi-grade. The clear implication is that the effort over the last 40 years has only ensured that we are barely managing to keep afloat.

The Kothari Commission felt that education could not be considered in isolation or planned in a vacuum, that being a powerful instrument of social, economic and political change, it would have to be related to our long-term national aspirations. It felt that unless proper steps were taken immediately, the gap between us and the industrialised countries would become too wide to be bridged. This, therefore, demanded a large-scale nation-wide programme for the discovery and development of talent and the creation of centres of excellence where such talent could be nurtured.

According to the Commission, India had to raise herself from her existing standards of living, which were amongst the lowest in the world, and take her rightful place in the comity of nations as soon as possible—a task which it felt had to be completed within the lifetime of a generation at the most. It considered that the development of a nation depended upon:

(a) the development of its physical resources and infrastructure, and in some senses, more importantly,

(b) on the development of its human resources through a properly organised system of education.

It was of the opinion that if this massive change was to be achieved without a violent revolution, education was the one instrument that could do it because of its potential for reaching all the people. This direct link between education, national development and prosperity, the Commission believed, could only come about if the national system of education was properly organised. The then prevalent system of education, still based on a design that was meant to meet the needs of an imperial administration within the limitations of a traditional feudal society, would need radical changes if it were to build a modern democratic and socialistic society—changes in objectives, in content, in teaching methods, in the size and composition of the student body, in the selection and professional preparation of teachers, and in its organisation. In fact, the Commission desired nothing short of a revolution in education, which in turn, it hoped, would set in motion the much desired social, economic and cultural revolution.

## Developments Since the Kothari Commission

A National Education Policy was formulated in 1968 based on the recommendations of the Kothari Commission. This specified among other things that facilities for technical and vocational education should be suitably diversified to cover a large number of fields, including agriculture, industry, trade and commerce, medicine and public health, and arts and crafts.

During the period from 1948 to 1968, a series of recommendations had similarly been made by several policy-making bodies to promote women's education in the country. In addition to the Radhakrishnan Commission and the Mudaliar Commission, the Durgabai Deshmukh Committee in 1958, the Hansa Mehta Committee in 1961, in the Bhaktavatsalam Committee in 1963 and the Kothari Commission in 1966—all emphasized the promotion of women's education, and the removal of gender based discrimination.

The first curriculum framework for schools was produced by the National Council for Educational Research and Training (NCERT) in 1975. The major thrust of this document was that the higher secondary stage should be regarded as a period for preparing some students for university education and a progressively increasing number for different vocations in life.

Post-Independence, school education remained a state subject till 1976, when the Constitution was amended to bring education on the Concurrent

List. In 1986, the National Education Policy of 1968 was revised and the country as a whole had a uniform National Policy on Education (NPE 1986). This policy, in the absence of any evidence that the promised universalization of education was ever likely to occur, specified that all children who attained the age of 11 years by 1990 would have had five years of formal education or its equivalent. Following this the first National Curriculum Framework for School Education was prepared by the NCERT in 1988 (NCFSE 1988). These two documents visualised a national curriculum framework, not as an instrument for imposing uniformity throughout the country, but as a means of evolving a national system of education. This was endorsed by the Program of Action formulated in 1992. The NPE (1986) had also sought to bring women's education at par with the education for men. Unfortunately, very few of its recommendations were successfully implemented.

In response to the widespread concern voiced by many educationists and parents about the increasingly heavy curriculum, a report entitled "Learning without Burden" was prepared in 1993 under the chairmanship of Professor Yashpal in an effort to reduce the curricular load on school children. Its recommendations emanated from the realisation that information should not be treated as knowledge and that using the explosion of information as a reason for burdening school children with an ever heavier curricular load displayed a fundamental lack of understanding of the nature of knowledge and of the process of the development of conceptual understanding in the education of children.

The National Curriculum Framework for School Education (NCFSE 2000) was an attempt to review the NCFSE prepared in 1988 in the light of the Yashpal Committee report. It incorporated many of the recommendations made in earlier reports without particularly trying to find out why those recommendations continued to languish on paper. This process has culminated in 2005 in the National Curriculum Framework (NCF 2005)—the latest contribution to this body of literature by the NCERT—which lays down the guidelines within which the new school textbooks will have to be written. It will also act as a document, which embodies the new vision of school education that will inform educational practice for the next five years or till such time as it is politically expedient to produce a new national framework.

The NCF 2005 dwells at length on the educational rationale for undertaking the revision of the National Curriculum Framework, although many suspect that it was initiated as a result of power changing hands at the Centre and the desire of one political party to undo what it perceived as the wrongs of another in the field of school education. The avowed aims of the NCF 2005 are to:

- connect knowledge to life;
- shift education away from rote learning;

- enrich the curriculum with materials other than textbooks;
- introduce a flexible system of examinations; and
- help nurture a caring identity within the democratic imperatives of our national Constitution.

It proposes to do this by making a distinction between knowledge and information, by promoting activity-based education, by the reduction of stress in students, by making education more relevant to the environment of the child, by promoting a plurality of textbooks and curricular materials, by incorporating local knowledge and traditional skills in the curriculum, by introducing flexibility in the management of schools and by promoting community participation.

Both the NCFSE 2000 and the NCF 2005, which is intended to be a review of the earlier document in the light of the Yashpal Committee Report of 1993, perforce address a number of common issues like language education, medium of instruction, the need for a common school system at all stages, of social cohesion, secularism and national integration and the relevance of these issues to the entire educational process. They both talk of the need for healthy, enjoyable and stress-free early childhood education, for the sustenance and nurturing of talent and a reduction of the curricular load, for inculcating trust in teachers, of their empowerment by ensuring their participation in the planning, implementation and evaluation of the curriculum as well as in the development of curricular material. Both documents mention the participation of parents and the community in the educational process and the need to root education in the Indian milieu.

Given that these ideas are not new and can certainly be traced back at least to the Kothari Commission Report, if not earlier, one would have expected that the NCF 2005 would have analysed why these desired features are not to be found in our current system of school education and enumerated the reasons why despite inclusion in the previous version as well as in many previous reports, they could not be implemented and nurtured in our system. The lack of any attempt at such analysis, therefore, leaves the reader with the nagging doubt that these legitimate and desirable features will continue to be merely voiced and never implemented. Although political regimes may have changed in the interregnum, there has been little systemic change and unless the constraints to implementation are identified and carefully analysed, little progress is likely to be made in any effort at meaningful curricular reform in schools.

There is also hardly any attempt to locate the NCF 2005 in the context of the prevailing reality of Indian education. There is no recognition of the urban-rural divide, or of the varied conditions to be found in public and government schools. It is, therefore, not clear what kind of school the document is addressing. One expected a broader analysis of not only the situation we are in but also an informed critique of why we are in the state we are at present. In addition, one would have expected the document not only to take positions but also present a critique of such positions and cite the research or analysis on which these positions are based. Why have we not succeeded in bringing about the changes that have been enumerated in many such documents in the past? The Mudaliar Commission Report, the Kothari Commission Report, the Yashpal Committee Report are all full of a great many good ideas, yet they remain pious wishes on paper. What is the point of repeating many of the recommendations of these and other past reports, of listing the outcomes that are desired, without any analysis of why they have not yet been implemented? There is little attempt to understand the feasibility of what is proposed in the document in our present context. Therefore, it is legitimate to ask, what is the guarantee that the fate of the recommendations of this document will be any different from the fate of the earlier ones, and consequently, why should one take the document seriously at all?

One has been informed in the Foreword that the current version of the curricular framework is the result of "a remarkable process of social deliberation initiated by the NCERT to focus public attention on what should be taught to our children and how". It ostensibly draws upon the views and opinions of a large number of people. However, it is moot as to what extent it is representative of the views expressed in the various position papers that were prepared as backgrounders and to what extent it is a product of the compilers' personal affinities for the ideas embodied in these papers. Be that as it may, the document has to be judged on its own merits and it is disappointing to note that it is not a more nuanced document. One may be in broad agreement with the overall vision of the document, but this vision remains undifferentiated—what is the long-term vision and what can be achieved in the immediate short term? There is also little discussion of the processes and structures that need to be put in place to take us from where we are to where we want to be.

There is hardly any discussion of what people expect from the education system and how these expectations—success in examinations, greater expectations of employment for their children, etc., will impact on the implementation of the vision that the document is trying to push. If parents want their children to, above all, become doctors and engineers or IAS officers, how will the teaching process be reformed unless the nature of the public entrance examinations to these professions itself changes. Many children nowadays are being encouraged to take a year off after graduating from school to join coaching centres and prepare for such entrance examinations in preference to joining a regular course of study at a university. What, if anything, do we propose to do to free children and their parents from the tyranny of the entrance examinations, whether to Business Schools, Engineering Institutes, Medical Colleges or the Civil Services? Though there is passing mention of reforms of the examination system, no great effort has been expended on formulating any concrete proposals. Discussions of curricular reforms will remain empty rhetoric if we do not take stock of the stranglehold that examinations have on pedagogy and what is taught and work purposefully towards breaking this unhealthy relationship.

A lot of needs have been pointed out in the document—of resources, both human and financial, of research studies and investigations as preludes to proper implementation. There is an inherent assumption that the expenditure on education will go up to six per cent of the GDP. We have heard such promises *ad nauseam* in the past. Is there any guarantee that the Government can be persuaded to deliver on this latest promise, and if it does not, what is the alternative plan the NCERT has in mind?

The shortage of resources, the non-availability of qualified and motivated teachers, the problem of inclusion of values (whose values?)—how is this all to be overcome? One can continue in this vein, but it will be more useful to consider in somewhat greater detail the contents of the first two chapters of the document, particularly as they set the agenda for what follows later. The first called "Perspective" and the second entitled, "Learning and Knowledge", delineate the curricular structure embodied in the new initiative. The major thrusts are (a) a constructivist view of education, (b) community participation in the management of education, (c) a common system of schools, (d) inclusion of work experience as an integral part of school education, and (e) a programme of national service. We will now take up these issues one by one.

## Constructivism and Other Pedagogical Issues

Although the constructivist paradigm seems to have enjoyed some measure of success in middle school science education, I believe that adopting Constructivism as the paradigm for the whole of school education—for all classes and all subjects, reveals a vision, which is both limited and limiting, particularly if we consider higher classes and older children. Success in middle school science teaching does not *ipso facto* guarantee that Constructivism would be successful as a universal pedagogy for all subjects and for children of all ages. Many strands make up a successful pedagogy and these are dependent on a variety of factors—the age of the child, the subject that is being taught, the level at which it is being taught, etc. The role of instruction has, for example, been stressed by Vygotsky (1985) who many believe to be the father figure of Constructivism. He says: "Instruction is one of the principal sources of the school child's concepts and is also a powerful force in directing their evolution; it determines the fate of his total mental development."

Critiquing Constructivism, Weil-Barais (2001) observes that "The teacher serves as a guide.... The aim is co-construction (pupil and the teacher construct together) and not just the construction of the pupil."

Belief in Constructivism as a universal pedagogy is the intellectual equivalent of believing that every child is capable of re-inventing the wheel, that every child can discover for herself, for example, Newton's Laws of Motion or Maxwell's theory of electromagnetism. However, as Wolpert (1992) says, "Scientific ideas are, with rare exceptions, counter-intuitive: they cannot be acquired by simple inspection of phenomenon and are often outside everyday experience." The progress from Aristotelian ideas to the physics of Galileo and Newton is the release of thinking from the bond of direct, sensual experience and channelling it into appropriate avenues by carrying out suitably designed experiments and by critically observing physical phenomena.

Science cannot be learnt by merely playing around with objects. Such an articulation, observes Matthews (1992), emerges from an inadequate appreciation or understanding of the scientific method. To expect students to learn anything Newtonian by playing around with objects is to underestimate the epistemological revolution initiated by Galileo and Newton; and also to underestimate the problems children face in internalising the classical scientific worldview. Playing around with, or prolonged looking at, real material objects will not generate point masses, inertial bodies, force definitions, geometry and calculus. There has to be formal guidance and informed instruction to help children develop accepted and useful concepts.

As has been pointed out, pleading for Constructivism to be the paradigm for all learning does not recognise the fact that very often children's own constructions of knowledge are flawed and at odds with more accurate constructions generally accepted by scientists. In Physics, children's natural constructions have been studied since the 1970's and many have by now been well documented. Interestingly, they have been found to be almost universally held. However, even though they are often at odds with currently accepted scientific understanding, they have been shown to be very resistant to change through formal instruction across cultures. Also, to the best of my knowledge, there have been no attempts at constructing a whole curriculum for physics, based only on addressing such misconceptions or alternative conceptions, as some investigators prefer to call them, even though many attempts have been made to identity and address these misconceptions as a route to developing better understanding of some selected concepts in children.

Thus, before Constructivism is accepted as the preferred universal pedagogy, extensive studies need to be carried out to discover the existence of such misconceptions in other subjects and at other levels and also to test them for their universality. It can by no means be considered to be as yet established that misconceptions or alternative conceptions in subjects other than science are universal; and if no universals are identified, how can one build a common curriculum that is based on addressing these misconceptions? Only if such universals are shown to exist and are also shown to exist in sufficient number of children, can we hope to build a pedagogy, which uses these misconceptions as a basis and shows teachers how to proceed towards the development of acceptable concepts in children.

The NCF 2005 talks of inclusive education as a means of teaching children with varied abilities, varied intelligence, as well as the differently abled. It is, of course, desirable that the curriculum should cater to them all, but how will it be done? Who will develop teaching material sensitive to such issues and on what basis? Where are the researches on which the development of such materials will be based? Where will the teachers come from, who will use these materials with sensitivity and concern in their classrooms? There is no evidence that the NCERT is even considering the training of teachers on anywhere near the scale this would require.

Also, this inclusiveness of multiple intelligences and multiple abilities, should, one would have expected, also have been extended to an inclusive pedagogy. On the contrary, the pedagogy that is being advocated is exclusively Constructivism. As a practitioner, my experience over the last 30 years has shown that the best position to adopt may not be an extreme or exclusive one, but rather one which is eclectic, choosing the most useful from a variety of pedagogies. Otherwise, how do we accommodate the varying and varied needs of all children with a wide range of needs and abilities? A specific approach on a specific topic may work with some children and not with others. Sticking to a particular pedagogy will probably prove too linear and unimaginative an approach to cater to the needs of all children.

There is strong advocacy in the document for teaching in the mother tongue, at least for the first 2 years of schooling. Yet there is no analysis of the difficulties in the implementation of such a proposal and how these difficulties would be overcome. First—how many mother tongues will be recognized as fit for being media of instruction? Who will produce the materials in the different languages, since they cannot and should not be mere translations of each other? Where will the teachers be found in sufficient numbers, who can handle classes of students with a mixture of so many mother tongues together? For example, in my class in the school where I studied, there were native speakers of Bhojpuri, Maithili, Magahi, Hindi, Urdu, Bengali, Punjabi, Assamese, Tamil and Garhwali. There are almost certainly schools with students with many more different mother-tongues. How will such situations be handled? If we say that we will use the regional language rather than the actual mother tongue for instruction, theoretically we are back to the same situation of imparting instruction in a language other than the mother tongue of the child. There is, therefore, need to look again at our basic premises, to examine whether we are merely parroting ideas from times past because they were once voiced by eminent thinkers.

A related issue is that although, in principle, all languages have the potential to serve as the medium of instruction in schools, not all are, as of today, equally equipped to do so. Thus arguments for the efficacy of instruction in the mother tongue in early classes based on evidence from Spanish speaking children in California do not hold much relevance in our context. Spanish is a well-developed language with a rich body of literature and a long tradition of discourse on intellectual and academic issues. The same is far from true for the majority of our mother tongues. Clearly more research in the Indian context needs to be done before we take a stand on such a critical issue, particularly in the light of the changing circumstances.

## Community Participation

The Kothari Commission had made a strong plea for the involvement of the community in the management of our educational system. In fact, the history of recommendations for community empowerment and decentralization in the administration of school education dates back to Freedom Movement, when it was conceived as part of the rhetoric of "power to the people" and "grass roots level democracy". The National Policy on Education in 1986 resulted in the setting up of an institutional framework for community participation at the district and sub-district levels in the form of District Boards of Education and Village Education Committees (VECs). This process was further strengthened by the constitutional amendments relating to the Panchayati Raj institutions by which time considerable experience with implementation of these ideas in different states had been accumulated. However, this experience has shown that the mere formation of the VECs does not ensure that the benefits are equitably distributed among the poor and the marginalized, particularly if they happen to be girls or women. For this it is necessary to ensure real participation at each level of the decision making process—in the identification of the problem, feasibility studies, planning, implementation and evaluation of solutions. Observers are also not sure whether increased community participation has led either to effective community empowerment or to improvement in education. It is not easy to alter the feudal mindset of much of our society, and its caste and gender based discrimination, particularly as the political and administrative elite would appear not only to have no stake in, but also be actively opposed to, improving the quality and reach of basic education.

Fears have been expressed, for example, by Sadhna Saxena (Govinda and Dewan, 2003) that the State may actually be abdicating its responsibilities for providing universal primary education in the name of community participation. She stresses that if this participation is to involve commitment of resources, then the community of the deprived certainly has no resources to support the education of its children.

Anjali Noronha (Govinda and Diwan, 2003) points out that in Madhya Pradesh, the introduction of the Education Guarantee Scheme and Alternative Schools staffed by *Shiksha Karmis* and *Gurujis*, has paradoxically had an adverse impact on government schools, because the *panchayat* representatives have no stake in such schools (their children usually study elsewhere) and very often have a direct stake in the personal interests of the teachers, who teach there.

It has also been noticed that the enthusiasm generated by the promise of community participation is invariably dampened by government inaction and apathy, and delay in the sanctioning as well as the release of funds. A point worth bearing in mind is that even if such empowerment forces teachers to come to school, how can it force an unwilling teacher to teach well?

Any apolitical notion of participation in empowering the community is deeply flawed and the outcome of such initiatives may, according to Vinod Raina (Govinda and Diwan, 2003), actually be the widening of the gap between the rich and the marginalized, as has been found to be true of development programmes in general, unless the state builds in appropriate safeguards. This implies that one must be prepared either for greater power vesting in the bureaucracy by virtue of the state intervening to ensure that local governance structures are more inclusive and representative, or for the engagement of supportive NGOs' indirect political activity to loosen local power structures. Neither of these two alternatives would appear to be free of problems.

Nevertheless, the NCF 2005 strongly advocates community participation in the management of school education—to decentralise decision making, to empower teachers and give them a voice in what they teach, to make them more accountable by strengthening the role of local bodies.

While subscribing to such proposals, one would nevertheless have expected that there would be some discussion in the document of the possible dangers of greater community involvement and the checks and balances that need to be built in. How is quality to be maintained, and some measure of uniformity? What problems would arise if you ask local bodies to define their own school curriculum? How would clashes between the modern and the traditional viewpoints be reconciled? How are we going to ensure that local vested interests and obscurantist views do not come to govern what is taught in the school? Let us not fool ourselves into thinking that these are only matters of concern for rural schools and rural communities. In some states in the USA, the value of *pi* is fixed to be 3 instead of 3.142... because somewhere in the Bible, the ratio of the diameter to the circumference of a circle is implied to be so. Or consider the debate that reached the courts of law in the USA as to whether Creationism should be given equal time as Darwin's Theory of

Evolution in the classroom. Can you imagine that our religious groups will not lap up the opportunity provided by community participation to have included not only their preferred views in mainstream courses but also prevent the teaching of anything in schools that they may perceive to be subversive to their beliefs?

Let us also not forget that the underprivileged are underprivileged because the existing power structures including the *Panchayati Raj* institutions are controlled by the privileged or the neo-privileged. How do we expect them overnight to become agents of change which will empower the disempowered? This is a conundrum, which requires much deeper thought and analysis, particularly of *Panchayati Raj* institutions, *nigrani* committees, and existing power relations, than has been done in any of the reports or curriculum documents.

Related to this is the question of the role of local knowledge. Before we can even begin to think of including local knowledge in the formal curriculum, we must necessarily address the question of its validation—how is it to be done, who will do it and what exactly is the local knowledge that we are talking of? Without answering such questions, all discussions regarding inclusion of local knowledge in the curriculum will remain in a state of intellectual vacuum.

Among the other issues that have either received short shrift or have been mentioned only in passing are multi-grade schools. What exactly is the document's stand on this issue? Are they a necessary evil that we have to endure, because we cannot remove the causes or are they the preferred answer to the chronic shortage of qualified and trained teachers? Similarly, if teaching is to become activity oriented and we wish to promote a critical pedagogy, we must find time for activities, investigations, discussions and brain storming sessions in the school curriculum. As a consequence, we must be prepared to prune the existing curriculum—not as easy a task as one may imagine. And again where are the extra resources to be found to train teachers in such pedagogy, as well as to provide the extra infrastructure that will be required to support such pedagogy?

Consider next the teaching of values. How is this to be done? There is no discussion as to who will decide and how it will be decided, which are the values that are nationally acceptable and, therefore, deserve to be included in the national curricular framework for schools. What is the mechanism by which we propose to decide such issues?

## The Common School

The Kothari Commission had noted with concern the segregation prevalent in education—the minority of private, fee-charging, supposedly better schools, meeting the needs of the upper classes and the vast bulk of free, publicly maintained, but poor schools being utilised by the rest. What was worse, it had noted, the segregation was increasing and tending to widen the gulf between the different classes.

There is probably no better example of an issue that has been recommended so often in the past and about which so little has been done in practice as that of the Common School System. The suggestion is repeated yet again in the NCF 2005, with absolutely no effort to explain or analyse why the proposal has never taken off. It is probably the most glaring example highlighting the fact that the NCF 2005, in its ostensible effort to appear superficially apolitical, makes no attempt to acknowledge that the most important factor constraining the improvement of curricular practices in the country is primarily the lack of political will to do so.

## Work Experience and National Service

It was the opinion of the Kothari Commission that all good and purposeful education should consist of at least four basic elements:

- 'literacy' or the study of languages, humanities and social sciences;
- 'numeracy' or the study of mathematics and the natural sciences;
- work experience; and
- national service.

Work experience, it believed, was the method of integrating education with work. This was not only possible but essential in a modern society. The need to provide some corrective to the over-academic nature of formal education was widely recognised. In the curricula of most contemporary school systems, a place has been found for what is variously called manual work or work experience. In our own country, the revolutionary experiment, *Nai Talim* that had been launched by Gandhi, emphasised the integration of education with productive work. It sought to make the distinction between intellectual and manual work less marked as also the social stratification based on it. It strove to make the entry of students into the world of work and employment easier, and promote social and national integration by strengthening the links between individuals in the community and by creating bonds of understanding between the educated and the masses. Clearly, the Kothari Commission hoped that Gandhi's vision would help bring about the revolution in education, what it saw as a precursor to the social, economic and a cultural revolution it dreamt of.

To bring the new elite created by modern education close to the people, the Kothari Commission also recommended that some form of social and national service should be made obligatory for students and should form an integral part of the educational process. The National Service Commission under the chairmanship of Dr. C.D. Deshmukh had, in fact, suggested that national service should be a full-time programme of 9 to 12 months for all young persons. However, there has never been any serious effort to act on such recommendations.

## The Current Scenario in Science Education and the New Science Textbooks

I am not sure how many of us are aware that there is a full blown crisis in science education worldwide. Enrolments are falling, as is the quality of the students, who are opting to study the sciences in general and physics in particular. In Britain almost 30 per cent of all Departments of Physics have either closed down or been amalgamated. In our country as well enrolment in science courses is falling, as is the quality of the students opting for them. There is a popular perception among students that Physics is boring, difficult and abstract, and most importantly in the present context, does not lead to well-paid jobs. Curriculum framers and textbook writers are, therefore, caught in the middle of what may be considered to be the seemingly opposed twin goals of science education: to produce new scientists as well as to promote scientific literacy for all, to increase appeal without compromising basic content, to emphasise application and relevance as well as hard-core theory—the problem is that the kind of curriculum that suits one, usually militates against the other.

The crisis in India should be worrying our planners, our policy makers and our curriculum developers. A shortage of good students in science classes in schools ultimately leads to a shortage of good science teachers and of good research scientists. And this shortage has already begun to be noticed—both in the teaching profession as well as in research institutes, funded so generously in comparison to university departments in recent years by the government. One result of this policy and of the operation of market forces has been that India's percentage contribution to world science has fallen sharply both in numbers and in the quality of research papers. According to CNR Rao, writing in the 'Scientific American', India contributes less than three per cent to world science compared to China's 12 per cent and our share of high impact papers has fallen to less than one per cent.

Of course, there are many causes for this decline—misplaced government policies and shortage of funds not being the least. Although procedures for the training and recruitment of teachers are other major culprits, it is also true that in recent years we have failed to make science teaching interesting enough to attract and retain young talent. To reverse this trend it is important to present science, particularly to young minds, not as an abstract body of knowledge but integral to understanding the world they live in. There needs to be an emphasis on practical work, investigation and exploration over textbook teaching and rote learning. In our schools, even in our 'best' urban public schools, there is very little experimental work actually done by students. In other countries, even four-year olds are involved in simple experiments like making a 'volcano' using baking soda or softening the shell of an egg by placing it in vinegar, while our schools seem to believe that experimental work is a distraction from the main business of learning science and doing well in examinations.

Recently, it has been proposed that in addition to the 40 per cent marks already reserved for internal assessment in practicals in the Class X Board Examinations, a further 20 per cent would be reserved for objective style questions, which would test whether students have actually performed the experiments they are supposed to have done during the course. Ostensibly, this is being done to make students take Practicals more seriously. In effect, what it will do is to spawn a host of '*kunjis*' to pass such tests and further devalue the role of experimentation in science classes. A related phenomenon, which defies all logical understanding, is that although teams of eminent scientists were brought together to write the new science textbooks, none of them had any say in the set of experiments that would accompany the texts. It would appear that the curriculum planners at the NCERT believe that science teaching can be compartmentalised into theory and experiment and that it is not necessary for the two to have anything to do with each other.

Since the proof of a pudding lies in its eating, an effective way to evaluate the impact of the NCF 2005 on our educational practices would be to look at the textbooks that have been prepared as the culmination of the most recent reform of the national curricular framework. Being a physicist by training, I will look at the new science textbooks that have been prepared for the lower classes, viz., Looking Around (Class 3 Environmental Science), Science and Technology (Class 6) and Science (Class 9), especially the Physics textbook for Class 11. I must hasten to add that the comments I make about these textbooks will not necessarily be applicable to the textbooks in the other disciplines. With this important caveat, let us proceed.

There is a strong plea made in the NCF 2005 for greater community involvement in the management of the school system. Firstly, nothing of this is to be seen either in the syllabus or in the textbooks that have been prepared. In fact, the very notion of a single, centrally produced set of textbooks to be used throughout the length and breadth of the country is the strongest possible sabotage of such a proposal and serves to highlight the lack of seriousness with which the recommendations have been made. In the same vein, although the NCF 2005 makes a strong pitch for Constructivism as the new universal pedagogy for all classes and all subjects, the new science textbooks seem to be completely innocent of any influence of constructivist pedagogy.

Basically, the new textbooks seem to be hardly affected by the many ideas embodied in the latest curricular framework document and the associated syllabi. Personally, I am not at all convinced that they should be. I believe that, in teaching science to younger children, what is actually taught is not as important as *how* it is taught, with experiments and investigations being used to ignite young minds to make them aware of the importance of the empirical basis of the discipline, instead of stuffing information into unwilling minds and merely emphasising its rationality. But this begs the question, is it really useful to go through this great exercise of framing national curricular frameworks if their influence stretches no further than the pages they are written on?

If we look at the actual books and start with the new textbook for Class XI, even a cursory perusal shows that it is almost a reprint of the previous Class XI NCERT textbook—identical in the running text, in the equations, diagrams, worked out examples, chapter summaries and exercises. In principle, there is nothing wrong with the NCERT reprinting an older book but then it should be up-front about it and not wipe out the old authorship to give the impression that the book is new and in consonance with the ideas enshrined in the new curricular framework.

The Class IX Science textbook is substantially different from its previous *avtâr*, although the structure of the chapters in Physics remains similar to that of the earlier one. The content is somewhat reduced and the diagrams are usually much clearer. There is a considerable increase in the number of activities included, but how many students will actually get to perform them? There are two concerns here which need to be addressed—the availability of the required equipment in schools and the ability of teachers to help students to perform the experiments. It would have been of some help if a comprehensive list of equipment required for the activities had been prepared so that teachers at least could try and procure those that were missing in their schools. Alternatively, the NCERT has an in-house workshop with a sanctioned strength of over a hundred persons. Why cannot it get a suitable kit of equipment manufactured in this workshop for distribution/sale to the schools, which adopt its textbooks? As for ensuring that the experiments are actually performed in class, nothing short of a massive teacher training programme to change mindsets and familiarise teachers with the activities suggested will succeed-and I don't see any sign of that happening.

The Class VI textbook on Science has a fair number of activities for children to do, but many are of the paper and pencil variety. However, its merits are marred by shortcomings in the language used, which is characterised by lack of precision, indifferent grammar and the occasional typographical errors. There are the occasional inaccuracies in the illustrations and some instances in which chapters could be improved and made more relevant to our circumstances.

The Class III textbook on Environmental Studies stands out as it is probably the best illustrated of the new textbooks. The pictures are relevant and imaginative, and so is the text. It contains a number of interesting activities that can be easily done by children. The language of the textbook could do with improvement, but notwithstanding that, it is a great step forward from the previous version of the Environmental Studies textbook.

The uneven quality of the science textbooks is surprising, particularly as many members of the writing teams are reputed scientists and teachers. That such a distinguished team can produce material of such quality can only point to the existence of systemic barriers in the NCERT to the production of good textbooks. One major contributing factor has been the totally unrealistic time frame in which the authors have been forced to work by the NCERT, but it is also worth examining whether committees are the best way of writing good textbooks.

One can see the point of a national curricular framework and, may be, justify a national syllabus, but I can see little merit in writing a single set of national textbooks in science for the whole country, at least for the lower classes. The NCERT would be doing the country a great service if it were to actually promote what it preaches—allow a multiplicity of textbooks with a multiplicity of approaches so that teachers and schools can choose the one they find most suited to their needs. It should also, in keeping with its mandate, promote quality research in education to guide it in its policy formulations and pedagogical recommendations.

## Programmes of Curricular Innovation

Let us conclude with a description of curriculum development programmes that seem to have embodied practices which are worth emulating. These programmes of innovation and improvement of elementary education were run by Eklavya—a voluntary agency based in Bhopal, with field centres spread out in different districts of Madhya Pradesh. One of these programmes, the Hoshangabad Science Teaching Programme (HSTP), which was initiated by Kishore Bharati and Friends' Rural Centre, ran at its peak in over 500 government schools, which were situated mainly in rural areas, involved nearly 3,000 teachers and engaged with something like 50,000 students every year.

The HSTP was a response to the challenge posed by the conditions prevalent in government schools which may be summarised as:

- A government school in a rural area is characterised by a building in poor condition with no library, no laboratories, no equipment and no facilities. This means no experiments can be done in class and science is taught as a body of received knowledge to be transmitted to children, validated by the authority of the textbook and the teacher, neither of which can be questioned.
- Teachers are often untrained in teaching science. They have no

resources and no support from the system. They often teach large numbers of children of mixed abilities and have no inputs into the curriculum. Yet, they are supposed to be the repositories of all knowledge. It is not surprising then that they adopt an authoritarian mode of teaching.

- Children are docile and submissive. This is almost a cultural imperative dictated by the fact that elders have to be respected and their authority can never be questioned. There are no rewards for displaying any initiative in class. All independent enquiry by children is suppressed in the name of maintaining discipline.

The HSTP was envisaged as a small beginning to counter this situation. It sought to bring experiment and observation to the centre-stage of science learning in middle schools. Experimental observations would provide the data for analysis and discussion, which would lead to a gradual building of phenomenological and conceptual understanding. The HSTP insisted on learning science through observation by doing experiments. Given that most schools in the programme were rural, learning from the environment became a guiding principle. The learning material that was developed consisted of detailed guidelines to do experiments, record and analyse observations followed by a series of questions, whose answers were expected to emerge from discussion among students guided by the teacher in the classroom. It was a major curricular and pedagogic breakthrough in a stagnant and hierarchical government school system in whose dominating paradigm "to know" had become synonymous with "to know by heart", where respect for all inherited knowledge was assiduously cultivated and wherein the assimilative faculties tended to be emphasised to the neglect of the critical and creative ones.

From the very beginning of the programme, school teachers and university faculty were involved in developing the curriculum. Out of an intense and protracted interaction between the organisers, university faculty and the participating school teachers, grew a philosophy of educational change, which can be characterised by:

- A resolve to operate within the framework of the existing government school system and to try and change it from within.
- A commitment to teach science through experiments. This was elevated almost to a guiding principle that nothing which could not be demonstrated by experiments that children could themselves perform in class would be included in the middle school curriculum. This meant, for example, that atomic theory and chemical formulae were not taught in the middle school. That this did not lead to a deprived curriculum was ensured by spending time on topics like

probability and positional astronomy for which suitable experiments could be devised for children of this age.

- A guarantee that all the equipment necessary for children to perform the experiments and activities in the curriculum would be provided to each school in sufficient number in the form of a special kit developed by the group. To reduce the cost of this kit, as much use was made of locally available material as possible. The experiments were also specially devised keeping this aim in view.
- All teachers in the programme were specially trained in not only doing each of the experiments in the curriculum but also in discussing with children the implications of their results. This was ensured by organising special three-week training programmes for every teacher every year for three years, by holding monthly meetings of teachers to discuss their difficulties and through regular school follow-up by trained personnel to help teachers with problems they encountered in the day-to-day implementation of the programme.
- Feedback was constantly collected from teacher training sessions and classroom experiences and used to modify the curriculum.
- End of the year and final middle school examinations were made less intimidating for children by getting the programme teachers to set the papers, in contrast to the standard practice of getting them set by a special board for all schools in the state. Permission was also obtained to make the examinations open-book and of unlimited duration. This meant that children could take with them their workbooks and class records to the examination and could take as much time as they wanted over the questions.
- The curriculum required children to do all their own experiments, working co-operatively in groups, and discuss their findings among themselves and with their teachers. It encouraged them to go on field trips, gather information about their surroundings and put up exhibitions of their work at village fairs.
- The major thrust of the programme was to focus on how learning could take place by scientific enquiry of phenomena rather than by the memorisation of scientific facts. Since, for many children, middle school would be the end of their formal education, emphasis was laid on teaching them to learn for themselves so that they could carry on learning even when they left the school.

One of the strategies of learning that was adopted on many occasions was to address the misconceptions or rather the alternative conceptions that children bring with them into the classroom, arising from their own attempts to make sense of the data that they constantly receive from their immediate environment. For example, many rural children believe that flies are born spontaneously from cattle dung. Instead of directly contradicting this belief or ridiculing it, we got children to cover fresh cattle droppings with polythene bags. They were asked to observe them over a period of time during which little flies would appear in similar droppings which have been left uncovered and had been visited by flies. This formed an interesting prelude to the study of the life cycle of a fly.

Similarly, rural children often believe that butterflies suck the goodness out of flowers and the flowers die as a result. Children were, therefore, asked to enclose some flowers in perforated polythene bags as soon as the flowers had budded but had not started to bloom. This allowed the flowers to 'breathe' but prevented butterflies from visiting them. In time, children saw that these flowers shrivelled up and bore no fruit while those that had not been so covered gave rise to fruit. This activity was used to introduce pollination and the role that insects play in the life cycle of plants.

To take one other example, the unit on astronomy starts by asking children what the minimum length of the shadow cast by a vertical stick is and the time of the day at which it occurs. Invariably the answer is that the stick casts no shadow at 12:00 hours. You can imagine how surprised children are, and for that matter many adults too, when they discover that neither of these beliefs is correct.

For the smooth functioning of the programme, the state department of education was persuaded to set up special structures in its offices and many administrative procedures were altered to bring them in consonance with the needs of the programme. Resource persons were drawn from universities, research institutes, local colleges and high schools to help with teacher training, monthly meetings, school follow-up and curriculum development.

Almost from the inception of the programme it was realised that improvement in science teaching could not be brought about in isolation. How other subjects were taught fed into the science classroom. Teachers could not be expected to become less authoritarian and more child-friendly in the science classes if they were not also trained to teach the other subjects in school in the same manner. If children were not taught mathematics and language properly, it was unrealistic to expect that they would either be able to analyse properly the data they collected in their science experiments or be able to adequately record or describe their experiences in their own words.

The interventions in language and mathematics were informed by the same philosophy of producing "thoughtful" teachers and "active" students. They attempted to create curricula taking a holistic view of education, in harmony with the educational and cognitive development of children, resulting in a programme for teaching social sciences in the middle school and an integrated programme for the teaching of language, mathematics and environmental studies in the primary school.

In the social science programme, children were helped to develop skills of historical analysis, engage in comparative studies, learn how to collect, tabulate, display and analyse data. They learnt skills in practical map making—of the neighbourhood of their school, of their village and its surrounding area. They learnt about the causes of the seasons and its effect on the environment, about local history, the different ways societies have been organised and the multicultural strands of the society they live in.

In the primary school programme, children were engaged in a variety of activities involving art, rhythm, music and dance. In the initial months of Class I, there were no textbooks and no written work. Children slowly started developing language and mathematical skills in an integrated manner through play and by the manipulation of concrete objects. They were encouraged to explore their potential for creativity. The individuality of each child was respected. A variety of teaching strategies were adopted so that each child could find some approach, which suited her. Topics were visited and revisited with progress in the form of an expanding spiral so that children had the opportunity to consolidate what they learnt and also pick up skills they may have missed the first time around. Children were encouraged to talk about their ideas so that they could develop confidence in their abilities and also learn by listening to the articulation of their peers. Teachers were encouraged to use errors that children made as teaching opportunities, exercising care so as not to hurt the sensibilities of the children in the process.

By common consent, Mathematics is considered to be the most intimidating of the subjects taught at school. It strikes fear in the hearts of many students and is also the subject with the highest rate of failure in our schools. Even adults often own up to a phobia for mathematics and boast how, despite such phobia, they manage successful careers in business or administration. The root cause of this is the way mathematics is taught in schools, not just in our country but, it would appear, throughout the world. Thus when in a survey in France a seven year-old boy was asked "If you have 10 red pencils in your left pocket and 10 blue pencils in your right pocket, how old are you?" and he answered 20 years, it was not as if he didn't know that he was seven years old. It was just that he was so overwhelmed by the dominant paradigm of school mathematics, in which answers to problems must be obtained from the numbers that are provided, however meaningless these answers may turn out to be, that he found nothing incongruous in what he said. It is this context-free nature of school mathematics that makes it such a sterile experience to many young minds. Contrast this situation with the mathematics that is done by ordinary men and women in their daily lives. Why is it that the woman, who sells fruit in the market and has probably never been to school, is able to do multiplication and addition connected with her trade, mentally and without error, when the same sums on being posed to children in class often leave them floundering? The answer cannot be unconnected to the fact that the oral methods she uses are clearly non-algorithmic and firmly rooted in her daily experience, and that any errors she makes could result in financial loss to her. She, therefore, has a stake in getting the answer right, a stake which is often missing in the classroom.

In the programme of teaching Mathematics, there was, therefore, an effort to make the teaching and learning of mathematics more relevant to a child's environment, to root it as much as possible in the child's experience. There was emphasis on activity, on concrete manipulands, on a slow progression from the concrete to the iconic to the symbolic and then to the abstract. There was no written work in the initial months of school. Adequate time was found in the curriculum for non-numeric work: work with shapes, with geometrical puzzles, with the graphical representation of data, with symmetry and patterns. Some of the other perceptions that evolved during the course of the programme which are worth recording are:

- Children are not blank slates when they enter school. They come equipped with a certain awareness of number and operations ('initial mathematics') that is independent of formal instruction.
- There is a natural pace at which each child picks up new concepts and skills in mathematics. Riding roughshod over this in an attempt to maintain a pace of learning dictated solely by an externally imposed pre-determined curriculum leads to frustration and the development of fear of mathematics.
- Learning does not take place suddenly. It is a slow process involving many loops and feedback cycles. Children must have opportunities to use emerging concepts in as diverse situations as possible. The curriculum must allow for creative repetition to enable children to deconstruct and reconstruct concepts that they come across. The school environment should provide a rich experience base for the child to make this possible.
- Children should be encouraged to do investigative work because it has been found that as a result they understand more, enjoy mathematics more and become more confident. The challenge here is to think of projects that are simple enough for children to undertake, yet interesting enough to keep them engrossed.

## Epilogue

Learning is inherently beautiful and a potential source of joy. However, only if the teacher feels this, can s/he communicate it to children. Our experiences have reinforced our belief that the teacher is the lynch-pin in any programme of educational improvement. If the teacher is not convinced of the need for change, no curricular change will work. Teacher training is, therefore, not just a matter of training teachers in new concepts and techniques but of changing their attitude to teaching especially in their relationship with children. This cannot be done by imposition and may be possible only through involvement and association.

Although it is ultimately the teacher, who has to transact the curriculum in the classroom, it is neither possible nor desirable to spell out exactly how everything should be done. It is, however, necessary to provide the teacher all possible support in the classroom. In addition, it is important that the teacher feels that s/he "owns" the programme. This can only happen if the curriculum is developed in conjunction with and in continuous interaction with teachers, who are actually engaged in teaching children, with feedback from the classroom constituting an integral part of the development process. The curriculum must also provide space for teachers to include topics, activities and investigations of their choice, should they wish to do so.

One of the most important realisations to emerge from these experiences is that of the intellectual isolation of the school teacher in India. This is why it is necessary to encourage the involvement of teachers from high schools, colleges and universities in programmes of education at the elementary school and to stress in-service training, orientation and continued academic and intellectual support for our elementary school teachers. It would be no exaggeration to state that in our experience, every instance of success in programmes of innovation can be traced to an involved, committed and capable schoolteacher. We must, therefore, commit ourselves to the idea of developing a network of persons actively involved in education to act as an intellectual resource and a source of inspiration to our teachers in the field. It is time education planners in this country realised that good teachers can salvage the worst curriculum and compensate, to some extent, for the most deprived conditions, and bad teachers can ruin the best curriculum and waste the best facilities.

## References

Brossard, Michel (2001). Construction of knowledge and writing practices, *Prospects*, 31(2).

Govinda, R. and Rashmi Diwan, (eds.), (2003). *Community Participation and Empowerment in Primary Education*, New Delhi: Sage Publications.

Government of India, (1986). *National Policy on Education (NPE)*.

Kothari Commission, (1966). Education and National Development, *Report of the Education Commission 1964-66-(Kothari Commission)*, New Delhi: Ministry of Education, Government of India.

Matthews, Michael R. (1992). History, Philosophy, and Science Teaching: The Present Rapprochement, *Science& Education* 1.

NCERT, (2006). Looking Around, *Environmental Studies, Textbook for Class III*,

NCERT, (2005). *National Curricular Framework (NCF)*,, New Delhi.

NCERT, (2000). *National Curriculum Framework for School Education (NCFSE)*, New Delhi.

NCERT, Physics, Parts I &II, *Textbook for Class XI*, New Delhi.

NCERT, (2006). Science, *Textbook for Class VI*, New Delhi.

NCERT, (2006). Science, *Textbook for Class IX*, New Delhi.

Nola, Robert (1998). Constructivism in Science Education: A Philosophical Critique, in *Constructivism in Science Education: A Philosophical Examination*, Michael R Matthews,(ed.) London: Kluwer Academic Publishers.

Rao, C.N.R. (2006). Overcoming the Crisis in Indian Science, *Scientific American India*, 1(15).

Suchting, Walls A. (1998). Constructivism Deconstructed, in *Constructivism in Science Education: A Philosophical Examination* Michael R Matthews, (ed.), London: Kluwer Academic Publishers.

Varma, Vijaya S. (2005). How should Physics be taught to facilitate understanding? in *Construction of Knowledge*. Udaipur: Tista Bagchi and Ramakant Agnihotri, (eds.) Vidya Bhawan Society.

Vygotsky, L.S. (1985). *Thought and Language*, Cambridge: MIT Press.

Weil-Barais, Annick (2000). Constructivists approach and the teaching of science, *Prospects* 31(2).

Yashpal Committee Report, (1993). *Learning without Burden*, New Delhi.

# Part IV

# Planning and Governance

# 16

# Rethinking Educational Governance for Social Transformation

SHARAD CHANDRA BEHAR

## Introduction

The report of the Education Commission (1964-66) is in every way a product of the Nehru era, though the Commission was constituted soon after the demise of Jawaharlal Nehru,. It is rooted in the then prevailing ethos, reflects the dominant ideology of the time, accepts unquestioningly the beliefs, understandings, theories, approaches, values, strategies, and ideas evolved and considered axiomatic during the charismatic and overwhelming leadership of Nehru. This essay seeks to address the major national concerns, and some of the global concerns of the time within the established framework of thinking.

Dr. J.P. Naik, Member Secretary of the Commission, who played a major role in drafting the report, had published his book, The Education Commission and After in 1979 in which he carefully examined the implementation of the recommendations of the Commission, revisited their rationale with an admirable open mind and found many of them questionable, while continuing to accept the validity of others.

The Commission "looked upon educational administrators as important change agents" and "laid considerable emphasis on improvement of educational administration". Let us see how he looks at each of these proposals with the wisdom of the hindsight in the following excerpts from his book (1979):

- *Institutional Reforms*: "But looking at the various suggestions made by the Education Commission on the subject and the reactions they evoked, I am left with two uneasy feelings. Firstly, I do realize, as a matter of hindsight, that educational administration has been a neglected area of study and that we did not then have adequate specialized knowledge to go into depth and make concrete proposals which could have been implemented with advantage. Unfortunately, we do not have this expertise even today. Secondly, I do realize that we over-emphasized the role of institutional structures. In fact, our reaction to several problems was merely to suggest the creation of an institution to look after it.... I also do not think that it would have made a radical difference to the overall situation if some or even all these institutions had been brought into existence.... *I have no regrets that these proposals have been mostly side-tracked"* (emphasis added).

- *The Indian Education Service (IES):* "I must also confess that I do not feel as enthusiastic about it now as I did in 1966. While ...the issue may be kept open in theory, I do not see any chance of the revival of the I.E.S. and even if it were to be revived, it will only make a marginal contribution to the solution of the basic issues."
- *Reorganization of the Ministry of Education and the State Education Departments:* "The present position is that the Education Commission has not been able to make any contribution to the improvement of the educational bureaucracy, either at the Centre or in the States; and in view of the decision not to revive the proposal for creating an I.E.S., *the whole problem will have to be examined afresh"* (emphasis added).
- *District and Municipal School Boards:* "It was of the view that a time has now come to administer all school education from the district level and to associate the local people closely in planning and implementing educational reforms.... *Unfortunately, this far-reaching proposal has not been accepted so far. This is one of those areas where the proposals of the Commission are on a sound footing and there is need to pursue them relentlessly"* (emphasis added).
- *Private Enterprise:* "It (is) still maintained that the growing educational needs of a modernizing society can only be met by the state and that *private enterprise can have only a limited and minor role* in the national education system of the future. The Committee of Members of Parliament was more inclined to flatter and please rather than hurt private enterprise. The National Policy on Education (NPE) 1986 also avoided all discussions of the subject.... This merely underlies the fact that there is a close relationship between voluntary organizations and political parties and politicians. For the same reason, all inconvenient issues about private enterprise have been side-tracked throughout the past 12 years. No problem can, however, be solved by being swept under the carpet; and *the precise role of private enterprise in a national system of education will be one of the major issues to be tackled in the reconstruction of education in the days ahead"* (Emphasis added).

In the following paragraphs, some of the proposed institutional reforms, including district boards, bureaucratic reforms including, Indian Education

Service and reorganization at all levels, and the role of private enterprise in the era of globalization, are being revisited.

## Education for Social Transformation

The Education Commission reposes great faith in education as the one instrument, and the only one instrument that can be used to achieve change on a grand-scale without a violent revolution (Para 1.14). Challenge of Education: A Policy Perspective (1985), approvingly quotes the Commission's view about the close correlation between education and social justice (Para 1.15). The NPE 1986 sees education as a tool of furthering the goals of socialism, secularism and democracy enshrined in our Constitution (Para 2.2). It also believes that the core curriculum will help promote values, such as, India's common cultural heritage, egalitarianism, democracy and secularism, equality of the sexes, protection of environment, removal of social barriers, observance of the small family-norm and inculcation of the scientific temper (Para 3.4), and to create awareness on the inherent equality of all. In fact, Chapter IV of the report is titled, Education for Equality, though lamentably, the chapter only outlines policies and programmes to achieve equality in education and fails to design education for equality or a system that will promote egalitarian attitude.

These documents only express the widely held belief that education is a strong means of social change. However, the system of education that existed in the 1960s or the current system, can be said to be the most appropriate for the purpose. It has to be transformed, or as the Education Commission puts it, an "educational revolution" has to occur. However, as Naik admits in retrospect, in the excerpts given above, even if its recommendation regarding educational administration were accepted and implemented, their contribution would have been negligible. Hence, we will have to totally re-conceptualize education and its governance, which can be an effective change agent. Mere improvements in the existing structure and culture of administration will not suffice. Focus has to be shifted to the totality of governance. The Education Commission also concentrated only on central, state and district levels. Although it strongly recommended a school complex system, it did not pay adequate attention to the governance at the level of school or sub-district, which are as crucial as any in a transformatory education and, therefore, needs to be integrated in the policy formulation.

## Role of State, Civil Society and Private Enterprises

Without going into the thorny question of whether globalization is beneficial to all and inevitable or whether it is a neo-liberal, neo-capitalist, neo-imperial design for a hegemonic world order, it should be possible to analyze a few relevant issues inextricably linked with the general trend of what is popularly known as liberalization, globalization and privatization.

There is a clear apprehension on the part of many perceptive observers that the state seems to be shying away and withdrawing from its role and responsibility in education. Passing on the buck, of enacting a central law for free and compulsory education, to the states with a very poor model draft is one indicator of this. There is a firm belief in the Education Commission's stand that in the existing unequal society, the State has to be fully responsible for ensuring high quality education to all at all stages—totally free up to elementary and secondary levels and highly subsidized at tertiary level. This has become all the more critical in the wake of globalization. With only about nine per cent of the relevant age-group participating in tertiary education, the State cannot shy away form its full responsibility. Education being directly linked to privileges, remuneration, social prestige and power-sharing in society, the state's total responsibility will continue in the foreseeable future—until a more egalitarian socio-economic order is established in the country, which looks like a distant dream. In hastening the process towards this, education, as repeatedly mentioned, has to play a critical and pre-eminent role. That is all the more reason why the State cannot withdraw even to the slightest extent from this sector, even if it does so from other sectors.

Common School and neighbourhood school system is an important step in ensuring "*level playing field*" for the deprived and privileged. Space for private schools and accompanying principle of freedom of choice makes the field uneven *ab initio* for the deprived, disadvantaged and underprivileged. There should be no compromise on this. Almost all models of educational organizations we have been presented with are consistent with this. A few private enterprises may be given a space but it should be ensured that the objective of, the disadvantaged getting similar or higher quality of education, is in no way compromised.

State responsibility and State monopoly are not integrally linked. While total State responsibility in education is to be favoured, its monopolistic control can be questioned. The Education Commission, as also all policy documents that exist up to date, conceive of the civil society as a support to the state-controlled, state-managed and state-planned education. There are statements like *non-governmental and voluntary effort, including social activist groups, will be encouraged,* and *steps will be taken to prevent* commercialization of education (NPE 1986-Para 10.9) or *giving pre-eminence to...association of non-governmental agencies and voluntary effort,* (NPE 1986—para 10.1), which make it amply clear that civil society will play only a secondary, supportive and marginal role. It is largely seen this role being played by managers of some institutions or innovators within the framework laid down by the government. The Challenge of Education (1985) also similarly suggests giving responsibility for children's and adult education to voluntary agencies (para 4.81). Even the draft Free and Compulsory Education Bill (which now has been converted into a model Act for the states) is deficient in this respect. It does not give any space to civil society except in establishing educational institutions.

There is no space for civil society to develop its own curricular framework. Even after accepting the *national curricular framework* it cannot make use of the *components that are flexible* in its own way. In recent years, private Universities are being allowed, but for the elementary and secondary education, the state control continues to be tight and iron-fisted, (with the exception of Indian School Certificate Examination, for historical reasons.) If recent news reports are to be believed, there is a move to establish a central council to regulate textbooks: the teaching-learning material. A Board of Secondary Examination with authorities to have its own educational paradigm to be established by civil society, currently, is unthinkable. If this vista is opened for the civil society, not commercial private enterprise, the scenario can radically change with encouragement to plurality of educational philosophies and perspectives in finding space.

There is an urgent need to consider this issue more deeply and intensely and adopt measures to loosen the control and monopoly of the State apparatus over education. Allowing academic and examining bodies and autonomous institutions of the civil society at levels other than higher education, with conditions, procedure for monitoring compliance with the conditions, provision for revocation in the event of non-compliance is one way, which of course will require fine tuning and detailing. While the state has to continue to be responsible for quality education for all, it should move away from total control and monopoly to effective regulation.

The Education Commission was categorically against commercialization of education. In the globalizing world of today, private enterprise, with its commercial orientation and concept of education as a trade, should be distinguished from the non-profit organizations, aiming at social welfare or social change and with a service-oriented concept of education. Distinguishing organizations on these criterion, admittedly is difficult and challenging, but not beyond human ingenuity and systematic rational approach. Private individual initiatives should also be treated differently, where reasonable remuneration is expected and justified like the professional's fees. Like the Education Commission, we should have been totally against the WTO regime's conceptualization of education as a trade. That is why there is need to be highly cautious and vigilant. Private enterprise should not be allowed up to the stage where the common school/neighbourhood school system is introduced. It is suggested that up to class X should be treated as part of the elementary education, while the higher secondary can merge with the higher education. Even in the rest, a transparent and participatory accounting and audit system should ensure that no profit is earned and only the cost and required investments are being realized. Private enterprise for profit and trade should be completely ruled out, not even on plea of competition resulting in quality improvement. Freedom of choice should be an accepted principle within the state and civil society managed education, which should have comparable costs. Mechanisms, like the voucher system or fees subsidization by the state, are attempts to promote and prop-up private enterprise on the fallacious argument of providing quality education to disadvantaged children. They are based on the unacceptable assumption, that (a) private institution only can and do provide quality education and (b) the state cannot or should not attempt to provide comparable or even higher quality education. Many of the models of governance, suggested in this paper open up the possibility of high quality education by the state system.

## Governance of Education-Scope

The Education Commission, deliberated upon and made recommendations on "planning and administration" of education—not on the totality of governance. The Challenge of Education (1985) and its aftermath—the National Policy on Education (1986) moved to the concept of management of education. The political executive, which is an integral and crucial part of administration or management, has not got the attention it deserves. *Governance has far richer and wider connotation than administration or management. It is inclusive of political executive in parliamentary democracy*, where administration (permanent executive) is separated conceptually from government (political executive), which changes with the change of its head (Prime Minister or Chief Minister). It is formed at least after every election and can be voted out of power. Government and accordingly governance, in this context of political executive, has primarily a political denotation. With the democratic decentralization attaining constitutional status and sanction, one can validly, logically and legitimately conceive of, and in reality there is existence of, political executive at district, village, town, city and the intermediate (Block, Tahsil, Mandal or whatever unit has the elected body in a particular state) levels because they have elected bodies comprising political personnel with decision making powers and strategic implementation authority.

The bureaucracy, as permanent executive, is a part of the wider concept of government, though generally referred to as administration, the expression used by the Education Commission. That is why it confined itself to the nitty-gritty of administration in this narrow sense. The NPE 1986, though using a then fashionable expression, management, did not touch upon educational governance in the context of political executive. *Good governance* in recent years has come to mean the totality of government functioning—its effectiveness, efficiency and benevolence including fair-play, transparency and respect for the people—the governed. In a democracy, the conceptualization should include the idea of the empowered people, who as the ultimate and real masters are also a part of the government—not just the governed. While designing governance systems, structures, processes and culture for a revolutionary education, the empowered people should be both the starting point and ultimate objective. It should, in fact, permeate the whole design.

The idea of multiple systems of governance, attempted to analyze in this paper, flows from an optimistic perspective and is grounded on the firm belief that its contours, design, values and culture play as vital a role in contributing to social change as the core of education.

## Core Values of Educational Governance

Educational governance, to be an effective change agent, must be based on some non-negotiable, un-compromisable values:

- *Plurality*: In the multicultural, multi-linguistic, multi-religious and highly plural society, multiple paradigms of education and governance shall be given space, allowed to flourish, shown full respect and shall be promoted. Suggestion to curtail the role of Ministries and formation of Commissions representing all political hues as the Apex body at National and State levels is to achieve this purpose. Decentralization with flexible patterns being allowed to be established and to exist also is a mechanism for this.
- *De-politicization of Education*: The adverse impact of politics entering the arena of educational institutions has been identified as a major problem in the Challenge of Education (1985), which also goes on to wish for self control by political parties in eschewing use of education for narrow political ends. It also suggests the need to evolve consensus and even contemplates constitutional amendment, if required, for the purpose (Para 4.135). While agreeing with this, one has to propose the de-politicization of educational governance by over-politicization, as explained later, and by taking it away from the area of confrontational politics to those of consensual and competitive politics.
- *De-bureaucratization of Education*: De-bureaucratization in reality encompasses many things; a kind of a culture, structure, certain tenets, method of functioning and associated attitudes and values. Some of them are briefly mentioned below:

### *(a) Non-hierarchical*

Hierarchy is one of the major characteristics of a bureaucratic system. It is based on inequality—a relationship of superiority and inferiority in role, status, authority, remuneration and prestige. Currently, educational governance also strictly adheres to this. Such a system cannot be expected to manage transformatory education, which will lead towards an egalitarian society. Even class room organization and practices, as also the culture of educational institutions have a hierarchy from students through all functionaries up to the head of the organization.

### *(b) Flat Organization*

Educational governance and administration from one end to the other will have a flat structure. There will be no bosses and subordinates, but only colleagues who are equals, who have complementary capabilities and roles.

Performance appraisal will be by all of all others. As per need, task forces (not in the degenerated sense of a committee to produce a report, which unfortunately has become its commonly understood connotation) that will have some challenging tasks to perform may be formed with leaders chosen by the group by consensus and based on the kind of expertise most critical for that range of tasks. They will work on the principle that, the leader is only the first among equals. Rotation of leader can also be adopted as a method of developing the culture of equality in an organization.

This basic value of equality and the leader being first among equals will be followed at every level from the classroom to the Commission. The class room in this conceptualization is a learning task force, the teacher being the leader and hence first among equals. The Head of an educational institution also will have a similar role and status. Every level—cluster, school complex, Block, District—will follow the same core value and principle, although structures and other details may vary from district to district or state to state or even school complex to school complex.

### *(c) Professionalization*

To establish and cultivate this culture of equality, which will also include fraternity and dignity of the individual, professionalization of the educational structure would be essential. There will be no distinction between educators (teachers and academics) and educational administrators. All would have to undergo a specially designed professional course of 5 years duration (or any other duration) after Higher Secondary education or after recruitment and would be required to work in both the categories of functions, rotation within fixed periods being unexceptionable rule, both during internship and while on the job.

*De-concentration/Dispersal of Authority*: For a variety of historical and practical reasons, including conservatism, inability or unwillingness to innovate and experiment, distrust of the ability of the people to use authority with maturity and responsibility, and above all the vested interests of those who enjoy authority and power in the name of people, all democratic systems, institutional structures and processes have led to the concentration and centralization of authority at various levels, institutions and groups of people. Educational governance, as change agent, will decentralize and even disperse authority at every level. Plurality and multiplicity being the most important principle, there is infinite scope for experimentation of dispersed and decentralized governance system, some of which will be outlined presently.

*Autonomy and Accountability*: Since at least in theory, autonomy and accountability are two sides of the same coin, the dispersal of authority should not be misconstrued as leading to chaos and an absence of accountability. On the contrary for every task, the task force will have authority and accountability first towards the educational community and then to the society at large. Enough authority—neither more nor less—to be able to experiment with, innovate and try diverse strategies, methods and working systems to complete the task successfully, is the essence of autonomy.

Accountability is to the beneficiary group or if multiple tasks together lead to tangible benefits to a group, then primary accountability will be to other task forces, so that synchronization and integration takes place within time and in the right way to achieve the final objective, or benefit to the beneficiary group.

*Federalism*: In democracy power flows from the people to the state. This basic principle is totally ignored today both in theory and practice and it is unquestionably accepted that power rests with the state. Education governance will be based on the basic value that the people and the learners are sovereign and wield power. They delegate limited power with clear mandate to a group, a bigger unit or a larger geographical unit to perform certain functions mandated by them.

To take an example, a village school is a unit formed by the people to perform assigned functions and shall be accountable to them. The schools need some support to discharge their responsibility. They may, therefore, form a federation of schools—a school cluster or a school complex—to provide that support. School complexes may federate into Block resource centers, which in turn could federate into the DIETs. In the same way the SCERTs and NCERTs would be the federations of the DIETs & SCERTs, respectively. In this model, the composition of each successive unit is determined by the federating units, as they are the creators. They will delegate the necessary authority and demand accountability from the members of the federation.

For administrative and financial needs similar arrangements will be made. The Block unit will be accountable to the schools, the District to the Blocks and so on including the State and the National Commission.

*Transparency*: Bureaucracy believes in secrecy, which has also been sanctified by the Official Secrets Act. The Right to Information Act and the underlying principle challenge the original culture, but the conflict has yet not come into the open with all its ramifications. Experiments in Gujrat and Andhra Pradesh to bring in transparency in transfers, postings etc., of teachers have shown encouraging results.

The duty will be cast upon the administration and the wider education system to be transparent, to act in such a manner that all can see and know what is happening and why. There should be no need to *ask for* or *apply* for information. It should be available to all those who care to or need to have it. Transparency is also important in the educational philosophy and processes, which currently is a black box for most parents and students.

*Corruption-free Governance*: While transparency can be a major instrument to fight against deep-rooted corruption in the bureaucracy, which seems to have acquired gigantic proportions with externally aided projects, we have to explore and adopt other mechanisms also. One of them can be social audit. Civil society organizations, any citizen forum, should have the right to take up audit—not only financial but also of performance—prepare and disseminate its report widely for all to know.

Grievance-redressal machinery also will have to be re-conceptualized. The person, who has a grievance, should have the right to request for independent jury or assessors to look at the genuineness of her grievance and recommend relief, which the government should be obliged to accept.

These and similar other innovative devices and procedures are feasible. Selection and training processes also shall be transformed to bring about a more honest system. Selection, which is usually based on the principle of merit, can be combined with that of integrity, with higher weightage to the latter.

*Respect for Dissent*: "Vidya Dadati Vinayam."—Knowledge makes one humble, is an ideal rarely practiced. Since education is in the business of knowledge, open-ness to and respect for different point of view, and providing space to those should be a non-negotiable core value.

*Functioning Model of the Vision Society*: If Education has to play the transformatory role, as so fondly wished by the Education Commission, every unit, from classroom to the National Commission, should be the functioning model of the larger society that education seeks to build. Every unit should function on the basis of the principles and culture of equality, liberty, fraternity, dignity of the individual, just and humane to everybody. The classroom, the school-community, the CRCs/School Complexes, the BRCs/DIETs/State and National Commissions, the Universities, the Colleges, the educational governance units at various levels—whether as a part of the PRIs, Local bodies, Government departmental units, or Universities—should present this social structure and values.

Education can be a strong weapon of social change, only if in addition to what goes on in the educational institutions in the name of education today, the entire education system, including the class room, the institutions and the administrative organizations are geared up to inculcate a value system in the students that is in consonance with, and conducive to, the democratic, equitable and just society visualized by the Constitution. This is possible, with appropriate recruitment and orientation policy, risk and reward system, a vigilant civil society facilitated by transparency in working.

## Educational Governance—Talent Power Management

The Education Commission, as also the NPE, favoured the formation of an Indian Education Service. The former also made recommendations on a State Education Service, which has acquired greater importance in the emerging scenario where PRIs and local bodies will be and are playing increasingly important role in education. Both these services will prove to be useful in providing continuity, quality and unifying thread in an era of decentralized governance, provided they function within the value-framework outlined for which different kind of recruitment, induction training, placement system and performance-appraisal will have to be put in place.

Recruitment to the services can be combined with the respective Combined Civil Services Competitive Examinations. This will imply generalists, who have no background in education being recruited. The merit of this system is the possibility of higher quality of entrants, since a large number of bright young persons from all disciplines aspire for and compete in the Civil Service Examination. Like the Indian Forest Service, separate competitive examination with requirement of background in any of the identified disciplines like Education, Management, Psychology, Sociology and other behavioural sciences may be considered. This, however, will exclude science, technical and many professional degrees, which are equally important in education, as domain knowledge plays not an insignificant role. Moreover, many bright persons, who join professional courses, will be debarred, the loss being of the proposed services. The balance of advantage, therefore, seems to be in favour of recruitment of generalist candidates. Another option is to set up a professional education system of a long duration for educators, comparable to engineering and medicine and recruit through a separate competitive examination, like the one for the Indian Engineering Service.

The recruitment process should however aim at testing not only the academic competence or the so-called personality through the interview, but also the values and commitment for the societal vision of the Constitution. Group discussions, field assignments, situational tests and many other techniques psychometrics has developed and can develop, should be used as they are used for recruitment to Armed Forces. Those who do not do well in these tests and do not fulfill special requirement of education services may still qualify for other services. A more rigorous process in this regard is essential, if we really want to convert educational edifice to be the functioning model of the society the Constitution aims at. Indeed, for selection of teachers and all other functionaries in the education sector, this additional qualification will have to be kept in mind to assess the suitability of the prospective teacher.

For teachers in publicly managed schools (State, PRIs, Local bodies), the question of recruitment in a cadre where transfer from one institution to the other is permissible or only for a school or college has been a controversial one. A cadre has the advantage of flexibility, scope for in-service career-advancement, large-scale recruitment, attracting better talent and the possibility of equitable distribution of talent between disadvantaged rural and better-endowed urban areas. In practice, however, a cadre-based system seems to have worked against the rural, backward and tribal areas. For this reason, as also on the argument that continuity of teachers in the same school builds a culture and better local community-relations, establishes desirable traditions and generates a feeling of community and shared responsibility leading to higher quality of education, the institution-based recruitment may have an edge. Demerits of this system often mentioned are: stagnation (both because of absence of opportunity for promotion as also for want of wider exposure), involvement in local politics adversely impacting on the health of the school and the difficulty in getting talented teachers in backward and remote areas. If there can be stability and schemes of career advancement in the universities, there is no reason why the same principle cannot be followed for a publicly managed school. This can help the de-bureaucratization, and withering away of the administrative wing. Further, more accountable and transparent administrative processes also can lead to remedy of many ills of the current administrative system.

There can be many blends of the two systems, where advantages of both can be combined to avoid many of the ills. Recruitment for a place in a cadre with the possibility of transfer only on promotion or for equitable distribution of talent is one such way. There is also a possibility of misuse, which can be reduced by a regime of transparency. In the decentralized system of educational organization and governance, the district units may have the discretion to adopt any of the options or their blends, within the broad guidelines.

In such a situation, the design, duration and quality of induction process for the persons in the service should aim at developing an education-social activist for which it should:

- Acquaint them with the numerous facets of the discipline of education in such an engaging manner that it becomes their passion to update their knowledge and understanding.
- Equip them to continue to acquire new insights into the intricacies and emerging trends in education.

- Provide real—not just symbolic—experience of teaching at different stages of education.
- Provide them skills and knowledge of Management along with competence to apply them in the field of education.
- Provide a thorough understanding of the current social structure and dynamics.
- Ignite and inspire them with the constitutional social vision, which should be facilitated by the process of recruitment, which also tests their social vision and commitment.

This process would take a long duration. For practical reasons if it has to be shorter, it should be designed keeping in view the ideal requirement with provision for a series of distance education learning modules that can be managed while on the job, interspersed with face to face interactions.

The initial jobs must be in a rural area as a teacher or/and head of the school complex so that she gets a proper understanding of the rural community—its structure and dynamics, as also its distance from the vision society. Her major task would be to reflect over the possible role of education in the bridging of this gap, in a shift towards the vision society. The duration of the initial rural placement should be long enough to accomplish this ambitious project.

Like the field training of other services, the new recruits should be required to perform for varying periods at all the positions that impinge upon the performance of a responsible education functionary. The educational institutions like BRCs, DIETS, SCERTs, SIEPA, Board of Secondary Education, Universities, BEO and DEO can be included in this system. Approximately, five years would be necessary for such an on-the-job learning, which will also be accompanied by study and learning through both distance mode and face-to-face interaction. Thus actual job-performance, reading-writing on the subject of education and face-to-face interaction would be so integrated as to create a continuous cycle of action-reflection-learning-action. Theories learnt will be applied, tested, evaluated and modified by each educator. Hopefully, this will provide a very thorough and sound grooming for working as an education activist—a social activist.

Professional education system for educators, when set up, should also be on the above lines, except that the field postings on all positions not being feasible, may be provided soon after the recruitment. In the states, where the support and partnership of the entire system can be obtained for the purpose of field postings, it should be adopted for the professional course.

Performance appraisal should be of 360 degrees. All those who impact or are impacted upon by a functionary's performance should have an opportunity to appraise her work. This is a principle being proposed for the assessment of the learner's performance. They have to be in sync.

While every job will have a different job-profile and, therefore, the criteria will have to be appropriate to the profile, apart from the general criteria. The extent to which the values of vision-society are practiced by her and in her organization will be an important criterion.

Appraisal system will also move away from target achievement to objective-achievement, from quantitative indicators, like the number of teachers trained to the number of teachers, who have achieved the objective of the training—acquiring the capacity to undertake diagnostic testing and adopt assessment as a tool of learning (formative assessment). This again is in sync with the suggestion to move away in learning assessment from marks to meaningful articulation of what has been learnt.

In the jobs that impact on or interact with the community, its appraisal should also be obtained for which there are some techniques and some can be developed and refined.

## Educational Governance: Political Dimension

Education is a highly political phenomenon. It is an immensely powerful instrument for the political parties for expansion of their ideologies as also for recruitment to their parties. Any idealistic demand that the political parties should leave education alone is highly unrealistic and unacceptable. For many other sectors like co-operatives, health, livelihood, similar sentiments and demands of keeping them out of politics are expressed from time to time. In a democracy, those who are competing for power in electoral politics will leave no sector, or opportunity to gain an upper hand over, and denigrate the opponent.

It is quite interesting to note that Naik felt that "It is unfortunate that the Education Commission did not highlight the role of political parties in educational reconstruction", and also that "politicians remain largely ignorant of basic educational problems" because of the educationists' desire of "political support without any political interference" and "what we need is better education of the politicians, the training of party cadres in education and the preparation of an educational programme by each party to which it is committed" (The Education Commission and After, page 239). The situation has changed dramatically—for better or worse, nay, both for better and worse. Better because education is receiving the attention of political parties it deserves, which is a long way from the ignorance noted and lamented by Naik. Therefore, there is a possibility of engaging the political policy and decision makers, which provides the scope for evolving consensus on major issues after real application of their minds and due deliberations by them. Education, being vital for the society and requiring long-term continuity and sustained implementation for achieving its goal of social transformation, can then be a part of a consensual politics so that vagaries of political change do not adversely impact its transformatory role. Worse, because even now the contested arena and issues are too narrow, like the History text books, while more vital and critical issues like the National policy, curricular framework, decentralized governance, writing of text books in diverse-pedagogy-friendly manner and space for free, flexible class-room processes that give students the ability of independent logical thinking, continue to be out of focus.

Guidelines on these could be arrived at by consensus, while their fine tuning through implementation mechanisms could remain in the domain of competitive politics. A concrete example is the NPE 1986, which was unanimously approved by the Parliament where all the major parties were represented, although its implementation has been vastly different under different leadership.

The area of consensus can be further expanded and the domain of competition in implementation through varying interpretations, strategies and programmes can be substantially narrowed, if a new NPE is attempted now, when education has acquired such a pride of place in both the confrontational and competitive politics that no political party can afford to neglect it. Under the circumstances, each will marshal its array of educationists and academics to join the task of drafting, engage in animatedly (even bitterly) debating but ultimately arrive at a broad area of consensus and a narrow area of dissent, hoping that the consensus area can always be interpreted to suit their perspective and ideology when they are in power.

That takes me to another important and distorting characteristic of politics—patronage overtaking merit and suitability in key appointments. In most—if not all—key appointments the mechanism of search committee has been provided. However, it is common knowledge that the composition of the search committees, the panel of names they recommend, and the final appointment from the panel, are manipulated. In fact, in most cases the whole process has proved to be a smoke screen for and a mechanism to gain respectability to the blatant favouritism and nepotism, resulting in—more often than not—key positions being held by people not on account of their merit but because of their allegiance to the powers that be. This is one of the factors leading to the demand for de-politicization of education. So long as current form of parliamentary democracy, electoral processes and associated principles like the unfettered rule of majority characterized by confrontational, competitive, and nepotistic politics continue, de-politicization is a distant, unrealizable dream. The remedy lies in deepening and widening the process of politicization, which hopefully will have to be achieved by de-politicization since it will expand the area of consensual politics.

All key appointments in education sector should be by a committee consisting of representatives of all political parties recognized by the Election Commission at the relevant level (National, State, District, Block, Village).

## Education Governance: National and State

With this perspective and the core values, let us look at the educational governance structure that should be put in place.

### *Advisory Boards of Education*

Central and State Advisory Board of Education can play a useful role in formulating policies and implementation strategies, in monitoring progress, reviewing the policies and generally guiding the course of educational change. They should become more federal in character, representing their federating units better. Currently, only the Ministers of Education of the states are members. Leaders of the opposition or their nominees should also be included. Expert members are nominated only by the Central Government. The states should also have a say. Either each state should be able to nominate one or if the number is likely to be too large, other means can be adopted. For example, a larger panel of experts prepared by the Central Government could be circulated to the states and only those are selected that find favour with most states. Methods of proportional representation can also be adopted. There should be a co-chairperson. A minister of a state in rotation can occupy this position.

Similarly, the State Boards can adopt a more federal character by giving similar space and importance to District Panchayats, Universities and other federating units.

### *Permanent Education Commission*

For historical reasons, in India, Education Commission has come to acquire the connotation of a committee or group of persons constituted for a short period to deliberate upon and make recommendations on the specified terms of reference.

However, like the UGC there can be a permanent Commission, assigned with responsibilities and duties to discharge and clothed with necessary authority, power and legal sanction. It can work within the framework of law, independent of the government and, in fact, demand accountability from it. Human Rights Commissions, Women's Commissions, Minority Commissions, S.C./S.T. Commissions at the national and/or state levels are examples of such legally constituted commissions.

To de-politicize education, it is imperative to constitute such a permanent Commission for the whole of education, not just one stage—elementary, secondary or higher or sub sectors like technical or agriculture education. The Kothari Commission had considered and delineated the role of then existing Ministry of Education (now renamed as MHRD). This should be drastically modified. The Ministry should restrict itself to laying down broad policy of a kind that would enable the ruling party to fulfill promises made in its election manifesto. Even this would be reduced to a symbolic exercise if representatives nominated by all political parties frame a consensus policy that is approved by the Parliament after due consideration.

The ministry then will be a symbolic unit with a very skeleton and lean staff. Almost all its current functions, responsibilities, authority and power should be transferred to the statutory commission, which will have a chairperson (the first among equals) and members nominated by the committee comprising representatives of all political parties recognized by the Election Commission at that level. It will also have representations of the State Commissions, the federating units, to provide the federal character. Hopefully, the Commission thus will be composed of people acceptable to all parties. Alternatively, it can have representation of each party in proportion to its numerical strength in the central and state legislature, somewhat on the lines of the Cabinet in Switzerland that has proportionate representation of the legislature.

Such a mechanism will drastically change the scenario. All controversies and major differences will be debated and be settled within the commission. In order to avoid bulldozing by the numerical majority, the commission will function not on the basis of majority but on consensus. If consensus is not achievable on a highly contentious issue, the decision shall be deferred at least twice. If even on the third or subsequent occasion, consensus cannot be arrived at and the matter brooks no delay, both or all the differing views will be accepted as authentic decision—with both or all options being available and be equally legitimately implementable by those responsible for implementing. Suppose the contentious issue is about the curriculum or text books or pedagogy to be adopted or the assessment method or the conditions for recognition of schools or methods of supervision, inspection, or of ensuring accountability, the Commission will incorporate in its decision, policy and communications all the options or different points of view which remain unresolved. The decentralized governance system that we favour will make this feasible since every unit can choose its own option for implementation. A comparative study after a reasonable period can provide empirical evidence validating one or more approach(es) and the conditions under which each proves to be effective or otherwise.

This approach will give respect to multiple options and views and it is essential because the status of human knowledge today on any of the contentious issues on education is not of that finality as to arrive at the one *ultimate truth*. It will also help in moving towards one or more options on the basis of a comparative study and empirical evidence.

If the issue is of a nature where one method has to be adopted and multiple options are likely to create chaos, the *instrument of referendum* (a potent process of direct democracy) can be adopted. The differing views will be referred to all those who are going to be affected and the results of the *referendum* will be final and binding on the Commission.

The Commission being suggested here will incorporate within itself the U.G.C., which in the circumstances will have no rationale for separate existence. In some South East Asian countries like Thailand and Indonesia, permanent Education Commissions do exist, although they are not necessarily conceptually what is being suggested here.

The one Commission for all stages of education will make integrated and holistic view of education real and feasible. The Kothari Commission seemed to be referring to such a view but remained contented with considering all *stages separately* by the same Commission.

Even if the fully integrated view, I am arguing for in this paper, is considered as too radical and unacceptable, the Commission can function through Committees for each stage or sector of education, each headed by a member of the Commission, so that the Commission can effectively integrate all stages. Identified important, as also contentions, issues relating to each stage can be reserved for deliberation and decision only by the full Commission. In effect there will be limited delegation in respect of each stage to the sub-committees and all matters necessary for integrated and holistic view of education will rest with the Commission.

This will be a considerable improvement over the current system, where now even the Central Ministry is fragmented into separate Secretaries for School and higher education, and the U.G.C. and NCERT also have no effective linkages. Multiplicity of statutory regulatory bodies like the AICTE, Bar Council, Pharmacy Council, Rehabilitation Council, Distance Education Council and the National Council of Teacher Education make the scene far for more complex and fragmented underlining the need for effective integration. Central Advisory Board of Education, because of its size, composition, the periodicity of its meetings cannot be expected to discharge this responsibility, effectively.

The Commission will be the real functional apex body at the national level. Similar Commissions at the state level will also be established with similar composition, mandate and method of functioning.

For the levels other than national and state, multiple approaches and models will be presented but all of them can be within the rubric of the National and State Commissions, which have been conceived to de-politicize education through deeper and wider political engagement. The design of this Commission aims at promoting multiple paradigms in education. It has been made inclusive of diverse philosophies of, and perspectives on, education independent of, or in tune with, competing political ideologies and societal vision—the non-transgressible boundary lines of the society, and the values enshrined in the Preamble and other provisions of the Constitution that elaborate, concretize and articulate it in a variety of contexts, primarily in the Chapters on Fundamental Rights, Directive Principles of state policy and some others relating to the SCs, STs, OBCs, minorities and marginalized groups.

### Project Specific Organizations Vs Mainstream

An increasing trend of creating new organizational structures, separate from the mainstream educational organization has been noticed in recent years. Partly, it is in compliance with the dictates of the donor agencies, which find neat separation more satisfying and comfortable. It makes their task of appraisal of the progress in the project easier. I also suspect that there is also an unarticulated but solid desire to create their own empire, which is visible on the ground. It helps in substituting the more difficult task of appraising the achievement of the objectives by more quantifiable superficial indicators. Regrettably, indigenously funded, Sarva Shiksha Abhiyan also continues to follow this model. In many sectors other than education, one can notice this questionable trend.

Partly, this is used as a solution to the cumbersome and highly dilatory procedure of flow of funds through the budget of the Central and State Governments. The States also tend to use such funds to tide over temporary set-back in their ways and means position, which in some states and in certain periods of the year when sources of income, by their very nature, are slow to yield, is not too infrequent. Registering a society and creating a parallel organization, in addition to being costly, also makes the gains, if any, of the project, too transient. The task of making it a part of the mainstream and converting the effective strategies and components integral to the usual educational processes and practice is very complex, arduous and tedious and is rarely achieved. During the period of the project it gives rise to avoidable intra-sectoral tensions, jealousies and heart-burning. The *marginalized mainstream* develops an indifferent, if not hostile, attitude towards the project. It, without accepting openly, in fact, becomes resistant to adoption of the lessons of the project, thereby defeating the major objective of the project.

Advocates and perceptive observers of democratic decentralization also perceive in this a sinister design to by-pass and denigrate the PRIs and local bodies, which is the inevitable consequence of creating a parallel organization from the state to the grass-roots. Such perceptions are strengthened by the move of all sectors to develop their own community organizations. Formation of Water-shed Development Committee, School Development and Monitoring Committee or Village Education Committee or Joint Forest Management Committee or Forest Protection Committees distinct from the PRIs are illustrations of organizations that are perceived as designed to by-pass the elected bodies, which can and should be entrusted with the task. This also betrays the distrust of the local elected representatives and elected PRIs and local bodies, on the parts of the powers that be—both bureaucrats and politicians at the state level. It is certainly a manifestation of the deep-seated prejudice and bias against democratic decentralization, whatever be the rationalization offered.

In view of the above, it is very critical to take a policy decision not to create parallel organizations and to build capacity in the existing system to take up the challenges of the project or a new innovative programme. Problems of fund transfer and similar genuine ones can be tackled in a variety of ways, once the prejudice and underlying motives are given up.

## Educational Governance–District and Sub-District

### *(a) Role of PRIs/Urban Local Bodies*

The Commission had favoured increasingly important role of local bodies and closer community involvement but was clearly against their control over educational institutions and functionaries, particularly the teachers (Para 18.17). The NPE 1986 (as amended in 1992) also proclaims decentralization, autonomy of educational institutions, (para 10.1) people's involvement and association of non-governmental agencies and voluntary effort,(para 10.1) as the guiding principles of management of education. They have all been clubbed together as if there are no tensions or contradictions amongst them. Only the document, the Challenges of Education (1985), circulated by the Government of India for discussion before finalizing the NPE 1986, recognizes the likely resistance from those who stand to gain by the current centralized system of educational management.

The concept of de-centralization and its instrumentalities seems to have a very narrow focus on management and planning only, excluding the academic aspects like curriculum, pedagogy, evaluation, etc. It is ironic that while ideas like empowerment of teachers and schools, local specificity in teaching-learning material are accepted by progressive educationists and reflected in the NPE 1986, academic decentralization is kept out of bounds. I would favor inclusion of this in the decentralization framework.

There is considerable variation in the extent, nature and genuineness of the decentralization regime. As per the constitutional and statutory design, the three-tier Panchayati Raj Institutions do not have a hierarchical relationship, although administrative and financial arrangements have gradually evolved to project the hierarchical relationship. In this context the relative role of each tier in education, particularly in the management of educational institutions, has been a complex and thorny issue. Some states have given each tier powers relating to the three stages of schools—Primary schools to be managed by Village Panchayats, middle schools by intermediate Panchayats and Secondary and Higher Secondary schools by District Panchayats. A few have given the real authority and responsibility only to the district Panchayats, and the other two tiers are involved marginally in local committees. Some states have empowered the PRIs by transferring to them functions, funds and functionaries, while others have given them cosmetic roles and responsibilities.

While ideally, education should be effectively and fully transferred to the PRIs and useful local bodies and let them learn through governance; this can be achieved gradually by making them earn it with demonstration of capacity of good governance in the sectors already under their domain.

Their authority and nature of involvement can be to the extent each unit deserves it for which the criteria, to assess their capacity to be fair, transparent, open, accountable and socially committed, can be evolved. In this approach, flexible decentralization will acquire a constantly changing dynamic character in which the pattern of administration, management and governance in a Block or District will also keep on changing as the Local Bodies & Community get empowered or become mature, tested through a *maturity barometer*.

The most practical solution in the long run would be to fully delegate to the District Panchayats full authority and accountability in respect of totality of education including higher education, while the state should play a similar role vis-à-vis the Centre, (as education is in the concurrent list), in the division of power between the state and the Panchayats and local bodies. It can influence the education sector by state sponsored schemes, externally funded projects and broad policies and guidelines. In establishing this regime the states should give up the approach of uniformity. Decentralization to each District Panchayat or Urban Local Body can be in stages based on the maturity barometer. They will be assessed by the State Education Commission—a depoliticized body—to avoid political considerations and unreasonable discrimination between districts and local bodies. Thus at a point of time, in each state, different districts/local bodies will have different extent and nature of power and responsibility in education though in the long run—say 10 years—all districts/ Urban Local Bodies would have earned full autonomy and accountability in education.

Giving management of education to the PRIs and local bodies has the huge advantage of integration in planning and implementation of programmes of other development sectors, since they are now the main institution of development in the field. Both education and other development sectors can benefit if the school can be made the unit for community and development activities. An innovative idea is to have an additional faculty member in the school who plays the role of the multipurpose worker and is also a community educator. She can manage even the continuing education center, which can be located in the school. The narrow concept of adult education as literacy, which has become a travesty of education, can be transformed by integration of development concerns with continuing community education. Community empowerment should be the function of the school, education being the most critical empowering process.

### (b) District Boards of Education

Both the Kothari Commission and the 1986 NPE suggest the establishment of a District Board of Education. Their conceptualization is of an administrative body. The NPE wants it to manage education up to the higher secondary level. Naik continued to believe that in this regard the commission's proposals are on a sound footing and there is need to pursue them relentlessly. The Commission had also suggested its relationship with the then existing PRIs and local bodies. However, after the 73rd & 74th amendment of the Constitution, the whole issue requires reconsideration. If Boards have to be established, their relationship with the new constitution-mandated local bodies with jurisdiction in education will have to be delicately fine-tuned. One possible solution in this complex and uncertain scenario is to have a highly flexible pattern of decentralization in which in each Block or District, different pattern of governance may exist. The Central authority's desire, to have a uniform pattern to enable it to have a tight control, will have to be drastically curbed, or may have to be fully negated.

Another option is to establish District Boards of Education on the lines of the National and State Commission as powers are transferred to the PRIs/ Urban Local Bodies, on the basis of the maturity barometer so that the educational governance at district level is also depoliticized as in the case of State and National levels. Just as at those levels the powers, authority and functions are transferred to the commissions, at this level they will be transferred to the district boards constituted as federation of all the academic institutions and school complexes.

Under such an arrangement, the Education Commission's reservation about transferring the teachers' control to the district level will no longer be valid. The Commission's apprehension that locally elected representatives' control may degenerate into undue interference on local educationally irrelevant grounds adversely impacting on their performance will have no grounds because the District Board will be a depoliticized body.

The District Board can be given administrative as also academic and assessment responsibility so that the concept of decentralization becomes comprehensive enough as argued earlier. Such a concept of District Board has been an important suggestion while presenting multiple models of governance.

### (c) District Advisory Board of Education

A District Advisory Board of Education, federal in character, giving representation to not only the Block/Taluka/Mandal Panchayats, Urban local bodies but also the DIETS, BRCs, Universities, colleges, eminent educationists, private managements, other civil society educational and social organizations, lead banks, industries, media and other stake holders, should be established on the lines of the National and State Advisory Boards of Education as a think-tank at the District level.

It may function as the education-expert sub-committee of the District Planning Committee, a body created by the Constitution both to derive legitimacy and for integrated planning and development in the District.

### *(d) School Complex*

The Commission had greatly favoured the concept of school complex for sharing of resources, in-house academic support through integrating all stages of schools, administrative decentralization and ensuring accountability across stages. The NPE 1986 also hopes that *a developed system of school complexes will take over much of the inspection functions in due course* (10.7 of NPE). Like many other recommendations of the Commission, it did not receive the deserved attention for implementation. On the other hand, as a consequence of a project implemented in a state with the aid of a foreign donor agency, there has been a contrary trend of establishing cluster resource centre only for the schools of the same stage. The concept of School Clusters has very different premises and principles. This deviation has been brought about without synchronizing it with the School Complex concept. The rationale and philosophy behind this model is that peer group interaction is more effective, while in the School Complex model the apprehension is that the teachers of high and higher secondary schools may dominate and the hierarchical relationship will be counter-productive to teachers' continuing education. Experience shows that cluster resource centers have not proved to be useful for academic enrichment, since academic resource persons are not available. The coordinator of the centre is primarily performing administrative tasks, more specifically, collecting statistics, monthly reports and information.

School Complex has a tremendous advantage over the school cluster arrangement because of availability of resource persons in the form of secondary school teachers. The core values we considered non negotiable, once realized in the complex system, the question of hierarchy and inequality will not arise. It would also have all other advantages like resource sharing, etc., suggested by the Education Commission. An additional feature is that cluster approach can be incorporated within the complex system. Every complex, having several institutions of the same stage, can also have clusters enabling peer group interaction and experience sharing periodically. Also, it will enable enrichment with the help of resource persons and the whole complex—institutions of all stages can intermingle and interact adhering to the core values. Looking at the substantial advantages of the complex arrangement we suggest even expanding the concept to include institutions of higher education. A college can be the nucleus of secondary and higher secondary schools in its catchment area. Thus there will be full integration of all stages of education. We have used this concept of education complex in the various models of governance that follow.

### *(e) Community Involvement/Participation/Control*

Both Education Commission and NPE 1986 have strongly and passionately argued for community participation in education as indicated in (a) above. For some time now it has also been advocated by all planners and donor agencies.

Hence, community involvement has become a creed, though the instrumentalities in different states, like Village Education Committee, School Development & Monitoring Committee, and Parents-Teachers Associations vary considerably in the way they implement the creed.

The relationship between locally elected representatives and the teachers continues to be a contentious issue. A view favours their control while the other argues for teachers' autonomy and higher status in the community for higher motivation and morale.

The solution lies in the culture and core values we are advocating. After all the root of the contention is who is superior and who will control whom. Once equality and mutual respect becomes the plank of relationship—schools and teachers in close interaction with, in fact, as an integral part of the community—the distinction, the mutual suspicion, and desire to dominate no longer remain an issue. Hence, the school embedded in a community, rather than a grafted institution shall be the concept to be promoted.

To enable this, a school should become the nerve-centre of village development and community activities. Any apprehensions of such an approach shifting focus arise partly from the lack of adequate appreciation of the wider concept of education, partly from inability to appreciate the educational gains of development activities and are partly misplaced because the integrated and multi-stranded nature of village community is not fully understood.

Community involvement and participation should not be symbolic. Their active association requires proper mobilization and empowerment. I have already suggested else where that school should play a critical role in empowering the community for community development. Once empowered and aware they can meaningfully participate in the educational activities of the schools and the village. Such a participation should give adequate representation to all stakeholders especially to the deprived and socially discriminated groups, lest community participation becomes a mask for the control of school and education activities by the privileged to further their own interest and perpetuate the socio, political, economic stratification of the village. Such deprived groups have to be the major focus of the school in pursuing the empowering process.

## Multiple Models of Educational Governance

Adhering to the core values outlined above, diverse models of transformatory educational governance can be designed. They range from various kinds of reform of the current system to radically alternative paradigms—challenging the orthodox concepts of class room to the concept of university campus or the *school* itself, the most micro units of educational organization and governance. In presenting some of the paradigms inevitably discussion on pedagogical practices will creep in. I believe that organization and governance of education cannot neatly be separated from educational perspectives and pedagogies.

While a few models as illustrations are presented her, there can be many more if we carefully look at all these models, since their components are more like blocks. Blocks from different models can be combined to create many other models. Also, using only some of these blocks or not using any of them but only with absolutely new blocks not included in any of the models presented here, many more absolutely new and different models of governance of education and corresponding system of education can be conceived. We firmly believe in this multiplicity of creative diversity.

Since we believe in decentralized and dispersed authority structure, the multiple models can simultaneously be functional and operative in different parts of the country. After all, the national spirit and defining characteristic of India is the existence of and respect for plurality and diversity of cultures, languages, religions, ethnicity, etc.

### *Model 1: University Based Integrated Governance*

In order to move from fragmented to integrated and holistic education, and to de-bureaucratize, de-politicize and decentralize education, the universities can be brought center-stage. The narrow concept of universities being responsible only for higher education will have to be given up. Every state has many regional universities (with territorial jurisdiction to affiliate colleges) that should be responsible for pre-primary to higher education. Each will have to establish an education resource center, which can play the role of present day SCERT and Board of Secondary Education. These centers will be constantly taking up fundamental, applied and action research on comprehensive non-threatening, learning-supportive assessment, curriculum development, pedagogical issues and all the aspects of education. It will be an amalgam of the Academic Staff College, State Institute of Educational Planning and Administration, University Department of Education, SCERT, Board of Secondary Education, with responsibility for all facets of education and at all stages of education.

The DIETS and BRCs also will be re-conceptualized in this context. District Boards of Education and School Complexes/clusters will be the next link in the chain. They will be out-posts of the University performing in its area all the functions that University Education Resource Center would perform in its entire jurisdiction.

Schools and colleges will be managed as today, by the state & private trusts and societies or PRIs and local bodies

Appointment of key persons in the University will be by an all-party committee. Consistent with the principle of federalism, the University will have adequate representation of the federating units—School complexes, BRCs, and DIETS.

A variation can be the expansion of the concept of school complex into educational complexes in which colleges form the nucleus of the higher secondary schools. Such complexes may be only for academic & assessment aspects but also can have an organic relationship including the administration.

### *Model 2: PRI and Local Bodies Based*

This model can combine with the first, with only the conceptual shift that the Universities, under whose umbrella the entire education is organized, will be established by the PRIs and local bodies. Another option is that while universities may have the academic and assessment responsibility for all stages of education, the PRIs and local bodies establish, run and manage educational institutions, including affiliating colleges. The concept of educational complex—extended form of school complex concept—can still hold good. If colleges are excluded from the purview of the PRIs and local bodies the school complexes can be the main organizational formation, yet within the academic umbrella of the University. Further, if District Boards of Education are established, there can be partial delegation of academic and assessment functions to them, as determined by the Universities. Such an arrangement combines the merits of National and State curricular frameworks being implemented with the elements of local specificity brought in by the District Board under the overall supervision, support and guidance of the University.

This and the first mode are the only ones, which have the merit of fully integrating all stages of education under one umbrella. The fullest integration is achieved when academic assessment and administrative responsibility are vested with the University for the entire system. Entrusting assessment responsibility also can reduce the need for external public examination at Secondary and Higher Secondary level. It can be optional only for those who are not continuing further education and want certification. There can be greater emphasis on formative assessment, as a tool of learning. This model can also have some variations:

- The present system of Boards of Secondary Education may continue and the schools—with or without the school complex structure—can be managed by the PRIs & local bodies.

- District Boards of Education may be established for Academic and assessment functions, which may act as the decentralized outposts of the Boards of Secondary Education with the advantage of providing space for academic decentralization and autonomy to accommodate local specificity.
- Autonomy, accountability and cost effective administration through school complexes can be achieved if the authority and responsibility for schools of all stages vest only in the District or Block Panchayat.

### Model 3: Autonomous or Self Managing Educational Institutions

Educational institutions can be managed only by local managing committees. They will not have a superior authority in terms of administering them. There will be an MOU between the Autonomous Institution and the funding agency, the Government or its substitute the PRIs and local bodies, as to what are they expected to achieve, how their performance will be assessed, at what intervals and what will be the indicators. The institutions will follow the curriculum laid down by the appropriate authority, the University, Board of Secondary Education or District Board. An assessment team will visit at least at pre-determined intervals to assess the performance in a participatory manner, offer comments and, guidance for improvement. So long as the institution is performing in the manner and up to the standard agreed upon in the MOU, its autonomous status and funding will continue. Where expectations are not fully met, but the performance is within tolerance limit, guidance will be provided on the basis of which a plan of action to reach the expected level is made by the school. It is discussed and approved with appropriate modifications, mutually agreed. Its implementation is monitored and assisted by the Assessing Team. On successful implementation, the autonomous status continues. Failure can entail curtailment of autonomy. The Government/PRI/Local Bodies or appropriate authority takes up the responsibility to bring the school up to the standard and make it sustainable, hand over to another local group, identified at the time of take-over, so that they are participating in the process of developing the plan for improvement and acquire the capacity to sustain the process when the *authority* withdraws.

### Model 4: Fully Autonomous Experimental Institutions

I have come across a number of institutions, which have radical alternative philosophy and perspective on education. They organize learning on that basis, have their own curricula, attract children who do not fit into the mainstream schools or children of highly progressive parents who can afford to ignore the mainstream. They are idiosyncratic institutions, currently admired by some and viewed with suspicion by others. They should be given full space. They should have also academic and curricular autonomy. The *Academic authority* should discuss with them their perspective and approach and approve them within its umbrella as autonomous schools or colleges; continue certification following the mutually agreed assessment process. In the long run they will be emulated by other institutions, with their assistance or on their own. Alternatively, they can continue to be institutions to watch with interest, awaiting their ability to demonstrate the success of their approach. Meanwhile, their experiment can go on with such modifications, as experience necessitates, until they finally succeed or give up.

Mainstream can benefit from such experimental institutions, if they are given space as suggested instead of being considered an outcast. To enable transferability to mainstream equivalence can be established.

### Model 5: The Pyramid Reversed

The Government education system is gigantic in size, hierarchical in nature and authority—driven in culture. Ideals of democratic leadership, management styles and spirit either do not work or work for short spans of time in small segments, which are wiped off sooner than later in the avalanche of the systematic flow, pressure and overpowering impact of the status-quo.

In this context, any of the models of autonomy visualized and presented here will require reversal of the pyramid and concomitant changes in the culture of functioning to be effective. Let me present some outline of the new picture that should emerge and become the order of the day.

The teacher should be fully accountable to perform which will be judged by the achievement of the objective of at least 85 to 90 per cent of the children achieving the prescribed package of learning or its equivalent in all the competencies, concepts and domain knowledge areas by following child-centric, activity-based, challenge-providing and joyful pedagogy.

She, therefore, will be responsible not only for the final achievement but also for the processes followed, as they are critical in the all round development of the personality of a child. Although current testing does not test the processes and focuses on achievement alone, testing techniques and methodologies can be changed to assess the extent to which the desired processes have been followed by the teacher.

In this manner, the teacher can be made squarely accountable if she is allowed the autonomy that we have argued for. There is a further condition of the reversal of the pyramid—an expression that requires elaboration. It is being elaborated by way of illustration in the current state-run school system. It is however, applicable *mutatis mutandis* to any pyramid-like centralized system, that exist or that we have suggested in the various models.

In the current system, the entire educational bureaucracy bosses over the teacher. Even the academic resource institutions like the CRC, BRC, DIET or Academic Staff College have a relationship of being superior to a teacher. This is what has to be reversed if the teacher has to be made accountable.

For the kind of precise performance of the teacher outlined above, certain minimum conditions have to be met by the educational administration and the academic support system.

If the conditions are not fulfilled the administrator or the academic institution/person with the necessary authority and responsibility should be held accountable and punished. The autonomous and accountable teacher should have the right to demand from appropriate officials, fulfillment of the unfulfilled conditions after she has made the best possible efforts to surmount such deficiencies through creativity improvisation and community support. The annual performance appraisal of those officials should be made by the teachers functioning in their official jurisdiction, who at the end of the year will indicate how many conditions have been fulfilled, how promptly and in what manner and how many remain unfulfilled, *despite demands*. This should be treated as the assessment of the officials' work by the teachers and should lead to appropriate risks and rewards for the official.

When all conditions are met, the teacher would be held squarely responsible. Whenever conditions are not met, the concerned defaulter will be accountable. In this manner an autonomous and accountable system of education will become a reality.

### Model 6: A Transparent Accountable System Promoting Plurality

Education has become a matter of faith like religion and, therefore, beyond questioning, critical reflection and rational scrutiny. Even most of those, who are very keen and eager to send their children to educational institutions, adhere to the *new religion* and very few critically reflect on the philosophy/ vision and processes of the institution where they are sending their children, although every teacher or institution has a view of education whether articulated or not.

This has to change. Education has to be transparent. This will mean full open disclosure of their perspective on the following which are essential components of any educational practice by every institution—whether a school, a college, a board or a university:

1. Vision of the society for which their educational package is designed.
2. A clear social, political and economic philosophy on which their vision of the society is based.
3. Their model of human being? This will include their understanding of:

(i) the innate (inherent) nature of human beings
(ii) the respective roles of genes (heredity) and environment (nurture) and
(iii) the kind and domains of knowledge, values, attitudes, abilities and personality characteristics they propose to develop in the children to evolve into their model of human being.

4. Their understanding of and approach to child development.
5. Their understanding of the role of different agencies in the development of the child.
6. What do they mean by education?
7. Goals and objectives of education including prioritization and relative weightages to clarify which of them will get higher focus in actual practice and in case of conflict amongst objectives which will be preferred and which will be marginalized.
8. Their perspective and understanding on the processes of learning.
9. Their image of the learner, her potentials and limitations (if any).
10. Role of adults, teachers, parents, peer group community and others like media in learning.
11. Their views on the nature, character and structure of knowledge, acquisition of knowledge, relationship of knowledge, learning and real life.
12. How non-cognitive, psycho-social abilities and other personality dimensions and characteristics will be developed?
13. Their organizational culture including its cherished values.
14. Their philosophy, understanding, objectives and processes of assessment
15. How will they satisfy the children, parents and the community that their professed goals and aims of education are being achieved?
16. Their beliefs on, and modalities of, ensuring their own accountability to the learners, parents and the society at large.

*Mōnitoring By Parents:* The parents will have the right to periodically monitor and asses the holistic progress of their children and the contribution of the institution in it. The school will have to devise methods and mechanisms, whereby parents can assess the progress of the student and intimate their comments including level of satisfaction and dissatisfaction along with suggestion for future improvement to be undertaken by the school.

### *Model 7: Challenging Institutional Structure Learner-Centric*

Today education is institutionalized. Institutionalization anywhere is accompanied by, routinization and rigidities—both sworn enemies of creativity. Further, when the institutions are meant for large numbers, they tend to be management-centric, not purpose-focused. Organizational dynamics overtakes the paramountcy of the objectives. Only amorphous masses, not individuals can be seen through the prism of a macro-organization.

Educational institutional structures are management-centric, not learner-centric. In order to engage with a large number of children, it adopts principles, tenets, processes that are based on the faulty assumption that education of a learner wholly depends upon the system and the institution. Therefore, it dominates issues, dictates and brings into being a highly rigid framework, irrespective of its impact on learning and despite it being counterproductive to the principal objectives for which it has been set up. The educational system ought to be learner-centric. This will imply challenging the basic principles, procedures and beliefs which constitute the foundation of the current system. Let us question some of the basic tenets and look at alternatives.

## Withering Away of Administrative Structures

The systems of educational complexes, school complexes, university-based integrated governance, functioning through task forces, non-transferable institution-based recruitment, self-managing autonomous institutions requiring only periodic visits to ensure proper exercise of autonomy and transparency, which can be accomplished through task forces and social audit can make the administrative offices at Block and District levels redundant. There are also many functions, which can be out-sourced. Taking the list of functions performed by each administrative office, it can be shown how they can be made to wither away.

Where they have to exist in a limited way, they can be de-bureaucratized by developing the democratic culture, radical change in the recruitment, induction training and orientation procedures, as elaborated earlier.

## Flexible Learner-Centered Education System

All behavioral scientists agree that individuals differ in their interests, pace, process, style and focus of learning and all these vary over space and many other factors that constitute the totality of the context of the learner as also of the learning situation. Despite this, the organized system of education is uniform and rigid in almost all of its dimensions. This mismatch between the needs and demands of flexibility of the individual learner and a rigid system created for all, hinders the growth, development and self-fulfillment of the learners, instead of facilitating it.

A learner-centered arrangement will have to be totally flexible, and have to abandon the current basic features. If we examine these features dispassionately, scientifically, and completely free from the beliefs and stereotypes deeply stamped on us by the system, (we are ourselves a product of the system) they appear arbitrary out-dated and completely out of tune with the latest research and knowledge of learning, education and human development.

The concept of Open University and Open School had the potential of presenting a model of flexible institutions. However, while providing some openness, most of them continue to be management-centric and closed (rigid) in many respects. They have neither fundamentally questioned all the rigidities, defects and maladies of the present systems nor have they attempted to explore alternatives.

Genuine learner-centric and flexible education will not have a fixed academic year, attendance requirement, fixed minimum duration for each course, boundaries of disciplines and faculties or fixed campus. Admission and assessment will be as per individual learner's convenience. The concept of a class itself is redundant. The teachers will be available in their chambers to the learners who seek their facilitation and guidance which can be of any duration and size depending upon the issue and the number of students seeking support of the teachers on such an issue.

Libraries, internets, peer discussions will be as much methods and tools of learning as seeking support of a teacher. It does not mean that a teacher will be inactive or free. She will have to continuously study, research, design numerous projects, assignments, tasks, that the students have to complete for obtaining certain credits and certification.

Project or Group assignment mode of learning will develop social skills, team spirit, leadership qualities, desirable personality characteristics and knowledge, breaking the artificial boundaries of departments and faculties.

In such an arrangement, stereotype of campus also will wither away. Whenever and wherever the students come together to learn and accredited teachers are available to provide guidance, it would be a campus. In that sense there will be as many campuses as the locations of teachers and knowledge seeking students.

A flexible, transparent education system will clearly articulate its own philosophy, perspective, and strategies on all aspects of education mentioned above and open the gates of affiliation or association to only those who subscribe to the same philosophy and approach because it believes that different views and methodologies deserve space for demonstrating their utility and effectiveness and that the students and parents should have the opportunity of informed choice and decision making. Such an approach will make the whole society engaged with all major issues of education. It will be in clear contrast with the present when both the students and parents choose an institution almost blindly or at the best on the basis of reputation which, in turn, depends upon its ability to enable students to secure high marks in the examination or obtain employment with fat salaries. Other higher objectives of education like developing a fine sensitive human being, who believes in a just, equitable and humane society gets totally neglected.

There will be an educationally aware and vibrant society where education is not left, to the whims and fancies of the few who happen to be in a position of authority and whose philosophy, views and approach prevail over equally valid diverse philosophies, views and approaches.

Since this system promotes multiple paradigms of education there will be widely diverse curricula, teaching-learning material, pedagogies and assessment procedures with the only condition that the basic principles of flexibility and transparency must be adhered to.

The extent of achievement of the declared objectives of education will be assessed, not just bits of information or knowledge relating to the specific disciplines. The written mode will be supplemented by other modes like assignments to be completed in a library or in the field or a particular task achieved in a real life situation. Even when written mode is used, the scripts will be valued by the student herself, then by the peer group, and finally, by the teachers and the combined evaluation will hold good. Writing of the script will be un-supervised. The nature of questions framed can exclude copying from books and other examinees since they will require reflection and signature of each individual's persona. Assessment will not be converted into meaningless numerical scores but will be elaborately communicative of the strengths and weaknesses of the student in respect of each objective of the course.

## Flexible Learning Centres

The mushrooming coaching institutions and their popularity provide an indication of the way in which education system can be deinstitutionalized with considerable autonomy and flexibility. In coaching classes, the teachers' accountability is directed towards the students and their income is also directly dependent upon her success as a coach, upon the reputation she/he can build and maintain. The autonomy of a competent coach is not interfered with, restrained or restructured by any external agency so long as the students are keen to join and pay for being coached by her, which is so long as she delivers.

Based on the highly accountable flexible and autonomous system of coaching that has come into existence to fulfill a felt need, let us explore alternative models, which have built in flexible autonomy and accountability.

There should be a system of licensing to work as a teacher, just like medical practitioners. The kind of qualifications, experiences, skills and knowledge that a person should possess as a perquisite for becoming a teaching practitioner will have to be substantially different from what they are today.

### *Private Teaching Practioner*

A licensed teacher should have a system to offer her expertise like a private medical practitioner at a place of her choice. Students and parents should have the options to choose any learning place set up by the teacher for any subject or aspect of learning. They can choose to be members of different learning groups for different aspects of learning. Teachers can also have their own fixed timings for different individuals or groups of students depending upon their assessment of the need based educational package required by a student or a group. The parents and learners should be able to access support of a recognized consultant for exercising their choice.

### *Poly Learning Centres*

A variation of this model can be based on the model of polyclinics where an entrepreneur sets up a place that facilitates many specialists to come and practice. Each one of them is independent. Inter-relationships among them are not formalized or institutionalized but may or may not grow depending upon the synergy amongst them. Students and parents will have the option to utilize the expertise of the licensed teacher working in a Poly-learning center. They can choose one or some of the specialists for some aspects and for others they may go to a different poly-learning center.

### *Education Homes*

A third variant of this can be modeled on the pattern of establishment of Education Homes like Nursing Homes, where many teachers come together to work as a part of an organic unit. One may call them schools or colleges or universities. However, to signify the in-built flexibility of the proposed system, they may be better called Education Homes. However, even in such an arrangement, the students and parents will have the option to use some of the facilities and services of one or some specialist of an Education Home and for other requirements go to another Education Home or a poly-learning center or even another formal school or college or university, which will have to adopt this pattern to survive in the proposed scenario.

## Institutionalized Flexible Learning System

A formal institution will have to transform itself if it has to survive by ensuring autonomy and accountability of the teacher in the manner similar to the poly-learning centres or Education Homes.

Many different arrangements are possible. Some of them are:

(a) Teachers may form a cooperative society, or a similar registered legally recognized body and jointly run the institution and be jointly responsible for the institution as a whole but each one of them will have the freedom to organize the activities relating to her domain and to offer her services in the manner she considers best.

(b) A senior teacher may establish an institution and choose her own colleagues so long as they are also willing to accept her as head teacher, share her vision and philosophy and work with her. Then it will become an integrated institution where the Head Master is accountable to the students while the teachers are accountable both to the students and the Head Master.

(c) The Government, PRIs and civil society organizations can also establish institutions with the aforesaid flexibilities built in. It can be on the poly-clinic model as a poly learning center or can be an institution where only the Head is appointed by the government and is accountable to the government and the students. The team of teachers will be selected by the Head based on her contacts, confidence and trust, but she along with her team will continue only so long as she performs and enjoys the confidence of the students and parents.

(d) Another variant may be in the form of appointment of the teachers by the management where the Head's position is rotated. The accountability will rest with the teachers, who will have the autonomy to organize teaching-learning and other areas of specialty in the manner they like. Non-performance will entail a group censor and finally separation from the group resulting in instability and unemployment.

(e) Another variant may provide for election of the Head by the teachers following electoral processes with adequate safeguards to avoid politicking.

(f) Formal institutions somewhat akin to the existing ones may also continue to be run by government PRIs or other private bodies where the option to the students and parents to join a part/subject/activity is available.

## Adaptation for Free Education

These alternatives are straightway feasible for the higher and secondary education. Elementary education that has to be free and compulsory can also adopt this model, provided innovative ways of paying teachers is worked out making education free for the child. This can be achieved by designing a National Elementary Education Scheme, on the lines of national health scheme of the U.K. and Scandinavian countries. The teachers, in that case will be paid, as the General Practitioner, in the National Health Scheme of the U.K. is paid, based on some criteria like the number of students enrolled with and requiring special support. This approach can be extended to all the stages of education the State decides to make free.

## Ray of Hope

Rethinking educational governance in order to revisit the Education Commission with eyes focused on social transformation necessitates challenging boundaries. The entire vast expanse of education then looks like a limitless phenomenon, inextricably merging with the society, culture its values, structures, processes and the larger goals—the Utopia every thinking society seeks to move towards. Their relationships then can be visualized afresh and feasible pathways can be charted. Such an attempt in this paper—though with limitations of the Kothari Commission being the stimulation—leads us to believe that it is possible to develop a blueprint for an educational revolution—as so passionately desired by the Commission, which will initiate peaceful multiple processes, for social transformation. Some faint leads to such an educational revolution can be discerned in this paper, which encourages me to conclude that another concerted effort by a large number of socially and educationally committed thinkers, rooted on the ground and realities but eyes fixed on the sky can present a fresh vision and agenda before this country for intense debate and dialogue so that education moves away from the domain and preserve of a few experts to the people, who then can adopt their own educational constitution which may truly in words and spirit start with: "We the people of India hereby adopt and give to ourselves......"

## References

Department of Education, (1966). *Education and National Development 1964-66,* Government of India.

Department of Education, (1985). *Challenges of Education,* New Delhi, Ministry of Human Resource and Development, Government of India, New Delhi.

Department of Education, (1986). *National Policy on Education 1986,* New Delhi, Ministry of Human Resource and Development, Government of India.

Department of Education, (1992). *National Policy on Education, Programme of Action, 1992* New Delhi, Ministry of Human Resource and Development, Government of India.

Naik, J.P. (1997). *The Education Commission and After*. New Delhi: APH Publishing House.

# 17

# Autonomy, Privatization and Commercialization in Higher Education

MADHU PRASAD

## Introduction

The concept of autonomy plays a central role in issues relating to theory, practice and policy-making in the field of higher education. It evokes strong responses as a "desirable" value within academia, and the need for an in-depth examination of the concept cannot be underestimated.

This study focuses on the notion of autonomy endorsed by the report of the Kothari Commission[1] and views it as being representative of a significantly democratic phase in the history of policy-making for higher education in India, following the unmaking of colonial empires in Asia and Africa. The Commission's report identifies autonomy not only as being expressive of, but also as being the enabling condition for, independent inquiry and self-development. Consequently, a concomitant political and financial responsibility on the part of the state forms an integral part of this conception.

However, a more recent conception of autonomy, which has been favourably received by policy-makers and some sections of the academic community, sees the financial autonomy of institutions, subjected only to market regulation, as the sole sustainable means for achieving academic autonomy with efficiency and accountability. The present study argues that it cannot be assumed that such a financial "autonomy" of institutions would necessarily promote academic autonomy, as markets are also institutions with in-built preferences and functional norms. Further, financial autonomy, which is undoubtedly an important component of autonomy in higher education, can also be effectively exercised through public funding, i.e. independently of market pressures. This independence is viewed as being necessary for providing the space within which academic goals can be adequately articulated and pursued. Finally, the issue of accountability is examined with reference to the divergent norms and values associated with the differing conceptions of autonomy in higher education.

The distance between the two concepts of autonomy outlined above is elaborated and enriched by drawing upon the experience of different countries and varied systems of higher education. In conclusion, the study commends the relative merits of the concept proposed in the Kothari Commission's report, and argues for its continuing relevance to a necessary national debate on the future of higher education in India.

## Historical Perspective

The Radhakrishnan Commission on Higher Education (1948-49)[2] identified many evils present in our universities, as arising from the fact that they had "no real autonomy whatever, and have proved incapable of resisting pressure from outside." It asserted that while "universities should be sensitive to enlightened public opinion, they should never let themselves be bullied or bribed into actions that they know to be educationally unsound or worse still, motivated by nepotism, faction and corruption." At the same time, the Commission also recommended that university education be placed in the concurrent list of matters within the purview of the central government, as a national guarantee of minimum standards of efficiency and the interchanges necessary and desirable between universities, made it impossible for higher education to remain a purely "provincial subject". Faced with the possibility of friction between the above requirements, the Commission's report proposed that the autonomy of institutions of higher learning be protected by creating "the best possible constitution, securing among other things the inclusion, of wisely chosen external members of its governing body and then to leave it free from interference" (p. 406).

The Kothari Commission report displayed a remarkable awareness of the risk posed to academic freedom by organizational structures that were not adequate to its requirements and goals. Observing that principles of administration or governance (clear chain of responsibility, delegation of function and authority, economy and efficiency) only appeared to be common to all good organizations, it emphasized that the specific nature of the concerned activities would determine how and through what measures these would be achieved in particular fields. "The character of a university as a society of teachers and students engaged in the pursuit of learning and discovery, distinguishes fundamentally the regulation of its affairs from, say, the profit-motivated management of commercial or industrial concerns or the administration of a government department or municipal corporation, or a unit of the armed forces.... Rules, regulations and techniques that hamper the achievement of the real purposes of the university should be modified or scrapped—they should not be allowed to become strait-jackets into which all university activities must be fitted" (p. 299).

The Commission's portrayal of a university as a "society" highlights the *shared* goals of the teachers and students, who constitute the academic community. Drawing an important distinction between institutional autonomy and academic freedom, the Kothari Commission clarified that teachers and students must have the freedom "to hold and express their views, however radical, within the classroom (and outside) provided they are careful to present the different aspects of a problem without confusing teaching with 'propaganda'." Advocating that "we would like to see teachers practice more of it (autonomy) and vigorously", the Commission recommended that a teacher (or student) "should receive all facilities and encouragement in his work, teaching and research, even when his views and approach be in opposition to those of his seniors and the head of his department or faculty" (p. 300).

This perspective continues to inform contemporary analyses to a significant extent. Educational pursuits, it has been agued, require "adoption of the procedural principle.... The conditions for the development of self-determination are the same as the conditions for its exercise. In education, this means the creation of free associations of people in learning communities".[3] An empirical study of faculty perceptions conducted in U.S. institutions over a three-year period, found that "self-regulation" among professionals was associated with high levels of performance. "Autonomy appears to contribute to higher-order needs for achievement and accomplishment."[4]

The Kothari Commission identified three overlapping levels of autonomy to promote, facilitate and protect academic autonomy:

- Within the university—autonomy of departments and colleges, and of the teachers and students working in them;
- Of the university within the system of higher education—independence from administrative and financial institutions, e.g. the Ministry and the University Grants Commission (UGC);
- Of the system of higher education as a whole in relation to other agencies/influences—this would involve autonomy from (i) political and market forces, such as Governments (both central and state) on the one hand, and corporate and commercial interests on the other; and (ii) religious institutions, and discriminatory socio-cultural tendencies e.g. casteism, communalism, racism, cultural hegemony and gender prejudice.

The necessity for evolving "attitudes and conventions which will do justice" to issues of autonomy and the "valid claims of society", at all levels was emphasized so as to handle these complex issues "with great skill and imagination" (p. 302).

The Commission's report contended that the claim for autonomy was not advanced as a "privilege", but on the grounds that it was the precedent condition for the discharge of their duties by the academic community. Autonomy for institutions of higher education, if based on the freedom and involvement of their constituent elements, was envisaged as the *enabling condition* for achieving their true aims. Only under conditions where such freedom was guaranteed to academicians, could institutions of higher education—*whether autonomous or affiliated, state-funded or privately financed*—be expected to contribute to strengthening habits of independent thinking.

Prof. Kothari had earlier headed the Committee on Model Act for Universities, (1961)[5]. The issue of autonomy was even more definitively addressed in its report: "the proper functioning of a university depends on the all-round acceptance of two basic principles...*autonomy for universities from external controls together with a democratic administrative system*, and *effective participation of the academic community in the formation and implementation of university policy and programmes*.... If such a community (teachers and students) is to discharge its duties to itself and to the nation, its governance of the university must essentially be in its own hands. The teachers should have in practice an effective voice in the determination of the policies and the management of the affairs of the university; their participation should be real and meaningful and not merely formal and constitutional" (p. 8).

The priority given by the Kothari Commission to the capacity for independent thought as the proper end of higher education is significant. It draws attention to the fact that the academic community constitutes an important section within the wider society, a section that is *trained* to reflect upon and critically respond to the latter. "The University is an autonomous institution at the heart of societies."[6] The concept of academic autonomy derives its strength and legitimacy from the nature of academic activity, and the Commission recognized that the creation of an environment that encouraged innovation and dissent was central to promoting intellectual dynamism. Consensus, which facilitated standardization of methods and processes resulting in attainment of competence, was certainly not underestimated, but it seemed clear that activities of understanding and learning required an independence that created space for a critical examination of prevalent ideas and values. The social responsibility and relevance of the academic community and of higher education for society was seen as resting firmly on this foundation. The perception of higher education as a public good also formed the basis of its relationship with the state. Institutions of higher education were to remain sufficiently responsive to societal needs to sustain official support, yet they were to be sufficiently protected against external pressures to safeguard their societal critique.

In the decades prior to India's independence and up to the late 1970's, opinion among academicians and policy-makers appeared to be fairly harmonized on questions of the importance of higher education and of the direction that should be given to its institutions. Higher education was seen as a vehicle for preferred social values, and the aspiration towards a democratically unified polity and society was unambiguously expressed in educational policy. "The function of the universities is not only to preserve, disseminate and advance knowledge but to furnish intellectual leadership and moral tone to society."[7] However, pluralism, not uniformity, was its basic premise. Pluralism encouraged a view of autonomy in which the preferred values advanced the awareness among the academic community that, "some, at least of the values on which their society is based, are properly open to questioning and that they have some responsibility for choosing which values they adopt."[8] Delivering the Convocation Address at the Allahabad University in 1946, Jawaharlal Nehru had reposed confidence in a similar approach: "A University stands for humanism, for tolerance, for reason, for progress, for the adventure of ideas and for the search for truth.... If the universities discharge their duty adequately, then, it is well with the nation and the people." The report of the Committee on Model Act for Universities (1961) underlined the fact that, "an autonomous university may not always achieve these ideals; but it is certain that a university, which is not autonomous, is hardly likely ever to achieve these great objectives" (p. 8).

The Kothari Commission Report remains the nation's most comprehensive articulation of an independent educational vision and policy. Within the structural framework it advocated, democratizing the structures of internal governance was coupled with an increased responsibility on the part of the University Grants Commission (UGC) to support and strengthen university autonomy precisely, as the *quantum of public funding* of the system of higher education *increased*. The Committee on Model Act for Universities (1961) had already called for an examination, by the UGC or an appropriate agency, of grant-in-aid codes operating in different states, "so that these may not only be liberalized, but brought into some uniform pattern for the whole country. A liberal system of grant-in-aid will make it easier to check questionable methods of raising funds that are sometimes adopted by some institutions" (p. 30). Further, in order to attract and encourage competent faculty across different types of institutions, it strongly recommended removing undue hierarchies so that "the 'gap' in conditions of service (including salary scales) of teachers (with similar qualifications) in the affiliated colleges and the university departments should be reduced". The Report of the Gajendragadkar Committee (1971)[9] reiterated this demand. It also recommended student participation in academic and administrative decision-making to further enhance the "sense of belonging" within the academic community, and favoured autonomy both within the university and in relation to external agencies.

The *Preamble of the Lima Declaration (1988) on Academic Freedom and Autonomy of Institutions*,[10] marking the 40th anniversary of the Universal Declaration of Human Rights, endorsed a perspective and concerns similar to those of the policy for higher education evolved in India after Independence. It emphasized the significance of differentiating between the social goals of education and of the market, and the responsibility of the State in ensuring this condition. The *Preamble* asserted that "academic communities have an obligation to pursue the fulfillment of economic, social, cultural, civil and political rights of the people", and that the right to education is a prerequisite for the enjoyment of all other human rights, which can only be "fully enjoyed in an atmosphere of academic freedom and autonomy of institutions of higher education". Recognizing the essential vulnerability of the academic community to political and economic pressures, it affirmed that every human being has the right to an education that "shall enable all persons to participate effectively in the construction of a free and egalitarian society, and promote understanding, tolerance and friendship among all nations and all racial, ethnic or religious groups. Education shall promote mutual understanding respect and equality between men and women...and contribute to the achievement of the major goals of contemporary society such as social equality, peace, equal development of all nations and the protection of the environment". Consequently, it identified the primary responsibility of the state to act as guarantor of the right to education without discrimination of race, colour, sex, language, religious, political or other opinion, national or social origin, economic condition, birth or other status. "Every State should make available an adequate proportion of its national income to ensure in practice the full realization of the right to education."

## The Spirit of Liberal Inquiry

Autonomy is a term commonly associated with the higher levels of education but, as a vital component of the learning process, it should characterize all stages of the system, including the elementary and the secondary, if it is to bear fruit at higher stages of learning. "Education is not a discipline imposed from above on an apathetic if acquiescent nature.... All true development is self-development."[11] Independent thinking cannot be induced at the university level, if curiosity and questioning have been stifled at school. This is commonly recognized in theory and policy, even when it is not implemented in practice. However, what is frequently underestimated is the contribution made to this process by providing access to quality education for *all* children of school-going age.[12] The heterogeneous composition of a student body poses a pedagogical challenge that does not lend itself to resolution by "memorize and recall" modes of learning. This is a problem faced not only by "alternate" sub-standard schools for the under-privileged, but one that even 'elite' institutions, carefully selecting students to preserve a homogeneity of social character and learning skills, are usually unable to overcome. The far-reaching ramifications of this debate are, of course, beyond the scope of this paper, but the importance of an interactive linking between the notions of autonomy and equality deserves to be acknowledged. The idea of "equality" is thereby spared the pedagogical discredit of being equated with uniformity, and "autonomy" can be seen to constitute an intrinsic aspect of processes of social transformation that are effectively initiated at all stages through the education system. The grounds for sustaining a strong social consensus in support of higher education as a public good are thus easily established.

Education cannot be divorced from the needs and requirements of social beings, by segregating the theoretical from the practical, or the academic from the vocational. All education involves the acquisition of skills, but it must simultaneously enable the fullest development of the personality in preparation for living a responsible life in a society that encourages freedom of choice. "Liberal education is preparation for the student for independent thinking, for critical inquiry and appraisal, and for creative and constructive thought and action. Liberal education does not call for separate institutions, nor always for separate teaching programmes. The spirit of liberal inquiry should inspire all teaching."[13] Education has to simultaneously encourage competence and critical thinking. The compartmentalization of learning activities into the rational-critical, encouraging an independent choice of goals and questioning of ethical and social values, on the one hand, and the vocational, on the other, appears plausible only when "education" itself is narrowly defined as the preserve of well-heeled elites. In fact, the one cannot be opposed to the other without defeating the point of what is understood by the term *educating* oneself. "Self-determination" has been identified "as the fundamental educational aim.... which is consistent with contemporary theory of human development and knowledge about the conditions for optimal learning". [14]

## Publicly Funded Institutions vs 'Entrepreneurial Universities'

It is clear from the range of issues raised above that questions relating to autonomy—of persons, disciplines, procedures and institutions—in higher education, cannot be properly addressed unless they are articulated systematically. A selective approach, focused upon current expediency, may end up doing more harm than good. In particular, the prevailing emphasis on promoting financial autonomy of higher education institutions as a means of effecting cost efficiency, given dwindling public funds for deployment in this sector, is a doubtful strategy. The main provider of public funds, the state, is increasingly unwilling or unable to provide the resources needed for an expanding higher education sector.[15] Higher education is being privatized at a great pace but in a chaotic, ad hoc fashion with no real conviction as to the purpose and conditions of this process. The issue is closely linked with the increasing dominance of a changed perception of what constitutes "public interest", and hence, of the social structures and relationships that defend it. For, if we recognize that the performance of the public sector has a high degree of specificity, and is guided by a primary reference to social concerns, then it should lead to the acknowledgement that *different standards*, other than those applicable to corporate interests, must be employed to assess efficiency in the provision of public services. The failure to do so, underestimates the social and political consequences of allowing public services to deteriorate and decline.

In a Memorial submitted to the Education Commission (1882), Jyotiba Phule had argued that government financing of higher education, *under circumstances where the masses were left in ignorance and poverty,* "tended to educate Brahmins and the higher classes only".[16] A hundred and twenty-five years later, the fundamental weakness has still not been remedied. The passage of legislation making nine years of schooling a fundamental right for all children notwithstanding, prevarication over the Right to Education Bill, (currently suspended somewhere between being an actual and a "model" bill that the central government wants to be rid off, but state governments have neither the finances nor the will to take off its hands), offers little hope unless a widespread social movement can be launched. However, the argument that only privileged groups have benefited from higher education is disingenuously offered today to advocate privatization and withdrawal of the state from this sector. A related line of reasoning claims that since the benefits of higher education, unlike those of primary and secondary education, accrue largely to individuals who receive it, there is little justification for burdening the taxpayer with the cost of providing it. Higher education should become financially "autonomous", although provision can be made for loans and scholarships for talented students from the weaker sections. This approach confuses the symptom with the cause—elites dominate the publicly funded system of higher education, when there is a failure to universalize quality elementary and secondary education—and then recommends a solution that would further aggravate the problem by *commercializing* higher education.

In recent years, higher education has been subjected to a barrage of research, proposals and mandates urging structural change. "There is a concerted effort in many countries to reduce the reliance on state funding and move towards market-friendly reforms."[17] "Policy prescriptions, particularly from the World Bank, have argued against the expansion of higher education.... Many developing countries have showed apathy towards higher education, deliberately ignored it, reduced public investments in it, allowed laissez-faireism, and even adopted policies towards marketization of higher education."[18] "There is a widely-held view that the days of public-funding of higher education are over. Many governments see education expenditure as a drain on the public purse, rather than an investment. Institutions like the World Bank make no secret of their view that the best way to fund education is to put the whole cost on students....*They concede that the likelihood of such a policy being implemented is 'very distant'. However, the prevalence of such views at a time when public finances are under strain could condemn state-funded education to death by a thousand cuts under the guise of promoting 'alternative funding sources'*."[19] With the intrusion of values of the marketplace into the higher education sector, it seems justified that users should pay for this "service" as they would for any other. The pursuit of knowledge becomes a commercial transaction, and universities and other postsecondary institutions are expected to think less like educational institutions and more like businesses in order to generate their own funding.

In Asian countries, and the campaign has intensified in India over the past fifteen years, the basic thrust has been that governments can no longer be relied upon to solely or even substantially finance this sector because the demand for its expansion exerts an unviable pressure on budgetary resources. Hence, the argument that institutions of higher education require to become "autonomous", i.e. financially independent of public funding, and increasingly, of state regulation. It is often assumed that other aspects of autonomy would follow automatically from this step and the assumption that institutional autonomy is coupled with faculty autonomy has been promoted as the basis of the "revolution in academics".[20] However, although financial *independence* is an important component of the "key element of academic freedom", the *autonomy of institutions from public funding*, with which it has frequently been confused, has been demonstrated to count for little by itself. Such autonomy, "depending on how autonomy regulations are set up and administered, may actually be used to diminish academic freedom".[21] Studies relating to the British experience have indicated a de-coupling of institutional and faculty autonomy. "As institutions, universities are more autonomous; their academic members are increasingly less able to direct their working lives."[22] The submission of the All India Federation of University and College Teachers Organization, contained in the report of the Acharya Ramamurti Committee (1990)[23], had also noted how the undemocratic character of decision-making within the universities, "allied to...the problem of Autonomous Colleges...have played havoc with higher education in a number of states" (p. 4). In Taiwan, the repeal of martial law in 1987 led to student and faculty movements for autonomy. However, despite the favourable circumstances, the revised University Act of 1994, which decentralized curricula design, financial flexibility and powers for relocation of funds, "did not specify which roles and responsibilities accrue to faculty members and which are within the domain of administrators....(Relations were) uniquely defined on each campus."[24]

The culture engendered by increasing commercialization radically alters the character of institutions of higher education. In the first instance, they are geared to cater to the private needs, mainly vocational and monetary, of the students, but as the process advances, the "mission" of the system of education itself becomes serving the vested interests of clients and owners. There is a failure to take into account the significant social contribution made by higher education to important sectors like elementary and secondary education, the medical services, the development of democratic consciousness, etc. The current crisis in systems of education and public health, triggered by an acute shortage of teachers and nurses, in some of the developed countries is instructive for understanding how distortions occur in the provision of socially significant services when there is a decline in the "market-value" of the professions that feed them. "Now with privatization, all these functions are being replaced by financial motives, such as financial efficiency, measured in terms of revenue generation. In short, the emerging higher education system can be summed up as a transformation of academic institutions into "entrepreneurial universities" and "commercial institutions", whose single most important objective seems to be mobilization of more resources."[25]

Experience over a wide range of countries has revealed a similar pattern. "Efficiency in operation implies reduction of cost of production", with the end result, according to an assessment based on the impact of the Norwegian university reforms process, that higher education itself is being perceived as "a producer of graduates and research outputs".[26] An analysis of the reforms process in Canada not only reaches similar conclusions, but also marks out the phases through which it has proceeded.[27] Universities are not simply undergoing a technological transformation because of the new "knowledge-based" industries (space, electronics, computers, materials, telecommunications, and bioengineering) and the attention focused on them as the chief source of the new intellectual capital. With the identification of the campus as a significant site of capital accumulation, there has been a major change in social perception that has allowed the systematic conversion of intellectual activity into intellectual property. The transformation has occurred through two general phases. The first, which began more than two decades ago, entailed the "commoditization" of the research function of the university, transforming scientific and engineering knowledge into commercially viable proprietary products. The second phase, now being witnessed, results in the "commoditization" of the educational function of the university, transforming courses into courseware, and the activity of instruction into commercially viable proprietary products that can be owned, bought and sold in the market.

Following these changes, faculties at institutions of higher learning now have much more in common with the historic plight of other skilled workers than they care to acknowledge. Their activity is being restructured via the technology in a way that reduces their autonomy, independence, and control over their own work. Workplace knowledge, and hence control, are being increasingly transferred into the hands of the administration. Once the faculty and courses go online, administrators gain greater direct control over faculty performance and course content and the potential for administrative scrutiny, supervision, regimentation, discipline and even censorship increase dramatically. The proliferation of industrial partnerships and new proprietary arrangements have facilitated efforts of industrialists and their campus counterparts to find ways to socialize the risks and costs of creating knowledge (higher fees and poorer instruction), while privatizing the benefits. In Canada, reforms in patent laws in 1980 gave universities automatic ownership of patents resulting from federal government grants and converted their executive boards into patent holding companies. The initial result was a reallocation of university resources towards its research function at the expense of its educational function. Eventually, however, tuition fees soared to subsidize the creation and maintenance of the commercial infrastructure and a correspondingly bloated administration. The study concludes that, in the view of capital, the universities had become "too important to be left to the universities".

## Autonomy and the Accountability Debate

One of the main issues at stake here appears to be the changing attitudes towards higher education among the "stakeholder" sections of society and the state. The change is seen in the "great deal of interest in accountability", while at the same time, "there is also a great deal of confusion about what this chameleon word means".[28] In colleges and universities, accountability "appears two faced, with sponsors and stakeholders demanding more services while supplying less support. To many outsiders in government and business, higher education seems more interested in autonomy than accountability—in demanding support than supplying services."[29] The resistance to interference, mounted by the academic community in the name of autonomy, is frequently treated as a fig-leaf, aimed at protecting "un-audited", and hence, undeserved privileges.

Academicians have argued that the difference between higher education and other public services arises from the special character of the profession and its responsibilities, and so it must be conceded that *it is their peers, who can most adequately assess their conduct and performance*. "Universities have generally had ambivalent relations with their surrounding societies: both involved and withdrawn; both serving and criticizing; both needing and being needed."[30] These dual roles demand a fine balance of autonomy and accountability. Too much accountability produces dependent institutions that are subservient to political, stakeholder or client whims. The situation has clearly become more complex now as even the traditional balance between "civic" and "collegiate" interests is being mediated by a dominant "commercial" interest. However, it is crucial to clarify confusions, because the escalating conflict over accountability is fast eroding what had earlier been a widespread consensus, that higher education was a public good and a social responsibility, and not just a private benefit for sponsors or students. The issue of how much public investment should be allocated to higher education depends on what the government and society take to be the social goals and benefits of higher education. Whether this funding should be treated as a subsidy that can be pruned at will, would depend largely on the extent to which commitment to higher education as a social good has lost its primacy or not.

## Reforming Higher Education in India

In India, the public commitment to protecting academic freedom notwithstanding, policy makers today are advocating administrative and financial "autonomy" of institutions of higher education to resolve problems of greater efficiency and accountability. In fact, over the past decade and a half, the view of university autonomy that earlier characterized higher education policy, has often been seen as having become dysfunctional on the whole, and has even been held responsible for a crippling lack of accountability among teachers, students and university administrators.[31] It has also been argued that the contemporary dynamic of market-driven economies has rendered the system hopelessly out-dated. Universities, including their faculties, should now be viewed as providers, and students as consumers, of a commodity called "knowledge". Social forces that contribute to the support of the education system—government, communities, parents etc.—are now viewed as "stakeholders", who can be expected to demand and receive tangible short-term and long-term returns on their investment. Market considerations and criteria are asserted to be the sole reliable determinants of the efficient deployment of investment in the educational sector.

To facilitate adjustment of the university system to the new order, *privatization of the system of higher education* is seen as the key motivator, the magic wand to set the forces of profit mobilization at work and "turn around the sick industry" that is higher education today. It is essential that this form of privatization be distinguished from that prevalent in traditional, indigenous schools of higher learning that were characteristic of India before the Woods Despatch of 1854, and from which historical legitimacy is sometimes claimed for current trends. The earlier institutions were privately endowed and maintained, usually by a community, or by wealthy patrons motivated by notions of piety and philanthropy. Educational policy makers can ill afford to lose sight of the distinction between philanthropic educational institutions and commercial, or profit oriented ones, although both are commonly referred to as 'private'.

Privatization in reference to higher education today refers to the on-going process of colleges and universities (both public and private) taking on the characteristics of, and the operational norms associated with, business enterprises. "Trend towards private higher education may be categorized as follows: (i) move towards self-financing courses in (a) government and (b) government-aided institutions; (ii) higher number of self-financing institutions in professional disciplines; (iii) granting a status of deemed university to increasing number of private institutions; (iv) increasing number of private universities being established by state legislation; and (v) multiple private providers of higher education not recognized (affiliated) by the university system and often collaborating with foreign universities."[32] Public funding and regulation decline as one goes down the list, and the last category is the "newly emerging" sector "guided by pure profit motive". Student enrolment, however, is seen to be moving in the reverse order. Figures for Tamil Nadu show that whereas growth of Arts and Science Colleges in the government (54 to 60) and government-aided sector (132 to 133) have remained more or less stagnant over the period 1993-94 to 2005-06, the expansion of self-financed colleges has been phenomenal—up from 54 to 251.[33] UGC Reports show a similar all-India trend. Government and aided institutions increased by 151 over the period 2000-01 to 2005-06, while private unaided institutions registered an increase of 3497. Student enrollment for the former category during the same period went up by 4.15 per cent, while the latter registered an increase of 76.70 per cent.[34]

Although the term is not a precise one, (any more than the distinction between the public and the private college or university), 'privatization' connotes a greater orientation to the student as a consumer, and includes the concept of college education as a product. Attention to image, competitor institutions and market niches, to pricing and the enhancement of net-earned revenue and a general framework of aggressive marketing gradually become dominant. Privatization also suggests the adoption of management practices associated with private business, such as contracting out, 'outsourcing' (i.e. turning to private firms to perform non-academic services such as printing, food services, bookstore operations, or general building maintenance), or leaving units providing these services to 'freely' compete with private players; aggressive labor relations and minimization of payroll expenditures; decisive decision-making and top-down management; widespread use of audits and accountability measures, and an insistence that each unit (department or academic program) contribute to profitability, or at least to the organization's particular metric of 'success'. Proponents of more privatized higher education claim that it makes colleges and universities more responsive to the needs of students and employers alike, in addition to generating efficiencies that can enhance the institution's "goals", *whatever these goals may now have become*. For, unfortunately, the recourse to managerial practices of market-oriented organizations has been seen to exert a deleterious impact on institutions of higher education. Firstly, "authority and power over university affairs is separated from disciplinary competence", and secondly, "university administrators have gained influence at the expense of disciplinary committees".[35]

*As the critical and transformatory purpose of education recedes into the background*, and the market model becomes dominant, the choices offered by the education system appear genuine enough and monetary criteria apparently guarantee a 'fair' exchange between quantum of fees and quality of learning. However, Indian conditions emphasize the inherent barriers to achieving a satisfactory expansion of higher education with the use of this strategy. The absence of a level playing field in a highly stratified society with wide disparities in regional and sectional access to resources would be compounded by a reduction in public funding, (which alone could ensure a sufficiently broad base for the applicability of the relevant norms and standards to all institutions), and is cause for serious concern.[36] The demand for making institutions of higher education financially autonomous to a greater and greater degree is a strategy aimed at facilitating the emergence of unit-based `providers' of a commodity, `knowledge', of varying quality. The consumer's ability to pay would determine, as in any shopping mall, the quality of the goods that are to be delivered.

## Articulating the Difference

How far this perspective has moved away from the concept of autonomy that once dominated the policy for higher education in India is often minimized by a selective use of formulations and recommendations made by the earlier commissions and committees. However, fundamental differences require to be emphasized. In the first place, the current concept does not recognize the specificity of academic pursuits as it reduces them to income generation, on the one hand, and protection of consumer or stakeholder rights, on the other. This is not merely an instance of using jargon that is currently in fashion. The terminology itself reflects the fragmentation into distinct, and potentially confrontational, vested interests of that "society of teachers and students", espousing the shared values of independent thought, on which the Kothari Commission had premised the *enhancement* of academic autonomy as higher education spread in the country. Secondly, "consumer choice and *stakeholderism* as instruments of voice and accountability are available only to stakeholders and consumers", but if services are supported with public resources then "any model of democratic government requires that instruments are also available to those who are not presently consumers or stakeholders of a particular public service".[37] It is also often difficult to identify exactly who are the appropriate consumers of a service—this is certainly the case with education, and particularly so in a highly stratified society. Finally, the question of social accountability within the framework of the current concept proceeds as if it were purely a matter of finance. Now only that education has value, or "excellence", which allows the student-consumer to fetch a good market price for the skills she has acquired. Again, the "excellence" of the institution providing the skills is to be judged by its being adequate to the fees charged. Those who pay less, get less. "But", as a contemporary social philosopher argues, "our interests in our fellow citizens extend beyond our concern as to how they spend their money; their behaviour in other respects affects our well-being. If others in our society fail to flourish or flourish in an inappropriate way, then this has repercussions for us. The interests of others affect us more directly as well, through the allocation of positional goods...."[38]

Proposals advocating autonomy for institutions of higher education often attempt to distance themselves from the prevailing neo-liberal strategy of promoting privatization in the social services sector.[39] A common strategy has been to draw "inspiration" from one of the recommendations of the Kothari Commission. The Commission did recommend autonomy for "outstanding colleges" or "clusters of very good colleges". This is frequently projected as the motivation for initiating a nation-wide spread of autonomous institutions of higher education. However, the Commission's recommendation was intended to utilize achieved academic excellence for both support and emulation, on the one hand, and on the other, to find solutions to problems posed by the fact that "historically the development of university education in different states has not been uniform...circumstances, both educational and social, led to certain distinct features.... A certain amount of variety in the pattern and organization of universities may be desirable in the interest of the development and progress of higher education in a large country like India."[40] The report of the Dr. G.S. Mahajani Committee on Colleges, 1964,[41] also took the position that granting autonomy to colleges was "*one* of the *practical* methods", of improving standards in higher education in India by selecting a few colleges "on the basis of past work, influence, traditions, maturity and academic standards and give them what might be called for want of a better phrase an 'autonomous status' with freedom to develop their personalities". However, and the report quotes from the earlier Robbins Report[42] to emphasize this, "there should be no freezing of institutions into established hierarchies; on the contrary there should be recognition and encouragement of excellence wherever it exists and wherever it appears." The Mahajani Committee's "anxiety was that the excellence shown by some distinguished postgraduate colleges should be the rule, rather than the exception" (p. 21-22).

The Ambani-Birla Report[43] explicitly gave expression to the reductionism inherent in the changed education policy initiatives. With the companion Model Act for Universities 2003, prepared by the UGC, it was intended to restructure higher education on the model of market-oriented enterprises promoting corporate values. The attempt was shelved because of strong opposition from academicians and teachers unions, but it is important to recognize that their opposition was well-founded:[44]

- The character of higher education, which is directed towards the long-term goals of a knowledge-based society, needs autonomy not only from governmental-bureaucratic institutions but also from market pressures;
- Higher education is the site for innovative foundational research and growth of knowledge. If it is reduced to mere transmission of operational technologies, the national society will remain at the mercy of external "providers";
- A growing, autonomous higher education system is an indication of a mature society. At present, India has amongst the lowest percentage, even among developing countries, of the relevant age group studying in its universities. State funding is essential to ensure that adequate talent from all sections can gain access. The attempt to privatize higher education on the present narrow educational base would not present a viable alternative.

The context of contemporary debates on institutional autonomy has been enormously influenced by the neo-liberal economic agenda, adopted by successive governments since the early 1990's. The motivation for recommending autonomy is the decline in public funding for higher education, resulting in its concentration in select areas, on the one hand, and in creating space for institutions that are 'free' to fend for themselves, on the other. It must be emphasized that when autonomy means that an institution is expected to mobilize its own financial resources and maximize student returns on investment in fees by focusing on acquired skills that command high market prices, the Rubicon has indeed been crossed. The Kothari Commission, like the commissions and committees that preceded and followed it, had been concerned primarily with academic and decision-making autonomy, not with financial "self-sufficiency, and certainly not with the idea that institutions of higher education ought to be primarily motivated by, and concerned with, courting markets as sources of finance for academic programs.

## In Lieu of a Conclusion

"Autonomy with respect to the state is nowadays only part of the total picture of institutional freedom. Universities are increasingly subject to pressures from sources other than the state—market forces, competition for staff and students, commercial interests in commissioned research."[45] It has become necessary to recognize that "the 'place', or 'space' for practicing authority in education is multi-dimensional. The changing relationships between governments and universities are reported to point to converging tendencies of more market-like effects on the higher education enterprise worldwide" but with "the ever-desperate need for revenue combined with the forced decentralization in general education, policy-making in higher education becomes charged politically".[46] Indeed, in the Indian context, it has been argued that even the understanding and strategy of the government has been influenced by a report of the World Bank entitled, Higher Education: The Lessons of Experience (1994).[47] This accentuates the need for widespread national debate on changes in policies for education in general, and higher education in particular. It cannot become the ground for pushing through 'schemes' that are either foisted on policy makers by international agencies or copied unimaginatively from the experience of countries that differ widely from India in socio-political and economic terms.

The question has acquired greater urgency because of the entry of the World Trade Organization (WTO) and the General Agreement on Trade in Services (GATS) into the arena of higher education. Within the format promoting financially autonomous institutions, the panacea of foreign direct investment is being endorsed almost as a free lunch-investment without tears—that would ensure both the spread and quality of higher education without any hard economic decisions or policy choices on our part. But as the commercialization of higher education has now reached the global marketplace, the importance of retaining the system's independence from the control of global political and economic vested interests, particularly in the context of the pressure to 'open up' the Indian education 'market' to foreign direct investment, can hardly be overlooked.

In the year 2000, the WTO considered a series of proposals to ensure that the import and export of higher education be brought under the complex rules and legal arrangements of WTO protocols and be made free from existing national restrictions. Prof. Nigvekar, then UGC Chairperson, presented the position paper, "Trade in Higher Education: Impact of GATS on Higher Education, Research and Knowledge Systems in Selected Contexts in Asia and the Pacific Region", at UNESCO's second regional meeting. "The overall thrust of the presentation was that higher education itself has become a tradable product and knowledge has become commodified. The important point was made that as of yet, there is little, if any, empirical evidence that GATS and the trade in education service per se is compromising national systems of higher education."[48] However, by January 2005, the conclave of education ministers from the states of the union expressed concern that "the national values and concerns of the host country may be undermined by the presence of foreign providers not sharing such values". In a world divided into centers and peripheries, questions of sovereignty have become pertinent as inequalities grow more pronounced. The increasingly competitive and fast moving global higher education scene is dominated by world-class universities in the industrialized countries, mainly in the English-speaking countries of the North (the United States, the United Kingdom, Canada), in the larger countries of the European Union (notably Germany and France), and in Australia. These countries are home not only to the dominant universities and research facilities but also to the multinational corporations so powerful in the new global knowledge system. As a result, the norms, values, language, scientific innovations, and knowledge products of countries in the center crowd out other ideas and practices.

Developing countries have special academic needs that require to be protected. Their universities are even now involved in many international partnerships, but these arrangements, based on perceived national needs, are open-ended and allow choice among programs and partners. If higher education worldwide were to be subjected to the strictures of the WTO, the idea that universities serve a broad public good would be significantly weakened. The ability of institutions of higher education to contribute to goals of national development and the strengthening of civil society, both necessary components of India's unfinished agenda of democratic transformation, would be hindered. Universities would be subjected to all the commercial pressures of a market regime defined by treaties and legal requirements that would be internationally enforced. Institutions of higher learning have a special place and a societal mission that deserve support. Submitting to a WTO-enforced trade practices regime would destroy one of the most valuable institutions for the transformation of contemporary Indian society.

## Notes

1. *Report of the Education Commission (1964-66): Education and National Development.* Ministry of Education, Government of India. New Delhi, 1966. The Commission was chaired by Prof. D.S. Kothari.
2. *Report of the University Education Commission,* (1948-49). Ministry of Education, Government of India. New Delhi, 1951. The Commission was chaired by Dr. S. Radhakrishnan.
3. James, C. Walker (1999). "Self-Determination as an Educational Aim" in Roger Marples (ed) *The Aims of Education.* Routledge, London, p. 123.

4. R. Perry, V. Menec, C. Struthers, F. Hector, D. Schonmeter, & R. Menges (1997). "Faculty in Transition: A longitudinal analysis of the role of perceived control and type of institution in adjustment to post-secondary institutions." *Research in Higher Education*. 38(5), p. 519-556. Those who "reported high levels of autonomy were more satisfied with their teaching, had less job stress and were less likely to consider quitting their jobs."
5. *Report of the Committee on Model Act for Universities*, (1961). Ministry of Education, Government of India, New Delhi.
6. Bologna Magna Carta Universitatum 1988 signed by University Rectors of European Universities to celebrate the 800th year of the Bologna University.
7. *Report of the Committee on Model Act forUniversities*. p. 5.
8. Christopher, Winch (2005). "Autonomy as an Educational Aim" in Wilfred Carr (ed) *The Routledge Farmer Reader in Philosophy of Education*. Routledge, London, p. 68.
9. *Report of the Committee on Governance of Universities and Colleges*. University Grants Commission. New Delhi, (1971). The Committee was chaired by Dr. P.B. Gajendragadkar.
10. Passed at the sixty-eighth General Assembly of World University Service meeting in Lima from 6-10th September 1988.
11. Radhakrishnan Commission Report. p. 37.
12. Report of the Central Advisory Board of Education's sub-committee on Autonomy in Higher Education (2005) states that the CABE, in its "pivotal role" of reviewing, improving and monitoring implementation of educational development, "made recommendation towards establishment of 'Common School System' as the bedrock of educational quality, social cohesion and national integration calling for moving towards a common admission policy, tuition-free school education, parity among all teachers, involvement of the community and adoption of the concept of 'neighbourhood school' to eliminate segregation. Unfortunately this stipulation has remained unimplemented despite its inclusion in the NPE (1968, 1986, 1992)" (p. 1).
13. Radhakrishnan Commission Report. p. 119.
14. James C. Walker. *Op cit*. p. 112.
15. The share of Government expenditure on education as a percentage of Gross National Product (GNP) which had risen from 0.67 per cent in 1951-52 to a modest high of 4.40 per cent in 2000-01, still well below the proposed target of 6 per cent, has actually declined to 3.54 per cent in 2004-05 (budget estimate). This is lower than the 3.71 per cent spent in 1985-86. [Report of the National Seminar on "Privatization and Commercialization of Higher Education". NUEPA. New Delhi. 2006. Table 8. p. 24.]
16. *Education Commission*, (1884). Bombay, Vol.II. Calcutta, p. 140.
17. N.V. Varghese (International Institute for Educational Planning, France), (2004). "Incentives and Institutional Changes in Higher Education". *Journal of the Programme on Institutional Management in Higher Education*. Vol. 16. No: 1. OECD, p. 27-40.
18. Jandhyala B G Tilak: "Are We Marching Towards Laissez-faireism in Higher Education Development?" Paper presented at IAU Sao Paulo Conference,

July 25-27, 2004. 12th General Conference: The Wealth of Diversity. Parallel Workshops – Session II.

19. Conclusions of the first World Conference on Higher Education, Education International (incorporating the European Trade Union Committee for Education, ETUCE) 19-21 March 1997. Reproduced in *IFUT News*, periodical of the Irish Federation of University Teachers, Vol. XXVI, Autumn 1999.
20. Jencks & Reisman. *The Academic Revolution.* Garden City, N.Y. Doubleday. 1968.
21. Report of the Second Round Table Meeting on Higher Education Autonomy in ASEAN and the European Union held at Pompea Fabra University, Barcelona, Spain, 13th-4th January 2005.
22. E. Tapper & B. Salter. "The Changing Idea of University Autonomy". *Studies in Higher Education.* 20(1), 1995. p. 59-71.
23. *Towards an Enlightened and Humane Society: Committee for Review of National Policy of Education 1986.* Department of Education, Ministry of Human Resource Development. Government of India. New Delhi, 1990.
24. Jay R. Dee, Alan B. Henkin & Jessica Hsin Hwa Chen. "Faculty Autonomy: Perspectives from Taiwan". *Higher Education.* 40. 2000. p. 213-216
25. Tilak. *Op cit.* 2004.
26. Bleikei, I.R. Hostaker & A Vabo. *Policy and Practice in Higher Education: Reforming Norweigian Universities.* Jessica Knightly Publishers. London 2000.
27. *David F. Noble.* Digital Diploma Mills: The Automation of Higher Education. *Monthly Review Press Books,* 1997.
28. Day, Patricia & Klein, Rudolf. *Accountabilities: Five Public Services.* London & New York, Tavistock. 1987. p. 1.
29. Joseph C. Burke. *Achieving Accountability in Higher Education: Balancing Public, Academic and Market Demands.* John Wiley & Sons Inc. 2004. p. 1.
30. Robert Berdahl. "Academic Freedom, Autonomy and Accountability in British Universities". *Studies in Higher Education.* Vol.15, No. 2. p. 169-180.
31. The report of the CABE sub-committee on Autonomy in Higher Education (2005) states, "every fresh assault on the university autonomy always comes as a reaction to some fresh failure on their part", (p. 24).
32. Sudhanshu Bhushan. *Privatisation and Commercialisation of Higher Education in India.* National Seminar on "Privatization and Commercialization of Higher Education". NUEPA. 2006.
33. Anandakrishnan, M. *Higher Education in Regional Development: Some Key Pointers.* Indo-UK Seminar on Regional Development. UGC. 2004.
34. Anandakrishnan, M. *Privatization of Higher Education: Opportunities and Anomalies.* National Seminar on "Privatization and Commercialization of Higher Education". NUEPA. 2006. Tables 4(a) & 4(b) p. 39.
35. N.V. Varghese. 2004.
36. Existing figures of regional disparity in higher education speak for themselves. Maharashtra, Tamil Nadu, Karnataka, Kerala and Andhra Pradesh have 32 per cent of the country's population, but 46% of general education colleges and almost 60 per cent of professional colleges are located there. Concentration of availability of certain courses in selected cities is also evident. With 34 per cent of the population, Bihar, Jharkhand, U.P. and M.P. account for 23 per cent of

general colleges and only 14 per cent of professional colleges. In Orissa, there are more than 50 government colleges in urban centers but not a single one in rural areas (Figures provided by Dr. Rohini Sahni, Dept. of Economics, University of Pune). The concentration in the five states listed above is due to private institutions locating themselves in developed regions with adequate public infrastructure. Even in a less developed state like Chhattisgarh, private universities set up with a generous use of the state government's regulatory powers, were delivering what little benefit they could, to students outside the state by constituting themselves as 'off-campus centers'.

37. B. Guy Peters and John Pierre: *Governance Without Government? Rethinking Public Administration.* Journal of Public Administration and Theory. Vol. 8, No. 2, 1998, p. 223-243.
38. Christopher Winch: "*Autonomy as an Educational Aim*" in Wilfred Carr (ed) *The Routledge Farmer Reader in Philosophy of Education.* Routledge. London, (2005). p. 65-73.
39. See the Report of the CABE Committee on Autonomy of Higher Education Institutions (2005), particularly the conceptual framework presented in Chapter 3.
40. *Report of the Kothari Committee on 'Model Act for Universities'*, 1961.
41. *Report of the Committee on Colleges.* University Grants Commission. New Delhi, 1967.
42. *Report of the Lord Robbins Committee on Higher Education.*
43. Mukesh Ambani and Kumaramangalam Birla: *A Policy Framework for Reforms in Education.* Prime Minister's Council on Trade & Industry, Government of India. New Delhi, 2000.
44. This is emphasized as a necessary corrective to the widespread and disparaging opinion of faculty as being resistant to change. "Academics everywhere are conservative when it comes to institutional change and have generally opposed reform." Philip G. Altbach: "The Dilemma of Change in Indian Higher Education". *Higher Education Reform in India.* (Eds.) Seema Chitnis & Philip G. Altbach. Sage Publications. New Delhi, 1993, p. 25.
45. Per Nyborg. Head of Bologna Secretariat. "Implications of Bologna Process in South East Europe." Council of Europe Conference, Strasbourg. 2-3 Dec. 2003.
46. Olga Bain. "University Autonomy: Utopia & Paradox". Journal of Centre for Comparative and Global Studies in Education. Vol. 3: Issue 1. 1999.
47. Devesh Kapur & Pratap Bhanu Mehta. *Indian Higher Education Reform: From Half-Baked Socialism to Half-Baked Capitalism.* CID Working Paper No. 108, September 2004. The World Bank report states that, "it is arguable that higher education should not have highest priority claim on incremental public resources available for education in many developing countries, especially those that have not achieved adequate access, equity and quality at the primary and secondary levels. This is because of the priority these countries attach to achieving universal literacy; because the social rates of return in investments in primary and secondary education usually exceed the rates of return in higher education..." (p. 3).
48. UGC website.

# Part V

# Resources and National Economy

# 18

# The Kothari Commission and Financing of Education

JANDHYALA B.G. TILAK

> "[W]e should strive to allocate the largest proportion of GNP[1] possible to educational development."
>
> — Education Commission (1966, p. 889).

## Introduction

The contribution of the Education Commission (1966), popularly known as the Kothari Commission, after the name of its chairman Professor D.S. Kothari, whose birth-centenary year was 2006, to the issue of financing of education is very significant. The monumental work of the Commission that runs into more than one thousand pages is regarded as a landmark in the history of education in post-Independence India and as a "turning point in India's educational life" (Adiseshiah, 1979)[2]. One can dig out a mine of relevant recommendations from this report on financing of education in India. There are (a) a few clear recommendations, (b) a set of norms used by the Commission which may also be considered as valuable recommendations, and (c) several general intuitive normative observations, which would suggest the need for a change in the approach of the policy makers and planners in education in India. Many of these recommendations and the premises on which they are based may still be relevant. Without claiming to be exhaustive, this short article revisits their premises, implementation and current relevance. The article is also narrowly focused on issues relating to financing of education, though some aspects that are closely related to financing are also briefly referred to.

Reviewing the Report of the Education Commission, J.P. Naik (1979), who was the Member-Secretary of the Commission and who had played an important role in drafting the voluminous Report, classified the several recommendations into three categories: (i) recommendations that attracted wide attention, (ii) recommendations that were opposed and rejected and (iii) 'other' recommendations. Other recommendations include: (a) those that did not excite any major controversy and were accepted but implemented indifferently;[3] (b) those that were simply ignored; and (c) other recommendations. Though Naik did not exactly refer to, there is yet another category of recommendations, viz., (iv) recommendations agreed upon and approved, but not implemented. Some of the major recommendations on financing of education made by the Commission belong to this last category of recommendations that were approved and accepted but not implemented; some belong to the first category that received wide attention, but were followed by little action; many to the second category that were opposed and rejected; and a few to the category of (iii) which were either simply ignored and/or are of no significance. The attempt here is to examine a few major recommendations of these various categories, offer a critical review of some of them, how are they implemented during the post-Commission period and comment on their relevance for the present context.

At the very outset it is important to note that the Education Commission, perhaps for the first time in India, had emphasized the critical role of education in social and economic development, as indicated by the title of its Report. It was clearly recognised that "[I]n a science-based world, education and research are critical to the entire developmental process of a country, its welfare, progress and security."[4] It is more emphatically noted that education "*determines* the level of prosperity, welfare and security of the people" (p. 3; emphasis added). The Commission seemed to have been influenced by the 'human investment revolution in economic thought' created by Schultz (1961) which was quite fresh at that time. It emphasized that investment in education leads to human capital formation, which in turn contributes to economic growth. The whole approach of the Commission to educational development in general and financing of education in particular was strongly influenced by its conviction on the role of education in development. Apart from spatial disparities, the Commission also recognized the need to ensure equity among several socioeconomic classes in India. Accordingly, the Commission argued, "we should accord the highest priority to education and allocate the largest proportion of GNP possible to it" (p. 873). It also warned: "In an age of science, there can be no greater risk than a policy of drift and niggardliness in education" (p. 892). Second, the Commission was very much concerned with the wide gap between India and the advanced countries, and the need to reduce it in education and through education in development between educationally and economically advanced countries and India on the one hand, and among several states and regions within India.[5] It resolved, "the gap between India and other rich countries needs to be reduced" (p. 873). Third (and this was an important aspect), it was the first commission that was required to carefully look into the entire spectrum of education. This it did, and adopted a comprehensive and holistic approach.

This approach of the Commission assumes particular importance, as it worked in the backdrop of a politically fluid situation caused by the demise of a popular Prime Minister, a major war with a neighbouring country, agricultural drought and the accompanying severe economic problems, including high rates of inflation and increasing unemployment—all this in a developing economy. Given this, the Commission was courageous in arguing for large investment in education and at the same time pragmatic in using austere and modest parameters and in recommending regulated expansion of higher education. Action on many of the recommendations of the Commission was to be decided at a worse time of political and economic uncertainty, characterized by the defeat of the ruling Congress party in many states, currency devaluation, powerful inflationary trends and a plan holiday.

An important contribution of the Commission is a detailed analysis of financing of education in India. The financial analysis attempted in the Report, particularly in Chapter XIX, was first of its kind in the country. In fact, there were very few studies on the economics and financing of education even in other countries at the time of the Commission.[6] The Commission has made (a) a detailed expenditure analysis—total, by levels and objects, (b) a detailed source-wise analysis of funds, (c) unit cost analysis, and (d) a detailed estimate of resources required for education for the next 20 years in constant prices. Both the detailed framework provided and the insightful analysis made were of great significance and use for the researchers in economics and financing of education and for educational planners as well.[7] The Commission in fact, noted the absence of studies and the critical need for such studies, and recommended support to universities for research in these areas.[8]

## Allocation of Resources to Education: Six Per cent of GNP

The most important recommendation made by the Commission on financing education refers to allocation of six per cent of national income to education.[9] Since this is one of the most important and most-often cited recommendations, we may discuss this in slightly greater detail. The Commission made a detailed analysis of the trends in financing education in the post-independence period, estimated the financial requirements of the educational system in India up to 1985-86, and recommended that "if education is to develop adequately,... the proportion of GNP allocated to education will rise... to 6.0 per cent in 1985-86" (p. 893). Moreover, this is one of the recommendations that was accepted and resolved by the Government of India (1968) in the *National Policy on Education 1968* "to increase the investment in education so as to reach a level of expenditure of six per cent of the national income as early as possible" (p. 9). Since the goal could not be reached, the Government of India reiterated in 1986 its commitment to reach the target and stated in the *National Policy on Education 1986*: "It will be ensured that from the Eighth Five Year Plan onwards it (the *outlay* on education) will uniformly exceed to six per cent of the National income" (Government of India, 1986, p. 29). Given the inadequate performance, the goal was to be reiterated again in the *National Policy on Education (Revised) 1992.* The Review Committee on National Policy on Education (also familiarly known as the Acharya Ramamurthy Committee, 1990), and the several reports of the CABE have repeatedly made it clear that six per cent of national income should be devoted to education. The repeated under-accomplishment of the goal led the government to repeatedly reiterate the promise in subsequent years in every five year plan, in every policy statement, Economic Survey(s), reports of the Ministry of Education/Human Resource Development, reports of several committees/commissions on education, and even in the Independence Day speeches of the Prime Minister from the ramparts of the Red Fort. Almost all political party manifestos and other agendas also endorsed this recommendation. All this shows some kind of a national consensus in the country towards fulfilling the recommendation of the Education Commission.

However, the most-often cited recommendation was also subject to some controversies. Attempts were made to provide subverted definition and scope to the terms such as 'national income', 'educational expenditure', and 'six per cent' and to misinterpret the letter and spirit of the recommendation of the Commission, the resolution of *National Policy on Education 1968*, and the *National Policy on Education 1986.* Arguments were also made to suggest that India already spends about or more than six per cent of GNP on education, and need no more to worry about this target. Significant attempts of this kind include, among others, a paper circulated by the Planning Commission (Kolhatkar, 1988),[10] the National Agenda of the BJP & Alliance Partners (1988)[11], the draft ninth five year plan of the Planning Commission (1999, p. 101) and the *Economic Survey* of the Ministry of Finance (1999).[12] They tried to argue that the six per cent of national income, as recommended by the Education Commission, consisted of not just government expenditure, but also all private expenditure including family expenditure on education and private sector expenditure, and even to show that as the goal is already over-achieved, it becomes redundant, and that it does not deserve any more attention.

As Tilak (1990, 1999, 2006) has shown, all these were attempts to misinterpret the facts, to quantitatively under-define the goals, to cover our dismal failures and to boast at our (pseudo) achievements! Tilak has further shown that these attempts have deliberately ignored the fact that the Commission had referred mainly to public expenditure, and that the UNESCO figures and other international statistics that the Commission used as a yardstick for comparison also refer to government expenditure only, and the recommendations made by the UNESCO, UNDP, the Delors Commission etc, in subsequent years refer to government expenditure only. Anand Sarup, former Education Secretary, who was involved in the preparation of the critical review of education in India, titled *Challenge of Education* (Government of India, 1985), and in the formulation of the *National Policy on Education 1986* made the point clear. In a paper, circulated in a meeting at the Planning Commission, and later published elsewhere, Anand Sarup (1988) stated: "Since it is public policy on education that is the crucial determinant of available educational places and opportunities in our country, *it (6 %) is the Centre and State expenditure on education* that is used for policy planning and implementation. This includes both plan and non-plan outlays" (p. 253; emphasis added). Thus, it is clear that the attempts to redefine and reinterpret the Commission's recommendation were to divert the public attention from the very need to substantially increase the public allocations to education. Finally, the controversy seems to have been buried recently with the *Common Minimum Programme* of the UPA Government (2004) pledging "to raise public spending in education to at least six per cent of the GDP."[13]

The second criticism of this recommendation is that this was not based on any sound basis and hence no sanctity needs to be attached to this recommendation. A careful look at the Report shows that such a criticism is not tenable. The Commission carefully reviewed in detail the trends in the expenditure on education in the past and, based on certain reasonable assumptions regarding economic growth (6%) and population growth (2.1% per annum) during the next 20-year period, it estimated the magnitude of the resources that should be available for educational development in India during this period. It is a detailed analysis that estimates the requirements of the system. The Commission noted, "The proportion of national income devoted to education in India is small in comparison with that in educationally advanced countries of the world" (p. 860). It compared the estimate of requirement with the corresponding figures of some specific countries, available in the UNESCO statistics: "Japan and the USA and the USSR are spending considerably more than 6 per cent of GNP on education" (p. 860); and they spent no more than a small fraction of their GNP on education at the beginning of the century. The Commission also felt that these countries might be spending about ten per cent of GNP by 1986, and in fact, more than ten per cent, if comprehensive disarmament takes place. Hence the need for India to increase its public expenditure at least to the level of six per cent of GNP by 1985-86. The Commission further noted that "the absolute amount of per capita spent by us on education is about one-hundredth of that by a highly industrialized country like the USA." Thus, the six per cent target recommended by the Education Commission is based on the estimated actual requirements of the system for the next 20 years and the need to reduce the wide gap between India and other rich countries in the levels of education development. (p. 873) Methodological, including conceptual and definitional aspects of educational expenditure and the details of the analysis and the targets of the Commission are unambiguously clear. The rationale provided by the Commission for its recommendation was also sound and the Commission also gave enough time to the government for reaching the goal, providing a 20-year period. Hence the criticism that the recommendation has no more sanctity at all is not valid.

Some also found that the target of the six per cent of GNP was an ambitious one. But the Commission felt differently. In fact, the Commission argued that it was a very modest target. Normally, expenditure on education should be double the rate of economic growth in the early stages of educational development. But the Commission set a modest target of ten per cent growth in educational expenditure, compared to six per cent rate of economic growth. Ideally, it could be 12 per cent in educational expenditure.

However, in a sense, the Commission's recommendation does not have much sanctity on its own, as the estimate was made long ago, based on somewhat austere estimates of growth in enrolments, per student expenditure and other parameters. The austere estimates and assumptions may not be much relevant today. In fact, the Commission itself observed that taking into consideration the changing circumstances, "the estimates will have to be continually revised" (p. 892). Nevertheless, it assumes importance mainly as the goal remained unaccomplished so far.

The only valid criticism of the Commission's recommendation could be that the estimate was based on somewhat austere parameters, such as high pupil-teacher ratio at primary level though it actually desired a lower ratio, earmarking only a smaller proportion of the total expenditure for construction of buildings and other items of capital expenditure, no provision for free uniforms, free stationery, free school meals, and health services and free and compulsory education. In the case of higher education, the 1965-66 unit costs were used in estimating resource requirements and recommended less expensive part-time and correspondence courses for about 30 per cent of the students. Essentially, due to resource scarcity, the Commission recommended carefully planned expansion of higher education on the basis of manpower needs. It meant lower rate of expansion, reduction in the total enrolment in higher education and in the number of institutions for full-time education, and economizing physical and financial investments without affecting standards.[14] Therefore, any exercise that attempts afresh at estimating the resource requirements may put the figure at much above six per cent of GNP.[15]

The main recommendation of the Education Commission on allocating six per cent of GNP to education made in 1966 has been endorsed later by several international organisations. For example, the Delors Commission (1996) has clearly argued: "Increasing *public spending on education*, in place of expenditure under other budget heads, should be regarded as a necessity everywhere, and especially in developing countries, since it is a vital investment for the future. *As a rule of thumb, not less than six per cent of GNP should be devoted to education*" (p. 165; emphasis added). UNESCO and UNDP also favoured it, as a desirable level for the developing countries. Thus in retrospect, the recommendation of the Education Commission could be seen as an important visionary exercise, based on sound calculations and understanding of the Indian education system and the world system.

Despite the wide acceptance of the recommendation and despite making it a part of the *National Policy on Education* in 1968 and in 1986, which were approved by the Parliament, the implementation of the recommendation has been very tardy, as Figure 1 indicates.[16] The proportion of GNP spent on education was nearly trebled from 0.6 per cent in 1951-52 to 1.7 per cent in 1967-68. The slope of the line of increase was relatively reduced during the post-1968 Policy period: the proportion was nearly doubled to 3.5 per cent in 1985-86 from 1.7 per cent in 1968-69; it further flattened, as the corresponding proportion increased to 3.8 per cent in 2004-05 from 3.4 per cent in 1986-87. Though one does not expect a steep increase in this ratio for a long period, the fact is, the rate of increase came down during the post-Commission period, and further reduced during the post-1986 Policy period.

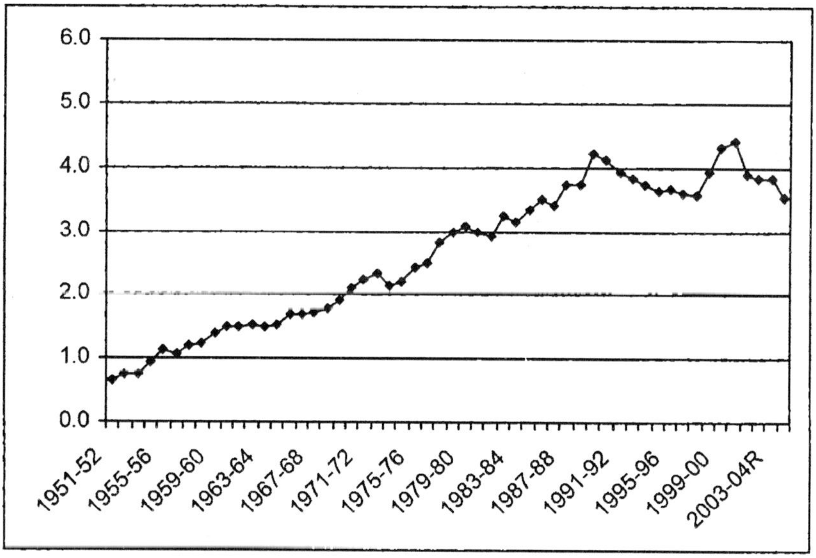


**Figure 18.1: Share of Public Expendiutre on Education in GNP (%)**

As Shah (2006) commented,," the more unfortunate and disturbing long-term trend in this regard is the slackening of government effort to mobilise required resources during the period of high economic growth (1986-87 to

2001-02) compared to that of low economic growth (1966-67 to 1985-86)."[17] An analysis of such trends in India and in other countries led Tilak (1984, 1986) to conclude that the percentage of national income a nation allocates to education is not determined by the level of economic development, but by other factors, most important of which being political will.

The proportion of national income allocated to education in India crossed four per cent in the early 1990s, but the level could not be maintained. We are still very far away from reaching this goal. Thus the major recommendation of the Commission is one that belongs to the category of 'Recommendations approved and received wide attention, but not implemented.'[18] After all, no detailed financial plan of reaching the goal was ever thought of. In the absence of any plan and efforts, the general trend of slow and reluctant growth in the share of education expenditure in GNP continued. Tilak (2006) has shown that if the trend continues and no significant efforts are made, the situation might worsen and the goal would remain elusive for a long period to come.

Interestingly, one may also note that the relative importance given to education in the five year plans has also declined during the post-Commission period, as shown in Figure 2.[19] While during the first three five year plans, on an average about seven per cent of the total five year plan expenditure was spent on education, the corresponding proportion declined to five per cent in the fourth five year plan, the very first plan after the Report of the Commission was submitted and the *National Policy on Education 1968* was formulated. The proportion further declined to 3.3 per cent in the fifth five year plan and further down to 2.7 per cent in the sixth five year plan.

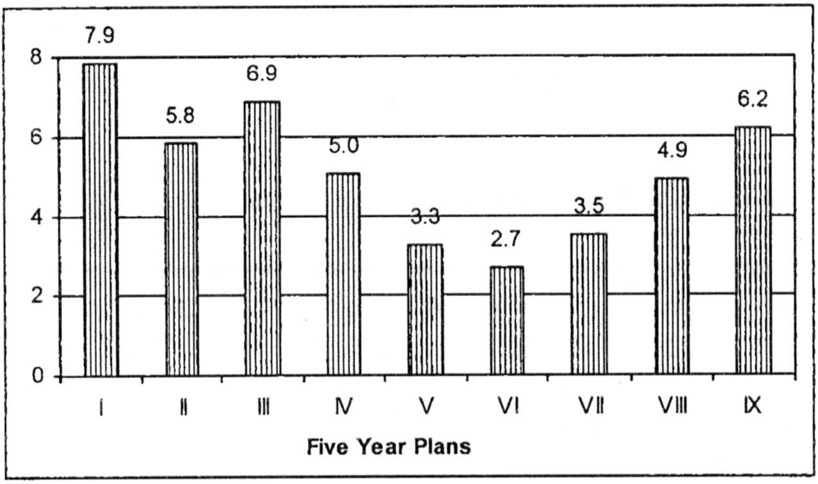


*Source*: Tilak (2003).

**Figure 18.2: Expenditure on Education in Five Year Plans (% of Total)**

While there may be several factors, such as the war, drought and inflation that led to this trend, it is clear the Commission's strong recommendation that "the efforts to increase allocations to education should be intensified" (p. 872) could not be given adequate attention. It is only after the *National Policy on Education 1986* was approved by the Parliament, this trend reversed. The allocation in the ninth, and probably in the tenth plan, is still much below the allocation made in the very first five year plan!

## Allocation of Resources to Different Levels of Education

The Commission not only estimated the requirements of resources for the education sector as a whole, it also recommended "the best" pattern of intra-sectoral allocation of resources in education, i.e., allocation of resources between different levels of education. At the outset, it should be noted that the Commission has acknowledged the inter-dependence of various levels of education and had adopted a balanced and holistic approach to educational development.

By referring to Japanese experience (pp. 863-65), the Commission has indirectly advocated some kind of sequencing in the pattern of allocation of resources among different levels of education—primary, secondary and higher education, in that order. Looking at the historical trends in India over the years, particularly during the post-independence period and the levels of development for the next 20 years, the Commission felt that from 1965 to 1975, the relative emphasis should be on a larger expenditure at the school stage; during 1975 to 1985 it will be on universal elementary education, vocationalisation of secondary stage etc, and then the 'emphasis should begin to shift in favour of higher education'. "After 1985, there will be increased emphasis on the development of higher education and research" (p. 893). It further stated: "As societies become industrialized, the total expenditure on education begins to grow and an increasingly larger part of it comes to be devoted to higher education and research" (p. 861).

But it appears that the pattern of intra-sectoral allocation followed was exactly the opposite. During the immediate post-Commission period, the importance given to elementary education in the total five year plan expenditure on education either remained stable at around 30 per cent, or declined marginally, and the share of higher education in the five year plan expenditure increased from 15 per cent in the third plan to 25 per cent in the fourth plan (and 22 per cent in the fifth plan), as shown in Figure 3.[20] When the pressures on secondary and higher education were increasing in terms of increased demand, the allocation to higher education was drastically reduced from the seventh five year plan onwards.

Further, while the recommendation seems to be logical and hence appealing, it is increasingly becoming clear that the traditional sequencing of primary, secondary and higher education may not work any more; higher education cannot wait until primary and secondary education is completely universal or well-expanded (Tilak, 2001). In a sense, the Commission has recognised this when it emphasized the importance of universal primary education[21] along with improvement of quality in higher education and research, and recommended allocation of resources for various aspects of higher education and research. In the long run, the Commission favoured equal distribution of resources, as in 1965-66, approximately one-third to the first level of education, one-third to secondary and the remaining one third to higher education (p. 868).

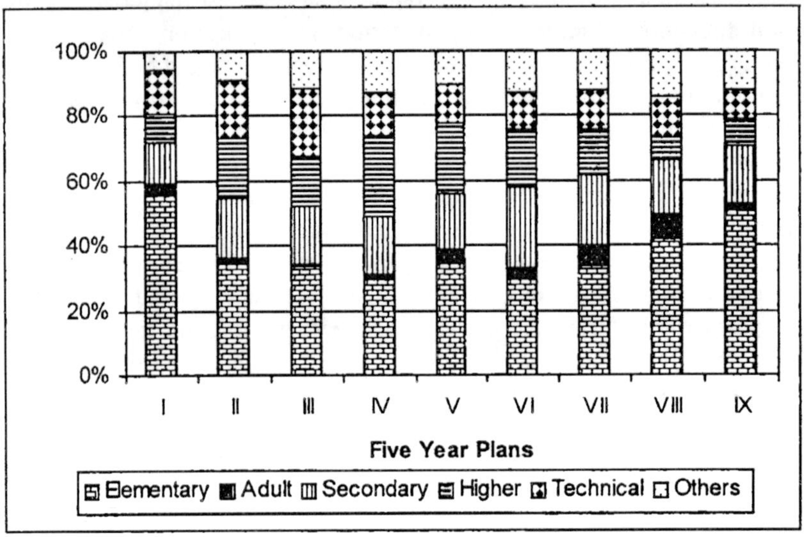


**Figure 18.3: Intra-Sectoral Allocation of Resources in Education in Five Year Plans**

A point worth noting is that the Commission recognized the importance of all levels of education, particularly primary education on the one side and the higher education and research on the other, and did not pose one level of education against another in recommending allocation of resources. It stated: "We realize the need for the development of higher education and the allocation of more resources to it. But it would not be proper to cut down for this purpose the expenditure on primary education" (p. 876). The Commission repeatedly stressed that "the provision of universal primary education is vital on grounds of social justice and to help the process of transformation of the national economy. Again, development of higher education and research is central to the entire developmental programme; and without an adequate provision for higher education there will be no adequate supply of competent teachers for primary and secondary education. What we want is *a balanced growth of education*" (p. 876; emphasis added). This is exactly what Surendranath Banerjee, stated in his Presidential address to the Congress Party in Pune in 1895: "We are not in favour of higher education *vs*. primary education. We are in favour of all education, high and low. They act and react upon each other. They are part and parcel of a common and indissoluble system."[22]

The government, however, seemed to have ignored this wise dictum altogether and often juxtaposed one level against another in the allocation of resources in the five year plans, saying that the government can finance either elementary education, nowadays EFA, or higher education, but not both, and thereby adopted different and even contradictory, approaches to development of different levels of education and their financing. Basically instead of a holistic and integrated approach to education, the government has adopted a fragmented approach, looking at different levels of education as fragments, as if they compete with each other for resources from the same basket.

## Inter-Functional Allocation of Resources: Items of Priority

The Commission has recognized the importance of not only teacher salaries when it has recommended a significant raise in teachers' salaries, but also non-teacher items and their costs. The small proportion of non-teacher costs was regarded as the main reason "why our primary schools are so dull and drab" (p. 878). The Commission recommended that non-teacher costs should be of the level of 20 per cent of the teacher costs at primary (lower and upper primary) level; and such costs should form one-third of the teacher costs at secondary level. The Commission recommended that at least 2.5 per cent of the total expenditure on education should be devoted to buildings and other items of capital nature including major equipment in school education and 20 to 25 per cent in the case of higher education. It also recommended providing at least four per cent of the total expenditure on school education for direction and inspection.

The Commission has placed great faith in teachers in educational reform and in the transformation of the society through them. It emphasized the need to raise the economic status of the teachers, proposing an upgradation of teacher salaries (p. 90 and p. 117). It felt that salary of the primary school teacher should be comparable to that of a public servant; it should be three to four times the per capita GNP. In case of teachers in higher education, the Commission recommended a national salary structure. University teachers should receive equivalent to what senior (IAS) officers in government services get. The government acted upon this recommendation rather promptly, though not to the extent suggested by the Commission.

The Commission also considered the need to provide schools within reach of the children and evolved a reasonable criteria like maximum distance a child can travel to reach a school. The Commission recommended that an amount equivalent to 20 per cent of the teachers' salaries should be allocated to non-teacher costs, but it did not seem to have paid sufficient attention to the provision of facilities within the schools, though it recognized the fact that schools are not adequately equipped to avoid dropout of children. In fact, the Commission felt poverty as a major reason for children dropping out of schools. As a result, the Commission did not mind recommending continuation and setting up of new single teacher schools, part-time primary education, etc., and did not feel the need to improve the school environment substantially. It was, in fact, left to district boards and municipalities to provide for infrastructure facilities; or they were simply taken for granted. As a result, many single teacher schools and schools with poor infrastructure facilities continued to grow even during the post-Commission period. Consequently, the deficit in expenditure on these items went on bulging, necessitating the government to launch country-wide the massively expensive operation blackboard programme, as recommended in the *National Policy on Education* 1986.

Among the major items the Commission paid attention to were the scholarships for students and research and improvement of quality in higher education.

## Scholarships

One of the important items of expenditure that the Commission paid serious attention was scholarships for students—as a mechanism of searching and nurturing talent, and as a mechanism of equalization of educational opportunities. The Commission favoured expansion of scholarship programme—specifically expansion of the programme of national scholarships and scholarships for the backward classes (pp. 206-221and pp. 918-19). It has recommended clear quantitative norms on the percentage of students to receive scholarships and the amounts as well – 2.5 per cent of the students at primary level (at the rate of Rs. 60 per annum), at least five per cent of the students at secondary level (at the rate of Rs. 150 per annum), and 30 per cent of the students enrolled in vocational education (at the rate of Rs. 300-400 per annum). In higher education, the Commission recommended that 25 per cent of the students in under graduate courses in arts and commerce (at the rate of Rs. 75 per month), 50 per cent of the students in under graduate courses in science and professional courses (at the rate of Rs. 125 per month), and 50 per cent of the students enrolled in post graduate courses (at the rate of Rs. 300 per month) should be provided with scholarships. In addition, the Commission recommended an increase in the number of national (merit) scholarships to about ten per cent of the students, and a wider coverage of university scholarships.

Though the amounts may vary, given the change in the value of the currency, the proportion of students to receive scholarships, suggested by the

Commission seems to be still relevant. At present, only an insignificant portion of students receive scholarships. The purpose of the scholarship programme, as envisaged by the Commission was to search and nurture talent and also to promote equity in the system. On both counts there is need to expand the present scholarship programme.[23]

In higher education, though the Commission did not find any advantage of loan scholarships over that of outright scholarships and felt that "an exclusive programme of loan scholarship is non-egalitarian", it recommended a liberal programme of loan scholarships to supplement the national and university scholarships (p. 218). A national loan scholarship scheme was launched in the subsequent years on the lines suggested by the Commission. The Commission was aware of the innumerable problems loan scholarships might create in recoveries and also the hardships that they cause to students. The problem of recovery was later found to be so severe that the programme was to be abandoned in late 1980s and was to be replaced by a normal student loan programme in the early 1990s, operated by commercial banks.[24]

## Higher Education and Research

The Commission has laid special emphasis on higher education and research, as it strongly believed that it is higher education and research that will contribute to economic development, and to bridge the gap between the rich countries and India. It suggested larger allocations to the UGC for specific programmes that will promote quality and excellence in higher education and research. For example, the Commission recommended (p. 905) creation of new centres/schools in universities, and extra financial support to some specific activities. The important ones that received the attention of the Commission include (a) creation of Centres of Advanced Study and major universities, (b) creation of Schools of Education in selected universities, (c) promotion of post graduate education and research, (d) provision of maintenance grant to state universities, (e) establishment of Central Testing Organization, (f) development of literature in modern Indian languages, (g) development of agricultural, engineering and medical education, and (h) promotion of educational research on all sectors of education. The Commission also recommended that UGC and state governments share the responsibility of providing development grants to universities (p. 634).

Some of these recommendations were followed up, though there might be still a lot to do. The Commission's recommendations that UGC provide maintenance grants to state universities, and that both UGC and state governments provide development grants to state universities did not receive any attention. UGC continues to provide only development grants to state universities and state governments tend to limit their grants to maintenance purposes.

## Role of the State and Other Sources of Funds

The Commission was emphatic in stating that most of the responsibility for education should be squarely placed on government funds (p. 870) and one should not depend upon the private sector. It rightly predicted and favoured, a big fall in the total revenue from fees. This was because the Commission rightly stressed the need to provide free and compulsory education—free education up to Grade X (up to lower secondary) and provision of free-studentships in higher secondary and higher education, and expansion of scholarships at all levels of education. The Commission also predicted that income from other sources (donations etc.,) would not rise much and that local bodies would not be able to provide more than a very small percentage of the total expenditure, howsoever best efforts they may make to raise their contribution. As a result, "the funds of the Central and State governments would have to bear about 90 per cent (or even more) of the total educational expenditure (p. 870)."

Over the years these predictions came true as far as the decline in the relative share of fees and other sources is concerned. The relative shares of fees of the local bodies and 'other' sources declined while that of the government increased. However, the latter has not reached the level of 90 per cent as recommended by the Commission. Though in case of school education the share of the government seems to be around 90 per cent, this is not the case in higher education, as the trends shown in Figure 4 indicate.[25] In recent years, it appears, the trends are further disturbing, with the decline in the relative share of the government and a steep increase in the share of student fees, particularly in higher education (Tilak and Rani, 2003).

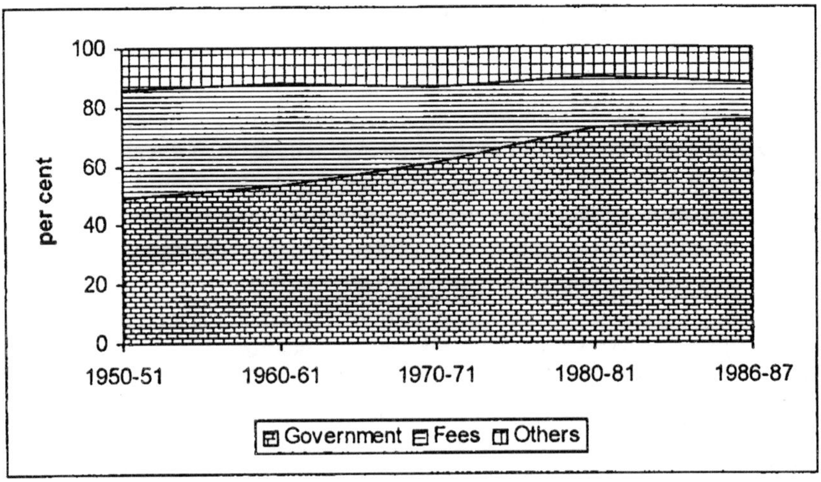


**Figure 18.4: Sources of Funds for Higher Education in India**

The Commission went further and pleaded for a larger role for the union government in financing education. While the Centre and states should meet 90 per cent of the total expenditure on education, the Central Government should assume primary responsibility and the states to have the "residual responsibility to finance education" (p. 904). Though elementary education was in the state list, the Commission favoured a larger role for the central government in funding elementary education. As Naik (1975, p. 92) reiterated, drawing from the Report of the Commission, "it will not be possible for any State Government to raise all the resources required for a programme of universal elementary education. It is, therefore, necessary to introduce a Central grant earmarked for elementary education on the basis of equalization."

Though the Commission argued for a larger responsibility to the Central government in financing education, it was not in favour of changing the constitutional provisions regarding the role of Centre and states in education. It clearly favoured continuation of education in the *State list* in the Constitution and felt that "there is plenty of scope, within the present constitutional arrangement, to evolve a workable Centre-State partnership in education and this has not been exploited to the full" (p. 830). The Commission took a holistic view on every aspect of education, rather than looking at different levels of education in different compartments. The Commission stated this clearly in the context of Centre-State relations in education: "We are not in favour of fragmenting education and putting one part in the concurrent and the other in the State list; education should, under any circumstances, be treated as a whole" (p. 829).

Contrary to what the Commission suggested, education was made a concurrent subject with the 42nd amendment to the *Constitution of India* in 1976, though one fails to note any significant increase in the role of the Centre in financing education in the following years (Tilak, 1989). It was only since 1986 after the formulation of the National Policy on Education, the Centre began assuming increasing role in financing of elementary education and contrary to the constitutional provisions there has been a diminution in the relative role of the Centre in higher education in the areas of policy formulation, planning and financing! (Tilak, 2004)

## Centrally Sponsored Sector

The larger responsibility of the Central Government should take, according to the Commission, the form of expansion of the central and centrally sponsored sectors (pp. 894-895). The Commission advocated that for any programme to be included in the Central and in the centrally sponsored sectors (pp. 908-09), it should be of crucial importance and national in character. Programmes which need the adoption of a common policy in all parts of the country should preferably be included in the centrally sponsored sector. The Commission also advocated dividing the total funds available in the centrally sponsored sector into two parts: half of them for national programmes, and the other half to the states. The states should be free to use these funds, with the approval of the union government, for any scheme which is significant and urgent in nature. The Commission made yet another important recommendation: the central assistance for centrally sponsored schemes should be non-relapsable and should be available to the states on a five year basis rather than on the basis of a plan period. In the case of important schemes in the centrally sponsored sector, the assistance may even be continued for a longer period, say ten years.

## Grants-in-aid to Local Bodies

In a Supplementary Note, the Commission has suggested a detailed mechanism of grants-in-aid to local bodies—district level bodies and municipalities (pp. 902-09), in such a way that grants-in-aid to local authorities would stimulate local contributions to education. It recommended that "the assistance of the local communities should be fully harnessed for improving the physical facilities in schools" (p. 872). The State government should provide for 100 per cent teacher grants, block grants per child to meet non-teacher costs, and separate grants for non-recurring expenditure. The Commission nevertheless realised that the local bodies may not be able to generate much funds on their own, despite their best efforts. The objective of the grants to the local bodies should be to ensure equality in expenditure per student and thereby to equalise educational opportunities. The Commission also suggested that every school should continue to receive the maintenance grant (with a provision for cut if the institution fails to perform) on some egalitarian basis, so that all schools come up to a minimum level of performance, and those schools that do good work should receive a special 'jam' grant (Naik, 1979, p. 143).

Experience shows that the state grants to local bodies have not been able to stimulate generation of resources by these bodies. The Commission was thus right in predicting that local bodies would not be able to mobilize any significant amount of resources on their own, given the limited resource base, and competing needs of various other sectors. Also, there are wide disparities in educational development in general and per capita or per student educational expenditure among districts and blocks.[26]

## Fees and Cost Recovery

The Commission had a clear and progressive understanding of the role of fees in education and its implications. The Commission stated, "It is undesirable to regard [fees] as a source of revenue. They are the most regressive form of taxation, fall more heavily on the poorer classes of society and act as an anti-egalitarian force" (p. 202). It also dismissed a 'progressive' or a discriminatory fee system based on economic levels of the students/their families as it "would not be administratively feasible and... their yield would be almost negligible" (p. 202).

Recognising the constitutional provisions, the Commission reaffirmed the importance of providing free and compulsory education of a common school system. There was no case of levy of any fees at the primary stage, though the Commission was confronted with arguments in favour of levying fees. After all, it was a constitutional commitment. The Commission was not happy that free education meant only tuition fee-free education and provision of free textbooks, but felt constrained to recommend (a) abolition of all kinds of fees in primary schools and (b) provision of incentives such as free stationery, uniforms, school meals etc. The then prevailing economic conditions seemed to have prevented the Commission from making such recommendations. It however, recommended free education up to Grade X (up to lower secondary) and provision of free studentships in higher secondary and higher education. It also recommended free vocational education. With respect to other levels of education also, the Commission did not actually favour levy of fees; but it was helpless. In case of secondary education, though it agreed to the suggestion to levy of fees at higher secondary level as a pragmatic solution to the problem of resource scarcity, it did note very clearly that "the levy of fees in secondary schools prevents several children from the poorer classes of society, and particularly girls, from receiving education" (p. 203). So it argued that in higher secondary and higher education, every attempt should be made to extend free education to cover all needy and deserving students.

With respect to higher education, the Commission found that the then existing levels of fee contributions (as a proportion of total revenues) were much higher in India than in the educationally advanced and richer countries such as the USA and Great Britain. The Commission's forward-looking progressive policies with respect to fees in higher education are worth noting: "We do not advocate the immediate general abolition of fees in higher education, although *this should be the ultimate goal of educational policy*...for the next ten years, the main effort with regard to fees in higher secondary and university education should be to expand the provision of tuition (fee)-free education to cover all the needy and deserving students. To begin with, the proportion of free-studentships should be increased to at least 30 per cent of the total enrolment. We also commend, for general acceptance, policies which have been adopted in some areas to provide tuition (fee)-free higher education to underprivileged groups" (p. 204; emphasis added).

Nowadays student fee is considered as one of the most common measures of mobilising finances for education. In fact, it is seen as a major potential source of funds. But confronted with the need to avoid neglect of the weaker sections of the society a system consisting of levy of fees along with concessions and exemptions to needy students is proposed. But the Commission did not find merit in such arguments. The Commission observed, "such a system does not have much to commend itself and involves several administrative difficulties" (p. 203).

The Commission also felt that there was no need for any cost recovery mechanisms. In fact, in the long run education would become *self financing*, not of course as being contemplated now. The Commission observed, "in the long run education to some extent is self-financing because the increased incomes generated by a relatively better educated labour force would provide resources for greater allocation to education... additional resources are generated through the process of economic growth" (p. 889) This is what Mishan (1969) also observed in a similar context, "higher education is an investment and will pay for itself; and will increase the earnings of the beneficiary students and the government will recover its costs through consequent higher tax receipts." The Commission has clearly recognised the significant economic contribution of education, when it observed, "the fact that education tends to augment the flow of national product, though with some time-lag, [and this] is of crucial importance" (p. 889).

Taking into account the 'very heavy expenditure' that parents incur on education, the Commission suggested quite a few mechanisms for mitigating their difficulties, such as strengthening of the provision of free textbooks at primary stage, launching of a programme of book-banks at secondary stage and provision of book-grants in higher education.

The evidence on levying fees in education in the post-Commission period is contrary to what the Commission recommended. Fee of all sorts, including tuition fee, were continued to be charged in government, local body and government-aided schools at primary level (Tilak, 1996a); fee levels in secondary education have been on the rise; and fees in higher education are on a steep increase (Tilak and Rani, 2003).

The Commission also argued against over dependence on private sector in education development (Naik, 1979, p. 30). The Commission felt that private sector has a limited and minor role in the national education system. It pleaded for control of private enterprise in education. Again, this suggestion is also not cared for very much by the government and, in fact, this was opposed strongly. An unbridled growth of private education at all levels of education has been allowed, with all its ramifications.

## Other Norms and Recommendations

A few other norms that were adopted by the Commission, which have serious financial implications may be noted as follows:

**First**, the pupil-teacher ratio. Though for pragmatic reasons, the Commission had adopted higher pupil-teacher ratio in estimating the resource requirements, it desired that to ensure reasonably good quality of education, the pupil-teacher ratio in primary education be 30 and 35 in higher primary schools. In lower secondary education it should be 25 students per every teacher and 20 in higher secondary education. In the case of secondary/ vocational education the desirable ratio suggested was one teacher per every 11 students. The Commission suggested such norms for higher education as well—one teacher for every 15 students on an average in under-graduate courses and eight students in post-graduate courses. Many of these norms are relevant in contemporary educational planning. The present norms and the current actual pupil-teacher ratios are much higher than the norms suggested by the Commission.

**Secondly**, the Commission realised the importance of vocational education for its own and to reduce pressures on higher education. It recommended a high degree of vocationalisation of education: 20 per cent of the total enrolments at secondary level, 50 per cent at higher secondary level and 30 per cent at higher education level. Further, it argued that 60 per cent of the students in higher education should be enrolled in professional and science courses.

Though the government often expressed in subsequent years its desire to vocationalise secondary education, the progress is not satisfactory. The reason is, fundamentally vocational education has been looked down and planned as a second rate, cheap education for the poor. As a result, it suffered from both demand and supply constraints. Vocational courses were introduced in colleges in recent years. In fact, the targets set by the Commission seem to be elusive even after forty years, as no serious attempts were made in this direction.

**Thirdly**, the Commission favoured promotion of excellence at all levels of education. Ten per cent of the schools at every level were to be provided with additional resources so that they function at optimal level of quality to become 'pace-setting' institutions! This was recommended by the Commission as "the highest priority programme" (p. 463). Similarly, the Commission favoured development of five or six 'major' universities where "first class post graduates work and research [become] possible" (pp. 506-07). This seemingly elitist idea was not favoured in the case of university education, though the recommendation relating to school education was followed-up in the following decades. The scheme of *Navodaya Vidyalayas* recommended in and set up after the *National Policy on Education 1986*, can be regarded as close to the proposal of the Commission. The proposal on universities was not received favourably by many, as it was felt that "better results would be obtained if minimum standards can be maintained in all institutions and special additional assistance, on the basis of proper criteria, given to institutions which show a high level of performance and promise" than from concentrating the efforts and resources on ten per cent of the institutions.[27] While the proposal of the Commission *per se* was not accepted, some universities did receive support for their excellence in education and research, and centres of excellence and inter-university centres were created and supported with extra funds that offer first class post graduate education and research, meeting to some extent the very objective that the Commission had in mind.

In addition to the above, there are several prescriptive observations made by the Commission in the Report which are of great significance in the present context. A few of such observations on financing of education are cited here:

The Commission rightly noted that "in the early stages of educational development the rate of growth of educational expenditure ought to be approximately twice the rate of growth of national income" (p. 873). It is important to note that this is a desirable practice. For example, Schultz (1986, p. 5) stated, "during the process of economic modernisation the rate of increase in human capital is higher than that of reproducible physical capital." If we follow the dictum and the educational expenditure increases at twice the rate of growth of the economy, reaching the goal of allocating six per cent of GDP to education will not be difficult at all, as noted by a committee of the Government of India (2005).

The Commission also recommended analysis of education expenditure by converting the figures into the constant prices. Though official documents of the government still do not present expenditure on education in constant prices, researchers have begun attempting analysis of education expenditures in real prices, using national income deflators or price indices.

The Commission stressed the need for efficient utilisation of resources. It repeatedly made the plea to eliminate under utilisation and wastage of resources in education and to introduce measures of economization.

All these are valuable suggestions of relevance at all times.

## Concluding Observations

The Report of the Education Commission was considered as a landmark in the history of Indian education. The Commission made several important suggestions, which are, even after forty years, relevant for educational development. They are relevant not just because their implementation is due; they are relevant today for their intrinsic value, essentially because the Commission had looked into the distant future, being firmly on the ground, adopted a visionary approach, built its recommendations on strong empirical evidence and knowledge—national and international—with a strong conviction on the role of education in national development, and above all with a strong commitment to national development. This short article could concentrate on a few selected aspects relating to financing of education. Even within the restricted area of finances, the paper could not be exhaustive in even listing all the recommendations made by the Commission. They are too many to cover in such a short paper. A few major recommendations of the Commission were selected for revisiting their premises, vision, implementation and current relevance.

Despite realising the need to be austere due to several reasons, as it worked under the overall atmosphere of austerity, the Commission did not compromise on a few vital issues. For instance, the Commission strongly advocated a national system of education; and it pleaded for universal full time education of the common school type to all children, though development of alternative channels of education was also suggested, as full time universal education was not immediately possible. It has argued for a free common school system of public education up to the end of Grade X and the adoption of neighbourhood school concept at the elementary stage (p. 458). It also suggested that all private schools must be brought into the common school system.[28] Third, it has recommended a large expansion of scholarship programme. It has also recommended a significant expansion of the centrally sponsored sector in education. Above all, it strongly recommended increase in the allocation of resources to education to the level of six per cent of GNP.

Unfortunately, while the Commission recommended a package of reforms, the government looked at the recommendations as piecemeal suggestions. As Naik (1979) observed, "It is thus a tragedy that the recommendations of the one Commission which was directed to look *comprehensively* at education were considered mostly in a *piecemeal* fashion" (p. 38; emphasis original). Many of the recommendations of the Commission on education in general and financing of education in particular were not acted upon with the seriousness they required. Some of them were accepted and some were rejected; some of them were paid lip-service; and many of them were ignored. While there can be several factors for the inaction of the government, the lack of strong political will seems to be the most important one. As a result, the Indian education system is still characterised with conspicuous failures—in eradicating illiteracy, in universalising elementary education, in vocationalisation of secondary education, in ensuring excellence and high standards in higher education, in allocating adequate resources for education, in improving the financial efficiency of the system, etc. Despite all these failures, some spectacular achievements in terms of student numbers, in building one of the largest reservoirs of scientific and technical manpower in the world, in 'exporting' manpower, etc., cannot be overlooked. The reason for widespread discontentment with the education sector is obvious. The Commission itself warned, "A report which is shelved or does not lead to action is worse than no report because it leads to frustration by arousing hopes that remain unfulfilled" (p. 897).

## Notes

1. Gross National Product.
2. Malcolm Adiseshiah: 'Foreword' to Naik (1979).
3. In the case of such recommendations, there is a wide difference between the Commission's recommendations and their actual implementation. See Adiseshiah (1994).
4. Letter of Submission of the Report by D. S. Kothari, addressed to M. C. Chagla, Minister for Education (*Report*, p. v).
5. The members of the Commission included 11 Indians, and one each from France, Japan, UK, USA and the USSR. This enabled the Commission to review the Indian situation in a comparative manner.
6. Economics of Education was formally born only in 1960, with the Presidential Address of Theodore W Schultz (1961) to the American Economic Association. Many studies were conducted only later.
7. The manpower planning exercise presented in the Report, as a Minute of Supplementation (pp. 937-92) was also first of its kind in India and was found to be of great significance. It was separately published Burgess et al (1968). Chapter XIX and the Minute of Supplementation form two very important contributions of the Commission to Economics and Financing of Education in India.
8. Following this recommendation, a series of studies on costs and financing of universities were later sponsored/conducted by the University Grants Commission, the Indian Council of Social Science Research, the National Council of Educational Research and Training, etc.
9. A similar recommendation was made by the Kher committee (1951) as early as 1950 that the Government of India should spend about ten per cent of its total revenue on education.
10. This was also circulated as a paper from the Planning Commission.
11. The *National Agenda for Governance* (BJP & Alliance Partners, 1998, p.5) has promised to "formulate and implement plans to gradually increase the governmental *and non-governmental* spending on education up to six per cent of the GDP" (emphasis added).
12. The *Economic Survey* (1998-99) stated: "Financing of education—increase in government and non-government spending on education, and bringing this up to six per cent GDP level" (p. 150).
13. For the first time, the terms 'national income' and 'GNP' were replaced by GDP (gross domestic product) in the statement. This was also mentioned in the *Economic Survey 2004-05*.
14. Interestingly, the recommendation to regulate the growth of higher education was opposed by many, but this figured as an important objective of educational planning in the fourth and fifth five year plans, given the rising rates of graduate unemployment, which was also noted by the Commission. The concern of the Commission on unemployment led to a full-fledged study on the problem (e.g., Blaug et al, 1969).
15. For Example, Tilak (1994) estimated that it would be above eight per cent.
16. Author's calculations based on *Education in India* and *Analysis of Budget*

*Expenditure on Education* (various years) of the Ministry of Education/Human Resource Development, Government of India.

17. That the proportion declined during the economic reform period is noted by many. For example, see Tilak (1996b) and Sadgopal (2004).
18. Naik (1979), however, lists it among the recommendations that attracted *limited* attention (pp. 59-60).
19. Based on *Five Year Plan(*s), and *Analysis of Annual Plan*(s) of the Education Division, Planning Commission, Government of India.
20. Based on *Five Year Plan*(s) and *Analysis of Annual Plan*(s) of the Education Division, Planning Commission, Government of India.
21. Primary education, according to the Commission, includes lower primary and higher primary education, i.e., up to Grade VII/VIII, which is nowadays being referred to as elementary education.
22. Quoted in Desai (1953, p. 57).
23. It is only in the most recent months that the UGC has launched a special research fellowship programme for weaker sections.
24. For a review of the national loan scholarship scheme, see Tilak (1992).
25. Based on *Education in India* (various years). New Delhi: Ministry of Education/ Human Resource Development.
26. See several papers in Tilak (1986b).
27. Committee of Members of Parliament. [quoted in J. P. Naik, 1979, p. 140).
28. Unfortunately many of these recommendations, including the strong recommendation of the Commission for the adoption of the common school system have been conveniently relegated to the dustbin. See Kamat (1985, p. 133).

## References

Acharya Ramamurti Committee, (1990). Government of India: *Towards an Enlightened and Human Society: NPE 1986: A Review, Report of the Committee for Review of National Policy on Education 1986* [Chairman: Acharya Ramamurti]. Faridabad: Government of India Press.

Adiseshiah, M.S. (1994). Education: The Normative (Kothari) Frame and the Actual, in *Education, Science and Human Values: Essays in Honour of Professor D.S. Kothari* (eds. R.C. Mehrotra and R.K. Arora). New Delhi: Wiley Eastern, pp. 120-38.

BJP & Alliance Partners, (1998). *National Agenda for Governance: Closing the Gap between People's Aspirations and Government's Performance*. New Delhi.

Blaug, Mark Richard Layard and Maureen Woodhall (1969). *The Causes of Graduate Unemployment in India*, London: Allen Lane the Penguin.

Burgess, T., Richard Layard and Pitambar Pant (1968). *Manpower and Educational Development in India 1961-1986*, London: Oliver & Boyd.

Delors Commission, (1996). *Learning the Treasure Within: Report to UNESCO of the International Commission on Education for the Twenty-First Century* (Chairperson: Jacques Delors). Paris: UNESCO.

Desai, D.M. (1953). *Universal, Compulsory and Free Primary Education in India*. Bombay: Indian Institute of Education.

Education Commission, (1966). *Education and National Development: Report of the Education Commission 1964-66*. New Delhi: Government of India, Ministry of Education [Reprint by the National Council of Educational Research and Training, March 1971].

Government of India, (1968). *National Policy on Education 1968*. New Delhi: Ministry of Education.

Government of India, (1985). *Challenge of Education*, New Delhi: Ministry of Education.

Government of India, (1986). *National Policy on Education 1986*. New Delhi: Ministry of Human Resource Development.

Government of India, (2005). *Report of the Committee on National Common Minimum Programme's Commitment to Six Per cent of GDP to Education*. New Delhi: National Institute of Educational Planning and Administration.

Kamat, A.R. (1985). *Education and Social Change in India*, Bombay: Somaiya.

Kher Committee, (1951). *Report of the Committee on the Relationship between State Governments and Local Bodies in the Administration of Primary Education* (Chairman: B.G. Kher), New Delhi: Government of India.

Kolhatkar, M.R. (1988). Education Expenditure in India in Relation to National Income (1980-88): Trends and Implications, *Journal of Education and Social Change* 2(2).

Ministry of Finance, (1999). *Economic Survey 1998-99*. New Delhi: Ministry of Finance, Government of India.

Mishan, Edward J. (1969). Some Heretical Thoughts on University Reform: The Economics of Changing the System, *Encounter* 32 (3) (March 1969): 3-15.

Naik, J.P. (1975). *Elementary Education in India: A Promise to Keep*. Bombay: Allied, 1975.

Naik, J.P. (1979). *The Education Commission and After*. New Delhi. [Second edition, New Delhi: A.P.H. Publishing Corporation, 1997].

Planning Commission, (1999). *Ninth Five Year Plan 1997-2002* (Draft). New Delhi: Government of India, Vol. II.

Sadgopal, Anil (2004). Globalisation and Education: Defining the Crisis, XVI Zakir Husain Memorial Lecture, New Delhi.

Sarup, Anand (1988). Planning for Educational Development, in Amrik Singh and G.D. Sharma (eds.) *Higher Education in India: The Social Context*, Delhi: Konark, pp. 252-62.

Shah, K.R. (2006). State Inaction in Education in India, *Journal of Educational Planning and Administration* 20 (3) (October 2006): (in press)

Schultz, T.W. (1961). Investment in Human Capital, *American Economic Review*, 51 (1) (March): 1-15.

Tapas Majumdar Committee, (2005). See also the *Report of the Committee on National Common Minimum Programme's Commitment to Six Per cent of GDP to Education*. New Delhi: Ministry of Human Resource Development (November) [Chairman: Tapas Majumdar] [http://niepa.org/download/mhrd%20report.pdf]

Tilak, J.B.G. (1984). Political Economy of Investment in Education in South Asia, *International Journal of Educational Development* 4 (2):155-66.

Tilak, J.B.G. (1986a). Political Economy of Investment in Education in South Asia: A Reply, *International Journal of Educational Development* 6 (3): 209-14.

Tilak, J.B.G. (ed.) (1986b). *Education and Regional Development*, New Delhi: Yatan Publications.

Tilak, J.B.G. (1989). Center-State Relations in Financing Education in India, *Comparative Educational Review* 33 (4) (November): 450-80

Tilak, J.B.G. (1990). Expenditure on Education in India, *Journal of Education and Social Change* Volume IV, No. 2 (July-September): 62-69;

Tilak, (1992). Student Loans in Financing Higher Education in India, *Higher Education* 23 (4) (June): 389-404.

Tilak, (1994). *Resource Requirements of Education in India: Implications for the Tenth Finance Commission* (Report prepared for the Government of India). New Delhi: National Institute of Educational Planning and Administration 1994. http://shikshanic.nic.in/cd50years/g/U/18/toc.htm

Tilak, J.B.G. (1996a). How Free is 'Free' Primary Education in India? *Economic and Political Weekly* 31 (5 & 6) (3 & 10 February): 275-82; and 355-66.

Tilak, J.B.G. (1996b). Higher Education under Structural Adjustment, *Journal of Indian School of Political Economy* 8 (2) (April-June): 266-93;

Tilak, J.B.G. (1999). National Human Development Initiative: Education in the Union Budget, *Economic and Political Weekly* (March 6): 614-20

Tilak, J.B.G (2001). Education and Development: Lessons from Asian Experience, *Indian Social Science Review* (ICSSR, New Delhi) 3 (2) (July-December): 219-66.

Tilak, J.B.G. (2003). *State, Households and Markets in Education*, 2003 Malcolm Adiseshiah Memorial Lecture. Chennai: Madras Inst of Development Studies.

Tilak, J.B.G (2004). Absence of Policy and Perspective in Higher Education, *Economic and Political Weekly* 39 (21) (22 May): 2159-64.

Tilak, J.B.G. (2006). On Allocating 6 per cent GDP to Education, *Economic and Political Weekly*, 41 (7) (18 February): 613-18.

Tilak, J.B.G., and Geeta Rani: Changing Pattern of University Finances in India, *Journal of Services Research* 2 (2) (October 2002-March 2003): 5-46.

UPA Government (2004). *Common Minimum Programme*, New Delhi: United Progressive Alliance, May [http://pmindia.nic.in/cmp.pdf].

# Part VI

# Education Commission's Perception of Knowledge

# 19

# Knowledge for National Development

PUSHPA M. BHARGAVA

## Introduction

Two scenarios can be painted on the use of knowledge for development of a country such as ours. In the first, knowledge that is used for development would be confined to a small percentage of the population—the rich and the powerful—and so would, largely, the products of development. The rest of the people—the unprivileged and the deprived—would surely benefit but to a much smaller extent and entirely on account of a trickle-down effect. In such a scenario, one could have a high rate of growth of GDP that makes the rich richer and the poor generally poorer, with at the most only a marginal benefit (which cannot be helped) coming to them. This is the situation today in our country and in many parts of the developing world. They are living examples of use of knowledge by a few to exploit the many, who are denied access to knowledge.

In the second scenario, the entire society will be a knowledge-based society, where all members of the society would not only have access to knowledge but would also be actually in possession of a certain minimum amount of knowledge that would enable them to claim their rights and discharge their duties effectively. The challenge, therefore, is how to achieve the second scenario. To be able to do that, we must, first understand the attributes of knowledge.

## Attributes of Knowledge

I believe, the following attributes of knowledge, which define knowledge, are noteworthy in the context of a knowledge-based society:

- For a citizen of any country to protect his rights and discharge his responsibilities, he/she needs to have a certain minimum amount of knowledge.
- For anyone to survive gainfully in the wake of ever-increasing competition, and maintain his self-respect and escape exploitation, he will, today need to be both a specialist and a generalist.

- There is a hierarchy of data, information, knowledge and wisdom. For information, one needs data. For knowledge, one needs information. For conversion of information into knowledge, one needs wisdom. Knowledge requires collation of information from multiple sources and of multiple kinds. Conversion of knowledge into wisdom requires weaving of experience (one's own as well as collective) into the fabric of knowledge.
- Ignorance comes as a package, while knowledge comes in bits. Ignorance is thrust on people; knowledge is acquired. Ignorance is like sand; knowledge is like rock.
- Today, knowledge knows no boundaries, and is a continuum. Man compartmentalizes knowledge as an alibi for ignorance.
- There is a direct relationship between a knowledge-based society and good governance; neither have any relationship to affluence. As there is no country in the world today that has a truly knowledge-based society, in no country governance is anywhere near ideal.
- The higher we go up in the hierarchy of power, greater is the demand for knowledge—not of just one discipline but of the whole continuum—but, generally, the lesser is the knowledge-base. This opens up doors for exploitation by self-interest groups operating nationally or internationally.
- It is not enough to be knowledgeable or have access to knowledge; it is more important to use it when required to ensure equity.
- Religious fundamentalism and terrorism, obscurantism, superstition, and irrational practices, are a consequence of vested interests that insulate people from knowledge.
- A knowledge-based society is easier to govern, provided the Government intends to be honest, fair, transparent and people-oriented. On the other hand, a selfish and/or totalitarian Government does not want its people to be truly knowledgeable.
- Today, knowledge dissemination, not only in the developing countries but also in the developed countries is extremely uneven. This unevenness provides, perhaps, the largest base for exploitation.
- Mechanisms of knowledge generation, dissemination and use around the world are faulty to various degrees, creating a fertile ground for growth of exploitation.
- Knowledge evolves and multiplies when shared. It remains stagnant and decays when kept confined.
- Knowledge equity within a country and between countries is essential for world peace. Knowledge inequity is the most important avenue of exploitation and neocolonialism.
- Globalization of knowledge equity will lead, in succession, to:

globalization of rights and responsibilities; globalization of access, of employment, and of facilities; breaking of barriers that divide people arbitrarily; globalization of peace; and, thus, progress towards one world.

A large number of examples can be given in support of the above statements. I shall, however, confine myself to making just two statements about religious fundamentalism and terrorism:

(a) I believe that all religious fundamentalism and terrorism, be it Hindu, Islamic, Zionist or Christian—now or in the past, is a consequence of what I have termed elsewhere as "seven deadly sins of the clergy" [1], one of which is to keep people insulated from knowledge.
(b) Prince Ghazi of Jordan, who is the special envoy of King Abdullah of Jordan, and has a Ph.D. from Cambridge, has, in his scholarly book [2] written under the pseudonym of Vincent Oliveti, attributed Islamic fundamentalism and terrorism to lack of knowledge and deliberate misinterpretation of the teachings of the Prophet as documented in the original Quran, by the Wahabi-Salafi sect of Muslims that is largely controlled by the clergy.

To make our country become a knowledge-based society, in which, all its people, cutting across our numerous man-made divisions, would be able to contribute towards national development through knowledge, I believe, we would need to look at a number of areas concurrently. Some of these areas would be: education, science and technology, agriculture and rural sector, traditional knowledge, governance, civil society, health, industry, social sciences, innovation and entrepreneurship, and patent and intellectual property rights. We would need to come up with integrated and coordinated programmes in all these areas that would be implementable and people friendly. In fact, this is meant to be the primary objective of the National Knowledge Commission set up by the Prime Minister of India in 2005. In this paper, I would deal with certain (not all) aspects of education, agriculture and rural sector, and traditional knowledge, in some detail. In these areas I will mention some important issues that we would need to look at or questions that we would need to answer.

## Education

For India to evolve into a knowledge-based society, one of the most important actions that our Parliament would need to take is to pass a bill de-commercialising school education, college (+2) education, and all higher education leading to an under-graduate or post-graduate degree. Before we proceed further, we must distinguish between commercial private institutions, which we must eventually ban, and non-commercial private institutions, which we should encourage. The commercial private institutions are set up with the idea of making profit that would go to the individuals, who have invested in the institution, exactly as happens in a company. Non-commercial private institutions may also—of course—make profit; however, the profit they make would be reinvested in the institution and no one would benefit from the profit the way that shareholders benefit by investing in a company. We must also recognize that today we have a number of educational institutions registered as societies or as trusts on paper; however, a detailed scrutiny of their real accounts would show that their primary objective is to siphon off money for those who promoted the institutions. This must stop. For this to happen, a new system of assessment, accreditation, supervision and auditing of private institutions would need to be set up.

I am not ruling out the setting up of private educational institutions in specialized areas—such as for training air hostesses or in the area of hotel management—which would not grant any kind of degree. The value of their certification would be determined by the quality of their products as assessed by the market.

In education, we would also need to look at the choices we provide, the kind of citizens we wish to produce, and the steps that we must take to rejuvenate our moribund school, college, vocational, university and professional education and research. Our strength is that we have some outstanding world class institutions; our weakness is that our average is abysmally low in comparison to that in countries that we must compete with to gain our rightful position in the community of nations.

We must also look at, squarely and boldly, the problem of the medium of instruction at various levels and increasing demand for democratizing the ability to read, write and speak English fluently.

I will here deal with the kind of citizens we should consider having, the question of choice, school education, university education, and the language issue.

## What Kind of Citizens?

We state below our perception of the values that would be important for our fellow citizens to cultivate, the minimal knowledge that they should have, and the concepts of which they should have a fair understanding so that they could appreciate their implications:

(i) Concept (and advantages) of a pluralistic society.

(ii) *Secularism*

- National integration
- Equality of sexes, castes, religious groups (untouchability)
- Internationalism

- Interdependence of nations
- Difference between "discrimination" and "making a distinction"
- Impartiality

(iii) Concept of common good

(iv) Socialism and democracy

- Understanding their implications
- Fight against exploitation
- Fight for social justice

(v) Awareness of our Constitution

(vi) Why lasting peace at various levels?

(vii) Commitment to UN declaration of human rights

(viii) Family planning

(ix) Cleanliness

- Personal cleanliness (the scientific view)
- Civic sense

(x) Health and sanitation (the scientific view)

(xi) Balanced nutrition (the scientific view)

(xii) Organisation vs chaos

(xiii) Social consciousness: advantages of social organisation

(xiv) Team work

- Group accomplishment
- Cooperation
- Networking

(xv) Freedom vs constraints

- Rights and privileges vs duties and obligations
- The right to question
- The responsibilities associated with this right

(xvi) Not to make an exception of oneself to a rule

(xvii) Respect for others and their rights

(xviii) Concern for problems of the future

(xix) Making the best use of our real accomplishments in the past, while recognising our failures during the same period

(xx) Modernity

- Contemporanity
- Amenability to change (acceptance of useful new knowledge and inventions and ability to discard)

(xxi) Efficiency

- Ability to organise one's thoughts and actions

(xxii) Need to work

- Dignity of labour
- Meaning and value of leisure

(xxiii) Commitment to excellence

(xxiv) Creative and innovative thinking
- Healthy curiosity
- How to find an answer to a question (the use of the method of science)

(xxv) Relationship between education and work
- Recognition that both are interdependent and continuing processes

(xxvi) Conservation of environment
- Prevention of pollution
- Understanding that the earth is a common heritage

(xxvii) Importance of ecology

(xxviii) Conservation of natural resources, flora, fauna

(xxix) Prevention of waste

(xxx) Need for understanding the environment we live in
- Ecology
- Science and technology
- Law
- Government
- Political systems
- Economics
- Planning

(xxxi) Attitude towards ostentation and show

(xxxii) Scientific Temper
- Objective and rational thinking
- Clear thinking
- Open mindedness
- Amenability to reason
- Construction of viable arguments
- Problem solving
- Decision making

(xxxiii) Scientific attitude towards
- Obscurantism
- Dogma, irrational beliefs
- Custom, convention, tradition
- Age, authority

(xxxiv) Understanding and knowing our history and geography

(xxxv) Aesthetics
- How it helps us

(xxxvi) Codes of behaviour

(xxxvii) Personal qualities
- Endurance
- Courage

- Compassion
- Consideration
- Kindness
- Helpfulness (not derived from patronage)
- Modesty
- Truthfulness
- Honesty
- Faithfulness
- Loyalty
- Tolerance
- Confidence (arising out of knowledge)
- Fairness
- Self-discipline
- Self-control
- Sense of responsibility at various levels

(xxxviii) Attitude towards winning or losing in a competition

- Recognition of merit and excellence greater than our own

(xxxix) Importance of

- Quantification and abstraction
- Estimation
- Accuracy

One of the important objectives of our formal education system (especially up to the +10 level) should be to ensure that the commitment of our future citizens includes what has been mentioned above.

## Choices

Suggestions for choices are given in Figure 19.1.

## School Education

School education is the foundation of all development in any culture or civilization today. There is no country in the world which has done well socially and economically that does not have a sound school education system. *Our* school system is far from being satisfactory. To make it serve as a foundation for national development, we must make education up to high school a fundamental and justiciable right implementable fully by the end of a specified period, say seven years.

We would need to give all children in the country full opportunity to go from class 1 to at least class 10 (if not class 12) in good schools, without their having to pay any fees. This can be achieved by having enough (say, 400,000) high schools of the caliber of good Central or *Navodaya* Schools and having them funded by the Central Government but run by the local-self-government as neighbourhood schools that would be a part of a Common School System.

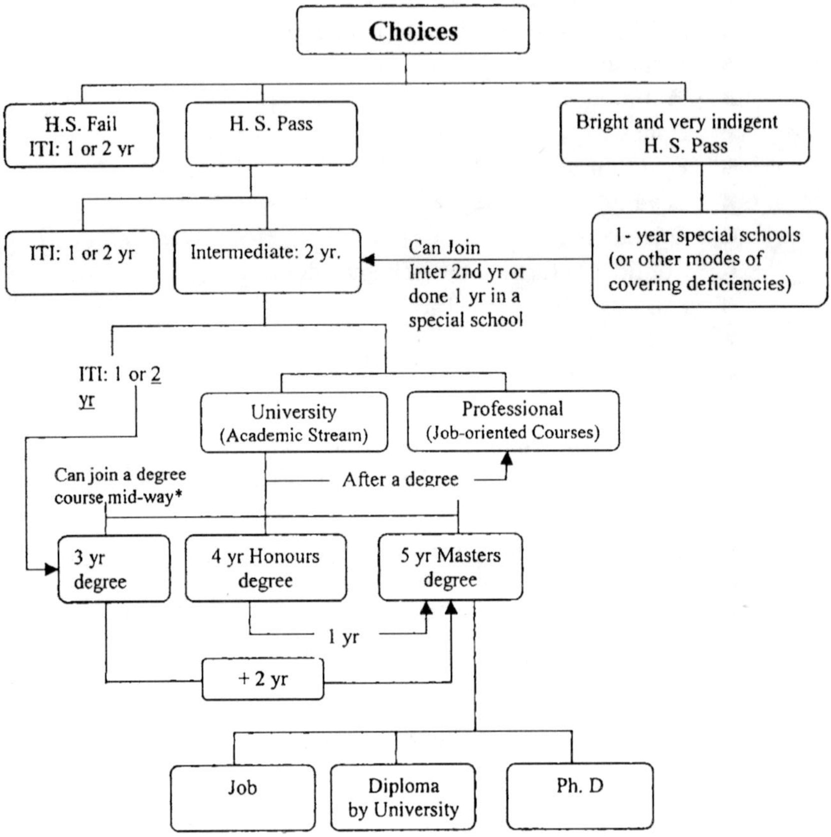


* get a degree in 1 or 2 yr depending on credits

**Figure 19.1: Education Choices**

This is the only way to eventually end reservations in academic institutions or jobs. (This would also help implement laws against child labour.) We would need to design government schools in a way that they serve as community centres outside of school hours. In the villages these schools can house public libraries and other activities that relate to acquisition, dissemination or use of knowledge. Adequate provision for pre-school educational facilities for those who wish to avail them should also be made.

We would need to ensure that all private, non-commercial schools fall in the pattern of free, neighbourhood schools, if need be through government support.

Some of the other steps that we need to take to make our school system responsive to social needs are the following:

- It should be noted that the Right to Education Bill, suggested by the Central Advisory Board for Education (CABE), was partially altered before presentation to the GOI. This "mutilated" bill was further mutilated/diluted in 2006 when it was decided not to have it come up in the Parliament but to send it to the States. This bill (sent to the States) does not have any of the features of an appropriate Right to Education Bill, some of which are detailed below. Therefore, the Central Government must immediately rescind the order through which the "doubly mutilated" Right to Education Bill was sent to the States. As legally, morally and ethically, universal quality school education is the responsibility of the Central Government, an appropriate Right to Education Bill should be passed by the Central Government as a means to discharge this responsibility. Steps should, therefore, be taken to have an appropriate Bill prepared for submission to the Central Government for follow-up. In the proposed Bill, education up to high school (10 years of school) should be made a fundamental, justiciable right. Mechanisms for implementing justiciably must be formulated and stated in the Bill, which should also incorporate the relevant points mentioned earlier in Sections (iii) to (v) and in the paras that follow:
- Government schools cannot work on the scale on which they are required in the country, and deliver quality education, if there exists, concurrently, a provision for private schools to charge tuition fees. Therefore, we need a law not only to prohibit commercialization of school education but also to prohibit charging of regular tuition fees by private schools. As already mentioned, private schools set up with an altruistic or philanthropic motive (as has happened in the past) should be integrated into the proposed Common School System, and supported financially by the Government to the extent required. A separate system for the auditing of accounts of private schools, referred to earlier, could be set up by the State School Regulatory Authority mentioned later.
- The maximum number of students in each class must be stated. All schools must have provision for nutritionally satisfactory mid-day meals. Participation of children in the regular chores of the school should be encouraged.
- The management of schools should vest with the local-self-government and civil society, even though funding for the school may come from the Central Government. Thus *Panchayats* could

run a high school in their area with the help of members of the civil society selected by the *Panchayats* from within or from outside the community the school covers. Thus, the management of schools should be decentralized.

- Stated minimum infrastructural requirements must be met by every school (be it in the private or the public sector); these requirements should be in accordance with the report of the Tapas Majumdar Committee, for example in respect of facilities such as buildings, toilets, drinking water, library, and facilities for the physically (including visually) challenged. The model of a good Central School or a *Navodaya* School could be followed.
- It should be ensured that there is equity in terms of quality of teaching and of teachers in the school to the extent possible.
- As regards qualifications for school teachers, they should be flexible with emphasis on concern, commitment, knowledge and communication skills necessary for the teaching that is expected to be done by the teacher, rather than on mere educational qualifications. Thus, for teaching of art, music or skills such as carpentry and weaving, what should be required is expertise in the area and the ability to communicate the skill to young students, rather than a degree or diploma. Suitable teacher-training programmes should be instituted, which the teachers could attend during the vacation. Their participation in such programmes should be financially supported. [*Suggestion*: the salary and grade (and avenues for promotion or career advancement) of teachers should be at least that of a provincial civil service officer.]
- There should be multiplicity of text books from which teachers could choose; concurrently, there should be flexibility in terms of the methodology of teaching.
- The process of framing of syllabi must be decentralized so that maximum use is made of local features and potential. Only the principles of framing the syllabus should be stated in the policy document. For example, the emphasis should be on concepts rather than on facts. Emerging new and exciting areas such as earth sciences, weather forecasting, bio-diversity—and useful areas such as acquisition of life skills—should find appropriate slots in the traditional disciplines; where possible new disciplines should be identified. The syllabus could state what we expect from a child; how these expectations are met must be left entirely to the teacher-student combine. This would bring to fore (and integrate into the formal system of education) our traditional knowledge, e.g. in respect of algorithms for calculation.

- For an appropriate curriculum and syllabus to be prepared, it would be necessary to state as to the kind of citizens we wish to produce in the country and what the purpose of the "+10" education should be. In my opinion, the emphasis in school education should be not on providing jobs but on producing responsible and knowledgeable citizens and developing skills that would allow one to use his/her hand to make a product or provide a service later in one's life. Thus every child getting out of high school should have acquired a skill on which he or she can subsequently build to earn a livelihood. The content of high school education and the mode of its delivery, should prepare a person to exercise one's rights and discharge one's obligations as a citizen reasonably adequately, even if the individual does not wish to study further. The options open for one who passes through a high school must be made known to the child—as also the options if the child drops out before finishing high school or does not pass through the high school.
- The assessment of students should be continuous, and the concept of a board examination to be taken at the end of a specified number of years, should be progressively abandoned. Every evaluation activity during continuous assessment must be regarded as a learning activity. As the emphasis would be on concepts and not on facts, open book examinations should be encouraged.
- A massive re-prioritization of funds should take place to ensure appropriate allocation of funds for the national school system. Deadlines for this to happen should be set up. For example, the Central Government should commit to spend six per cent of its GDP on education by the financial year 2008-2009.
- An appropriate School Regulatory Authority at the national level should be set up. To make it effective, systems such as the CBSC and ISC should be wound up so that there is just one school system in the country. While policies could be laid down by the Central Authority mentioned above, while the funds may come from the Central Government, and while the management of the school may be in the hands of the local-self-government and the civil society, the overall supervision of the school system and its regulation and monitoring should be in the hands of an appropriate body of the State (State School Regulatory Authority). There should be no accreditation permitted of Indian schools run by a foreign body. The appointment of teachers should vest totally with the school management and should be for a particular school, or a small number of schools such as a set of primary schools and a high school run by the same local authority. School teachers must not be burdened with

duties such as election duties for which part-time students could be engaged. The job of teachers should not be transferable except between schools run in the same area by the same local authority, e.g., a primary school and a high school run by the same group of *Panchayats*. State School Regulatory Authority should have the right to close a school.

- Even though, teachers' guides may be available, teachers must be free to teach as they consider appropriate. The assessment of teachers must be partly done by the students. The performance of the students could be another indicator of the extent and the manner in which the teacher has exercised his/her responsibility. While assessing the performance of the students their background should be taken into account.
- The country perhaps needs some 600 district institutes of educational training (DIET) where the teachers could be sent for periodical updating. The setting up of these institutes must be on a time-bound basis.
- Incentives should be provided for private investment in the school system in accordance with what has been mentioned above.
- School students should be encouraged to create interesting new data while learning, e.g. on micro-biodiversity as suggested by Dr. Madhav Gadgil of the Indian Institute of Science.
    - In the school system, a compulsory course should be introduced on basic information for citizens such as traffic rules, human rights, religions of the world, our administrative system, waste disposal, public health issues, agents causing contamination of water, land and air, and the like.
    - The present examination system in schools should be replaced by a system in which only objective (multiple choice) questions are asked and the answer sheets can be evaluated mechanically. No student should be failed up to Class X. In Class X (and later), the results should have a clause of "Re-examination" instead of "Fail". The examination system should be such that a failed student can take an examination every few months. Eventually (after, say, ten years), public examinations should be replaced by internal examinations based on course systems, marks (grades) being awarded for work and performance all through. At the high school level, the proposed objective of public examinations till they continue should be to test knowledge of concepts more than that of facts.
    - A system of extramural courses/lectures for students/parents/public on interesting/new areas, should be introduced.

- Bright, indigent students at high school level (as is being done by some NGOs, such as BREAD) should be identified, and a special system (including financial support and facilities for "deficiency" make-up, such as summer and holiday training, evening classes of six months to a year in a special school) set up for their further education.

## Higher (University) Education

### *(a) Objective of Higher Education*

If the higher education is in a professional course, the objective should clearly be to prepare a person for a profession. This would be true also of vocational education at all levels. However, the objective of university education in basic disciplines, such as physics, chemistry, sociology, economics, biology, history or languages, should be to produce experts in the area who are knowledgeable and excited about the field, and who are capable of engaging in research to push the frontiers of knowledge. Such people, if they turn out to be true experts in the field, would rarely be without a job; history shows that for such people, jobs are always created and that is how knowledge advances and new disciplines come into existence.

### *(b) Nature of Higher Educational Institutions*

There should be a substantial investment in higher education (ideally, over one percent of GDP). While private institutions granting degrees should be encouraged, it should be ensured by a suitable legislation (an Act of the Parliament) that they are *de facto* and *de jure* not commercial institutions (that is, like companies). All profit made by such institutions should be put back to meet the objectives of the institution within the country. They should be set up following the same procedure as a publicly funded institution, and they should submit themselves to the same regulatory mechanism as the publicly-funded institutions would need to do.

As regards foreign institutions setting up campuses in the country, the CNR Committee recommendations should apply. In brief, this would mean that they should follow all the above provisions, and that the degree given should be an Indian degree and not the degree of a foreign institution.

There should be no bar to private profit for organizations in the technical sector that provide specific training in an area of interest to the country and its people; they should not be authorized to provide a degree (but can provide a diploma or a certificate), and must operate ethically. They should be regulated by a separate authority that will ensure, through appropriate mechanisms (such as a security deposit with the government), that the students are not taken for a ride and get a reasonable return on their investment.

There should be a higher education regulatory authority (HERA) consisting of academicians of high public credibility, vision and strong commitment to the country and to excellence, that would set up systems of accreditation of all institutions of higher education and license testing and monitoring organizations.

### *(c) Who Gets in?*

Details in Figure 19.1.

### *(d) Access*

- Admission must be means-blind and made on the basis of merit and not on the basis of a student's ability to pay—be it in private or in the state-run universities.
- Poor students must be supported financially and schemes must be worked out for this to happen, including bank loans through an arrangement between a bank and the university.
- In principle, every student's fee should be paid, be it by the student (through one's own source or through a university-arranged bank loan), by the State or by the university.

### *(e) How may Students Get in?*

- There should be national tests like those conducted by Educational Testing Service of Princeton, but testing both scholastic ability and social experience and sensitivity, for admission to a university, which the student should take during the last year of his pre-university education.
- The Test should be conducted 4-6 times a year, and a student should be able to take the test as many times he/she wishes, and ask for any test score to be sent or not to be sent to the universities of his choice.
- There should be a nominal fee for the test. During the test the student should give preferences of universities all over the country. The universities can then decide whom to take on the basis of the test score.
- If a person has succeeded in obtaining admission to more than one university, he or she must indicate by, say, January, the university of his or her preference—so that all universities finalize their admissions, by say, May. All this can be done easily using ICT.
- The above test should cover all private universities too.

### *(f) Quantity*

We need 3,000 good universities (that is, universities that satisfy all the criteria laid down by the proposed Higher Education Regulatory Authority), each with not more than 10,000 students. This can be achieved in the following way:

- Upgrade existing universities by, for example, providing a certain percentage of their budget as extra grant every year, that would ensure that they follow the new norms of the regulatory authority.
- Convert good colleges into universities—private or State-run—ensuring that they are not commercial institutions.
- Have small colleges in a city that are good and are not *de facto* or *de jure* commercial institutions, come together to form a university in which, for example, the faculty appointments would be transferable from one constituent college to another; one college could have one department and another college another department.
- Set up new universities (to begin with, perhaps 20) in the next five years.

### (g) Employment of Those Coming Out of the Universities

Employers may conduct their own tests to ascertain suitability of the output of institutions of higher learning.

### (h) Quality (Teachers, Infrastructure, Students, Management)

— Institute a new stringent, objective and fair system of appointment and promotion of university teachers.

— Increase proportion of non-tenure, contract appointments.

— Introduce transparency and accountability in regard to the above mentioned. Any university appointment should be open to all citizens of the country as well as to citizens of other countries if suitable persons are not available in the country.

— Prevent inbreeding by using suitable conventions.

— Remove barriers to involving appropriate people from outside India in teaching and assessment at various levels.

— Make retirement age flexible for outstanding academicians, satisfying stringent criteria.

— Make provision of compulsory retirement with (more than?) full benefits for non-performers of today—after the new system takes root.

— Set up a code for university teachers, say, in regard to attendance, and number of teaching hours. The most famous and the best-known members of the faculty should teach undergraduates.

— Dissociate salary from position and function in the academic world (examples are available).

— Provide liberal incentives for proven and recognised accomplishments of teachers. Abrogate existing system of time-bound promotions. Link career prospects for the staff of academic institutions with performance evaluated stringently.

— Set up a stringent (but fair and objective) system of evaluation of institutions based on specific but dynamic criteria. Higher Education Regulatory Authority may accredit appropriate organisations for doing this and reporting to HERA, which would have the authority to give punishment or reward.
— Introduce salary differentials (within a specified range) within a department, within a university, and between universities.
— Make provision for regular part-time employment (e.g., one could have two half-time secretaries instead of one full-time, or a university teacher could draw part of his/her salary from the university and part from an industry. Thus, encourage multi-institutional affiliation of academics (including a public-private mix).
— Encourage multiple appointments for outstanding academicians (e.g. in a university and a research lab, or an Indian university and a foreign university, or a university and an industry) of university teachers. Frame appropriate rules that would encourage consultancy.
— Make the national accreditation system ensure that appropriate and adequately professionalised infrastructural facilities are installed in the university that is being accredited (examples: workshop, instrument repair, water, power, library, dispensary, bank, cleaning, security, etc.). A list of some 60 such "tested" facilities is available.
— Bring back undergraduate courses to universities.
— Abolish over a period of 10 years, all affiliated colleges in all areas (including professional ones). Replace them with (not necessarily convert them to) universities as already mentioned. A bill to that effect will need to be passed.
— Revise procedure for selection of vice-chancellors.
— Restructure management structure of universities to decentralize power and decision-making, and encourage collegiate management. Minimise the roles of vice-chancellor, registrar, heads of department (HOD) and the UGC. Change the system of rotation of HODs. Make compartmentalization into "department" or "faculty" or "schools", dynamic instead of being rigid, and create "virtual departments" to represent emerging areas of knowledge.
— Adopt course and credit system in universities, thus changing the examination system. Provide flexibility so that a student can complete the requirements for a degree in any period he wishes. Thus an indigent student can work part-time and complete his degree in, say, five years instead of the minimum of three years. Contents of the course should be determined by the teacher but the outline should be included in the information booklet of the university to be published annually, a year in advance and put on the website.

- — Ensure that research publications (articles, journals) from the country adopt the open access system.
- — Encourage the use of free and open source software.
- — Revise the procedure for Ph. D examination. For example, have at least one examiner from one of the, say, 1000 best universities and research institutions abroad; the viva could be conducted through a conference call.
- — Change the accounting systems of academic and research organizations to make it more result-oriented. Increase real accountability (professional, social and financial).
- — Set up a ICT-based system for maximizing national benefit from the visit of foreign visitors, who are often invited by one organization.
- — Remove fragmentation of education (e.g. as of today, medical and agricultural colleges are often under Ministries of Health and Agriculture with no coordination with education ministries, and unwarranted transfers).
- — Set up a system of interaction with civil society to maximize their involvement. This could be done, for example, by offering extramural courses to members of the public—say, in the evening—and having public lectures.

## Language

Both English and the home language/regional language should be taught primarily as tools to access knowledge and for communication from the first grade. In our school system, all Indian languages, including English, should be treated on par. To bridge the current divide between English-medium and regional language-medium schools, and recognizing that language learning is not confined to the language class, all schools should teach some non-language subjects chosen by the school, in English, and some others in the regional language. In view of shortage of English teachers, graduates with high efficiency in English and good communication skills may be inducted for teaching English, through an appropriate selection procedure and then given a short-term orientation; they need not have a formal teachers training qualification.

As one goes up the educational ladder, there may be an increasing use of English as the medium of instruction so that by the time a person reaches the college (+2) level, he is in a position to receive all his instruction through English. This policy alone will be able to dissolve the divide that exists today between those who are proficient in English and those whc do not know the Language—a divide that may become the most important in the country if not handled appropriately now.

## Agriculture and Rural Sector

I will deal with two issues here: (a) identifying areas where existing information should be disseminated in the agriculture sector and/or where new information needs to be generated and disseminated as above (these could be called research-cum-extension areas); and (b) designing information packages for *Panchayats* that would make them—and, through them, the Gram Sabhas—knowledgeable and capable of exercising their rights and discharging their rights effectively. These issues will be dealt with one by one.

*(a) Research-cum-extension areas:* The following topics (randomly arranged) that relate to the felt needs of farmers are suggested for further research and extension work by ICAR (Indian Council of Agricultural Research) and other organizations:

(1) Post-harvest technologies, including technologies for value addition such as food processing.
(2) Water harvesting using traditional technologies.
(3) New agriculture-product storage technologies, particularly for decentralized storage.
(4) Veterinary genetics and pathology (including microbiology and virology), for example, sequencing of genomes of animals specially and widely used in India, such as buffaloes; and developing genetically engineered vaccines for diseases such as FMV and rinderpest.
(5) Organic agriculture and associated activities such as vermiculture.
(6) Developing methodologies for quick marker-aided selection.
(7) Integrated pest management and bio-pesticides.
(8) Introduction of hybrid vigour into pure-breeding varieties.
(9) Setting up of commercial DNA fingerprinting of plants and seeds. Also, appropriate and easily accessible documentation to help farmers ensure that they do not get spurious seeds.
(10) Development of osmo-resistant varieties.
(11) Better weather prediction models.
(12) Identification of varieties of medicinal plants that would have high amounts of markers correlated with activity.
(13) Development of technologies for use of agricultural waste products.
(14) Technologies that could increase productivity and release time, labour and resources of farmers which could be utilized for additional employment.
(15) Identification of avenues for additional employment and research on making them attractive and lucrative enough for farmers to engage in them.
(16) A socio-economic analysis of the use of energy in agriculture, along

with energy saving mechanisms and strategies for energy management.

(17) Development and propagation of technologies for controlled release of fertilizers and pesticides.

(18) Systems approach towards commercialization of existing technologies such as for orchid tissue culture in Arunachal Pradesh or production of vanillin by tissue culture.

(19) Metabolic engineering to generate more value (e.g. transferring genes of maize for enzymes such as phosphoenol pyruvate carboxylase/ oxygenase and orthophosphate dikinase into rice for increasing yield).

(20) An in depth study of 'shifting agricultural practices', for example in Arunachal Pradesh, to increase its efficiency.

These areas should be pursued by carefully selected, competent and committed scientists in a mission mode, with clear time-targets, appropriate funding based on milestones, freedom from bureaucratic hassles but professional, social and financial accountability.

Dr. Mangala Rai, Director-General of the Indian Council of Agricultural Research, a visionary, has recognized the validity of the above areas for research and extension work. As of writing this article, four brainstorming sessions have been held on post-harvest technologies, organic farming, integrated pest management and bio-pesticides, and energy use in agriculture, under the auspices of the ICAR. A fifth one on seeds is on the anvil. If the recommendations of these brainstorming sessions are implemented, which the ICAR has already started doing to the extent it can, it could very well transform our agriculture and agricultural economy.

(b) *Information packages for Panchayats*: The Secretaries to the Government of India or to the State Governments, essentially, run the country. However, the power of a Secretary to the Government of India or to the State Government is confined just to the area that he/she is concerned with, such as education, health or industry. On the other hand, a *Panchayat* has to deal with virtually every aspect of governance of the area and of the people it represents. In a way, therefore, the duties of the *Panchayats* are far more varied than those of a Secretary to the Government, even though the area in which they are discharged and the number of people affected, are much smaller. This variety calls for knowledge and skills which, one would expect, qualitatively exceed that of a Secretary to the Government of a State of India or even a Secretary to the Government of India at Delhi. The fact, however, is that a Secretary to the Government of India or to a State Government is highly educated, well-trained, and has had enormous opportunities (both formal and informal) to learn, besides being financially extremely well of. On the other hand, the members of the *Panchayats* have none of these advantages and yet they are expected to do in their geographical area far more than what a Secretary to the Government is expected to do in his/her area.

To give the readers an idea of the variety of responsibilities of the Indian *Gram Panchayats* from 1993 onwards, when the new *Panchayati Raj Act* was passed by the Government of India, I list below some of the functions, powers and duties of the *Panchayats* in India:

1. Power to make general order.
2. General functions.
3. Construction, repair, maintenance of community assets.
4. Agriculture, including agricultural extension.
5. Animal husbandry, dairy and poultry.
6. Fisheries.
7. Social and farm forestry, minor forest produce, fuel and fodder.
8. Khadi, village and cottage industries.
9. Rural housing.
10. Rural electrification including distribution of electricity.
11. Non-conventional energy sources.
12. Poverty alleviation programmes.
13. Education, including primary and secondary school education.
14. Adult and non-formal education—promotion of adult literacy.
15. Cultural activities.
16. Fairs and festivals.
17. Public health and family welfare.
18. Women and child development.
19. Social welfare, including welfare of the handicapped and mentally retarded.
20. Welfare of weaker sections, particularly the "scheduled castes".
21. Public distribution system.
22. Judicial powers.

How could we empower *Panchayats* with knowledge that would equip them to handle the above mentioned responsibilities, keeping in mind the fact that rural India, where 70 per cent of India lives, is largely uneducated and disadvantaged in many ways? We can do so by resorting to the following steps:

(a) Developing and testing appropriate information packages.
(b) Training the trainers. For example, for the State of Punjab that spearheaded the Green Revolution in the country in the 1960s and has a little over 12,000 *Panchayats* and about 100,000 *Panches* and *Sarpanches*, we would need about 150 trainers. These trainers could, when trained, convey the information packages to local core groups, who can then take the information package to the *Panchayats*.

All this can be done within five years at a meagre cost. The above mentioned programme will, of course, need to be supplemented with an updating mechanism using information and communication technology to ensure that the information base of the *Panchayats* is kept updated.

Coming to the content of information packages, the *Panchayats* would need both specialized information that is immediately relevant to the work of the community that they represent, and general information that would make them real and informed citizens of India and of the world. I give examples of both these types of information that, I believe, should be communicated to the *Panchayats* through information packages mentioned above.

For our *Panchayats* in the villages to operate optimally, they would need to have relevant specialized information at least in the following areas:

- The provisions of the *Panchayati Raj Act.*
- Judicious use of pesticides and alternatives to chemical pesticides. (In many parts of the country, excessive use of pesticides has led to extensive contamination of ground water.)
- Appropriate use of fertilizers and their traditional alternatives. (In some parts of the country, the amount of nitrogen in the synthetic fertilizers used is as much as 15-fold in relation to the prescribed requirements of phosphorous and potassium. The excess nitrogen leaches out during irrigation and contaminates ground water.)
- About seeds and the way to test them, including places where these tests can be carried out.
- Understanding business, for example, marketing.
- Awareness of the rights of farmers, especially the provisions of the farmer-friendly Plant Varieties and Farmers' Rights Protection Bill of the Government of India that was passed a few years ago but notified only in 2005.
- Water harvesting and water conservation, using both traditional and modern methods.
- Understanding enough about soil, for example, the role of micronutrients which appears to be a problem in many parts of the country today.
- Food storage, preservation and processing.
- Disaster management.
- New materials.
- Importance of statistics.
- Waste-land and grass-land development.
- Development of fisheries.
- Techniques to improve breed of cattle, poultry and other livestock.
- Fuel plantations that would provide fire-wood to a group of villages.

(Three such plantations of trees that would mature in three years have been suggested for each group of villages so that one of them can be harvested and re-sown each year.)

- Forestry.
- Methods of indigenous and low cost construction.
- Use of non-conventional energy sources.
- Development of dairy/animal products (One of the ten or so major revolutions that have occurred in the country after its Independence is the milk revolution, making India the largest producer of milk in the world; this revolution was largely directed by cooperatives of milk producers, ably led by now the legendry Dr. V. Kurien.)
- Prevention and management of epidemics.
- Understanding the potential of marketing our creative, cultural and heritage industries, which are largely village-based and which have the capacity of generating a great deal of additional employment besides significant full-time employment, discussed in some detail later.

Examples of areas where general information could be provided to the members of the *Panchayats* to make them knowledgeable and real citizens of the country who have the ability to provide informed opinion on various issues at different levels of governance, are given here. Some of these areas (or often asked questions that need to be answered) are as follows:

- The basic concepts of hygiene, sanitation, nutrition and disease.
- What is electricity? The need for earthing.
- What is electronics? How does a radio or television operate (why an aerial)?
- Various materials available today.
- Our origins and evolution; reproduction.
- What is a satellite: its uses?
- How does our banking system/stock market operate?
- The globe and us.
- Landmarks in world history.
- Conservation versus development.
- Major issues that relate to population.
- How is our country managed? (The basic structure of our administration).
- Our assets (natural, human, man-made, social).
- Our problems and weaknesses.
- Human rights and civil liberties (the UN Charter of Human Rights).
- Consumer awareness.
- Our 4,500-year old tradition of art and culture.

- The human body.
- Scientific method: conflicts with superstition.
- Natural marvels.
- Man-made marvels.
- Some exemplary extraordinary lives.
- Key technological innovations.
- Religions of the world and communal harmony.
- Issues relating to environment.

If the above-mentioned information is conveyed appropriately—and I believe this can be done over a period of 40 hours (that is, during one working week)—it is most likely that the recipients of this information would obtain answers to or acquire an understanding of the following:

- Education: why, what and how?
- Freedom versus constraints.
- Rights versus responsibilities.
- Scientific temper and decision-making.
- Accountability.
- Equality amongst people.
- The need to narrow the gender gap.
- The need to fight and eliminate corruption.
- Realization that there is no hierarchy amongst professions—from cleaning to agriculture to electronics. (What the society needs are high-quality professionals in all fields.)
- The need for courage, integrity and confidence.
- The various linkages in contemporary society.
- The need to have a vision and to be able to peep into the future.
- The need and mechanisms for keeping up-to-date.
- The hierarchy between data, information, knowledge and wisdom.
- Way of networking with higher levels of administration, both horizontally and vertically.
- Resourcefulness: the need to raise resources on our own.
- Identifying and implementing sustainable long-term developmental programmes.

The country has a fairly large number of Government-funded rural development programmes, a national horticultural mission, and some 500 *Krishi Vigyan Kindras* (centres for acquiring knowledge of agriculture). Hopefully, in the future, the number of high schools in the country that would provide 10-year of schooling (for children aged 6-16) would be sufficiently large to give equal opportunity to every child in the country to have good school education. The highly respected M.S. Swaminathan Research

Foundation has been working towards setting up 250,000 village resource centres. We, perhaps, also need to set up 50,000 knowledge clubs in our villages. It seems only appropriate that all these efforts are integrated. Such an integration could play a crucial role in making our rural society knowledge-based.

## Traditional Knowledge

India has had an unbroken tradition, built over five millennia, of unusual varieties of arts, crafts and practices that collectively go under the name of "traditional and cultural knowledge". Some of this knowledge is documented while the rest of it is not adequately documented. Further, wherever documentation exists, in many cases, it does not allow one to immediately cull out information that one would need today to optimally utilize our traditional or cultural knowledge in the area. In spite of valiant efforts of the Government of India after Indian Independence some six decades ago, and equally important efforts of a number of highly talented, knowledgeable and committed individuals, the fact remains that, in its engagement with mediocrity, India has far from optimally utilized its traditional knowledge for social and economic gain. Not only has this knowledge the potential of providing full employment or additional employment to over 200 million people, it can also generate revenue for the country of over 600,000 crores of Indian Rupees, and provide products and services of great social and economic value, thus enhancing the prestige of the country. Further, the traditional wealth of India has the potential of serving as a vehicle for expression of the creative ability of Indians in diverse fields, generating new areas of tourism, and providing opportunities for research in new areas, besides of course adding to the repertoire of knowledge for the peoples of the world. The fact is that all this is possible, and it is only when that happens that India would be an effective knowledge-based society, for it would have then encompassed both modern and traditional knowledge and married the two where necessary.

I would now make some comments on the following areas of our traditional knowledge:

(a) Plant-based drug formulations,
(b) Traditional agricultural practices,
(c) Traditional water-harvesting practices,
(d) Our creative and cultural traditions, and
(e) Some new aspects of tourism.

However, before I discuss about these traditional knowledge areas, I would like to mention some principles and basic premises that relate to traditional knowledge (from its documentation to use) that we must accept and adopt. This statement of "principles and basic premises" was worked out at a meeting on traditional knowledge under the auspices of the National Knowledge Commission in Hyderabad on December 5, 2005. The participants in this meeting included Prof. Anil Kumar Gupta of the Indian Institute of Management, Ahmedabad; Dr. Darshan Shankar of the Foundation for Revitalisation of Local Health Traditions, Bangalore; Mr. Rajiv Sethi, Vice-Chairman, Indian Planning Commission's Task Force on Creative Industries, New Delhi; Dr. A.K. Gogai of the Indian Council of Agricultural Research, New Delhi; Prof. M.P. Ranjan of the National Institute of Design, Ahmedabad; Mr. Neetu Loond of Ishwar, an Indian textiles corporation, Paris; Mrs. Chandana Chakrabarti of the National Knowledge Commission; and the author. This group felt that the following principles and basic premises must be recognized and followed while commercializing traditional knowledge:

(1) In all commercialization of traditional knowledge, there must be equity in respect of distribution of profits. Thus, the producers or the traditional keepers of the knowledge must be considered as equal partners along with others in the commercial exploitation of traditional knowledge. A code of fair trade practices in this area must be evolved by the designated organization.

(2) It must be recognized that traditional knowledge does not need to be collective; it can be with an individual. Similarly, it should not be taken as being static. It must be recognized that innovation takes place constantly even in what we label as traditional knowledge. National Innovation Foundation that takes care of innovation in the unorganized sector, and the newly set up National Agricultural Innovation Foundation, must be fully supported.

(3) Where a marriage of traditional knowledge with what is commonly perceived as modern knowledge, is likely to yield better results, it should be ensured that the traditional knowledge component is not lost sight of, either in practice or in publicity.

(4) We must recognize both tangible and intangible variations in any traditional knowledge item, stemming from underlying traditional taxonomy.

(5) Where traditional knowledge comes from identifiable groups or individuals and is not in public domain, prior informed consent of the contributors of the traditional knowledge or innovation must be obtained.

(6) A legal framework should be created for establishing proprietary rights for traditional knowledge holders—be they individuals or a community.

(7) A system should be set up for urgent scientific investigation of traditional practices, including survival strategies, for which there is strong prima facie evidence.

(8) The definition of work for employment purposes must include all activities that relate to the use and application (not just manual but also mental) of traditional knowledge.
(9) A system should be created for support to those who are involved in formal transmission of traditional knowledge—especially women and older people in communities where young people have been migrating to urban areas in large numbers.
(10) A system should be set up, which would provide incentives for inter-community transmission/transfer of traditional knowledge, to ensure that the knowledge is not lost—remembering that knowledge multiplies when shared and decays when kept secret or confidential.
(11) The results of all research and development, based on traditional knowledge, must be shared with the providers of the initial knowledge package.
(12) Whatever infrastructure is created to document, standardize, validate and/or commercialize traditional knowledge, must be cross-sectoral and cross-ministerial; the system set up must operate in a mission mode with cross-sectoral and cross-ministerial powers, for traditional or cultural knowledge is almost always cross-sectoral.

I will now deal with the use of traditional knowledge in the areas of plant-based drugs, traditional agricultural practices, traditional practices of water harvesting, our creative and cultural tradition, and tourism in this order.

## Plant-Based Drug Formulations

There seems to be little doubt that if mankind did not have any cures for any ailments with which it may have suffered since we appeared on our planet, we would have been extinct by now, just as, if we had all the cures we have today, the world population of today would have been reached several millennia earlier. The most likely modes of treating ailments in ancient and mediaeval human history would have been plant-based drug formulations, which exist virtually in every culture around the world. In fact, some of the effective drugs we have today were derived from such traditional formulations. Examples would be quinine, reserpine, vinblastin, and artimesin that have come to us from Latin American, Indian and Chinese traditions. An example of a plant-based drug formulation that does not consist of a single chemical entity like the ones mentioned above, but which is an ethical (that is, prescription) drug in several parts of the world, including the Western world, is Liv-52 for liver disorders. However, just as one can be sure that at least some of the traditional plant-based drug formulations must be effective, one can be equally sure that all of them are unlikely to be as effective as they have been claimed to be.

The advantages of plant-based drug formulations in comparison to conventional drugs used in modern medicine are many. They are far cheaper to validate and produce; they would, therefore, cost much less to the consumer. And their lack of toxicity has been often established through centuries of usage. Further, their manufacture would be totally non-pollutive and environment-friendly.

There are, perhaps, some 40,000 unique traditional plant-based drug formulations available in the country in the documented Ayurveda, Sidhha, Unani and Tibetan systems of medicine and the undocumented tribal systems of medicine. They need to be (a) appropriately documented, using modern information technology, in such a way that we can retrieve answers to as many questions as possible from the computerized data; (b) prioritized for further work on the basis of stated criteria; (c) standardized to obviate variations in the chemical constituents on account of soil or climatic conditions; (d) validated using, first, in vitro techniques and then the usual techniques commonly used for validation of drugs, including clinical trials; and then (e) manufactured and marketed. All this should be done using good laboratory practice, good clinical practice, and good manufacturing practice (GLP, GCP and GMP). I believe that at least 4,000 out of the 40,000 plant-based drug formulations mentioned above, will be found to work and be marketable, if tested systematically.

We have prepared a detailed project outlining the above and giving a detailed financial analysis. It projects marketing of one hundred tested and validated formulations over a period of ten years, with an investment of a few hundred crores, which should at the end of 10 years, lead to a turnover of Rs. 10,000 crores per year with a net profit of more than Rs. 5,000 crores (one billion US dollars) at the prices of the year 2000. India has the capability, including infrastructure, of implementing ten such projects in the next 20 years. This would be significant in view of the fact that less than 35 new chemical entities (NCEs or new drugs) have been added every year in the last ten years, to the repertoire of drugs in the modern system of medicine, with each new drug costing on an average one billion US dollars (Rs. 5,000 crores) in research and development. The above number has been decreasing over the years with only 20 NCEs being approved in 2005.

Two major initiatives have taken place recently in India in regard to documentation of traditional drug formulations and plants used in such formulations, in the country. One initiative has been taken by the CSIR (Council of Scientific and Industrial Research, the premier federal-founded scientific research agency in the country) in which they have attempted to document the formulations. The second initiative has been taken by Dr. Darshan Shankar, belonging to the well-known non-governmental organisation, the Foundation for Revitalisation of Local Health Traditions in Bangalore. Dr. Shankar had earlier done a superb job of documenting over 7,000 plants (out of, perhaps, 10,000) used in traditional plant-based drug formulations in India. He is now documenting the formulations themselves. Documentation of formulations in a way that we can use it today poses several problems, especially of language equivalence. However, ways and means of overcoming this problem have been worked out. In summary, we have taken the first step in marrying traditional knowledge with modern technology—a marriage that has the potential of augmenting substantially, rapidly and at much less expense, our repertoire of drugs. Indeed, more than 50 percent of the new drugs of tomorrow (by 2025) may well be plant-based drug formulations that have been standardized and validated, and India can make a major contribution to this area.

## Traditional Agricultural Practices

The Indian Council of Agricultural Research (ICAR) has recently brought out a series of volumes [3] that document 4,502 traditional agricultural practices, out of which 86 have been validated and 38 cross-validated as of December 2005. In addition, there is a similar documentation of such practices by Dr Anil Gupta of the Indian Institute of Management in Ahmedabad. I believe that the following should be done to ensure that validated traditional agricultural practices find a place in today's agriculture around the world, and add substantially to either economic or social gain:

- We should set up a consolidated, cooperative system of documentation of such practices, appropriately computerized and indexed, to which anyone can contribute and which anyone can access.
- The cross-validated practices mentioned above, should be commercialized and an appropriate mission set up for this purpose by the Government of India. However, we should keep in mind what I have already said in Section 9, that before the above commercialization takes place, appropriate consent of those who contributed to the practice (individuals or communities) should be obtained and a system set up for fair sharing of profit as a result of such commercialization.
- A set of strategies for validation should be worked out. For example, one should be able to use and encourage expert farmers to be a part of the validation process. They should be appropriately supported with adequate staff.
- An appropriate venture fund that would support the above-mentioned validation should be set up.
- The above process of validation should not be confined to what has

been documented till now. It must be recognized that innovation by farmers, even the illiterate ones as is the case with many farmers in India, continues to take place all the time. Such innovation could be in areas as diverse as new agricultural implements, pesticides, veterinary medicine, animal and plant growth regulators, food processing and so on. A nation-wide system should be set up that will ensure that all such innovations are fed in the system of documentation mentioned above.

An example of an area where traditional agricultural practices are already poised to make significant contribution in India, is organic farming using traditional practices within the framework of a modern scientific paradigm.

## Traditional Water Harvesting

Detailed information on traditional modes of water harvesting is already available in a book [4] authored by the late Anil Agarwal and Sunita Narain, who is at present the Director of the Centre for Science and Environment (CSE), New Delhi. [Sunita Narain is a winner of the World Water Prize. The CSE, under her leadership, was the organisation that brought out the contamination of soft drinks in India, most of them produced by multinationals, with unacceptably high levels of pesticides. Earlier, the CSE, through a decision of the Supreme Court of India, was responsible for all public transport in Delhi to shift to Compressed Natural Gas (CNG) as the fuel, leading to a dramatic reduction in air pollution.] The book is a superb documentation of traditional practices in this area. If an agency can be established in which both the Government and the NGOs (non-governmental organizations) such as the CSE participate, the application of these practices all over the country can probably take care of our water problem in possibly the most inexpensive way, obviating the need for the proposed, extremely expensive and environment—unfriendly project of interlinking of rivers in which, unlike in the popularization of validated traditional practices, there would also be a tremendous scope for corruption which, unfortunately, is as much a hallmark of today's India as is its scientific and industrial development.

## Creative and Cultural Traditions

To give the readers a flavor of the richness of creative and cultural traditions of India, I give below a partial list of such traditional endeavours that have the potential of commercialization and raising revenue, both for the producers or keepers of such work as well as those who create a set-up to commercialise them, in addition to the Government through its participation in commercialization or through appropriate taxation. This list is based on information provided by Mr. Rajiv Sethi, Vice-Chairman of the Task Force on Creative Industries set up by the Planning Commission of the Government of India. This list is only indicative and not exhaustive:

(1) *Handicrafts*: Bead and bangle making; blowing glass; carving/etching/engraving; casting; cutwork/trellis; enamelling; ephemeral expressions; filigree/wire work; footwear; furniture assembly and carpentry; glazing; inlay; lacquering/lac turnery; lapidary; moulding and shaping; paper making; plating; embossing; setting/fixing; throwing; turning; traditional painting and frescoes; assembly skills (e.g. toy making and book binding); pottery (including the disposable *kulhars* for serving drinks such as water); *papier mache*; various indigenous uses of plant material such as making of disposable and totally hygienic *pattals* (plates) to serve food, from leaves; and cloth from parts of banana tree.

(2) *Textiles, clothing materials, and related activities*: Felt making; spinning/drawing of thread; weaving; cording, knotting and tasselling; dyeing, printing; embroidery/applique/quilting; lace work/crochet work/knitting; tailoring; costume accessories (turbans, bags, belts); traditional apparel and accessories; wool preparation and processing.

(3) *Household and rural community-based manufacturing*: Herbal preparations; utility products (chalk, incense); sericulture; honey making.

(4) *Design*: Graphic design; inter-media design; industrial/product/commercial/packaging design; artistic direction, scenography, museography; fashion, costume and accessories design.

(5) *Architecture and building arts*: Planning and survey; traditional architectural design and features; building services including building material; construction skills (e.g. masonry, welding and soldering); interior design; landscape design; community-based systems of transportation; sanitation; irrigation; conservation and restoration.

(6) *Fine arts and studio arts*: Painting; sculpture and installations; cartoons and caricature/calligraphy.

(7) *Performing and ritual arts*: Dance; music; theatre and dramatic arts; itinerant/street/circus arts and entertainment; folk performances; festivals and rituals.

(8) *Literary arts*: Oral literature and story telling.

(9) *Antique arts and trade.*

(10) *Cultural education and training:* Libraries and archives (both private and public); museums and galleries (both private and public); cultural centres.

(11) *Advertising and marketing*: *Haats* (a place where the producer brings and sells his/her products without an intermediary) and bazaars.

(12) *Leisure and entertainment*: Traditional games and sports.
(13) *Food and culinary arts*: Vegetables, fruits, food processing; organic food (already discussed).
(14) *Beauty, health and healing*: Yoga, meditation, massage, and bone-setting; cosmetics; jewellery; martial arts.

Under each of the above categories we would need statistical information and identification of individuals, associations and NGOs for:

(a) content/idea creation and development;
(b) manufacture/production;
(c) distribution and marketing; and
(d) regulatory and quality protection mechanisms.

It is noteworthy that all of the above traditional arts and crafts are practised on a substantial scale in the country today, each activity involving thousands to millions of people. As examples, I mention below some impressive facts and possibilities:

- Both traditional and modern Indian paintings and sculptures have now come of age in the international market. A 9th century Chola bronze (a statue not more than 10 inches in height) is likely to fetch in the international market ten million dollars.
- Paintings of well-known Indian artists, such as Husain, routinely fetch one crore of rupees each. Indian contemporary painters have never had it so good. In fact, it is now been realized all over the world that an investment in paintings done by some Indian painters who are living today or who lived in the last century, may be one of the best investments that one can make today.
- As of today, it is estimated that some twenty million people may be involved in weaving cloth on handlooms or doing something on cloth by hand before marketing. There is a mind boggling variety of weave, texture and design which identify to a discerning eye the place (including, often, the village) where the cloth was woven or processed. Such variety in textiles which makes every piece that one wears unique for all practical purposes, has been unparalleled in human history. If an Indian women buys a handloom sari, the chance is that she will *never* meet any other women wearing the same sari. Similarly, most of us can identify paintings done by women (often illiterate) of a little village in Bihar called *Madhuban*. These *Madhubani* paintings were discovered by the so-called intelligentsia of the country only a few decades ago. At that time one could buy a good one for twenty rupees (forty U.S. cents). You cannot buy one of the same quality today for a thousand times that price. It is clearly in the country's

interest to make these women go to school and become a part of the real world and yet continue to be engaged in the traditional craft that they have loved, which today has a tremendous market.

## Food

India has some extremely unusual vegetables and fruits—and an unparalleled variety of them. Thus, there are some 150 documented vegetables for which all the nutritional information is available, and perhaps another 50 used by tribals that have not been systematically documented so far. The same is true of fruits. Many of the Indian vegetables and fruits have been shown to have amazing pharmacological effects and medicinal properties as documented both in our traditional literature as well as recently in some of the world's best-known scientific journals. It is, therefore, a matter of great concern that even our five star hotels serve no more than some 10 vegetables, and very rarely fruits such as custard apple or guavas!

India has thus the potential of making an important contribution to the world vegetable and fruit market, if it could only appropriately publicized its rich heritage in this regard. In this connection, we should recall that there was no (what we call) mineral water available in the United States or in Britain till the 1960s. It was the French high-power marketing that made bottled water (beginning with Evian and Perrier) so popular in these countries, even though in all of them the water that comes through the tap is perfectly drinkable. In our country itself we have seen how South Indian snacks have invaded the North Indian market where they were unknown till the late 1940s. There is, therefore, no reason why India should not exploit its tremendous heritage in regard to foods and vegetables and attempt to popularize them all over the world. That would be sharing of knowledge!

## Tourism

India, perhaps, has the potential of raising the number of tourists and, consequently, the revenue through tourism, by one order of magnitude by leveraging our creative, cultural and legacy traditions. The four suggestions given below in this regard were arrived at the meeting mentioned earlier of experts held under the auspices of the National Knowledge Commission late last year.

- Attempts must be made to empower, through information, local people to serve as guides. They could also be the custodians of our biodiversity heritage. This would be in consonance with the provisions of the proposed tribal rights bill of the Government of India. [The Scheduled Tribes (Recognition of Forest Rights) Bill, 2005.].
- We should identify tribal art centres where they exist, and open new

ones where possible, with competent and trained guides from the local population. We must recognize that local people have information and anecdotes that the tourists will enjoy. (Eight per cent of India is tribal)

- Similarly, we should set up a system by which tourists are able to witness real and authentic local performing arts without adulterating them in any way, and ensuring that the respect and dignity of the performer is fully maintained. The objective should be to share a tradition and not to make an exhibition of our people.
- Our country has some extremely unusual sites and practices which can become a major tourist attraction. For example, there is a place where birds commit suicide. Similarly, the whole process of picking up the raw betel-nut branches from a cluster of more than 50 feet tall trees, by a person who climbs up one tree to the top and then jumps by swinging the tree to another tree, without a safety net, is absolutely stunning. Such places could become major tourist attractions following the principles mentioned above. The revenue from the visit of tourists to such places could be shared with the communities involved.

## Other Areas

Finally, I list below very briefly some of my concerns about certain other important issues not mentioned above.

*Professional Education:* What kind of medical education system do we have that has no course on medical ethics and that does not produce quality family physicians? What is the use of engineering education that produces unemployable engineers as is the case with numerous engineering institutions? Do we allow a system of accreditation of professional colleges that employ event managers to organize, against payment, teachers, equipment, patients and what have you for the day of the visit of the accreditation committee?

*Science and Technology:* What short-term/long-term steps do we need to take to make the quality of scientific research better and technological research more relevant? Do we permit directors of research labs to have their names on almost all the papers published from the laboratory, only because they are Directors? How do we bring in ethics in doing, administering, communicating and using science?

*Governance:* Do we need to professionalize our civil services? And how could the government make use of the enormous professional talent in the civil society?

*Civil Society:* We have an abundance of never-ending soaps on television that revolve around the question, who is who's child, an issue which could be settled in one episode by DNA fingerprinting. How do we give housewives better options so that they may spend their afternoons fruitfully?

*Industry:* How do we introduce ethics in industry and break the MNCs-government-bureaucracy nexus?

*Health:* When over 90 per cent people suffer from less than 0.1 percent of known diseases for which standard cures are available, can we provide reasonable medicare in our villages with appropriately trained personnel who do not have an MBBS degree?

*Patents:* Must we continue to be a victim of TRIPS and GATT that are loaded heavily against us? If not, what strategies must we adopt?

*Innovations:* We have an inadequately funded yet reasonably efficient National Innovation Foundation and we have just set up a National Agriculture Innovation Foundation. How do we help these foundations to optimally utilize the tremendous innovative abilities in our unorganized sector, including agriculture? Remember, a large number of the world's most widely used innovations (such as the zipper or the shoe-lace holes) were not made in the organized sector.

## Conclusion

In conclusion, recognition of the attributes of knowledge and weaving them into the social fabric, setting up systems of disseminating and communicating knowledge that would make a country's citizens informed citizens (not only through formal education but also through non-formal means on a continuous basis), and judicious use of both new and traditional knowledge, would be, in my opinion, important ingredients of a policy that would make India a knowledge-based society. It is only then that the country, which has all through history been committed to peace and has never had colonialist tendencies, would be able to renew its role as a major participant in the process of developing a peaceful and prosperous world—a world with no man-made borders.

## References

A. Agarwal, S. Narain and I. Khurana, (2001), *Making Water Everybody's Business: Practice and Policy of Water Harvesting*, New Delhi: Centre for Science and Environment.

Indian Council of Agricultural Research, New Delhi, Inventory of Indigenous Technical Knowledge in Agriculture, Document 1 (2002), Document 2 (2003), Supplement 1 to Document 2 (2003), Supplement 2 to Document 2 (2004), Document 3 (2004), Document 4 (2004), Document 5 (2004).

P.M. Bhargava, (2006), Seven deadly sins of the clergy, *The Tribune (India)*, 2nd January 2006.

Oliveti, V. (2002), *Terror Source: The ideology of Wahhabi-Salafism and its consequences*, Birmingham: Amadeus Books.

# Part VII

# Contemporary Concerns and Future Challenges

# 20

# Vision of Institutionalizing New Ideas of the Education Commission: Focus on Open and Distance Learning

RAM TAKWALE

## Introduction

The Education Commission Report (1964-66) is the first comprehensive study of the Indian System of Education right from the pre-schooling to research stage and is titled, 'Education and National Development'. The members of the EC were guided by the provisions in the Indian Constitution and by the aspirations and expectations of leaders of the Indian freedom struggle.

The Constitution, essentially tried to decentralize the political, knowledge and economic power concentrated in the traditional Indian Society in the hands of some sections of the people and to redistribute the powers to all people including the *women*, and the marginalized in Indian society. The constitutional rule in India is a great continuing process of democratization and is expected to influence all subsequent socio-economic changes and transformation.

During the freedom struggle, an alternative to the education system promoted by the British Rule had evolved in the form of *Rastriya Shikshan* (National Education) guided more by Mahatma Gandhi's idea of Basic Education (*Buniyadi Shiksha*) and Life Education (*Jeevan Shiksha*). The main approach of the Education Commission (EC) emanates from this background and aims at creating a National System of Education linked to the life and development of the people of India. The Education Commission was expected to bring in a revolutionary change covering all people aimed at a radical reconstruction of the Indian society.

The EC Report guided subsequent development in Indian education and resulted in two major policy documents, National Policy on Education 1968 and 1986/1992 and numerous policies and programs that have changed the education system in the country and helped achieve impressive progress in education.

India has one of the biggest systems of education with a total enrolment of 189.2 million, with 81.1 million girl students and 5.45 million teachers in schools, nearly ten million students in 350 universities and 15,000 colleges with 420,000 teachers. This includes 11 open universities and 104 distance education institutions of dual mode; and the open university system has an enrolment of about 20 per cent of the total. The rate of growth since Independence is quite high, coverage has increased, dropout rate has got reduced, and the percentage of girl students in education increasing.

The focus of the paper is on the EC recommendations on the correspondence education or home study, which later on took the form of open and distance education, and added non-formal mode to the system of formal education. The Commission could not have anticipated the rapid development of the information technology (IT) leading to networking of people and places all over the globe, which has created a situation for the development of the post-industrialization society. The new technology offers tools and technologies, which enable decentralization and mass participation on an unprecedented scale. These processes are typical of the information age and have no resemblance to any of the industrial and agrarian era. However, the ideas of the Commission rooted in the development of people, democratic decentralization, people's participation, and the bottom up approach have greater relevance in the Information Age. The issues related to the quality, quantity and equity—the illusive triangle of Indian education,—were addressed by the Commission. This forms the main focus of this paper.

## EC Recommendations Related to Open and Distance Learning (ODL)

The Education Commission has considered educational reconstruction as the most general problem faced by the nation, and proposed programs that fall into three broad categories:

- *Internal transformation of the educational system* so as to relate it to life, needs and aspirations of the nation;
- *Qualitative improvement of education* so that the standards achieved are adequate, keep continually rising and, at least in a few sectors, become internationally comparable; and,
- *Expansion of educational facilities* broadly on the basis of manpower needs and with an accent on equalization of educational opportunities.

The Commission starts with a faith that "*The destiny of the nation is now being shaped in the classroom*" and considers education as the main *instrument of change*. It believes that in a "*world based on science and technology, it is education that determines the level of prosperity, welfare and security of the people*". The most important and urgent reform needed in education is to transform it, to endeavour to relate it to the life, needs and expectations of the people and thereby make it a powerful instrument of social, economic and cultural transformation necessary for the realization of the national goals. For this purpose education should be developed so as to increase productivity, achieve social and national integration, accelerate the process of modernization and cultivate social, moral and spiritual values (Page 613 of EC Report, 1966).

This paper focuses on *Open and Distance Learning (ODL)* and in this context the EC recommendations are grouped under three headings:

1. *Expansion* of educational facilities through non-formal education,
2. *Transformation* of existing system into National System of Education, and
3. Initiating major changes and generating movement for radical reconstruction by creating *'Educational Revolution'*.

In all the three areas, the recommendations that are directly linked with Open and Distance Learning and, those recommendations that are linked with planning, financing, managing, etc., that support the development of ODL in the country are included.

## Expansion

*Non-formal Education*: The major restriction observed by the Commission was the nature of full-time education then existing with the typical culture of academic studies, concentrating mostly on cognitive development of the individual. The Report recommends that "*part-time and own-time education*" should be developed on a larger scale at every stage and in every sector of education and should be given the same status as full-time education (Recommendation 13 on p. 617 of EC Report). The Commission distinguishes between part-time education as offered by the formal institutions and own-time education as that given through correspondence education.

In Chapter XVII on Adult Education, the Commission recommends eradication of illiteracy throughout the country within a shorter period reaching a literacy level of 80 per cent by 1976. Under the mass approach to eliminate illiteracy, EC recommends mobilisation of all educated men and women, all educational institutions to participate in a mass movement to eradicate illiteracy (p. 665, EC Report 202).

The Commission also proposes Continuing Education programs to be started by educational institutions by throwing their doors open, outside their regular working hours, to all those who wish to continue the education. It expects to create a *parallel part-time system of education for adults* for obtaining the same type of diplomas and degrees as students in schools and colleges (Recommendation 203).

Under EC recommendation 204, the Commission proposes to bring the education to those who are unable to take advantages of part-time education offered by an institution by organizing correspondence courses, which should provide:

(i) Contact centers to interact with teachers, to use library and other facilities in the existing colleges, and the correspondence students should be given equal status as that of regular students.
(ii) Support through radio and television programs.
(iii) Courses in agricultural and industrial areas that would help workers to improve productivity.
(iv) Courses to enrich lives by studying subjects of cultural and aesthetic value.
(v) Courses for teachers in schools to keep them abreast with new knowledge, new methods and techniques of teaching.
(vi) National Council of Home Studies to be established by the Ministry of Education in collaboration with other Ministries, for the purpose of accreditation and evaluation of agencies, which provide correspondence courses, for identification of the areas in which different types of correspondence courses would be of benefit, for promoting creation of such courses through proper agencies and for conducting evaluation and research.
(vii) Opportunity to take examinations conducted by the Secondary Education Board and universities in the country should be made available to those who wish to work on their own without any assistance.

The Commission expects the universities to assume a much larger role and responsibility for educating adults.

## Educational Planning and Administration

The EC has the following recommendations on Educational Planning and Administration that are in the nature of ideas related to the organisation and management of ODL:

***Planning*** (Recommendation 208, p. 667 of EC Report):

1. There has been an overemphasis on achievement of targets in enrolment and expenditure and there is, therefore, a need to take a more comprehensive view and evolve a broader pattern of goals, especially those relating to qualitative improvement.
2. The purpose of educational planning in a federal democracy has to be the right blend of centralization (*and decentralization?*—added) in the appropriate sectors and especially in administration. One useful

suggestion, which can be made in this context, is to adopt a system of priorities at different levels—national, state and local.

3. School education is predominantly a local-State partnership and higher education is a Center-State partnership. It is this basic principle that should guide the evolution of the delicate balance between centralization and decentralization, which is essential for planning.

***The Role of Private Enterprise*** (Recommendation 209, p. 667 of EC Report):

The future role of private enterprise in education should be broadly on the following principles:

(a) As the private enterprise has played an important role in the development of education in modern India, the State should make all possible use of the assistance that can come from the private sector for the development of education.

(b) The State has now rightly assumed full responsibility to provide educational facilities and private enterprise can, therefore, have only a limited and minor role.

***The Role of Local Authorities*** (Recommendation 210, p. 667 of EC Report): The normal practice should be that of entrusting the right to administer the education with a local authority on two conditions—good administration and promote the cause of education. This privilege would be withdrawn if any of these conditions is violated:

1. As an ultimate objective it is essential that schools and their communities should be intimately associated with the processes of education.
2. The ultimate goal to be reached is the establishment, at the district level, of a competent local education authority, which may be designed as the District School Board and which would be in charge of all education in the district below the university level. This should also be accepted as a national policy.
3. In all cases of association of the local authorities with the education system, adequate safeguard should be provided to ensure that the teachers are not harassed and that they do not get involved in local factions and politics.

District and Municipal Boards should have separate School Boards with jurisdiction of the corresponding administrative areas of the Boards.

## Educational Finance

The EC recommendations are:

1. *Total Expenditure on Education* (Recommendation 223, p. 672 of

EC Report): The proportion of GNP should rise from its value of 2.9 per cent in 1965-66 to 6.0 per cent in 1985-86.

2. *Sources of Educational Finance* (Recommendation 225, p. 672 of EC Report): Although most of the responsibility for the support of education will be placed on governmental funds, a total centralization of all financial responsibility for education in the Government will not be desirable. Attempt should, therefore, be made to raise contributions from local communities, voluntary organisations and local authorities for this purpose.
3. *Economies and Utilization* (Recommendation 229, p. 673 of EC Report): Even with the mobilisation of maximum resources for education, the funds will still be inadequate to meet even the minimum needs of educational reconstruction, if conventional techniques involving large wastage and stagnation continue. It would, therefore, be necessary to adopt measures for economy, for eradication of wastage and for most efficient utilization of funds. All measures that promote economy consistent with efficiency should be adopted.

## Transformation

***Features of National Education:*** The educational institutions of a national character established by the leaders of the Freedom Movement—Rabindranath Tagore and Mahatma Gandhi—like the Rastriya Shala/Vidyapeet (National School/University), based on basic and life-related education linked with people were the alternative to the educational institutions under the colonial rule. The Education Commission accepted the idea and formulated it in the form of a National System of Education. The basic thrust of the recommendations of the Commission is to restructure and transform the system of school, college and university education in the country into a comprehensive National System of Education.

The ***National System of Education*** (Naik, 1982) should have the following features:

1. It should be based on our own traditions and be suited to the life, needs and aspirations of our people.
2. It should emphasize education of all people.
3. It should use regional languages as medium of instruction with Hindi as a link language and English as an academic language for access to universal knowledge.
4. It should eliminate difference between individuals educated in the modern education system and that of people's education.
5. It should emphasize science and technology education for modernization and elimination of poverty,

6. It should inculcate a spirit of patriotism and pride in our cultural heritage, and
7. It should emphasize moral and aesthetic values.

## Educational Revolution

***Education as an Instrument of Change:*** If this *change on a grand scale* is to be achieved without violent revolution (and even then it would still be necessary) there is one instrument, and one instrument only, that can be used: EDUCATION. Other agencies may help, and can indeed sometimes have a more apparent impact. But the national system of education is the only instrument that can reach all the people (p. 4 of EC Report).

The direct link between education, development and prosperity, which the Commission has emphasized and in which it deeply believed, "*exists only when the national system of education is properly organized, from both qualitative and quantitative points of view*". All education is necessarily not good, both for individuals and for society, and the faith that education will necessarily lead to progress can be harmful as it is misplaced. History shows numerous instances that the social groups or elites having control over power—political, economic or knowledge—have used it as their prerogative and tool to maintain their hegemony and perpetuation, often in collusion with other power groups. The social and cultural revolution has often brought about changes in an educational system that offer educational opportunities to people and harness their potential and talent in solving problems of development and progress. A system of university education that produces large proportion of graduates, with high competency and professionalism, with high quality is of great value in development of manpower that is used for higher productivity and prosperity. However, university education, which produces majority of its graduates without proper development of manpower in terms of competencies, professional skills and quality, adds to the large number of unemployed graduates. In such cases when the education is indifferent and not linked with national development, it will have the opposite result.

"The main concern of the Commission is to *achieve radical reconstruction and transformation in education and development* in terms of higher quality, quantity and equality with high transformative value in terms of social, economic and cultural changes. When such changes are brought about with unprecedented speed, coverage, inclusiveness and impact, the change then is not an evolution but amounts to a revolution".

## Implementation of the EC Report

J.P. Naik, the Member Secretary of the EC and virtually the writer of the Report, has reviewed the Education Commission Report in his book 'Education

Commission and After' (Naik, 1982) and categorized the recommendations into *three* groups; namely those that:

(a) Attracted wide attention,
(b) Limited attention, and
(c) Opposed or rejected or just ignored.

J.P. Naik includes Non-formal Education, Education of the People and the Common School System (Restructuring into 10 + 2 + 3 years in school and university education for the first degree) in the first group (wide attention) and includes in the third group (rejected or opposed) recommendations related to major universities, selective admissions at the higher secondary and university stages, selective improvement of schools, etc. Recommendations related to work experience; vocationalisation, value education and character building, decentralization, etc. are in the middle category that received moderate attention.

In the expansion of the education system, the "home study and own-time education" received the widest response and during the last four decades, the open learning system expanded beyond expectations. It has not only expanded to increase access and quality education, but now has become one of the major policies to promote non-formal education for increasing access and coverage. One of the major factors that received attention is its lower unit cost and openness. We review the ODL as it developed through Open Schools and single and dual mode universities.

## Non-formal Education: Home Study and Own-Time Education

During the last four decades, the home study and own-time study expanded as non-formal education at three levels:

1. *Primary level*: Non-formal school education for school drop outs.
2. *Secondary level*: Open School programs
3. *Tertiary level*: Open university programs

In fact, the non-formal education is the only program that has received so much attention of the state and people that it has now become an important component of the Indian Education System. As in many other countries, the reason for this liberalization and introduction of newer mode of education is more because of political initiative and pressure that called for expansion of access to education. Later on, the economic benefits of correspondence courses for supporting formal education also became an important motivational factor in the expansion of the correspondence and distance education.

## Major Steps in Establishing Open School System

1. The first Correspondence Course started by the Delhi University in

1962 was motivated by the then Soviet Union system of correspondence education for working adults. However, it was started at the university level rather than at the school level for evolving the program with quality (Dewal and Biswas, 2006).

2. In 1965 the use of correspondence courses was started for secondary students by the Madhya Pradesh Government at the instance of the Council of Boards of School Education to improve the academic status of private candidates appearing for Board examinations. The other two boards that followed were Rajasthan Board of Secondary Education and the *Patrachar Vidyalaya*, Delhi, in 1968 (Dewal and Biswas, 2006).
3. The UNESCO Report (1972), "Learning to Be", advocated important ideas of learning society, life-long-learning (L3) and use of alternative schooling systems, which changed thinking of educationists and policy makers. The Satellite Instructional TV Experiment (SITE) in 1975-76, with the help of satellite ATS-6 launched by the USA for a year, and the establishment of the Center for Educational Technology by the Space Application Center of the Indian Space Research Organization (ISRO), Ahmedabad, created not only a partnership of two departments, the MHRD and ISRO, but also ensured the ISRO participation in the development of communication technology for education.
4. The Parthasarathy Committee Report 1975: Obviously impressed by the UK Open University, the first single mode university in the world, the Report proposed that a National Open University should be established in India. Since the universalisation of primary education was the key national policy and its provision a constitutional obligation of the Government, there was a shift in decision from the Open University to open school. And the pilot project of the Open School of the Central Board of Secondary Education was started in 1979.
   (a) The Pilot Project: The Open School program started with a pilot project had the following objectives (Dewal and Biswas, 2006).
   (b) To offer opportunities of education to children who complete class VIII but are unable to remain in a regular school;
   (c) To meet the demand for secondary education consequent upon fulfillment of the target of elementary education;
   (d) To serve the drop-outs, left-outs, and the push-outs in order to bring them back to the mainstream;
   (e) To offer an opportunity to girls and women who have no previous qualification but are desirous of receiving education;
   (f) To offer a programme of supervised self-learning for those adults

who have entered the world of work but wish to improve their career prospects;

(g) To equip children and adults of rural areas and to enable them to receive the benefits of latest technologies so that they can contribute to maximization of production and improvement of standard of living;

(h) To serve those children who belong to the disadvantaged sections of the community, and

(i) To provide a process of continuous life-long-learning.

5. The responsibility of the Open School was to evolve an alternative school system—a non-formal mode of education—to serve the school drop-outs as well as adults, thereby increasing access and coverage including the disadvantaged ones by evolving flexible entry requirements, offering wider choices to meet the needs of learners, and by evolving flexible and appropriate system of examination and certification.

   The Pilot Project of Open School was quite a success in getting the idea of open school wider acceptance throughout the country, in developing multi-level courses, in creating syllabi with self-instructional learning materials, in evolving a flexible student support and examination system with a certification process equal to the formal certification offered by various boards. The Central Government also gave all the necessary support to make the non-formal stream acceptable to institutions and people.

6. National Open School: After a decade of the pilot project, a National Open School (NOS) was established in 1989 under the Ministry of Human Resource Development as an autonomous body, which included the programs and activities of the CBSE Pilot Project. Since its establishment, the NOS have expanded its programs to include senior secondary education, vocational education, regional language programs, Urdu language programs, open basic education programs, etc. It also started giving academic, economic and technical support to the State Open Schools. The NOS has started using ICT in its operations since 1989, and has now a well-developed Computer Division, which handles most of the NOS operations of materials development and publishing, management of databases, software development and installation, etc. (www.nos.org). Applications such as on-demand and on-line examinations are taken up for development. The NOS has thus played an important role as the apex organisation for giving support to research, development, training and extension activities of open schooling in India. As an apex agency for Open Basic Education (primary education), the NOS provides the broad

learning outcomes, high quality study materials, text-free sample questions and blue print of examination paper with suggestive marking schemes to the Accredited Agencies carrying out the basic education program. The NOS was converted into the National Institute of Open Schooling (NIOS) in 2005-06 (website: www.nios.ac.in).

7. State Open Schools: Since India is a Union of 29 states and six union territories, with different languages and dialects, with socio-cultural diversities, it is obvious that a single National Open School cannot serve the purpose of giving access to school education to students from all over the country. So far, 10 State Open Schools have been established: Tamil Nadu (1982), Andhra Pradesh (1991), Punjab (1991), Haryana (1994), Madhya Pradesh (1996), Karnataka (1996), West Bengal (1997), Kerala (1999), Jammu & Kashmir (2001) and Rajasthan (2005). Thus the NIOS and the ten State Open Schools form quite a large system of imparting education through distance mode.
8. National Consortium for Open Schooling (NCOS) and National Institute of Open Schooling (NIOS): With the expansion of the open schools in states, a need was felt to coordinate and promote the open schooling program in the country. The NIOS is expected to provide program and resource support to the open schools at the state levels. A National Consortium for Open Schooling was formed in 1997 consisting of the NOS and all the state open schools and other related agencies; and the NOS served as the secretariat of the NCOS (Williams, 2006). The NOS was, therefore, re-christened as National Institute of Open Schooling in 2002 to cover its additional functions (website: www.nios.ac.in). As an apex organisation, the NIOS carries out the same activities as its state counterparts, but has a leadership role to play in open schooling.

## Major Steps in Establishing ODL: Open University Programme

1. Since the beginning of the correspondence course program of Delhi University in 1962, the Open and Distance Education (ODE) has grown initially as correspondence education in a dual mode, and later on with an addition of a single mode Open Universities starting with the Andhra Pradesh Open University (now Dr. B.R. Ambedkar Open University), a state open university, in 1982.
2. At present there is one National Open University (IGNOU) and 12 State Open Universities with 8,93,000 students registered and 27,43,000 on rolls as in 2004. The IGNOU plays a double role, a university for the whole country offering distance education through English and Hindi as media of instruction; and also as an agency, the

Distance Education Council, for coordination, promotion and maintenance of standards in distance education in India.

3. The dual mode education has also expanded substantially in India. The former Departments of Correspondence Education were transformed into Distance Education Institutes (DEI) of the universities; and today there are 73 dual mode universities with a total of 7,45,000 students registered in 2002 through DE mode (DEC, 2004).
4. The ODL system enrolment is included in the total enrollment figures given above for higher education in India. The ODL system accounts for nearly 18 to 19 per cent of the total enrollment of higher education institutions. The Open University system and DEIs have nearly the same enrollment. However, the DEIs have recorded a growth rate of 30 per cent during 1999-2004, whereas the open university system has shown a faster, 98 per cent growth.
5. Use of ICT: The IGNOU has pioneered the use of satellite communication and broadcasting in open and distance education. Since 1995, the IGNOU had used the distributed classroom with one-way video and two-way audio for distance education. It is supporting and coordinating broadcasting of four national channels for education in India.

**Table 20.1: National Media Capacity of IGNOU**

| *Media and Technology* | *Number* | |
|---|---|---|
| Satellite Transponder | 1 | |
| Teleconferencing centers | 790 | (to increase to 2000) |
| National TV channels | 6 | (including teleconferencing channel) |
| All India Radio Stations | 186 | (interactive radio counseling) |
| Tele-learning centers | 22 | |
| FM Radio stations | 17 | (to increase to 40) |
| Satellite | 1 | (EduSat) |

*Source*: Panda *et al.,* (2006)

The Indian Educational Satellite (EduSat, launched by the ISRO) in September 2004 with 13 transponders with 5 beams in ku-band covering 5 regions of India (Central, eastern, western, northern and southern) and one for all India coverage, which makes Direct To Home (DTH) education possible. The EDUSAT would help creating distributed classrooms and network of school and higher education institutions for offering quality education for all. However, this vision and perspective created is yet to be realized. Besides the IGNOU, there are three state open universities which are getting up-linking and TV channel support from the ISRO.

**Table 20.1: State and National Open University Resources (2003-04)**

| *Indicators* | *IGNOU* | *Other State OU's (10)** | *Total* |
|---|---|---|---|
| Programs | 101 | 340 | 441 |
| Courses | 900 | 2963 | 3863 |
| Students Registered ('000) | 366.1 | 557.6 | 923.7 |
| Students on Rolls ('000) | 1311 | 1562 | 2873 |
| Regional Center's and Sub-Regional Center's | 54/23 | 57/88 | 111 |
| Study Centers | 1257 | 3131 | 4388 |
| Academic counselors/tutors | 33,366 | 31472 | 64838 |
| Audio | 1293 | 1011 | 2304 |
| Video | 1792 | 496 | 2288 |
| Staff | 1369 | 2208 | 3577 |

*Note*: * Ten State Open Universities covered are: Dr. B R Ambedkar Open University (BRAOU-1982), Vardhaman Mahavir Open University (VMOU, formerly Kota Open University,-1987), Nalanda Open University (NOU-1987), YC Maharshtra Open University (YCMOU-1989), MPBOU, KSOU, NSOU, UPRTOU, TNOU. Source: Panda *et al.*, (2006)

## Quality Assurance in ODL and Distance Education Council

The EC recommended establishment of a *National Council of Home Studies* for the purpose of accreditation and evaluation of agencies, and also for supporting research, development and deployment of content. The establishment of the IGNOU and NOS is a major step in implementing the EC recommendations. The provision of Distance Education Council was made in the IGNOU Act and the DEC came into existence after a few years of successful working of the IGNOU. Similar provision does not exist for open schooling.

The Distance Education Council (DEC) has the responsibility of coordination, promotion and maintenance of standards in distance education. The DEC is also another arm of the IGNOU, which functions as an open university and also as a promotional agency. This role has created many problems due to conflict of interests with the State Open Universities due to the IGNOU's dual role of a university and a promotional agency for all distance education in India. The DEC has evolved a framework for Quality Assurance and Accreditation in partnership with the National Assessment and Accreditation Council (NAAC). However, the DEC has followed a different path of quality control by evolving different process of quality control (Garg *et al.*, 2006). Because of the conflicts of interests of the state and national open universities, it is proposed to separate the DEC from IGNOU and form it into a national agency responsible for quality and standards in distance education. It appears that the separation is being done when convergence of formal, non-formal and informal education is taking place, when entirely different and integrative approach is essential due to the emergence of e-education or distributed education.

## Achievements, Issues and Concerns of ODL

In this section we consider the achievements of open school and university education system briefly and also the fulfillment of the ideas of EC Report.

### Achievements of NIOS and Open Schooling: Main Features

The NIOS has implemented practically all the aspects of the self and own-study suggested by the Education Commission and has succeeded in creating efficient, effective and alternative open school system.

1. By adopting a policy of institutional accreditation for imparting open school education, NIOS has roped in quite a large number of public and private schools and NGOs to increase access to variety of target groups.
2. With a large number of accredited institutions giving delivery of education, the coordination and maintenance of standards becomes an important issue. The training of center-coordinators and teacher-tutors is undertaken with usual cascading approach. It would be essential to develop systems for ensuring quality of education imparted at the accredited centers and progress of learners. The NIOS is trying to do this by using networking and using IT in its administrative and academic functions.
3. Since giving free primary school èducation is the constitutional responsibility of the Governments, both of the Union and State, and there is a ban on employment of children for earning up to the age of 14 years, a full-time school education is going to be the main and dominant formal mode of education. In such a situation, the open school system becomes a corrective mechanism for schooling system up to standard VIII, and assumes the role of an alternative mode for students over 14 years of age and adults.
4. The school system in India is more of a social nature and not a professional system. Hence, it is the concern of quite a large section of the Indian society, involving parents, communities and private enterprise, which offer supplementary help to students in their studies. The total size of the society involved in education including students is nearly 20 per cent of the population. The proportion of students covered by the open schooling is quite small as compared to the total number of learners in schools.

### Achievements of Open University System

The ODL has impressive achievements to its credit. It has not only established alternative educational system (non-formal system), but also created a nationally accepted alternative for India for increasing access and coverage with quality and cost-efficiency. Following are the main outcomes of the ODL:

1. The ODL has increased outreach in terms of coverage, numbers, subject disciplines, age of learners, occupational background, etc.
2. The ODL has helped in reducing unit cost of education, which is quite substantial in general as well as in professional courses. It is up to one-half in case of professional courses requiring laboratories and one-fifth to one-tenth in case of general and liberal courses. The cost also depends on the quality maintained in the development and delivery of the programs.
3. The ODL is now using ICT in various administrative and management processes for increasing efficiency of communication and achieving cost-reduction. The ODL has created a vast network of physical facilities such as study and regional centers spread all over the country, a large number of teachers-facilitators in the ODL along with a local student support system.
4. One of the greatest achievements is the creation of quality learning materials prepared by the open universities. It has raised the quality of instructional materials by adopting excellent pedagogic designs and has enhanced the quality of study texts by employing best expertise, experience and teachers. The learning is supplemented by audio and videotapes, and by radio and TV lessons as well as distributed classroom of the type of one-way video and two way audio. This has helped in raising the quality of education.

India has already accepted the ODL as an alternative for increasing access and outreach. It is expected that the proportion of the ODL students in higher education system is expected to increase to 40 per cent by 2012.

## Limitations and Shortcomings in ODL

1. *The Same Form & Structure of Degree Programs*: The ODL in Open University system has evolved an alternative delivery mode with a lot of flexibility. However, it has maintained the same form and structure leading to degree or diploma certification. This is possibly to have recognition from employers and acceptance from society. The goals and objects of degree programs remain the same and have not advanced to make the system a National System of Education.
2. *Linkages with Workplaces*: The emphasis on people's education with a focus on productivity is yet to get developed and built-in in the system for high school, senior secondary and vocational education. Linking education with productivity demands linking learning with work-place based training and education and its linking with value addition in terms of socio-economic development.
3. *Limited Coverage and Access*: The existing size of the ODL in school

system is too small and forms a very small fraction of the total size of school education. At the university level it is appreciable, but not enough to call it a people's system.

4. *Lack of Access to Media*: Study text forms the main study materials for large majority of students. Use of electronic media in study is yet very limited.
5. *Lack of Coordination*: There is an overlap of target groups to be covered by the open schooling and Open University education. The OU education is for mature adults and many OUs have brought down the age from 21 years to 18 years for open admission for the preparatory course essential for open degree programs without 12th pass. Since open schools also cater to mature adults, it is essential to have coordination in the programs to serve the mature adults.

## EC Recommendations and ODL

The Education Commission's faith that "The destiny of the nation is now being shaped in the classrooms" is not assuming a different form in which conventional classroom or formal education has to accept the partnership of the ODL due to the development in ICT.

What has not happened as per the recommendations of the EC Report is as follows:

*EC Recommendation 203*: The Commission proposed Continuing Education programs to be started by all the educational institutions by throwing their doors open, outside their regular working hours, to all those who wish to continue education. The EC expects to create a *parallel part-time system of education for adults* for taking the same type of diploma and degrees as students in schools and colleges.

*Comment*: This has not happened, partly because of restrictive policies and also due to unsuitability of the existing ODL system to fulfill the needs and demands of the large sections of people. It is still very much *'teacher-centric'* and does not respond to the needs and requirements of the people.

*National Council of Home Studies* was expected to be established by the Ministry of Education in collaboration with other Ministries, for the purpose of accreditation and evaluation of agencies, which provide correspondence courses. The purpose of educational planning in a Federal democracy has to be the right *blend of centralization and decentralization* in the appropriate sectors and especially in administration.

*Comment*: The Distance Education Council was created within the IGNOU and MHRD domain. It does not cover the education and training programs offered under different ministries. The island tendency of the authorities and institutions dominates and there is no effective mechanism to coordinate continuing education across all the ministries at the central and state levels.

The present top-down approach of planning and development carried out centrally through various agencies has strong limitations of involved interests and structures.

*Role of Private Enterprise* (Recommendation 209, p. 667 of EC Report): The EC recommended that:

(a) The state should make all possible use of the assistance that can come from the private sector for the development of education.

(b) The state has now rightly assumed full responsibility to provide all the needed educational facilities and the private enterprise can, therefore, have only a limited and minor role.

*Comment:* The State has adopted a policy of promoting private sector in school as well as university education. This has led to the stratification of educational systems according to the cost and quality accessible to the people, thereby creating stratified society according to the level and quality of education.

In fact, the public system of education created for all with the state support has been neglected and is languishing. Quality institutions of education, such as the IITs and IIMs, have been created either with the state support as a national policy or with the private support. A quality alternative is made available to those who can afford, whereas the quality and standards of education institutions for public is deteriorating fast. The country is following dual policies; the first is to create quality institutions, even by inviting private contribution, to compete with developed countries particularly in the present scenario of global competitiveness essential for national progress, and the other is to expand existing public facilities, mostly of poor quality, for providing wider access. Currently, even the poor are paying heavily for the education of their children to enable them rise in the quality hierarchy. What is essential in the present circumstances is not only education for all but *quality education for all* for reducing disparities and divides in the society.

*The Role of Local Authorities* (Recommendation 210, p. 667 of EC Report): As an ultimate objective it is essential that schools and their communities should be intimately associated with the processes of education.

*Comment:* Close linkage of the education system with society and industry is yet to be established on a scale that would impact the society in its development. The education has always remained a weak subsystem of the total socio-economic system and has yet to play a 'center-stage' role.

*Educational Finance: Economies and Utilization* (Recommendation 229, p. 673 of EC Report): Even with the mobilisation of maximum resources for education, the funds will still be inadequate to meet even the minimum needs of educational reconstruction, if conventional techniques involving large wastage and stagnation continues. It would, therefore, be necessary to adopt measures for economy, for eradication of wastage and for most efficient utilization of funds.

*Comment:* A stage has now developed wherein '*more of the same*' is not going to change the system. The transformation has to go far beyond the drive for efficiency and productivity. The system needs a paradigm shift or entirely new paradigm to address the concerns of quality and equality and equity.

*The EC expected to create National System of Education* (Naik, 1982) for people's education on a scale and coverage that would serve the purpose of a learning society. The EC proposed many measures with a goal for creating '*Educational Revolution*'. The National Education System should become a powerful instrument of social, economic and cultural transformation necessary for the realization of the national goals. It should also emphasize moral and aesthetic values.

*Comment:* This is yet to be achieved. The change expected should emphasize education of people, should eliminate differences between individuals educated in the modern education system, formal or non-formal. In fact, what is essential is a system that would unite and integrate the people and nation and not stratify the society. Some of the issues, particularly of quality education for all for evolving a system of people's education, is dealt with in the further part of this paper.

## Education and National Development

The EC had a certain vision of India of tomorrow and of national development. It looked forward to the creation of a democratic, secular and egalitarian society, which should be based on science and spiritual values and wherein evils of poverty, ignorance and ill health would be eliminated through a humane use of scientific and technological knowledge (Naik, 1982)

The nature of vision of India of tomorrow has now radically changed and the EC recommendations on national system of education have to be reformulated on the basis of the emerging knowledge, economy and knowledge society. This brings in subjectivity for vision and perspectives, an unavoidable factor in perspective building. We follow here the analysis given by J P Naik in his book, Education Commission and After (1982) and consider the third model of development based on Gandhian thoughts, besides, of course, the other two models of capitalist and socialist development already being tried and implemented in India.

The EC Report was titled, Education and National Development. However, it suffers from some inadequacies. The first is that its formulation, based on many positive statements for productivity and prosperity of the nation to be achieved through the system of education, is rather naïve and unsatisfactory. Secondly, the EC does not refer to the many crucial aspects of development. The relationship between education and society is also not clear in as much as development is linked with social reconstruction. The EC expected that the change should be brought about in a big way.

## UGC Policy Frame

Since the EC Report, many policies and programs were adopted that added to the developmental concerns of the society. Addition of extension as the third dimension in the Policy Frame of the UGC (1976), the programs of adult and continuing education, National Social Service scheme started in every university and college are some activities that have become now a part of higher education. In schools too, the introduction of socially useful productive work tried to link school education with community development. However, all these activities have remained peripheral and did not get integrated with the "classroom" or mainstream education. In some universities these subjects have become academic disciplines, followed well-trodden path of teaching courses and curriculum leading to degrees. However, it is not commensurate with the needs of the society for productivity and has little employability.

## UNESCO and Development

The international community, after a series of regional and international seminars organized by the UNESCO, had approved in the United Nation's General Assembly two major programs of development:

- Millennium Development Goals (MDG) adopted in 2000, and
- Decade of Education for Sustainable Development (DE4SD) for the period 2005-2014 adopted in December 2002.

The MDGs is an overarching framework for development and for cooperation; and provide targets for international actions to bring such visions into reality by overcoming poverty; improving child, maternal and sexual health; expanding educational provision; redressing gender inequalities in education; and developing national strategies for sustainable development. The MDG program is followed by all developing countries and is regularly monitored internationally by the UNESCO with a goal of eliminating poverty, providing health and livelihood security for all.

The DE4SD emphasizes that education is an indispensable element for achieving sustainable development and stresses the necessity to improve educational systems and the design of learning programmes for sustainable development. Sustainable development is a dynamic and evolving concept with many dimensions and interpretations, and reflects locally relevant and culturally appropriate visions for a world in which development "*meets the needs of the present without compromising the ability of future generations to meet their own needs*" (UNESCO, 2004).

Both these programs are the outcome of aspirations, needs and requirements of the new knowledge society emerging in the 21st Century. The two programs, therefore, can form the goals to be achieved along with cultivation of life-long-learning (L3) process for development.

## Developmental Models and Sustainability

One of the major issues in linking education with development is its model and its suitability to Indian needs, context and culture. Indian Constitution adopted the socialist model of development with many programs that aim at social welfare, support to the weaker and the disadvantaged and provide minimum essential living standards to common people. However, the policies of social welfare and support to the weak and disadvantaged are without any developmental model. Simultaneous processes of liberalization and privatization are going on to be competitive and progressive in the context of globalisation. The two processes of privatization and social empowerment are not apparently compatible, and often clash in goals, approaches and interests. However, the power of Indian democracy that decides the polity to govern the state, has made the leadership accountable to the people, at least once in a few years. This has enabled the pursuit of two apparently contradictory processes that pull in opposite directions. The developmental pulls in opposite direction has to be understood in terms of bi-polar objectives—both being essentially positive in character but tending to pull policy projections in opposite directions. As pointed out by Moonis Raza, the model of Indian education has "essentially been based on decisions relating to trade-off between 'so to say' two 'goods'. What appears, as directionless meandering of educational policy in Independent India should be appreciated as the operationalisation of compensatory mechanisms generated by the turbulence of transition from underdevelopment to development. Some of the important pulls have been identified as those of quantitative expansion to qualitative improvement, of equity and efficiency, of value and utility, of commitment and detachment, of integration and differentiation, of concentration and dispersal, of autonomy and accountability, and lastly of the 'pure' academic and the 'involved' teacher" (M. Raza, 1991).

The major issue is whether there exists a way to bridge the two parts pulling in opposite directions by some mechanism that would integrate and create a level playing field for all to offer quality with quantity, equity with efficiency, integration with diversity, centralization with dispersal and autonomy with accountability. The answer is no in the models of the 20th century, but yes in the context of emerging information society and knowledge economy of the 21st century; and has to be searched in appropriate application of Information Communication Technology (ICT).

## Growth and Promotion of IT in India

The Makinley Report based on the studies conducted at the behest of the National Association of Software & Service Companies of India (NASSCOM-www.nasscom.org) predicts robust growth for the Indian IT services and IT Enabled Services industry. It may grow to US $ 57 billion in exports by the year 2008. Further, it is expected that the Indian companies would eventually move up form the BPO (Business Process Outsourcing) or Call Centers to KPO (Knowledge Process Outsourcing). In the near future India would be the third largest economy after the USA and China.

The IT industry's growth has multiple effects on India (The Economic Times, 2005) because of the rising class of younger consumers with high disposable income. The IT has helped spawning of ancillary businesses such as transportation, real estate, communication and catering, and created quite high employment opportunities, particularly for the engineers, graduates and for the professionally qualified. Reasons attributed to this growth are due to leadership with strong foundation of:

- Large pool of English speaking manpower, and
- Emphasis on quality at significantly low costs.

Information Technology applications are fast spreading in India. Mobile telephony is one of the sectors witnessing very fast growth and is expected to reach nearly 500 million Indians by 2010. The broadband connectivity is expanding fast through optical fiber as well as through wireless Internet. The Indian Government is supporting the IT industry by creating infrastructure development, attracting investment by reducing corporate taxes and creating a stable tax system, and by setting up Knowledge Commission to support IT related development.

The ICT application and promotion in India are so rapid that a great impact is expected in all areas of the economy and society. The changes are already being seen and amount to a revolution—the *Information Revolution*. The IT is developing in such a way that convergence of telephony, broadcasting and computing would occur on two 'screens'—TV screen for home use and cell-phone screen for mobile use. The Triple Play Broadband Technology has started its applications in India, and would offer the services through telephone wire to every TV screen in a house within 5-10 years.

The rapid development of newer and versatile technologies in IT is expected to change the nature of communication. The technologies such as development of *high fidelity Internet that can deliver "immersive" technologies and nano technologies* are going to change the communication industry and help in raising the overall quality of life. The major direction of development visualized by 2020 is of personalization of mass technologies and linking with local, contextual and need-based aspects of developmental processes. The IT can help humanization lost in the industrial society (R. Venkateshan, 2005).

All these developments would have a profound impact on education. The IT would enable development of mass-personalized education with just-in-time learning services. Education could be linked with places of working and living of anyone anywhere. Education, if developed properly with ICT support, could be a great equalizer.

Wider applications of IT in all walks of life are creating an information society and knowledge economy. Applicable knowledge is going to drive development and, with all the communication technologies enabling access to various services, it is likely to help reversal of centralization processes started in industrial society with concentration of industries and services in urban cities. By providing urban infrastructure in rural areas essential for cultural and healthy life, the ICT may help in accelerating the decentralization, and may bridge the rural-urban divide in India.

Information Technology promotes three main processes:

- *Virtualization* in which any organisation or institution or group of institutions could be developed as a distributed system working together and communicating with each other as if they are on a single campus.
- *Digitization* in which content could be digitized and communicated to anyone, anywhere linked with e-network.
- *Mass-Personalization or Customization* is a process in which products and services could be customized or personalized besides their *massification.*

These are entirely new processes typical of Information Technology and did not exist in earlier technologies that helped form the industrial or agrarian society. The IT could be used effectively for techno-social transformation by innovating tools & techniques and by creating new organisations to help shaping of a new society on a value system that we use to create organisations and institutions. Following are some of the tools and technologies that would play a vital role in evolving new paradigms:

### Platform for Level Playing Field for All

*The Learning Management System (LMS) and network platforms* that enable to offer learning and developing services for working individually and in a group.

### People's Tools and Technologies

*Open Education and Development Resources* created centrally and globally through open participation for free use by all (Approach of Wikipedia-www.wikipedia.org).

### Open Education Resources

*Local Knowledge Creation Platform and Tools* that help generate local databases, which would enable locals to get information, knowledge and apply useful knowledge for creating wealth and prosperity.

### Technologies to Create Virtual Communities with Specific Interests

*Virtual Private Network (VPN)* on global platforms for L-groups and L-communities for development organized on the basis of common purpose and interest and run with democratic principles of participation and decentralization.

### Distributed Systems for Learning, Educating, Working Together and Developing

*Distributed Systems* for enabling production companies & provider groups/ agencies and customers to partner in production and services and share outcomes and wealth, not monetary alone.

Many of these technologies and tools are available, and the IT industry is in the process of developing newer ones. This process of technology development may last for two-three decades till the IT maturates or reshapes itself in a completely new form. The development is on the basis of market forces and is competitive in nature. Alternative model of development with cooperative working to fulfill felt and perceived needs of the stakeholders needs to be evolved in such a way that customers and users also participate in the productive and service processes (Distributed industries and agencies).

## Third Model of Development

Besides the two models—capitalist or privatization model and socialist or public model of development, a third model, the Gandhian Model of development, could be conceived and developed in the context of information revolution to solve the illusive triangle of quality, quantity and equality in education. The third model should address the problems of equality and justice on the basis of liberty, equality and fraternity, the trinity of human values evolved in the French Revolution and adopted by the Indian Constitution. A principle of Private-Public-Community Partnership with a win-win approach has the force and potential in a system of democratic governance to integrate the first two models and help evolve the third one in the context of the Knowledge Society.

### Elements of the Third Way

Mahatma Gandhi's concept of *education for life, from life and throughout life* is the basis of Life Education (*Jeevan Shikshan*) and could form the foundation for the Indian National System of Education expected in the EC Report.

Elements of the Gandhian Developmental models that are amenable to Information Revolution are:

1. *Trusteeship concept* expressed through private-public-community partnership with a win-win approach.
2. *Self-supporting and sustainable village* expressed through sustainable locality of the group of villages or a block (corresponding to PURA [APJ Abdul Kalam, 2003])
3. *Participatory democracy at local and central levels*—regional, national and international—created through global and local networks, enabling individuals/locals to form groups and communities and to participate in development and progress with autonomy.
4. *Economy based on surrounding nature* and its abundance changed to central-local open learning and development resources openly available for locality development with global markets accessible to all.
5. *Handicraft with appropriate technologies for giving livelihood to everyone* to be replaced by development of personalized/ customized need-based products and services to be offered by locals to anyone, anywhere by forming learning and developing communities with sustainability and by having local as well as global participation.
6. *System of Values based on openness, transparency, fairness, sharing and caring along with search for truth and satyagraha as a form of protest and agitation against exploitation and injustice* being common to both old and new models.

The purpose of considering these points is not to develop the Gandhian Model, which itself is a very difficult and complex task, but to consider those technologies, organisations and values that would empower the common people and their groups (Learning Groups/Self-Help Groups) to achieve sustainable development through Information Communication Technologies. They would, it is hoped, be enabling to identify basic elements of locality development and progress for common people in consonance with the global direction of development. Identification of these components and processes, it is hoped, would lead to formation of Gandhian Model of Education for sustainable and autonomous locality development or Indian Model of National System of Education. In this transformation, education would obviously be playing the central role.

## Educational Revolution for Developing National System of Education

***Educational Revolution:*** The idea of educational revolution for radical social transformation for developing a National System of Education proved to be a dream of the Commission. J.P. Naik (1982) has analyzed the reasons for its failure. Firstly, in the EC Report, the change agents for the Educational Revolution were supposed to be teachers, students, managers of education and the state and central governments. This was a wrong identification. The people who form the part of the power structure with vested interests cannot be expected to bring about revolutionary changes wherein there is devolution of power and sharing of benefits on the basis of equality.

J.P. Naik identifies five reasons for holding up the Educational Revolution from take off:

1. Separation of education for students and adults.
2. Wrong use of tools and techniques—preservation of formal rigid system
3. Non-involvement of people
4. Failure in improving the living standards of masses—poverty eradication.
5. Cooling down of missionary zeal of educational intelligence.

No revolution existed in the 20th Century. The only revolution available now is a Communication Revolution, with which Education Revolution could be started.

The Change Agents now should be all "teachers": all those who participate in educating and training teachers, tutors, trainers in industry and parents and community could become the teachers and change agents for educational revolution. It would be essential to empower the people—the "teachers—to undertake the socio-economic transformation with the help of education for development. The process for revolution, rather total revolution, was once developed in India without success by the movement of J.P. Narayan, a political leader, and involved processes of education, organisation, creation and agitation. This is possible only when education gets linked with socio-economic transformation of the society. Development is always a participatory work, involving students and people, and is carried out successfully through cooperative working under a suitable leadership. The process of empowerment is enhanced and accelerated with networking of people, knowledge, developmental and technology resources and the success requires a leadership system that would be committed to the people for safeguarding their interests. Examples of such an empowerment are the success stories of Grameen Bank of Bangladesh or Lijjat Papad in India working for socio-economic development. In fact, mobilisation of learning and developing groups with specific interest like women's self-help groups can become part of a larger organisation of a learning and developing community to give organizational support for protecting their interests, vis-à-vis private and public institutional interests.

## A Model of ODL for Development

Information Technology is bringing about changes that amount to an information revolution with the emergence of Information or Knowledge Society. The ICT has changed the entire basis of communication needed for teaching, learning and teacher-learner interaction. Many new paradigms could be designed and developed including the existing one in which teacher-centricity could be retained with top-down flow of knowledge or the so-called 'donor' model.

Education for development changes the whole scenario. It brings in not only learning usually promoted to achieve knowledge, actionable or non-actionable, but also the processes of development through actionable knowledge. Application of actionable knowledge to create new products or services or to add value to the existing products and services is a process of development essential for achieving progress and prosperity. The process is specific to the group or institution or people involved, has a local context as well as the use of universal knowledge and old or new tools and technique appropriate to the tasks undertaken. The process essentially is of continuous development generated to achieve higher quality of outputs and outcomes. It is also a capability building process for a group or institution to rise to higher levels of achievements and gets repeated cyclically till one reaches the best in the class or type of work.

The concept of quality is defined in many ways. Usually the definitions are objective or perspective in nature. The objective definitions of quality includes the concept of exceptional as well as those that conform to the highest norms and standards, The perspective definitions of quality include the concepts such as *fitness for the purpose, value for the money* or *transformative value* expected. In the case of developmental education, the idea of transformative value is used to find the outcomes and impacts of the efforts of learning and development.

## Capability Development Model for Learning and Development

This model is based on Baldrige Model of Education for Performance Excellence (www.baldrige.com) and uses terms and concepts that form the basis of the Baldrige Model for education. The terms used here are taken from the Baldrige Model with a constraint that they are used for development of individuals, small groups and organisations (I-CONSENT, 2006).

1. *Situational Tasks* in case of Education, the learning situations are class, school or college and society and learners are individuals, small groups, and their virtualization. The *Goals and Objects* are obtained from the needs analysis of students, stakeholders and market focus.
2. *Approaches* refer to methods, their appropriateness, effectiveness and systemic nature.

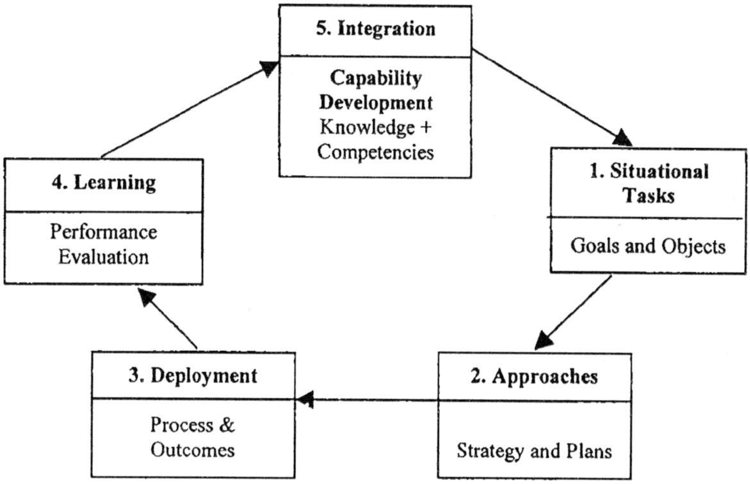


**Fig. 20.1: Capacity Development Model for Learning and Development**

3. *Deployment* refers to the extent to which the approach is made relevant to local situation/organisation, applied consistently to all related works in the tasks.
4. *Learning* refers to refining the approach adopted through cycles of evaluation and improvements, encouraging breakthrough changes and innovations through approaches, and by harmonizing actions, processes and methods, and by obtaining outcomes and impacts through group/organization wide systemic changes.
5. *Integration* refers to aligning approaches selected for the local situations to those that are relevant to regional/national/global goals and approaches, making measures, evaluation and improvements complimentary to other processes and work outcomes/impacts in other situational tasks, and harmonizing learning and improvements across group/organisation wide goals.

The model offers continuous process of improving and developing the situations and adding more and more transformative value with continuous building up of capabilities of students, stakeholders and organisation. This is a cyclic process of locality development for achieving excellence.

Mobilisation and continuous improvement processes implied in the model need:

- *Organisation and management system* for stakeholders, partners and resource management system.
- *Leadership system* at all levels in wide variety of situations for forming, managing groups and their interest specific communities through sharing and collaborative learning.

A learner would need a different culture—a culture of Knowledge Society of the 21st Century, with Life-Long-Learning (L3) and continuously developing through Learning (L)-groups and L-communities. Every learner has to be equipped with:

1. Learning to Learn for knowing (self study)
2. Learning by doing (Active Learning)
3. Learning through virtual processes such as Distributed Classroom.
4. Cooperative Learning—Group Learning and Developing.
5. Learning through experimenting and innovating—*Prayog Pariwar*.

The learning processes imply a shift from teaching to learning; and the role of teachers and educational resources would be to support learning and personalization essential for the learner or their group to follow their learning path to achieve goals of learning and development.

## Needs Total Innovation

A program of big changes envisaged in the Education Revolution can happen only when we solve the puzzle of iron triangle of quality-quantity-equity or achieve success in providing quality education for all. This is not possible by any means and methods of agrarian or industrial society. It needs tools and technologies of Information Age. It involves organisation or mobilisation of people into learning and developing groups and their communities. What is needed is a total innovation in techno-social organisation of ODL for Development with following features:

1. *Technology use* for giving total e-governance support both in administration and academic programs.
2. *Content organisation and deployment* on pedagogic principles for learning and developing.
3. *Organisation of stakeholders* for Life-Long-Learning (L3) and developing.
4. *New System Design* with goals and approaches for promoting creativity, innovation and entrepreneurship leading to productivity and prosperity.
5. *System with Core Values* for helping cooperative working and consortium building of provider organisations and institutions as well the user groups and communities.
6. *Built in Quality Assurance and R&D* for linking knowledge creation at central and local levels with their use in developing institutions and locality.

These are also the basic components for Technology Mediated Open and Distance Education (Tech_MODE) (I-CONSENT, 2006 www.mkcl.org/iconsent)

Emphasis is laid on the *technological and organizational innovation* with following components for:

### *Technology Applications*

1. *e-Networking* of providers, learners and educational functionaries and their facilities.
2. *Internet use for communication and for working together.*
3. Mobile Telephony and *Internet for linking* anyone, anywhere, anytime.
4. Learning Management System to manage learners and their learning.
5. Tools and *frameworks for assignment and evaluation* essential in assessment processes.
6. *Content Development* and Integration framework for creating cooperative teaching and learning products and services.
7. *Distributed Classroom* with audio graphic and video conferencing facilities.
8. Mass-personalization/customization.
9. *Meta-database* with Sharable Content Object Reference Model (SCORM) compatibility essential for personalization of curricula and content.
10. *Neural Network* to offer one-to-one training through artificially learning computer connected through networks.

### *Organizational Applications*

1. Mobilisation of Life-long *Learning Groups and L-Communities* with special interests.
2. Creation of *global knowledge and developmental resources* and their delivery to all users.
3. Gathering *local data and information for generating local knowledge* for locality development (Approach of Wikipedia).
4. Creating *processes of empowering groups and communities* at local and central levels and their linkage with locality and institutional development.
5. Nurturing *local and central leadership system* with open, participatory and democratic processes of decision-making.
6. Creating *public-private-community partnership* with win-win approach for consortium building of all stakeholders.
7. *Sharing and institutionalizing learning* and knowledge with creation of common wealth of knowledge and educational resources.
8. Developing *system for quality and excellence* built in the working of individuals, groups and organization.
9. *Linking outcomes with markets* where products and services of the consortium could be utilized and benefits obtained.

10. *Creating productive endeavors* in which producers/teachers and consumers/learners participate in creating, innovating and 'marketing' together.

In order to strengthen the partnerships and consortium formation following cementing forces are essential:

- *Core values*, based on universal human values and ethics in the consortium and organisation such as openness, democracy, transparency, and accountability etc.
- *Culture of learning and working together*—for developing and sharing, with cooperation rather than competition, etc.
- *Common goals* of sustainable development of all partners and creating new approaches and methods for development.

Applications of technology and organization for creating network of groups, communities and consortia would form and shape society in a different organizational structure. The process of decentralization is achieved through virtualization and personalization. The program of ODL for development with local and global knowledge access for all would accelerate the march towards knowledge society faster and systematically. The processes of empowerment could be generated with interest based organisation and promotion with knowledge and technology learning and up-gradation continuously. With these processes, the society could slowly be taken to a higher level of knowledge and performance. With emphasis on ethics and morality as core values, it is possible to develop a Gandhian Model for cooperation, peaceful coexistence and sustainable development. However, there is one major contextual difference; the whole world has to be treated as a single village in which various communities could live with autonomy and achieve prosperity. Creating such a social order is a great challenge. The approach suggested would also enable achieving quality education for all with ever increasing capability. Although these concepts and ideas are in the initial stage of formulation, there is no doubt that they lead towards the formulation of a Third Model of Development.

## IT Mediated National Education System: Features

The Technology Mediated Open and Distance Education (Tech-MODE) (Workshop, 2005) had the following main features:

1. Distributed Education with convergence of formal, non-formal and informal modes of education.
2. Solves the problems of quality, quantity, cost reduction, and speed simultaneously. Education System for anyone, anytime, anywhere learning.

3. Mass education system with personalization—high and unlimited scalability.
4. Shift from learning for knowledge to learning for development.
5. Enables to pool best experts, quality content and services for all.
6. Enables shift from content learning to innovation, creativity and entrepreneurship development.
7. Enables to create open educational and developmental resources for personalized, customized and contextualized development.
8. Enables to create level playing field for ensuring quality education for all.
9. Creates developmental culture of cooperative learning with inclusion of core values in working together. Helps develop partnerships and new organisations.
10. Helps develop many localized and globalised paradigms and developmental models that could enable search of unity in diversity.

The National System of Education has to choose its developmental model correctly with appropriate values essential for democratic and participatory development. It would also need appropriate policy and resource support from the state if it is to succeed in bringing in people and their institutions together in their efforts to achieve sustainable development and prosperity.

## Education for Our People

The Commission expected the education to become a strong force for equalization and generate quality, wide access and equality for education of Indian people. The expectation of the EC to develop such a National Education System created through Education Revolution was not realizable in the 20th Century framework. It is now possible to develop appropriate paradigms with specific value system to start Educational Revolution by employing Information Revolution. The whole approach has to be people-centric utilizing the developed consciousness of the Indian people after working with the Indian democracy for nearly 60 years. The major shift lies in emphasizing bottom-up models of development and empowerment in the society and polity with centralized power structure. The constitutional goals of creating new Indian society based on equality and justice by sharing of social, economic and knowledge powers and by creating level playing fields on which weaker and stronger would have the equal opportunity for access and success is a great challenge for India and its educational system. The leadership and resources have to be searched, not in the existing power structure but in the democratic participation of the people. All those who are committed to the constitutional goals and vision of society should help in creating and supporting right policies and programs for people's empowerment.

National policies and strategies should support not only technological convergence, but also convergence of modes of education, help shift focus of education towards sustainable national development, help people's participation for creating common wealth of open educational and developmental resources, create networks with access to all disadvantaged and help nurture leadership from people, who would lead an Educational Revolution for developing the Indian National System of Education. The existing system of education has to undergo a radical transformation to make itself a suitable instrument for developing the Knowledge Society on the basis of equity and justice. Forming consortia at local, regional, national and international levels would be helpful in creating a change movement outside the Government but by ensuring public-private-community partnership with a win-win partnership.

## References


APJ Abdul Kalam (2003) Address on Convergence of Technologies at the dedication function at the International Institute of Information Technology, 28-05-2003: Pune (www.presidentof india.nic.in)

Dewal, Onkar Singh, Bishwas, Gopa (2006) *Evolution of the Open School System in Four Decades of Distance Education in India, Reflections on Policy and Practices*, New Delhi: Viva Books Pvt. Ltd.

Distance Education Council (2004) *Information Base on Distance Higher Education in India*, New Delhi: Published by IGNOU, Maidan Garhi, 110 068, India.

EC Report-1966 (1966) *Report of the Education Commission (1964-66): Education and National Development, Vol. I*; New Delhi: Ministry of Education, Government of India.

Garg, Suresh and Kaushik, Madhulika (2006) *Quality Assurance in Distance Education: DEC Initiatives in Open and Distance Education in Four Decades of Distance Education in India,* New Delhi: Viva Books Pvt. Ltd.

GOI Educational Statistics, (2004) and Elementary Education in India: Where do we stand? District Report Cards, (2004) by Arun C. Mehta, Volume I and II, NUEPA.

I-CONSENT (2006) Document under development as an outcome of the Workshop held in Mumbai during Sept. 24-26, 2006 on development of e-B.Ed. program based on situational learning (ref. www.mkcl.org/iconsent) (Unpublished).

Naik, J.P. (1977) *Convocation Address in Precious Thoughts*, Pune: University of Pune publication.

Naik, J.P. (1982 a) Educational Development in India during the next twenty years: 1981-2000, *Bulletin of the India Institute of Education, J.P. Memorial Issue, Vol. III*, Pune: IIE Publication.

Naik, J.P. (1982) *The Education Commission and After*, Bombay: Allied Publishers Pvt. Ltd.

Naik, J.P. (2006) To Begin a Revolution with a Revolution. Originally published by the New Era in *Indian Education of People's Welfare Ltd., India*, Communicated by Dr. Chitra Naik of IIE, Pune.

NASSCOM- National Association of Software & Service Companies (NASSCOM, < www.nasscom.org>

Panda, S., Venkaiah, V., Garg, Suresh and Puranik Chambi (2006) *Tracing the Historical Development in Open and Distance Education in Four Decades of Distance Education in India*, New Delhi: Viva Books Pvt. Ltd.

Ravi Venkateshan, NASSCOM Newsletter, February 2005

Raza, M. (1991) *Preface to Higher Education in India, Retrospect and Prospect*, New Delhi: Moonis Raza, (ed.) AIU publication.

The Economic Times, March 15, 2005.

UGC (1976) *Policy Framework of UGC for Higher Education*, Publication of UGC.

UNESCO (2004) *United Nations Decade of Education for Sustainable Development*, UNESCO Publication, Oct. (www.unesco.org)

Williums, V.J., and Kaushal, Savita (2006) *National Consortium for Open Schooling in Four Decades of Distance Education in India*, New Delhi: Viva Books Pvt. Ltd.

Workshop (2005) Report of the National workshop on Evolving New System of Education: Tech-MODE for Learning and Development and Consortium Approach to Teacher and School Transformation at Pune, 9-10 April 2005.

# 21

# The Vision of Institutionalizing New Ideas of the Education Commission: Focus on Open and Distance Learning

H.P. DIKSHIT

## Introduction

The beginning of the Higher Education System, as it exists today, seems to have been made about 125-150 years ago when the four oldest institutions of Higher Education, viz., the Universities of Calcutta, Bombay, Madras and Allahabad came into existence. These institutions provided high quality education to selected and talented students from different parts of the country and at times from abroad also. Professor D.S. Kothari, who was a product of the University of Allahabad, held in high admiration the fine traditions that he witnessed and training that he received at the University. There are still some talented teachers and students in these universities but there is a general feeling that the old glory and excellent campus environment suitable for academic pursuits are not the same as before. This has attracted attention of all concerned during the last several decades without any reasonable degree of success in reviving the old campus life and excellent environment conducive to academic transactions and advanced research. Similar concerns and challenges perhaps led the Kothari Commission to make the following observation: *"Indian Education needs a drastic reconstruction; almost a revolution"*'

In order to understand the historical perspective of the need for a revolution we need to remind ourselves about some of the unfulfilled promises that were made to our countrymen on the eve of Independence. We realized as a nation, at that juncture in the transition of our history, that we had to urgently deal with some serious challenges concerning social transformation of our communities. During such a period of transition, any developing country has to handle successfully some important and initial tasks like confidence building capabilities, creating awareness and empowering people for active and meaningful participation in the process of national development and reconstruction. The complexity of the problem, the difficulties in achieving our cherished goals for a total transformation of society, for the general betterment of quality of life of our people, is reflected on the fact that at that stage just 20 per cent of our people were literate with only two per cent of literate women. We well understand that education liberates, empowers, enlightens and enables successful reconstruction of free civil societies. However, the following observation amply highlights the contemporary scenario prevailing in the country at that time.

> "The chief cause of India's ruin has been the monopolizing of its education and grabbing of the land by a handful of men. If we are to rise again, we shall have to do it by spreading education among the masses."
>
> —Swami Vivekananda

The vast potential of human resource had to be properly educated and trained with some priority. Jawaharlal Nehru, the first Prime Minister of India, declared that the most important task for the country was to focus on educating every Indian. In addressing this task of educating the nation we have been consistently realizing all these years that our efforts have been inappropriate to the task. We took several major and successful initiatives but we are still far from the target of achieving even total literacy. Nevertheless, without bothering too much with what did not happen in the past, we have to look to the future and develop capabilities to handle education and training of large target groups of learners under tight time frames. This is very effectively reflected in the following quotation:

> *"In India, we face many difficult problems. Don't be worried. Don't be frustrated by the immensity of the problems. The problems are immense, no doubt, but so is our will and our determination and so is the will of the innumerable people of India"*
>
> — Jawaharlal Nehru, the first Prime Minister of Independent India.

In the contemporary scenario of rapidly growing international competition and global development we are compelled to move fast with greater priority and urgency to develop knowledge base around us. Dr. Abdul P.J. Kalam, a distinguished scientist and former President of India, in his inspiring book: *Wings of Fire*, highlighted this as follows:

> "If you want to leave your foot prints on the sands of time do not drag your feet".
>
> — Dr. Abdul P.J. Kalam,

The Kothari Commission fully understood that one of the essential requirements for quality education was the availability of well trained and highly qualified teachers in our campuses, whether in schools or institutions of higher learning. It, therefore, attached great significance and importance to Teacher Education and Training. Before we dwell more on this crucial matter we would like to examine some unique case studies related to the issues raised by the Commission that have direct relevance to the theme of this paper. With reference to State Studies on Teacher Education—Teacher Education in Bihar (NCTE) [21], on p. 8 of this study (Bengal Education Report 1907-1908) reference is made as to how the students of the state suffered because of setting up of Medical and Engineering Colleges outside the state. It is strongly advocated there that the educational disadvantage under which the people of Bihar have suffered will get further accentuated unless new institutions are set up in the state itself. It is further observed that the people of the state are home loving and will certainly not go for a course of training in a foreign city.

About the infrastructure and academic faculty including Principal, the report mentioned that the building consisted of well developed classrooms, academic faculty of five with one room and an additional room for Tutorials for every faculty member. All these arrangements were made for a total number of 12 students in the beginning which was raised to 15 and 40 in the years 1913 and 1915 respectively. It is interesting to observe and reflect on the fact that the total number of seats were reduced by 50 per cent due to financial constraints in the year 1916 and was again brought to the original level of 40 in the year 1918 when the Government could revive appropriate funding. *This is an excellent example of not compromising with standards if the appropriate resources were not available.* The following extracts from the Educational Policy Declaration of 1913 as given in the study ([21], p. 18) reflect a firm determination for ensuring quality education:

Eventually under modern system of education no teacher should be allowed to teach without a certificate that he is allowed to do so.

The subsequent growth in number of institutions and seats in Teacher Training Institutes was not enough to meet the contemporary requirement. This is a problem that we encounter more gravely today mainly due to the fact that any expansion in the "Modern System" of education involved substantial amount of additional cost, which the Government was unable to bear. The following extracts of a communication sent by the Inspector of Schools at Bhagalpur ([21], p. 28) is indicative of the anguish, helplessness and despair in the minds of practitioners of education for their inability to enhance access to education as per the requirements of the learners:

> To turn away 90 per cent of the candidates eager to qualify themselves for the work of teaching and to debar them from holding teachership,

> because they have not qualified (in entrance test) is an evil by far greater than the one such limitation to admission is designed to cure. Expediency requires that the Education Policy be influenced not only by the theoretical consideration of efficient training but to some extent by the actual needs of the day.

It is amazing that such concerns and considerations to facilitate training of in-service untrained teachers reappeared nationally as late as the turn of this century when the Government of India, state governments, national organizations and institutions like the National Council for Teacher Education (NCTE) and the Indira Gandhi National Open University (IGNOU) encountered the same problem on a much higher scale and greater degree of complexity. The only difference is that today we are well equipped with some new systems of education, which are capable of handling such situations more conveniently, efficiently and effectively. As of today, it seems that in the absence of such newly developed systems, we would have found ourselves more helpless and anguished than what the Inspector of Schools at Bhagalpur felt about hundred years ago. In fact, as visualized in the above noting of the Inspector, the NCTE, the Government of India, the IGNOU and a few state governments in the North East and Sikkim jointly took a practical view only a few years ago and offered a truncated Training Programme for the in-service teachers of those states through the distance mode.

Several issues, concerns and challenges covered in the foregoing observations are as relevant and important even today for any part of the country as they were at that time and subsequent stages of development of education system in the country. Equity in access and equal opportunity for education to all the citizens of our Republic in reasonable neighbourhood of their dwellings, whether in rural or urban areas, is an important goal that is highlighted by the Kothari Commission. This received focused attention of the Planning Commission and the University Grants Commission (UGC). Finally, in 1961 the Central Advisory Board of Education (CABE), the highest policy making body of the Government of India decided to get the possibility of the system of Correspondence Education examined before its introduction in the country. There were misapprehensions about the new system and it was considered necessary to thoroughly evaluate the system. The Government of India set up a Committee of experts with Prof. D.S. Kothari, then Chairperson of the UGC, to study all aspects of the new system. This Committee favoured introduction of the Correspondence Education system for experimenting a pilot run. Thus, Correspondence Education was introduced in the University of Delhi in the year 1962. Subsequently, the Kothari Commission highlighted the necessity of increasing access to meet the increased demand for education by introducing new systems in the form of part-time education and private or own time education. These recommendations crystallized in the form of education through Evening Colleges and Correspondence Education, respectively.

## Recommendations that Contributed to Shape a Revolution

As mentioned above, any tangible solution to substantial up-scaling of access to education to meet the requirement of mass education in a vast country like India with growing population, had evaded for more than a century. It was necessary to supplement the existing systems with new systems of education. However, bringing in major changes in the education system and their universal acceptance has been a difficult task especially for developing countries. Therefore, the bold recommendations of the Kothari Commission to implement new systems are considered as a path breaking and futuristic initiative that gradually complemented the prevailing system of education. We believe this motivated the beginning of a successful revolution in education that we are witnessing today with admiration, pleasure and satisfaction. This great event in our educational history amply fits in with the following observations made by two great Indians, a few decades ago:

> "When old words die out on the tongue, new melodies break forth from the heart; and where the old tracks are lost, a new country is revealed with its wonders."
>
> —Rabindranath Tagore

> "A moment comes, which comes but rarely in history, *when we step out from the old to the new...*"
>
> —Jawaharlal Nehru

The Commission also strongly recommended that the students passing out of these systems should be treated at par with the students of the conventional system. This still remains unfulfilled and we would discuss this issue a little later. Keeping the theme of this paper in mind, it is apt to refer to the following recommendations of the Commission: ([17], p. 8, [1]):

1. In order to bring education to those who are unable to attend part-time courses widespread organization of correspondence courses should occur.
2. Students taking correspondence courses should be provided opportunities to meet the teachers occasionally.
3. Correspondence courses should be supported by well coordinated radio and television programmes.
4. Correspondence courses should not be confined to preparing students for the University degrees but should also provide agricultural,

industrial and other workers such special courses of instruction as would help them to improve production.

5. Correspondence courses should be made available for those who desire to enrich their life by studying subjects of cultural and aesthetic value.
6. Correspondence courses should be developed for the teachers in schools to keep them abreast with the new knowledge as well as with new methods and techniques of teaching.

The basic issue emerging out of the foregoing scenario and observations, perhaps, is common to almost all sectors of education, especially in developing countries with large populations. *Therefore, it is essential to evolve and depend on new systems, which optimizes up-scaling of education at low costs while maintaining quality.* But if we refer to the Bihar case study the intake capacity of the institution had to be reduced by 50 per cent when the Government funding to the institution got reduced. Further, the magnitude of infrastructure indicated above is unaffordable even now. The classroom based "modern system" of education or the traditional system of education, as it was perceived in our country nearly hundred and fifty years ago, continues to co-exist with other systems of education. In the traditional system there are, of course, several institutions maintaining high quality of education, recognized the world over, but there are a large number of other institutions which suffer from credibility about quality of education and research being conducted in them.

Sir John Daniel, the former Vice-Chancellor of The Open University of U.K. and currently President and Chief Executive Officer of Commonwealth of Learning explains the paradox of increasing access at sustainable costs while maintaining quality with the example of triangle, the three sides of which represent costs, quality and access [24]. If the length of the side representing quality is retained then any increase in the length of the side representing access would necessarily lead to increase in the remaining side representing costs by basic geometrical construction. Thus it is clear that in the traditional system, if one wants to increase access one has to spend on additional infrastructure and faculty to retain the quality. This means that increasing access is directly dependent on increased costs and that is why in the case study of Bihar it was decided at one point of time to decrease the access by 50 per cent when the financial support got decreased. It is believed that under the influence of a strong and biased feeling against any new system, which differed greatly from the traditional system, a major problem of deficient (or at times even surplus) gaps between supply and demand for education was created. This is especially true of the crucial requirement of trained and appropriately qualified teachers.

## Rapid Growth and Transformation of Correspondence Education

Starting in 1962 with the Delhi University, 11 more conventional universities and one institution of higher education had transformed to dual mode education system by the year 1972. Subsequent to the recommendations of the Kothari Commission and declaration of the Education Policy of 1968, a Working Group was appointed in the year 1971 with Mr. G. Parthasarthi as the chairperson to examine the feasibility of setting up an Open University. The Working Group made the following important recommendation, which outflows from the observations of the Kothari Commission about introducing new systems in the form of part-time education and private or own time education:

> *In a situation of this type, where the expansion of enrolments in higher education has to continue at a terrific pace and where available resources in terms of men and money are limited, the obvious solution, if proper standards are to be maintained and the demand for higher education from different sections of the people is to be met, is to adopt the Open University System with its provision for higher education of part-time or own time basis* (GOI, 1974).

By the year 1982, the number of institutions of higher education operating in dual mode rose to 34 and percentage of students receiving education rose to 6.16 per cent of the total students in higher education. The following Fig. 1 provides an interesting comparison between the annual growth rate for students studying through the conventional and the correspondence modes of education during 1977-1982 (Annual Reports of UGC and [25]).

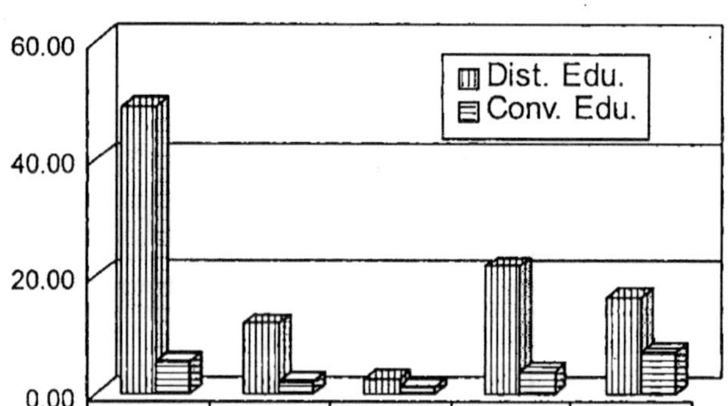


| | 1977-78 | 1978-79 | 1979-80 | 1980-81 | 1981-82 |
|---|---|---|---|---|---|
| Dist. Edu. | 49 | 12 | 2.4 | 21.7 | 16.4 |
| Conv. Edu. | 5.4 | 2.1 | 1.1 | 3.9 | 7.2 |

**Figure 21.1: Percentage Annual Growth of Students During 1977-82**

It is interesting to observe that during the period under study the growth rate for correspondence education is relatively higher than the conventional system of education. As we would see this has been growing ever since at a very fast rate.

These encouraging developments led to the setting up of the first Open University by the Government of Andhra Pradesh in 1982, while the Government of India created the National Open University viz., the Indira Gandhi National Open University by an Act of Parliament in 1985. From the system of Correspondence Education to the system of Open and Distance Learning (ODL) that was mainly provided by the Open Universities, there was a quantum leap forward in increasing credibility, effectiveness and acceptance of the new system. The ODL system was flexible enough to suit education of heterogeneous groups of learners with varying capabilities, constraints of time and locations, expectations and requirements for education. The important recommendation (2.2 p. 4) of making provision of teachers to meet the students face to face was also fulfilled. The up-scaling of the system was cost effective and its reach was extensive to meet the expectations (2.1 p. 4) of the Kothari Commission. The ODL system has been consistently growing since its introduction. Fig. 21.2 provides a comparison between the annual percentage growth of students in the Conventional and Distance modes of Education during 1988-1989 (Annual Reports of UGC and [25]).

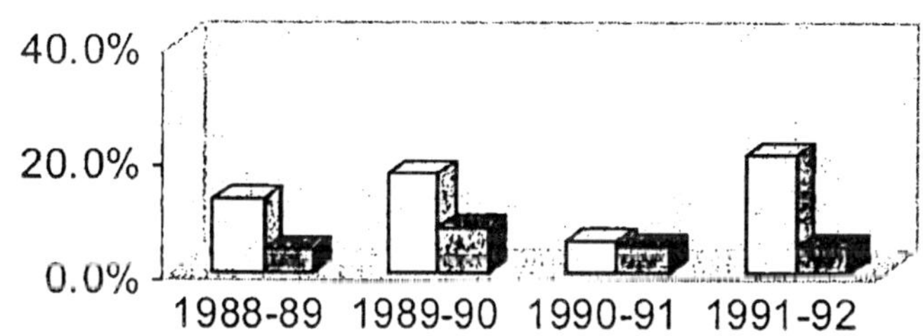


| | 1988-89 | 1989-90 | 1990-91 | 1991-92 |
|---|---|---|---|---|
| Dist. Edu. | 12.8% | 17.4% | 5.5% | 20.5% |
| Conv. Edu. | 3.5% | 7.5% | 4.2% | 4.2% |

Dist. Edu. Conv. Edu.

**Figure 21.2: Percentage Annual Growth of Students during 1988-92**

Open Schooling was initiated by the Central Board for Secondary Education in 1979. This was experimented up to 1989 and then amalgamated with the National Open School as an autonomous organization set up by the

Ministry of Human Resource Development. This is now known as the National Institute of Open Schooling ([17], p. 10).

It is now well understood that the ODL system is capable of handling a variety of large target groups of learners with different levels of understanding to meet their multidimensional requirements and expectations. Starting with education for awareness, school education to higher education and research are being covered by several of our ODL institutions successfully and efficiently. In the process of the very dynamic growth of the ODL system, unfortunately, some weaker systems have also emerged. In order to transform such systems, the Distance Education Council (DEC, the apex statutory body created under the Act of IGNOU), which has the responsibility to determine and maintain standards in Distance Education and promote it nationally, has aggressively carried out a massive campaign by extending financial and professional supports. The goal is to encourage development and sharing of quality content globally and to improve the quality of student support to learning.

## Knowledge-Based Revolutions in India with Global Impact

Instead of revolutions, which emerge from conflicts between communities and nations, a meaningful revolution in the contemporary global scenario has an entirely different shape and form. This is based on acquiring knowledge and its useful applications for the general well being of the people. In the community of nations there is a serious concern about the major divide in participation rates of people of relevant age group in higher education for developed and developing countries. For developed countries this rate is around 50 per cent, whereas for majority of developing countries like ours it is even below 10 per cent. If we have to aim at developing knowledge society, this percentage has to go up at least to 40 per cent. In the past few decades, however, we have fortunately witnessed three very visible and vibrant revolutions in our country with global impact. These are knowledge intensive and have complemented success of each other in our country. These have also led to interesting and useful global competition even in cross border education [22] in developing knowledge societies and generating new capacities and capabilities which have direct relevance to the nations' needs and requirements. *In this context it seems that there is some urgency in redefining and repositioning education* which, in terms of the Kothari Commission, needs to be revolutionized and new systems capable of meeting the foregoing challenges evolved. This is perhaps the time for us to act under a tight time frame.

## The ICT Revolution and the ODL

One is, of course, in the area of Information Technology that has placed our country as the most favoured destination for IT applications in the world. It is indeed very satisfying to observe that in achieving this success and placing India among the few most advanced nations in IT, Distance Education played a very crucial role. As we advanced in IT we urgently needed the support of a large number of trained manpower and it is very satisfying to mention that the Open University system very well fulfilled this national requirement. Indeed, the National Open University alone provided education to nearly 150 thousand students in Master's Level programmes in IT to meet this crucial and massive manpower requirement.

## The Revolution in Space Technology and ODL

Our country is credited with a similar revolution with global impact in Space Technology and its applications. We are thrilled to observe that the Indian Space Research Organization (ISRO) has successfully achieved indigenous capabilities to design, develop and launch satellites. We are now rated among the top six countries in the world with such capabilities. The ODL system in our country has greatly benefited from the strides made by the ISRO. It is strikingly interesting to observe the following vision of the founder of the Indian Space Programme in our country complementing the recommendation 2.3 of the Kothari Commission (p. 4) for use of radio and television for education.

> "We are to play a meaningful role nationally, and in the community of nations, we must be second to none in the application of advanced technologies to *the real problems of man and society.*"
>
> —Dr. Vikram Sarabhai, the founder of Indian Space Programme

The ISRO has always focused its strides in Space Technology and its applications to provide support to initiatives aimed at development of our society. Thus, the research and exploration of the outcomes of research for applications in the ISRO were oriented towards space technology for rural development and education from the very beginning. As far back as 1975-76 Satellite Instructional Television was conducted using the Application Technology Satellite (ATS6) of the United States of America. This pioneering effort was the first successful experiment in development, testing and management of satellite based instructional television system especially covering the rural areas. 2400 locations in six states were networked through satellite communication to receive instructional television programme in the field of education from August 1, 1975. The duration for telecast of the programmes consisted of 4 hours. The ISRO took the responsibility of overall system management and also had specific responsibility for the hardware elements. The ISRO also produced 160 science education programmes for children, of 10-12 minutes duration each. Major responsibility for programme production was with the National Television Broadcast Organisation supported by the Ministry of Information and Broadcasting. The Ministry of Education, in collaboration with concerned State Governments and other organizations, handled the Teacher Training programme. Nearly 24,000 teachers were trained in October 1975 through multimedia packages specially developed for primary school teachers in science. In the following year, the programme was further extended to include more teachers. The programmes were first produced in Hindi and then dubbed into other languages like Telugu, Kannada and Oriya. The success of this initiative led to further interventions made by the ISRO in providing satellite communication for education and community development programmes of different ministries and organizations. Starting from the 1970s, within a period of nearly 30 years, the ISRO has emerged as one of the international giants in satellite capability for various applications with direct impact on the quality of life of the people—a mission that the founder of ISRO had envisaged.

Once the Open University system got established, greater responsibilities of content generation and its dissemination for education fell on the ODL system, while expensive technological support continued to be coming forth from the ISRO. Gradually, a universally acclaimed synergy of cooperation and understanding between the ISRO and the national Open University, IGNOU, developed due to foresighted observations of the Kothari Commission and Dr. Vikram Sarabhai. The Commission's recommendations 2.4 to 2.6 (p. 4-5) seem to have greatly influenced inclusion of an important mandate given to the IGNOU by an Act of the Indian Parliament in 1985, which includes *inter alia* emphasis on education for the well-being of the people. Thus, we see great commonality between objectives of the ISRO and IGNOU working for the common cause of improving the quality of life of the people. This is very unique and different from the mission of any other institution of higher learning in the country. Thus, ISRO and IGNOU have been collaborating in use of satellite communication to enrich learning processes and increase access to education through distance mode. Distance Education, which is dynamic and innovative, successfully absorbed the technology to provide more effective learning support. Thus capability for four TV-channels and two interactive networks dedicated for education had been developed under the ISRO-IGNOU collaboration by 2002.

In order to fulfill the requirements of education for all, the Government of India introduced Sarva Shiksha Abhiyan in 2001, a massive but important task that had to be accomplished by 2015. The people and the government were conscious of consequent pressures for increased access to higher education in the near future. The massive educational set up and systems required to handle such large numbers led the country to plan *inter-alia,* development of effective satellite communication systems with extensive point to point reach covering the whole country. Thus, some successful joint interventions between the ISRO and IGNOU and other educational institutions and organizations propelled the idea of designing and developing a dedicated satellite for education by the ISRO. It is fascinating to observe that within a short period of less than two years, the ISRO successfully designed, developed and launched a dedicated geo-stationary satellite for education known as EDUSAT on September 20, 2004. India is unique in the world in this respect and this capability is immensely helpful to support our mission to provide seamless education and to accomplish the target of education for all. The following observation about the potential use of EDUSAT for education is very encouraging and illuminating:

> "Democratization of knowledge indicates knowledge for anyone, any time, any place. EDUSAT will be extremely helpful in making this shift possible and decreasing the digital divides."
>
> — Dr. A.P.J. Abdul Kalam

Soon after the successful launch of EDUSAT by the ISRO two parallel coordinating and monitoring agencies were put in place one each by the Ministry of Human Resource Development (MHRD) and another by the ISRO. The IGNOU was nominated on both the committees. A National Core Group on EDUSAT utilization and coordination with members from different national organizations in education, ministries and the ISRO was constituted. As we started working on utilization of unprecedented capabilities for education both for national organizations and all the State Governments, we realized that design, development and successful launch of EDUSAT could be accomplished scientifically under a very tight time-frame but utilization of these capabilities by different users was a much more difficult task; efforts are still continuing. The IGNOU has been actively coordinating this activity with the MHRD, ISRO, State Governments and different national organizations from the inception of EDUSAT from September 2004 to June 2006. Reference to the large number of presentations made at different levels in the meetings of chief ministers of the states in the North East & Sikkim, Ministers of School Education, Higher Education and Technical Education of different states, State Secretaries of these Departments have been given in the list of references ([4]-[16]).

The EDUSAT has six transponders each for Ku and Extended C Band networks. The transponders for Ku Band provide one National Beam and 5 Regional Beams for the East, West, North and South and Central Regions of the country and even beyond. The national beam supports 5-6 Ku Band national networks with a footprint covering almost the whole country (except the

Andaman and Nicobar islands), but including our neighbouring countries like Bangladesh, Bhutan, Nepal, Sri Lanka and Maldives. The eastern part of Pakistan is also reachable by this network. This capability is seen as an important means for development of regional educational networks for sharing our resources and capacities for the cause of educational development and advancement of our region leading to better understanding and friendship. A request received from Sri Lanka for usage of the national EDUSAT network is being processed. The Extended C band network has a larger footprint than even the national Ku band beam covering the whole country including Andaman and Nicobar Islands. The greatest advantage of these satellite networks is that we can ensure point to point two way audio and video communication from the teaching end to learning end located anywhere under the footprint of the satellite beam. State level networks are in different stages of development. The following figure gives the status of National level Satellite Interactive networks as in July 2006:

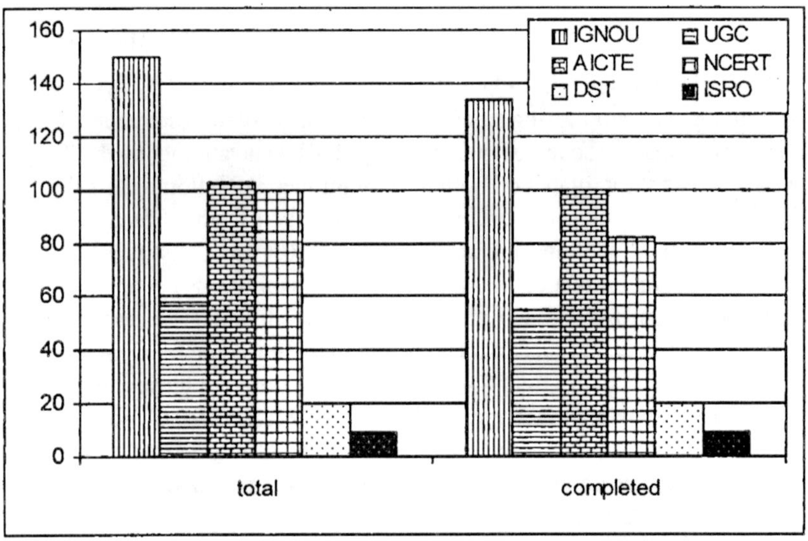


**Figure 21.3: Status of Edusat National Interactive Networks**

It is indeed very satisfying to highlight the crucial role of a few functionaries in IGNOU who carried out the integration of equipment at different locations throughout the country by distance mode employing available networks. This resulted in a short term programme of training for users jointly developed by the ISRO and IGNOU. The following enlist the capabilities of EDUSAT networks:

- Satellite communication enabled education
- Virtual classrooms

- Video on demand
- Database access
- National and State level repositories
- On-line operations
- Linking FM radio stations of IGNOU for simultaneous broadcast.

### IGNOU Leads the Revolution through ODL

We now turn to the third major revolution which, as already observed, has been greatly influenced and even complemented by the other two revolutions in the Information and Space Technology sectors. This is in the form of emergence of Open and Distance Learning system with global impact, which has revolutionized the education system of the country. This revolution has emerged silently but very rapidly, successfully and effectively during the last two decades. In support of this claim we could observe that as of today, nearly 25 per cent of the total number of students in higher education is in the ODL system. The National Open University alone provides education to nearly 13 per cent of students in higher education. Similarly, several State Open Universities are providing massive education in the country primarily focused on their regions. The system is dynamic with modular approach, which provides multilevel entry and exit to suit the convenience of learners. It is cost effective and has ensured excellent understanding and cooperation with the conventional system in terms of sharing of facility and faculty to optimally utilize the existing infrastructure support and manpower. Open Universities in our country have registered a phenomenal increase in enrolment with the current average rate of growth of students at nearly 24 per cent per year.

A very successful dent has been made by the IGNOU and State Open Universities through the ODL system to fulfill the recommendation 2.6 of Kothari Commission about training of School Teachers. As an illustration we place the following table giving information about recent programmes conducted by the IGNOU in the North East region.

The Recommendation 2.4 gives a very unique and special mandate for the ODL system, which perhaps leads the system to the process of redefining education and repositioning the objectives of educational institutions. It has great potential for transformation of an extensively large manpower into manpower skilled with knowledge under a tight time frame. We also understand that such a transformation will completely change the concept of viewing large population as a serious problem under resource crunch to an extremely useful human resource with significant and visible contributions for the cause of national development. There cannot be any dispute about the importance of the foregoing goal and the national priority that it deserves. We encounter this requirement in almost all areas of human development.

As a first step any process of implementation of nationwide projects and plans we require as an essential prerequisite training of large numbers of master trainers, who in their turn carry out the process to educate, motivate and create necessary awareness for further target groups of people. The IGNOU has undertaken many such initiatives. One is jointly with Hero Honda Company for training of mechanics and a few others with the Ministry of External Affairs, Ministry of Power, Ministry of Agriculture and international organizations like the UNESCO, WHO, WIPO, UNICEF etc. The Kothari Commission laid special emphasis on training in Agriculture sector. Taking the lead from this recommendation, the Yashwantrao Chauhan Maharashtra Open University did a pioneering work in this direction which had its impact on improved agriculture production. The IGNOU has also set up a new School of Agriculture, which is developing customized open learning educational/training packages to meet the emerging needs of productivity enhancement, improvement in quality, sustainable intensification and diversification of agriculture, community participation and creation of job creators, rather than job seekers. Some of these involve education and training of several hundreds of thousands of people. This is what is meant by redefining of education system leading to a very purposeful and directed education. This is very different from tailor-made, prescription-based education, which is often quite independent of the learners' varying capacity, capability, aspirations and expectations. Thus the IGNOU emerged with the following vision statement in the year 2003 along with somewhat similar vision for the DEC:

**Table 21.1: Teacher Training Programmes of IGNOU in NE-Region**

| *Location* | *2005* | | *2006* | |
|---|---|---|---|---|
| | *B.Ed.* | *CPE* | *B.Ed.* | *CPE* |
| Itanagar | 91 | 104 | 85 | 291 |
| Guwahati | 78 | — | 87 | — |
| Imphal | 35 | — | 36 | — |
| Shillong | 148 | 1172 | 195 | — |
| Aizawl | 16 | 232 | 87 | 395 |
| Kohima | 51 | 212 | 87 | — |
| Gangtok | 265 | — | 146 | — |
| Agartala | 11 | 2348 | 36 | 1293 |
| Total | 695 | 4068 | 759 | 1979 |

Indira Gandhi National Open University, the national resource centre for open and distance learning with international recognition and presence, shall provide seamless access to sustainable quality education, skill up-gradation and training to all by using innovative technologies and methodologies and ensuring convergence of existing systems for massive human resource required for promoting integrated national development and global understanding.

## A Pilot Project with Grassroots Reaches

It seems that with the new technology-enriched capabilities available to us we are privileged and empowered to effectively utilize these to extend the ODL system to provide access right up to the grassroots locations of the country. In order to go beyond the existing reach a joint project of IGNOU-ISRO-MHRD-State Governments of 9 Hindi-speaking states is being implemented through a national EDUSAT network with a HUB at Jabalpur. This is made accessible to all the primary schools in one remotely located district of Sidhi in M.P. and one block each of a few other Hindi speaking states from Arunachal Pradesh to Rajasthan and Himachal Pradesh to Chhattisgarh. The project was conceived in January 2005 and starting from December 2005, it has been expanded in stages. As of now nearly 1500 schools are linked to this educational network with systems supported by solar cells. The content is generated by motivating teachers from the participating schools. Initial report about the success of the project is encouraging, in spite of encountering some unexpected challenges. Initially, the focus of the project is on basic education in Mathematics and Communication Skills through the Hindi medium. It is perceived that this extensive network costing nearly Rs 15 crores, can have a variety of applications in areas like tele-medicine, confidence building and other such programmes contributing to the overall development of the people living in least developed settlements in future. We are very optimistic about the success of this most challenging task but we are encouraged by our successful efforts and experiences of using IT capabilities for empowering students in a few thousand primary schools located in remote and less developed areas under the Headstart project ([5], [23]) and nearly 400 schools under the CLASS project.

## Global Impact of ODL and Pan African Network for Education

In terms of international impact of ODL system of India we may like to mention that the IGNOU alone has presence in thirty five countries and this is expanding. The IGNOU is currently hosting the secretariat and chairing the SAARC Consortium of Open and Distance Learning (SACODiL), created under a decision of Heads of Government of countries in the SAARC region and Global Mega Universities Network that was created under an initiative of the UNESCO. Several countries are using ODL material produced in India for their students. Globally, south-south collaboration in ODL is growing. In many developing countries ICT networks are being used extensively for education, community health and many other aspects related to improving the quality of life of the people [19], [20]. Dr. A.P.J. Abdul Kalam, the President of India in his address during the inaugural session of the Pan African Parliament held at Johannesburg on September 20, 2004, proposed the development of a Satellite and Fiber Optic network to provide communication and connectivity for all the 53 member countries of Pan African Parliament with India. The members of the Pan African Parliament greatly appreciated and supported the idea. As a follow up, the Prime Minister's Office decided to identify the Ministry of External Affairs as the nodal agency for project implementation. The ministry got a project report prepared by experts and officials of Rashtrapati Bhavan, Prime Minister's Office and External Affairs Ministry along with experts from the ISRO, Telecommunication Consultants India Ltd. (TCIL) and the Indian Institute of Science, Bangalore [3]. The IGNOU was assigned the responsibility of providing its courses and programmes either as such or in transformed version to suit local requirements and context through the Pan African network. Tele-education programme of the IGNOU is believed to commence shortly with Ethiopia.

## Emerging Applications of Technology in ODL

The concern in the ODL system for the convenience and requirements of learners has propelled the system to be more dynamic with greater contemporary relevance. Some of the best systems in the ODL have, therefore, kept pace with new dimensions of technology and are able to successfully absorb them in expanding access and improving quality of programme delivery. Satellite Communication, which we have been using extensively, requires very heavy initial expenditure in developing infrastructure and it also requires optimal utilization of the capability, which is available round the clock for economic viability. Our experience with the IGNOU shows that it takes quite sometime before Satellite networks are fully utilized. It takes time to acquaint the learners in usage and benefits arising from the new technology. Further, some minimal local expertise has to be developed and put in place for ensuring uninterrupted usage of the network. It is from this point of view that the fiber optic connections, if available, are preferable because one is required to pay for the precise usage of the connectivity as per one's requirement. Thus, starting with connectivity for a shorter period we can expand its usage as the learners get accustomed to it and feel convenient with the system. However, the viability of the fiber connectivity to some of the most remote places is the main issue due to which Satellite Communication, which is point to point, has its significant advantages. It is, therefore, advisable that we should use a convergence of all technologies available to suit our requirement and learners' convenience.

Mobile cell phones provide a very significant and relatively newer technology support. Besides their easy access and convenient handling, the new mobile phones are empowered with enormous technological capabilities.

The new technologies are empowering tiny mobile phones with several useful features such as, pocket radio, pocket PC, internet connectivity, remote television, SMS, e-mails, etc. The cost of both the mobile phones and charges for their usage has been declining very fast, besides increase in their technical capabilities. Nearly 760 million people across the world are buying mobile phones per year. The number of people using mobile phones has been increasing in India at a very fast rate. Nearly 24 million people buy mobile phones in India per year, which means that five mobile phones are being bought in India every minute. The profile of buyers also represents all sectors of our society. It is estimated that by the end of the current year about 70 million Indians will have Mobile Phone facility. Besides the convenience in using these phones, in many areas, the reliability of mobile phone over landline phones is comparable, if not better. It would, therefore, be advisable to use Mobile Technology for education; some open universities in India have started planning for it.

Several private providers are also launching Satellites for world wide coverage and it is expected that these providers will further bring down the cost to attract more customers. One such initiative is being undertaken by London-based INMARSAT, which has already launched INMARSAT 4 F1 Satellite, followed by another satellite INMARSAT 4 F2, which covers one third of the earth surface including North and South America. It is expected that the availability of this Satellite will greatly accelerate transfer of files through mobile phones at low costs. With such facilities, perhaps we can think of providing education to countries like Brazil where some interest has been shown by the Government for cooperation with the IGNOU.

A meeting of the Secretaries to Government of India in the Planning Commission, Department of Higher Education and Department of Information Technology has agreed that during the 11th Plan substantial funds should be made available for a robust network for education using a combination of Satellite/Fiber/Wireless Communication. A very rough estimate of the finances required for the projected network would be around Rs. 10,000 Crores.

## From Unfulfilled Tasks to the Road Ahead

We have already highlighted the promises that were made to the nation at the time of Independence, which are very crucial for our national development. Serious efforts have been made to achieve the desired goals from time to time but unfortunately the targets have been missed and we cannot afford to continue with such a situation anymore. The generation, expansion and meaningful applications of new knowledge are growing at a tremendous rate and they would continue to grow even faster. Never before, have we witnessed such committed and strong efforts of developing countries (however weak their current stage of development) to achieve the status of developed countries by acquiring sound knowledge base as quickly as possible. As mentioned earlier we in India have also to pitch the participation rate of relevant age group of learners in higher education to at least 40 per cent from the current rate which is around seven per cent. All resources—Government, Private and even cross border—have to be employed to achieve this target in a reasonable timeframe and with some cautious and rational choices and combinations. The systems that have to be put in operation should be capable of providing education with equity in quality and access. In spite of the Kothari Commission's specific observation about equal recognition of different forms of education, the same has not happened even after 40 years of the recommendations because of closed mindsets and inertia in accepting change. In Israel, the Everyman's University has been providing technical and professional education for the last 40 years. There are several other such instances the world over but it is an irony that in our country there are still reservations, hesitations and misapprehensions about capabilities of any system other than the conventional mode in providing quality education.

A new era, which appears to be in the form of twilight before sunrises, seems to be around the corner in the form of some recent new developments in the higher education sector. Indeed, we could succeed in making a successful dent when the DEC-NCTE, DEC-ICAR (Indian Council of Agriculture Research), DEC-Dental Council of India signed a Memorandum of Understanding for making joint efforts to ensure mutual recognition and maintenance of quality of education with increased access. These efforts gained momentum when the chairpersons of the AICTE, DEC and UGC jointly signed a communication to all the Heads of Institution in the country in early 2003. The UGC even issued a regulation in support of quality education through the distance mode. Some well credited and world class institutes have started using the ODL system with the help of the ICT. These include delivery of some programmes by the Kanwal Rekhi Centre for Information Technology, Indian Institute of Technology (IIT) Bombay, National Institute of Technology (NIT) Nagpur and the G.S. College of Technology at Indore. Programmes for Government Engineering College Raipur by the IIT, Kanpur and a programme under Indo-French Cyber University by the Indian Institute of Science, Bangalore, are transmitted through broadband connectivity. The IGNOU, of course, started providing Bachelor of Information Technology degree Programme on line a few years ago. Going a step further, the IIT Madras is ready to launch a programme involving five better institutions around it to improve the quality of education and even give the IIT Madras degree to the students passing out from such institutions. This project is supported by the MHRD and is almost ready for launch. Thus the beginning is very encouraging and reassuring, but we have to go miles ahead to achieve our cherished goal of education for all.

The MHRD has been working on development of a single portal for education in India. Open source education has been growing after the Massachusetts Institute of Technology (MIT) started hosting lectures which could be accessed by anyone, anywhere through e-connectivity. We are also aware of work on drug design through Virtual Laboratory using open source for biological details and parameters. In India, most of the institutions providing quality education are funded by the MHRD and it should be easier to encourage them or even mandate them to make available the learning material in the open domain. The IGNOU has started putting its educational content both in print and multimedia mode in the open domain.

As yet another new initiative to address the problem of increase in access to quality education, a National Knowledge Commission (NKC) was set up on June 13, 2005 by the Prime Minister of India, with the mandate of devising and guiding reforms that will transform India into a strong and vibrant knowledge economy in coming years. The timeframe assigned to the NKC is three years, that is October, 2, 2005 to October 2, 2008. Some urgency is apparent in the working of the NKC, which has sent encouraging signals and given firm assurances for a total overhaul of the education system, which may hurt, shake and even create tension to some people accustomed to the existing system (Observations of Sri Sam Pitroda, Chairperson, NKC, in an open house organized by the Confederation of Indian Industry at Delhi as quoted in the English daily, The Hitavada, October 12, 2006). There is striking similarity in a few areas identified to be given focus by the NKC (website: www.knowledgecommission.org) and corresponding recommendations of the Kothari Commission. Distance Education is one such area and the NKC websites reads as follows.

> "*Distance Education*: While formal education is useful for building human capital, not all individuals are able to participate in it. Enough resources must be invested to ensure that distance education is developed as a viable alternative to formal education".
>
> —National Knowledge Commission

We are looking forward to an extremely extensive and robust fiber network connecting all institutions even in the most remote areas of the country and use them for highly interactive education by best available teachers, irrespective of the location of students. The difference in the present ODL mode and the new mode, which in the meeting organized by the NKC has been termed as Distributed Education (or Equally Distributed Education?) would be that the interactive component would be increased to the level of the conventional system. This will increase costs but would certainly be more effective. In such a system students would be exposed to strong components of Virtual Laboratory and Virtual Library.

## References

Ahmed, Firoz and Garg, Suresh (2006). *Forty Years of Kothari Commission: Reforms and Reflections,* Viva Books Private Ltd.

AIU, *Handbook on Distance Education,* (2004). Seventh Edition, Association of Indian Universities Publication.

Bhaskarnarayan, A. *et al.*, (2005). *PAN-African Network through Satellite and Fiber-Optics for Tele-Medicine and Tele-Education,* A project proposal jointly developed by officials of the Rashtrapati Bhawan, Indian Space Research Organisation, Ministry of External Affairs, Government of India and TCIL and an expert from Indian Institute of Science, Bangalore.

Bhatia B.S. and Dikshit, H.P. (2004). *A Dedicated Satellite for Education,* A paper presented at a meeting of the State Ministers of School Education chaired by the Union Ministers for Human Resource Development, Govt. of India.

Dikshit, H.P. (2002). Multidimensional strategy and capability of ICT to reach the most distant and deprived, *Proceedings of UNESCO-LEARNTEC 2002 Conference*, Karlsruher, published by Karlsruher Messe—and Kongress-GmbH.

Dikshit, H.P. (2002). *Vice-Chancellor's Convocation Report*, presented in 13th to 17th Convocations of IGNOU, April 2002, February 2003, 2004, March 2005 and February 2006.

Dikshit, H.P. (2003). *Quality Education: Challenges and Tasks Ahead*, 90th Annual Conference of Indian Science Congress Association, Lucknow, (January)

Dikshit, H.P. (2003). *Mission and Prospects of Distance Education in India, Action for the Future of Distance Education—Innovation and Collaboration*, Shanghai: World Summit of GMUNET. (November).

Dikshit, H.P. (2004). *Building capacities of education through cross boarder provision*, Sydney: UNESCO-OECD Australia Forum on Trade in Educational Services. (October).

Dikshit, H.P. (2004). *Key Note Address* Thiruvananthapuram: Tele Learning Conference organized by Department of Space, Government of India. (October).

Dikshit, H.P. (2005). *Using Space Technology For Societal Needs-Space Based Education*, Ahmedabad: 92nd Annual Conference of Indian Science Congress Association, (January).

Dikshit, H.P. (2005). 13th Convocation Address of Dr. B R Ambedkar Open University, Hyderabad, January, 2005, *University News-Association of Indian Universities*, (October).

Dikshit, H.P. (2005). *Technology enabled learning in the context of small island states*, Mauritius: Public Lecture, (August).

Dikshit, H.P. (2005). *Dedicated ICT Networks for Education*, New Delhi: GMUNET-Second World Summit, (September)

Dikshit, H.P., *Knowledge Revolution Through Satellite Based Education*, pp. 244-262 in Garg *et al.* [17 ].

Dikshit, H.P., *Re-engineering Social Transformation Through ICT-Enabled Education: IGNOU Perspective*, pp. 63-79 in Garg *et al.* [18 ].

Garg, Suresh Venkaiah, V., Puranik, Chambi and Panda, Santosh (Eds.), (2006). *Four Decades of Distance Education In India: Reflections on Policy and Practice,* New Delhi: A collection of papers, Viva Books Private Ltd.

Garg, Suresh, Panda, Santosh, Murthy, C.R.K. and Mishra. Sanjay (Eds.), (2006). *Open and Distance Education in Global Environment: Opportunities for collaboration*, New Delhi: A collection of selected papers submitted for the ICDE International Conference on the theme: Open and Distance Education in Global Environment: Opportunities for collaboration, held at Indira Gandhi National Open University, New Delhi. Viva Books Private Ltd.

Khan, A.W. and Dikshit, H.P., *Emergence of Distance Education Media Networks*, pp. 181-194 in Garg *et al.* [17].

Kulandaiswamy, V.C. and Ponnevaikko, M., *Tamil Virtual University: Some Experiences*, pp. 263-274 in Garg *et al.* [17].

NCTE, (1999). *State Studies on Teacher Education: Teacher Education in Bihar*, New Delhi: National Council for Teacher Education, and similar Reports for the States of Kerala and Tamil Nadu.

NUEPA, (2006). *Report on a National Seminar on Privatization and Commercialization of Higher Education,* New Delhi: National Institute of Educational Planning and Administration, (June).

Sharma Amita, *et al.*, (2001). *Headstart: Computer Enabled Education and Development*, Collection of Workshop Papers on Information and Communication Technology for Professional Development of Primary Education Personnel of DEP-DPEP. Edited by Sitansu Jena *et al.* (February).

Sir John, Daniel (2006). *Technology in higher education: How to avoid failure and achieve success*, New Delhi: Lecture in a seminar on Technology Enabled Blended Higher Educations: Visioning of University of 21st Century.

Yadav, M.S. and Panda, S. (1995). Open and distance higher education: policy and development, in Panda, S. (ed.) New Delhi: *Open and Distance Learning: Policies, Practices and Quality Concerns,* ABI.

# 22

# Adult Education

HRIDAY KANT DEWAN

## Introduction

What is Adult Education? This is a question that evoked varied responses from scholars, commissions, philosophers, political leaders and social re-constructors. The manner of this articulation affects the way the programme gets conceptualized and translated into action. These articulations have been varied in their basics as well as in details.

The Kothari Commission considers education to be a major instrument of change. It also emphasizes the need for developing human resources through a well organized educational programme. This is stated to be a more important task than the development of physical infrastructure. It argues that for a country to reach its aspirations the process must include a change in the knowledge, skill, interest and values of its people. There is need for science-based education to bring the farms out of their stagnation and encourage the farmer to experiment and adopt mechanisms that increase production. In the context of industrial development as well the Commission emphasizes the need for education to develop skilled employees. The following extracts from the Commission's Report underlines this: (para. 1.13):

> "The realization of the country's aspirations involves changes in the knowledge, skills, interests and values of the people as a whole. This is basic to every programme of social and economic betterment of which India stands in need. For instance, there can be no hope of making the country self-sufficient in food unless the farmer himself is moved out of his age-long conversation through a science-based education, becomes interested in experimentation, and is ready to adopt techniques that increases yields. The same is true of industry. The skilled manpower needed for the relevant research and its systematic application to agriculture, industry and other sectors of life can only come from a development of scientific and technological education. Similarly, economic growth is not merely a matter of physical resources or of training skilled workers; it needs the

> education of the whole population in new ways of life, thought and work".

The Commission clearly perceived that education of each individual is the pre-condition for economic development. It also saw this as a mechanism to bring in a social metamorphosis, a reorientation of values and a continuous evolution of the form of life in the Indian society. In subsequent paragraphs, the document articulates further how it sees education transforms the social forces and processes and also spells out to some extent the nature of transformation and the mechanism it advocates for it. Education without violent revolution can bring the transformation. Look at the following extract from the document: (para. 1.14, p. 8):

> "If this 'change on a grand scale' is to be achieved without violent revolution (and even for that it would be necessary) there is one instrument, and one instrument only, that can be used: EDUCATION. Other agencies may help, and can indeed sometimes have a more apparent impact."

The Commission realizing the over-emphasis on the national goals in the above articulations adds in paragraph 1.15, a caution indicating its awareness that education is also a process of developing the potentialities of the person to the fullest, but reiterates that the national goals and societal goals subsume the goals of education for an individual:

> "In a democracy, the individual is an end in himself and the primary purpose of education is to provide him with the widest opportunity to develop his potentialities to the full. But the path to this goal lies through social reorganization and emphasis on social perspectives".

This importance to education as a means of change as well as being the critical input for the economic and productive development of the country is evident throughout the document. There is also an underlying faith in science as an agent that would help the country to get rid of stagnation and under-development. For example, in the beginning of the Chapter on Education and national objectives it says:

> "The destiny of India is now being shaped in her classrooms. This, we believe, is no mere rhetoric. In a world based on science and technology, it is education that determines the level of prosperity, welfare and security of the people."

The emphasis and the particular choice of terms notwithstanding, we can see that the document can be said to have three strands of reasons for the question 'why adult education?'. These include:

(a) Education as a continuous and life-long process to help citizens cope with the world becoming more complex and to enable the citizens to participate in the development process willingly, intelligently and efficiently.
(b) To provide the citizen with the means to personal enrichment, professional advancement and effective participation in social and political life.
(c) For social transformation and participation in the democratic process of the country within the purview and restrictions of the national goals.

It may be noticed that out of these, the document emphasizes the first strand repeatedly. It looks at education as a means to promote modernization and overcome resistance to change and clinging to the traditional forms of life. This role of education and the underlying philosophy behind it have been often contested. It has been argued that the so-called educated is oblivious of the knowledge and wisdom the so-called illiterates have and their life experiences and skills must be kept in mind in the process of educating them. Narulkar, S. and Sykes, M. state this in the following words:

> "It would be far nearer the truth to say that it is the peasant who by his solid worth, wisdom and stability stands between us and the chaos and ruin that would otherwise threaten our social order. It is not the peasant who needs to learn from us, it is we of the so-called 'educated classes' who need to learn from him" (Narulkar S. and Sykes M. (1956) A picture and programme of Adult Education Chapter 1: Adult Education in Nai Talim, p. 3).

They also argue that one of the major purposes of Adult Education (AE) should be to empower the villagers to feel more confident of themselves, have a sense of worth and dignity along with the will and motivation to change their living conditions. They contest the modernization as purpose of education and squarely hold the educated responsible for causing misery to the rural poor.

> "The central purpose of rural adult education must be to restore this self-respect, to reawaken in the villagers the sense of their own worth and dignity. A desire for better living conditions, a new will to achieve them, a new confidence in their own power to achieve them, will be the natural consequences of reawakened self-respect" (p. 4).

> "The first aim of adult education should be the release of energy, not the increase of knowledge" (p. 11).

This position, the underlying assumptions and the consequent programme and strategy emerging from it have been severely criticized, indeed ignored as irrelevant by most interventions of scale. The points raised have, however, come up again and again in discourse at the national as well as the international forums. The instructor needs to teach the adult with the feeling that they are helping them to improve their life, giving them guidance as how to lead their life.

The endeavour of adult education should be to use the language of the people, who are being 'educated', be sensitive to their cultural ethos and ways of thinking, and not to impose knowledge on them but to reconstruct it with them, using their context and their needs as a basis for choosing content, etc.

The variety of people, ideas and intent has brought many organizational forums, structures and processes in adult education. The document emphasized the need to be conscious of the fact that the content and programme of education has to be examined before we support a process as being sound education. In para. 1.16 it states categorically the need to examine what education are we talking about and perhaps, as a corollary, look at who is, therefore, providing this education. It argues that all education is not necessarily liberative and good:

> The naive belief that all education is necessarily good, both for the individual and for society, and that it will necessarily lead to progress, can be as harmful as it is misplaced...History shows numerous instances where small social groups and elites have used education as a prerogative of their rule and as a tool for maintaining their hegemony and perpetuating the values upon which it has rested. On the other hand, there are cases in which a social and cultural revolution has been brought about in a system where equality of educational opportunity is provided and education is deliberately used to develop more and more potential talent and to harness it to the solution of national problems.

The position articulated by the Commission differs from other documents of that period. The position is interesting in many ways. For one, it has tried to limit the issues in question by keeping the articulation in the framework of enlightenment and modernization. It has also taken a position on the relationship of work and education and on the model of economic and social development and the place of adult education in it. The strong point of the Kothari Commission is that it has (however adequately or inadequately) recognized education, including adult education, as a social and political intervention rather than a welfare-based 'nice' activity.

## 'Why Adult Education' in other Key Documents

The CABE Report of 1944 argues that adult education should not be a mere compensatory effort and should aim to give continuous life long education. It also emphasizes education that may benefit each learner according to his/her inclination and background. The document, however, hastens to add that in India, the context and the situation is very different from the situation in western countries and, therefore, we should look at modest goals in the beginning. It defines adult education as being a goal in the long term and not an immediate action area. The report suggests a gradually evolving adult education programme that will eventually mean opening of avenues and providing opportunities for each adult to enhance his/her abilities and not remain an effort to ensure literacy:

> In India so far the general attitude has been to regard adult education as connoting adult literacy. The reason is obvious...an adult must be literate before be can hope to derive any benefit from facilities for education in the wider sense. For this reason the Adult Education Committee recognized that the main emphasis in this country must, for some time to come, be on literacy, although from the very beginning some provision must be made for adult education proper, so that those made literate may have an inducement as well as an opportunity to pursue their studies [CABE Report, 1944, p. 48].

This, although distancing adult education from mere adult literacy, eventually erases the distinction and accepts that for the time being in India adult education can only go up to attempting literacy as the first step.

In paragraphs 17.08 and 17.11, the Commission describes the problems illiteracy poses for the nation as well as for the individual. Both pay a heavy price for it even though because of the persistent illiteracy we can become insensitive to the harm done. The circumstances of the modern life condemn the non-literate to a life of inferior existence.

> He has little prospect of a reasonable income. He remains isolated from sophisticated social processes, such as democratic government and commercial marketing. The uneducated is not in reality a free citizen. Illiteracy as a mass phenomenon blocks economic and social progress, affects economic productivity, population control, national integration and security and improvement in health and sanitation [17.08].

Later, in paragraph 17.11 it says that the pace of industrialization and modernization of agriculture is inhibited by the large number of illiterates. The reason for this is that the work force that they constitute is unable to take up responsibility that requires technical competence and they tend to resist change and cling to traditional forms of life. It argues that untrained minds cannot receive new ideas and new practices. In the same paragraph later it talks about the resistance to change as well as the need for conviction on the part of the national leadership and points out the lack of political commitment to such programmes. It also says that to some extent that may be due to a large number of illiterates and perhaps inadequate resources but that is not the only reason. It clearly indicates the need for a political movement and pressure on the system that would provide the social will [p. 780-781].

The position of Sykes and Narlukar as articulated in the Hindustani Talimi Sangh document of 1956 is very different from the ideas represented in the Kothari Commission and distinct from the position in the CABE report. They argue that the practice of education needs to be rethought and that 'modern' education is not liberal. They suggest that while an educated community was essential for democracy, yet the manner in which these terms were interpreted betrayed a misleading explanation of the situation in India. They argued that unless the problems of the village are tackled by the villagers themselves and they feel empowered to provide for their own primary needs and set a standard of living for themselves, it is not sound education. They also argued that there was no need for attempting revolutionary changes in the villagers' pattern of life. The new order needs to be built with the old materials which includes the cultural traditions. The entire formulation of the Talimi Sangh shows an understanding of the economy that relies on containment and contentment rather than on achieving more. This is in contrast to what the Kothari Commission states to be the role of education and what it presented as the view of a developed society.

This issue of adult education and its relationship with poverty, social transformation and the village economy is still contentious and unresolved. The Talimi Sangh document and the Kothari Commission refer to and draw inspiration and seemingly advocate very different strategies from the ideas of Gandhi.

The Commission does not recognize conflicting tension between oppression, exploitation and domination on the one hand and education for greater knowledge on the other. While mentioning the need for equity and justice in milder terms than those in the CABE report, it did not dwell on the question of Adult Education any further. This absence of a statement on the socio-political and economic perspective is even starker in the 1986 policy. It did not stress the need of Adult Education either from equity or social justice point of view. Instead it argued that adult education would increase productivity. It emphasized that the industrial houses should be partners in imparting adult education. The whole population should be literate because the country was at the threshold of industrial revolution. The following from the NPE 1986 *Program of Action*, is illustrative: (p. 133, point 8).

> Adult education is both a process through which effective delivery mechanisms are created for the deprived sections of society and a forum through which such sections secure information and understanding regarding the processes of development. Hence it is of importance that effective linkage is established between adult education and development programmes.

And again, the Technology Mission on eradication of illiteracy (p. 136) says:

> Eradication of illiteracy will be launched as a Technical and Societal Mission. Such a Mission approach presupposes that we are at the threshold of momentous scientific, technological and pedagogic changes, which may, besides augmenting the range of the communication system, make the process of acquiring literacy quicker and easier.

The formulation here is that eradication of literacy is a technical and societal mission. The principal components that are to be worked upon include the infrastructure and teaching-learning materials using technology. The emphasis is on facilitating the technological gadgets and their use in the classroom and on bringing in new ideas of pedagogy. The dominant recommendations and the discussions were around infrastructure and technology usage.

This is the view point severely criticized by Brian Street in *Literacy and Development* (Eds. Aditi M., Vasanta D., p. 54, 55). This is also different from the view point in Adult Education in a Free Society. The argument is that the rural poor illiterate cannot be considered to be ignorant, a burden and a retardation. Brian Street points to this attitude being a reason for failure of adult education effort in a big way:

> In development contexts the issue of literacy is often represented as simply a technical one: that people need to be taught how to decode letters and they can do what they like with the literacy after that. The argument about social literacy challenges this simplification by suggesting that engaging with literacy is always a social act even from the outset.... It is therefore important that those working in the field of literacy and development engage equally in the theoretical and conceptual debates being described here and challenge the dominant conception of literacy work which sees it as simply applied, obvious and not in need of such theory. It is precisely the lack of such explicit attention to theory, I would argue, that has led to so many failures in development of literacy programmes.

This is a criticism of both the modernization view and the view that literacy is only a technical issue.

It is to be remembered that while the policy document and the structure of the government considered the above questions in preference to any other, those posing the question from outside the government-structure were constantly bringing up issues laden with philosophical and sociological dimensions. For example, not only was the modernization view severely questioned but also emphasized the need to use the knowledge of the learners and the instructor to learn from it. It was also being recognized that literacy did not by itself give an ethical world view and by itself was not necessarily liberating the individual.

The other aspects of the modernization plan including the ethical strength of science were also questioned. The argument that science provided a means of rational enquiry and that it was not responsible for its use as harmful technology was not universally unacceptable. The relationship of science, technology and society also threw up many challenges for the view that looked at scientific temper as the most crucial factor for a just and equitable social order.

It may be pointed out that this debate is not just restricted to the Indian situation. In fact, as in India, also elsewhere, the political underpinnings of adult education programmes and their strategies continue to be repeatedly discussed. In Nicaragua also the role of adult education was perceived as a part of the larger challenge to overcome inequity and create more egalitarian structures:

> Fundamentally a problem of poverty and power, the challenge to overcome illiteracy often becomes part of the larger challenge to overcome inequity and to create more egalitarian social structures through which the poorer members of a society can participate in the exercise of both economic power and political decision making [*Between Struggle and Hope, The Nicaraguan Literacy Crusade, pp. 4, 5 & 6*].

The view states that the effort in Nicaragua stood for an interconnected and comprehensive process of development in which adult education and literacy was a strand. The effort was seen in the context of providing power to the poor and the deprived and strengthening the human values that had been denigrated. The effort was aimed at participation of the poor in the exercise of economic power and political decision making. The program did not intend to make them catch up and learn ideas generated elsewhere but break the shackles on their thoughts and way of living. They considered that intervention to be political first rather than merely education:

> Development activities in different areas such as health, agriculture, industry, education and community organization were thought of as threads to be woven into an integrated plan for transformation, a plan that would facilitate the creation of a more equitable, more productive society. As such, the literacy crusade was considered an important beginning to this many-faceted national program [Between Struggle and Hope, p. 23].

Clearly, the view is different from the modernization and consequent 'trickle-to-the-powerless-and-illiterates' view. It is also different from the containment and denial of Sykes & Narulkar. Adult education for them is an affirmative political action to transform the social structures by breaking and reconstructing them. The process has to free people from cultural and social oppression.

It is clear that one of the ingredients of the educational process adopted is the socio-political understanding of the people engaged in it. While some people may believe that education is a neutral intervention and meant for the benefit of the entire society, there are many who believe that education is not a neutral intervention, as we can see from the above excerpts also. Most of the government documents and policy statements look at education within the framework of the state and its constitution. Their emphasis is on sharing knowledge and modern ideas with the communities deprived of such an opportunity. Even though in some of them, the mention of awareness, empowerment and organization is made, their primary driving force remains the attempt to develop more modern citizens, who can participate in the process of development and move forward with the changing conditions. The emphasis is not on giving them mechanism to transform but to become participants in the process of transformation that is being brought on in an effort to modernize the state.

It is clear that in the 1986 policy, we are looking at adult education at best as means of uplifting and not even as a mechanism for providing opportunities to widen the learning and participate in the democratic process. The elements of equity, active citizenship and transformation of society that were included in the CABE document to some extent and were reflected obliquely even in the Kothari Commission, are not evident any more. These changes are also reflective of the changed political environment. What do these changes reflect? How do we analyze the journey from CABE report of 1944 to the Hindustani Talimi Sangh document of 1956 to the Kothari Commission and subsequent documents?

It is clear that the Kothari Commission in its section on adult education had (even if weakly) pointed out the need to continue education beyond schooling as a fundamental aspect of a democratic society. The thrust was, yet, for adult education for willing and informed participation in the economic development programme. In its articulation of the literacy programme in paragraph 17.14, the Commission argues that eventually the skills of reading and writing arithmetic should be such as to enable the learner to continue his education. It says that literacy cannot be equated with the mere ability to read and write. Literacy must be functional—that the literate not only have sufficient mastery of "tools of literacy" but also be able to acquire relevant knowledge that will enable him to pursue his own interests. As the meaning of the word, functional has remained a major point of contention, let us, look at what the Kothari Commission has said:

1. It must be, as far as possible, 'work-based' and aimed at creating attitudes and interests and imparting skills and information which will help a person to do efficiently whatever work he is engaged in.
2. It must help the non-literate to interest himself in vital national problems and to participate effectively in the social and political life of the country.
3. It must impact such skill in reading, writing and arithmetic as would enable him, if he so wishes, to continue his education either on his own or through other available avenues of informal education.

   It follows that literacy programmes will have three stages. The initial stage will consist of acquaintance with reading, writing and arithmetic and some general knowledge relating to civic and national problems in which the entire society is involved and to the profession in which the learner is engaged. The second stage should deepen the knowledge and skills gained in the initial stage and train the adult in using literacy gained for solving personal problems and enriching personal life. The third stage should lead the adult to one of the programmes of continuing education" (Chapter XVII, p. 783, Section 17.4).

The perspective of the 1986 policy can be said to be focusing primarily on the first stage. These three points represent the major strands of thought for the macro formulations of adult education policy in India. All programmes have incorporated the three points in different proportions and in different ways.

Dr. Mohan Singh Mehta, a pioneer in the adult education movement, and other people of the Seva Mandir, who have spoken about adult education repeatedly, emphasized the need to ensure that the programme resulted in empowering the poor to become more conscious of themselves and stand on their own feet. In 1978, the programmes of adult education carried the strands of modernization as well as empowerment. The Seva Mandir's documents at this point were encouraging dialogue on the need to empower and include the adult. While there was criticism in the Seva Mandir of the belief that villagers were ignorant and needed to be made sensible, there was also a clear need felt to bring to the people some information about how to make clean drinking water possible, contain water-borne diseases, and ensure infant and mother vaccination and other such concerns.

In subsequent years, the programmes also included attempts to generate additional income and to work with village groups in order to encourage them to seek more benefits from the government schemes. In a sense, it included certain kind of organization building all the time even though the role of the organization kept changing. There was a cautious reinterpretation of the

Gandhian principles of education that in order to sustain adults' interest in education, some useful programmes that would motivate them were required. These could be enhancing their work skills and communication skill. Those who were working with the adult learners realized that the villagers had a lot of knowledge, which was practical and useful and often had the wisdom that the educated lacked. The Seva Mandir also drew a distinction between literacy and practical education and felt that in terms of values there are numerous things that the adult villagers, who were illiterate, could teach the educated society.

We also must consider the work in other regions and recognize that as early as in 1976 even the UNESCO in its evaluation of the literacy effort (*Experimental literacy program, a critical assessment*, UNESCO/UNDP 1979) questioned some of the premises of the reigning theory of development—the trickle down model—in terms of both productivity and motivation. It challenged the assumptions that illiterates hinder development and production because of their lack of education and pointed out that lack of "opportunity structures" might be the more fundamental reason [quoted in *Between Struggle and Hope (The Nicaraguan Literacy Crusade)*, p. 8-9].

The Nicaraguan Crusade looks at the effort to reach adult literacy as a mission impossible unless the participation of the poor in socio-economic decision making is simultaneously ensured *[The Nicaraguan Crusade WA 1]*. For this view, literacy is not an intrinsically positive event. It can even lead to further subjugation and greater misery for the poor unless combined with a socio-political movement. This would logically lead to the argument that it is only after a sufficiently large socio-economic movement has been built that we can talk about macro adult literacy to consolidate the gains; otherwise it has to be a part of the building up of the movement.

The dominant point of view in India, of course, has been that programmes of adult education can be conceived and implemented at macro level and can impact the lives of the people positively. While some argue for movement in the socio-economic conditions first (Sykes and Narulkar, Mehta etc.) and others (NFE 86, CABE 92, etc.) have emphasized the need for literacy first. The CMSS made adult literacy a part of its movement and emphasized that such efforts not only required empowerment but also comprehensive intervention in development of better living conditions. An effort at literacy would simultaneously require better health and physical facilities.

The 1986 Policy Document and the National Literacy Mission in the nineties concentrated on the need of literacy drives and campaigns.

The question is whether adult education has to have itself a tinge of conscientization or it should be at the opposite end with no politicization. We also need to argue what we choose and how we make it possible.

The extent of politicization and its nature is, however, determined by those who will be giving direction to the effort. At any given point, there are a variety of political forces and all of them try to service their own interest. The programme of adult education is a part of this struggle and, therefore, the reasons why different individuals promote it or encourage it arise from different social and political aims. The society that the Gandhian vision sought had at its base shades of equity and empowerment for the rural poor but the others perceived social structure based on rationality.

The basic questions can, therefore, be formulated as: Is adult education a process of political education where different forces would attempt to educate in different ways? Would that also include literacy? Or is it that literacy is a precursor to development and can be separated from the philosophical dimensions of education and society and be treated as a skill to be acquired and used? There is no clear answer to this. What is, however, clear is that it does not seem possible to teach people even reading and writing as there has been continual redefinition of what it means to read and write. There is also the question of motivation of adults; the argument is that unless the programme has some gain for them they will not attempt to make the effort to learn to read and write. So, on the one hand, there is the question of respecting the adult learners and their ideas while keeping their culture and language in mind. On the other, the question is of providing them knowledge and information that would provide economic and social gains to them. So it seems that if the adults have to be motivated we cannot do so without bringing in a social, economic and political perspective and neutral literacy—just skill of reading and writing—is not a possible goal.

## The Content and Method

The 'why' of adult education is reflected in each aspect of the concrete steps and both content and method are affected by it. The question whether the adult education programmes need to focus on providing reading, writing and arithmetic skills or aim at organizing and empowering people to struggle for equity and justice? What is the correct strategy to adopt? Do we begin by attempting to do a very small part of what we consider relevant and meaningful adult education programme or should we work in a manner where we look at a comprehensive intervention? Embedded in the above are many sub-questions like whether the success or failure of the programme of adult education depends upon the pedagogy and methodology used or the poor relations, attitudes and structures that were engaged in the exercise of reaching education to everyone.

The Kothari Commission document identified Science as a rich source of knowledge and indicated that the content of adult education programme is to be determined in that framework. It does not spell out anything else and is silent on many of the issues raised by the CABE document of 1944 and the 1956 paper of Sykes and Narulkar. It restricts itself to talking about how materials would reach and the pedagogy and nature of the materials rather than their content. It also admits that teachers cannot be expected to transact the kind of ideas that are meaningful and, therefore, they need to provide materials which they would be using. Speaking broadly, it articulates the concept of literacy as not restricted to reading and writing but to be, as far as possible, work based. It has no other comment on the content, language or the other aspects considered subsequently very important. It rather focuses on how these materials will be made available in sufficient quantities and the need for having variety in them:

> There should, however, be inter-State cooperation in order to ensure that the literature produced furthers national policies and strengthens national integration and patriotic sentiment. Inter-State cooperation may also help in certain cases to reduce cost of production. We feel that the Ministry of Education should take the lead and organize inter-State and inter-departmental cooperation for production of literature required for literacy and adult education programs [Kothari Commission, p. 792].

This statement has taken positions of some basic concerns of adult education programmes. First, it says that the content of the material should have some useful information. The word 'useful' requires to be defined further—useful for whom and useful for what and useful in what way. The other statement it makes is that voluntary teachers would need guide books and other literature. It also speaks about forms of audio-visual aids to help in communication. It says that the language of the material can be decided at the State level and materials also be developed at the State level.

Sykes and Narulkar argue that there can be no pre-conceived content. The content has to emerge from the interaction of the facilitator with the learner and that the educator's job is to decide how much can be shared with the adult.

> No subject of instruction, however useful and desirable in itself, can be effective in adult education unless the adult himself is first stimulated and awakened so that he sees his need of it and asks that his need be met....He must decide what sort of knowledge he wants to enable him to cope with these situations, and his demands, will vary from place to place and from person to person. The educator's job is to decide how the content of the instruction can best be arranged for presentation to the adult mind [Narulkar and Sykes (1956), A picture and programme of Adult Literacy and Education p. 35].

It further adds that you cannot standardize adult education. It cannot be fixed in terms of syllabus; each class instructor has to evolve its own content and method centred around the economy and the society with local knowledge. The language has to be what the adults speak.

The content is clearly a question of socio-political understanding and any material that is produced reflects that (e.g., whether to use the word 'water' or 'revolution' to begin engagement with adults). The understanding of education that Sykes and Narulkar argue for includes spiritual education and Dharma as a part of the programme.

All this has to be compared with the arguments at other places where the question of *whose* knowledge has been forcefully raised. The Seva Mandir also brought out many materials in the local language, *Mewari,* and tried to negotiate the difficult line between the need for staying close to the mother tongue and the aspiration to master the dominant language.

Those who have followed Paulo Freire's framework have a more serious question to raise on content. The popular education movement in Latin America adopts an epistemological approach "in which knowledge is continually socially constructed by the learning subjects as a personal and social act of (self-) understanding and (self-) liberation." In popular education, reality is the true source of knowledge and we cannot simplify it by isolating it from its socio-economically, culturally and politically changing context.

This raises a very important question regarding how we should decide on the content for a programme of adult education. For popular education the process has to be a part of the life and a socially dialectical process.

In the Indian context, the NPE 1986 Review Committee re-examined the view in the Policy and emphasized the need to make the content and process of adult education distinct from that of literacy alone and underlined the need for education to be work-based. This implied an emphasis on finding areas of interest for the adults and helping them learn those and wherever possible bring the literacy effort. It criticized the over emphasis on literacy and emphasized that the focus of adult education should be on fundamental rights and social justice. It recognized the probable conflict such education would have with the system and emphasized the need for participation of voluntary agencies, community groups, political parties and their mass organizations to supplement the work of the government:

> Adult education programmes should be accompanied by a wide range of measures relating to health, nutrition, housing, and employment needs. They should also address themselves to issues of fundamental rights, laws, secularism and democracy.... Instead of starting with adult literacy, the start should be in respect of creation of awareness for essential needs and from there work backward to adult literacy [Review of 1986 policy: 1990, p. 200].

The 1992 *Programme of Action,* which is based on both the 1986 Policy and its 1990 review, categorically states that there is nothing that needs to be substantially changed in the policy document. In the section on 'adult education' the Plan of Action only reiterated the position of the National Literacy Mission arising out of the 1986 policy and reemphasized the pace of the total literacy campaign approach. It had a very carefully defined structure of the literacy effort and included the development of materials which were based on experts' advice so as to make the adults literate in the minimum time.

1. Basic literacy for about 200 hours spread over about six months which will basically be a guided learning programme;
2. Systematic post-literacy programme for about 50 additional hours spread over two months which will start with guided learning and will culminate into self-learning by making the learner self-reliant; and,
3. Self-directed continuing education in the perspective of life-long learning through library service, newspapers for neo-literates, charcha mandal, and such other activities. This may also include the skill development programme for personal, social and occupational development [POA 1992; p. 21].

It is also useful to look at the Education for All document of 2000 wherein, again, adult education means adult literacy and the chapter on adult education only speaks about reducing rate of illiteracy. The document talks about literacy as an ability to read and write as defined in the National Literacy Mission.

To understand this in perspective, we need to realize that the document argues that the first priority in literacy planning has to be on vision for 6-14 age group and ensure that new illiterates do not enter the adult age (EFA 2000, p. 59, Strategy for reduction of Literacy bound effort).

The Plan of Action was implemented all over the country. The Bharat Gyan Vigyan Jatha was the nodal agency of the National Literacy Mission that spear-headed the total literacy campaigns.

There are many questions that are brought up by the combined reading of the POA document and the BGVJ document of 1990 in conjunction with other documents. The first one relates to what it means to be literate. The term has been incisively discussed and interpreted in many different ways. The content and methods relate to this description of 'who is literate?' This eventually gets linked to what is adult education and why we want adult learners to get education and/or literacy. As we have seen, very different meanings have been ascribed to this word. Each of these would generate a different focus in both the content as also in method. Even within the total literacy campaign different districts used different shades of the word 'literacy' as Menka Roy points out (Afterword in *Paradigm of Learning: The Total Literacy Campaign in India*, edited by Malavika Karlekar). In some places it was literacy alone and in some others it was linked to other activities, the content and method following the principle that it needs to be meaningful. She writes that the literacy campaign only took ground where it was linked with development activities.

The emphasis in literacy programmes does not squarely articulate the need for developing in the adults the confidence of speech and thought, the confidence to articulate their experiences and share lives without hesitation.

D. Vasanta, S. Gupta and P. Devi (*Practice and Research in Literacy*, by Aditi Mukherjee & Duggirala Vasanta, 2002) also argue that literacy cannot be treated as a given state, skill or action. Literacy is what learning understands:

> Instead, as suggested by Lange (1988) we need to rethink the concept; 'literacy' as something that incorporates all these three dimensions; something whose meaning is given by the learners...something which makes the learners use their language...to bring about socio-political and economic transformation of their society in the way they have envisaged it...(p. 161).

Brian Street in the same book also criticizes looking at the literacy as simply a technical issue. As already discussed, he argues that engaging with literacy is a social act and therefore, requires a theory of society. It cannot merely be a question of pedagogy and techniques using technology or without it but more a question of sharing our social, political and ideological thoughts.

The preparation of the materials for the adult learner is important and they need to be generated at the local level. One of them obviously is related to the political perspective of the materials.

The other issue, which perhaps should be more manageable, is of language of the materials. This also is an area which has different philosophical positions and questions that the ground realities pose. It must, however, be recognized that the issue of language is not merely an issue of words and sentences. It is an issue of the culture, the social dynamics and the historical relationship of the communities. There are also some difficulties related to the print media as well as to the availability of literature in different languages. They are labeled as dialects sometimes even denying the historical reality of predecessors' language. As has been argued by Aditi Mukherjee (Language and Literacy in *'Practice and Research in Literacy'*, p. 90), language is a medium for social negotiations and dealing with the power structure. She raises the question of language use in the primers and contests the pragmatic argument, which purportedly wants to restrict primers to only a few languages. She points out that the positioning of some languages as dialects and some as languages is not a linguistic question but has many other dimensions related to the power balance at that historic point of time. Further, the reasoning that primers should be only in certain languages is the recognition of the hegemony of the dominant section and arguments of homogeneity as a preferred answer to equity are to the benefit of the dominant world view.

Where does this lead us? It is a very sound position to hold that the social experience and self-respect of the community can be consolidated and preserved by giving space to the language of the community and for adult learners to learn through that language. This view has also been voiced by Mahatma Gandhi, Sykes and Narulkar as well as proponents of popular education of the Nicaraguan Literacy Crusade. The perspectives in these and the implications are very different but they all talk about the language of the learner as the language to work in. On the other hand, we have the Kothari Commission, the NLM and the CABE report all pointing towards the use of a standard language at least in the written materials. We have also the experience of the Seva Mandir struggling to create materials that could be in the language of the community and hunting for community knowledge that could be codified. Many of the documents by the Seva Mandir in village communities are brought out in *Mewari*. While it is true that most of the people speak *Mewari* in other regions they speak *Bagari* and at some areas a mixture of these in different proportions. All these pose the question: What is the language that we should use for materials and at what level can the material be prepared to be close enough in the language of the community?

There is another issue that is difficult to resolve and that relates to the aspirations of the community leaders. Most efforts of promotion of local language have experienced resistance from local leaders. They see the use of local language as a device to prevent their community from joining and dominating the mainstream. Rajesh Sachdeva ("Attitude of Mother Tongue" in *Practice and Research in Literacy*) tells the story of the MLA, who opposed the teaching of *Vagari* at the cost of Hindi in an area where *Vagari* and not Hindi is generally spoken. This, as Rajesh Sachdeva points out, raises the question of how we deal with the use of local language; it also raises the question whether a programme of adult education conceived at a macro level can even be expected to address this issue.

Just like the issue of 'why adult education?', the issue of content and method does not have a simple or clear path. Should adult education be merely literacy or it should include work education? If it is literacy then what is the meaning of this term literacy? If it is to be work based then what kind of work form it should take and what should be the form of the classroom? There is also the wider question of the content including elements of understanding social injustice, exploitation, organization, group interest and struggles.

What should be the knowledge that forms the basis of the program? Should it only come from the local context constructed with the learner community or should it be knowledge that modernizes the learner community? In these debates the Kothari Commission and the subsequent policy documents placed their faith on literacy, scientific knowledge, technological awareness and the state language.

The creation of materials that need to be interesting and attractive as well as easy to transact is a difficult task. The attempts for engaging adults so that they find the learning interesting have also been intense. The mis-match between some of the skills being elementary and the maturity of the adult poses challenges for the content of the materials.

The experiences so far clearly point out that in whatever way we define literacy, as yet, it has not been possible to engage a large number of adult learners with more than the ability to decode. And if this decoding happens and is even achieved it does not lead to sustained learning. While choosing content we need to remember the formulation that the villagers have intrinsic, appropriate and proper knowledge and that should not be tampered with. So, while you may be teaching a few things that are obviously correct you cannot contest what they know. The different strands of opinion on this can start from the need to be sensitive to the learner, to respect their experience. The content, of course, needs to be meaningful and engaging for the adults.

The question of methods is both a pedagogic question, which itself is very difficult to communicate and struggle with and also a social and political issue with a large cultural input as well. If we believe that dialogue is a good way to learn and that only through dialogue can knowledge be shared and the learner provided the opportunity to construct her own understanding then clearly the methods need to ensure dialogue. The purpose of adult education then becomes widening the scope of discourse that the community engages in and to create platforms for sharing of views and ideas. Without such possibilities being created and a little bit of its reflection in a wider society, it may be difficult to ensure that the dialogic method is used in the classroom. If the methodology is based on sharing and construction by the learner, it is also appropriate that learning to write also includes some elements of this kind. It may be argued that the content and method of teaching people to decode is the first step and appropriate methods need to be adopted for it. Once this happens then subsequent post literacy program would result in adults being able to learn. This has, however, not happened as studies in different parts of the country have shown. If we think that the objective of the exercise is to enable adult learners to be capable of reading whatever they want to then it is clear that we need a better programme that may be longer. The method and the content have to be such that they overcome the sociological and cultural barriers that prevent learners from exercising their choice.

## Where do We Get Teachers from?

Transacting education with learners requires instructors or teachers. These have to be capable of not only understanding the goals and the method but also be able to function according to their understanding. They have to be able to bring adults together and judge them as well as scaffold their learning even while dealing with their inflexibility, adult temperament and struggling with their fixed relationships, beliefs and self image.

It is clear that the large number of adult learners need a large number of teachers as well. It is also recognized that these instructors need to do a difficult job and, therefore, must have certain qualities and preparations. Many formulations consider the question of adult education as being centred around the teacher and argue that only when we have an appropriate person to work with the adult learners can the engagement be meaningful. The CABE report points out that adult learners required greater stimulation and placed a greater demand on the teacher than children:

> A high degree of tact, understanding and ability to inspire and lead is required of the teacher, for he has to deal not with a child, who is mentally raw and receptive and who has compulsorily to attend school, but with a grown-up person who requires more stimulating and interesting instruction and who is likely to leave the class the moment he finds the lessons not worth while (p. 51-52).

While the CABE report thinks that visual and mechanical aids such as pictures, illustrations, cinema, gramophone, radio and forms like dancing, music can be more pleasant accomplishment and recreational activities, it considers them as activities that will attract and stimulate adult students. It is clear that the report recognizes the problem of engaging the adult learners over a reasonable period of time and the need for an appropriate instructor, who could by using her own capability as well as aids to sustain the interest of learners. Sykes and Narulkar, however, do not consider this to be adequate. For them the teacher is the saver and the activist that brings life to the village and to the adult learner. They view the teacher as friend and guide to every member of the society. They accept the teacher to be capable of awakening the inner soul, awakening goodness and the dreams; that bring cooperation, trust and faith. He is supposed to be the pivot around which the village community will come together and become an entity that cooperates and supports each other. Sykes and Narulkar also point to the need for teachers to be volunteers. They hint at avoidance of the need for paid workers to do the task of adult education. Their role for the adult education worker is a part of the "*Samagra Gramsevak*".

It is clear that the kind of teachers that is being discussed above can neither be prepared by training and nor can be easily available. It is because of this that Sykes and Narulkar view adult education as an organic growth process and does not look at literacy as a goal. It is another matter whether it is possible to find such volunteers even though L.D. Mishra (*'Practice and Research in Literacy*, by Aditi Mukherjee

& Duggirala Vasanta) argues that there can be millions of volunteers, who are selfless and committed with an understanding of education and the ability to mobilize and lead like Gandhi.

The Kothari Commission and the subsequent documents, however, were looking towards the eradication of literacy in a time bound manner. In paragraphs 17.23 and 17.24, the Commission points out the requirements of communicating adult education programme and points out the kind of people who could be made available for it.

> A mass literacy campaign depends largely upon the voluntary services of all educated people, including government servant, employees in public organizations, lawyers, doctors, engineers and students in schools and colleges ... We recommend that the students in the higher primary, secondary, higher secondary, vocational schools and those in the undergraduate classes of the universities and colleges should be required to teach adults as a part of the compulsory national service programme.... It is equally necessary to require the teachers in schools of all types to teach and to participate in the campaign when they are called upon to do so (p. 786, 787).

There seems to be, however, a large gap between what is expected from the adult education programme and the articulation in 17.24 of the people who can be considered as probable teachers for it. It is not clear how a normal school student would be able to motivate the adult learner or be able to find ways to make discussions around issues of national security, environment, health and general welfare interesting for adults. For the preparation of such volunteers the Commission talks about short-term training in the methods of teaching and dealing with adults. It also talks about providing a guide book and other helpful materials. We know, however, that the use of guide book is always minimal and does not aid the development of motivation. The Commission appears to be conscious of this and, therefore, limits the scope to methods. The Commission also talked about awareness and motivation generation through such materials. It is clear that the need of large resource pools of teachers has resulted in all such efforts overlooking the expectations from the person who, is to perform the task of adult educator. The demand that Sykes and Narlukar had from the teacher in their content society is being placed on the adult educator in the materialistic and technological society of the Kothari Commission. This could not be sustained as shown by subsequent experience. Adult learning requires sustained effort; even if it is considered to be only as complex as that for children, the nature of resources allocated and the expectation from the adult educator are of a much higher magnitude.

Identification and capacity building of those who will be engaged with the adult learner is, therefore, an important concern. For a programme dealing with adult learners systematically, it becomes imperative to address the issue of identifying volunteers as well as ensuring that they have the abilities to engage the adult learners meaningfully. Since most of the people, who are educated, lack the capacity to appreciate the anxiety and emotions the learner is going through and also do not appreciate the way in which human beings learn, it becomes very difficult for them to sustain interactions. In an attempt to quickly prepare a large number of instructors to engage with the learners most of the programmes have cobbled up short-cuts.

It is obvious that these short-cuts can only attempt to address issues like decoding in engagement with adult learners. We certainly cannot address the needs that the adult learner has in terms of why all this is relevant to him/her. As various people who have thought about adult education have pointed out adult learning has to have an element of opening the mind of the learner to fresh ideas as well as helping him/her articulate experiences more vividly and cohesively.

It is clear that all this is not an easy task for the instructor. It is also not easy when he/she does not have a wide variety of stories in mind or the ability to construct problems that emerge from the experiences of the adult learners he/she is working with. Most instructors also lack the ability to create an environment of music or other forms of artistic expressions in such a way that they can find the foundation for the dialogue and the engagement.

There have been many efforts in training and preparing the adult educators to perform this difficult task. However, unlike for school education, there are no adult education training courses and the institutions engaged in research in adult education are also extremely limited. It is clear that adult education has not been a priority and efforts have been made only in a sporadic manner. From the CABE report of 1944 till the most recent documents, adult education has been left to either poorly equipped centers or to mass campaigns.

## Structure and Mechanism

The question of structure and mechanism has two aspects. One is related to a group of people wanting to engage in continuous learning. Adult education in some of the developed countries has this dimension where many of those who have had some education need to learn again to update their knowledge or need to have the opportunity to add more degrees or diplomas to their names. These require structures and mechanisms that would make possible their participation in universities and colleges. It would also require vast numbers of public libraries, which are accessible. These structures would, of course, need to consider the time at which the learners would be free to continue their learning. It has been observed that over the last few decades the need for mechanisms to make this possible have also been increasing and while there is no sustained attempt at the State level to do it, there are many private initiatives that have started making it possible for those aspiring to continue learning.

The nature of the problem in the Indian context has been the large number of people who cannot read and write. As we have seen, there has been debate about what they know, what kind of knowledge they need and the nature of the teacher, who will keep them engaged. The CABE report of 1944 pointed out that in the 1940s, literacy figures changed from 7.83 per cent to 14.6 per cent. This was a large jump but as the CABE report reasoned, at this rate, the country would take 140 years to become fully literate and argued the need to change the pace. It is, however, clear that to change the pace we need to have resources available. And as we have seen these resources are not just financial resources. The report also recognized this and pointed out that one of the major constraints would be the people who would undertake this task.

The issue of structure, means and mechanism, as suggested by the CABE report of 1944 as well as of the other policy documents is to move faster towards making people able to read and write. We cannot forget the intense debates that have been mentioned in the section where various kinds of literacy have been presented. If we look at literacy as a socially driven programme, which will seek and obtain support of the State if it so desires, then we need only to make enabling provision so that these efforts can flourish. Alternatively, we can also argue that the process of education of any community whether small or large is dependent upon social, economic and cultural situations and would change over a period of time riding over the currents emerging in society and, therefore, first there should be demand for such provisions. The macro perspective has looked at adult education as State or at best State and Non-government organization driven with the support of social organizations and individuals. Therefore, in the Indian context, while we may argue about the extent of support provided in adult education, it has been a concern of the Government.

The two major requirements for engaging with the learners are the materials and the place where the classes will take place apart from the person who will be able to make this possible. Finance is the major constraint in building an adult education centre. While we have an Operation Blackboard scheme that spoke about additional classrooms, teachers and materials for primary education, we have no corresponding arrangement for adult education. The CABE report of 1944 while emphasizing the need to increase the pace of reading and writing ability dismissed the need to provide separate buildings for the adult education centres. It argued that the school buildings would offer reasonable premises for the adult education centres and if such buildings are not available, other local buildings could be used as adult education centres.

This statement of adults not needing a space like a school has persisted in all subsequent formulations and programmes. During the period where adult education centres were run in villages on borrowed spaces like the Non Formal Educational Centres, their appearance were largely dismal. The major battles were around finding lanterns and basic reading materials to the adults. The government policies, programmes and sanctions did not reach the ground with adequate speed thus hampering the functioning of the system.

Adult education has always been perceived as a temporary programme and, therefore, permanent structure has not been built. The financial sanctions were for a limited period, often resulting in gap between one sanction and the other. The organizational structure and the instructor they engaged clearly needed continuity. The expectation that the teachers would be volunteer gods who needed nothing for their subsistence is clearly without foundation. As a result, the programmes of adult education on the ground always struggled and even non-governmental organizations like the Seva Mandir found it difficult to run the programme.

The Kothari Commission (para 17.25) adds to the responsibility the CABE report (1944) had placed upon the school. It expected school to be the centre of the life of the community and desired that it functioned as a place for education for the whole community and became a people's school.

The Commission, however, also added some more facilities for it to function like the Adult Education Centre of a community. These included aids like library, radio set, exhibition posters and modules etc. It also laid an elaborate programme and conditions for adult literacy. The commission emphasized the need for comprehensive planning and preparations in any drive towards literacy. It saw the use of all kinds of mass media in this; it also emphasized the need for mobilizing political, social and other leaders as well as all government departments. While it looked upon teachers as the major group to be engaged with learners, it emphasized the need for using social services of universities and other departments for this purpose. The document also emphasizes the need for continuing post-literacy effort and recognizes that the programme needed to be developed in accordance with the local conditions and requirements. It spoke about the need of training of the volunteers and pointed out that the training period should be short. It emphasized on the involvement of voluntary agencies apart from emphasizing supervision and vigilant evaluation. It proposed that those involved in literacy programme should continue to learn and form study groups or other forms of association. It also emphasized the need for public commitment and enthusiasm (EC Report, 17.26).

The document's formulation has three major assumptions. The first is that adult education is not an easy task and requires mobilization not only of structures and learners but of the community as a whole to sustain the process. The second is the formation of informal groups that will maintain the links and the process of continued learning. The purpose behind this is literacy and needs a sustained effort. The third is that even while recognizing the need for careful planning, the programme design is meant to be frugal. Aiming to utilize existing structures and institutions the emphasis is on setting up of a mechanism that would ensure the possibility of the persons in the existing system taking on the task.

Both the Kothari Commission and the CABE report of 1944 emphasized the participation of voluntary effort and non-governmental organizations. The CABE report informs us that the participation of voluntary effort in adult education is increasing. It also, however, emphasized that the problem is so vast that it cannot be considered to be within the capacity of unaided voluntary effort.

One of the major concerns of the massive adult education effort is to educate the women learners; the percentage of literacy among women has always remained much lower than that of men. There is reluctance in both the society and family in getting women to learn to read and write. The 1944 CABE report spoke about social customs more unfavourable for women to pursue education. It also pointed out the fact that the limited number of women teachers further complicates the issue.

The Kothari Commission, 22 years later, also reiterated the distressing situation of literacy among women and emphasized the urgency of initiating bold and imaginative efforts for increasing literacy among them. It also pointed out the low motivation among women as well as the hostile social environment in literacy organization. It also pointed out that women who attend the programmes have learnt less and cannot be certain when they will find time to learn. Both the CABE report and the Kothari Commission suggests that high school and college girls as well as women teachers should be specially made to undertake this responsibility. The Kothari Commission recommended condensed courses that would also include training in some special skill like teaching or nursing. It had also recommended village sisters for teaching village women. This village sister was to be a local woman who was paid a small salary, trained and periodically retrained. In the urban areas this could be done by the retired government employees and others. It is a fact that in spite of other developments the number of women involved remained proportionately limited. There were never enough women participants in the adult education centres or in the campaigns. Even in places where the number of women was larger it was lower in categories of supervisors or block coordinators (Menka Roy, *Paradigms of Learning: The Total Literacy Campaign in India, p. 28)*.

There is nothing very different from this situation in the 1986 and subsequent policies except that in the 1990 review there is an emphasis on bringing in work experience and training to encourage and motivate adult learners. The 1986 policy and the CABE report of 1992 argue for literacy as the first step in mobilization campaign. It is also obvious that even though the centre-based approach was tried for many years and many new centres opened in the campaign of 1978, the idea always was that these are not permanent structures. It was always believed that the efforts of adult education required huge mobilization, which can only come through a massive campaign. Similarly, the Kothari Commission also suggests mass approach for the large number of adult learners, who do not know how to read and write. Recognizing the fact that the previous efforts of removing illiteracy had failed, the Commission argued that this was because there had been no direct attack on mass illiteracy and no massive campaigns had been launched till then. It felt that the programmes had been started at the State level or on local basis; they were launched with considerable drive and enthusiasm but petered out in apathy. They felt that this was because the campaigns were limited in scale and were not able to achieve significant advances. Besides this, efforts were also uncoordinated (Para 17.10, p. 780). The Commission proposed that to end this situation we should have a coherent and sustained effort without asking for a lot of resources. The campaign should bring together voluntarily everyone and gave the example of the effort in Russia after the Revolution.

The BGVJ document of 1990 and L.D. Mishra (*'Practice and Research in Literacy'*, by Aditi Mukherjee & Duggirala Vasanta) spoke about the unfinished task of Independence and looked at the Jatha as a crusade against dependence to make democracy more meaningful for the millions.

It is clear that this massive effort saw a degree of organization and commitment that had not been witnessed before. The organizers of the Jatha were aware, like the Kothari Commission, which hesitated to say what BGVJ articulated, that all kinds of people including political parties and mass movements are brought together. They were walking the thin line between involving everyone and opposing what they called the obscurantist forces. The mechanism proposed by the Jatha relied on motivation generated from spirit of volunteering and commitment to rational beliefs. It is important to consider what the dream entailed. The Jatha was also borne out of the realization that the massive movement of setting up of adult education centres in 1978-79 had failed to make a significant dent and that to go forward we needed more time than has been planned in policy documents. There was also a strong movement in Kerala that involved different kinds of people to promote science and rationality. P.K. Ravindran writing in *Practice and Research in Literacy* spoke about the National Adult Education Programme as a historically important step and points out the experience of the first articulation of NAEP and concludes that it is very difficult to maintain ideological commitment that runs counter to the interest of the ruling class.

This view is also supported by the writings of Mohan Singh Mehta in

1978-79 who was full of hope about the programme. The effort was not limited to knowledge of the alphabets but aimed at wider education, which helped them in their adult life and also empowered them. However, he was disappointed with the manner in which the campaign had been conducted—the government functionaries did not work wholeheartedly; sanctions were taking a lot of time causing the people to lose enthusiasm; centres were not functioning appropriately in most places and instructors were hired without any training. He points out that being entirely dependent on the kindness or good samaritan spirit of the government is like becoming incapable of standing on our feet. The task of adult education should be carried out by the society and not depend on the sweet will of the government (Bhaisahabra Patra Nov., 1983).

In the 1990's, given the problems of resources and the need for urgency, there appeared to be no other way forward other than launching another campaign. The efforts led by Kerala Sastra Sahitya Parishad (KSSP) and some BGVJ group led to hopeful projections that these could be replicated in other areas as well. Coupled with the arguments that have already been underlined in the Kothari Commission document the effort was aimed at reaching as many districts in the country as could be possible.

The experience of the NAEP had made clear that any effort at adult education needed to rely heavily on voluntary and social reformers. The massive effort, therefore, needed people to dream that it would be possible to generate a lot of enthusiastic and committed volunteers who would work without keeping their self interest at the forefront.

It is difficult to asses what the Jatha achieved. There is conflicting evidence as each district had a different story. What is, however, remarkable is that a large number of people were mobilized for various reasons and that in many districts strong literacy campaigns and other movements sprung up symbiotically. There has been a lot of argument whether the movement came first or the local movement regarding an issue that was pinching started earlier. It is, however, clear that the enthusiasm to declare districts literate and inadequate appreciation of the complexity of the task led to inadequate achievement.

Several studies have been conducted revisiting districts where very strong and vibrant literacy movements are said to have taken place. What the researcher found was that not all of what was claimed could have happened and very little of what happened survived over a period of time. While the assessment procedures were detailed out to the last and the expectations from the learners also spelt out, they were continuously modified and diluted from the original goal of ensuring that the learner is able to read and write. Many, who have revisited districts that had been declared totally literate, have found that the achievements were extremely exaggerated and manipulated. They also speak about the fact that the movement did not have a natural social base and was largely driven by the bureaucratic whip. Wherever the collector was energetic and forceful, the programme took all the steps mentioned. The teachers who were selected for the task were often supervised strictly. The entire education department, much more than ever before, at the district level came within the control and authority of the Revenue Department. It can be argued that one of the major outcomes of the BGVJ was to give the collectors both the responsibility and the authority to intervene in educational process. The analysis of the total literacy campaigns and the achievements can be seen in *'Paradigm of Learning: The Total Literacy Campaign in India*, edited by Malavika Karlekar, and the whole effort throws up many issues.

As Sadhna Saxena points out, the responses to the TLC have been uneven across the country and these variations could be correlated to the differences in chances, "socio-economic conditions, state of development and history of social movements". She concludes that "there was disappointment as the mobilization neither transformed into a sustained social movement nor into a learning process (Paradigm of Learning). The campaign was a mixed bag involving many people but sustaining very little at the end. The reasons for that include the kind of people involved in the process and the kind of trainings that was given. While the mechanism for setting up structures were clear, and the processes for reaching of the structures laid out, the mechanism for preparing people to take up challenge at each level was inadequate. There was neither sufficient time for it nor clarity on how this could be reached. The Jatha perhaps had hoped that from this could emerge structures that would continue to exist as social and educational entities gradually leading to build up of movements, which would do more than educate the people and would transform the community and the society.

While analyzing the campaign in partnership with the government we cannot do without considering the role of the bureaucracy. As has been pointed out earlier, the design of the programme that made the collector the main focal point of the movement at the district level had many ramifications. Most of the policy documents have argued the need to coordinate and use government departments in a focused manner to struggle with illiteracy. The collector as the chairperson of the TLC was, therefore, a major step in that direction. The collectors were able to involve various departments while making it possible to facilitate their movement. All this helped to fulfill the programme of the campaign as a priority task. However, as with the other aspects, the role and the functioning of the collector were varied across different districts. Some were very keen and interested, others passive or, some were not enthusiastic. For many the program was an effort that was needed and hence drew a lot of their energy while for others it was a burden. Therefore, the programme was successful where the collectors were active.

## Literacy Campaigning

The Jatha had hoped that the middle class people going to the villages would get sensitive to the economic situation and become sympathetic to the plight of the poor. It had also hoped that the rich and the poor would be able to come together and rub shoulders. The design of the programme and the pace set, however, made this difficult. The rich from the cities associated up to the district level or at the most the block level. There was no sustained interaction with the villagers. The pace of the campaign and the nature of the programmes also led to most of the effort and time being spent in completing the programme rather than exploring and understanding the local conditions and situations. A learner in order to sustain the ability to read and write needs time and the programme was not designed for a long duration. As has been argued elsewhere also there was limitation in making this entire effort a programme of pedagogy and of method. The total literacy campaign in many places was initiated without adequate preparations with many people joining it with unclear motivation and direction. Since budget expenditure targets had to be met and results shown, projects were rushed through without adequate scrutiny.

It is important to see the rationale of the argument that any mass campaign would find districts at different stages of literacy and preparedness. It is also true that the Kothari Commission had reasoned that unless the whole country or a substantial part of it is galvanized together into making a move it may not be as effective. The question that emerges is what should be the bench mark for preparation and how does one balance the whole nation being galvanized against the un-preparedness at many places.

Malavika Karlekar argues for more sustained efforts towards adult literacy and points out that an effort like a campaign may not be sustainable without making sufficient preparation. She says:

> TLC is not a magic wand; nor can its incumbent euphoria be sustained unless the regional differences and contexts are factored in. In many cases, this means taking cognizance of the local language and its nuances, and of methods and techniques of pedagogy which assign an appropriate place to indigenous forms of expression and local knowledge. This will mean reassessing attitudes towards orality—and indeed, redefining ways of viewing literacy and illiteracy. In the growing environment of global competitiveness and the deification of the market, it becomes particularly important not to lose sight of the wood for the trees.

The key questions emerging from here are how does one sustain the movement and the participation it generates, take into account the local language and deal with the cultural diversity and create alternative definitions of oral culture and literacy in such a way that there is no disrespect attached to be illiterate. The consequence of huge mobilization effort in the total literacy campaign should be to question the modernization principle as an argument for adult literacy and to give space and place for other articulations keeping in mind that the modernization theory need not be discarded entirely. We obviously need to keep track of bringing new ideas to the community but respect and value local knowledge and customs as well and this, not as a pedagogical tool, but as the purpose and aim of adult education. The content of the programme needs to be sensitive to the requirements of the community and based on their life experiences rather than on decoding expertise.

There is another issue that emerges from the experiences of total literacy campaign. Menka Roy points out that many of the negative features of TLC were due to its programmatic structure. There were very specific details laid out for each step of functioning and not enough steps for local initiative and local modifications. She writes that it is necessary to reject the very nature of time bound programmes and the focus on achieving a target very quickly. The Seva Mandir proposal to implement total literacy in two blocks had to struggle with the limitations imposed by the TLC provisions and had to go beyond them. It needs to be explored whether there was too much planning in the total literacy campaign and an attempt at too much coherence. The pace of the programme demanded reaching solutions quickly to the field, particularly, where people were not confident enough or could not reach a consensus on the steps to be taken. As a result, the uniformity of action, even though the situations of districts were very different, itself became a constraint for effective functioning. This in a sense reposes the concern of Sykes and Narulkar already referred to.

The people in the literacy campaign were from very different backgrounds and had very different view points. Though critical of total literacy, from the beginning a large number of organizations did participate in it in some way or the other. The nature of their participation and extent, however, varied because of many reasons. The ideological positions and political stances of these organizations were very different. Their purposes of participation were not identical. We can, therefore, ask whether the total literacy campaign (which replaces the earlier schemes which allowed different organizations to move to different approaches) was not limited by the effort to promote too much coherence. People from different shades and hues were forced to wear a common garb.

It is clear that along with the policy statement, the country has also to present a plan of action. Currently, the nature and structure of governance and functioning place a lot of power and authority in the hands of the government officers belonging to the administrative services at the central level as well as the district level. While the policy formulations and the district programmes were developed in consultation with others it was the understanding of the bureaucrats that governed, how the system would unfold. At the district level, the role and personality of the district collector played a crucial role in setting literacy campaigns in motion. Menka Roy points out that sensitizing the district collector brought the official into contact with the local community. This was largely because such interactions on relatively equal terms had not happened before. She, however, also points out that this did not necessarily bring any lasting challenge in the bureaucratic attitude or style, and once the momentum died down or the district collector was transferred, the pattern changed. She also argues that the campaign was too dependent on the personal interest of someone who was actually an "outsider". In terms of the way forward she suggests the need for greater participation of NGO's and Local Self-Governments and that any policy needs to be aware of the difference between North Indian States and the South Indian States with regard to ground situations of institutions. There is also need for institutionalization of the adult education with adequate infrastructure. All this needs to be done with adequate decentralization with each region with its own history, culture and development needs being responsible for itself [Menka Roy in her Afterword, p. 338-340, Paradigm of Learning: The Total Literacy Campaign in India].

## Conclusion

Looking at the effort of providing adult education in India we recognize the need to address the following key questions: What is education? Why adult education? Who is an adult? What are the resources needed? We then need to ask whether education can be conceptualized in the same manner for adult learners, who are illiterate and adult learners who are literate but need to continue with their learning. Is it the case that in situations where a large number of people are illiterate there is greater need for a simultaneous social, political and economic transformation? What are the kinds of structures that we can build? Should these structures be permanent, well-equipped even though they develop slowly? Or should we use the resources to create a mass movement in which every one gets involved in some way or the other?

The next major question is: What are the motivations that can bring the adult learner to acquire literacy and further education? Are these motivations and responses different from those of children in some fundamental way? The adult learners should be engaged in doing what? Is there some importance to the content? What kind of content should be chosen and who should choose it? What is the link between content and process and is there any place for pedagogy at all?

The other critical questions are related to the teachers: Who can these be? What should be their capabilities? Can it be reasonably demanded that they are capable of doing everything, that too without adequate compensation and constant struggle to survive? If we feel that it is not feasible then we need to think about an alternative by which they can be empowered to perform a role that can be reasonably expected from them. In this we also need to look at the problems of cascading and, therefore, the time span for massive effort.

All these questions are to be examined under the key question, what is education. Is the purpose of education to prepare the learner for a struggle to improve his/her life and fight injustice and oppression? Or is the main purpose to give them modern ideas and gradually lead them towards a globalized society and globalized economy? Or is there no conflict between these and a harmonious mixture of the two can be developed?

We also need to ask whether literacy leads to increased disparity and decrease in cooperation, deference and sensitivity to the others or, to the contrary, it increases the democratic spirit and freedom. In terms of the role of the government and the State there are questions like: whether it is possible for a State itself to actively pursue literacy or it should stop at allowing and nurturing independent organizations and programmes promoted by them.

What should be the level of centrally directed ideas and space for local ideas to grow? Can the planning be such that we use the resources in concentrated manner over a period of time and then move on to other areas?

## References

Bharat Gyan Vigyan Samithi (n.a.), *Perspectives, Achievements, Tasks & Dreams*, New Delhi.

CABE (1944), *Report.*

Government of India (1992), *CABE Report, Chapter 10 : Adult and Continuing Education.*

Karlekar, Malavika (2004), *Paradigms of Learning—The Total Literacy Campaign in India*, Sage Publications, New Delhi.

Kothari, D.S. (1966), *Education and National Development*, Report of the Education Commission, National Council of Educational Research & Training, New Delhi.

MHRD, (1986), *National Policy on Education, 1986*, Government of India, New Delhi.

Miller, Valerie (1985), *Between Struggle & and Hope—The Nicaraguan Literacy Crusade.*

Mukherjee, Aditi and Vasanta, Duggirala (2002), 'Practice and Research in Literacy,' *Research in Applied Linguistics*, Vol. 5, Sage Publications, New Delhi.

Narulkar S. and Sykes M. (1956), *A Picture and Programme of Adult Education, Adult Education in Nai Talim.*

National Council of Educational Research and Training (2000), *National Curriculum Framework for School Education* , New Delhi.

National Council of Educational Research and Training (2005), *National Curriculum Framework for School Education* , New Delhi.

Seva Mandir (1978 & 1989), *Meaning of Adult Education*, Bhai Sahab Ra (Part-2), Udaipur, Rajasthan.

Seva Mandir (various years), *Annual Reports*, Udaipur, Rajasthan.

# 23

# The Challenge before Indian Agricultural Universities: Impact and Relevance of Kothari Commission's Vision and Strategy

DINESH ABROL AND L. PULAMTE

## Introduction

The Education (Kothari) Commission (1964-66) gave its most detailed recommendations on the system of education for agriculture. Its key recommendations were meant to achieve the reorganisation of the Indian agricultural higher education institutions with the aim of tackling the scientific and technological challenges the country faced in enhancing agricultural productivity. The vision and strategy of the Kothari Commission served as a core statement in the case of agricultural universities; its major recommendations were faithfully implemented. The members of the Kothari Commission comprised all those who were critical to the institutional reorganisation and policymaking in the case of Indian Agricultural Universities. Their strengths and weaknesses are, therefore, to a large extent clearly attributable to the Commission's detailed recommendations.

India's food security was in an acute crisis when the Kothari Commission[1] made its recommendations. It was in search of a solution to the problem of food security that the Kothari Commission decided to transform the then existing agricultural and veterinary colleges into Indian agricultural universities as organizations providing research, education and extension under one roof. It is significant that today, when we are revisiting the results of the implementation of the Commission's recommendations, the state of agriculture remains the most important challenge to the system of agricultural education in India. Not many among the policymakers and scientists have been bold enough to admit that the system of education for agriculture needs to be radically transformed to devise the post-green revolution strategy. However, a few have tried to suggest to the agricultural universities to abandon the vision and strategy of the 1970s agricultural development and higher education[2].

This article points out that, in the context of the rapidly deepening agrarian crisis, the current challenge for the system of education in agriculture is far more complex. For the planners of the system of education, the challenge is that they are required to decide on whose side they are and for whom do they want to plan in respect of the system of agricultural education. Even today, when the contribution of agriculture to gross domestic product is around twenty per cent, India has still a large rural population (69 per cent of the total population) continuing to sustain itself from the farm, off farm and non-farm rural employment. Today, the challenge facing the nation is, therefore, one of not just increasing food production to provide food security to the nation but of how to sustain the livelihoods and incomes of the surviving rural population[3]. The earlier technological strategy of the green revolution, that was the basis for educational planning in the case of the Kothari Commission, has mostly exhausted its possibilities and is becoming highly unsustainable in terms of ecological and social justice dimensions. It is to be noted that powerful forces are driving the process of change in the system in a very different direction in which corporate control of technology is a significant element and the farmers' risk is known. It exhorts the educational planners to create a new vision and strategy for the agricultural higher educational institutions in the interest of larger common good.

This article argues that experience of the implementation of the Kothari Commission in the case of Indian agricultural universities is very clear. Currently, in the case of agricultural universities, the community of practitioners of agricultural education, research and extension, has a mandate as well as the culture of diffusing largely the technology of green revolution, which is increasingly becoming costly to sustain for even the large farmers and well endowed regions of the country. It suggests that this time the educational planners would have to keep the "who-whom" of the vision and strategy clearly in focus. It is stressed that the new vision and strategy of the system of education for agriculture must not become unidirectional to benefit only the big business and those resourceful farmers, who are capable of mobilizing external inputs and access distant markets in collaboration with the foreign partners from the global agribusiness. The new vision and strategy should be so formulated that those who have plans for the benefit of the small producers too have technical citizenship and sufficient space for knowledge production and utilization in the system of agricultural education. It is noted that to work for the benefit of the rural population as a whole the system of education should be able to focus on the systemic development of the resources, capabilities and markets that are easily accessible to the small producers in the rural economy. It is pointed out that the system of knowledge production in agricultural universities would have to be capable of handling the prevailing ecological and social diversity.

## Part I: Revisiting Commission's Vision and Strategy for Agricultural Education

In this part it is proposed to investigate to what extent the causes of agrarian crisis relate to, a) the emerging systemic failures in respect of knowledge production; and, b) the inherent drawbacks in the recommendations of the Kothari Commission[4]. We enumerate in this section a large number of failures and connected structural rigidities created on account of the implementation of the vision and strategy of the Education Commission. These structural rigidities are today coming in the way of further progress in the generation and implementation of appropriate agricultural technology.

### *Failures Experienced during Implementation of the Kothari Commission*

The failure to deliver on the front of generation and implementation of appropriate technologies for the existing agricultural knowledge production system is dealt with here. The needle of breakdown points to the direction of the failure of policymakers to undertake the required systemic changes in education and putting in place the necessary innovation for agriculture in India. It is also clear that there are important structural rigidities in the existing system of innovation and that quite a few of these rigidities are mostly attributable to the nature of social engineering undertaken by the policymakers for the purpose of the introduction of "green revolution" technology in agriculture.

Take the aspect of technology implementation. It is itself today an important factor in the continuing stagnation in yield levels. Even the latest publication entitled, "Measures of impact of Science and Technology in India: Agriculture and Rural Development", (M.S. Swaminathan Research Foundation, 2007, p xxiii) recognises the failure of technology implementation system and its consequences for the Indian agriculture. It states, "We cannot be silent on-lookers to the continued co-existence of mountains of affordable technology and acute agrarian distress". Whether or not there exists ready-made mountains of affordable technologies, the fact of the matter is that these technologies continue to exist only on the shelf as potentially transferable technologies.

If the yield gap in the case of cereals is remaining high, it is due to the lack of capacity for transfer of appropriate technologies for agro-ecological management. In India, food supply is dominated by rice and wheat, which account for about 90 per cent of the region's total cereal production[5]. Growth in the area of rice and wheat cultivation in India has reduced considerably. Future production gains will have to come mainly from yield increases. Although average rice and wheat yields rose at about two per cent per year between 1960 and 1990, evidence is accumulating to suggest that the impressive rates of yield growth achieved earlier are no longer being sustained.

In some intensively cultivated areas, yields of rice and wheat have actually begun to decline. This is alarming, especially since the use of productivity-enhancing inputs now seems to be approaching saturation levels. Fertilizer use on rice and wheat is now close to optimal, and use of additional fertilizer is unprofitable.

Although causes of the slow down in productivity rate are still in the process of being analysed by researchers, their preliminary conclusions are clearly in the direction of pointing out that soil-related problems[6], problems relating to declining water tables, problems of salinity and sodicity[7], increase in the incidence of pests and diseases, build-up of grassy weeds[8], delayed planting of wheat following rice that reduces yield[9], are the key reasons.

In different parts of India, the rapid spread of canal irrigation has resulted in the development of the problem of large-scale water logging (2.45 m ha) and soil salinity/alkalinity (3.30 m ha). Intensive cultivation of the high-input responsive varieties of crops remove substantial quantities of major nutrients such as nitrogen, phosphorous, potassium, iron and sulphur, and minor nutrients such as zinc, manganese, boron and copper. Nitrogen and phosphorous are removed in large quantities when grain yields of the order of 7 to 8 t/ha are harvested in a year, as in many double-cropped irrigated areas[10]. There is evidence that farmers have been removing more nutrients from the soil than they have been adding by way of fertilizers.

The ICAR (1998) study indicates the aggravation of imbalances for Haryana during the period of 1966-96. In Haryana, there is also evidence that the organic carbon content has declined from 0.5 per cent to 0.2 per cent. Consequently, nitrogen-use efficiency by the crops has been adversely affected and more inorganic nitrogenous fertilizers are required to harvest the same yields as 20 years ago. It is said such imbalances are continuing to evolve today at a higher rate than before because of the rising costs of chemical fertilizers. All of these factors point to the lack of sustainability of growth in crop yields in the long run.

The latest estimates reported by National Bureau of Soil Survey and Land Use Planning (NBSS&LUP), Nagpur using Global Assessment of Soil Degradation Guidelines (GLASOD) indicate 187.8 million hectares (M ha) of land degraded to various degrees and by various degrading processes. Ministry of Agriculture estimates indicate the degraded land area to be in the range of 107.43 M ha by eliminating duplication of area reclaimed which is also included in the other estimates. Whatever is the extent of the area, the fact remains that soil degradation is the most serious problem and maximum degradation is by water erosion. The NBBS&LUP estimates of water erosion indicate 132.5 M ha losses of topsoil and 16.4 M ha of soil terrain deformations.

It is clear that the current practices of technology management must change even if we want to reduce the yield gap between the laboratory and farms. It would involve the development of technologies of agro-ecological management for diverse agro-ecological resource endowment situations. It is not that knowledge for the development of such technologies cannot be created. The fact of the matter is that presently the system is not able to provide space to the development of technologies for agro-ecological management. It is our case that the "as existing" system of technology implementation is just not geared to handling the issues arising out of the diversity in the agro-ecological regions and farmers' resource endowments.[11] Later, we provide more details of how come this kind of failure in the system is persisting and why the managers are unable to correct it at least for more than one decade.

Take the aspect of technology generation for the agriculture sector. Even in the technology component, in which the agricultural universities were considered to be strong in research outcomes, have been extremely disappointing during the nineties. In the case of crop husbandry sector, the Varietal Improvement Programme, focusing on development of superior crop varieties through plant breeding, has been a vital component of the technology system chosen for introduction in the Indian agriculture during the green revolution phase. In this very technology component the nineties was a period of complete stagnation in respect of research outcomes and knowledge utilisation; the Indian agricultural universities could not develop any new superior technological solutions needed to overcome the situation of persisting stagnation in agricultural productivity.

In the case of wheat, the gain in yield declined significantly, from 3.17 per cent in the 1980s to 1.67 per cent in the 1990s. This decline has been attributed to lack of development of genetically high yield varieties In the case of Wheat Varietal Improvement programme, in 1963-65 Kalyansona, gave yields up to 5.3 t/ha in experimental plots in northwest India. The latest best yielding variety, PBW-343 yields 5.6 t/ha. Other factors contributing towards this have been water scarcity and lack of moisture efficient genotypes, as well as increase in soil temperature (Nagarajan, 2006).

The situation is not in anyway better for the other crops. For the last twenty-five years, no genotype of rice has been developed with yield potential greater than IR 8 and Jaya (Nagarajan, 1998). The annual increase in yield declined in the case of rice from 32 kg per hectare in the period 1970-71 to 1990-91 to 20.6 kg per hectare in the 1990s. During the period 1965-2000 the number of varieties of rice released from different states/institutions of India was 620. Among the released modern varieties (MVs), 54 per cent were recommended for the favourable irrigated ecosystem, 27 per cent for the rain-fed lowlands, and 19 per cent for the rain-fed upland favourable irrigated eco-system. Though even during the second phase of green revolution breeding for shorter duration MVs has received a considerable attention, most of the MVs were developed to meet the increasing demand for better quality rice.

Similarly, though development of MVs with multiple resistant to insect pests and diseases has remained a priority in the breeding strategy since the eighties, only four per cent of total MV releases are resistant to more than one insect pest. The share of MVs with multiple resistant to diseases has declined from 10 per cent during 1965-75 to 4 per cent in the late 1990s.

Experiencing the yield plateau is already a real problem for the introduction of MVs and for the system of agriculture that the Indian agricultural universities have been promoting till this day. The potential boundaries of this technology system have been arrived at. Beyond these boundaries yield levels cannot be increased in the case of MVs. However, it is also clear that the challenge posed before the system of knowledge production is far greater than before. Kumar (1998) has estimated the required production and productivity targets for individual commodities. His estimates show that the productivity of rice needs to improve from 1.85 to 2.9 t/ha in 2020, wheat from 2.42 to 3.92 t/ha, and total food grains from 1.5 to 2.4 t/ha.

The issue of sustainability of agricultural development has also come to the fore now in a big way. The question to be asked is whether the strategy of focusing on the existing system of agricultural universities on the Varietal Improvement Programme itself is an appropriate strategy. For even the irrigated regions and well-endowed farmers, the system has proved to be myopic. If the strategy of introduction of high yielding varieties, which are also external input intensive including water as well as energy, is not working for the irrigated regions, it is even less likely to work for the regions and farmers, which are less favourable from the standpoint of the management of soil and water resources.

It is clear from the above discussion that the management limits of technological system of intensive agriculture are already serious enough to cause a major decline in the viability of intensive agriculture in the leading states of Haryana and Punjab and other green revolution areas of the country. The Indian agricultural universities have so far managed agriculture without taking into account the farming system perspective (limited to addressing the biophysical dimension of sustainability), regional natural resource management perspective (supposed to accommodate the social dimension of sustainability), regional-ecosystem-health perspective (expected to address the ecological, health, aesthetic and ethical dimension of sustainability). The fact of the matter is that the "as existing" system of agricultural universities is in no position to handle the issues of diversity pertaining to agro-ecological regions and farmers' resource endowments.

It is our understanding that the Commission created a top-down system of technology implementation. It would have to be radically restructured if we wish to ensure an adequate agricultural growth rate in the country as a whole. The system the Kothari Commission recommended worked well only with regard to the immediate objective of increasing food production for a small set of farmers in selected regions. But for it to be radically transformed to tackle the problems of diversity, we will have to also ask why the system has not been able to change gear even when the agricultural universities were subjected to severe criticism for the same reason for quite some time now[12].

### *Kothari Commission's Vision and Strategy Results in Structural Rigidities*

The system developed structural rigidities because the Kothari Commission was instrumental in endorsing a system in which alternate technological and market niche had very little space or scope to get protection and time to stabilize. During the first two decades, the space for alternate technological approaches was very little because the proposed programme was also bearing the mission of dissemination of a borrowed technology package at a very high pace. There was hardly any space for the cultivation of basic sciences in the system. However, in our view, the space for work on technological alternatives was less not only due to the absence of emphasis on basic sciences but also on account of the way the role (s) of education, research and extension were integrated too tightly through a highly centralized system functioning under the influence of an extremely narrow mandate of how to increase the area under high yielding varieties.

In fact, the integration of the system of knowledge production and reproduction was for a narrower mandate of the Varietal Improvement Programmes for cereals like Wheat and Rice. Even in the development of new varieties, the incorporation of local germplasm in the plant breeding work was a highly neglected area. Too much accent was placed at least during the initial period on yield with little emphasis on quality, consumer acceptance, adaptability to local conditions, resistance to pests and diseases etc. Yield potential (or high yield) was the breeding objective for 89 per cent of the crosses carried out in rice breeding programmes in India, while only nine per cent of the crosses were for drought tolerance and only two per cent for deep water tolerance. According to a study conducted by Janaiah and Hossain (2004) the percentage of varieties adopted by the farmers in their fields over the fourteen major rice growing states accounted for only 35 per cent of total varieties released till 2000.

The unfortunate part of the story is that the warnings from concerned scientists were ignored and the situation was allowed to drift for a long time in the system[13]. This happened because of the new system where the functions of research, teaching, extension and even adult education of farmers and related persons are combined into a single institution. The research facilities under the control of the state government departments were to be transferred to the agricultural universities. But this networking and integration into a strictly regimented and centrally coordinated national technology transfer system built for the modernization of Indian agriculture with the help of a very specific technology system turned out to be its strength in the short run but its weakness even in the medium run. It is not that the Indian scientists were incapable of doing original work but it was the system that prevented them from pursuing a work of this nature. The peer groups and top authorities were well in the grip of the new package strategy and they saw to it that much effort was not "frittered away" on problems, which were not pertinent to the new package strategy.

Many examples can be given to illustrate the point of how these rigidities have come about and what accounts for their resilience in the case of the SAUs and ICAR. Take the case of All India Coordinated Research Projects (AICRPs). For the transfer of high yield variety (HYV) technology to succeed, both adaptive and protective research was required to some extent to change the original characteristics of HYVs to suit local conditions. For this, the national research capacity had to be spread over the various regional centres located in different ecological regions. Adaptive research work started in India with varieties imported from CIMMYT (Centro Internacional de Mejoramiento de Maíz y Trigo), etc. Dinesh Abrol (1984) suggests, "Given the fact that the starting point was the foreign varieties and the charter was to modify the original characteristics only to a minimum, the effort did not have to go beyond the fostering of institutional structures required for adaptive research, field experimentation and tests for suggesting the requirements of complementary inputs.

Thus, as far as research is concerned, networking into all-India coordinated projects directed and controlled by a few institutions was its strength only in the short run. This is because it permitted strict implementation of established crop improvement procedures for non-local internationally transmitted germplasm without much diversion. It also produced demonstration effects in quite a short time, judged by the general standards of efficiency of national technology transfer systems in other areas in the country.[14] But it was also a weakness because it was geared to doing mainly adaptive research, testing and demonstration for HYVs, and had neglected fundamental research, leaving the initiative to international agricultural research centres, which provided the germplasm for plant-breeding work and strategies for the new farming system.

Changes have occurred and continue to occur, even today, in the system of research, education and extension, but it is evident that deeper structures prevent the system from making the required correctives. Incremental innovations characterize the system of research and education. The forces directing the content of agricultural sciences are even today the forces that do not have the local conditions of the farmers in any way uppermost in their mind. Structures that the system initially fostered to get the best results for green revolution technology package have got rigidified; though their relevance for the current concerns is being increasingly questioned at all the levels now. Even the National Commission on Agriculture (1976) pointed out, "the undue concentration of coordinated projects in the ICAR institutes like the IARI and the IVRI is another undesirable feature and could have been avoided.... Only a very limited number of coordinated research projects have their headquarters located at the agricultural universities.... The same is true of ad hoc research schemes. The IARI alone accounted for more than half of the total number of ad hoc schemes in crop sciences for all the ICAR institutes in 1974-75. While all the agricultural universities put together accounted for 162 schemes, the IARI alone had 125 schemes in the area of crop sciences in the year 1974-75". This kind of centralization had made an adverse impact on the quality of education and extension and was observed in the Report of the National Commission on Agriculture (1976).

Furthermore, it is also important to recognize that the rigidities of deeper structures were inbuilt into the strategy of the collaborative programme itself. Priorities were clearly articulated to favour a system of adaptive research and training for the diffusion of a technology system that had already completed its development phase. But as the technology system needed adaptations to enable even the farmers, who were not resource poor to adopt the high yielding varieties in the well endowed regions, the agricultural universities were required to carry out their tasks for the diffusion of these high yielding, high input-responsive varieties in an integrated way. It wrote, "They should begin with and for some time concentrate on the traditional agricultural specialties such as agronomy, plant genetics, animal breeding, animal husbandry, veterinary science, plant pathology, soil science, microbiology, horticulture, entomology and parasitology."

Research was concentrated mainly on individual crops and their productivity. Research on farming systems, which would take into consideration all the inputs, was either scant or totally absent. Recycling of agricultural wastes—as practised in many parts of the country—was absent as an objective in the agronomic experiments whose incorporation could provide nutrients. Soil microbiology, biological nitrogen fixation, microbial decomposition in soil, use of algae, etc., received relatively little emphasis in the research system because of obsession with high yielding varieties sensitive to chemical fertilizers. Neglect of water management emerged as the single most important consequence of the new strategy[15]. The fourth evaluation report of the Intensive Agricultural District Programme (IADP) identified the lack of adequate research information and the non-availability of trained staff as the main difficulties in organizing work in the area of water management[16].

Distortions were quite serious in the case of fundamental research in the established system of institutes and agricultural universities. The National Commission on Agriculture had to say the following with regard to the fundamental research being conducted in Indian agricultural universities: "What often passes as fundamental research in agriculture but a variation of similar study done elsewhere having little or no relevance to our conditions.... Owing to continued lack of encouragement, this category of research has not gained growth in agricultural universities. The basic science faculties are too weak to sustain the desired leadership"[17].

The role conceived for the National System of Agricultural Research, Education and Extension was on the one hand, to strengthen adaptive research, protective research and testing and on the other, to provide the manpower needed for the package dissemination in the country. In the international division of labour in the research network, fundamental research was assigned to international agricultural research centres financed by the United States. Moseman, member of the first joint Indo-American team and director of the Rockefeller Foundation's Agricultural Sciences Program wrote, "Although these international centres cannot meet the specific national or local needs for research they will modify the nature of programmes and organisations required in individual countries and *will permit an orderly phasing and evolution of national systems. Stronger initial emphasis can be placed on adaptive, protective and applied research within each country with emphasis on basic fundamental studies postponed until later.*"[18] *(emphasis added).*

The fact that the research, education and extension got geared to pushing mainly the HYVs package is not because there was any conspiracy hatched but because it was structurally evolved by conceiving a well defined division of labour between the international, national and regional structures. Control through peer groups, which determined the system of reward and recognition, was a key mechanism for influencing the system. Whenever there was a need to rationalize the structures in order to solve the emerging conflicts, centralization and bureaucratic structures came handy. Reinforcing factors included exchange programmes for foreign travel. The National Commission on Agriculture (1976) wrote, "The craze (for foreign travel) has been so great that quite a few had to be warned recently and some suspended and dismissed".

But all of this was happening to a large extent because of the lack of indigenous assessment of priorities. Influential peer groups trained in the US, financed in many cases quite heavily in respect of their research programmes, directed the choices of curricula, research problems and extension strategies in different agro-ecological regions. All this, combined with the ambitions of the young scientists to be able to work with those who have not only influence and authority because of their links with funding agencies but also status in the international community, stood in the way of a positive development.

The existing system of agricultural higher education lacks in all those characteristics that would allow integrating the system of education, research and extension for the cultivation of objectives pertaining to diversity, critical inquiry and self-reflection. The responsibility of not being able to provide the correctives to the farmers with regard to the technique lies squarely with the system of agricultural universities as it was made responsible for not only education but also for research and extension. The recommended system of integration was insufficiently modern. It should have had enough space for the creation of technological alternatives and self-reflection.

### *American Involvement and Kothari Commission*

If we are serious about correcting the system of education for agriculture and innovation today, it needs to be recognized that the vision of the system that the Kothari Commission approved was a programme being evolved in the process of Indo-American collaboration on agriculture. In fact, the Education Commission was responsible for providing legitimacy to the programme being already worked out to the last dot amidst the administrators of agriculture through the Indo-American collaboration. It was a first full-fledged nod from the side of educationists and education planners as a whole to the system of agricultural higher education already under construction.

The first Joint Indo-American team was formed in 1955 and had examined the entire field of agricultural higher education and research in India and to recommend improvements. An Indian delegation spent three months in the United States examining "land grant universities" while an American team of three examined the situation of agricultural higher education in India. The joint team had urged that agricultural universities similar to those in the United States be established and that these institutions not offer postgraduate education unless their faculty conducted research. The team also recommended close ties between colleges of agriculture and technology (i.e. engineering) in each of the universities.

The central point in the Education Commission's recommendation, the establishment of at least one agricultural university on the suggested lines in each state, was in fact a recommendation of the Second Joint Indo-American team (ICAR 1960). Since the Indian Government had formed this joint team with the U.S. with a view to evaluate progress made since the first team report in 1955[19] and to review the relations with the U.S. land-grant universities, which had already made the recommendations regarding the system of agricultural higher education to be established, the Kothari Commission was merely reinforcing it. It is indirectly admitted in the Kothari Commission Report when it states that the programme is not new. All the additional suggestions that the Kothari Commission made on agricultural education in schools, polytechnics, universities and IITs are discussed later. They are shown to have been ignored by the system planners to a large extent.

The Education Commission (1964-66) had not only adopted a virtually ready-made programme, it appears that while formulating its vision and strategy regarding the system for agricultural education, but also legitimized the ready-made programme without an appropriate scrutiny. There was an already set direction created by the government in respect of the planning of agricultural education during the 1950s. And the reason for this lapse is obvious if one goes through the process of formulation and implementation of the Kothari Commission's own vision and strategy. It could not think afresh because the processes it followed were also not free from the direct influence of the US interests. The influence of the US interests would become sufficiently clear if we mention about their direct involvement in the vision and strategy formulation and later in the programme implementation. For example, Dr. Ralph W. Cummings, the Director of Rockefeller Foundation in India, was not only a member of the Kothari Commission but also had a direct involvement in the programme implementation. It is true that the Kothari Commission had some very eminent educationists and scientists as members in the Task Force on Agriculture formed by it and that Dr. Ralph. W. Cummings was not alone in deciding on the issue of the vision and strategy. But what is often forgotten was that he was also in-charge of the programme implementation. It is a matter of history that Dr. Cummings also served later as the chairperson of the committee that planned the structures and criterion of performance for the Indian agricultural universities.

The report of the Agricultural Universities Committee (Cummings Committee) was the basis on which the ICAR developed the Model Act, which was designed to guide state legislation concerning the creation of agricultural universities. First made available to the states in 1966, the Model Act enumerated the following four goals for the State Agricultural Universities (SAUs): i). To impart education in different branches of study, particularly agriculture, horticulture, veterinary and animal sciences, and other allied branches of learning and scholarship; ii) To advance learning and research, particularly in agriculture and other allied sciences; iii) To extend knowledge gleaned from such sciences, especially to the rural people of the state; and iv) To achieve such other purposes as the university may determine from time to time (ICAR 1981, 6).

The Cummings Committee visited the states of Punjab, Orissa, Rajasthan, Andhra Pradesh, Madhya Pradesh, Karnataka and Tamil Nadu. The committee visited a state only upon a request from the state, forwarded through the Government of India, Ministry of Agriculture. Its principal aim was to review the proposals for agricultural universities in various states with regard to the adequacy of the proposed enabling legislation and the adequacy and soundness of the detailed implementation plans in terms of organizational, administrative and educational criteria. But there comes the catch now and also a key lesson of policymaking. *Central support was to be made available for only those agricultural universities that met the criteria developed by the Agricultural Universities Committee.* The USAID—US university assistance in agricultural education—was restricted to those states that established agricultural universities in line with the recommendations made by the Agricultural Universities Committee (Cummings Committee).

During the 20-year period (1952-72), six US universities were involved in programmes that had the objectives like improvement of teaching, establishment of research and extension activities in the new universities and in the existing agricultural colleges. During these twenty years, more than 300 staff members from the six US universities came to India, on either short or long term assignments and more than 1000 faculty members and graduate students from India studied in the US. This number does not include significant number of Indians who were supported through various fellowship programmes or through their own funds and who received US university degrees at both cooperating and other land-grant institutions. Nor does it include the many Indians trained at home at public and private agricultural colleges. Their primary mission was and remains teaching. During these twenty years, about 700 man-years of US staff were devoted to help India build the present system of agricultural research and education, including the creation of nine new agricultural universities.

Lawrence Busch (1988) states, "The 20-year period of intensive assistance to the SAUs can be described as the single largest agricultural education project ever undertaken by AID.... Unlike the land-grant system in the United States, which developed over 125 years into a system that came to embrace research and extension as well as teaching, India's SAU system sprang up virtually overnight as a full-fledged, comprehensive system." Except for a few hitches here and there, from both the sides the participants of this program implemented it in a single-minded fashion. In those states where no agricultural university developed, all activities under the Agricultural Education and Research projects were phased out with the end of current commitments. The result was that each and every university tried not to deviate from the proposed model and criteria provided by the Central Government. Lawrence Busch (1988) adds, "This was in part a response to pressure from AID-Washington to show that clearly demonstrable impacts were being felt."

However, an important lesson that we must once again take into account today is that the concept of institution building that was developed in the United States in the 1960s was a form of "social engineering" not limited to the system of education but also extended to the society and economy as a whole. Lawrence Busch (1988) also writes, "What went unnoticed, even by Hannah in his Blueprint (1956) was that the US land-grant universities were embedded in a complex institutional matrix that included organized farm groups that lobbied at the state and federal levels for funding for agricultural research and education; a diverse far-flung system of agricultural credit; effective suppliers of agricultural inputs and processors of agricultural outputs; a farm constituency that was virtually entirely market oriented; an efficient system of transport of agricultural commodities; and well organized markets."

Very little resistance was experienced by the system at the time of its establishment. As far as the forces that opposed the establishment of the model of new institutions is concerned, there were only those forces of opposition, who had vested interests in the old order and had very little to contribute to the development of alternatives and corrections. It seems that the forces of resistance to the proposed specific technology system, with which the fate of agricultural universities was linked, were rather weak; organized powerful voices in both regional and class terms that could be said to also favour a different form of agriculture were missing from the agricultural scene at the time of establishment of the agricultural universities. The aspect that got highlighted in the early seventies was on the technology being resource intensive and, therefore, the need to undertake land reforms and augment irrigation and credit facilities to allow them to benefit from the new technology. In the eighties, when the farmers had sufficient experience with the technology, these forces also demanded that the scientists must not be content with the results obtained from the experimental stations; they must also undertake on-farm research, change the extension system and solve the problems of smaller farms in a targeted way.

In the nineties, the situation was one of uncertainty and of even leading the country and the system to accepting a position that the state need not step in to solve the problems of Indian agriculture. Let the private sector come into the system including research where the SAUs and the rest of the system should become a partner. Certainly, for the last few years there is a change in the way the country now feels about the "green revolution" technology and has become concerned about the state of agricultural education, research and extension in a very different and radical way. Some of these forces are again demanding from the agricultural universities that they also devote energy to the problems of small farmers and become more pluralistic in approach to the production of knowledge[20].

It would not be out of place to mention here that the model of agricultural higher education that the Education Commission approved in 1964-66 was also quite different from the one that the Radhakrishnan University Education Commission (UEC) had envisaged for implementation in the country in 1948-49. It is to be noted that the Radhakrishnan Commission was not in favour of borrowing a readymade model because it believed that India should develop a model of her own kind after a thorough study. It was interested not only in taking the best features of the models of agricultural universities available in the world but also in selecting and adapting them for the development of a system of agriculture connected appropriately with the local resources, capabilities and markets. It was of the view that the system of education for the transformation of agriculture and village industries should be undertaken in an interconnected way by the rural university.

Even in the midst of all these distortions, the SAUs and the rest of the national research and extension system have been able to generate several scientists, teachers and student outturns that have very different ideas about the priorities of Indian agriculture. There is a lot of churning going on at the level of both official and non-official programmes in the country. The resistance is coming from within the system, though it is only a minority in terms of overall numbers within the system, it is putting up a contest. The language has also changed and it is reflected in the recommendations of the committees set up officially by the ICAR and other official arms of the Government of India. There is also a contest from the influences arising on account of the changing international agriculture regime. Today, the corporate sector is far more important in research and production of agricultural inputs such as seeds. It is doing its best to force the public sector research and education system in India to get into a partnership with the business entities active not only in agricultural biotechnology but also in all other areas of conventional technologies. The Indo-US Knowledge Initiative for Agriculture has succeeded in putting Monsanto and Wall-Mart in command once again within the public sector agricultural research, education and extension system. This contest of the forces is visible in the recommendations of the committees as well as in the community of scientists and teachers.

## Part-II: Contemporary Concerns and Challenge of Institutional Reforms

The official evaluation undertaken until very recently was also mostly an exercise in rationalization within the framework of the Kothari Commission's recommendations. An important consequence of this rationalization is that while the nation has been successful in achieving the targets fixed in respect of establishment of the system of agricultural universities, the progress made in respect of establishment of the agricultural schools and polytechnics has not been realized.

The Education Commission recommended the establishment of Agricultural Polytechnics for imparting vocational education in agriculture. After the Planning Commission and inter-Ministerial Committee considered the issue, the Indian Council of Agricultural Research (ICAR) appointed Dr. Mohan Singh Mehta Committee in 1973 for formulating the institutional design for vocational training in agriculture. The National Policy on Education 1986 also highlighted the need for vocationalization of education at different levels.

The Scheme of Community Polytechnics was started in 1978-79. The community polytechnic is a wing of an existing polytechnic and is mandated to undertake rural/community development activities through application of science and technology in its proximity, using infrastructure existing in polytechnics. At present, there are 669 community polytechnics in the country (MHRD Annual Report, 2005-06). The Scheme has been reviewed twice at the national level and both the reviews recommended the expansion of the scheme to cover all AICTE-approved polytechnics, besides suggesting a multi-skill competency-based training, a special programme for women, handicapped, street children and functional linkages with other rural development skills of the central/state governments. The 168th Report of the Parliamentary Standing Committee on Human Resource Development (December 2005) observes that the Scheme has failed to make the desired impact so far. The Committee feels that the under-utilization of funds must have affected the training programmes, thereby defeating the very objective of the Scheme. In an attempt to further improve the funds utilization, a series of State-level review meetings/workshops have been organized at various locations in the country, in the months of April and May 2005, by the Regional Resource Institutions i.e. National Institute of Technical Teachers Training & Research (NITTTRs). The Committee also feels that the regional distribution of Community Polytechnics is uneven. The Committee is of the opinion that the Department should try to open more Community Polytechnics in the eastern region (it has only 97 out of a total of 669 Community Polytechnics), which is a backward area with the highest concentration of rural population.

The Review Committee of Agricultural Universities in 1978 recognized continuing education as a mechanism to keep self-employed graduates abreast of the latest developments and technical advice. The National Academy of Agricultural Sciences (NAAS) too put emphasis on distance education in agriculture for farmers and small agri-entrepreneurs; regular specialized training for rural youth with wide use of IT, digitalization of course content, virtual universities, *e*-learning and video conferencing. The Fourth Deans Committee in 2006 also put emphasis on this aspect by suggesting organization of non-formal education programmes and in establishing centres of distance education in all SAUs for reaching out to the youths who are not benefiting through the regular system.

The Committee suggested establishment of Farm Science Centres, later named as Krishi Vigyan Kendra (KVK). Almost a decade after the Education Commission's recommendation, the first KVK was finally established in 1974 in Pondicherry. During the Eighth Plan the mandate of the KVK was further enlarged to include technology assessment & refinement and assessment of its impact through On-farm trials and Frontline demonstration (ICAR, 2005). The present activities of the KVK are: (i) On-farm trial to identify the location specificity of technology under various farming systems, (ii) Frontline demonstrations to its production potentials on the farmers' fields; (iii) Training of farmers to update their knowledge and skills; and, (iv) Training of extension personnel to orient them in the frontier areas of technology development.

Till the end of the Ninth Plan, the total number of KVKs sanctioned was 276. For the Tenth Plan period, it has been decided to cover the remaining rural districts of the country with one KVK each on 100 per cent funding basis. This is in fulfillment of one of the strong recommendations of the Parliamentary Standing Committee on Agriculture (PSCA). According to 'India-2002' there were 578 rural districts in the country and it was decided to have one KVK in each of the 578 rural districts by the end of the Tenth Plan. Ten additional districts are created during 2002 to 2005, raising the number of rural districts to 588. It is envisaged to consider these additional districts as well for support to establish the KVK.

As of now, 492 KVKs have been sanctioned including 128 during 2004-05 and 41 during 2005-06. Provision of e-linkage is also made to 200 KVKs, and also for provision of Soil and Water testing facility in 326 KVKs during the Tenth Plan. During the last three years of the Tenth Plan (2002-03 to 2004-05), the KVKs organized 60,025 training programmes benefiting 15.14 lakhs farmers, 15,262 training programmes benefiting 3.15 lakhs rural youths, and 6,926 training programmes benefiting 1.61 lakhs extension personnel. During the same period the KVKs have conducted on-farm trials on 1236 technologies and 80,907 frontline demonstrations, besides organizing 52,986 extension activities, and production of 18,609 ton seeds and 95.46 lakhs planting material.

Introducing agricultural vocational courses in agriculture, horticulture, crop production, poultry and dairy production, fisheries, agro-processing, conservation, afforestation, etc., would help meet the need for required trained change agents at the village level and also provide employment opportunities for the rural youths. Around 20 States/UTs have introduced agricultural vocational courses. Establishing polytechnic schools under SAUs will also help in meeting the requirement of trained manpower at the grass root level. The agricultural universities can easily establish polytechnics without incurring much financial burden by adding a few more technical staff and some laboratory facilities in their research stations and the *Krishi Vigyan Kendras*. There are more than 30 polytechnic schools in five SAUs-17 in Maharashtra, 13 in Gujarat and five in Andhra Pradesh, etc. (Sulaiman, 1996).

Similarly, though there has been a little more progress in respect of the establishment of agricultural education and allied sectors in the rest of the higher education system (which means in the IITs and Universities), it is clear that the nation needs to do much more. Linkages of the rest of the system with the agricultural universities continue to be weak and would have to be strengthened. Later in this part we take stock of the developments in relation to the system outside the agricultural universities.

The agricultural universities are yet to attract the best and appropriate talent for the established system of education as recommended by the Kothari Commission. In spite of the biological sciences boom, the problem of attracting the best talent to the system of agricultural universities is yet to be tackled. The best students continue to opt for engineering and medicine, and it is difficult to get qualified and motivated faculty members. It may be mentioned that these two problems were identified almost thirty years back by the Report of the Review Committee on Agricultural Universities (ICAR, 1978).

### *Concerns and Challenges Identified in the System during the Post-seventies*

The Review Committee on Agricultural Universities in 1978 reiterated the Education Commission's policy of "at least one agricultural university in each state" when it evaluated the system officially for the first time. It clearly stated that the ICAR should not deviate from this. This has been fulfilled except in the case of North-east India. In this region, with the exception of Assam, where a full-fledged agricultural university has been established. Campuses of the Central Agricultural University are located in different parts of the rest of the North-eastern States. The Working Group on Agricultural Research and Education for the Tenth Plan (2001) however, noted that several States have more than one SAU resulting in thin distribution of the limited resources. Some States have also opened "discipline" based universities. This too is against the concept of the SAUs.

In order to avoid duplication and confusion between agricultural universities and the State Departments of Agriculture, the Education Committee recommended that the former should take over all research, education and extension programmes. As evident from the Report of the Review Committee on Agricultural Universities, these transfers were not that smooth up to 1978. The Report noted that as far as the transfer of education function to agricultural universities is concerned there was no serious problem except in the case of Uttar Pradesh. Transfer of research responsibilities presented serious problems in a number of states such as West Bengal, Bihar, Tamil Nadu, Rajasthan, Uttar Pradesh, Orissa and Madhya Pradesh. The transfer of extension education has been incomplete in the states like Kerala and Bihar, particularly in the case of Gram Sewak and Gram Sevikas Centres and Farmers Training Centres.

### *Expansion of Facilities for Agricultural Education*

Before Independence, there were only 17 agricultural colleges, three veterinary colleges and one agricultural engineering college in our country. The first SAU was set up in 1960 at Pant Nagar. Now there are 38 SAUs (including four Veterinary and Fisheries Universities), five Deemed Universities (four of these are ICAR Institutes), one Central Agricultural University and three Central Universities having agricultural faculties. There are 121 agricultural colleges, 38 veterinary and animal science colleges, 22 agricultural engineering colleges, 17 home science colleges, 13 fisheries colleges, 10 forestry colleges, 14 horticultural colleges, 11 dairy science colleges, 7 colleges of basic science and humanities and three colleges/faculties on agri-business management in the family of institutions relating to agricultural research and education. There are also 31 agricultural schools established only in the Universities of Andhra Pradesh, Gujarat and Maharashtra.

Presently, the Under Graduate (UG) level education in agricultural and allied sciences is imparted in eleven broad disciplines; viz., Agriculture, Horticulture, Forestry, Home Science, Sericulture, Agricultural Engineering, Food Science and Technology, Agricultural Marketing, Banking and Cooperation, Fishery science, Dairy Technology and Veterinary Science. The academic programmes offered at the Master's level at various colleges of SAUs, as recommended by the Accreditation Board of ICAR, consist of as many as 46 Programmes. At present, 52 universities (including 19 general) offers M.Sc. Programme and 41 universities (including 9 general) offers Ph.D. programme in 95 and 80 disciplines at postgraduate and Ph.D. level respectively. At present the intake capacity is 13,500 graduates, (8,600 in agriculture, 2,000 in veterinary, 750 each in Agricultural Engineering and Home Science streams), 6000 M.Sc. and 1,550 Ph.D.

New institutions have come into existence only in the fields of agricultural engineering, home science, horticulture, dairy science and fisheries. The Education Commission recommended that beginning with the traditional agricultural specialties, these universities should gradually extend their scope of studies to cover a wide range of specialized courses to fulfill the emerging needs. An analysis of the dates of establishments of the colleges in the agricultural universities shows that most of these colleges were in existence before the concerned system of agricultural universities was established. Almost all the universities started educational programmes in the faculty of Agriculture and Veterinary perhaps because of their primary importance.

When many of the agricultural universities are now granting degrees in diversified fields such as Horticulture, Agricultural Engineering, Home Science, Fisheries, Forestry and Dairy Science, adding specialized courses has been a difficult challenge for the system. In recent times, specialized courses such as Agricultural Business Management, Agricultural Biotechnology, and Environment Science & Technology have been started. Agricultural universities are also now offering Food Science & Technology, and Food Processing Technology.

When the Working Group on Agricultural Research and Education for the

Tenth Plan (2001) began to evaluate the gaps, it recommended that education in the neglected areas like basic sciences, biodiversity, environment, fisheries, forestry, veterinary sciences etc., and the new areas like biotechnology, information technology requiring cutting edge science, should be strengthened to meet the growing demand of trained human resource in such important areas. Development in the basic science is the backbone of applied sciences. The SAUs, by and large, have ignored the question of balance of applied and basic sciences and gone to implement applied science courses far more rapidly.

### *Concerns Regarding the Patterns of Outturn and Intake*

The outturn of students in agriculture and allied sciences for the period 1980 to 2000 is presented in Table 23.1. A steady growth of outturn is observed in the case of graduates during 1980 to 1990 but it stagnated after 1990. A similar trend is also seen in the case of post-graduates but this suddenly increases in 2000-01. The Institute of Applied Manpower Research study (IAMR, 2001) appears to suggest that the higher the educational level of agricultural graduates the more is the employment rate. Probably this phenomenon might have triggered this significant increase in the outturn of post-graduates in 2000-01. The outturn of doctorates started declining from 1990-91. The period between 1970-90 shows a growth rate of about 2.2 to 2.3 per cent in the outturn of agricultural UG, PG and Ph. D students. This is comparatively less than the overall growth rate for all disciplines in science and technology (DST, 1993). Undergraduate education deserves a special remark as it registered growth in all streams except in agriculture.

**Table 23.1: Growth of Students Passed in Agriculture and Allied Sciences**

| *Year* | *Diploma* | *Under Graduate* | *Post Graduate* | *Ph.D.* | *All* |
|---|---|---|---|---|---|
| 1980 84* | — | 7420 | 2044 | 502 | 9966 |
| 1984-85 | 16 | 7691 | 2950 | 713 | 11370 |
| 1985-86 | 15 | 7879 | 3026 | 736 | 11656 |
| 1986-87 | 18 | 8077 | 3336 | 884 | 12315 |
| 1987-88 | 145 | 8731 | 3471 | 730 | 13077 |
| 1988-89 | 366 | 9761 | 3651 | 616 | 14394 |
| 1989-90 | 110 | 10165 | 4155 | 954 | 15384 |
| 1990-91 | 1015 | 10114 | 3870 | 790 | 15788 |
| 1991-92 | 1093 | 10110 | 3725 | 790 | 15718 |
| 1996-97 | 1214 | 11230 | 4137 | 877 | 17458 |
| 2000-01 | — | 13000 | 6000 | — | 19000 |

*Sources*: Ramarao, D., Nanda, S K, and Sriram, C. (2004). Forecasting Trained Agricultural Manpower, NATP Project Report, NAARM, Hyderabad, India; Data for 1980-84 are the averages for the four-year period; Data for the period 1980-89 from CSIR, 1993; Data for the period 1990-92 is from Rama Rao & Muralidhar, 1994; Data for the year 1996-97 is from Rama Rao and Sandhya Shenoy, 1998; Data for the year 2000-01 is estimate and taken from IAMR, 2001.

The intake of students to various courses in agricultural universities by broad specialization in the year 2004 is shown in Table 23.2. Altogether about 20,763 students were admitted into various courses; UGs comprise 65 per cent, PGs 27 per cent and 7 per cent in Ph.D. The admission pattern shows that PG admission capacity is about 42 per cent of UG capacity. The admission pattern can also be interpreted as follows. About 42 per cent of the UGs go for PG programmes and 27 per cent of the PGs go for Ph.D. programmes. The proportion of UGs going for further studies appears to be high. This could be due to the fact that the employability of graduates in agriculture and allied sciences is low as compared to those with PG degrees in the same disciplines.

**Table 23.2: Level-wise Annual Intake of Students in Agricultural Sciences in India in 2004**

| *Faculty* | *UG* | *PG* | *Ph. D.* | *All* |
|---|---|---|---|---|
| Agriculture incl. Environmental Sciences | 5238 | 2579 | 847 | 8664 |
| Agriculture Engineering | 669 | 241 | 50 | 960 |
| Agricultural Marketing/Banking and Co-op/Agricultural Business | 94 | 60 | 0 | 154 |
| Dairy Sciences Technology | 290 | 77 | 42 | 409 |
| Fisheries | 290 | 175 | 54 | 519 |
| Food Science and Technology | 33 | 48 | 5 | 86 |
| Forestry | 235 | 47 | 18 | 300 |
| Home Science | 753 | 231 | 34 | 1018 |
| Horticulture | 441 | 331 | 87 | 859 |
| Sericulture | 27 | 26 | 0 | 53 |
| Veterinary and Animal Sciences | 1979 | 1355 | 407 | 3741 |
| Total of SAUs | 10049 | 5170 | 1544 | 16763 |
| Others* | 3500 | 500 | — | 4000 |
| Total in the country | 13549 (65.3%) | 5670 (27.3%) | 1544 (7.4%) | 20763 (100%) |

*Source*: IASRI, 2004 taken from www.iasri.res.in

* Others include colleges outside state agricultural universities and deemed universities.

## *Employment Pattern and Impact on Intake*

The students and faculty are a key resource in the system of education for agriculture and rural transformation. Changes have to take place at their level in respect of competence and attitudes. It would not be possible to bring about the changes without their reorganization and participation in the structures that can generate the appropriate kind of competences and attitudes. Needless to say, these changes have a connection with what finally also happens in the society and economy regarding the use of their competencies and attitudes.

As early as in October 1969, Alice Stone Ilchman deliberated on the often-raised concern regarding the tendency of young farm graduates to migrate from farms to seek employment in towns and cities. She pointed out that though the Education Commission correctly assumed that agricultural education usually results in graduates remaining connected with agriculture, but what it failed to understand was that this continuing association depends on the availability of jobs. In the environment of research and extension, the envisioned graduates would pursue professional and specialized careers in such fields as agronomy, animal breeding, plant genetics and parasitology, as well as in such "new" professions for India as agricultural engineering, nutrition, administration of agricultural services and resource conservation. Postgraduates were expected to enter agricultural research and teaching. Clearly, graduates of agricultural universities (and, to some extent, agricultural colleges) were not expected to return to the farms. In her view, "Correct in its assessment of appropriate curricula, correct in its assumption about the behaviour of graduates, the Education Commission may have floundered on a persistent and growing problem for all Indian education: youth are more easily educated than jobs are created".

The intake and outturn trends also confirm that the concerns and challenges facing the system are systemic. Inadequate employment opportunities for agricultural graduates reflect on the students' low preference for degrees in agriculture. The system of education for agriculture needs revamping through the development of a new vision as well as strategy of implementation, especially when working out a new vision and strategy for the implementation of appropriate reforms in the system of agricultural education. It is necessary to bring reforms in structures and state policies and be made favourable to the programme of social re-engineering of agricultural higher-education institutions.

The phenomenon of rising unemployment among agricultural graduates and postgraduates speaks of the poor quality of the present education system in agriculture and allied sciences. It also indicates the education system's inability to equip the manpower with knowledge and confidence to cater to today's requirements. The symptoms of unemployment can be seen in the rising number of Research Assistants and continuation of the agricultural graduates in temporary employment for more than five years. There is need to convert our agricultural education from the current "producer of unemployable graduates" to one that is "employment oriented".

The IAMR study (IAMR, 2001) is analyzed here to reflect on the employment scenario of agricultural graduates. The activity status of those who graduated in 1996 shows that employment rate increases with the increase in the level of education leading to a subsequent decline in the unemployment rate. Among the graduates, only 38 per cent of them were employed. In the case of PGs and doctorates, 57 per cent and 92 per cent respectively, were employed. The unemployment rate was high among graduates (43 per cent) and low among doctorates (5 per cent). Of the sample, only 78 (4.46 per cent) were self-employed, of which 58 were graduates and 20 post-graduates. Among the self employed, as many as 65 per cent were engaged in rural areas and the remaining 35 per cent in urban areas. The rate of absorption in terms of time taken for their absorption in first paid employment was highest among the doctorates followed by post-graduates and graduates. Only 24 per cent of the graduates were absorbed during the first year, whereas for the post-graduates and doctorates it was 50 and 84 per cent, respectively. By the third year of passing their examination, three fourth of the graduates could be absorbed, whereas, in the case of post-graduates about 90 per cent of them were employed and almost all the doctorates were employed.

Discipline-wise data show that at graduation level, the incidence of unemployment was highest in Agriculture, whereas Veterinary & Animal Science, Agricultural Engineering, and Dairying have emerged as the disciplines with good potential for employment. A majority of the post-graduates in subjects like Agricultural Economics, Agronomy/Tea Husbandry, Plant Breeding & Genetics, Soil Science and Water Management, Horticulture, Plant Pathology, etc. were absorbed in various jobs in the initial years of passing the examination. Also, in certain subjects such as Computer Applications, Agricultural Physics, Floriculture, which have low outturn, the applicants were employed soon after completing their PG programme.

A majority of the agricultural graduates (48 per cent) employed got employment by applying directly to the employing organizations whereas a few of them through Employment Exchange and Placement Office. Similarly, most of the post-graduates (45 per cent) and doctorates (54 per cent) secured employment by applying directly to the employing organizations. The Employment Exchanges and Placement Offices either appeared to have lost their relevance or were unable to provide efficient services to those seeking employment.

Majority of the graduates and post-graduates were employed in the State Government followed by the Private Sector, the Public Sector and the Central Government (Table 23.3). The sector-wise employment pattern of the doctorates differs from that of the graduates and post-graduates. It appears that the avenues for employment in the Central Government increases with the increase in education level. To illustrate, only five per cent of the graduates and 11 per cent of the post-graduates were employed in the Central Government departments/ministries while the percentage of doctorates was 19 per cent. Alternatively, with the increasing level of education, either the preference of the people to work in the Private Sector or avenues for employment in this sector falls significantly.

**Table 23.3: Existing Pattern of Employment of Agricultural Graduates and Post-graduates**

| *Sectors of Employment* | *Graduate* | *Post-graduate* | *Doctorate* | *Total* |
|---|---|---|---|---|
| 1. Central Government | 23<br>(4.91) | 28<br>(11.20) | 15<br>(18.52) | 66<br>(8.26) |
| 2. State Government | 188<br>(40.17) | 110<br>(44.00) | 29<br>(35.80) | 327<br>(40.92) |
| 3. Public Sector | 59<br>(12.61) | 29<br>(11.60) | 17<br>(20.99) | 105<br>(13.14) |
| 4. Private Sector | 130<br>(27.78) | 50<br>(20.00) | 4<br>(4.94) | 184<br>(23.03) |
| 5. Cooperatives | 29<br>(6.20) | 5<br>(2.00) | — | 34<br>(4.26) |
| 6. Others | 39<br>(8.33) | 28<br>(11.20) | 16<br>(19.75) | 83<br>(10.39) |
| **Total** | **468**<br>**(100)** | **250**<br>**(100)** | **81**<br>**(100)** | **799**<br>**(100)** |

*Note*: Figures in parentheses are percentages to the total.

The IAMR study also throws some light into the patterns of migration by education and employment. It is interesting to note that with the increase in the level of education, the inter-state migration increases significantly. For example, among the graduates, only 9 per cent of the students have come from other states whereas as many as 91 per cent belonged to the same state. A similar trend is observed in the case of post-graduates. However, the pattern of migration changes significantly in the case of doctorates, 53 per cent of them belonged to the same state and 47 per cent have moved in from other states for their education. With regard to migration for employment, a large majority of the respondents were employed in their native place. Sixty seven per cent of them were employed in their state of residence, whereas the remaining found employment in other states.

Finally, the issue of matching the demand with supply is also critical to the future development of education for agriculture. Way back in the mid 60s, the Education Commission laid emphasis on the importance of manpower projections by stating that "Steps should be taken for preparing more accurate estimates of the requirements of manpower in the agricultural development" and had put a rough indication of the requirements of agricultural manpower—double the output of graduates and an equal number of diploma holders—for the next ten years. In spite of this good start of the practice of manpower projection in agriculture, of late there has been indiscriminate enrolment in various undergraduate and postgraduate degree courses that led to overproduction of agricultural manpower. This subsequently resulted in unemployment. On the other hand, there is also underproduction of manpower and low enrollment in certain emerging disciplines, such as Agri-business Management, Biotechnology, Information Technology, etc. The demand for graduates trained in food sciences, nutrition, food processing and marketing is expected to increase. Commercial aspects of purchase, marketing, organization theory and management, business statistics and accounting should be offered as topics. Taking into account the future needs, courses in ecology, waste and wastewater analysis, environmental impact methods and analysis, renewable energy and non-conventional energy sources, biotechnology and IT in agriculture should be introduced.

While talking of surplus at the post graduation level, we also hear reports of shortage of teachers in agricultural universities and colleges. The IAMR study (2001) reveals that in eight out of the eighteen universities and 67 colleges surveyed reported shortage of teachers. Seven institutions reported shortage of teachers at the post-graduate level while 11 at the doctorate level. The main reasons attributed for this shortage are administrative delays (39 per cent), unattractive remuneration (33 per cent) and shortage of qualified staff (22 per cent).

The projection of the demand and supply of agricultural manpower for the year 2010 made by IAMR (2001), shows that the Service Sector has the highest demand for Agricultural and Allied Scientists followed by Agricultural and Allied, Mining and Quarrying Sector. The country will have a stock of about 3.8 lakh graduates and above in Agriculture and Allied Sciences by 2010. In the case of postgraduates and above and doctorates it would be 1.45 lakh and 19,000, respectively.

The data on matching of demand for and supply of post-graduates by disciplines during 2005 and 2010 as worked out by IAMR (2001) are presented in Table 23.4. The approaches applied to work out here the supply of agricultural manpower certainly have limitations but the results are indicative. There would be a surplus of 53,657 in 2005 and 55,657 in 2010 at the post-graduate level. The surplus assumes significance in the discipline of Agriculture where 65 per cent of the total surplus comes from this discipline. Significant surpluses to the tune of about 10 per cent were also observed in Home Science and Horticulture & Forestry.

An analysis of data of Agricultural Scientist Recruitment Board (ASRB) for the period from 1993-94 to 1997-98 indicates a high proportion of applicants to candidates who were finally selected. This is particularly true in the case of Agriculture, Horticulture and Home Sciences. It is comparatively low in Veterinary and Dairy Science. The total number of applicants for ARS examination increases from 2,305 in 1999-2000 to 18,796 in 2001-02. This figure touches 20,676 in 2003-04. It is observed that in four years the number of applicants has increased nine-fold. This is a clear indication of the fact that employment opportunities as scientist in ASRB are not growing substantially

**Table 23.4: Matching of Demand for and Supply of Post-graduates in Agriculture and Allied Sciences by Discipline in the Year 2005 and 2010**

| *Discipline* | *2005* | | | *2010* | | |
|---|---|---|---|---|---|---|
| | *Demand* | *Supply* | *Surplus* | *Demand* | *Supply* | *Surplus* |
| Agriculture | 41,116 | 76,841 | 35,725 | 58,733 | 95,238 | 36,505 (65.31%) |
| Horticulture and Forestry | 5,639 | 10,430 | 4,791 | 8,248 | 13,373 | 5,125 (9.16%) |
| Animal Science & Dairy | 3,819 | 7,094 | 3,275 | 5,547 | 8,995 | 3,448 (6.16%) |
| Veterinary Science | 3,420 | 6,394 | 2,974 | 4,905 | 7,953 | 3,048 (5.45%) |
| Fisheries | 885 | 1,719 | 834 | 1,196 | 1,939 | 743 (1.32%) |
| Home Science | 6,970 | 12,650 | 5,680 | 10,576 | 17,150 | 6,574 (11.76%) |
| Miscellaneous | 476 | 854 | 378 | 730 | 1,183 | 453 (0.81%) |
| Total | 62,325 | 1,15,982 | 53,657 | 89,935 | 1,45,831 | 55,896 (100 %) |

to be able to absorb the increasing outturn of post-graduates in agriculture and allied sciences. This ultimately affects both agricultural education and research.

In view of the new and emerging pattern of demand for qualified manpower there are also new proposals afloat to add some courses pertaining to quality control, feed formulation, artificial insemination, and animal/fish products technology in veterinary and fisheries sciences. In pharmaceutical sector, manufacturing veterinary medicines, the concepts of bio-equivalence and bioavailability of drugs; patents of veterinary drugs; and stress on veterinary microbiology, pharmacology and pharmaco-kinetics are also proposed to be included in the curriculum.

The IAMR study undertaken at the behest of ICAR also mentions the emerging occupations in Agriculture and Allied Sciences, which are listed below:

- Agriculture: Strategic Agriculture Extension Planning Expert; Data Analyst; Web Administrator; Pesticide Formulation Expert; Biochemist; Biotechnologist; Integrated Nutrition Management Expert; Quarantine Officer; Agricultural Meteorologist; Silkworm Breeding Farm Manager; Bio Control expert; Quality Control Officer; Plant Genetic Resource Officer; Bio farming Expert; Agricultural Economist.
- Horticulture: Floriculturist; Landscape Expert; Tissue Culture Expert; Micro propagation Expert; Post Harvest Technologist.

- Fisheries: Fish Process Technologist; Pollution/Quality Control Officer; Fish Microbiologist.
- Veterinary: Animal Breeder; Animal Feed & Nutrition Expert; Fodder Technologist.
- Animal Husbandry: Diagnostician; Animal Disease Surveillance Expert; Wild Life Conservation Expert; Embryo Transfer Technology Expert; Veterinary Surgeon; Veterinary Immunologist; Veterinary Epidemiologist; Veterinary Biochemist; Veterinary Biotechnologist.
- Dairy Technology: Dairy Microbiologist; Dairy Technologist; Quality Control Officer.
- Forestry: Agro-forestry Expert; Timber Processor.
- Home Science: Dietician; Community Welfare Officer; Parent Counselor.
- Agricultural Engineering: Irrigation Expert; Green House Expert; Systems Engineer; Packaging Technologist; Plasticulture Expert; Energy Management Expert; Software Professionals.
- Others: Environmental Manager; Remote Sensing Expert; Ecologist; Food Technologist; Sustainable Agricultural Expert; Value Addition Expert; IT Expert.

In order to make out the future demand of agricultural manpower there is a need to establish linkages of agricultural universities/institutions with the employing organizations such as Development Departments, R&D organizations, Government Departments of Agriculture, Animal Husbandry, Horticulture, Fisheries, Forestry, etc, Agro-Processing industry, Food Processing industry, Dairy industry and Veterinary Pharmaceutical industry, both in the Public and Private sectors. The absorption pattern of graduates in agriculture and allied sciences shows a shift from the government to the private sector as a major source of employment. This is due to the liberalization of the economy. There is then the need for grooming our future agricultural manpower according to the demand and requirement of all the parties and the emerging occupations. The academic requirements of agricultural graduates needed for the public and private sectors are different. Also, the present curriculum of agricultural education does not satisfy those requirements. Attention has also to be paid to the ecological, social and sustainable concerns and requirements.

## Curriculum Development and its Delivery System

In India, the Government has been the main employer of agricultural graduates and post graduates. Since the Government is not able to employ the same strength as before, the private sector is now the only hope of agricultural graduates. Therefore, employability is now a key concern for agricultural education. The process and aims of curriculum development are in transition.

The ICAR appointed the first Deans' Committee in 1965 with the aim of developing guidelines for curriculum of the first degree in Agriculture and for laying down the pattern of education to be adopted by Agricultural Universities. These guidelines served as the basis for the educational programmes development in SAUs for a decade. The suggestions made by the second Deans' Committee were submitted in 1981 and were examined by each of the SAUs and discussed in a workshop at the National Academy of Agricultural Research Management (NAARM) in 1985, where periodical review once in every ten years by the Dean's Committee was suggested. The third Deans' Committee on Agricultural Education revised the curriculum adopted by the agricultural universities during 1995 keeping in view the employment opportunities at that point of time (ICAR, 1995). The Committee recommended bringing uniformity among the Agricultural Universities, keeping regional requirements in view and to allow inter-state mobility, avoid inbreeding, improving quality of education and turn out quality graduates for facing challenges in sustaining Green Revolution and bring about White, Blue and Yellow Revolutions in coming years. Analysis of this representative syllabus suggests that about 80 per cent of the total credits are devoted to imparting technical (subject-specific) skills whereas about 20 per cent are marked for developing soft skill (Ramarao *et al.*, 2004).

The Review Committee of Agricultural Universities, in 1978, recognized practical training as an important component of the curriculum. It recommended introduction of crop production programme for agricultural graduates and similar programmes for graduates of other faculties on a compulsory basis from the academic session 1978-79 for at least final year students in two crop seasons. It suggested that the other agricultural universities should adopt, with suitable modifications, the pattern of practical training followed for agricultural graduates at the GB Pant University of Agriculture and Technology and the Punjab Agriculture University. The ICAR should contribute initial capital required for setting up of a revolving fund from which advance can be given to students for operation of the crop production courses and "Earn-while-you-learn" schemes. Also, it recommended review of the existing curricula so that field practical training constitutes about one third of the entire course load in addition to laboratory practicals. Practical assignments should be given to solve specific field problems.

The practical component in the syllabus and periodic revision of curriculum has assumed importance as it was in the agenda of many review committees. The Review Committee of Agricultural Universities (ICAR, 1978) recommended that the ICAR should assist agricultural university to develop curricula for "self-employment" elective programme with emphasis on managerial, financial and practical aspects. The ICAR should pay greater attention towards schemes for improvement in the quality of education, periodic revision of courses and curricula and production of textbooks and teaching materials. The Task Group on Revamping and Refocusing National Agricultural Research (GOI, 2005) suggested adding more courses on post-harvest handling, processing and value addition. The National Academy of Agricultural Sciences (NAAS 2005) also suggests periodic review and revision of curriculum consistent with national and global scenario, market trends, self-employment avenues and requirements of the industry. In 2006, the fourth Dean's Committee (ICAR, 2006) advocated the restructuring of UG programmes for increased practical and practice contents and the inclusion of courses on entrepreneurship development, agri-business, biotechnology and environmental science in all disciplines. It came out with several other recommendations to effect major changes in course curriculum and syllabus. This major revision in course curriculum would necessitate investment in infrastructure, faculty training and procurement of state-of-the-art equipments. The recommendations are summarized as follows:

- Three-year (6 semesters) course work and one-year (2 semesters) Rural Agricultural Work Experience (RAWE) Programme including hands on training and electives in inter-disciplinary courses.
- Existing courses strengthened by adding relevant latest information in each discipline.
- Introduces new courses like Introductory Agriculture, Renewable Energy, Project Development appraisal and monitoring and Entrepreneurship Development under various disciplines.
- Electives in eight areas of specialization identified to impart practical skills to the students.
- The minimum course load prescribed for each of the six semesters is twenty credits; a student has to register twenty credits with the major load in one area of electives and the rest is split among one or two areas of electives either in seventh or eighth semester.
- RAWEP can be implemented either in seventh or eighth semester as per convenience.
- The Universities have the flexibility of changing the courses and their contents to an extent of 30 per cent to 40 per cent.

The Education Commission (1964-66) suggested exploring the possibilities of providing one-year internship on a well-managed State university demonstration farm before awarding the degree to the students. This suggestion started to see light when Agricultural University Review Committee in 1978 came out with the recommendation that it would be necessary to introduce internship for degree for UG courses in veterinary sciences. It however, observed the impracticability of implementing internship for the graduates in other streams and recommended that for Agriculture,

Home Science, Horticulture, Fisheries and Agricultural Engineering integrated practical training should be built into the course programme. The UG Programme of the ICAR now requires one semester or equivalent period to be spent by each student to gain work experience in rural areas, field, factory or other works related to his field of study as part of the graduate programme. Internship is now required for veterinary UG students to complete their course in B.V.Sc. The Fourth Deans Committee suggested two years of professional programme with one year of industrial attachment in Home Science discipline.

Several committees have recommended, for example, that strengthening of entrepreneurship component in the syllabus and course content could lead to more graduates taking up self-employment in agriculture and allied occupations. A study undertaken by the National Institute of Agricultural Extension Management (MANAGE) Hyderabad, observes that there were few takers for the agri-business and agri-clinic scheme. Out of 18,885 applicants, only 3,762 (19.90 per cent) turned out for training and just 676 set up agri-business ventures. A success rate of 18 per cent is observed for this self-employment programme (MANAGE). This study also made its recommendations to the authorities to ensure that "Our graduates should be made 'job providers' rather than leaving them as 'job seekers'. Stress should be given to incorporate the component of market relevance in the curricula so as to produce knowledgeable and skilful professionals".

The latest Deans' Committee has also stressed on its inclusion in the syllabus. It recommends 1-2 years of experiential learning in the new curriculum wherein emphasis has been laid on developing skills for career in agri-business and agri-clinic with the aim of competence development in all aspects of enterprise management. But the fact of the matter is that lack of education in entrepreneurship is one of the relevant factors where the education system can provide a remedy by including the component in the syllabus and courses. Equally important is the fact that the bridging organizations are ignored and they are being left to fend for themselves in the field. System designs favouring local production of the knowledge—intensive agri-inputs and services would have to be experimented with to create business models for the success of small business entities. The system of SAUs is certainly not geared up for such an approach. Though it is another matter that the 1978 report of the Review Committee on Agricultural Universities too had identified the requirement of supporting the consulting activity through the SAUs in the form of a recommendation on the task of incubation of business through consulting, but even after thirty years the system is considered to be not yet ready for the task.

Similarly, the delivery system of knowledge to students too needs change. The Review Committee of Agricultural Universities 1978 recommended that the ICAR should organize regional summer institutes on teaching methods and techniques. We should adopt the strategy of effecting change in the format from teaching to learning and from passive delivery of lectures to active work on projects, interactive, case-study-based learning through multi-media tools and multi-faculty teaching instructions (Katyal, 2005).

## Evaluation and Grading

Pressures and tensions are also evident in the sphere of evaluation and grading. The Review Committee (1978) recommended that at the end of each academic year, instructors of courses should meet to review aspects like contents, evaluation, grading, etc. Also analytical studies in respect of grading and examination pattern should be undertaken. The Second Deans' Committee noted that the internal evaluation by the teacher, who has taught the course, has led to incomplete coverage of courses. It suggested to the universities that a teacher other than the one who taught the course should set the final examination paper. The Third Deans' Committee recommended external evaluation in all degree programmes to the extent of at least 40 percent. The Fourth Deans Committee 2006 still notices wide variation in examination and evaluation system among the SAUs and suggested examination reforms at the UG and PG levels.

## Determination and Maintenance of Standard and Quality

Accreditation is a process of assuring an acceptable institutional quality. It is a tool for improving educational standards and for improving transferability and marketability of students nationally and internationally. The ICAR has been promoting the quality of agricultural education in the country through Education Panel (1952), Standing Committee on Agricultural Education (1965) and Norms and Accreditation Committee (1974). The Norms and Accreditation Committee has very little role in determining the norms and accreditation of SAUs and periodically assessing their performance, as ICAR is not a statutory body like the UGC. The ICAR Review Committee (ICAR, 1988) then suggested for a reconstitution of the Norms and Accreditation Committee with suitable authority. The Committee observed that since agricultural education is a state subject and the universities are 'autonomous' institutions, new colleges are opened and educational programmes started without adequate facilities and trained manpower. These institutions later sought the ICAR's financial support deviating from the priority set during the beginning of each Plan period.

The All India Council of Technical Education (AICTE) and the Veterinary Council of India (VCI) regulate technical education including agricultural engineering and veterinary education, respectively. Actually, there was no statutory body to regulate education in agriculture, forestry, horticulture, dairy science, fisheries and home science. In 1996, an Accreditation Board—a new process of accreditation that is comprehensive, rigorous & periodic, and aimed at improving the quality and relevance of higher agricultural education—was established.

Accreditation in agricultural education is voluntary in nature and not mandatory as in the case of the AICTE, MCI and VCI. The ICAR at the most can withhold developmental assistance to those universities that do not comply with its instructions. This assistance in any case is only around 15 per cent on an average (Sulaiman, 1996). Till August 24, 2004, twelve SAUs (with a total of their 79 constituent colleges) and two Deemed Universities that provided agricultural education were given accreditation by the Accreditation Board of the ICAR. It remains to be seen how far the Board performs its role, as it does not have the statutory powers to enforce the standards. The Fourth Deans' Committee in 2006 recommended that the norms and standards of departments, faculty positions and minimum infrastructure for different faculties at UG level be developed.

## Faculty Improvement and Intellectual Inbreeding

Problems relating to teaching personnel are manifold. There could be heavy workload for teachers due to shortage of qualified teachers, recruitment of poor/unqualified faculty, lack of opportunities for teachers' refresher courses, seminars and conferences, teachers' inability to update their knowledge in current trends and opportunities in world agriculture as a result of globalization. It is reported that only 87, 76 and 79 per cent respectively of faculty positions at the Assistant Professor, Associate Professor and Professor levels were filled up (Katyar, 2003). Shortage of faculty to this magnitude has led to overloading of the teachers with routine teaching work. Since investment in building faculty competence is a good investment for the future of agricultural education, developing an HRD policy to ensure training and retraining of teaching faculty becomes indispensable.

Simultaneously, a system of evaluation of teachers needs to be developed to ensure teacher's academic accountability. There is need to quantify the output of individual teacher, college or university. Teaching aids used and teaching methodologies employed may be given weightage. Preparation of referral reading material and books, bulletins and practical manuals and efforts made in improvising course contents and revision of syllabi are also important criteria. At the post-graduate/doctoral levels, the quality of theses evaluated in terms of papers published, technologies developed and awards/recognitions received can be another set of criteria. Feedback from the students on the performance of teachers is also essential for ensuring teachers' academic accountability. Assessment of teachers by students has been started in some universities like the CCS Haryana Agricultural University. To ensure that qualified faculty is employed, National Eligibility Test (NET) is continued to be made mandatory requirement for initial recruitment at the Assistant Professor or equivalent level.

The Review Committee on Agricultural Universities had suggested that the Central Staff College for Agriculture should be quickly developed to provide training courses for the staff of agricultural universities, particularly in project planning and preparation, institutional management, monitoring and evaluation. The scientists of the National Academy of Agricultural Science also recommended in 2005, the setting up of Teachers Training Institute in agriculture at the national level to impart specialized courses in teaching skills. The Fourth Deans' Committee made it mandatory to give training of 20 per cent faculty nationally and four per cent internationally each year in the best institutes.

In 1978, the Review Committee on Agricultural Universities recommended that at least one centre of excellence in each of the major disciplines should be set up in selected agricultural universities during the next two plan periods. During the Eighth Plan, 36 Centres of Advanced Studies (CASs) (Table 23.5) were established in different State Agricultural Universities and Deemed Universities (DUs) with the objective of strengthening the faculty development and to undertake research in frontier and strategic areas and impart advanced training to the faculty members from SAUs and other institutions. The CASs will now be charged with development of textbooks in each of the areas so as to develop the much needed instructional material. The Quinquennial Review Team (QRT) under the chairmanship of Dr. M.V. Rao reviewed the CAS scheme for the period 1995-1999 and suggested several new areas for CAS, which include Environmental Pollution and Pesticide Residues, Post Harvest Technology and Product Development for Agriculture, Horticulture, Animal, and Fisheries products, Medicinal and Aromatic Plants, Feed Technology for Cattle, Poultry and Fish, Wildlife Management, Fish Pathology, Fish microbiology, Tea, Taxonomy of plants, animals, insects, micro-organism, International agriculture, trade and marketing (ICAR Annual Report 2001-02).

In 2005, the Task Group on Revamping and Refocusing National Agricultural Research even went to the extent of recommending specialized sub-sections within departments to promote super specialization.

To avoid intellectual inbreeding among scientists, the ICAR Review Committee Report 1988 recommended that both the ICAR and SAUs should encourage students and teachers to obtain at least one of the degrees from the SAUs other than those from which the candidates had obtained UG or PG degrees, and these Universities should reserve 25 per cent of seats in PG degree programmes for candidates from outside the State. The inbreeding as a result of State policies for recruiting staff basically form the region and product of the university has resulted in having less competent faculty and

**Table 23.5: Centres of Advanced Studies in Agriculture Established during Eighth Plan**

| *Name of Universities* | *Centres of Advanced Studies* |
|---|---|
| Andhra Pradesh Agricultural University, Hyderabad | Home Science (F&N) |
| Central Institute of Fisheries Education, Bombay | Fisheries |
| CSUAT, Mathura | Veterinary Pharmacology |
| GB Pant University of Agriculture and Technology, Pantnagar | (i) Agronomy<br>(ii) Plant Pathology |
| Haryana Agricultural University, Hisar | Veterinary Microbiology<br>Entomology |
| Indian Agricultural Research Institute, New Delhi | (i) Agricultural Extension<br>(ii) Agricultural Economics<br>(iii) Biochemistry<br>(iv) Plant Biotechnology<br>(v) Plant Pathology |
| Indian Agricultural Statistical Research Institute, New Delhi | Agricultural Statistics & Computer Application |
| Indian Veterinary Research Institute, Izatnagar | (i) Animal Biotechnology<br>(ii) Animal Physiology<br>(iii) Animal Nutrition |
| Jawaharlal Nehru Krishi Vishwa Vidyalaya, Jabalpur | Soil Science |
| Kerala Agricultural University, Thissur | Veterinary Pathology |
| Mahatma Phule Krishi Vidyapeeth, College of Agriculture, Pune | Agricultural Meteorology |
| Mahatma Phule Krishi Vidyapeeth, Rahuri | Horticulture (Fruits) |
| National Dairy Research Institute, Karnal | (i) Animal Genetics & Breeding<br>(ii) Dairy Technology |
| Narendra Dev University of Agriculture and Technology, Faizabad | Plant Physiology |
| Punjab Agricultural University, Ludhiana | (i) Farm Machinery & Power<br>(ii) Genetics and Plant Breeding<br>(iii) Soil Science<br>(iv) Veterinary Gynaecology & Rep.<br>(v) Veterinary Surgery and Radiology |
| Tamil Nadu Agricultural University, Coimbatore | (i) Agronomy<br>(ii) Entomology<br>(iii) Genetics & Plant Breeding<br>(iv) Microbiology |
| Tamil Nadu Veterinary & Animal Sciences University | (i) Clinical Medicine & Therapeutics<br>(ii) Poultry Science |
| University of Agricultural Sciences, Bangalore | Veterinary Parasitology |
| Dr. Yashwant Singh Parmar University of Horticulture and Forestry, Solan | Horticulture (Veg.) |

absence of introduction of expertise in new areas of science. Such policies have deprived the universities of the opportunities for cross hybridization of ideas required for the growth and academic improvement of the universities. Nevertheless, the situation has not improved. The Fourth Deans' Committee (ICAR, 2006) suggested that recruitment of 15 per cent of the posts at entry level to be made mandatory on the basis of open national selection from outside the state to reduce inbreeding.

It is proposed that besides agricultural universities, other universities can also play a role in imparting agricultural education. This has been recognized by the Education Commission when it clearly spelt out the possibilities in three ways, viz., (i) other universities wishing to introduce agricultural studies should be given all assistance; (ii) an academic relationship between some of the agricultural universities and the IITs should be developed. This can take the form, among other things, of an exchange of students and staff, and arranging common programmes of study and research and (iii) the possibility of organizing agricultural faculties in one or two of the IITs and in some leading universities should be explored. So far as fostering academic relationship between agricultural universities and the IITs is concerned not much headway has been made. However, significant progress has been made with regard to introducing agricultural studies and faculties in general universities and IITs as is evident from the following account.

In IIT-Kharagpur, the following programmes are being offered in the Department of Agricultural and Food Engineering: B.Tech.(H) in Agriculture and Food Engineering and Water Resources Development and Management; MS (Agricultural & Food Engg.), M.Tech. in Farm Machinery and Power, Soil and Water conservation Engineering, Dairy and Food Engineering, Applied Botany, Water Resources Development and Management, Aquacultural Engineering, Agricultural Systems and Management, Post Harvest Engineering and Ph.D. in Agricultural & Food Engineering. The IIT-Delhi offers courses in general microbiology, hydrology and water resource management. The Centre for Technology Alternatives for Rural Areas of the IIT-Mumbai offers short term courses in farm machinery, food processing and water management. The IIT-Roorkee offers PG Diploma, M.Tech and Ph.D. programmes in Hydrology and Water Resources Development and Management.

Some of the general universities also have centres, faculties or institutes offering UG, PG and Ph.D. programmes in agriculture and its allied subjects. M.Sc.(Agri) is offered at the Aligarh Muslim University, Banaras Hindu University, Annamalai University, Dr. Bhim Rao Ambedkar University, Guru Nanak Dev University, Mahatma Gandhi Gramoday Vishwavidyalay, Nagaland University, University of Allahabad, University of Calcutta and Visva-Bharati. The universities such as Andhra University, Goa University, Marathwada

University and Osmania University offer B.Fish.Sc and M.Fish.Sc. Annamalai University offers M.Sc. (Agril. Engg.) and University of Allahabad offers both M.Sc. (Agril. Engg.) and M.Sc. (Dairy Technology).

### Tenth Five Year Plan and its Response to Contemporary Concerns

Perhaps for the first time during the Tenth Five Year Plan the policymakers came to officially recognize some of the concerns being now openly expressed regarding the challenges facing the system of Agricultural Universities in India. The Tenth Five Year Plan document is the last official comprehensive statement available on the status of SAUs, the concerns and challenges of which are summarized below:

*Lack of Adequate Financial Resources*: The SAUs are charged with complete integration of research, teaching and extension, for the holistic societal development. Most of the SAUs have not been able to achieve integration of these functions due to the limited resources.

*Lack of Support to Colleges*: The opening of new campus colleges without adequate financial resources or faculty has adversely affected the quality of HRD programme.

*Opening of New SAUs*: The original concept was to have one agriculture university in each State, but several States have more than one SAU resulting in thin distribution of the limited resources. Some States have also opened 'discipline' based universities. This too is against the concept of SAUs.

*Extensive Inbreeding*: Inbreeding as a result of State policies for recruiting staff basically form the region and product of the same university has resulted in having less competent faculty and absence of introduction of expertise in new areas of science. Such policies have deprived the universities of the opportunities for cross hybridization of ideas required for the growth and academic improvement of the universities.

*Poor Infrastructure*: Most of the SAUs have poor infrastructure, out-dated equipment, poor lecture halls, poor libraries and amenities required for frontline educational institutions, as funds are not available for maintaining and upgrading the infrastructure.

*Faculty Competence*: This is one area which has been neglected. Most of the institutions have no career development plans. The kind of opportunity for training of faculty, which existed during the early part of their establishment, is no more available. Faculty competence is critical since faculty is the key resource for academic excellence. Unless the faculty keeps abreast with the new developments, it is hardly possible to impart the necessary skills to the students.

*Neglect of the Holistic Societal Developments*: The SAUs at the time of their establishment were considered as the engine for societal development particularly in rural areas. This role, however, has been neglected.

*Neglect of Basic Sciences*: Development of basic science is the backbone of applied sciences. The SAUs, by and large, have ignored this concept.

The above mentioned description makes it fairly clear that the existing system of education and research is once again in need of thorough revamping. In the sixties, when the Kothari Commission discussed the quality of agricultural education in the existing agricultural colleges, the premise of the Commission was that "the existing system of education in agricultural colleges is largely unrelated to life and there is a wide gulf between its content and purposes and the concerns of national development"[21]. The challenge is no different; as already suggested it is even more complex.

## Revamping of Infrastructure and Increase in Investments

The ICAR assists the SAUs by way of development grants, coordinated projects, ad hoc projects from the cess funds and assistance to KVKs, etc. The State governments contribute the maximum share to the funds made available for the SAUs. However, today several universities are incurring huge deficits due to the State Government's inability to provide enough funds and also the universities are not able to generate their own resources. This financial crunch has adversely affected the universities in terms of development of laboratories, acquisition of books, journals and teaching aids and the availability of funds for travel to attend seminars, workshops, trainings, etc., within and outside the country. So the Fourth Deans' Committee in 2006 strongly recommended increase in developmental assistance by the ICAR to SAUs and Deemed Universities (DUs) to the extent of 20 per cent of its budget. Earlier, the ICAR had increased support from 8.9 per cent in the Eighth Plan to about 14 per cent in the Tenth Plan to SAUs and DUs. There are also suggestions to allocate a clear proportion of funds for agricultural education, research and extension education.

Implementation of the Agricultural Human Resources Development (AHRD) Project with World Bank Credit assistance to help India modernize its agriculture sector through improved agricultural education system was completed on December 31, 2001. This project was initiated in 1995. Besides the ICAR, the States of Andhra Pradesh, Haryana and Tamil Nadu implemented it in their development departments and the SAUs. The AHRD Project covers only four universities i.e., the CCS Haryana Agricultural University, Hissar; Tamil Nadu Agricultural University, Coimbatore; Acharya N.G. Ranga Agricultural University, Hyderabad; and, the Tamil Nadu Veterinary & Animal Sciences University, Chennai. However, it is a matter of great satisfaction that the educational reforms under the project have spread to non-AHRD Project participating SAUs also. The major initiatives taken under the AHRD project by the ICAR include establishment of the Accreditation Board and new accreditation procedure for quality assurance in education, reducing inbreeding through All-India Competitive Entrance Examination for admission to SAUs, uniformity in UG and PG regulations, major revision of course curriculum at UG and PG levels, introduction of sabbatical leave, development of instructional material, faculty training for improving competence as a teacher, infrastructure development, modernization of laboratories and lecture halls, library strengthening and access to information through internet and delegations, women technological empowerment and bringing global competitiveness. In the project participating States initiatives put in place by the Development Departments included trainers training, establishment of Human Resource Management and Human Resource Development cells, establishment of Manpower Advisory Council, infrastructure development for training and transfer of technology to end users (ICAR Annual Report, 2001-02).

## A framework for Development of an Alternate Future Vision and Strategy

It is also clear that the State Agricultural Universities (SAUs) have to resolve far more complex problems—of natural resources management, policies and institutions concerning the incentives and performance evaluation, organization and management, and control and regulation of teaching, research and extension. Policies for the development of agriculture and rural economy will have to be conducive to the cultivation of a system of education for agriculture, which will value and allow and encourage the agricultural universities to create a new ideology of research, expertise and service. It is important that the strategy of agricultural transformation plays itself a complementary role and provides synergy to the changes to be brought about in the system of education for agriculture and rural development.

Although as early as 1970, the National Commission on Agriculture was of the view that more attention be devoted to fundamental research, that only one SAU be established in each state, and that better linkages be established between research and agricultural extension for dry land regions and to the benefit of farmers who are not well endowed. But the system of agricultural universities could not respond to these priorities positively due to the policies and institutions being not favourable to the proposals. There was a mismatch between the priorities of those who were directing and managing the SAUs and all those who administer these institutions. Synergy was missing from the framework of coordination set up for the purpose of finding solutions to the problems of either small farmers or dry land regions.

For example, in 1977-78, the ICAR undertook an internal review of the SAUs (ICAR, 1978). Its report recommended that all research facilities be transferred from the state governments to the SAUs; that the functions of teaching, research, and extension be better integrated; that each state has only one agricultural university; that high standards should be maintained in the appointment of vice-chancellors; and that new programs be established only when the requisite faculty and facilities were in place. The same ICAR report urged that practical training programs be instituted for all undergraduates that more emphasis be given to training for self-employment, that home science be made more rural in its orientation, and that the committees make faculty selection with larger number of outside experts. However, there was very little action on these proposals.

Even while recognizing that technical education is practiced differently as compared to general education in higher education institutions, it needed to be certainly farsighted and pluralistic in its approach to knowledge for problem solving. It is true that the system of technical education all over the world is oriented to problem solving. Even in India the system of agricultural higher education that the Kothari Commission endorsed was far less flexible and far more centralized. What the Kothari Commission endorsed was not pluralistic and knowledge production wise autonomous; it was completely oblivious of diversity in agriculture. It was not at all appropriately modern and updated in its approach. Although it created modern facilities for agricultural science in India, the system constrained and restricted research and generating appropriate technology.

Implicit in the story of agricultural universities, as it appears to have unfolded during the last four decades, is the fact that the system of agricultural education is being closely tied to the US universities and also largely limited to the adoption of a system of specific technology and institutions. The system has been built in such a way that in these organizations changes could only occur from the top down, not from bottom up, and persons with a measure of official authority or sanction must guide them.

It is also clear that the other critical factor was the balance of forces engaged in promoting and resisting the strategy of implementation of the proposed programme of agricultural education, research and extension during these four decades. In the initial period, as shown, the strategy of programme implementation was deeply embedded in the web of well cultivated linkages of integration with the forces promoting the change to a system of agriculture dependent on HYVs and inputs produced outside the system of local economy. Further, the Government of India was already in the process of implementation of the programme of establishment of agricultural universities. It was also in the creation of a system of input and output markets for the extension of the same specific technology, particularly with the assistance being provided by the US Agency for International Development (USAID) and the international agri-business supplying the technology for the production of relevant inputs. All these forces were integral to the social engineering for building new institutions for agricultural higher education.

Thus, against the above background, it is proposed that the change must come about through a new framework of coordination of both, technology as well as rural production. Although the state has to continue in this role as a short-term strategy with support to the farmers reeling under the current crisis and faced with the problem of food security, it is not possible for the Indian state to keep the system of agriculture as a prisoner of the specific technology and production system, which is becoming too costly for it to sustain. In the long run, the nation must switch to a sustainable system of agriculture. What that system would be is becoming clear now; it will have to be a system of chemical pesticide free or independent green agriculture in some regions and organic agriculture in other regions.

Unlike the Kothari Commission that ended up endorsing a centralized system of education, research and extension, the new system of education for agriculture would need to be flexible and pluralistic. It would have to be integrated and embedded in a system of sustainable development of rural areas. Its approach to produce location specific technologies would be systemic in character. It would have to rely far more on natural and social sciences that care for ecological and social justice.

However, it is also quite clear that the forces favouring a pluralistic, flexible and more rooted in rural economy are even now in contest with the forces favouring further integration with the emerging international agricultural regime. By signing the Indo-US Knowledge Initiative for Agriculture, the government has made it clear that the forces favouring further integration with the agri-business are still very powerful. It is also a fact that more strength will have to be gathered by the forces favouring sustainable development of agriculture and rural industries and services as a part of the process of developing the local economy as a system in itself without breaking its connections with the national and international Science and Technology (S & T) system. In fact, some of the latest recommendations of the Planning Commission make it clear that the system planners are going through a process of internal struggle and many are interested to transform the system of SAUs in the country as per the national requirements.

In such a situation of contest; our proposals are aimed at an institutional reform, which would give space to the forces interested to follow an agricultural strategy that would promote agricultural production make use of the local resources and enhance productivity without compromising sustainability. Technology systems for non-pesticide management compatible with green agriculture, low external input system of agriculture, biological agriculture, organic agriculture and other such systems would have to be integrated through the cultivation and promotion of an alternate set of forces through the development of an alternate policy for rural industrialization in which the development of local economies as a system is itself valued. Even the National

Commission on Farmers reflects today the emerging issues to a large extent; the question is how we are going to strengthen the relevant forces in favour of an alternate strategy of sustainable development of rural economy and agriculture in the midst of changes taking place in the national and global economy.

In the Radhakrishnan Commission (UEC) 1948-49, the educationists had thought about a system of rural universities where a similar vision guided them in respect of agriculture and rural industrialization. This vision valued local artisan, peasant and agricultural labourer in a manner that comes quite close to the directions that the system of education as a whole has to take. The system favoured a strategy of using the advances of science to create such technology systems, which were to upgrade the village industries and agriculture as a system in itself. It means that the system would have allowed the nation to cultivate and promote an alternate set of forces in which the rural universities and professions to be created were to combine their energy with the farmers, artisans and agricultural labourers. It favoured not only the establishment of the courses for agriculture in secondary schools but also the integration of these schools with the rural universities for both research work and supply of motivated students for graduate and post graduate education.

But the forces working in favour of the model of rural universities were not very strong is also clear from the experience of rural institutes set up by the Gandhian forces in the country through the Ministry of Human Resource Development. The 150th Report of the Parliamentary Standing Committee on Human Resource Development (August 2004) states that the National Council of Rural Institutes has not become functional ever since it was established in 1995. It is clear that what we have today in the form of rural institutes is by no means the alternative to the existing system. It can play a complementary role. The nation has not been supportive of the existing system of agricultural schools and polytechnics. This needs to be integrated by the system planners into a new framework of coordination of technology and production for the development of local economies as a system in itself.

Linking of SAUs with several research and educational organizations will yield rich dividends in terms of faculty exchange and utilization of facilities. The linkage between traditional universities and SAUs could be fostered in area of fundamental research. Even within the agriculture sector, mobility within and between NARs/SAUs/DUs and networking of ICAR/SAUs should be encouraged. The exchange of students and faculty with foreign institutes and outsourcing of faculty and networking among SAUs and national institutes could be tried out. Given the fact that the Government has limitations in carrying out extension activities, the small-scale units manned by agricultural graduates/post-graduates, who will have back up from and access to the agricultural universities and KVKs, need to be given a bigger role in agriculture extension policies/activities being planned/implemented by the State and Central Governments.

Linking SAUs with agro-industries to optimize resource utilization, and proper harnessing of technologies generated in the SAUs is another measure. The Fourth Deans Committee 2006 made it mandatory for each SAU to have linkage with at least one ICAR institute for formal research guidance and vice versa. It suggested that development grant should be linked with adoption of this reform.

As discussed in Part I of the article, a lot is required to be done to improve the management of the system of agricultural education in respect of academic, administrative and financial autonomy. It is undeniable that the Indian system of agricultural universities has not been able to strike a balance between autonomy and accountability. It is a recognised fact that the system could not grant space to those practitioners who were required to be supported by the institutions for the exploration of technological alternatives and scientific knowledge needed for the management of diverse agro-ecological regions. Even the Fourth Deans' Committee has primarily focussed on the determination of infrastructure and manpower and maintained silence on all the other aspects. It is clear that the concerns discussed in Part I are yet to enter into the process of accreditation and evaluation. Similarly, when the leadership recommends that the quality of individual institutions be critically assessed, and the accreditation system be made more stringent to enforce accountability (NAAS, 2005), the issue is what kind of message does the scientific community conveys on the concept of quality and relevance in terms of the challenges remains an open question. In our view, this issue still needs an appropriate resolution. Diversity, self-reflection, critical inquiry, commitment to the "who-whom" of research and extension would have to be valued in the processes of generation of autonomy and enforcement of accountability.

## Conclusion

To rework the vision of the existing system as a whole in line with the framework outlined, the system planners should be asked to take the bold step of involving the forces that are active within the peasantry, agricultural labourers, and artisans to organize them for a restructured innovation system to create a matrix of forces interested in the social engineering, favouring sustainable development of rural economy and agriculture. There is no alternative to strengthening of the forces and organizing them for the establishment of networks for a new system of agricultural education tied to the vision of transformation of national agriculture on the lines suggested above. Needless to state that the forces favouring the agri-business approach are stronger and far more organized and would have to be resisted through the establishment of a system of pluralistic and flexible institutions to allow the forces of resistance to gather far more strength at the earliest in respect of knowledge production for an alternate system of agriculture and rural economy.

## Notes

1. When in 1959 an Agricultural Production Team was created, which reviewed the institutions concerning agricultural administration, it had already urged to the planners that the food problem be made a top priority.
2. Even Late Prof. S.K. Sinha, Former Director Indian Agricultural Research Institute, who dared to call spade a spade, found himself in a minority in the Working Group formulated for the Tenth Five Year Plan. The Tenth Plan Working Group produced a fairly accurate picture of the state of Indian Agricultural Universities, which we elaborate later in this article, failed to do justice to the creation of a new vision and strategy about which he had himself written so eloquently in the year 2001 in Current Science. Prof. M.S. Swaminathan, who too now admits the problems plaguing the system openly, has not been able to get all the stakeholders to agree to undertake the necessary reforms to tackle the emerging problems of the system of agricultural education-research-extension. He has not been able to prevent the Government of India and the Indian Council of Agricultural Research (ICAR) leadership from entering into the Indo-US Knowledge Initiative for Agriculture, which purports to take the system in the directions of agribusiness corporations controlling the system from behind.
3. The characteristic features of this crisis are far more severe than what India faced in 1964-66, and are manifest in the resultant involuntary displacement of large masses of labour force out of the rural, agricultural hinterland, and the near absence of alternative means of survival with dignity for more than half of the rural population. Widespread phenomenon of farmers' suicides constitutes a cruel testimony to this state of affairs. The impact on the dependent landless people is equally severe. The exodus to urban centres in search of employment has accentuated, resulting in ever-increasing outgrowth of slums around all urban centres. The lack of employment opportunities and income have resulted in an unprecedented reduction in the per capita availability of food-grains for the rural poor, pushing as large as three quarters of the rural population below " the poverty line". The Indian peasantry as a whole is adversely affected by the crisis; the situation is explosive and threatens to destabilize the social and political fabric. The struggles for occupying available land and for securing a living wage for landless labour have become more intense and violent.
4. See the Tenth Plan recommendations on agricultural education, which we also review later in this paper. The Eleventh Plan is in the making; this is an appropriate time to revisit the Kothari Commission.
5. Over the longer term, most analysts believe production increases will be hard pressed to keep pace with even modest growth in demand, and they suggest that the challenge of development of improved production technologies is a formidable one. South Asia's rice-wheat cropping systems, which cover 12 million hectares, are concentrated on the Indo-Gangetic and Brahmaputra floodplains and the foothills of Himalayas. About 32 per cent of total rice area and 42 per cent of wheat area in the region comes under rice-wheat cropping

systems, which can also include legumes, oilseeds, fodder crops, vegetables, sugarcane. Crop production is often linked to livestock production (Hobbs and Morris, 1996).

6. Puddling of rice soils leads to the breakdown of soil aggregates, resulting in reduced pore sizes and the formation in some soils of a plow pan. Puddling restricts water movement and affects soil reactions that are favourable for rice but unfavourable for wheat. Puddling may be one of the major causes, linked to it is the problem of poor rooting. Poor rooting of wheat following rice (because of poor soil structure, water logging and root-restricting soil layers) may be a major cause of declining productivity in wheat. Soil biological actors are relatively less researched. Cassman and Pingali (1995) hypothesize that the main cause of declining rice yields has been a reduction in the soil's natural ability to provide nitrogen, which they attribute to interactions between organic matter and soil microbes.
7. Concern over water availability has mounted especially fast in Northwestern India. During the past decade, water tables have dropped at a rate of 0.5-0.8 m per year in the state of Haryana and at a rate of 0.2-1.0 m per year in the neighbouring state of Punjab. Declining water tables not only raise production costs, but such rapid rates of decline raise serious questions about the long-term sustainability of rice-wheat systems. In some areas, farmers are already being forced to cut back on the number of irrigations, and where water shortages are acute, they are sometimes forced to limit plantings. Poor water management practices are leading to the aggravation of the problems related to soil salinity and sodicity, which in turn are affecting soil productivity.
8. *Phalaris minor*, a grassy weed which poses problems on wheat, is a major problem of the rice-wheat cropping systems. If left unchecked, this can cause crop losses in wheat of nearly 100 per cent. Reports are that this weed is developing resistance to isoproturon, the most extensively used herbicide in India. The rice-wheat system has expanded the host environment for many insects. The result is the appearance of overlapping generations of insects. Leaf diseases in rice and karnal bunt and foliar blights in wheat are arising. Lack of varietal diversification is a serious problem.
9. Management decisions taken to increase the productivity of one crop have negative consequences for the productivity of other crop in the rotation. Reduced tillage considered to be a solution for fertilizer uptake efficiency and yield increase in wheat creates new problems; stem borer carryover in unploughed rice stubble.
10. For example, a rice-wheat cropping system yielding 6.95 tons/ha of rice and 3.86 tons/ha of wheat removes 316 kg of nitrogen and significant amounts of phosphorous, potassium and other secondary micronutrients (Yadav 2000)
11. In a recently published review of the soil sciences research undertaken in India during 1975-2001, Rajeshwari Raina (2006) writes, "Location specificity demands interdisciplinary team work with a range of local partners. Both are unfortunately features that are discouraged by the patrons of soil science research. Three sub-disciplines, soil science, soil chemistry and physics and soil fertility account for almost 82 per cent of the Indian journal publications in soil sciences. This may be interpreted as a dominant feature of Indian soil science—three of the most popular sub disciplines that contribute yield-enhancing technologies

in convergence with the green revolution paradigm and the commodity orientation in agricultural science in general.

12. Its vision and strategy was inadequately conceived for the dry land regions; it was clear and officially recognized by the National Commission on Agriculture (National Commission on Agriculture, 1976). See Dinesh Abrol, "American Involvement in Indian Agricultural Research", Social Scientist, New Delhi, August 1984, p. 8-27 for further details. But even in the long run as the system has failed to provide remedies to the problems afflicting the Indian agriculture across agro-ecological regions, it would not be wrong to state that the vision and strategy of the Kothari Commission should itself be questioned and given a fresh look. To reinforce the same point we also cite here late Suresh. K. Sinha, Former Director IARI, who wrote, "to ensure food security the country will have to give up the 1970s model of agricultural development" (Sinha, 2000).
13. See Dinesh Abrol (1984), p. 15 for further details of the treatment that the system meted out to Dr. Richaria, Director of Central Rice Research Institute (CRRI).
14. See Dinesh Abrol, American Involvement in Agricultural Research, Social scientist, 1984.
15. See Dinesh Abrol (1984), p16.
16. See Dinesh Abrol (1984), p17.
17. See also National Commission on Agriculture, Report on Research, Education Extension, 1976.
18. Albert Moseman, Building Agricultural Research Systems in the Developing Nations, Agricultural Development Council Inc (ADC), New York, 1970, p. 101.
19. Lawrence Busch writes, "The Second Joint Indo-American team urged that the process of university development be expedited and that one agricultural university similar to a U.S. land-grant university be established in each state. All agricultural research was to be coordinated by ICAR. The Community Development Program's broad focus was to be narrowed and the program was to be ceded to the Ministry of Agriculture, a point that was the subject of some dispute among the Indian members of the joint team (ICAR 1960, 72-74)
20. See the report of M.S. Swaminathan chaired National Commission on Farmers, Ministry of Agriculture, GOI, New Delhi, 2006.
21. For instance, it said that the educational system does not reflect the supreme importance of agriculture which is neglected at all stages and does not attract an adequate share of the top talent in the country; enrolment in the agricultural faculties of universities is extremely low; and agricultural colleges are comparatively weak and underdeveloped;

## References

Abrol, Dinesh (1976), *Agricultural Manpower Planning: A Review*, M. Phil Dissertation, New Delhi: Centre for Studies in Science Policy, JNU, August 1976.

Abrol, Dinesh (1984), American Involvement in Indian Agricultural Research, *Social Scientist*, New Delhi, August, pp. 8-27.

Busch, Lawrence (1988), Universities for Development: Report of the Joint Indo-US Impact Evaluation of the Indian Agricultural Universities. *AID Project Impact Evaluation No. 68*. Washington, DC: US Agency for International Development.

CSIR (1993), *Outturn of Scientific and Technical Manpower in India*, New Delhi: HRD Group, CSIR, Vol. 1-4.

DST (1993), *Research and Development Statistics*, New Delhi: Department of Science and Technology. India.

Easter, William; S. Bisaliah and John, O. Dunbar (1989), After twenty-five years of institution building, The state of Agricultural Universities in India face new challenges, *American Journal of Agricultural. Economics*, 71(5): 1200-1205.

GOI (1955), The First Joint Indo-American Team on Indian Agricultural Education, Research, Extension, Govt. of India.

GOI (2001), *Report of the Working Group on Agricultural Research and Education for the Tenth Five Year Plan*, New Delhi: Planning Commission, Govt. of India.

GOI (2005), *Report of the Task Group on Revamping and Refocusing National Agricultural Research*, Planning Commission, Govt. of India.

Hannah, Harold W. (1956), *Blueprint for a Rural University in India*, New Delhi: Indian Council for Agricultural Research.

Hannah, Harold W. (1966), *Resource Book for Rural Universities in Developing Countries*, Urbana, Illinois:, University of Illinois Press.

Hannah, Harold W. and Robert, R. Caughey (1967), *The Legal Base for Universities in Developing Countries*, Urbana, Illinois: University of Illinois Press.

Hobbs, P. and M. Morris (1996), *Meeting South Asia's Future Food Requirements from Rice-Wheat Cropping Systems: Priority Issues Facing Researchers in the Post-Green Revolution Era*, Mexico: NRG Paper 96-01, D.F.: CIMMYT.

IAMR (2001), *Assessment of National Manpower Needs in Agriculture and Allied Sector*, New Delhi: Institute of Applied Manpower Research.

ICAR (1960), *Report of the Second Joint Indo-American Team on Agricultural Education, Research and Extension*. New Delhi: Indian Council of Agricultural Research.

ICAR (1981), *Model Act for Agricultural Universities in India*. New Delhi: Indian Council of Agricultural Research.

ICAR (1988), *Report of the ICAR Review Committee*, New Delhi: Indian Council of Agricultural Research.

ICAR (1995), *Report of Third Deans' Committee on Agricultural Education in India*, New Delhi: ICAR.

ICAR (2005), Empowering KVKs with Technologies & Improving Effectiveness to be Focus Area, *ICAR Press Release* dated 25 Oct., 2005, New Delhi: Indian Council of Agricultural Research.

ICAR (2006) *Report of Fourth Deans' Committee on Agricultural Education in India*, New Delhi: ICAR.

Janiah, Aldas and Mahbub Hossain (2004), Partnership in Public Sector Agricultural R & D: Evidence from India, *Economic and Political Weekly*, Vol. XXXIX (50).

Katyal, J.C. (2003), Employment-oriented Agricultural Education, in Dhakar, L.L. and Mathur, A.N. (Eds.) *Proceedings of National Symposium on University Autonomy and Quality Improvement of Higher Education*, November 13-14, 2003, organised by Maharana Pratap University of Agriculture and Technology, Udaipur.

Katyal, J.C. (2005), Higher Agricultural Education in India—Implications of General Agreements on Trade in Services, in *Proceedings of the 29th Annual Convention of Indian Agricultural Universities Association*, January 12-13, 2005 at CCS Haryana Agricultural University, Hisar. pp. 1-14.

M.S. Swaminathan Research Foundation (2007), *Measures of Impact of Science and Technology in India: Agriculture and Rural Development* (*Measures of Progress of Science and Technology in India—Part III*), Chennai

Moseman, Albert. (1970), Building Agricultural Research Systems in the Developing Nations, New York: Agricultural Development Council Inc (ADC), 1970, p. 16.

NAAS (2005), Redefining Agricultural Education and Extension System in Changed Scenario, *Policy Paper No. 31*, New Delhi: National Academy of Agricultural Sciences.

Nagarajan, S. (1998), Perspectives on Wheat Demand and Research Needs, in Nagarajan *et al.*, *Wheat Research Needs beyond 2000 AD*. New Delhi: Narosa Publishing House.

Nagarajan, S. (2006), Sustaining Wheat Production and Ensuring Food Availability, Paper presented at the Seminar on Crop Biofortification for Alleviating Micronutrient Malnutrition, organized by the Department of Biotechnology, Government of India, and MSSRF, at the M.S. Swaminathan Research Foundation, Chennai, February 13-14.

National Commission on Agriculture (1976), Report on Research, Education, Extension, National Commission on Agriculture, Government of India, 1976.

Raina, Rajeshwari (2002), Agricultural Science and the Social Sciences: An Uneasy Relationship, in *Behind the Blackboard*, SFI Publications.

Raina, Rajeshwari (2006), The Soil Sciences in India: Policy lessons for Agricultural Innovation, *Research Policy*, Vol. 35, Issue 5, pp. 691-714.

Rama Rao, D. and Muralidhar, U. (1994), *A Study on Agriculture University Information System (AGRIUNIS)*, National Academy of Agriculture Research Management, Hyderabad.

Rama Rao, D. and Sandhya Shenoy, N. (1998), *Professional Women in Agriculture*, Hyderabad: DST Project Report, National Academy of Agriculture Research Management.

Ramarao, D., Nanda, S.K. and Sriram, C. (2004), *Forecasting Trained Agricultural Manpower*, Hyderabad: NATP Project Report, NAARM.

Report of the Two-day Regional Workshop on Rural Higher Education towards Sustainable Village Development and Gram Swaraj (June 2002).

Rockefeller Foundation (n.a.). *Working Papers on Strategies for Agricultural Education in Developing Countries*, p. 103.

Sinha, Suresh K. (2000), Education for Agriculture in India: Time for a Change, *Current Science*, 79(3):302-10.

Sulaiman, Rasheed V. (1996), Agricultural Education in India—Problems and Policy Imperatives, *Journal of Rural Reconstruction*, 29(2): 23-43.

*The IV IADP Evaluation Report (1978)*, Vol. 1, 6th Lok Sabha, March.

# Epilogue

The preceding pages give an account of the insights provided by eminent scholars on the various themes identified for the seminar on "Education Commission: Revisiting the Commission's Premises, Vision and Impact on Policy Formulation." The conceptual backdrop of the intended deliberations of the Seminar has been presented and elaborated. The papers contributed have been encapsulated in the form of a review which provides the quintessence of the wide spectrum of thoughts and critical observations made in the papers.

The 3-day seminar had a plenary session besides the inaugural and the valedictory sessions. A total of 26 papers from eminent educationists from across the country were received on the seven themes outlined earlier. However, 22 papers were presented in the various sessions of the seminar.

Prof. Andre Beteille, Chairman, ICSSR, New Delhi, inaugurated the national seminar. In his inaugural address, Prof. Beteille highlighted the equity concerns in the Indian education system, besides giving a brief account of his association with Prof. D. S. Kothari. He emphasized that it would be unwise to develop one level of education at the cost of the other, while making it clear that higher education cannot be developed without improving school education. He mentioned that it would be morally wrong to deny access to elementary education on the basis of caste, class and religion. However, he said that for access to higher education, while it should not be discriminatory on grounds of caste, class and religion, there should be a selection process on the basis of merit. He mentioned that "intellectual capacity should be one of the criteria for selection to have access to higher education". There is, therefore, a need to harmonize the challenges of social inclusion and discrimination on the basis of merit at the higher education level.

Shri Sudeep Banerjee, Chancellor, NUEPA, who chaired the inaugural session, observed that there has been a shift in the educational discourse in recent times and greater emphasis is made in these discourses on the creation of a knowledge society, and that the role of education in promoting democratic and egalitarian society has somehow been undermined over the years. During his address, he desired that educationists must regain their space in the policy planning process.

This seminar has provided a timely opportunity to revive the attention of the educationists and scholars on the ideals of the education system at a time when dangerous distortions are taking place in the name of "liberalization" and "market orientation". The deliberations during the three days have highlighted the need to launch quick, effective and concerted action, beyond just expressions of concern.

Cutting across all the major themes, the seminar emphasized the necessity to spell out unambiguously the national policy framework that will serve as the guiding force for development of education that will fulfill the aspirations of the Indian society. The Seminar focused on the underlying causes behind inequalities and disparities in the education system in access, institutional structures, curricular variations, affordability, and regional/sub-regional imbalances.

Even though the conditions prevailing during the 1960s were very different when the Kothari Commission looked into the education development issues, most of its recommendations stand highly relevant today. While the Commission recognized state as the primary agent of educational change at all levels, over the years with the neo-liberal development strategies, the role of the state is being increasingly undermined in the development of education. There is a need for paradigm shift in our educational discourse and policy planning, given our 40-year long experience of not being successful in implementing some of the critical recommendations of the national Commission.

Major highlights of the seminar (which constitute the discussions in the seminar on the papers developed by the authors) have been outlined below as endorsement of those elaborated in the papers in depth:

## Theme I: Perspectives, Goals and Values

- The national system of education should relate education to all relevant societal concerns which have a potential for national development. While education may have utilitarian objective, it cannot be devoid of values.
- Education is not an instrument; it is a process. It also means convergence of knowledge to developmental study. That is, knowledge component of education has utility to society but it should also be coupled with values. Linking education with work, life and cultivating values as widely propounded by Mahatma Gandhi should be taken up today when we are talking about education for sustainable development. This requires change and transformation in the basic concept of modernization of education.
- A balanced perspective on the development of science and social science is needed and, therefore, it warrants a balanced development of all facets of a knowledge society.
- Contrary to the Education Commission's perspective on the role of education in national development, unfortunately, education has become the periphery of national development thereby shifting the

very approach to development of education in the country.

- Most of the recommendations of the Education Commission are still relevant, their implementation need to be viewed in the context of changing educational terrain as also the changing political context.

## Theme II: Equity and Social Justice

- Although the Commission was very particular about making efforts to bridge regional imbalances, educationally backward states identified in 1978 continue to remain backward today even after so many interventions by the state as well as the central governments. Most of the illiterates and out of school children are found concentrated in nine educationally backward states.
- Projectization approach to educational interventions would not help address issues of regional imbalances. Most focused action plans for backward states need to be undertaken. States in collaboration with the Centre and not the vice-versa should design programmes and interventions for educational development.
- There is a need to put in place a regulatory mechanism to monitor the quality of education at all levels. This would greatly help addressing issues of regional imbalances in educational development.
- Inclusive education should not be seen in isolation. Education of girls and the disabled should aim at their empowerment rather than taking a mere utilitarian approach.
- Establishment of a Common School System that would provide the bedrock of social justice ought to be ensured as quickly as possible as it alone can address the issue of inclusion besides promoting national integration.
- Diversity in the classroom is both a treasure and a reality. But we need to evolve the pedagogy that should help us deal with the challenge of meeting the differential learning needs of children. This would be the key to overcome the problem of 'silent' exclusion, which is rampant in our schools.
- While differences in terms of ethnic groups, language, region and caste have to be understood, appreciated, and tolerated; there is an urgent need to chalk out a specific school curriculum to nurture national identity.
- There are basically two ways to deal with the issue of inclusion: Right Based Approach and Need Based Approach. There is a strong constitutional commitment to ensure rights and equity in education, at least at the elementary stage. However, there is very little appreciation in the policy making process to address the issue. In fact, the approach is riddled with fragmented programmes and

projects that treat children as objects in different groups.

- For the first time, an attempt has been made to estimate the number of children with disabilities in the country. The government has also flagged the importance of coordination and networking of different Ministries and NGOs as important partners to deal with the issue of inclusive education.
- Creation of space for voices of persons with disabilities for designing and implementing polices; ensuring a responsive governance, structure and equitable educational opportunities for the disabled are the urgent areas that need immediate attention.

## Theme III: Curriculum, Pedagogy and Knowledge

- Productive work should be seen as a source of knowledge rather than a mere correlation between work and education.
- The Commission perhaps went wrong in prescribing the strategies to implement work education, though it had given enough emphasis on the subject.
- There is a need to institutionalize the role of productive and community work as a medium of knowledge acquisition and for developing values and skills through school curriculum. Work experience should be introduced as an integral part of education. However, curricular reform cannot be detached from structural reforms in the school system.
- Improving teacher education continues to be a major challenge in the country. The changes brought about in teacher education during the last 40 years considerably fall short of the expectations of the Commission.
- Ensuring professionalism in teacher education; development of education as a discipline; bridging the gap between the school and the teacher education curricula; quality control in teacher education; capacity building of teacher educators; and above all removing the isolation of universities and teacher education system are keys to teacher empowerment.
- A policy of segregating teachers on the basis of recruitment procedures, reward structure and accountability would be damaging to the education system in the long run if we are really concerned about bridging the socio-economic disparities, and recognize education as an equalizer of social inequities.
- Commercialization of teacher education needs to be stopped. The organizations responsible for regulating teacher education system in the country need to focus more on providing academic support services to institutions engaged in teacher education.

- There is a need to build a culture of intellectual enquiry in teacher education. Forming multi-disciplinary study groups drawn from different state and national level organizations including the NCTE, NCERT and NUEPA would help diagnose and suggest measures to improve teacher education in the country.

## Theme IV: Planning and Governance

- The role of the civil society has been largely limited in planning and governance of education, which is a major cause for concern. There is a need to ensure accountability and transparency in educational governance besides, focusing on alternative models of governance of education.

## Theme V: Knowledge for National Development

- Flexibility in the choice of courses; merit as the criterion of promotion; differential salary structure to attract the brightest teachers; development of syllabi by teachers; and a national system of recruitment of teachers to avoid inbreeding; integration of teaching and research; and a sound accreditation and audit system should be some of the hallmarks of developing knowledge and excellence in higher education in the country.

## Theme VI: Resources and National Economy

- The Commission recognized education as an important determinant of the level of prosperity, welfare and security of the people and accordingly pleaded for increased allocation of funds to education. The Commission made several recommendations with regard to allocation of resources, provision of free education, fees and cost-recovery in education, scholarships, inter-functional allocation of resources and others like grants-in-aid to private schools, etc. All these recommendations were backed on sound premises, detailed empirical analysis, and wider and in-depth knowledge of issues involved.
- The most popular and important recommendation of the Commission was to allocate six per cent of GNP to education by 1986. This remains under achieved even though it was approved by the Parliament.
- The Kothari Commission's recommendations on financing education like the need to allocate six per cent of GNP to education, provision of free education, role of fees in revenue generation for education, cost recovery in education, role of state, scholarships etc., are still highly relevant.
- The Economics of Education and the role of education in increasing the productivity are being underplayed and education is beginning

to be viewed as a right that needs to be taken into account in any discussion on financing of education. A range of issues like the need to allocate more than six per cent of GNP to education in the changing circumstances, methodologies with regard to estimating resource requirements, ever increasing and cumulative gap in the allocation of resources, need to improve efficiency in utilization of resources, inter-sectoral reallocation of resources, regulation of private sector are major concerns for policy planning.

## Theme VII: Contemporary Concerns and Future Challenges

- Many recommendations of the Commission have not been implemented to the desired extent and many good initiatives could not be up-scaled to benefit the large target group of learners served by the distance mode.
- Education for agriculture in India is facing one of the biggest challenges, i.e. market-oriented agricultural education and extension along with changes in agricultural marketing policy for the national and international market. Kothari Commission and subsequent developments could not address the local needs through agricultural education.
- Agricultural education should be an independent subject at the school level. A clear policy for allocation of financial resources for agricultural education, research and extension need to be formulated.
- There is a need for establishing agricultural universities on the model of IITs and IIMs and students from rural areas should be encouraged to study in agricultural universities.
- There is an urgent need to re-conceptualize the role and functions of adult education in the country that is one of the important drivers of socio-economic and educational change.
- State retaining the authority to provide finance has also led to the erosion of administrative and academic autonomy of educational institutions. There is a need to restore academic autonomy to teachers.

## Conclusion

One of the most important outcomes of this seminar is that we all have agreed to change and change for better, and, therefore, there has been expressions of interest on the need for constituting another Education Commission to deal with the emerging challenges of education and building a new society, a society which would continue to be very Indian while making a huge presence in the global village. The deliberations have, indeed, provided a rich collection of valuable ideas for all the stakeholders to initiate an agenda for follow-up action in an effective and efficient manner.

# Contributors

**A. K. Sharma**, former Director of NCERT, New Delhi, has held various important positions. He was the Principal, Regional College of Education, Mysore, for over two decades. Subsequently, he moved to the NCERT headquarters where he served as the Head, Department of Teacher Education, and then, as the Joint Director, NCERT. He was instrumental in conceptualizing the Scheme of District Institute of Education and Training (DIET). He specializes in surface and coordination chemistry. He has also authored several papers and articles on various aspects of school and teacher education.

**Anil Sadgopal** retired as Professor and Dean, Faculty of Education, University of Delhi. He had undertaken a number of important assignments including Member of the National Commission on Teachers, the Acharya Ramamurti Committee and the Central Advisory Board on Education (CABE, 2005). He is the recipient of several awards including the Jamnalal Bajaj Award (1980) and Rathindra Puraskar (1984) for application of science and technology in rural areas. He has authored a couple of books and more than a dozen articles on policy analysis and various aspects of globalization and education.

**Anita Ghai** is Reader in Psychology at Jesus and Mary College, University of Delhi. Issues relating to education of persons with special needs are central to her areas of interest. She has authored a couple of books and several articles. She is on the editorial board of two journals, *Disability Studies Quarterly* and *Disability and Society*.

**Arjun Dev** retired from the NCERT in 2000 as Professor of History and Head of NCERT's erstwhile Department of Education in Social Sciences and Humanities. He had been the Member Secretary of the National Steering Committee on Textbooks Evaluation and of National Advisory Committee on Contemporary India set up by the Government of India in the early 1990s. He was associated with conducting various studies, including a study of the position of upper primary stage in Indian schools, a 17-country study of critical issues in secondary education in the Asia-Pacific region and, more recently, studies on human rights education. He is currently associated with the *Towards Freedom* project of the Indian Council of Historical Research.

**C. Seshadri**, a scholar in philosophy of education and an eminent teacher educator, had long association with the National Council of Educational Research and Training as Professor of Education and Principal at the Regional College of Education, Mysore. His major areas of professional engagement include: development of national curricular frameworks for school education and teacher education and the implementation of the centrally sponsored scheme of teacher education. He has served as consultant to the UNESCO and the DFID in their projects in literacy, basic education and teacher education in China and South Asian countries.

**Dinesh Abrol** researches on the issues of Science and Technology (S&T) Policy at the National Institute of Science, Technology and Development Studies, New Delhi. He has authored a number of books, research papers and articles. His research contributions extend to the themes of assessment of research and technology for development, development of systems of innovation (IS), management of industry-research institutions-university linkages and design of patent law. He has been associated with the People's Science Movement, a civil society network of organizations devoted to the task of organizing the scientists and technologists to link themselves with the people on the issues of science, technology and society.

**H. P. Dikshit** has been a Visiting Professor with a number of premier institutions, both within and outside the country. Recipient of the Ramanujan Birth Centenary Year Award of ISCA and Distinguished Scientist Award of MPCSc&T, Prof. Dikshit had been the Vice-Chancellor of IGNOU, Himachal Pradesh University, Shimla, MP Bhoj University, Bhopal and Rani Durgavati University, Jabalpur. He is known to have contributed significantly to the promotion of mathematics education.

**Hriday Kant Dewan** has been working in the field of education for over three decades in different capacities and in all its aspects. His areas of interest include development of study material for elementary schools as well as for adults. He is currently the Organizing Secretary-cum-Educational Advisor of the *Vidya Bhawan Society*, Udaipur, Rajasthan. He has led several evaluation studies at state and district levels and also provided support to and collaborated with different governments for production of textbooks, teacher training.He has also been working with the MHRD to evolve programs of alternative schools; and with the IGNOU for designing and developing courses, especially for Mathematics teaching techniques and on integrated teaching and learning.

**Jandhyala B G Tilak** is Professor and Head, Department of Educational Finance at the National University of Educational Planning and Administration (NUEPA). He is on the editorial board of several national and international journals in education and development studies. His publications include eight books and more than 250 research papers published in professional journals, focusing on theoretical, conceptual, empirical and advocacy aspects of education. He is the recipient of Swami Pranavananda Saraswati National Award of the UGC for outstanding research in education and Dr. Malcolm Adiseshiah Award for distinguished contributions to development studies.

**L. Pulamte** has been engaged in research on issues related to science and technology (S&T) policy and regional innovation system at the National Institute of Science, Technology and Development Studies, New Delhi. He has carried out action research projects in the area of technology implementation and research projects on technology evaluation and impact. He has presented several papers on S&T Policy, Regional Dimensions of STI (science, technology and innovation) at national conferences.

**M. A. Khader** is the Director of SCERT, Thiruvananthapuram, Kerala. Prior to his current assignment, he was a professor at the NCERT, New Delhi. His areas of professional interest and contribution cover curriculum development, teacher education and policy studies in education. He also headed the Curriculum Group at the NCERT, and was the Member Secretary, National Steering Committee set up for the formulation of National Curriculum Framework, 2005.

**M. Anandakrishnan** is the Chairman, Madras Institute of Development Studies, Chennai, Tamil Nadu. He was awarded Padmashri by the President of India in 2002 for his commendable service to the cause of education. His areas of professional interest include: civil engineering, environmental engineering, science and technology policy analysis and management of academic institutions, higher and technical education. He has held several important positions both at the national and state levels including the post of the Vice-Chairman, Tamil Nadu State Council for Higher Education, Advisor to the Chief Minister of Tamil Nadu on Information Technology and e-Governance and the Vice-Chancellor, Anna University. His publications include several books, articles and papers mainly focusing on various aspects of development of science, technology, technical and higher education.

**M. S. Yadav** retired as Professor and Dean of the Centre for Advanced Studies in Education at the M. S. University, Baroda. His areas of specialization are school education and teacher education. He has authored a number of books and articles.

**Madan Mohan Jha** had seen the functioning of Indian school system from up close during his field postings, as a member of the Indian Administrative Service as also Director of the UNICEF supported Bihar Education Project. His assignment as joint secretary in the Ministry of Human Resource Development (1998-2002) provided him perspective on policy as also opportunities for participating in numerous international seminars and conferences. He earned his D. Phil from the University of Oxford (2002-05) for his work on Inclusive Education in the Indian context for children labeled as having 'special' needs. His publications include the book entitled *School without Walls*. As a Member Secretary of the Common School System Commission, he was instrumental in developing a vision and a framework for common school system in Bihar. His untimely demise in 2007 has, indeed, been a big loss to the academia.

**Madhu Prasad** is a Reader in Philosophy at the Zakir Husain College, University of Delhi. She has several publications focusing on the impact of colonialism in higher education and issues of autonomy and the neo-liberal trend towards privatization of higher education. She is on the editorial board of the journal, *Social Scientist*. She is a founder member of the National Committee of the People's Campaign for Common School System, and the People's Study Group.

**Mohd. Akhtar Siddiqui** has served as a member of the faculty at the Jamia Millia Islamia, New Delhi for over two-and-a half decades. His research interests include commerce education, teacher education, educational management and education of deprived sections of society. He has published several books and articles in these areas. He is currently a Professor in Education and Dean, Faculty of Education at the Jamia Millia Islamia. As a member of various governmental and professional organizations, he has been contributing to the promotion of the cause of education, especially among the disadvantaged sections of the society.

**Pushpa M. Bhargava** is the founder and former Director of the Centre for Cellular and Molecular Biology, Hyderabad. He is currently the Director of Anveshna Consultancy Services, Hyderabad. He was awarded the Padma Bhusan by the President of India in 1986 and the Legion de Honeur in 1998 by the French Government for his scientific and social contributions.

**Padma Velaskar** is Professor and Chairperson of the Centre for Studies in Sociology of Education at the Tata Institute of Social Sciences (TISS), Mumbai. She teaches courses in Sociology, Sociology of Education and Women's Studies. Her research interests lie in areas of the relationship between caste, class and gender, education and social stratification, dalit women's social status and the state and education. She has published widely in these areas. She is currently Coordinator of new, collaboratively developed post-graduate programme in Education (Elementary) at the TISS.

**R. Govinda** is currently Professor and Head of the Department of School and Non-Formal Education at the National University of Educational Planning and Administration (NUEPA), New Delhi. He specializes in Policy Analysis,

Decentralized Management, Basic Education, Non-formal Education and Educational Evaluation. He had taught at the Centre of Advanced Study in Education, Baroda; was on the Faculty of International Institute for Educational Planning (IIEP), UNESCO, Paris and Institute for Social and Economic Change, Bangalore, Consultant for UNESCO, UNICEF, ACCU, NORAD, the World Bank and the Asian Development Bank. He has authored several books and professional papers in Indian and international journals.

**R. P. Singh** retired as Professor and Head, Department of Teacher Education, NCERT, New Delhi. During his long association with the NCERT, he served in different departments as Professor and Head, besides being the Principal, Regional College of Education, Bhopal and Head of the Journal Cell. His areas of interest include history of education, and teacher and comparative education.

**Ram Takwale** is Emeritus Professor, Director of MKCL and Chairman of the I-CONSENT. He has the background of a teacher, educational planner, administrator and developer. He was vice-chancellor of Pune University, YCMOU and IGNOU. He has worked for many national and international bodies and organizations. He now works with several voluntary organizations. His current interest is in the use of ICT for developing models of education for quality education for all. Towards this, he is engaged in developing an Indian Consortium for Educational Transformation (I-CONSENT) of partner institutions and is creating e-platform of MKCL for large techno-social systems. His specific interests are the development of Finishing Institute in partnership with industries, program of Virtual School and Learning Homes and e-teacher education.

**Sharad Chandra Behar** had been in the Indian Administrative Service (IAS) from 1961 to 1997. He has been simultaneously engaged in administration, activism and academics. He has held important positions in the educational hierarchy in the State Government before retiring as Chief Secretary to the Government of Madhya Pradesh. He had been the founder Director of the State Council of Educational Research and Training (SCERT), Madhya Pradesh, and the Eklavya. He has also served as the Vice-Chancellor of Guru Ghasi Das University at Bilaspur. He has been closely associated with a number of civil society organizations, campaigns and people's movements. His publications include several books and about 100 papers on education, administration and issues of social concern.

**Sudesh Mukhopadhyay** is Professor and Head, Department of Inclusive Education at the National University of Educational Planning and Administration (NUEPA), New Delhi. She had been a Visiting Fellow at Manitoba University, Canada; on the faculty of the NCERT, New Delhi; and

Director of the SCERT, Delhi. She specializes in education of the persons with disabilities and teacher education, and has several publications in these areas.

**Vijaya S. Varma** has served on the Faculty of Education, University of Delhi with great distinction for a long time. His areas of specialization include curriculum development and teacher education. He has authored a number of interesting readings.

# Index